NEW TESTAMENT: HISTORY OF INTERPRETATION

Excerpted from the
DICTIONARY OF BIBLICAL INTERPRETATION
Edited by John H. Hayes

ABINGDON PRESS
Nashville

NEW TESTAMENT: HISTORY OF BIBLICAL INTERPRETATION
Copyright © 2004 by Abingdon Press

Excerpted from the *Dictionary of Biblical Interpretation*,
edited by John H. Hayes, Abingdon Press, 1999.

This book is printed on acid-free paper.

ISBN 0-687-036860

Cataloging-in-Publication Data is available from the Library of Congress.

Scripture quotations, unless otherwise indicated, are from the New Revised Standard Version Bible, copyright © 1989 by the Division of Christian Education of the National Council of the Churches of Christ in the United States of America.

The Hebraica® and Graeca® fonts used to print this work are available from Linguist's Software, Inc., PO Box 580, Edmonds, WA 98020-0580
tel (206) 775-1130.

04 05 06 07 08 09 10 11 12 13 — 10 9 8 7 6 5 4 3 2 1

MANUFACTURED IN THE UNITED STATES OF AMERICA

CONTENTS

Appendixes
1. Apocrypha

2. Pseudepigrapha

FOREWORD

Fifty years ago New Testament scholars agreed that one studied a New Testament or other ancient text by using historical criticism to discover the meaning a text had for its original readers. After that one asked how what it meant back then related to what it means today. For all their differences in conclusions, there was agreement about methods. The goal was an interpretation that was historically accurate, that told what really happened or what a text really said, and that was free of the interpreter's assumptions or biases

Fifty years later there is little agreement about methods across the discipline. A look at any program book for the Society of Biblical Literature for the last five years reveals an amazing variety of approaches to a New Testament text, so much so that one can even speak of a "balkanization" of methods. The Society of Biblical Literature even sponsored a journal, *Semeia*, to explore new—and for many exciting or liberating—approaches to biblical interpretation. Approaches included modern literary criticism, rhetorical criticism, oral interpretation, Reader Response criticism, social scientific interpretation, African-American interpretation, feminist criticism, liberation theology, and the like. Some approaches sprang up and then died, e.g. structuralism and the "New Hermeneutic." Names of scholars, often from other disciplines, appeared as guides to interpretation: It does not surprise one to learn that L. William Countryman (2003, p.1) recently said that "The most basic problem [in biblical interpretation] is the tendency already well underway by the middle of the twentieth century toward a fragmenting of the field into distinct and narrowly defined 'methodologies,' each pursued in increasing isolation from the others." Not only is there a Balkanization of method but there is also a balkanization of the entire discipline of biblical studies.

Such developments are positive in many respects; they have enriched our understanding of biblical texts. They have taught us new questions to ask and brought riches to light. Biblical scholarship will continue to find new ways to read the Scriptures, stimulated by the needs of the modern world and the desire to mine the riches of the biblical texts. Such developments are to be encouraged. Their value is demonstrated by the new insights into the role of women in church and society that have emerged, by the richness of insight that social scientific criticism has brought to our understanding of ancient social structure, value systems, urban and village life, etc. Add what archaeology has contributed to our understanding and we could describe a "Copernican" revolution in biblical studies since World War II.

But these developments have also brought with them an unintended impoverishment with them. Two unfortunate results of this development are evident. On the one hand there is an increasing specialization in scholarship. One is a Paul scholar or even a specialist in the Corinthian correspondence, or a specialist in apocalyptic literature. The result is that there are fewer and fewer scholars who seem to control the entire field and so are able to produce the necessary works of synthesis that give coherence to the field.

The other result is a kind of methodological modernity that seeks always to look for the most recent interpretive model. One result is a burgeoning of guides to method in biblical studies—and to works on the theory of interpretation. Such works have become necessary to enable one to makes one's way through the maze of biblical interpretation today. (There are too many to list. Examples include Coggins and Houlden 1990; and Aune's outstanding work 2003) Scholars also tend to overlook the great scholarship of the past and thus at times repeat work that has been well done in the past. One might add that there is often an attitude that seeks to divorce interpretation from theological concerns.

And that is where this volume makes a major contribution to biblical studies. Three types of articles from the standard two-volume *Dictionary of Biblical Interpretation* edited by John H. Hayes are included here. The first section presents an article on each New Testament book written by an outstanding interpreter of each. The articles survey the history of interpretation, show how methods and interpretation changed over the centuries, and then give extensive bibliographies of commentaries and studies. The second, much smaller, group is articles on special topics: Sermon on the Mount, Parables, Synoptic Problem, Q, and Paul. Finally, what may prove to be most valuable for some, articles on the Jewish apocryphal and pseudepigraphic books. The reading of these articles will remind scholars of the valuable work of the past, pose questions that need further study, and provide references to resources that will give direction for continuing research.

Works Cited

D. E. Aune, *The Westminster Dictionary of New Testament and Early Christian Literature and Rhetoric* (Louisville, London: Westminster John Knox Press, 2003).

R. J. Coggins and J. L. Houlden (eds.), *A Dictionary of Biblical Interpretation* (Harrisburg: Trinity Press International, 1990).

L. W. Countryman, *Interpreting the Truth: Changing the Paradigm of Biblical Studies* (Harrisburg: Trinity Press International, 2003).

Edgar Krentz
Lutheran School of Theology
February 2004

PUBLISHER'S FOREWORD

This volume collects the articles on the history of critical research for the individual New Testament books and broad areas of New Testament study (the Synoptic Problem, Q, Jesus' Parables, the Sermon on the Mount, Paul, and New Testament Prophecy and Prophets) that originally appeared in the *Dictionary of Biblical Interpretation* (Abingdon Press, 1999) and is intended as a supplemental text for seminary and university classes on the New Testament or on the history of biblical research. It is also suitable for introductory level courses on biblical interpretation and for graduate students preparing for exams. The essays provide an overview of the history of research of a given New Testament book and five broad areas of New Testament study.

The emphasis throughout has been on the questions and issues posed by critical scholarship. Therefore, discussions of pre-Reformation interpretation have in most cases been substantially shortened or eliminated altogether. Discussion of early Christian and medieval exegesis have been retained regarding text criticism, the development of the canon, and when early scholarship addressed questions still under discussion in modern critical scholarship.

Many students of the New Testament have little knowledge of these books and limited access to scholarly resources, we have collected the articles on the Apocrypha and Pseudepigrapha from the *Dictionary of Biblical Interpretation*. A general knowledge of these books is fundamental to understanding "intertestamental" or Second Temple Judaism as the backdrop for New Testament interpretation. Because the apocryphal Additions to Esther are discussed in the context of the entire book of Esther, the essay "Additions to Esther (and Esther)" will also appear in our forthcoming volume, *The Hebrew Bible: History of Interpretation*.

With the major exception of substantially editing the information on early and medieval church interpretation, the essays have not been altered except to correct misprints, correct and update the bibliographies, make minor grammatical corrections, and adapt the abbreviations and other style matters to the *SBL Handbook of Style* (Peabody: Hendrickson Publishers, 1999). With several exceptions, the original phrase "Old Testament" has been consistently changed to "Hebrew Bible" throughout. In those articles, especially on the books of the Apocrypha, "Old Testament" was retained to indicate the shape of the canon developed by the Protestant reformers as based on the "Hebrew Bible" or the traditional Jewish canon of the Law, the Prophets, and the Writings. Given the purpose of the article by T. Stylianopoulos in the Orthodox tradition, "Old Testament," was retained throughout the article "Orthodox Biblical Interpretation."

In addition to the original essays, there are five newly commissioned articles by P. W. Flint, "Psalm 151"; R. DeMaris, "Archaeology and New Testament Interpretation;" A. Hunt, "Historiography of the Hebrew Bible;" S. Porter, "Linguistics and Biblical Interpretation;" J. Fitzgerald, "Lexicography Theory and Biblical Interpretation;" and L. Welborn, "Euro-American Biblical Interpretation." We thank these writers for their willingness to participate at very short notice.

N.B. *Dictionary* entries are identified by an asterisk * (subject or theme discussed), section marks § (discussion in a specific section), and dagger marks † ‡ (discussion in one or more entries).

ABBREVIATIONS

General

abr.	abridged	Heb.	Hebrew
approx.	approximately	HT	Hebrew Translation
Aram.	Aramaic	i.e.	*id est*, that is
art(s).	article(s)	ibid.	*ibidem*, in the same place
aug.	augmented	ill.	illustration
b.	born	inc.	incomplete
B.C.E.	Before the Common Era	intro.	introduction
bib.	biblical	Lat.	Latin
bk(s).	book(s)	lit.	literally
C.E.	Common Era	LT	Latin Translation
c.	circa	LXX	Septuagint
cent(s).	century(ies)	MS(s)	manuscript(s)
cf.	compare	MT	Masoretic Text
chap(s).	chapter(s)	NF	Neve Folge
comb.	combined	NT	New Testament
contr.	contributor	OG	Old Greek
corr.	corrected	OL	Old Latin
d.	died	OT	Old Testament
dept.	department	par.	paragraph
dir.	director	pl.	plural
diss.	dissertation	posth.	posthumous
ed(s).	editor(s)	pt(s).	part(s)
e.g.	*exempli gratia*, for example	pub.	published
Eng.	English	Q	*Quelle,* synoptic sayings source
enl.	enlarged	repr.	reprint
esp.	especially	repub.	republished
est.	established	rev. ed.	revised edition
et al.	*et alii,* and others	RGS	*Religionsgeschichtliche Schule*
etc.	*et cetera,* and the rest	sec(s).	section(s)
ET	English Translation	supp.	supplement
frg(s).	fragment(s)	tr.	translator/translation
Ger.	German	trans.	transcribed
Gr.	Greek	Vg.	Vulgate
GT	German Translation	v(v).	verse(s)
HB	Hebrew Bible	vol(s).	volume(s)

Biblical Translations

ASV	American Standard Version
CEV	Contemporary English Version
KJV	King James Version
NAB	New American Bible
NEB	New English Bible
NIV	New International Version
NJB	New Jerusalem Bible
NRSV	New Revised Standard Version
REB	Revised English Bible
RSV	Revised Standard Version
EV	Today's English Version (Good News Bible)

Books of the Bible
Hebrew Bible

Gen	Genesis	Song (Cant)	Song of Songs (Song of Solomon or Canticles)
Exod	Exodus		
Lev	Leviticus	Isa	Isaiah
Num	Numbers	Jer	Jeremiah
Deut	Deuteronomy	Lam	Lamentations
Josh	Joshua	Ezek	Ezekiel
Judg	Judges	Dan	Daniel
Ruth	Ruth	Hos	Hosea
1–2 Sam	1–2 Samuel	Joel	Joel
1–2 Kgdms	1–2 Kingdoms (LXX)	Amos	Amos
1–2 Kgs	1–2 Kings	Obad	Obadiah
3–4 Kgdms	3–4 Kingdoms (LXX)	Jonah	Jonah
1–2 Chr	1–2 Chronicles	Mic	Micah
Ezra	Ezra	Nah	Nahum
Neh	Nehemiah	Hab	Habakkuk
Esth	Esther	Zeph	Zephaniah
Job	Job	Hag	Haggai
Ps/Pss	Psalms	Zech	Zechariah
Prov	Proverbs	Mal	Malachi
Eccl (or Qoh)	Ecclesiastes (or Qoheleth)		

New Testament

Matt	Matthew	1–2 Thess	1–2 Thessalonians
Mark	Mark	1–2 Tim	1–2 Timothy
Luke	Luke	Titus	Titus
John	John	Phlm	Philemon
Acts	Acts	Heb	Hebrews
Rom	Romans	Jas	James
1–2 Cor	1–2 Corinthians	1–2 Pet	1–2 Peter
Gal	Galatians	1–2–3 John	1–2–3 John
Eph	Ephesians	Jude	Jude
Phil	Philippians	Rev	Revelation
Col	Colossians		

Apocrypha and Septuagint

Bar	Baruch	Ep Jer	Epistle of Jeremiah
Add Dan	Additions to Daniel	Jdt	Judith
Pr Azar	Prayer of Azariah	1–2 Macc	1–2 Maccabees
Bel	Bel and the Dragon	3–4 Macc	3–4 Maccabees
Sg Three	Song of the Three Young Men	Pr Man	Prayer of Manasseh
		Ps 151	Psalm 151
Sus	Susanna	Sir	Sirach/Ecclesiasticus
1–2 Esd	1–2 Esdras	Tob	Tobit
Add Esth	Additions to Esther	Wis	Wisdom of Solomon

Old Testament Pseudepigrapha

Ahiqar	*Ahiqar*
Ant. bib.	Use *L.A.B.*
Apoc. Ab.	*Apocalypse of Abraham*
Apoc. Adam	*Apocalypse of Adam*
Apoc. Dan.	*Apocalype of Daniel*
Apoc. El. (H)	Hebrew *Apocalypse of Elijah*
Apoc. El. (C)	Coptic *Apocalypse of Elijah*
Apoc. Ezek.	Use *Apocr. Ezek.*
Apoc. Mos.	*Apocalypse of Moses*
Apoc. Sedr.	*Apocalypse of Sedrach*
Apoc. Zeph.	*Apocalypse of Zephaniah*
Apoc. Zos.	Use *Hist. Rech.*
Apocr. Ezek.	*Apocryphon of Ezekiel*
Aris. Ex.	Aristeas the Exegete
Aristob.	Aristobulus
Artap.	Artapanus
Ascen. Isa.	*Mart. Ascen. Isa.* 6-11
As. Mos.	*Assumption of Moses*
2 Bar.	*2 Baruch (Syriac Apocalypse)*
3 Bar.	*3 Baruch (Greek Apocalypse)*
4 Bar.	*4 Baruch (Paraleipomena Jeremiou)*
Bib. Ant.	Use *L.A.B.*
Bk. Noah	*Book of Noah*
Cav. Tr.	*Cave of Treasures*
Cl. Mal.	Cleodemus Malchus
Dem.	Demetrius (the Chronographer)
El. Mod.	*Eldad and Modad*
1 En.	*1 Enoch (Ethiopic Apocalypse)*
2 En.	*2 Enoch (Slavonic Apocalypse)*
3 En.	*3 Enoch (Hebrew Apocalypse)*
Eup.	Eupolemus
Ezek. Trag.	Ezekiel the Tragedian
4 Ezra	*4 Ezra*
5 Apoc. Syr. Pss.	*Five Apocryphal Syriac Psalms*
Gk. Apoc. Ezra	*Greek Apocalypse of Ezra*

Hec. Ab.	Hecataeus of Abdera
Hel. Syn. Pr.	*Hellenistic Synagogal Prayers*
Hist. Jos.	*History of Joseph*
Hist. Rech.	*History of the Rechabites*
Jan. Jam.	*Jannes and Jambres*
Jos. Asen.	*Joseph and Aseneth*
Jub.	*Jubilees*
L.A.B.	*Liber antiquitatum biblicarum* (Pseudo-Philo)
L.A.E.	*Life of Adam and Eve*
Lad. Jac.	*Ladder of Jacob*
Let. Aris.	*Letter of Aristeas*
Liv. Pro.	*Lives of the Prophets*
Lost Tr.	*The Lost Tribes*
3 Macc.	*3 Maccabees*
4 Macc.	*4 Maccabees*
5 Macc.	*5 Maccabees* (Arabic)
Mart. Ascen. Isa.	*Martyrdom and Ascension of Isaiah*
Mart. Isa.	*Mart. Ascen. Isa.* 1-5
Odes Sol.	*Odes of Solomon*
P.J.	*Paraleipomena Jeremiou* or *4 Bar.*
Ph. E. Poet	Philo the Epic Poet
Pr. Jac.	*Prayer of Jacob*
Pr. Jos.	*Prayer of Joseph*
Pr. Man.	*Prayer of Manasseh*
Pr. Mos.	*Prayer of Moses*
Ps.-Eup.	Pseudo-Eupolemus
Ps.-Hec.	Pseudo-Hecataeus
Ps.-Orph.	Pseudo-Orpheus
Ps.-Philo	Use *L.A.B.*
Ps.-Phoc.	Pseudo-Phocylides
Pss. Sol.	*Psalms of Solomon*
Ques. Ezra	*Questions of Ezra*
Rev. Ezra	*Revelation of Ezra*
Sib. Or.	*Sibylline Oracles*
Syr. Men.	*Sentences of the Syriac Menander*
T. 12 Patr.	*Testaments of the Twelve Patriarchs*
T. Ash.	*Testament of Asher*
T. Benj.	*Testament of Benjamin*
T. Dan	*Testament of Dan*
T. Gad	*Testament of Gad*
T. Iss.	*Testament of Issachar*
T. Jos.	*Testament of Joseph*
T. Jud.	*Testament of Judah*
T. Levi	*Testament of Levi*
T. Naph.	*Testament of Naphtali*
T. Reu.	*Testament of Reuben*
T. Sim.	*Testament of Simeon*
T. Zeb.	*Testament of Zebulun*
T. 3 Patr.	*Testaments of the Three Patriarchs*

T. Ab.	*Testament of Abraham*
T. Isaac	*Testament of Isaac*
T. Jac.	*Testament of Jacob*
T. Adam	*Testament of Adam*
T. Hez	*Testament of Hezekiah* (*Mart. Ascen. Isa.* 3:13-4:22)
T. Job	*Testament of Job*
T. Mos.	*Testament of Moses*
T. Sol.	*Testament of Solomon*
Theod.	Theodotus, *On the Jews*
Treat. Shem	*Treatise of Shem*
Vis. Ezra	*Vision of Ezra*
Vis. Isa.	Use *Ascen. Isa.*

Periodicals, Reference Works, and Serials

AB	Anchor Bible
ABBL	J. G. Eichorn (ed.), *Allgemeine Bibliothek der biblischen Litteratur*
ABD	*Anchor Bible Dictionary.* Edited by D. N. Freedman. 6 vols. New York, 1992
ABR	*Australian Biblical Review*
ABRL	Anchor Bible Reference Library
ACNT	Augsburg Commentaries on the New Testament
ACCS	Ancient Christian Commentary on Scripture
AGJU	Arbeiten zur Geschichte des antiken Judentums und des Urchristentums
AKML	Abhandlungen zur Kunst-, Musik- und Literaturwissenschaft
ALBO	Analecta lovaniensia biblica et orientalia
ANRW	*Aufstieg und Niedergang der romischen Welt: Geschichte und Kultur Roms im Spiegel der neueren Forschung.* Edited by H. Temporini and W. Haase. Berlin, 1972-
AnBib	Analecta biblica
ANTC	Abingdon New Testament Commentaries
ANTF	Arbeiten zum neutestamentlichen Textforchung
AOAT	Alter Orient und Altes Testament
AOT	*The Apocryphal Old Testament.* Edited by H. F. D. Sparks. Oxford, 1984
APAT	*Die Apokryphen und Pseudepigraphen des Alten Testaments.* Translated and edited by E. Kautzsch. 2 vols. Tübingen, 1900
APOT	*The Apocrypha and Pseudepigrapha of the Old Testament.* Edited by R. H. Charles. 2 vols. Oxford, 1913
ASNU	Acta seminarii neotestamentici upsaliensis
ATD	Das Alte Testament Deutsch
ATLA	American Theological Library Association
BBB	Bonner Biblische Beiträge
BBB	*Bulletin de bibliographie biblique*
BBET	Beiträge zur biblischen Exegese und Theologie
BBR	*Bulletin for Biblical Research*
BCPE	*Bulletin du Centre protestant d'études*
BDAG	Bauer, W., F. W. Danker, W. F. Arndt, and F. W. Gingrich, eds. *Greek-English Lexicon of the New Testament and Other Early Christian Literature.* 3d ed. Chicago, 2000
BEATAJ	Beiträge zur Erforschung des Alten Testaments und des antiken Judentum

BETL	Biblioteca ephemeridum theologicarum lovaniensium
BEvT	Beiträge zur evangelischen Theologie
BFCT	Beiträge zur Förderung christlicher Theologie
BGBE	Beiträge zur Geschichte der biblischen Exegese
BHT	Beiträge zur historischen Theologie
BHWJ	Bericht der Hochschule für die Wissenschaft des Judentums
BIOSCS	*Bulletin of the International Organization for Septuagint Cognate Studies*
BJRL	*Bulletin of the John Rylands University Library of Manchester*
BNTC	Black's New Testament Commentaries
BSac	*Bibliotheca sacra*
Bib	*Biblica*
Bijdr	*Bijdragen: Tijdschrift voor filosofie en theologie*
BiBh	*Bible Bhashyam*
BR	*Biblical Research*
BRev	*Bible Review*
BibS(F)	Biblische Studien (Freiburg, 1895-)
BTB	*Biblical Theology Bulletin*
BWANT	Beiträge zur Wissenschaft vom Alten (und Neuen) Testament
BZ	*Biblische Zeitschrift*
BZAW	Beihefte zur Zietschrift für die altestamentliche Wissenschaft
BZNW	Beihefte zur Zeitschrift für die neutestamentliche Wissenschaft
ConBNT	Coneictanea biblica: Old Testament Series
CBQ	*Catholic Bible Quarterly*
CBQMS	Catholic Bible Quarterly Monograph Series
CCCM	Corpus Christianorum: Continuatio mediaevalis. Turnhout, 1969-
CCSL	Corpus Christianorum: Series latina. Turnhout, 1953-
CNT	Commentaire du Nouveau Testament
ConNT	Coniectanea neotestamentica
CP	*Classical Philology*
CRINT	Compendia rerum iudaicarum ad Novum Testamentum
CS	*Christliche Schriften*. J. G. Herder. 4 vols. 1794-98
CSEL	Corpus scriptorum ecclesiasticorum latinorum
CSCO	Corpus scriptorum christianorum orientalium. Edited by I. B. Chabot at al. Paris, 1903-
CSJH	Chicago Studies in the History of Judaism
CTJ	*Calvin Theological Journal*
CTM	*Concordia Theological Monthly*
CurTM	*Currents in Theology and Mission*
DBSup	*Dictionnaire de la Bible: Supplément*. Edited by L. Pirot and A. Robert. Paris, 1928-
DJD	Discoveries in the Judaean Desert
DSD	*Dead Sea Discoveries*
EBib	*Etudes bibliques*
EKKNT	Evangelische-katholischer Kommentar zum Neuen Testament
EgT	*Eglise et théologie*
EncBrit	*Encyclopedia Britannica*
EncJud	*Encyclopaedia Judaica*. 16 vols. Jerusalem, 1972
ETL	*Ephemerides theologicae lovanienses*
ETS	Erfurter theologische Studien
ExpTim	*Expository Times*

FB	Forschung zur Bibel
FBBS	Facet Books Biblical Series
FF	Foundations and Facets
FFNT	Foundations and Facets: New Testament
FRLANT	Forschungen zur Religion und Literatur des Alten und Neuen Testaments
GCS	Die griechische christliche Schriftsteller der ersten [drei] Jahrhunderte
Hen	*Henoch*
HBC	*Harper's Bible Commentary.* Edited by J. L. Mays et al. San Francisco, 1988.
HKNT	Handkommentar zum Neuen Testament
HDB	*Dictionary of the Bible.* Edited by J. Hastings
HJPAJC	E. Schürer, *History of the Jewish People in the Age of Jesus Christ* (3 vols., rev. G. Vermes et al., 1973-87)
HNT	Handbuch zum Neuen Testament
HNTC	Harper's New Testament Commentaries
HTKNT	Herders theologischer Kommentar zum Neuen Testament
HTKAT	Herders theologoischer Kommentar zum Alten Testament
HTR	*Harvard Theological Review*
HTS	Harvard Theological Studies
HUCA	*Hebrew Union College Annual*
HUT	Hermeneutische Untersuchungen zur Theologie
IB	*Interpreter's Bible.* Edited by G. A. Buttrick et al. 12 vols. New York, 1951-1957
IBC	Interpretation: A Bible Commentary for Teaching and Preaching
ICC	International Critical Commentary
IDB	*The Interpreter's Dictionary to the Bible.* Edited by G. A. Buttrick. 4 vols. Nashville, 1962
IDBS	*Interpreter's Dictionary to the Bible: Supplementary Volume.* Edited by K. Crim. Nashville, 1976
IOS	*Israel Oriental Studies*
IPAT	*Introduction aux pseudépigraphes grecs d'Ancien Testament*
IRT	Issues in Religion and Theology
JSem	*Journal of Semitics*
JAAR	*Journal of the American Academy of Religion*
JAL	Jewish Apocryphal Literature Series
JAOS	*Journal of the American Oriental Society*
JBL	*Journal of Biblical Literature*
JBW	*Jahrüch für biblische Theologie*
JE	*The Jewish Encyclopedia.* Edited by I. Singer. 12 vols. New York, 1925
JETS	*Journal of the Evangelical Theological Society*
JJS	*Journal of Jewish Studies*
JMRS	*Journal of Medieval and Renaissance Studies*
JP	*Journal of Philology*
JPT	*Jahrbücher für protestantische Theologie*
JQR	*Jewish Quarterly Review*
JR	*Journal of Religion*
JRAS	*Journal of the Royal Asiatic Society*
JSHRZ	*Jüdische Schriften aus hellenistisch-römischer Zeit*
JSJ	*Journal for the Study of Judaism in the Persian, Hellenistic, and Roman Periods*
JSJSup	Journal for the Study of Judaism in the Persian, Hellenistic, and Roman Periods: Supplement Series
JSOT	*Journal for the Study of the Old Testament*

JSOTSup	*Journal for the Study of the Old Testament* Supplement Series
JSNT	*Journal for the Study of the New Testament*
JSNTSup	Journal for the Study of the New Testament: Supplement Series
JSP	*Journal for the Study of the Pseudepigrapha*
JSPSup	Journal for the Study of the Pseudepigrapha: Supplement Series
JSS	*Journal of Semitic Studies*
JTS	*Journal of Theological Studies*
KBANT	Kommentar und Beiträge zum Alten und Neuen Testament
KEH	Kurzgefasstes exegetisches Handbuch zum Alten Testament
KEK	Kritisch-exegetischer Kommentar über das Neuen Testament
LD	Lectio divina
LJS	Lives of Jesus Series
LW	*Living Word*
Mus	*Muséon: Revue d'études orientales*
MGWJ	*Monatschrift für Geschichte und Wissenschaft des Judentums*
MNTC	Moffat New Testament Commentary
MSU	Mitteilungen des Septuaginta-Unternehmens
MThS	Münchener Theologishe Studien
NA²⁷	Novum Testamentum Graece, Nestle-Aland, 27th ed.
NABPR	National Association of Baptist Professors of Religion
NCB	New Century Bible
NEchtB	Neue Echter Bibel
NEB.AT	Neue Echter Bibel. Kommentar zum AT
NHS	Nag Hammadi Studies
NIB	*New Interpreters Bible*
NICNT	New International Commentary on the New Testament
NIGTC	New International Greek Testament Commentary
NISB	*New Interpreter's Study Bible*
NJBC	*New Jerome Bible Commentary*
NPNF	*Nicene and Post-Nicene Fathers*
NovT	*Novum Testamentum*
NovTSup	Novum Testamentum Supplements
NTAbh	Neuetestamentliche Abhandlungen
NTD	Das Neue Testament Deutsch
NTG	New Testament Guides
NTL	New Testament Library
NTOA	Novum Testamentum et Orbis Antiquus
NTS	*New Testament Studies*
OBO	Orbis biblicus et orientalis
OLZ	*Orientalistische Literaturzeitung*
OTL	Old Testament Library
OtSt	*Oudtestamentische Studiën*
OTP	*Old Testament Pseudepigrapha*. Edited by J. H. Charlesworth. 2 vols. New York, 1983
PAAJR	*Proceedings of the American Academy of Jewish Research*
PatMS	Patristic Monograph Series
PRSt	*Perspectives in Religious Studies*
PSBA	*Proceedings of the Society of Biblical Archaeology*
PTMS	Pittsburgh Theological Monograph Series

PVTG	Pseudepigrapha Veteris Testamenti Graece
RB	*Revue biblique*
RBL	*Ruch biblijny i liturgiczny*
REJ	*Revue des études juives*
RGG	*Religion in Geschichte und Gegenwart.* Edited by K. Galling. 7 vols. 3d ed. Tübingen, 1957-1965
RHR	*Revue de l'historia des religions*
RevQ	*Revue de Qumran*
RelSRev	*Religious Studies Review*
RSR	*Recherches de science religieuse*
Sem	*Semitica*
SAC	Studies in Antiquity and Christianity
SecCent	*Second Century*
SB	Sources biblique
SB(J)	Sainte bible traduite en français sous la direction de l'École Biblique de Jérusalem
SBAB	Stuttgarter biblischa Beiträge
SBB	Stuttgarter biblische Beiträge
SBEC	Studies of the Bible and Early Christianity
SBFLA	*Studii biblici Franciscani liber annus*
SBLDS	Society of Biblical Literature Dissertation Series
SBLEJL	Society of Biblical Literature Early Judaism and Its Literature
SBLNTGF	Society of Biblical Literature The New Testament in the Greek Fathers
SBLSCS	Society of Biblical Literature Septuagint and Cognate Studies
SBLSP	*Society of Biblical Literature Seminar Papers*
SBLTT	Society of Biblical Literature Texts and Translations
SBS	Stuttgarter Bibelstudien
SBT	Studies in Biblical Theology
SC	Sources chrétiennes. Paris: Cerf, 1943-
SE	*Studia evangelica I, II, III* (=TU 73 [1959], 87 [1964], 88 [1964], etc.)
SEÅ	*Svensk exegetisk årsbok*
SHCT	Studies in the History of Christian Thought
ScrHier	Scripta hierosolymitana
SecCent	*Second Century*
StEv	*Studia Evangelica*
StPB	Studia Post-biblica
StTh	Studia Theoloica
SNT	Schriften des Neven Testaments
SNTSMS	Society for New Testament Studies Monograph Series
SP	Sacra pagina
SPB	Studia postbiblica
SSEJC	*Studies in Early Judaism and Christianity*
STDJ	*Studies on the Text of the Desert of Judah*
SUNT	Studien zur Umwelt des Neuen Testaments
SUNY	State University of New York
SVTP	Studia in Veteris Testamenti pseudepigraphica
SVTQ	*Saint Vladimir's Theological Quarterly*
TazB	Texte und Arbeiten zur Bibel
TANZ	Texte und Arbeiten zum neutestamentlichen Zietalter

TBT	*The Bible Today*
TD	*Theology Digest*
TDNT	*Theological Dictionary of the New Testament.* Edited by G. Kittel and G. Friedrich. Translated by G. W. Bromiley. 10 vols. Grand Rapids, 1964-1976
THBW	Theologische-homiletisches Bibelwerk
THKNT	Theologischer Handkommentar zum Neuen Testament
ThJb(T)	Theologischer Jahrbuch, Tübingen
TKNT	Theologischer Kommentar zum Neuen Testament
TLZ	*Theologische Literaturzeitung*
TRE	*Theologische Realenzyklopädie.* Edited by G. Krause and G. Müller. Berlin, 1977-
TRev	*Theologische Revue*
TRu	*Theologische Rundschau*
TSAJ	Texte und Studien zum antiken Judentum
TS	Texts and Studies
TSK	*Theologische Studien und Kritiken*
TU	Texte und Untersuchungen
TZ	*Theologische Zeitschrift*
TZT	Texte zur Theologie
TUMSR	Trinity University Monograph Series in Religion
UBS^4	*The Greek New Testament* United Bible Societies, 4th ed.
UNT	Untersuchungen zum Neuen Testament
UTB	Uni-Taschenbücher
VC	*Vigiliae christianae*
VTSup	Vetus Testamentum Supplements
WATSA	What Are They Saying About Series
WBC	World Biblical Commentary
WMANT	Wissenschaftliche Monographien zum Alten und Neuen Testament
WUNT	Wissenschaftliche Untersuchungen zum Neuen Testament
WZKM	*Wiener Zeitschrift für die Kunde des Morgenlandes*
ZAW	*Zeitschrift für die alttestamentliche Wissenschaft*
ZBNT	Zürcher Bibelkommentor/Neves Testament
ZKG	*Zeitschrift für Kirchengeschichte*
ZKT	*Zeitschrift für katholische Theologies*
ZNW	*Zeitschrift für die neutestamentliche Wissenschaft und die Kunde der älteren Kirche*
ZTK	*Zeitschrift für Theologie und Kirche*

CONTRIBUTORS

David E. Aune
University of Notre Dame
Notre Dame, Indiana

Ernest Best
University of Glasgow
Glasgow, Scotland

George J. Brooke
The University of Manchester
Manchester, United Kingdom

William P. Brown
Union Theological Seminary
Richmond, Virginia

James H. Charlesworth
Princeton Theological Seminary
Princeton, New Jersey

Randall D. Chestnutt
Pepperdine University
Seaver College
Malibu, California

John J. Collins
Yale Divinity School
New Haven, Connecticut

Raymond F. Collins
The Catholic University of America
Washington, D.C.

Alexander A. Di Lella
The Catholic University of America
Washington, D.C.

Tamara C. Eskenazi
Hebrew Union College
Los Angeles, California

Peter W. Flint
Trinity Wesleyan University
Langley, British Columbia
Canada

Victor P. Furnish
Perkins School of Theology
Southern Methodist University
Dallas, Texas

John J. Hayes
Candler School of Theology
Emory University
Atlanta, Georgia

Martha Himmelfarb
Princeton University
Princeton, New Jersey

Morna D. Hooker
University of Cambridge
Cambridge, England

Frank W. Hughes
Codrington College
St. John, Barbados

John C. Hurd
Trinity College
University of Toronto
Toronto, Ontario, Canada

Luke T. Johnson
Candler School of Theology
Emory University
Atlanta, Georgia

Warren S. Kissinger
Library of Congress
Washington, D.C.

Robert D. Kysar
Candler School of Theology
Emory University
Atlanta, Georgia

Betty Jane Lillie
Pleasant Ridge, Ohio

Jennifer B. Maclean
Roanoke College
Roanoke, Virginia

J. Ramsey Michaels
Emeritus
Southwest Missouri State University
Springfield, Missouri

G. Tom Milazzo
Greensboro, North Carolina

C. A. Moore
Emeritus
Gettysburg College
Gettysburg, Pennsylvania

Robert Morgan
University of Oxford
Oxford, England

Frederick J. Murphy
College of the Holy Cross
Worcester, Massachusetts

Jerome Neyrey
University of Notre Dame
Notre Dame, Indiana

John C. O'Neill
University of Edinburgh
Edinburgh, Scotland

David B. Peabody
Nebraska Wesleyan University
Lincoln, Nebraska

William Poehlmann
St. Olaf College
Northfield, Minnesota

John F. Priest (Deceased)
Florida State University
Tallahassee, Florida

Heikki Räisänen
University of Helsinki
Helsinki, Finland

Bo Reicke (deceased)
University of Basel
Basel, Switzerland

Calvin J. Roetzel
Emeritus
Macalester College
St. Paul, Minnesota

Jürgen Roloff
Friedrich-Alexander-Universität
Erlangen
Erlangen, Germany

Lawrence H. Schiffman
New York University
New York, New York

Charles S. Shaw
Greer, South Carolina

Graham N. Stanton
Fitzwilliam College
University of Cambridge
Cambridge, England

Georg Strecker (deceased)
Georg-August-Universität
Göttingen
Göttingen, Germany

Charles H. Talbert
Baylor University
Waco, Texas

Walter F. Taylor
Trinity Lutheran Seminary
Columbus, Ohio

James C. VanderKam
University of Notre Dame
Notre Dame, Indiana

John S. Kloppenborg Verbin
University of St. Michael's College
Toronto, Ontario
Canada

Arthur W. Wainwright
Emeritus
Candler School of Theology
Emory University
Atlanta, Georgia

Frances M. Young
University of Birmingham
Birmingham, England

Matthew, Gospel of

The evangelist's purposes and the setting of his Gospel within first-century Judaism and Christianity raise numerous questions that have continued to fascinate and bemuse scholars. Was Matt a conservative Jewish Christian whose community retained its links with contemporary Judaism? Or was he a Gentile whose readers had abandoned completely their earlier links with Judaism? Did he understand "this gospel of the kingdom" (24:14) to be "true Judaism," "fulfilled Judaism," or a "new religion"? Did he intend to counter the views of some extreme Paulists? Why is his anti-Jewish polemic even more ferocious than it is in the sources on which he drew? These questions have been debated keenly since the development of historical criticism at the end of the eighteenth century, which led to a much deeper appreciation of the distinctive features of Matthew's Gospel. Until then Matthew's theological perspective and the historical setting of his Gospel had not been sharply differentiated from those of Mark and Luke.

1. *Early Interpretation.* Soon after its composition, the Gospel of Matthew became the dominant account of the life and teaching of Jesus[§]. Toward the end of the second century, John's Gospel began to rival Matthew's in popularity; but by then Matt had already created the climate of ordinary Christianity in most parts of the church. In the early centuries Matt was cited and commented on more frequently than the other Gospels were. With a few exceptions, Matt heads lists and manuscript copies of the four Gospels. The early widespread use of Matt is easy to explain: In the early church there was universal acceptance of the tradition that Matt the apostle had written it. Matthew's stylistic abilities and his full and carefully ordered collections of the sayings of Jesus in five discourses made his Gospel particularly useful for catechetical instruction. Its Jewish features encouraged Jewish Christian groups (of various kinds) to use it, and its pro-Gentile passages ensured its ready acceptance by the Gentile church.

The terse comment of Papias[§] on the Gospel's origin was influential from the middle of the second century until the early decades of this century. About 130 C.E. Papias stated that "Matt put together in the Hebrew language the discourses and each one translated them as best he could" (Eusebius *Hist. eccl.* 3.39.14). There is still no agreement on the precise meaning of these words, however. Did Papias think that Matt was written in Hebrew or in Aramaic? Or was he referring to Matthew's "Jewish forms of expression" in his Greek Gospel? Was he referring to the composition of the five discourses, to Q, or to the whole Gospel? Did Papias mean that the discourses were translated from one language to another or simply interpreted? Irenaeus[§] probably knew Papias's comment; he certainly accepted this explanation of the Gospel's origin, adding that Matt was written for "preaching among Hebrews" (*Adv. haer.* 1; Fr. 29). Tatian[§], who composed a harmony of the four Gospels (about 170 C.E.), thought that Matt provided the most reliable historical account of the ministry of Jesus before the passion. Most other early Christian writers assumed that Matthew's Gospel contained the very words of Jesus. The one great exception was Origen[§], who distinguished between the literal and spiritual (or allegorical) meanings of the text, but his position did not win the day. Almost all interpreters assumed (without discussion) the traditional view that Matt the apostle wrote the first Gospel in Hebrew and that he had provided an accurate account of the life and teaching of Jesus.

2. *Reformation.* Luther[§] frequently quoted verses from Matt, but in the 1522 preface to his translation of the New Testament, he singled out John, 1 John, Romans, Galatians, Ephesians, and 1 Peter as "the true and noblest books of the New Testament." Luther was aware of some of the problems facing the reader of Matt. For example, he knew that the infancy narratives in Matt and Luke could not be harmonized. He also recognized that Matt 27:9

mistakenly cites Jeremiah for Zechariah but commented, "such points do not bother me particularly" (1955, 20:125). Given his distinctive theological criterion for the interpretation of Scripture, his indifference is no surprise.

Calvin[§], on the other hand, parted company with the views of the origin of Matt that were almost universal in the early church. He claimed that since Matt cited the Greek translation of the Hebrew Bible, he could not have composed his Gospel in Hebrew. He firmly rejected Augustine's[§] opinion (which he mistakenly attributed to Jerome) that Mark is an abridgement of Matt and conjectured (cautiously) that Mark had not seen Matt when he wrote. Calvin did not explore the relationship between Matt, Mark, and Luke closely; but he insisted that it was impossible to expound properly any one of the evangelists without comparing him with the other two.

Calvin's commentary on his own harmony of the synoptic Gospels followed Matthew's order very closely; yet he did not suppose that Matt had provided a verbatim and chronologically accurate account of the life and teaching of Jesus. In several places Calvin suggested that both Matt and Luke rearranged the traditions to suit their own purposes. In his comments on Matt 23:34, Calvin conceded that Matthew's version of the saying of Jesus is "defective: its meaning must be supplied from the words of Luke" (1956, 3:101). These anticipations of modern Gospel criticism, however, are comparatively infrequent in Calvin's crisp exposition. More often than not he simply noted but did not account for the differences between the synoptic Gospels. Like Luther, and unlike several writers in the early church, he rarely attempted to explain the differences between the synoptic Gospels and John.

3. *The Rise of Modern Study of Matthew.* The development of historical criticism in the eighteenth century led to a thorough investigation of the origins and distinctive features of the four canonical Gospels. Although the traditional view that Matt was the first Gospel to be written was frequently challenged in the final decades of the eighteenth century, it was still widely supported in the middle of the nineteenth century. In 1847 F. C. Baur[§] set out his views on the "tendencies" of the four evangelists as part of his bold reconstruction of the development of earliest Christianity. Baur accepted J. J. Griesbach's[§] view (1783) that Luke used Matt (the first Gospel) and that Mark used both Matt and Luke. With the exception of passages that expected an imminent Parousia, Baur considered Matthew's "Jewish" Gospel as historically reliable. In contrast, just a few years earlier in 1838 C. Wilke[§] and H. Weisse[§] had independently defended Markan priority, but their case was accepted only slowly. In 1911 the Pontifical Biblical Commission still echoed Papias in its insistence that the apostle Matt wrote the first Gospel—and not merely a collection of *logia*. By then (with the notable exception of T. von Zahn 1897-99) most Protestant scholars, however, had accepted Markan priority.

Abandonment of the traditional view of Matthew's origin led to a reappraisal of its distinctive features and its setting in early Christianity. Once Markan priority was accepted, it became impossible to equate the "Jewishness" of Matt with its early origin in Palestine and authorship by the apostle. In 1918 B. Bacon[§] argued that the evangelist had gathered together teaching material from his sources into five great discourses that correspond to the five books of the commandments of Moses. Ten years later E. von Dobschütz[§] (1928) claimed that since Matt was primarily concerned with catechetical instruction, the evangelist was a converted rabbi who had probably been trained in the school of Johanan ben Zakkai immediately after the fall of Jerusalem in 70 C.E. The Gospel's structure, its overall purpose, and its relationship to contemporary Judaism have all been high on the agenda of Matthean specialists ever since.

4. *Modern Trends in Interpretation.* The period immediately after 1945 is particularly important for the modern interpretation of Matt. G. Kilpatrick, K. Stendahl[§], and W. D. Davies[§] each wrote influential books. Kilpatrick (1946) wrote a major study of the origins and purposes of Matt, some parts of which anticipated the later development of redaction criticism. His exposition of

Matthean style and of the Gospel's relationship to Judaism stimulated further discussion; however, his claim that Matt was written to be read liturgically has attracted less attention, although it is a plausible explanation of many of the Gospel's distinctive features. Stendahl (1954) claimed that in Matthew's "formula" quotations of the HB, the biblical text is treated in somewhat the same manner as in the Habakkuk scroll that had recently been discovered at Qumran (Dead Sea Scrolls[§]). In a lengthy and thorough study of the setting of the Sermon on the Mount in early Judaism and in early Christianity, Davies (1964) cautiously suggested that the sermon (and by implication, the whole Gospel) was a kind of Christian counterpart to aspects of the reconstruction of Judaism that occurred at Jamnia following the fall of Jerusalem in 70 C.E.

a. Redaction criticism. In the meantime a fresh approach to the interpretation of Matt had developed in Germany. G. Bornkamm's[§] 1948 essay (G. Bornkamm; G. Barth; and H. Held 1960) on the stilling of the storm pericope marks the beginning of the thoroughgoing redaction-critical approach that dominated Matthean scholarship for more than thirty years. Assuming that Matt had used Mark's account of the stilling of the storm, Bornkamm paid close attention to the additions, modifications, and omissions the evangelist made as well as to the different context in which the pericope had been placed. Bornkamm concluded that Matt had not merely handed down the Markan story but had expounded its theological significance in his own way. Thus Matt is the first exegete of the Markan pericope. Matthew's redaction of Mark (which often appears at first to involve changes to purely incidental details) shows "proof of definite theological intentions" with its references to discipleship and to "the little ship of the church."

This essay (which was not translated into English until 1963) paved the way for a number of redactional studies of Matthean themes or sections of the Gospel, all of which drew attention to Matthew's distinctive theological viewpoint. In the first phase of redaction criticism, outstanding monographs were published by W. Trilling (1959), G. Strecker (1962), and R. Hummel (1963). Although they have never been translated into English, in due course they encouraged many English-speaking scholars to use redaction-critical methods. The translation into English in 1968 of J. Rohde's thorough survey of the first phase of redaction-critical work on Matt stimulated further research from this standpoint. Careful isolation of the evangelist's redaction of his sources has been the basis of numerous expositions of Matthew's Christology, his ecclesiology, and the relationship of his community to contemporary Judaism.

In the first phase of redaction criticism, few scholars challenged the presupposition that Matt wove together Mark, Q, and some special traditions (see, however, A. Butler 1951). W. Farmer[§] (1964) and C. Tuckett (1983) have also expressed doubts about Markan priority. However, Markan priority remains the basis of most Matthean scholarship in the last decades of the twentieth century. Criticism of Q has been more rigorous. M. Goulder (1974), for example, claimed that apart from a handful of oral traditions Mark was Matthew's only source. Matt used midrashic methods (Midrash*[§]) and freely expanded Mark for liturgical purposes. Goulder's exposition of Matthean style has been warmly welcomed, but his midrashic and lectionary theories have been severely criticized. Goulder (1989) also published a thorough defense of the view that Luke used Matt and Mark but not Q. If so, then Luke becomes the very first interpreter of Matt! In order to advance his own particular views, Luke virtually demolished Matthew's carefully constructed discourses and abandoned Matthew's finely honed phrases and distinctive vocabulary.

Many scholars acknowledge that the Q hypothesis has difficulties, but consider these minimal in comparison with those faced by rival views of Matthew's and Luke's redactional methods. In their multi-volume commentaries on Matt, U. Luz (3 vols. 1985, 1990, 1997), J. Gnilka (2 vols. 1986, 1988), and W. D. Davies and D. Allison (3 vols. 1988, 1991, 1997) all accept that Matt used both Mark and Q and that redaction criticism remains the most fruitful way of uncovering the Evangelist's purposes.

Redaction critics of Matt must continue to address four important issues. First, they must recognize the possibility that some of the Evangelist's modifications are stylistic rather than theological. For example, Matthew's accounts of the feeding of the five thousand and of the four thousand have been said to reflect more clearly than Mark 6:41; 8:6 the institution of the Eucharist; yet, on closer inspection Matthew's alterations of Mark turn out to be completely consistent with purely stylistic modifications he makes elsewhere.

Second, they must be careful not to gloss over inconsistencies too readily and thus set aside one strand of the evidence as "pre-Matthean tradition" and accept another as the evangelist's own contribution. In 10:5-6, for example, the disciples are forbidden to go to the Gentiles but are sent to "the lost sheep of the house of Israel." How can this passage be related to the universalist, pro-Gentile and anti-Jewish sayings found throughout the Gospel? Matthew's attitude to the law is equally problematic. While most redaction critics agree that it is generally more conservative than Mark's, the evangelist included disparate or even contradictory statements. M. Suggs (1970) echoed the depair of many redaction critics when he concluded that Matthew's presentation of Jesus' attitude to the law makes jugglers of us all!

Third, redaction critics must acknowledge that Matt frequently used his traditions with little or no modification simply because he accepted them and wished to preserve them and make them part of his portrait of Jesus and of his message to his own Christian communities. Earlier traditions reflect Matthew's theological convictions just as much as his redactional modification; Matt used material from his tradition in the service of his own major themes and purposes.

Fourth, redaction critics must become aware that Matt is writing a Gospel, not a letter, and that it is most unlikely that he intended to counter the views of a particular group of Christians. Although several scholars have accepted G. Barth's view (Bornkamm, Barth, and Held) that Matt opposed Christian antinomian heretics who threatened the true life of the congregation, Matthew's references to "lawlessness" and to "false prophets" in key passages are general and not limited specifically to antinomians.

b. Literary-critical approaches. Literary-critical*§ and Social-Scientific*§ insights have become prominent in interpretation of Matt, but not as a result of a strong conviction that redaction criticism is a misguided method. Some scholars have felt that since that particular seam has, as it were, now been almost fully worked out, methods that have been fruitful in the study of other biblical writings should be explored. Other scholars, accepting that literary criticism and social-scientific criticism are natural outgrowths of redaction criticism, have used these methods to gain insight into the Gospel of Matt.

Literary-critical studies have taken several forms, including: Structuralism*§, Narrative Criticism*§, and Reader-Response Criticism*§. In 1987 D. Patte published a full structuralist commentary concerned with the evangelist's faith (or "system of convictions") rather than with the Gospel's first-century setting. He works with two basic premises. Since Matt has set out not only what he wants to say but also what he does not want to say, attention must be paid to "narrative oppositions" in the text. In addition, the interpreter must look for the tensions between the readers' "old knowledge" and the "new knowledge" that the evangelist is seeking to communicate. Patte lucidly expounds one form of structuralism and shows how it might be used in exegesis. He does not reject traditional methods—they are in fact used in his notes. However, he fails to show how a structuralist approach might be integrated with other methods to provide a fresh reading of the text.

In the mid-1980s, R. Edwards (1985) and J. Kingsbury (1986) used narrative-critical methods in order to elucidate the meaning of Matt for readers today. Their work has been developed further by a number of younger scholars, several of whom were Kingsbury's doctoral students (D. Bauer 1988; D. Weaver 1990). Narrative-critical studies of Matt have their roots in "composition criticism," a modified form of redaction criticism that set out Matthew's distinctive viewpoint without source-critical presuppositions. Attention was directed away from Matthew's redaction of his sources to his methods of composition, to the overall structure of the Gospel, to the structure of individual sections and sub-sections, and to the order in which traditions are placed. In his study of Matthew's fourth discourse in chap. 18, for example, W. Thompson (1970) insisted that Matt must be read "in terms of Matt," a method he dubbed "vertical analysis" in contrast to the "horizontal analysis" of redaction criticism. Narrative criticism also concentrates on the evangelist's methods of composition, but unlike composition criticism it draws explicitly on the insights of modern literary critics.

Like scholars who use structuralist methods, narrative critics are less interested in the historical context of Matt than in the ways the text elicits the reader's response. Matt is understood to be a narrative comprising a story and its discourse. The story of Matt is of the life of Jesus of Nazareth from conception and birth to death and resurrection. The discourse is the language, including the many devices of plot, characterization, rhetoric, and point of view that are the means by which the story is put across. Kingsbury's earlier redaction-critical study of Matt (1975) concentrated on the structure, Christology, and eschatology of the Gospel. In his narrative-critical study (1986) many of his conclusions are similar, but he does not integrate the two methods.

Edwards's and Kingsbury's (1986) books anticipated the use of reader-response criticism in Matthean scholarship. Howell (1990) used "selected aspects of narrative criticism and a type of reader response criticism" in order to increase appreciation of the way Matthew's narrative shapes one's experience of the story. The word "inclusive" in the title points to Howell's intention to show the ways readers are involved (i.e., "included") in the story and teaching of the Gospel. Howell's monograph has raised an issue that will almost certainly be keenly debated: the extent to which literary approaches can be combined with more traditional historical methods. Howell has insisted that the intention of the evangelist and the historical situation in which the text was produced are not a matter of indifference for the biblical literary critic. G. N. Stanton (1992) claims that although modern literary theory is stimulating and helpful, precedence must be given both to the literary conventions that influenced the Evangelist and to the expectations of his first-century readers: Interpretation of a text cannot be carried out in isolation from consideration of the social setting of its readers (whether ancient or modern).

c. Social-scientific approaches. Many New Testament writings have been studied fruitfully from several social-scientific perspectives. Unfortunately, Matthew's Gospel does not lend itself as readily to a social-historical approach as do many other New Testament writings. Whereas many details in Paul's[†§] correspondence with the Corinthians, for example, can be set firmly in the social setting of Corinth in the middle of the first century, we do not know for certain where Matt wrote. Although many writers accept that Matt was written in Antioch, the evidence is far from conclusive, even though we know a good deal about earliest Christianity in Antioch and also about the city itself. But even if we could be certain about the geographical setting of the Gospel, a further problem would remain. Whereas the social historian's eye often alights on incidental details, it is often difficult to know whether such details in Matt reflect the social setting of the earlier traditions used by the evangelist or his own social setting. These problems vitiate several of the essays edited by D. Balch (1991), some of which are written from a social-historical perspective, while others use sociological models (Sociology and New Testament Studies[†§]).

Sociological and anthropological theory regularly make use of "models" constructed on the basis of Cross-Cultural Studies*[§] of a wide range of phenomena from different historical periods. These "distant comparisons" are based on sets of similarities in the behavior of individuals, groups, and communities in a range of cultural settings. In spite of obvious differences, striking recurrent patterns can be observed that are not specific to a particular culture or historical setting. They offer students of first-century writings possible fresh ways of reading the text by encouraging them to keep a keen lookout for further relationships, analogies, and resemblances. This general approach is developed effectively by B. Malina and J. Neyrey (1988), who use anthropological models drawn from studies of witchcraft societies to interpret the accusations leveled against Jesus in Matt 12. In the second part of their book they draw on labeling and deviance theory in a study of Matthew's passion narratives in chaps. 26 and 27. In a stimulating essay in the volume of cross-disciplinary essays edited by Balch (1991), A. Wire employs macro-sociological analysis to reconstruct roles characteristic of scribal communities within advanced agricultural societies.

Sociological models built on the basis of distant comparisons of cross-cultural social settings will rarely be sharply defined. "Close comparisons," however, provide a useful complement to distant comparisons. Careful consideration of communities that have similar cultural and historical settings is often instructive. Here the differences (which are rarely significant when distant comparisons are used) cry out for explanation. The similarities in the social phenomena may provide confirmation of assumptions about a particular writing or community as well as a check against the obvious dangers in transferring insights drawn from studies of modern societies into first-century settings.

J. Overman (1990) and Stanton (1992) both use close comparisons to complement distant comparisons in sociological studies of Matt. Overman argues that social developments within the Matthean community frequently parallel and are analogous to the social and institutional developments within a range of first-century Jewish groups and sects. Stanton uses the Damascus Document from Qumran as a close comparison and suggests that both Matt and the Damascus Document come from strikingly similar settings: They were both written for sectarian communities that were in sharp conflict with parent bodies from which they had recently parted company painfully. Both writings functioned as foundation documents for their respective communities; they used several strategies to legitimate the separation. This understanding of the relationship of Matthew's readers to Judaism is in sharp contrast to the conclusions reached by A. Saldarini (1994), who insists that Matthew's Christian-Jewish group remained a deviant community within the diverse Judaism of the day.

Literary and social-scientific approaches have undoubtedly brought new vitality to the study of Matthew's Gospel, however, their strengths and weaknesses for interpreting Matt will need to be assessed critically, just as the usefulness of redaction criticism for Matthean studies has been reconsidered. Showing promise for the future of Matthean scholarship are studies that have used these approaches to focus on the role of women in this Gospel (J. Anderson 1983, 1987; E. Cheney 1996, 1998; A. J. Levine 1992; E. Schaberg 1987; E. Wainwright 1991, 1994).

Recent commentaries on Matt include Carter (2000) from a social science and liberation approach, Schnackenburg (2002), and Senior (1988). Recent studies of Matt include various forms of literary criticism (Brown 2002; Powell 2001; Repschinski 2000; Yamasaki 1998), social science analysis (Neyrey 1998; Scheuermann 1996), feminist critique (Levine and Blickenstaff 2001; Mattila 2002; Wainwright 1998), Matt and the Synoptic Problem (Krämer 1997), Matthew's critique of the Roman empire (Carter 2001), Jesus' conflicts with religious and political authorities (Gielen 1998), and various studies of Matthean theology (Cousland 2002; Gench 1997; Luomanen 1998; Yong-Eui 1997).

Bibliography: J. C. Anderson, "Matthew: Gender and Reading," *Semeia* 28 (1983) 3-27; "Mary's Difference: Gender and Patriarchy in the Birth Narratives," *JR 67* (1987) 183-202; *Matthew's Narrative Web: Over, and Over, and Over Again* (JSNTSup 91, 1993). **B. W. Bacon,** *Studies in Matthew* (1930). **D. R. Balch** (ed.), *Social History of the Matthean Community: Crossdisciplinary Approaches* (1991). **D. R. Bauer,** *The Structure of Matthew's Gospel: A Study* in Literary Design (JSNTSup 31, 1988). **D. R. Bauer and M. A. Powell** (eds.), Treasures New and Old: Recent Contributions to Matthean Studies (Symposium Series 1, 1996). **F. C. Baur,** Kritische Untersuchungen über die kanonische Evangelien (1847). **M. E. Boring,** "The Gospel of Matthew," NIB (1995) 8:87-505. **G. Bornkamm, G. Barth, and H. J. Held,** Überlieferung und Auslegung im Matthäusevangelium (1960; ET Tradition and Interpretation in Matthew [1963, 1983²]). **J. K. Brown,** The Disciples in Narrative Perspective: The Portrayal and Function of the Matthean Disciples (Academia Biblica 9, 2002). **R. E. Brown,** The Birth of the Messiah: A Commentary on the Infancy Narratives in Matthew and Luke (1977). **A. B. C. Butler,** The Originality of St. Matthew: A Critique of the Two-Document Hypothesis (1951). **J. Calvin,** Commentary of a Harmony of the Evangelists Matthew, Mark, and Luke (tr. W. Pringle, 1956). **W. Carter,** Matthew: Storyteller, Interpreter, Evangelist (1996); Matthew And The Margins: A Sociopolitical And Religious Reading (Bible and Liberation, 2000); Matthew and Empire: Initial Explorations (2001). **E. Cheney,** She Can Read (1996); "The Mother of the Sons of Zebedee," JSNT 68 (1998) 13-21. **J. R. C. Cousland,** The Crowds in the Gospel of Matthew (NovTSup 102, 2002). **W. D. Davies,** The Sermon on the Mount (1966). **W. D. Davies and D. C. Allison,** A Critical and Exegetical Commentary on the Gospel According to Saint Matthew (ICC, 3 vols. 1988, 1991, 1997). **E. von Dobschütz,** "Matthäus als Rabbi und Katechet," ZNW 27 (1928) 338-48 (ET "Matthew as Rabbi and Catechist," The Interpretation of Matthew, ed. G. N. Stanton, 1983). **R. A. Edwards,** Matthew's Story of Jesus (1985); Matthew's Narrative Portrait of Disciples (1997). **W. R. Farmer,** The Synoptic Problem: A Critical Analysis (1964). **R. T. France,** Matthew: Evangelist and Teacher (1988). **F. T. Gench,** Wisdom in the Christology of Matthew (1997). **M. Gielen,** Der Konflikt Jesu mit den religiösen und politischen Autoritäten seines Volkes im Spiegel der matthäischen Jesusgeschichte (BBB 115, 1998). **M. D. Goulder,** Midrash and Lection in Matthew (1974); Luke, a New Paradigm (2 vols. JSNTSup 20, 1989). **J. Gnilka,** Das Matthäus-evangelium (HThK, 1986-88). **R. H. Gundry,** Matthew: A Commentary on His Literary and Theological Art (1982, 1994²). **D. A. Hagner,** Matthew (WBC 33A, 1993; 33B, 1995). **D. B. Howell,** Matthew's Inclusive Rhetoric: A Study in the Narrative Rhetoric of the First Gospel (JSNTSup 42, 1990). **R. Hummel,** Die Auseinandersetzung zwischen Kirche und Judentum im Matthäusevangelium (BEvT 33, 1963). **G. D. Kilpatrick,** The Origins of the Gospel According to St. Matthew (1946). **J. D. Kingsbury,** Matthew: Structure, Christology, and Kingdom (1975); Matthew as Story (1986, 1988²); Gospel Interpretation: Narrative Critical and Social Scientific Approaches (1997). **M. Krämer,** Die Entstehungsgeschichte der synoptischen Evangelien: das Matthäusevangelium (1997). **A. J. Levine,** "Matthew," The Women's Bible Commentary (ed. C. A. Newsom and S. H. Ringe, 1992) 252-62. **A. J. Levine with M. Blilckenstaff,** A Feminist Companion to Matthew (Feminist Companion to the New Testament and Early Christian writings 1, 2001). **P. Luomanen,** Entering the Kingdom of Heaven: A Study on the Structure of Matthew's View of Salvation (WUNT 2/101, 1998). **M. Luther,** Luther's Works 20 (ed. H. C. Oswald, 1955). **U. Luz,** Das Evangelium nach Matthäus (3 vols. EKKNT 1-3, 1985, 1990, 1997; ET 1989, 2001, forthcoming); Matthew in History: Interpretation, Influence, and Effects (1994); The Theology of the Gospel of Matthew (NT Theology, 1995). **B. J. Malina and J. H. Neyrey,** Calling Jesus Names: The Social Value of Labels in Matthew (FF, Social Facets, 1988). **T. Mattila,** Citizens of the Kingdom: Followers in Matthew from a Feminist Perspective (Suomen Eksegeettisen Seuran julkaisuja 83, 2002). **J. H. Neyrey,** Honor and Shame in the Gospel of Matthew (1998). **J. A. Overman,** Matthew's Gospel and Formative Judaism: The Social World of the Matthean Community (1990). **D. Patte,** The Gospel According to Matthew: A Structural Commentary on Matthew's Faith (1987). **M. A. Powell,** God with Us: A Pastoral Theology of Matthew's Gospel (1995); Chasing the Eastern Star: Adventures in Biblical Reader-Response Criticism (2001). **B. Repschinski,** The Controversy Stories in the Gospel of Matthew (FRLANT 189, 2000).

J. Rohde, *Die Redaktionsgeschichtliche Methode* (1966; ET 1968). **A. J. Saldarini,** *Matthew's Christian-Jewish Community* (CSJH, 1994). **J. Schaberg,** *The Illegitimacy of Jesus: A Feminist Theological Interpretation of the Infancy Narratives* (1987). **G. Scheuermann,** *Gemeinde im Umbruch: Eine sozialgeschichtliche Studie zum Matthäusevangelium* (FB 77, 1996). **R. Schnackenburg,** *The Gospel of Matthew* (trans. R. R. Barr, 2002). **E. Schweizer,** *The Good News According to Matthew* (1975). **D. Senior,** *Matthew* (ANTC, 1998). **G. N. Stanton** (ed.), *The Interpretation of Matthew* (IRT 3, 1983, 1995[2]); *A Gospel for a New People: Studies in Matthew* (1992). **K. Stendahl,** *The School of St. Matthew and Its Use of the OT* (ASNU 20, 1954, 19682). **G. Strecker,** *Der Weg der Gerechtigkeit Untersuchung zur Theologie des Matthäus* (FRLANT 82, 1962). **M. J. Suggs,** *Wisdom, Christology, and Law in Matthew's Gospel* (1970). **W. G. Thompson,** *Matthew's Advice to a Divided Community: Matthew 17:22-18:35* (AnBib 44, 1970). **W. Trilling,** *Das wahre Israel: Studien zur Theologie des Matthäusevangeliums* (1959). **C. M. Tuckett,** *The Revival of the Griesbach Hypothesis* (1983). **E. Wainwright,** *Towards a Feminist Critical Reading of the Gospel According to Matthew* (BZNW 60, 1991); "The Gospel of Matthew," Searching the Scriptures, vol. 2, *A Feminist Commentary* (ed. E. Schüssler Fiorenza, 1994) 635-77. **E. M. Wainwright,** *Shall We Look for Another? A Feminist Rereading of the Matthean Jesus* (Bible and Liberation, 1998). **D. J. Weaver,** *Matthew's Missionary Discourse* (JSNTSup 38, 1990). **C. H. Weisse,** *Die evangelische Geschichte, kritisch und philosophisch bearbeitet* (2 vols. 1838). **G. Yamasaki,** *John the Baptist in Life and Death: Audience-Oriented Criticism of Matthew's Narrative* (JSNT 167, 1998). **Y. Yong-Eui,** *Jesus and the Sabbath in Matthew's Gospel* (JSNTSup 139, 1997). **T. Zahn,** *Introduction to the NT* (2 vols. 1897-99).

G. N. STANTON

Mark, Gospel of

1. *Early Church*. If Markan priority is assumed, the earliest interpreters of Mark were Matthew and Luke, who used it as the basis of their own work; Matthew, in particular, took Mark's account as the framework of his Gospel. The earliest comment on the Gospel, however, goes back to Papias[§], bishop of Hierapolis, writing c. 130 C.E. (possibly a little earlier), whose words are quoted by Eusebius[§] (*Hist. eccl.* 3.39.15). Papias referred to the testimony of John the Elder to the effect that Mark was Peter's "interpreter" *(ermēneutēs)* and that he wrote down "accurately" *(akribōs)* but "not in order" *(ou mentoi taxei)* what he remembered of the words and deeds of the Lord as transmitted by Peter. According to Papias, Peter intended to provide instructions to meet the needs of the moment rather than a complete exposition of the Lord's ministry; thus Mark was not guilty of any blunder in writing an incomplete account. That Papias found it necessary to defend Mark against charges of recording events in the wrong order and of incompleteness indicates that he was already receiving an unfavorable comparison with the other evangelists. Unfortunately Papias's *Exposition of the Oracles of the Lord* in five books has not survived.

Nothing more is known about the author of the Gospel since he is not necessarily to be identified with the John Mark mentioned in Acts. During the next two centuries several writers mention the tradition associating him with Peter: Justin Martyr[§] (*Dial.* 106.3); the author of the Anti-Marcionite Prologue (c. 160-180); Clement of Alexandria[§] (Eusebius *Hist. eccl.* 6.14.6-7); Irenaeus[§] (*Adv. Haer.* 3.1.1); and Origen[§] (Eusebius, *Hist. eccl.* 6.25.5). Undoubtedly this association preserved the Gospel for posterity, for it was somewhat neglected by commentators and appears to have been used less than the other Gospels. Yet from the beginning it was included in the Canon[§] (although sometimes it was placed last of the four—in Codex Bezae, Codex W, and OL manuscripts) and was sufficiently established to be included by Tatian[§] in his *Diatessaron* (ca. 170).

In 1958 M. Smith (1973) discovered a copy of a letter claiming to have been written by Clement of Alexandria. This letter refers to a second, "more spiritual gospel" composed by Mark and containing additional material, which the Carpocratians had misused and also supplemented with material. Controversy has raged about the authenticity of the letter and the origin of the additional material (which amounts to only a few sentences). If the letter is genuine, it is evidence for an early gnosticizing interpretation of the Gospel (Gnostic Interpretation[§]).

Early interpreters of Mark include Origen, whose commentary has unfortunately not survived, Jerome[§], who used allegory in his interpretation and noted that 16:9-20 is missing from many Greek manuscripts, and Augustine[§], who dealt with the problem of inconsistencies and examined in detail the question of the relationship between the Gospels.

2. *Middle Ages and Reformation*. The close relationship between Mark and Matthew led to the comparative neglect of Mark over the next few centuries. Comment on Mark at this time (with notable exceptions such as Bede[§]) was often confined to those brief sections that do not have parallels in Matthew. The work of Erasmus[§] in publishing the Greek text opened up a new era of interpretation, and he personally published a Latin paraphrase of Mark in 1524. Luther[§], although he wrote no commentary on Mark, often commented on the Gospel in his sermons; rejecting allegorical exegesis, he insisted on "one simple solid sense." Calvin[§] wrote a commentary on a harmony of the Gospels (1555) in which he suggested that the similarities among them were due to the work of the Holy Spirit, while J. Hoffmeister (an ardent opponent of Luther) wrote a commentary on Mark expounding the literal meaning of the text. A century later J. Lightfoot[§] (1663) made a notable contribution by looking at the Gospels in the light of contemporary Jewish literature.

3. *The Ascendancy of Critical Study.* Critical study of the text began a new phase when J. Bengel[§] (1734) and J. Wettstein[§] (1751-52) provided critical editions of the Greek New Testament. In 1773 J. Elsner published a critical philological commentary on the Gospel of Mark, maintaining that Mark was the companion and interpreter of Peter, not an abbreviator of Matthew. All three editors took the last twelve verses to be genuine in spite of their omission from many manuscripts.

In 1774 J. J. Griesbach[§] published the first complete synopsis of the Gospels (in place of earlier harmonies), thus initiating critical investigation of the relationship between the synoptic Gospels. In his subsequent commentary (1789-90) he argued that Mark wrote last of the three synoptic evangelists and used both the other Gospels, aiming to produce a shorter book. Although H. Owen (1764) had already put forward a similar solution, this theory is known by Griesbach's name. Griesbach also suggested that the "original ending of Mark's gospel" (presumed to have followed 16:8) had been accidentally lost. Many scholars in the early nineteenth century accepted Griesbach's theory of synoptic relationships; F. C. Baur[§] (1851), for example, believed that Mark was written to reconcile the differences between Jews and Gentiles reflected in the other Synoptics.

But rival theories abounded. G. Lessing[§] (1778) argued that the agreements between the three synoptic Gospels could be explained on the assumption that the evangelists had all used a written Aramaic gospel of the Nazarenes. Lessing's theory was developed by J. G. Eichhorn[§] (1794), who maintained that the hypothesis of a common source is the only possible explanation of the fact that none of the Gospels consistently offers the best text in comparison with the others. J. G. Herder[§] (1796-97) believed the primal gospel had been an oral gospel and had been best reproduced in Mark, whereas K. Lachmann[§] (1835) argued that Mark best preserved the order of the original source. J. Koppe[§] had already challenged Augustine (1782) by arguing that the shorter Gospel was probably chronologically prior to the longer, although he was still thinking in terms of the evangelists' using common sources. Then in 1786 G. Storr argued that Matthew and Luke had actually used Mark. This idea was not pursued, however, until 1838, when C. Wilke[§] and C. Weisse[§] independently of each other advocated Markan priority. Both are generally credited as the originators of the Markan hypothesis—namely, that Mark is the earliest Gospel, that Matthew and Luke both used Mark, and that Mark provides a reliable historical basis for the life of Jesus[§].

The importance of this debate lay in its relevance to the question of the nature of the Gospels and their value as historical documents. The rationalistic interpretations of the Gospel narratives by H. S. Reimarus[§] (1774-78) and H. Paulus (1800, 1828) were followed by D. F. Strauss's[§] (1835-36) argument that the Gospel material was primarily mythological (Mythology and Biblical Studies*[§]). In reaction to Strauss, B. F. Westcott[§] (1851) maintained that Mark was the earliest Gospel and a reliable historical source. Similarly H. Holtzmann[§] (1863), who argued for the priority of Mark on the basis of the Gospel's primitive style and diction, and whose advocacy of the two-source hypothesis (Mark and sayings source) virtually settled the matter for years, believed that Mark gave a mainly objective account of the historical Jesus, setting out the development of his messianic consciousness. After centuries of neglect Mark became the focus of attention for scholars intent on the quest of the historical Jesus. They felt that they were on firm ground with Mark and Q; the former provided a straightforward, historically reliable narrative while the latter supplemented this with early traditions of Jesus' teaching. Thus F. Burkitt[§] (1906) described Mark as a "historical document . . . in touch with the facts." The Gospel was assumed to be an objective, unsophisticated account of events.

This approach, however, did not go unchallenged. Arguing that the Gospels did not supply sources for the life of Jesus, M. Kähler[§] (1892) described them, and Mark in particular, as "passion narratives with extended introductions," while W. Wrede[§] (1901) maintained that Mark does not present us with a "life of Jesus," since the Christ of faith has been superimposed upon the historical Jesus. Wrede was the first to suggest that Mark was a theological work comparable to John, and in many ways Wrede's work foreshadows that of the Redaction*§ critics half a century later. He examined the "messianic secret" in Mark's Gospel and suggested that it represents a way of handling the tension between the belief of the early church in Jesus as Messiah and the unmessianic nature of Jesus' ministry. Wrede's book was not translated into English until 1971, but his influence in Germany was enormous. Although his explanation of the messianic secret has been found unsatisfactory, his recognition that history has been subject to theology is now widespread.

J. Wellhausen§ (1903) was the first to suggest that Mark deliberately ended his Gospel at 16:8. Meanwhile B. Bacon§ (1909) and A. Loisy§ (1912) argued that Paul†§ influenced Mark. During this time M. J. Lagrange§ (1910) wrote a notable commentary, the first truly scientific commentary on a Gospel written by a Roman Catholic; he believed that Mark was dependent on Peter and that Matthew used Mark. The problem of synoptic relationships led some scholars (e.g., E. Wendling 1905) to champion the idea of an Ur-Markus, or earlier version of Mark used by Matthew and Luke, while W. Bussmann (1925-31) suggested that the Gospel had been compiled in three stages.

4. *Form Criticism.* The most significant development at this time proved to be the rise of Form Criticism*§, which challenged the use of Mark as the basis of a "life of Jesus." W. Bousset§ (1913) had already emphasized the importance of the oral period for the development of the tradition while suggesting that the passion narrative had taken the form of a connected report from an early stage. Next, the work of K. Schmidt§ (1919), M. Dibelius§ (1919), and R. Bultmann§ (1921) turned scholarly attention to the individual pericopae that made up the Gospel. The evangelists were seen as collectors of the tradition whose contribution lay in choosing the material and linking it together. Questions were raised not only about the historicity of individual stories, which were now understood to reflect the beliefs and practices of the early Christian communities, but also concerning the historical value of the Markan outline. Whereas Bultmann and Dibelius analyzed the tradition, Schmidt examined the Markan framework and concluded that it was editorial.

The extreme skepticism of some form critics—notably Bultmann—caused many scholars to reject their views, but the value of their contribution to Markan studies was ultimately immense. It came to be recognized that the believing communities shaped (not necessarily created) the material in the oral period and that the material cannot, therefore, be used immediately as evidence for a "life of Jesus." Equally important was the recognition that the Markan framework did not represent a chronological outline (Chronology, New Testament§) for a biography. Opposing this view, C. H. Dodd§ (1932) argued that Mark's framework is also traditional and similar to the kerygma found in Acts. Although Dodd's view continued to be popular for many years (especially in England, where V. Taylor presented the traditional approach in his scholarly and influential commentary [1952] and where the Papias tradition linking the Gospel with Peter continued to be given great weight), it was subjected to damaging criticism a quarter of a century later. D. Nineham (1957) pointed out that even if Mark's framework were traditional rather than editorial, it would have little historical value since it was simply a summary outlining Jesus' teachings and healings.

5. *Redaction Criticism.* The recognition that the individual stories reflected the beliefs of the Christian communities and that they were not necessarily arranged in chronological order even when they embodied tradition that went back to Jesus meant that Mark's Gospel could no longer be appealed to as the basic outline for a "life of Jesus" or interpreted as the record of the development of his "messianic self-consciousness." A large part of the Markan hypothesis had thus collapsed. But interest in the testimony of the evangelist was about to revive in a new way.

The rise of redaction criticism turned scholarly attention from the small units that comprise the Gospels to the Gospels as wholes. If the framework is editorial, not historical, then perhaps it reflects the personal interests and concerns of Mark. The form critics had compared Mark's Gospel to a haphazard collection of beads on a string; however, if the evangelist Mark had arranged the beads in a particular order, then the evangelist should be seen as an author rather than a mere collector—an author who chose and arranged his material with particular purposes in mind, thereby expressing his own theology. From being regarded as a historian, then a compiler, Mark now came to be treated as a theologian.

In addition to W. Wrede, another precursor of redaction criticism was R. H. Lightfoot[§], whose primary concern was with the purpose of the evangelists, in particular Mark (1934, 1938, 1950). About the same time E. Lohmeyer[§] (1936, 1937) argued that in Mark's Gospel Galilee and Jerusalem are of crucial importance as places of both redemption and opposition; however, he traced this idea back to the pre-Markan community and believed that Mark was written in Galilee. Lohmeyer suggested that the place of writing influenced the Gospel. Arguing that Mark was totally unconcerned with Jesus' life, H. Ebeling (1939) interpreted the secrecy motif as a foil to the revelation of the truth about Jesus, which is now known to readers of the Gospel. Interest had now shifted from what Mark tells us about Jesus to what he tells us about the faith of his community. Nevertheless, as J. Robinson (1957) pointed out, Mark chose to write a history of Jesus and presumably found meaning in that history. What he records is not objective history, however, but the story of the cosmic struggle between the Spirit and Satan that inaugurates the eschatological reign of God—a struggle that continues in the life of the church.

The term redaction criticism *(Redaktionsgeschichte)* was coined by W. Marxsen, who is regarded as the initiator of this method in his study of Mark (1956; ET 1969). Redaction criticism is based on the belief that it is possible to distinguish between tradition and redaction and to analyze the way in which an author has arranged, edited, and modified the tradition and composed new material. If we assume Markan priority, then redactional work on Mark is much more difficult than on Matthew or Luke because we have no sources with which to compare it. Redaction critics, therefore, have concentrated on Mark's vocabulary and style (e.g., in the editorial summaries of 1:32-34; 3:7-12; 6:6b), on his ordering of the material and compositional technique (e.g., in his use of intercalation, 5:21-43; 11:11-25, etc.), and on his dominant concerns. Investigating the evangelist and his community, the redaction critic attempts to discover the situation at the time the evangelist was writing together with the beliefs, expectations, and problems of his community. The critic's concern is thus no longer primarily with the *Sitz im Leben* of the tradition or with that of Jesus but with that of the Gospel itself.

Marxsen believed that the Gospel was written shortly before 70 C.E. to urge the church in Jerusalem to flee to Galilee, where the Lord was to return; the story inevitably breaks off at 16:8 because the parousia had not yet taken place. This interpretation raises countless problems, but Marxsen's importance lies in his championship of a new method and his attempt to discover the original setting of the Gospel, not in the success of his theory.

A spate of redaction-critical studies followed. Many of these concentrated on particular passages (e.g., Mark 6:52: Q. Quesnell 1969; Mark 13: L. Hartman 1966, J. Lambrecht 1967, and R. Pesch 1968; Mark 11: W. Telford 1980) or themes (e.g., E. Best 1965, 1990[2]; D. A. Koch 1975; U. Luz 1965; H. Räisänen [1976; ET 1990]). E. Schweizer presented the redaction-critical approach to the Gospel to non-specialist readers in his masterly commentary (1967; ET 1970). While building on the results of form criticism, these scholars took for granted the creative role of the evangelist. Questions were now raised concerning the *Gattung,* or genre, of the Gospel. If Mark could no longer be seen as a biography or as the memoirs of the apostle Peter, was it to be understood as an aretalogy, portraying Jesus as a hero figure? Was it an apology, as suggested by S. Brandon (1969), who argued that it was designed to cover up Jesus' political involvement, or was it an apocalyptic message (Apocalypticism*§)? Was it modeled on Greek drama, or was it intended for use as a lectionary? One obvious reply to all these suggestions is that in writing a Gospel, Mark created a new literary genre designed to proclaim the good news. But since nothing can ever be entirely new, attempts to discover partial antecedents in various literary models have continued. Several scholars (e.g., R. Burridge 1992) have argued that the Gospels would, after all, have been understood in the first century as biographies. Too often it has been forgotten that the Gospel was intended to be read aloud and that a suitable model should suggest hearing rather than reading (M. Beavis 1989).

One issue is the nature and purpose of the "prologue." R. Lightfoot (1950) identified it as 1:1-13 and compared it with the Johannine†§ prologue; others have argued that it consists of vv. 1-15 (L. Keck 1966; J. Drury 1985). The Gospel as a whole has been compared with Greek tragedy (G. Bilezikian 1977 and B. Standaert 1978), and the opening verses seem to serve as a dramatic prologue, providing the information necessary for understanding the story that follows.

6. *Thematic Interpretations*. In trying to discover the genre of the Gospel, critics were searching for its central theme, which for many was basically christological. J. Schreiber (1961), following Bultmann, held that Mark's story was an amalgam of the Jesus tradition with a Hellenistic myth about a divine being who comes to earth. The obvious weakness of Schreiber's interpretation is Mark's omission of any reference to Christ's preexistence. T. Weeden (1971) suggested that the Gospel was an attack on a false Christology that depicted Jesus in terms of a *theios anēr*. After presenting this false understanding in the miracles in the first part of the Gospel, Mark then provides his own *theologica crucis* in the concluding chapters. The disciples, who come under attack throughout the Gospel, represent those who held this false view, playing down the suffering of Jesus and hence the need to suffer themselves. Weeden's interpretation failed to take into account the fact that Mark presents the miracles in a positive light. B. Blackburn (1991) has demonstrated the irrelevance of the idea of the *theios anēr* for Mark. N. Perrin§ also understood Mark to be attacking a false Christology, which he corrected with his own interpretation of the Son of Man. Others (e.g., Schweizer) have pointed to the fact that at crucial points in the story Jesus is declared to be "Son of God" (1:11; 3:11; 9:7; 15:39).

The identity of Jesus is inextricably linked with the story of his passion; it is no accident that he is confessed as "Son of God" at the moment of his death. Mark's story is indeed a "passion narrative with an extended introduction." The question is why there should be such emphasis on the cross. Is it to combat a false Christology—or simply because it was necessary for Mark to deal with the scandal of the cross by insisting that it was part of the divine plan? And why is there such emphasis on the need for the disciples to suffer? Was it because there were teachers in Mark's church who had false ideas about discipleship; or was it, as has traditionally been held, because Mark's readers were themselves undergoing persecution? Many scholars have argued that the disciples represented, not opponents of Mark, but members of his community; their reactions mirror the community's response to the call to Christian discipleship. The nature of discipleship is a dominant theme—especially in 8:22–10:52 (Best 1981, 1986)—and throughout the Gospel the disciples are portrayed as misunderstanding both the activity and the teaching of Jesus.

Linking the themes of Christology, suffering, and discipleship is the continuing puzzle of the messianic secret. If the secret is no longer seen as straightforward historical tradition, neither is it supposed, as Wrede suggested, that the ministry of Jesus was wholly "unmessianic." Many scholars stress the fact that the secret is bound up with the passion and that it is only through his suffering that Jesus' identity can be known (e.g., G. Minette de Tillesse 1968). The secret is perhaps to be seen as a Markan device for revealing the real significance of Jesus to his readers and for explaining the failure of Jesus' contemporaries to grasp the truth about him.

Increasingly, it has seemed likely that Mark's ending is not "lost" and that his enigmatic con-clusion at 16:8 is deliberate; it is only by responding to the summons to follow Jesus that one learns the secret of who he is (M. Hooker 1983).

B. Mack (1988), who has portrayed Mark's work as quite creative, has revived the idea that Mark combined two distinct types of material—the one representing memories of Jesus as a teacher of aphorisms, the other representing him as an eschatological Redeemer. Unexamined assumptions and the bypassing of important evidence make Mack's work unconvincing, how-ever (see, e.g., L. Hurtado 1990).

7. *Date and Place of Composition.* Concern to discover the original *Sitz im Leben* of the Gospel and to analyze the beliefs and situation of the Markan community led H. Kee (1977) to apply a sociological approach (Sociology and New Testament Studies*§) to the Gospel. He sug-gested that it was probably written shortly before 70 C.E. in Syria. In contrast, W. Kelber (1974) argued that it was written in Galilee some time after 70 C.E. M. Hengel (1985) has upheld the traditional belief that it was written in Rome shortly before 70 C.E. This debate has largely cen-tered on the interpretation of the eschatological discourse in Mark 13.

8. *Sources.* The study of Markan redaction is bound up with questions about Mark's sources. If he is the first evangelist, has he taken over previous collections of material? Following the form critics, many commentators have assumed, e.g., that Mark 2:1-3:6 represents a pre-Markan collection of conflict stories. The discovery that Mark was not simply a scissors-and-paste redactor but an author collecting material to make a particular point created the possibility that the sequence of stories might be his own, because he depicted the Authority*§ of Jesus and the growing opposition of those in power. Because of the overlaps in 4:35-8:26 (two significant miracles on the sea, two feeding miracles, two disputes with Pharisees, extended sections dealing with uncleanness, parallel healings of deaf and blind men, etc.), it has often been suggested that Mark inherited two parallel cycles of tradition, which he incorporated into his Gospel. If he was a careful author placing his material in order, however, then he might have deliberately arranged these stories in parallel. Mark 13 has long been regarded as a clear example of a separate source that Mark incorporated into his Gospel. The theory that he used an apoca-lyptic fly sheet that originally circulated among Christians warning them about the horrors of the coming Jewish war goes back to T. Colani (1864) and was developed by, among others, Bultmann and Pesch. This theory of a separate eschatological discourse had its origins in the problem of reconciling these sayings with the church's understanding of Jesus. G. Beasley-Murray (1956, 1967) boldly defended the chapter's authenticity as a discourse of Jesus. More recent studies have recognized the large role played by redaction in this chapter and have thus challenged both positions. Finally, the passion narrative, long believed to have had some kind of pre-Markan existence and thus assumed to be an exception to the form-critical analysis of the Gospel as consisting of independent pericopae, has come under scrutiny and has increas-ingly been regarded as being subject to the same kind of redactional activity as the rest of the Gospel (e.g., L. Schenke 1971; J. Donahue 1973).

In deciding whether Mark was a scissors-and-paste collector or a creative author, it is neces-sary to consider his vocabulary, style, and compositional techniques. F. Neirynck (1972, 1988[2]), for example, argued that "duality" is characteristic of Mark's style. It is essential in such dis-cussions to establish that something is either characteristic of the Gospel as a whole or of those sections due to Mark's redaction, since otherwise it could be a feature of his sources.

But what if Mark's sources were in fact neither individual pericopae nor short collections but the other two synoptic Gospels? Even after the two document "solution" to the Synoptic Problem[†§] had become generally accepted, some scholars (mainly Roman Catholic) had con-tinued to maintain the priority of Matthew. B. Butler (1951) put forward the most notable defense of this theory. Shortly afterward, the Griesbach hypothesis that Mark was dependent on both Matthew and Luke was revived. The foremost exponent of this view is W. Farmer[§] (1964), although it has received enthusiastic support from others, notably H. H. Stoldt (1977; ET 1980). Although the majority of scholars still think that the evidence supports Markan priority and that Matthew and Luke expanded the shorter Gospel (e.g., C. Tuckett 1983), this view has been increasingly challenged, so that it is no longer possible to describe it as an "assured result" of Gospel criticism. The relevance of this debate to the interpretation of Mark has changed dramatically since the nineteenth century: Then, interest in the priority of Mark was linked to the quest for the historical Jesus and concern for establishing reliable information about him; now, its primary importance relates to the search for the evangelist's message and the understanding of the way in which he has handled his tradition. If Mark in fact used Matthew and Luke, then redactional-critical studies have to begin from very different premises than those accepted by the majority of critics.

9. *Literary Criticism.* The difficulty of ascertaining Mark's sources encouraged the next stage in Markan studies—that of Literary*[§] criticism, which has no interest in such questions. ("Literary criticism" is used here in the sense familiar to students of literature and not, as has been common among biblical scholars, of the historical study of the text.) Earlier studies had concentrated on the structure of the Gospel. Those by A. Farrer[§] (1951, 1954), who changed his mind several times, illustrate the danger of subjectivity in this approach. P. Carrington had argued that the Gospel was intended as a lectionary (1952). M. Goulder (1978) has argued a similar view, while J. Bowman believed that it was a Passover Haggadah (1965). Then new methods of literary criticism were applied to the Gospel, and these methods were often indifferent to historical questions concerning the evangelist as well as those relating to Jesus and the faith of the early communities. Interest had now shifted from the evangelist's intentions and the situation of his community to the Gospel itself. This literary-critical approach has been especially popular in the United States. Composition criticism, Rhetorical Criticism*[§], structural analysis (Structuralism and Deconstruction*[§])—the varieties of new approaches seem endless—all have the advantage that they handle the text as it stands and are not dependent on questions about sources and how the evangelist has handled them. Whereas redaction critics have investigated the ways in which Mark handled the tradition, these new literary critics see him as a creative author; they are interested only in the finished work, and there is thus no need for a painstaking separation of tradition from redaction. What is important is the logic of the narrative as it stands, not the way in which the evangelist has handled the tradition or adapted his sources. This approach is particularly attractive in the case of Mark, since it is impossible to be certain how much we owe to Mark personally.

An example of the application of literary criticism to the Gospel can be seen in the work of a secular literary critic, F. Kermode (1979). Structuralist analysis has been applied by various writers (e.g., D. Via 1975). Typical of the new methods of literary analysis is the work of J. Dewey (1980), who explored the concentric structure of Mark 2:1–3:6; applying to this section the techniques of rhetorical criticism, she uncovers an intricate chiastic construction that she argues is due to the author's literary creativity. In concentrating on the way in which the stories are arranged and told, she has moved beyond the redaction critical approach. Similarly R. Fowler (1981), who has analyzed the two feeding narratives, maintains that the parallels between them are due to the creative activity of Mark, who used the second narrative as the model for the first. Others have explored the significance of the setting of the various stories—house, sea, desert, etc. (e.g., D. Rhoads and D. Michie 1982). M. A. Tolbert (1989) offers a literary-critical approach to the whole Gospel. F. Belo (1981) builds his political reading on a literary analysis. C. Myers (1992) uses what he calls a "socio-literary approach" in expounding Mark as a model for nonviolent resistance in the modern world. These are also all good examples of Reader-Response Criticism*[§] because so much depends on the response of the reader.

Some literary critics have little need to ask questions about authorial intentions; they cut the Gospel loose from its original moorings and examine it in its own right, so that its meaning now depends on its impact on the reader (e.g., S. Moore 1989). It is easy to see how subjective such interpretations must be: The reader is acknowledged to be more important than the writer. Nevertheless, it is important to remember that all interpretation is to some extent subjective. For example, in his study of the redaction-critical method (1989), C. Black shows how the presuppositions of various redaction critics have influenced their reading of Mark. Methods that claim to be objective are the more dangerous if their true nature is not recognized.

Additional studies have also looked at the way in which Mark constructed his Gospel and at the role of women. Using Narrative Criticism*§, some scholars have examined rhetorical devices (J. Camery-Hoggatt 1992); others have considered the way in which one section is integrated into the whole (T. Geddert 1989); still others have evaluated the way in which Mark tells his story (C. Marshall 1989). J. Marcus (1992), who examines Mark's christological exegesis of the Hebrew Bible, employs a somewhat different approach. Tolbert (1992), J. Dewey (1994), and others have examined the manner in which women function in the Gospel of Mark.

Recent commentaries on Mark include Broadhead (2001), Donahue and Harrington (2002), Dowd (2000), Eckey (1998), Edwards (2002), France (2002), Marcus (2000–), Moloney (2002), Tolbert (2003), Trocmé (2000), van Iersel (1998), and Witherington (2001). Herrero (2001) has written a commentary on Mark's passion narrative. Studies of Mark's redaction, compositional techniques, and community include Bonneau (2001), Orton (1999), and Peterson (2000). Studies of Markan theology and Christology include: Brandt (2002), Broadhead (1999), Chávez (2002), Dechow (2000), Feneberg (2000), Matjaz (1999), Naluparayil (2000), Rowe (2002), Sabin (2002), Santos (2003), Schildgen (1998), Trainor (2001), Trimaille (2001), (van Oyen 1999), and Watts (2000). Croy (2003) discusses the peculiar nature of Mark's opening (1:10) and closing (16:8). Kelhoffer (2000) discusses the origins and setting of the Longer Ending (Mark 16:8-20). Danove (2001), Palachuvattil, Pellegrini, and Rüegger (2002) have used linguistics, philology, and semiotics to analyze Mark. Some scholars (Dawson 2000, Horsley 2001) read Mark through specific political lenses. Geyer (2002), MacDonald (2000), Moeser (2002), Vines (2002), and Wilkens study Mark in comparison to Jewish and Greco-Roman literature. Hall (1998) reevaluates K. L. Schmidt's form critical analysis of Mark. Heckel (1999), Neville (2002), and Peabody (2002) discuss Mark's relationship to the other synoptic gospels. Hatina (1998) and Watts (2002) study Mark's use of Scripture. Incigneri (2003) addresses Mark's rhetoric in relation to Mark's original audience. Geyer (2002), Hanson (2000), Malbon (2000), Minor (2001), Rhoads, Dewey and Michie (19992), Svartik (2000), and van Iersel (1998) use narrative criticism, reader response theory, and other forms of literary criticism to analyze Mark. Klumbies (2001) discusses the relationship between myth and Mark. Feminist critique and use of Mark is in Levine and Blickenstaff (2001) and Mitchell (2001).

Bibliography: J. C. Anderson and S. D. Moore (ed.), *Mark and Method: New Approaches in Biblical Studies* (1992). **B. W. Bacon,** *The Beginnings of Gospel Story* (1909). **F. C. Baur,** *Das Markusevangelium: nach seinem Ursprung und Charakter* (1851). **G. Beasley-Murray,** *Jesus and the Future* (1956); *A Commentary on Mark Thirteen* (1957). **M. A. Beavis,** *Mark's Audience: The Literary and Social Setting of Mark* 4:11-12 (JSNTSup 33, 1989). **F. Belo,** *A Materialist Reading of the Gospel of Mark* (ET 1981). **E. Best,** *The Temptation and the Passion: The Markan Soteriology* (SNTSMS 2, 1965, 1990²); *Following Jesus: Discipleship in the Gospel of Mark* (JSNTSup 4, 1981). **G. B. Bilezikian,** *The Liberated Gospel: A Comparison of the Gospel of Mark and Greek Tragedy* (Baker Biblical Monograph, 1977). **C. C. Black,** *The Disciples According to Mark: Markan Redaction in Current Debate* (JSNTSup 27, 1989). **B. Blackburn,** *Theios Aner and the Markan Miracle Traditions* (WUNT

2/40, 1991). **G. Bonneau,** *Stratégies rédactionnelles et fonctions communautaires de l'évangile de Marc* (*Ebib* n.s. 44, 2001). **W. Bousset,** *Kyrios Christos* (1913; ET 1970). **J. Bowman,** *The Gospel of Mark: The New Christian Jewish Passover Haggadah* (StPB 8, 1965). **S. Brandon,** *Jesus and the Zealots: A Study of the Political Factor in Primitive Christianity* (1967). **P. Y. Brandt,** *L'identité de Jésus et l'identité de son disciple: le récit de la transfiguration comme clef de lecture de l'Evangile de Marc* (NTOA 50, 2002). **E. K. Broadhead,** *Jesus: Titular Christology in the Gospel of Mark.* (JSNTSup 175, 1999); Mark (Readings, a *New Biblical Commentary,* 2001). **R. Bultmann,** *Die Geschichte der synoptischen Tradition* (1921, 1931[2], 1995[10]; ET rev. ed. 1976). **F. C. Burkitt,** *The Gospel History and Its Transmission* (1906). **R. Burridge,** *What Are the Gospels? A Comparison with Graeco-Roman Biography* (SNTSMS 70, 1992). **W. Bussmann,** *Synoptische Studien* (1923-31). **B. C. Butler,** *The Originality of St. Matthew: A Critique of the Two-Document Hypothesis* (1951). **M. Cahill** (ed. and tr.), *The First Commentary on Mark: An Annotated Translation* (1998). **J. Calvin,** *Commentary of a Harmony of the Evangelists Matthew, Mark, and Luke* (tr. W. Pringle, 3 vols. 1956). **J. Camery-Hoggatt,** *Irony in Mark's Gospel: Text and Subtext* (1992). **P. Carrington,** *The Primitive Christian Calendar: A Study in the Making of the Marcan Gospel* (1952). **E. G. Chávez,** *The Theological Significance of Jesus' Temple Action in Mark's Gospel* (Toronto Studies in Theology 87, 2002). **T. Colani,** *Jésus-Christ et les croyances messianiques de son temps* (1864). **N. C. Croy,** *The Mutilation of Mark's Gospel* (2003). **P. L. Danove,** *Linguistics and Exegesis in the Gospel of Mark* (JSNTSup 218, 2001). **A. Dawson,** *Freedom as Liberating Power: A Socio-Political Reading of the Exousia Texts in the Gospel of Mark* (NTOA 44, 2000). **J. Dechow,** *Gottessohn und Herrschaft Gottes: der Theozentrismus des Markusevangeliums* (WMANT 86, 2000). **J. Dewey,** *Markan Public Debate* (SBLDS 48, 1980); "The Gospel of Mark," *Searching the Scriptures,* vol. 2, *A Feminist Commentary* (ed. E. Schüssler Fiorenza, 1994) 470-509. **M. Dibelius,** *Die Formgeschichte des Evangeliums* (1919; ET 1971). **C. H. Dodd,** "The Framework of the Gospel Narrative," *ExpTim* 43 (1932) 396-400. **J. R. Donahue,** *Are You the Christ? The Trial Narrative in the Gospel of Mark* (SBLDS 10, 1973). **J. R. Donahue and D. J. Harrington,** *The Gospel of Mark* (SP 2, 2002). **D. Dormeyer,** *Das Markusevangelium als Idealbiographie von Jesus Christus, dem Nazarener* (SBB 43, 1999). **S. Dowd,** *Reading Mark: A Literary and Theological Commentary* (Reading the New Testament, 2000). **J. Drury,** "Mark 1:1-15: An Interpretation," *Alternative Approaches to NT Study* (ed. A. E. Harvey, 1985) 25-36. **H. Ebeling,** *Das Messiasgeheimnis und die Botschaft des Marcus-Evanglisten* (BZNW 19, 1939). **W. Eckey,** *Das Markusevangelium: Orientierung am Weg Jesu; ein Kommentar* (1998). **J. G. Eichhorn,** *Über die drey ersten Evangelien* (1794). **J. R. Edwards,** *The Gospel According to Mark* (The Pillar New Testament Commentary, 2002). **W. R. Farmer,** *The Synoptic Problem: A Critical Analysis* (1964). **A Farrer,** *A Study in St. Mark* (1951); *St. Matthew and St. Mark* (1953-54 E. Cadbury Lectures, 1954). **R. Feneberg,** *Der Jude Jesus und die Heiden: Biographie und Theologie Jesu im Markusevangelium* (Herders biblische Studien 24, 2000). **R. M. Fink,** *Die Botschaft des heilenden Handelns Jesu: Untersuchung der dreizehn exemplarischen Berichte von Jesu heilendem Handeln im Markusevangelium* (Salzburger theologische Studien 15, 2000). **R. M. Fowler,** *Loaves and Fishes: The Function of Feeding Stories in the Gospel of Mark* (SBLDS 54, 1981). **R.T. France,** *The Gospel of Mark: A Commentary on the Greek Text* (NIGTC, 2002). **T. Geddert,** *Watchwords: Mark 13 in Markan Eschatology* (1989). **D. W. Geyer,** *Fear, Anomaly, and Uncertainty in the Gospel of Mark* (ATLA Monograph Series 47, 2002). **M. Goulder,** *The Evangelists' Calendar* (1978). **D. R. Hall,** *The Gospel Framework: Fiction or Fact?: A Critical Evaluation of Der Rahmen der Geschichte Jesu by Karl Ludwig Schmidt* (1998). **D. J. Harrington,** "A Map of Books on Mark (1975-1984)," *BTB 15* (1985) 12-16. **L. Hartman,** *Prophecy Interpreted* (ConBNT 1, 1966). **Thomas R. Hatina,** *In Search of a Context: The Function of Scripture in Mark's Narrative* (Studies in

Scripture in Early Judaism and Christianity 8, 2002). **Michael Hauser,** *Die Herrschaft Gottes im Markusevangelium* (1998). **M. Hengel,** *Studies in the Gospel of Mark* (1985). **J. G. Herder,** *Vom Erlöser der Menschen* (CS, 1796-97). **J. S. Hanson,** *The Endangered Promises: Conflict in Mark* (SBLDS 171, 2000). **T. K. Heckel,** *Vom Evangelium des Markus zum viergestaltigen Evangelium* (WUNT 120, 1999). **F. P. Herrero,** *Pasión y Pascua de Jesús según San Marcos* (Publicaciones de la Facultad de Teología del Norte de España, Sede de Burgos 67, 2001). **H. J. Holtzmann,** *Die Synoptischen Evangelien: Ihr Ursprung und geschichlicher Charakter* (1863). **M. Hooker,** *The Gospel According to St. Mark* (BNTC, 1991); *The Message of Mark* (1983). **R. A. Horsley,** *Hearing The Whole Story: The Politics of Plot in Mark's Gospel* (2001). **H. M. Humphrey,** *A Bibliography for the Gospel of Mark, 1954-80* (1982). **L. Hurtado,** "The Gospel of Mark: Evolutionary or Revolutionary Document," *JSNT* 40 (1990) 15-32. **B. J. Incigneri,** *The Gospel to the Romans: The Setting and Rhetoric of Mark's Gospel* (Biblical Interpretation 65, 2003). **M. Kähler,** *Der sogenannte historische Jesus und der geschichtliche, biblische Christus* (1892; ET 1964). **S. P. Kealey,** *Mark's Gospel: A History of Its Interpretation* (1982). **L. E. Keck,** "Introduction to Mark's Gospel," *NTS* 12 (1966) 352-70. **H. C. Kee,** *Community of the New Age: Studies in Mark's Gospel* (1977). **W. H. Kelber,** *The Kingdom in Mark: A New Place and a New Time* (1974). **J. A. Kelhoffer,** *Miracle and Mission: The Authentication of Missionaries and Their Message in the Longer Ending of Mark* (WUNT 2/112, 2000). **F. Kermode,** *The Genesis of Secrecy* (1977-78 C. E. Norton Lectures, 1979). **P. G. Klumbies,** *Der Mythos bei Markus* (BZNW 108, 2001). **A. Koch,** *Die Bedeutung der Wundererzählungen für die Christologie des Markusevangeliums* (BZNW, 1975). **J. B. Koppe,** *Marcus non epitomator Matthaei* (1782). **K. Lachmann,** "De ordine narrationum in evangliis synopticis, *TSK* 8 (1835) 570-90. **M.-J. Lagrange,** *Évangile selon Saint Marc* (EBib, 1929). **J. Lambrecht,** *Die Redaktion der Markus-Apocalypse* (AnBib 28, 1967). **G. E. Lessing,** "Neue Hypothese über die Evangelisten" (1778; ET in H. Chadwick, *Lessing's Theological Writings: Selections in Translation* [Library of Religious Thought, 1956]) 65-81. **A. J. Levine with M. Blickenstaff** (eds.), *A Feminist Companion to Mark* (Feminist Companion to the New Testament and Early Christian Writings 2, 2001). **J. Lightfoot,** *Horae hebraicae et talmudicae* (1663). **R. H. Lightfoot,** *History and Interpretation in the Gospels* (Bampton Lectures, 1934); *Locality and Doctrine in the Gospels* (1938); "The First Chapter of St. Mark's Gospel," *The Gospel Message of St. Mark* (1950) 15-30. **E. Lohmeyer,** *Das Evangelium des Markus* (KEK, 1937); *Galiläa und Jerusalem* (FRLANT NF 34, 1936). **A. Loisy,** *L'Évangile selon Marc* (1912). **U. Luz,** "Das Geheimnismotiv und die markinische Christologie," *ZNW 56* (1965) 9-30. **D. R. MacDonald,** *The Homeric Epics and the Gospel of Mark* (2000). **B. Mack,** *A Myth of Innocence: Mark and Christian Origins* (1988). **E. S. Malbon,** *In the Company of Jesus: Characters in Mark's Gospel* (2000). **J. Marcus,** *The Way of the Lord: Christological Exegesis of the OT in the Gospel of Mark* (1992); *Mark: A New Translation with Introduction And Commentary* (AB 27-27A, 2000-). **C. D. Marshall,** *Faith as a Theme in Mark's Narrative* (SNTSMS 64, 1989). **R. P. Martin,** *Mark: Evangelist and Theologian* (1972). **W. Marxsen,** *Der Evangelist Markus: Studien zur Redaktionsgeschichte des Evangeliums* (FRLANT NF 49, 1956; ET 1969). **M. Matjaz,** *Furcht und Gotteserfahrung: die Bedeutung des Furchtmotivs für die Christologie des Markus* (FB 91, 1999). **C. Meyers,** *Binding the Strong Man: A Political Reading of Mark's Story of Jesus* (1992). **G. Minette de Tillesse,** *Le Secret messianique dans l'é- vangile de Marc* (LD 47, 1968). **M. L. Minor,** *The Power of Mark's Story* (2001). **J. L. Mitchell,** *Beyond Fear and Silence: A Feminist-Literary Approach to the Gospel of Mark* (2001). **M. C. Moeser,** *The Anecdote in Mark, the Classical World and the Rabbis* (JSNTSup 227, 2002). **F. J. Moloney,** *The Gospel of Mark: A Commentary* (2002). **S. D. Moore,** *Literary Criticism and the Gospels: The Theoretical Challenge* (1989). **J. C. Naluparayil,** *The Identity of Jesus in Mark: An Essay on Narrative Christology* (Studium Biblicum Franciscanum

Analecta 49, 2000). **F. Neirynck,** *Duality in Mark: Contributions to the Study of the Markan Redaction* (BETL 31, 1972, 1988²). **F. Neirynck et al.,** *The Gospel of Mark: A Cumulative Bibliography, 1950-90* (1992). **D. J. Neville,** *Mark's Gospel—Prior or Posterior: A Reappraisal of the Phenomenon of Order* (JSNTSup 222, 2002). **D. Nineham,** "The Order of Events in St. Mark's Examination of Dr. Dodd's Hypothesis," *Studies in the Gospels: Essays in Memory of R. H. Lightfoot* (1957) 223-39. **T. C. Oden and C. A. Hall** (eds.), *Mark* (ACCS, 1998). **D. E. Orton,** *The Composition of Mark's Gospel: Selected Studies from Novum Testamentum* (Brill's Readers in Biblical Studies 3, 1999). **H. Owen,** *Observations on the Four Gospels: Tending Chiefly to Ascertain the Times of Publication* (1764). **J. Palachuvattil,** *"He Saw" : The Significance of Jesus' Seeing Denoted by the Verb Eiden in the Gospel of Mark* (Tesi Gregoriana. Serie Teologia 84, 2002). **H. E. G. Paulus,** *Kommentar über die drey ersten Evangelien* (1800); *Das Leben Jesu als grundlage einer reinen Geschichte des Urchristentums* (1828). **D. B. Peabody,** *One Gospel from Two: Mark's Use of Matthew and Luke,* (2002). **S. Pellegrini,** *Elija—Wegbereiter des Gottessohnes: eine textsemiotische Untersuchung im Markusevangelium* (Herders biblische Studien 26, 2000). **P. Perkins,** "The Gospel of Mark," *NIB* (1995) 8:507-733. **R. Pesch,** *Naherwartungen: Tradition und Redaktion in Mk 13* (KBANT, 1968). **D. N. Peterson,** *The Origins of Mark: The Markan Community in Current Debate* (Biblical Interpretation, 2000). **P. Pokorný,** "Das Marcus-Evangelium: Literarische und theologische Einleitung mit Forschungsbericht," *ANRW* II.25.3 (1986) 1969-2035. **Q. Quesnell,** *The Mind of Mark: Interpretation and Method Through the Exegesis of Mark 6:52* (AnBib 38, 1969). **H. Räisänen,** *Das "Messiasgeheimnis" im Markusevangelium: Ein redaktions Kritischer Versuch* (Schriften der Finnischen Exegetischen Gesellschaft 28, 1976; ET, The "Messianic Secret" in Mark's Gospel, [Studies on the NT and Its World, 1990]). **H. S. Reimarus,** *Fragmente des wolfenbuttelschen Ungenannten* (1774-78). **D. Rhoads, J. Dewey, D. Michie,** *Mark as Story: An Introduction to the Narrative of a Gospel* (1999²). **D. Rhoads and D. Michie,** *Mark as Story: An Introduction to the Narratives of a Gospel* (1982). **J. M. Robinson,** *The Problem of History in Mark* (SBT 21, 1957). **R. D. Rowe,** *God's Kingdom and God's Son: The Background to Mark's Christology from Concepts of Kingship in the Psalms* (AGJU 50, 2002). **H. U. Rüegger,** *Verstehen, was Markus erzählt: philologisch-hermeneutische Reflexionen zum Übersetzen von Markus 3,1-6* (WUNT 2/155, 2002). **M. N. Sabin,** *Reopening the Word: Reading Mark as Theology in the Context of Early Judaism,* 2002). **N. F. Santos,** *Slave of All: The Paradox of Authority and Servanthood in the Gospel of Mark* (JSTNSup 237, 2003). **L. Schenke,** *Studien zur Passionsgeschichte des Markus* (FB 4, 1971). **B. D. Schildgen,** *Crisis and Continuity: Time in the Gospel of Mark* (JSNTSup 159, 1998). **K. L. Schmidt,** *Der Rahmen der Geschichte Jesu: Literar-kritische Untersuchungen* (1919). **J. Schreiber,** "Die Christologie des Markusevangeliums," *ZTK* 58 (1961) 154-83. **E. Schweizer,** *The Good News According to Mark* (1967; ET 1970). **M. Smith,** *The Secret Gospel: The Discovery and Interpretation of the Secret Gospel According to Mark* (1973). **B. Standaert,** *L'Évangile selon Marc: Composition et genre littéraire* (1978). **H. H. Stoldt,** *Geschichte und Kritik der Markushypothese* (1977; ET 1980). **G. C. Storr,** *Über den Zweck der evangelischen Geschichte und der Briefe Johannis* (1786). **D. F. Strauss,** *Life of Jesus* (2 vols. 1835-36; ET 1855). **J. Svartvik,** *Mark and Mission: Mk 7:1-23 in its Narrative and Historical Contexts* (ConBNT 32, 2000). **W. Telford** (ed.), *The Barren Temple and the Withered Tree* (JSNTSup 1, 1980); *The Interpretation of Mark* (19952). **M. A. Tolbert,** *Sowing the Gospel: Mark's World in Literary-historical Perspective* (1989); "Mark," *The Women's Bible Commentary* (ed. C. A. Newsom and S. H. Ringe, 1992) 263-74; "Mark," NISB (2003) 1801-45. **M. F. Trainor,** *The Quest for Home: The Household in Mark's Community* (2001). **M. Trimaille,** *La christologie de saint Marc* (Collection Jésus et Jésus-Christ 82, 2001). **E. Trocmé,** *L'Evangile selon saint Marc* (CNT 2, 2000). **C. Tuckett,** *The Revival of the Griesbach Hypothesis* (1983). **D. Via,**

Kerygma and Comedy in the NT (1975). **B. M. F. van Iersel,** *Mark: A Reader-Response Commentary* (JSNTSup 164, 1998). **G. Van Oyen,** *The Interpretation of the Feeding Miracles in the Gospel of Mark* (Collectanea biblica et religiosa antiqua 4, 1999). **M. E. Vines,** *The Problem of Markan Genre: The Gospel of Mark and the Jewish Novel* (Academia Biblica 3, 2002). **G. Wagner** (ed.), *An Exegetical Bibliography of the NT: Matthew and Mark* (1983). **R. E. Watts,** *Isaiah's New Exodus in Mark* (Biblical Studies Library, 20002). **T. J. Weeden,** *Mark: Traditions in Conflict* (1971). **C. H. Weisse,** *Die evangelische Geschichte, kritisch und philosophisch bearbeitet* (1838). **J. Wellhausen,** *Das Evangelium Marci* (1903). **E. Wendling,** *Ur-Marcus* (1905). **B. F. Westcott,** *Introduction to the Study of the Gospel* (1851). **C. J. Wilke,** *Der Urevangelist oder exegetisch-kritische Untersuchung* (1838). **H. Wilkens,** *Kata Markon: Judenchristliches Evangelium in hellenistischer Kultur* (2000). **B. Witherington,** *The Gospel of Mark: A Socio-Rhetorical Commentary* (2001). **W. Wrede,** *Das Messiasgeheimnis in den Evangelien* (1901).

M. D. Hooker

Luke, Gospel of

1. *Introduction.* The interpretation of Luke has generally followed the cultural and religious currents of the times. In the early period interpretation was done within the church as a defense against heresy within the church and as an apology directed toward the world outside the church. During the Middle Ages, exegesis was either in the form of a sermon designed to move listeners or in the form of biblical commentary read by monks as part of their ascetic discipline. In general, such exegesis was devotional, concerned with living the Christian life and attaining salvation.

2. *The Interpretation of Luke in the Renaissance and the Protestant Reformation.* The development of humanistic scholarship and the fierce theological and ecclesial battles of this time period set the tone for exegesis. Erasmus§ produced not only the first printed Greek New Testament (1516) but also paraphrases and annotations on biblical books. His paraphrase of Luke (*In Evangelium Lucae Paraphrasis* 1523) was not a translation but a freer kind of continuous commentary that nevertheless maintained the integrity of the persons speaking. The *Annotations,* which went through five expanding editions in Erasmus's lifetime, are characterized by two principal features: Textual Criticism*§ (his primary concern) and consideration of the opinions of the fathers (like the medieval exegetes but with greater freedom). Thus he reported the opinions of the fathers who agreed with him, pointed out differences among them to justify his own departures from commonly held views, and criticized their errors. The focus of his interpretation was the moral meaning of Scripture. Humanists like Erasmus used Luke, as they used other Scripture, to expose the folly and corruption of the church. Erasmus's favorite subjects were the tragedy of the institutionalization of religion, the sophistical nature of scholastic theology, and the worldly aspirations of the clergy. Beyond his specific moral interpretation of Luke and other New Testament documents, he gave the Protestant Reformation a Greek text and a philological method to use in its theological exegesis.

If humanists like Erasmus used Scripture to expose the church's corruption, reformers like Calvin§ employed Scripture as a theological weapon. In his *Harmony of the Gospels* (1555 [ET 1972]) Calvin reclaimed an ancient form. Maintaining that no one can comment intelligently or aptly on one of the three Synoptic Gospels without comparing it with the other two, he treated Luke in connection with the other synoptic writers, focusing on Reformation theology. For example, when Luke 1:6 says, "They [Zachariah and Elizabeth] were both righteous before God," does it mean that they had no need of Christ? No! They were not perfect. They needed forgiveness. Their righteousness depended on the free kindness of God whereby God did not lay their unrighteousness to their charge because of the covenant God had made with them. On this point Calvin fought against both those who read justification by faith into the passage and those Roman Catholics who claimed to be justified by works. In Luke 1:46-50, did Mary say, "Henceforth all generations shall call me blessed" because she sought renown through her own virtue and efforts? No! She was celebrating God's work alone. Calvin held that this shows how completely Roman Catholics were mistaken in giving her titles like "Queen of Heaven" and in conferring on her the royalty that belongs to Christ, saying, "Ask the Father, bid the Son." The holy Virgin rejects them all, fixing her glory on the grace of God. "It follows that the praises of Mary, where the might and sheer glory of God are not entirely set forth, are perverse and counterfeit." Although Calvin, like Augustine, dealt with such difficulties as the different genealogies of Matthew and Luke, his major concern remained theological; and Luke served as a tool for his aim of the theological reformation of the church.

3. *The Interpretation of Luke in the Enlightenment.* H. S. Reimarus§, professor of oriental languages at the Hamburg academic gymnasium, worked in the context of developments in the

German Enlightenment's understanding of the relation between revelation and reason. The leading German philosopher of the period, C. Wolff, held that (a) revelation may be above reason but not contrary to reason, and (b) reason establishes the criteria by which revelation may be judged. The Wolffian synthesis was attacked from two directions. Neology, the middle phase of the Enlightenment, contended that (a) revelation is real, but its content is not different from that of natural religion in general and that (b) reason may eliminate those doctrines of Christian revelation that are not identical with reason. Rationalism, however, (a) agreed that reason establishes the criteria to judge revelation but (b) contended that reason's criteria prove revelation to be false, leaving reason to exist alone. Publicly Reimarus followed Wolff in saying that natural religion prepares for Christianity; privately he joined rationalism in saying that natural religion replaces Christianity. Wolff held that there are certain criteria by which any alleged revelation must be tested: First, revelation must be necessary, containing knowledge available only by miraculous means. Second, it must be free from contradictions. Privately Reimarus took Wolff's criteria and applied them to Christian origins, as set forth in the four Gospels and Acts, to show that it is possible to trace the natural origins of Christianity and that the supposed revelation is filled with contradictions. Reason's criteria thereby undermine the claims of the alleged Christian revelation.

Reimarus accepted the traditional view that Matthew and John were written by eyewitnesses, while Mark and Luke were not. He claimed that the evangelists constructed their own picture of Jesus after his death, but that they left, unintentionally and through sheer carelessness, traces of the historical reality of Jesus. From these traces one can see that Jesus did not espouse the three central doctrines of Christianity: spiritual deliverance through the suffering and death of Christ (atonement), Christ's bodily resurrection from the dead, and Christ's speedy return for reward and punishment. Jesus saw himself as a worldly Messiah, but his disciples turned him into a spiritual Savior after his death for economic reasons. It requires no miracles to explain the development of Christian origins; furthermore, the historical facts of Jesus' career contradict the claims made for him by his disciples after his death. Other contradictions are everywhere apparent, e.g., Matthew and John make no mention of the appearance on the road to Emmaus as Luke 24:13-32 does; Matthew knows nothing of the appearance in Jerusalem that is found in Luke 24:36-49; John and Matthew do not report Jesus' ascension as Luke 24:51 does; Mark 16:1 says the women buy spices when the feast day is past, whereas Luke 23:56 has them buy the spices in the evening before the feast day; Matthew and Mark report only one angel at the tomb, while Luke 24:4 says there were two. Reimarus used Luke only to illustrate contradictions in the Gospel accounts, contradictions that he believed show the falsity of the alleged Christian revelation.

Reimarus wrote as an academic, not a cleric, expressing his personal doubts in the form of an apology focused, not at the enemies of the church, but at Christianity itself. He sought to disprove its claims to have received truth through revelation. His interpretation of Luke, the other Gospels, and Acts both denied their essential historicity and exposed their creation by Jesus' disciples after his death. Reimarus is so important for biblical interpretation because on these two points his work set the stage for the subsequent interpretation of Luke and the other Gospels up to our day.

4. *The Interpretation of Luke in the Modern World.* Since 1800, interpretation of the Gospels, including Luke, has followed two very different lines. On the one hand, in response to Reimarus's denial of the essential historicity of the Gospel accounts (later reinforced by D. F. Strauss), there has been a drive to establish the historical basis of the tradition by means of source analysis and by appeals to authorship and Archaeology*§: the quest of the historians' Jesus. On the other hand, there has also been an attempt to interpret the meaning of the Gospels in their final form by relating the tendency of each to its historical context or occasion: the quest

of the evangelists' theology. The different ways Luke has been interpreted since 1800 have depended on which of these two approaches has been applied to the Gospel at any given time.

The impetus to establish the historical basis of the tradition about Jesus was sometimes undertaken on behalf of the aims of orthodox Christianity in the belief that, if the historicity of the tradition was validated, it would confirm the picture of Jesus in the Gospels. Sometimes the impetus came from the desire to overthrow Chalcedonian Christology in the belief that the historical tradition behind the Gospels would reveal a Jesus more intelligible to modern times, a Jesus of obvious moral superiority to all others and, therefore, self-validating to the modern conscience. Exponents of the latter approach to scholarship as it applies to Luke include A. von Harnack[§] (1907, 1908), W. Ramsay[§] (1905, 1915), B. Streeter[§] (1924), and V. Taylor[§] (1926, 1972).

In order to reestablish the value of the Lukan writings as historical authorities, von Harnack (1907) sought to prove that the Third Gospel and Acts were written by a fellow worker of Paul, Luke the physician. Von Harnack then (1908) reconstructed Q from Matthew and Luke, concluding that Q was a document of the apostolic epoch, more ancient than Mark and composed in Palestine. Ramsay took what is perhaps the most historically dubious passage in the New Testament, Luke 2:1-4, and attempted to establish its essential historicity on the basis of contemporary discoveries in Egypt that seemed to indicate a system of periodic enrollments in Syria and the East generally. Streeter, assuming the two source theory, argued for the existence of Proto-Luke, a synthesis of Q + L that was, in fact, a complete Gospel prior to the composition of the Third Gospel. Proto-Luke appears to have been a document independent of Mark and approximately of the same date—a conclusion Streeter believed to be of considerable moment to the historian. Taylor contended that behind the Third Gospel's passion narrative was a special source, an authority as old as Mark but independent of the Second Gospel. Such an independent pre-Lukan passion narrative would assist the historian in reconstructing the events of Jesus' final days.

The focus of all these efforts was to use the Third Gospel as a window through which to view something other than the Lukan text; interpretation consisted of treating Luke as a mine from which one could dig the ore of pre-Lukan historical tradition. This concern persists—in part at least—in I. Marshall (1978) and J. Nolland (1989, 1993a, 1993b), doubtless due to the authors' evangelical Christian conviction that "faith follows not feeling but fact." Since Luke was regarded as a secondary source by this line of interpretation, moreover, the Third Gospel received considerably less attention from scholars pursuing the quest of the historical Jesus than did Mark.

The attempt to interpret each of the Gospels in its final form was, initially at least, based on the assumption that the true meaning of a Gospel is determined by discerning its place in the historical development of early Christianity, as opposed to its canonical context (Canon of the Bible[§]). Interpretation, therefore, took the form of a history of early Christianity. F. C. Baur[§], in the first half of the nineteenth century, is the epitome of this approach. Assuming J. J. Griesbach's[§] order of the Gospels, with Matthew first, then Luke, and finally Mark, Baur read Luke as a reinterpretation of Matthew from a Pauline perspective. The Gospel of Luke arose in its final form after 70 c.e., motivated by the party relationships of that period. Luke's universalistic tendency was a Pauline antithesis to the particularism of the Jewish Christian Matthew; it was related to an alleged occasion in the historical development of early Christianity. Thus interpretation of Luke consists of the act of bringing tendency and occasion together. For Baur, such interpretive activity must be accompanied by indifference to result and freedom from subjectivity, the shining goal toward which every true scholar presses. It never occurred to the university-based Baur that his Hegelian presuppositions were a significant component of his own subjectivity.

R. Bultmann's[§] view of Luke in his *Theology of the New Testament* (1948-53 [ET vol. 1, 1951]) represents both continuity and discontinuity with the interpretive scheme of Baur. Like Baur, Bultmann was concerned to set the Third Gospel in its historical context. The tendency of Luke and its companion volume, Acts, is to substitute a history of salvation for the primitive Christian imminent eschatology. The occasion is the delay of the Parousia in early Christianity at the end of the first century. Faced with disappointments arising from the delay, the Third Evangelist told the story of Jesus as part of a history of salvation in which the gift of the Holy Spirit replaces the imminent end. Unlike Baur, Bultmann then engaged in content criticism: The New Testament contains two strata, the first embodying the early eschatological kerygma, the second reflecting an early Catholic fall away from the truth. Paul and John's Gospel represent the authentic stratum; Luke, among others, belongs to the early Catholic distortion of the original Gospel and as such does not have the same normative quality for the church that Paul and the Fourth Gospel have. Interpretation for Bultmann began with discerning Luke's alleged tendency and setting it in connection with an alleged occasion; it finished with a critical appraisal of the value of Luke's tendency for Christian faith.

H. Conzelmann (1960) further developed Bultmann's view of Luke as an account of Jesus that eliminates imminent eschatology in response to the delayed Parousia, although he refused to relegate Luke to early Catholicism (1969). Conzelmann's contribution lies in the methodology proposed to discern the Lukan tendency. By noting Luke's departures from his primary source, Mark, and by paying special attention to the overall narrative framework or pattern of arrangement, one can discern the Lukan tendency. This became, with some fine-tuning, the method of Redaction Criticism*§ that dominated Lukan studies for more than a generation. Even where the overall Bultmannian picture of Lukan theology is resisted, as in the commentaries by Marshall (1978), J. Fitzmyer§ (1981, 1985), and Nolland (1989, 1993a, 1993b), the German redaction-critical method is assumed. F. Bovon (1987) summarizes the results of such redaction-critical study of Luke under the headings plan of God, the interpretation of the Hebrew Bible, Christology, Holy Spirit, salvation, reception of salvation, and church.

At the end of the twentieth century, interpretation of Luke reflects a multiplicity of methods and approaches. In addition to those carried over from the past, five interpretive options may be mentioned in a logical, not chronological, order.

a. Interpreting Luke in light of Mediterranean parallels. From 1973 to 1983 the Society of Biblical Literature's§ Luke-Acts Group (1973-78) and Seminar (1979-83) broke with the construct of Conzelmann and developed an approach to Luke more akin to that of H. Cadbury§ (1927). Like Conzelmann, Cadbury assumed the two source theory and viewed Luke as a reinterpretation of Mark. Unlike Conzelmann, he did not believe it possible to detect a single dominating occasion for Luke's Gospel or a singular purpose formulated consciously in response to it; he was concerned to set Luke's literary techniques, no less than his theology, in relation to parallels from the Mediterranean world. The Luke-Acts working groups likewise eschewed an approach that depended on a dominant conception of the development of early Christianity and opted for a method of interpretation that depended heavily on parallels, especially literary ones, from the Mediterranean world. *Perspectives on Luke-Acts* (1978) and *Luke-Acts: New Perspectives from the Society of Biblical Literature Seminar* (1983), both edited by C. Talbert, reflect an approach that sees interpretation primarily as setting what is said in Luke and how it is said by Luke in its immediate context in Mediterranean antiquity. The Mediterranean milieu allows one to determine how Luke would have been heard by an ancient auditor and, therefore, to discern what it would have meant to him or her. The focus is on what Luke meant in the context of his own time. This stream of interpretation has yielded monographs like that of S. Garrett (1989) and a commentary by Talbert (1982).

b. Interpreting Luke in light of non-biblical literary criticism. The older New Criticism has been supplanted by a Narrative Criticism*§ based on a communications model like that of R. Jakobson, which regards texts as mirrors rather than windows. This way of reading focuses on the final form of the text and concentrates on such matters as plot, characters, and type of narration by an implied author. Something of the method was presented to historically oriented New Testament scholars by N. Petersen (1978). This type of literary study is devoid of references to the Mediterranean environment just as was that of the New Criticism; thus the narrative world of the Gospel text is abstracted from its time and place. This type of reading has borne fruit in monographs like that of D. Gowler (1991), which deals with the matter of characterization, and in the commentary by R. Tannehill (1986), a combination of New Criticism and modern narrative criticism in which there is an almost total lack of references to Mediterranean sources outside the Bible. Tannehill's thesis is that the author of Luke-Acts consciously understood the story of Jesus and his followers as unified by the controlling purpose of God.

  c. Interpreting Luke in light of anthropological and sociological models. J. Neyrey's edited collection (1991) is concerned with the question, What is the social system assumed by Luke? Issues addressed include: What is the typical economic system in a peasant society? What are the features of patron/client relations? What is the relation between city and countryside? Who benefits from labeling another as deviant? How do honor and shame operate in Mediterranean society? Given these questions and their answers, where does Luke fit and how does he react?

  d. Interpreting Luke in the context of ancient liturgical practices. M. Goulder (1978, 1989) contends that Luke wrote his Gospel as a cycle of liturgical/Gospel readings to be used throughout the year in Christian worship as fulfillments of the Hebrew Bible lections then existent in the synagogues.

  e. Interpreting Luke in the context of the canon. B. Childs[§] (1985) reflects what has come to be called Canonical Criticism*[§]. This approach tries to take account of the fact that as a result of the canonization process a new and larger context has been effected for originally independent material. Luke, for example, cannot be read canonically if it is interpreted in isolation from the other three Gospels. Read in connection with them, Luke can neither become part of a complete harmony of the Gospels (as with Tatian) nor be sifted to discover the real Jesus behind the levels of accretion (as with the quest of the historical Jesus). The plural form remains constitutive for the canonical critic, so the Lukan Gospel must be read as part of the canonical four. A large segment of Childs's book is given over to "A Canonical Harmony of the Gospels," in which he treats the final form of the text of Luke in its individuality but alongside the other Gospels read in the same way. Childs refuses either to harmonize or to attempt to establish the historical events behind the Lukan text.

  In large measure the diversity of methods proposed for interpreting Luke today is rooted in biblical scholars' openness to currents in fields outside biblical studies. Their inability to choose among the multiplicity of methods derives largely from the confusion over which community they represent: church or academy. What may be appropriate for the one may not always be appropriate for the other, as F. Dreyfus (1975) has convincingly shown. One's community determines what questions are deemed appropriate to ask of the text; methods of interpretation are chosen and/or developed in order to answer such questions. If there is anything the history of interpretation of Luke teaches us, it is this.

  Recent commentaries include Bovon (2002), Green (1997, 2003), Lieu (1997), and Tannehill (1996). Green and McKeever (1994) provide a bibliography for Lukan studies narrowly focused on historiography. Knight (1998) is a general introduction to the Gospel. Akaabiam (1999) and Hendrickx (1996-2001) represent the growing number of recent studies on Luke written from or to a particular contemporary (usually non-Western) socio-cultural context. Alexander (1993) has devoted special attention to Luke's preface to his Gospel (1:1-4). Boismard (1997) and Brown (1993[2]) analyze the sources and relationship of Luke 1–2 to the rest of the Gospel. Heil (2003), McNicol, Dungan, and Peabody (1996), and Peabody, Cope, and McNicol (2002), investigate Luke's place in the synoptic problem. Bonz (2000) studies the relationship between Luke and ancient epic, especially Virgil's *Aeneid*. Recent studies of Lukan theology include Bormann (2001), Buckwalter (1996), Byrne (2000), Cunningham (1997), Green (1995), Nave (2002), Phillips (2001), Phillips (2001), Pokorný (1998), and Prior (1995). Arlandson (1997) and Weissenrieder (2002) represent recent social science analysis of Luke. Feminist critique and analysis of Luke is represented by Bieberstein (1998) and Levine and Blickenstaff (2002). Cadwallader (2002), Elvey (2002), and Trainor (2000) present environmental interpretations of Luke. Darr (1998), Heil (1999), Roth (1997), Thompsons and Phillips (1998), Tuckett (1995), and Wasserberg (1998) provide recent literary studies of Luke. Johnson (2002), Kurth (2000), Moessner (1999), Rusam (2003), and Wetherly (1994) study Luke in relationship to the Hebrew Bible, the Jews, and Israel's legacy to the early church. Orton (1999) and Talbert (2003) contain assorted studies on Luke. Parsons and Pervo (1993) and Verheyden (1999) revisit the literary unity of Luke-Acts.

Bibliography: **T. H. Akaabiam,** *The Proclamation of the Good News: A Study of Lk 24 in Tiv Context* (1999). **L. Alexander** *The Preface to Luke's Gospel: Literary Convention and Social Context in Luke 1.1-4 and Acts 1.1* (SNTSMS 78, 1993). **J. M. Arlandson,** *Women, Class, and Society in Early Christianity: Models from Luke-Acts* (1997). **F. C. Baur,** *Kritische Untersuchungen über die kanonischen Evangelien ihr Verhaltnis zu einander ihren Charakter und Ursprung* (1847). **S. Bieberstein,** *Verschwiegene Jüngerinnen, vergessene Zeuginnen: Gebrochene Konzepte im Lukasevangelium* (NTOA 38, 1998). **M.-E. Boismard,** *L'évangile de l'enfance (Luc 1-2) selon le proto-Luc* (Ebib, n.s. 35, 1997). **M. P. Bonz,** *The Past as Legacy: Luke-Acts and Ancient Epic* (2000). **L. Bormann,** *Recht, Gerechtigkeit und Religion im Lukasevangelium* (SUNT 24, 2001). **F. Bovon,** *Luke the Theologian: Thirty-Three Years of Research (1950-83)* (PTMS 12; rev. ET 1987); *Luke 1: A Commentary on the Gospel of Luke 1:1-9:50* (Hermeneia, 2002). **R. E. Brown,** *The Birth of the Messiah: A Commentary on the Infancy Narratives in the Gospels of Matthew and Luke* (ABRL, 1993[2]). **H. D. Buckwalter,** *The Character and Purpose of Luke's Christology* (SNTSMS 89, 1996). **B. Byrne,** *The Hospitality of God: A Reading of Luke's Gospel* (2000). **H. J. Cadbury,** *The Making of Luke-Acts* (1927). **A. H. Cadwallader,** "Swords into Ploughshares: The End of War? (Q/Luke 9.62)," *The Earth Story in the New Testament* (ed. N. C. Habel and V. Balabanski, Earth Bible 5, 2002) 57-75. **J. Calvin,** *A Harmony of the Gospels* (ed. T. F. Torrance, 3 vols. 1972). **B. S. Childs,** *The NT as Canon: An Introduction* (1985). **H. Conzelmann,** *The Theology of St. Luke* (1960); *An Outline of the Theology of the NT* (1969). **S. Cunningham,** *"Through Many Tribulations": The Theology of Persecution in Luke-Acts* (JSNTSup 142, 1997).). **J. A. Darr,** "Herod the Fox: Audience Criticism and Lukan Characterization" (JSNTSup 163, 1998). **F. Dreyfus,** "Exégèse en Sorbonne, Exégèse en Église," *RB* 81 (1975) 321-59. **A. Elvey,** "Storing Up Death, Storing Up Life: An Earth Story in Luke 12.13-34," *The Earth Story in the New Testament* (ed. N. C. Habel and V. Balabanski, Earth Bible 5, 2002) 95-107. **J. A. Fitzmyer,** *The Gospel According to Luke* (AB 28-28A, 1981, 1985). **S. R. Garrett,** *The Demise of the Devil: Magic and the Demonic in Luke's Writings* (1989). **M. D. Goulder,** *The Evangelists' Calendar: A Lectionary Explana-tion of the Development of Scripture* (1978); *Luke: A New Paradigm* (1989). **D. B. Gowler,** *Host, Guest, Enemy and Friend: Portraits of the Pharisees in Luke and Acts* (1991). **J. B. Green,** *The Gospel of Luke* (NICNT, 1997); *The Theology of the Gospel of Luke* (New Testament Theology, 1995); "Luke," *NISB* (2003) 1847-1903. **J. B. Green and M. C. McKeever,** *Luke-Acts and New Testament Historiography* (IBR Bibliographies 8, 1994). **A. von Harnack,** *Luke the Physician: The Author of the Third Gospel and the Acts of the Apostles* (NT Studies, 1907); *The Sayings of Jesus: The Second Source of St. Matthew and St. Luke* (NT Studies 2, 1908). **C. Heil,** *Lukas und Q: Studien zur lukanischen Redaktion des Spruchevangeliums Q* (BZNW 111, 2003). **J. P. Heil,** *The Meal Scenes in Luke-Acts: An Audience-Oriented Approach* (SBLMS 52, 1999). **H. Hendrickx,** *The Third Gospel for the Third World* (4 vols. in 7, 1996-2001). **L. T. Johnson,**

Septuagintal Midrash in the Speeches of Acts (Père Marquette Lecture in Theology 2002, 2002). **J. Knight,** *Luke's Gospel* (New Testament Readings, 1998). **C. Kurth,** *Die Stimmen der Propheten erfüllt: Jesu Geschick und "die" Juden nach der Darstellung des Lukas* (BWANT 8, 2000). **G. Lafon,** *L'esprit de la lettre: Lectures de l'Evangile selon saint Luc* (2001). **A.-J. Levine with M. Blickenstaff** (eds.), *A Feminist Companion to Luke* (Feminist Companion to the New Testament and Early Christian Writings 3, 2002). **J. Lieu,** *The Gospel of Luke* (Epworth Commentaries, 1997). **I. H. Marshall,** *The Gospel of Luke* (NIGTC, 1978). **A. J. McNicol, with D. L. Dungan and D. B. Peabody,** *Beyond the Q Impasse: Luke's Use of Matthew* (1996). **D. P. Moessner** (ed.), *Jesus and the Heritage of Israel: Luke's Narrative Claim upon Israel's Legacy* (Luke the Interpreter of Israel 1, 1999). **G. D. Nave, Jr.,** *The Role and Function of Repentance in Luke-Acts* (Academia Biblica 4, 2002). **J. Neyrey** (ed.), *The Social World of Luke-Acts: Models for Interpretation* (1991). **J. Nolland,** *Luke* (WBC 35A-C, 1989, 1993a, 1993b). **D. E. Orton** (ed.), *The Composition of Luke's Gospel: Selected Studies from "Novum Testamentum"* (Brill's Readers in Biblical Studies 1, 1999). **M. C. Parsons and R. I. Pervo,** *Rethinking the Unity of Luke and Acts* (1993). **D. B. Peabody, L. Cope and A. J. McNicol** (eds.), *One Gospel From Two: Mark's Use of Matthew and Luke* (2002). **N. R. Petersen,** *Literary Criticism for NT Critics* (1978). **T. E. Phillips,** *Reading Issues of Wealth and Poverty in Luke-Acts* (Studies in the Bible and Early Christianity 48, 2001). **P. Pokorný,** *Theologie der lukanischen Schriften* (FRLANT 174, 1998). **M. Prior,** *Jesus, the Liberator: Nazareth Liberation Theology* (Luke 4. 16-30) (Biblical Seminar 26, 1995). **A. Rabil, Jr.,** *Erasmus and the NT* (TUMSR 1, 1972). **W. M. Ramsay,** *Was Christ Born at Bethlehem? A Study of the Credibility of St. Luke* (1905); *The Bearing of Recent Discovery on the Trustworthiness of the NT* (1915). **M. Rese,** "Das Lukas-Evangelium: Ein Forschungsbericht," *ANRW* II.25.3 (1986) 2258-328. **S. J. Roth,** *The Blind, the Lame, and the Poor: Character Types in Luke-Acts* (JSNTSup 144, 1997). **E. Rummel,** *Erasmus' Annotations on the NT: From Philologist to Theologian* (1986). **D. Rusam,** *Das Alte Testament bei Lukas* (BZNW 112, 2003). **A. Schweitzer,** *The Quest of the Historical Jesus: A Critical Study of Its Progress from Reimarus to Wrede* (1910; complete ET 2001). **T. K. Seim,** *The Double Message: Patterns of Gender in Luke-Acts* (1994). **B. Streeter,** *The Four Gospels: A Study of Origins, Treating of the Manuscript Tradition, Sources, Authorship, and Date* (1924). **C. H. Talbert** (ed.), *Reimarus: Fragments* (1970); (ed.), *Perspectives on Luke-Acts* (1978); *Reading Luke: A Literary and Theological Commentary on the Third Gospel* (1982); (ed.), *Luke-Acts: New Perspectives from the Society of Biblical Literature Seminar* (1983); *Reading Luke-Acts in its Mediterranean Milieu* (NovTSup 107, 2003). **R. C. Tannehill,** *The Narrative Unity of Luke-Acts: A Literary Interpretation,* vol. 1, *The Gospel According to Luke* (1986); *Luke* (ANTC, 1996). **V. Taylor,** *Behind the Third Gospel: A Study of the Proto-Luke Hypothesis* (1926); *The Passion Narrative of St. Luke: A Critical and Historical Investigation* (1972). **R. P. Thompson and T. E. Phillips** (eds.), *Literary Studies in Luke-Acts: Essays in Honor of Joseph B. Tyson* (1998). **M. Trainor,** "'And on Earth, Peace . . . ' (Luke 21.14)," *Readings from the Perspective of Earth* (ed. N. C. Habel, Earth Bible 1, 2000) 174-92. **C. M. Tuckett,** *Luke* (NTG, 1996); *Luke's Literary Achievement: Collected Essays* (JSNTSup 116, 1995). **J. Verheyden** (ed.), *The Unity of Luke-Acts* (BETL 142, 1999). **G. Wasserberg,** *Aus Israels Mitte—Heil für die Welt: eine narrativ-exegetische Studie zur Theologie des Lukas* (BZNW 92, 1998). **J. A. Weatherly,** *Jewish Responsibility for the Death of Jesus in Luke-Acts* (JSNTSup 106, 1994). **A. Weissenrieder,** "The Plague of Uncleanness?: The Ancient Illness Construct 'Issue of Blood' in Luke 8:43-48," *The Social Setting of Jesus and the Gospels* (ed. W. Stegemann, B. J. Malina, G. Theissen 2002) 207-22.

C. H. Talbert

THE NEW TESTAMENT CANON

John, Gospel of

The interpretation of the Gospel of John has led a double life. On the surface the text appears relatively simple; however, those who have read this Gospel more carefully are aware of its complexity. Interpreters inevitably must deal with a number of issues if they are to read with greater understanding. First and foremost among those issues is the uniqueness of this Gospel among the canonical Gospels (Canon of the Bible*§) and its distinctive Christian thought. Other issues include the identity of the Fourth Evangelist, the purpose for which the Gospel was written, the intellectual and religious milieu out of which it came, and the ambiguity of its teachings.

1. *The Early Church.* The earliest known instance of the interpretation of the Gospel of John may be found in 1 John (cf., e.g., the prologues of each). In that document the unnamed author appeals to themes found in the Gospel to address a schism in the first readers' church. Thus 1 John may be early evidence of two classic interpretations of the Fourth Gospel that were destined to dominate the early centuries of the church. The schismatics, it is argued (R. Brown 1982), understood the Johannine community's Gospel in terms that prefigured later Gnostic Interpretation*§, while the author of 1 John used the tradition embedded in it to defend views that would later become characteristic of early Christian orthodoxy (e.g., Christ's humanity, 1 John 4:2).

Beyond the canonical evidence, the existence and circulation of the Gospel of John are demonstrated by at least the middle of the second century. By ca. 180 C.E. it was widely held that the Gospel was the work of John, son of Zebedee, the "beloved disciple" of the narrative. By the mid to late second century, Gnostic Christians, the Montanist movement, and emerging orthodoxy hotly contested the interpretation of John. The Gnostics§ allegorized the Gospel for their spiritualizing and anti-material understanding of the faith. The Montanists in part derived their understanding of their own divine inspiration from the Johannine Paraclete texts (R. Heine 1987-88). Early Christian writers such as Irenaeus§, Origen§, and Clement of Alexandria§ used John to argue against the Gnostics and Montanists. Tertullian§, Athanasius§, Gregory of Nyssa§, and Augustine§ (M. Comeau 1930) all used the Gospel to argue their (emerging orthodox) positions on Christology and the Trinity. Origen also noted John's distinctiveness when compared to the Synoptic Gospels.

2. *The Middle Ages.* John Scottus Eriugena§, Alcuin§, and Thomas Aquinas§ represent medieval interpretations of John. Eriugena took the Greek text of John quite seriously and investigated John's use of symbolic language, a persistent concern among John's interpreters throughout the centuries. Alcuin relied upon a full-fledged allegorical interpretation and reflected the Mariological concerns of the age. Aquinas combined the complex use of the scholastic method with a sensitivity to the spiritual concerns of the text (Black 1986).

3. *The Reformation.* The period of the Reformation and the rise of humanism brought a new convergence of influences to bear on the reading of the Fourth Gospel. Among those disparate forces were a concern to preserve the tradition of interpretation established in the patristic period and continued through the Middle Ages, a new interest in rhetoric and philology arising from the humanism of the era (e.g., H. Grotius 1641), and the theological themes of the Reformation movement.

Erasmus§ (1991) noted the obscurity of Johannine language, which made paraphrasing difficult, if not impossible; and he concluded that the language is filled with riddles (a conclusion still echoed in contemporary scholarship). The Gospel's subject matter (the divinity of Christ) was also something of a riddle for Erasmus. The Reformers sought to clarify those riddles, reflecting Erasmus's interest in the Fourth Gospel's rhetoric (cf. M. Hoffmann 1997).

The reformers brought to the Johannine text newly revived theological issues. They also dared, however, to assess critically the relative value of the canonical books, not holding them to be of equal worth. Luther[§] (LW, 35:362) cherished the Fourth Gospel as "the one, fine, true, and chief gospel, and is far, far to be preferred over the other three and placed high above them." Among other things, Luther premised his view on the simple fact that this Gospel offered more of Jesus' words than did the others. He thought Scripture had one simple meaning and functioned to arouse faith in the reader by means of both law and gospel—that is, by both killing human self-confidence and bestowing new life. A contrast of faith and reason also figured prominently in his treatment of John. Luther persistently tended to refer the text to faith; e.g., he insisted that the sin referred to in 16:8 is unbelief.

The themes in Calvin's[§] commentary (1949) are similar. He maintained that the Gospel of John deals more with doctrine than with the narrative of Jesus' life and suggested that while the Synoptics disclose Jesus' "body," John reveals his "soul." Thus the Fourth Gospel provides the key for opening the first three. Thereby, the Reformation continued the emphasis on John as the "spiritual" Gospel. As well as stressing salvation by grace and the conflict of revelation and reason, Calvin was predisposed to find in the Gospel the sovereignty of God rather than the futility of human existence. However, both Luther's and Calvin's work on John betray apologetic and polemic features.

Not unlike its initial interpretation to define and defend proper doctrine against heresy, the reformers found in the Gospel of John some of the biblical basis for their efforts to redirect the church. John 6, for instance, figured prominently in the debates over the eucharist in 1520. Both Luther and Calvin insisted that the discourse in 6:22-71 was concerned with faith and denied that it was appropriately interpreted in the light of the Lord's Supper. They also disallowed the use of 3:5 as authority for the church's practice of baptism. Thus they opened an ongoing discussion over the symbolism of these two passages and the general problem of the role of the sacraments in Johannine thought.

Two examples of Reformation interpretation of John are found in the commentaries of P. Melanchthon[§] and W. Musculus[§]. Influenced by Luther's writing, Musculus left the monastery, became a pastor in Augsburg, and eventually settled in Zurich. His exegetical work *Commentariorum in Evangelistam Ioannem* (1547) displays the use of both patristic and medieval interpretative methods, yet also shows the influence of humanism (C. Farmer 1997). When a passage proved difficult, Musculus frequently sought insights from tradition. He seems to have regarded the text as rich in meaning and thick in reference, much as his predecessors had. Although appreciative of medieval interpreters, he was critical of how quickly they allegorized Johannine passages. He justified his own use of allegory only when he believed the literal meaning and context called for it; e.g., he treated the feeding of the crowd in chapter 6 allegorically because Jesus later in the chapter speaks of himself as "bread." Still, his allegorization of John is greater than that of other Reformation commentators, although the influence of humanism is evident in his careful consideration of linguistic matters. Clearly and profoundly affected by Erasmus, the only one of his contemporaries named in the commentary, Musculus was willing, however, to disagree with him. Most significant about Musculus's interpretative method is his concern to identify the relevance of a passage for his contemporary readers. Always regarding the text as a resource for individual Christian life and faith, he represents the best of Reformation interpretation.

Musculus's commentary also demonstrates his difference with the Roman Catholic interpreters of the time. His theological commitments surface in his discussion of the Sabbath controversy in 5:9-18 in which he carefully defined the true nature of Sabbath obedience and stressed the moral obligations of the healed man. Going further than his Catholic contemporaries, he allegorized the healing into a statement of human salvation and even the whole history of God's saving activity. His Reformation beliefs led him to see the paralyzed man lying near the pool as representative of the weakness of the human will to win its own salvation; he viewed Christ's healing as symbolic of God's grace and mercy.

Melanchthon's small commentary (*Annotationes in Johannem* 1523) is equally representative of the interpretation of John during the Reformation (T. Wengert 1987). Called the first "Protestant" commentary on John, it masterfully combines humanism, Luther's Reformation principles, and the patristic and medieval traditions of interpretation. Like Musculus, Melanchthon extensively used the early writers; like medieval exegetes, he allegorized the text where tradition had done so (e.g., the Lamb of God). However, where the patristic interpretations and those of the Middle Ages had tended to concentrate on the christological meaning of passages, Melanchthon shifted attention toward the soteriological implications of the text, often thereby honoring the simpler meaning. As the church had before him, he found trinitarian language in 1:1-18; however, along with Luther he emphasized that the Word is life that slays death and that divine grace motivated the incarnation, thus exemplifying the theological thrust of the Lutheran movement.

Similarly, he parted company with medieval interpretations and their influence on the dominant church of the day most notably on two issues: first, the power of free will and the merit of human behavior as opposed to justification by faith alone, and second, the authority of the papal office for Christian faith and piety. For example, he interpreted 15:16 in terms of the election of all Christians through grace and not the election of the apostles to their office. He expressed his humanism in attention to the rhetoric of the text and philological concerns as well as to the oratorical qualities of the Johannine Jesus. But always he favored theological issues; for Melanchthon the Fourth Evangelist was both a historian and a teacher of right doctrine.

The period of the Reformation reinforced the role of the Gospel of John as a source for sound theology, as the earliest interpretations had done. But the influence of humanism broadened the scope of Johannine interpretation once and for all. It anticipated the freeing of the Gospel from the grasp of the church by posing its Authority*[§] over the church and its teachings. Moreover, the influence of humanism hinted at the possibility that John was valuable beyond the shaping of proper doctrine; hence it opened the way for the Enlightenment.

4. *The Enlightenment.* This period brought a stream of critical questions and ushered in a period of interpretative creativity equaled only by the patristic era. Among the most vital questions, the pursuit of which occasioned pivotal points in the reading of the Fourth Gospel, are the apostolic authorship and historical reliability of the Johannine narrative, the relationship of the Gospel to the Synoptics, and the religious and philosophical setting for the origin of the Gospel.

The new issues first erupted around the questions of the apostolic origin and historical reliability of the Johannine representation of Jesus. R. Simon's[§] Textual Criticism*[§] (1689) combined with Deism*[§] to open the discussion of these issues. Simon, sometimes named "the founder of the science of New Testament introduction" (T. Zahn, *RE*, 5, 263), sought to defend the teachings of Roman Catholicism against the assault of the reformers but was in due course expelled from the priesthood. His insight that the names attached to the Gospels were not the work of the evangelists themselves invited study of the identity of the Fourth Evangelist.

Eighteenth-century interpretation of the Gospel, however, continued the early view that John was the "spiritual" Gospel penned by the apostle John. H. S. Reimarus[§] expounded this view, contending that John knew but corrected the Synoptics and that the two could not be harmonized; in fact, the historical reliability of each was dubious (1972, 2:582). Lessing expanded this view in *Neue Hypothese über die Evangelisten als blosse menschliche Geschichtsschreiber betrachtet* (1777-78). In the last decade of the eighteenth century, both Lessing and J. G. Herder[§] (*Christliche Schriften* 3 1797) were the first to question the apostolic authorship of the Gospel;

they argued that, compared with the Synoptics, the Gospel of John enhanced Christ's dignity. Herder saw John as an "echo" of the Synoptics that nonetheless clarified them. John stretched the reaches of Jesus' message beyond Judaism to the whole world.

In the nineteenth century the historical reliability of the Gospel of John received further attention. A former Anglican priest who had moved toward Unitarianism, E. Evanson[§] (1805) challenged the Gospel's apostolic origin and boldly used Luke-Acts to reject the reliability and apostolic origin not only of the Gospel of John, but also of Matthew and Mark and other New Testament writings. In his anonymously published *Der Evangelist Johannes und seine Ausleger vor dem jüngsten Gericht* (2 vols. 1801-4), E. Vogel (1750-1823) continued the argument against the traditional authorship of the Gospel. In his 1820 work K. Bretschneider (1776-1848) summarized the arguments against the Gospel's authenticity and for identifying its author as an Alexandrian gentile Christian of the second century; however, in light of F. Schleiermacher's[§] (1837) and others' defense of the Gospel, he later recanted his view. Schleiermacher staunchly defended the Gospel on which he had constructed his Christology, seeing in the Fourth Gospel a Jesus who was at the same time both human and divine.

D. F. Strauss[§] (1835) questioned the historical credibility of the Fourth Gospel and insisted that the evangelist had imposed his own speech in the style of Hellenistic philosophy on Jesus and John the Baptist. He offered, furthermore, a detailed analysis of the points at which the Synoptics and Acts disagreed with the Fourth Gospel on historical matters, concluding that the Gospel of John was wrong (e.g., Jesus did not have a mission among the Samaritans as John 4 suggests). Of the four Gospels, John's is the most mythological (i.e., ideas represented in objects) and hence suffered the most at the hands of Strauss's Hegelian construction. He posed an either/or alternative for interpreters: Follow either the Synoptics or John, for no harmonization between them is possible.

Other scholars also questioned the historical credibility of the Fourth Gospel. A. Loisy[§] (1903, 1921[2]), not unlike W. Wrede[§] (1903, 1933[2]), argued that the Fourth Evangelist was more a theologian and apologist against Judaism than a historian. The Gospel cannot be taken as a complement to the Synoptics but needs to be understood as an ecclesiastical witness indifferent to history. According to Loisy, the evangelist uses an allegorical method, provides a spiritual and mystical portrayal of Christ, and makes Christ into a theological dogma. C. Wiezsäcker (1902[3]) advanced the theory that the Fourth Evangelist was a secondhand disciple of the one called "the disciple whom Jesus loved" and, removed from an immediate relationship with the historical Jesus, repressed his life into an entirely didactic work. A. Jülicher[§] (1894) understood the Gospel of John to be a "philosophical prose-poem" without value as a source for discovering the historical Jesus. C. Weisse[§] (1838) argued that the Johannine discourses actually originated from the apostle John and were written down after his death. They were personal images of the apostle's view of Christ rather than historical reminiscences (so also D. Schenkel and A. Schweizer).

With increasing success in demolishing apostolic authorship came a movement to date the Gospel as late as 130-135 C.E. (Lützelberger) or even 170 C.E. (F. C. Baur). Although Baur[§] thought John contained nothing historical and was a post-Pauline (Paul[†§]) Christian reflection, he valued it because of its power to compel readers to make a decision for or against God. However, B. Bauer[§] (1840) appreciated its literary qualities in spite of its unreliability as a historical document. The Fourth Evangelist was an artist, even though the work is flawed. The discourses in particular demonstrate evidence of careless editing, Bauer argued. From his reading of John he developed a fanciful portrait of Jesus that led him finally to assert that Jesus was not a historical figure at all (1852).

Other scholars, however, disagreed. Schleiermacher staunchly maintained the apostolic origin of the Gospel and granted it priority over the Synoptics, regarding 1:14 alone as the basic text for the whole of theology. W. De Wette[§] (1824) defended the authenticity of the Gospel, even though he believed that portions of it had been revised by a later figure. K. Frommann (1839) made a gallant effort—however imprecise—to distinguish between the transmitted accounts of Jesus and the Johannine Christ by isolating what he thought might be redactional additions to the discourse materials. Even more gallant was the defense of the claim, mounted by F. Büchsel (1928), that the Fourth Evangelist was an eyewitness expressing genuine Christian ideas. He even ventured to assert the historical superiority of the Fourth Gospel to the other three. Still others sought to strike a compromise by claiming historical reliability for the narratives but not the discourses. Among these were B. Weiss[§], W. Bousset[§], and E. Renan[§].

Inevitably bound up with the question of John's authorship and historical reliability was its relationship with the first three Gospels. The common view that John represented a "spiritual" Gospel implicitly supposed that it was written as a conscious supplement to the Synoptics. Now that view was challenged. Even without necessarily casting doubt on historical reliability or apostolic authorship, reservations or outright denials that the Fourth Evangelist knew and made use of the Synoptics came from several corners (e.g., J. Semler 1771, 1772; G. Lessing; J. Wegscheider; F. Schleiermacher; and H. Weisse). The pursuit of a resolution to the uncertain relationship between the Synoptics and the Gospel of John carried well into the twentieth century, where its most vigorous debate is still found.

Other scholars raised questions that were also destined to be continued in the twentieth century. The Hebrew Bible scholar J. Wellhausen[§] (1907, 1908) questioned the unity and arrangement of the Gospel. Noting that 14:31 should be immediately followed by 18:1, he theorized that the discourses between the two passages were misplaced. The Gospel was, he concluded, the product of a process involving several stages. E. Schwartz (1907, 1908) studied the *aporias* in the Gospel and concluded that it is composed of numerous overlapping strata, although he despaired of the possibility of ever reconstructing its earliest form. The proposals of Wellhausen and Schwartz were later pursued by F. Spitta[§] and H. Wendt[§]. The former postulated a foundational Gospel written by John, son of Zebedee, which an editor expanded. Wendt favored the discourses over the narrative material, believing that the sayings of Jesus betrayed the knowledge of one who personally knew the historical Jesus. These studies launched what became a more widespread theory in the second half of the twentieth century.

The rise of the Religionsgeschichtliche Schule*[§] propelled Johannine interpretation into the question of the Gospel's religious and intellectual milieu. As a result, a general but not unanimous shift occurred away from proposals for a Jewish setting toward those suggesting Hellenistic or oriental contexts. A. von Harnack[§] (1927) continued to maintain that the Gospel was derived from Palestinian Judaism and that its author was doubtless born a Jew, but he conceded that Johannine theology is Christian mysticism. Early in the nineteenth century de Wette classified New Testament literature into Jewish, Christian, Alexandrian or Hellenistic, and Pauline and located the Gospel of John in the second of his categories. The Gospel is rooted in the soil of Hellenistic mysticism, claimed Bousset (1905). Out of those roots it presents a mysticism that seeks a vision of God leading to divinization.

J. D. Michaelis[§] (1788[4]) was apparently the first to see a positive relationship between Johannine thought and Gnosticism. Loisy thought that the Fourth Evangelist had been trained in Gnosticism before becoming a Christian and that in the second century the first form of the Gospel underwent revision to make it compatible with dominant Christian thought. H. Gunkel[§] (1903) proposed that Johannine thought is syncretistic in contrast to the simple message of Jesus. Given the Johannine emphasis on knowledge and dualism, the Fourth Evangelist must have had contact with an "oriental gnosis."

A new but related candidate for the setting of the Gospel arose in the form of the Mandaeans, born in the work of W. Brandt, who argued that Mandaeanism had Jewish roots. It was furthered first by R. Harris's publication of the Syriac Odes of Solomon (1909) and then by M. Lidzbarski's[§] publications of and reflections on the Mandaean literature (1915, 1925). The Odes attracted immediate attention since there were obvious parallels between them and the Johannine discourses. Harris argued that they were extant in their present form at the time of the writing of the Gospel, while von Harnack maintained that a Christian had revised them at a later time. R. Reitzenstein[§] (1919) and W. Bauer[§] (1925[2]) were among the forceful proponents of the theory that Mandaeanism and the Odes were influential in the composition of the Fourth Gospel.

Building on the work of Reitzenstein and Lidzbarski, R. Bultmann[§] (1919) argued that the Gospel was based on a redeemer myth taken over from Mandaean and Manichaean sources. The content of Johannine theology is shaped by oriental Mythology*[§], proving how oriental-Gnostic speculation penetrated early Christianity in general. The Fourth Gospel represents a special and unique form of Christianity focused on a revealer figure. Remarkably, however, the central thesis of this form of early Christian thought is that Jesus reveals nothing more than the fact that he is the revealer. Behind that, Bultmann was persuaded, is a pre-Christian redeemer myth that lacks the full identification of the redeemed with the redeemer. The evangelist is interested only in the fact of the revelation, not its content.

5. *Twentieth Century.* Bultmann provides a bridge from the energetic scholarship of the nineteenth century to that of the mid-twentieth century since, although he was in many ways a product of the nineteenth century, his influence cast a long shadow into the contemporary period. In large part the previous period set the agenda for Johannine interpretation in the twentieth century, and Bultmann's contributions to that agenda can hardly be overemphasized. He proposed that a pre-Christian Gnosticism shaped the environment out of which the Gospel was written and accentuated the Gospel's polemic against the followers of John the Baptizer, a group that most clearly manifested oriental Gnosticism.

With this assumption Bultmann fashioned an influential theory for the sources employed in the Gospel's composition (D. M. Smith 1965). Appealing to stylistic, contextual, and content evidence, he argued for the existence of three primary sources: For the discourses the Fourth Evangelist used a collection of *Offenbarungsreden* similar to the Odes of Solomon; the Semeia source resides behind the narrative of Jesus' wonders; and a passion source (independent of the Synoptic narratives) underlies the story of Jesus' death and resurrection. Beyond these three basic sources, as well as others, Bultmann posited a serious disruption of the arrangement of the original Gospel (e.g., chaps. 4, 5, 6, and 7) and additions by an "ecclesiastical redactor" (e.g., 6:51-58). This hypothetical redactor attempted to correct the theology of the Evangelist and to harmonize the Gospel with the Synoptics, especially in passages concerning the sacraments, eschatology, the eyewitness attestation of the Gospel, and the beloved disciple.

Equally important among Bultmann's contributions is his effort to construct a *sachlich* theology of the Gospel (e.g., his insistence that Jesus reveals no more than that he is the Revealer), at the heart of which is Bultmann's hermeneutic. At the point of convergence among his Lutheranism, Heideggerian existentialism, and *Religionsgeschichtliche Schule* commitment, Bultmann formulated his demythologization scheme. For him the Fourth Evangelist represented the first demythologizer of the Christian message, producing a document that emphasizes existential decision in response to revelation.

The nineteenth century ignited the doubt that the Fourth Evangelist knew and used the Synoptic Gospels, and Bultmann seems to have shared that doubt. In the twentieth century the sparks of doubt were fanned into a roaring fire of controversy (Smith 1992). In the first quarter of the century H. Windisch[§], B. Streeter[§], and B. Bacon[§] advanced convincing arguments for the Fourth Evangelist's use of at least Mark and Luke, a view that temporarily comprised something of a consensus. Shortly, however, P. Gardner-Smith (1938) amassed an impressive yet simple case for the independence of John from the Synoptics. While not unanimously success-ful, his study moved Johannine interpretation decisively away from the assumption that the evangelist knew and used the Synoptics to write a supplementary Gospel. For a time the rela-tionship of the Synoptics and the Fourth Gospel seemed almost settled, but arguments for dependence continued to persist (e.g., C. Barrett 1978[2]). Nonetheless, the formation of a con-sensus around Gardner-Smith seemed firm and was substantiated near the midpoint of the cen-tury by the work of C. H. Dodd[§] (1963). The consensus, however, was to be short-lived and began to unravel in stages.

The first stage of the demolition of agreement occurred as researchers explored parallels between Luke and John. J. Schniewind[§] (1958), J. Bailey (1963), and others mounted impres-sive evidence of literary connections between John and Luke. The second stage began with N. PERRIN's proposal (1974) that Mark's passion narrative was the composition of the Second Evangelist and not the reproduction of a pre-Markan narrative. If that is the case, then the sim-ilarities between the passion stories in Mark and John must be due to the Fourth Evangelist's acquaintance with the Gospel of Mark and not with a pre-Markan source. The final stage of the demise of the consensus of Johannine independence came from the European scene, where a new and vigorous effort to study Johannine and synoptic parallels was undertaken with some success (e.g., M. Boismard and A. Lamouille 1970; F. Neirynck 1992; A. Dauer 1984; and B. de Solages 1979). As a consequence of the carnage done to the Gardner-Smith consensus, by the first decade of the twenty-first century, views of the relationship between John and the Synoptics lack any unanimity whatsoever; and a pluralism of perspectives pervades contempo-rary scholarship.

Nonetheless, the theory of John's independence from the Synoptic Gospels has reopened the question of the Gospel's historical reliability. If the Fourth Evangelist did not know or use the Synoptic Gospels, then the Gospel could have been written at least contemporaneously with the Synoptics (although the predominant dating remains 90-95 C.E.). The relative value of the Gospel of John for access to the historical Jesus has been enhanced, too, by the acknowledg-ment that none of the canonical Gospels has historical reporting as its primary goal. The Fourth Gospel stands on common ground with the Synoptics in seeking to proclaim the existential importance of the historical event of Jesus of Nazareth.

On the one hand, some scholars still propose that the evangelist was an eyewitness to that historical event, if not one of the apostles (e.g., J. Robinson 1985; D. Carson 1991), and tend to date it earlier. On the other hand, the absence of such claims has made it possible for others to propose that the historical reliability of John is not as uncertain as scholarship had argued in the nineteenth century. Dodd (1963) contended that the Fourth Evangelist (independently of the Synoptics) employed an oral tradition that was the source from which all the evangelists drew material and represented the earliest Christian tradition. Consequently, the narratives of the Fourth Gospel are potentially as historical as are those of the Synoptics (so also B. Lindars 1972). The discourse material may also be understood in quite different ways than often pro-posed in the nineteenth century. They may be homiletical treatments of some kernel having its source in the historical Jesus (e.g., Lindars 1972; Brown 1966). The Gospel is not commonly regarded as a prime source for knowledge of the historical Jesus, but neither is it to be dismissed out of hand as devoid of historical value.

Since the middle of the twentieth century, scholarship has actually shown little interest in identifying the author of the Fourth Gospel. Instead, in the wake of Bultmann's influence, atten-tion has focused on the reconstruction of the sources used by the evangelist (R. Kysar 1975, 1984). Following the precedent set by late nineteenth-century investigations, the supposition that the Gospel entailed sources and/or a process of composition was often advanced (e.g., E. Hirsch 1936a). Proposals for the isolation of written sources behind the Gospel have especially focused on a "signs source" (e.g., R. Schnackenburg 1968; R. Fortna 1970, 1989; W. Nicol 1972) and have enjoyed some favor; however, as a whole they have been generally unsuccessful in winning wide endorsement. On the other hand, scholars have more readily embraced theories for the development of the present Gospel through successive stages of composition or editing and redaction (e.g., Brown 1966, 1970, 1979; Lindars 1972; and, in a limited way, Schnackenburg 1968, 1980, 1982). Such theories postulate that the original Gospel was expanded and edited a number of times before reaching its present form; some scholars (e.g., F. Segovia 1982) find traces of the language and situation of 1 John in the later redactions.

Attention to sources and the development of the present form of the Gospel drew scholarship to study the community responsible for the document's origin (Kysar 1981). R. A. Culpepper (1975) proposed that the community constituted a "school" in the classical sense, and R. Brown[§] provided a description of that group (1979; cf. Cullmann 1976). As the focus shifted away from the identity of the evangelist to the community involved in the Gospel's formation, studies of the situation of that church and the message of the Gospel to it emerged (e.g., D. Rensberger 1988). In addition to the community's dialogue with its social setting (R. Whitacre 1980), scholarship became interested in the possibility of an intra-community controversy in the Gospel (e.g., P. Anderson 1996). North American scholarship seemed for a time on the brink of a consensus on the community responsible for the Gospel, but after decades of scholarship there is little agreement on precisely what compositional process resulted in the present form of the Fourth Gospel. As a consequence of this lack of consensus about the process of composition, Redaction-critical*[§] studies have been crippled, although frequent.

The shift of views on the issue of the setting for the Gospel is less vague. The nineteenth century moved steadily away from a Jewish setting toward a Hellenistic and/or Gnostic one. In many circles during the first half of the twentieth century, Gnostic or Hellenistic hypotheses prevailed, not the least because of Bultmann's influence. E. Hirsch (1936b) argued that the Fourth Evangelist was more comfortable with classical Greek literature than with Jewish thought and style. Other examples include E. Käsemann's[§] (1968) Gnostic and Dodd's (1958) Hellenistic theses. Käsemann's efforts to identify the theology of the Gospel as a "naive doceticism" provoked considerable discussion, especially around the issue of the nature of the incarnation (1:14). L. Schottroff (1970) argued for a fundamentally Gnostic understanding of the world in the Fourth Gospel (cf. U. Schnelle 1992). Not universally accepted, this trend was dramatically reversed in the last third of the twentieth century.

The persistent advocacy for a Jewish setting for the Gospel accounts for this reversal. C. Burney[§] argued for an Aramaic origin; other scholars (e.g., Schattler 1930) recognized a Semitic quality in both its language and its thought. In his influential commentary J. Bernard (1928) proposed that the evangelist was a Jew who held much in common with Philo[†§]. Within that setting the first step of the reversal from a Hellenistic and/or Gnostic background to a Jewish one came with the obvious parallels between some of the Qumran documents (Dead Sea Scrolls*[§]) and the Gospel of John (e.g., the dualism of light and darkness) and the acknowledgment of the multiplicity of forms of first-century Judaism to which they witness.

The next and more significant step occurred when J. L. Martyn (1979[2], 1978) and Brown (1966) offered new proposals that significantly reshaped Johannine interpretation. Although Martyn's and Brown's proposals are different, together they suggest that the Gospel was written soon after the expulsion of the Johannine Christians from the Jewish synagogue and amid a vigorous debate between Christians and Jews in the locale where the Gospel was written. Their proposals were followed by a tidal wave of scholarship that built on their hypotheses and elucidated the Gospel from that perspective, or at least from the vantage point of a predominantly Jewish setting (e.g., W. Meeks 1972; R. Fortna 1970; and S. Pancaro 1975; see R. Kysar 1975). The Johannine discourses of Jesus too, P. Borgen proposed (1965), betray a homiletical pattern rooted in Jewish midrashim (Midrash§) common to both John and Philo. The theory of an expulsion from the synagogue and other studies have resulted in the reaffirmation of a basic (and perhaps heterodox) Jewish setting for the Gospel of John. Moreover, taken together these studies refocused understandings of the purpose of the Gospel on nurture amid crisis and not on evangelism, as 20:31 is sometimes interpreted to suggest (e.g., Carson 1991). The synagogue expulsion theory has nonetheless been challenged on a number of fronts, including the general question of the nature of Jewish-Christian relations in the first century as well as the adequacy of the textual evidence (esp. 9:22; 12:42; and 16:2) to sustain such a sweeping proposal.

While efforts to identify the author of the Fourth Gospel have subsided in many regions of contemporary scholarship, the question of the relation of the evangelist and the author of the Johannine epistles and Revelation continues to attract attention. Theories regarding the relationship of the Johannine Gospel and the epistles remain varied, including the persistent suggestion that at least 1 John was earlier than the Gospel (e.g., F. Büchsel 1928 and H. Wendt). Still, the proposal that the epistles were later products from and for the same community responsible for the Gospel is widely accepted (e.g., Brown 1979, 1982). There is less effort to argue for the common authorship of the Gospel and Revelation, although belief in the commonality of the Apocalypse with the Johannine corpus continues (e.g., J. du Rand 1991).

Finally, the last quarter of the twentieth century witnessed the emergence of several new interpretive methodologies, each of which has had an impact on the interpretation of the Gospel of John. The first was occasioned in large part by the Martyn-Brown hypotheses regarding the origin of the Gospel and employs social science methodologies for interpreting the text. Sociological (see Sociology and New Testament Studies*§) and anthropological models, it is proposed, provide insight into the community behind the text. The enterprise was begun by W. Meeks (1972) and carried forward in a very different way by J. Neyrey (1988) and even more markedly so by N. Peterson (1993). In general this effort has attempted to reconstruct the sectarian nature of the Johannine community and its social situation.

The more radical of the new methodologies is the new literary criticism (Literary Criticism*§). Social-Scientific*§ investigations continue to posit the value of understanding the historical origin of the Gospel. To some degree the new literary movement arose from dissatisfaction over the value of the older historical-critical methodology rooted in the previous several centuries and was spurred on by the new literary criticism used in other literature. It attempts to interpret John by means of the text without recourse to something that lies outside and beyond it (e.g., its historical setting) and to assume the text's unity against all source and redaction-critical procedures. Of course, the assertion that the Fourth Evangelist was a literary genius and the Gospel a poetic masterpiece was not the invention of late twentieth-century investigations. H. Windisch§ (1923) identified some of the dramatic qualities of the Johannine narrative, and H. Strathmann (1968) recognized the poetic powers of its language. Moreover, D. Wead (1970) anticipated the reversal that was about to occur. R. Culpepper (1983), however, opened a new frontier in the literary criticism of the Fourth Gospel. His work was followed by several investigations of the use of Johannine irony (P. Duke 1985; G. O'Day 1986), a Reader-Response*§ investigation of the implied reader (J. Staley 1988), studies of the Gospel's rhetoric (M. Davies 1992), a commentary on the farewell discourses (F. Segovia 1991), and finally several commentaries on the entire Gospel (e.g., F. Moloney 1993, 1996; M. Stibbe 1994). A. Dettwiler (1995) offers an intertextual literary reading (Intertextuality) of passages often understood as redactional. A variety of literary approaches and other new interpretations of the Gospel have emerged as well (Culpepper and F. Segovia 1991; Segovia 1996; see M. Gourgues 1995 for further bibliography). Especially significant are the recent studies that examine the role of women in the Gospel (e.g., G. O'Day 1992, 1995; A. Reinhartz 1994) and the relation of the Gospel to imperialism (Cross-Cultural Biblical Interpretation*§).

Old questions still remain unanswered. A multiplicity of hypotheses on central issues continues to exist, and new methods of interpretation now abound. All of these continue to make the interpretation of the Gospel of John as difficult and as crucial as it was when that initial interpretation in 1 John was written.

Recent commentaries on John include Beasely-Murray (1999), Dietzfelbinger (2001), the social science analysis of Malina and Rohrbaugh (1998), Moloney (1998), O'Day (2003), Schenke (1998), Schnelle (1998), Schwank, Smith (1999), and Wengst (2000-2001). Mills (2002) provides a bibliography of journal articles in Johannine studies. Boismard (2001) and Hofrichter (2002a, 2002b) both discuss the place of John in the Synoptic Problem. Recent collections of essays on various topics include Fortna and Thatcher (2001), Martyn (2003), Nissen and Pedersen (1999), Painter, Culpepper, and Segovia (2002), Orton (1999), and Schreiber and Stimpfle (2000). Kealy (2002), Larsson (2001), and Smith (2001) discuss the history of the interpretation of John. Discussions of the theological issues in John include Asiedu-Peprah (2001), Beenema (2002), Busse (2002), Brunson (2003), Cebulj (2000), Coloe (2001), Dayl-Denton (2000), Harstine (2002), Heise (2001), Ihenacho (2001), Kriener (2001), Kügler (1999), Labahn (1999), Lincoln (2000), Metzner (2000), Ringe (1999), Saeed (2000), Sasse (2000), Schmidt (2000), Scholtissek (2000), Schräder (2003), Theobald (2002), Thompson (2001), and Urban (2001). Gender issues in and feminist analyses of John are in Beirne (2003), Conway (1999), Fehribach (1998), Köstenberger (2001; a review of research), Lee (2002), Levine and Blickenstaff (2003), Ruschmann (2002), and Schneiders (1999). Studies of John's relationship to Judaism, anti-Semitism in John, Jewish Christianity in John, and Jewish interpretations of the Gospel include Bieringer, Pollefeyt, and Vandecasteele Vanneuville (2001), Diefenbach (2002), Lingad (2001), and Reinhartz (2001). Blomberg (2001) discusses the historical reliability of John. Postmodern and postcolonial studies of John include Chatelion Counet (2000) and Dube and Staley (2002). Recent literary studies of the Fourth Gospel include Koester (2003), Ng (2001), Nicklas (2001 implied reader), Popp (2001), Resseguie (2001), van der Watt (2000), and Webster (2003). Both Riesner (2002) and Therath (1999) study the intersection of geography and theology in John. Three cutting-edge approaches to John include the relationship between the Gospel and Freudian theory (Naegeli 2000), folklore analysis of John (Thatcher 2000), and environmental perspectives (Habel 2002, Wainright 2002, Balabanski 2002, Olajubu 2002).

Bibliography: E. Abbot, *The Authorship of the Fourth Gospel: External Evidences* (1880). **P. Anderson,** *The Christology of the Fourth Gospel: Its Unity and Disunity in the Light of John 6* (WUNT 78, 1996). **J. Ashton** (ed.), *The Interpretation of John* (Studies in NT Interpretation, 19972). **M. Asiedu-Peprah,** *Johannine Sabbath Conflicts as Juridical Controversy* (WUNT 2/132, 2001). **B. W. Bacon,** *The Fourth Gospel in Research and Debate* (1910). **J. Bailey,** *The Traditions Common to the Gospels of Luke and John* (NovTSup 7, 1963). **V. Balabansky,** "John 1—The Earth Bible Challenge: An Intra-textual Approach to Reading John 1," *The Earth Story in the New Testament* (ed. N. C. Habel and V. Balabansky, Earth Bible 5, 2002) 89-94. **C. K. Barrett,** *The Gospel According to St. John: An Introduction with Commentary and Notes on the Greek Text* (1978²). **B. Bauer,** *Kritik der evangelischen Geschichte des Johannes* (1840); *Kritik der paulinischen Briefe* (1852). **W. Bauer,** *Das Johannesevangelium erklärt* (1925²). **G. R. Beasley-Murray,** *John* (WBC 36, 19992). **J. Becker,** "Aus der Literatur zum Johannesevangelium (1978-80)," *TRu* 47 (1982) 279-306, 305-47; "Das Johannesevangelium im Streit der Methoden (1980-84)," *TRu* 51 (1986) 1-78. **M. M. Beirne,** *Women and Men in the Fourth Gospel: A Genuine Discipleship of Equals* (JSNTSup 242, 2003). **C. Bennema,** *The Power of Saving Wisdom: An Investigation of Spirit and Wisdom in Relation to the Soteriology of the Fourth Gospel* (WUNT 2/148, 2002). **J. Bernard,** *A Critical and Exegetical Commentary* *on the Gospel According to St. John* (ICC, 2 vols. 1928). **J. Beutler,** "Literarische Gattungen im Johannesevangelium: Ein Forschungsbericht, 1919-80," *ANRW* II.25.3 (1984) 2506-68. **R. Bieringer, D. Pollefeyt and F. Vandecasteele Vanneuville, eds.,** *Anti-Judaism and the Fourth Gospel* (2001). **C. C. Black,** "St. Thomas's Commentary on the Johannine Prologue: Some Reflections on Its Character and Implications," *CBQ* 48 (1986) 681-98. **C. L. Blomberg,** *The Historical Reliability of John's Gospel: Issues and Commentary* (2001). **M.-É. Boismard,** *Comment Luc a remanié l'Évangile de Jean* (CahRB 51, 2001). **M. Boismard and A. Lamouille,** *L'évangile de Jean: Synopse des quatre évangiles en français 3* (1977). **P. Borgen,** *Bread from Heaven: An Exegetical Study of the Concept of Manna in the Gospel of John and the Writings of Philo* (NovTSup 10, 1965). **W. Bousset,** "Der Verfasser des Johannesevangeliums," *TRu* 8 (1905) 225-44, 277-95. **C. Bretschneider,** *Probabilia de evangelii et epistolarum Joannis, apostoli, indole et origine eruditorum judiciis modeste subjecit* (1820). **R. E. Brown,** *The Gospel According to John* (AB 29, 1966; 29A, 1970); *The Community of the Beloved Disciple: The Life, Loves, and Hates of an Individual Church in NT Times* (1979); *The Epistles of John* (AB 30, 1982). **A. C. Brunson,** *Psalm 118 in the Gospel of John: An Intertextual Study on the New Exodus Pattern in the Theology of John* (WUNT 2/158, 2003). **R. Bultmann,** "The History of Religions Background of the Prologue to the Gospel of John," *The Interpretation of John* (Studies in NT Interpretation, ed. and tr. J. Ashton, 1997[2]) 27-46; *The Gospel of John: A Commentary* (tr. G. Beasley-Murray, ed. R. Hoare and J. Riches, 1971); *Die Reden des Johannesevangeliums und der Stil der gnostischen Offenbarungsrede* (FRLANT, 1919); *Theology of the NT 2* (tr. K. Grobel, 1975). **C. F. Burney,** *The Aramaic Origin of the Fourth Gospel* (1922). **F. Büchsel,** *Johannes und der hellenistische Synkretismus* (BFCT 2, 16, 1928). **U. Busse,** *Das Johannesevangelium: Bildlichkeit, Diskurs und Ritual* (BETL 162, 2002). **J. Calvin,** *Commentary on the Gospel According to John* (2 vols. tr. W. Pringle, 1949). **D. Carson,** *The Gospel According to John* (1991). **C. Cebulj,** *Ich bin es: Studien zur Identitätsbildung im Johannesevangelium* (SBB 44, 2000). **J. H. Charlesworth** (ed.), *John and the Dead Sea Scrolls* (1972, 1990). **P. Chatelion Counet,** *John, A Postmodern Gospel: Introduction to Deconstructive Exegesis Applied to the Fourth Gospel* (Biblical interpretation 44, 2000). **M. L. Coloe,** *God Dwells with Us: Temple Symbolism in the Fourth Gospel* (2001). **M. Comeau,** *Saint Augustine: Exégète du quatrième évangile* (Études de théologie historique, 1930). **C. M. Conway,** *Men and Women in the Fourth Gospel: Gender and Johannine Characterization* (SBLDS 167, 1999). **O. Cullmann,** *The Johannine Circle: Its Place in Judaism Among the Disciples of Jesus in Early Christianity* (NT Library, tr. J. Bowden, 1976). **R. A. Culpepper,** *The Johannine School: An Evaluation of the Johannine School Hypothesis Based on an Investigation of the Nature of Ancient Schools* (SBLDS 26, 1975); *The Anatomy of the Fourth Gospel: A Study in Literary Design* (Foundations and Facets, 1983). **R. A. Culpepper and F. F. Segovia** (eds.), *The Fourth Gospel from a Literary Perspective* (Semeia 53, 1991). **M. Daly-Denton,** *David in The Fourth Gospel: The Johannine Reception of the Psalms* (AGJU 47, 2000). **A. Dauer,** *Johannes und Lukas* (FB 50, 1984). **M. Davies,** *Rhetoric and Reference in the Fourth Gospel* (JSNTSup 69, 1992). **A. Dettwiler,** *Die Gegenwart des Erhöhten: Eine exegetisch Studie zu den johanneischen Abschiedsreden (Joh 13,31-16,33) unter besonderer Berücksichtigung ihres Relecture-Charakters* (FRLANT 169, 1995). **W. de Wette,** *Kurze Erkärung des Evangeliums und der Briefe Johannis* (KEH NT, 1852[4]). **M. Diefenbach,** *Der Konflikt Jesu mit den "Juden"* (NTAbh n.s. 41, 2002). **C. Dietzfelbinger,** *Das Evangelium nach Johannes* (ZBKNT 4, 2001). **C. H. Dodd,** *The Interpretation of the Fourth Gospel* (1958); *Historical Tradition in the Fourth Gospel* (1963). **M. W. Dube and J. L. Staley** (eds.), *John and Postcolonialism: Travel, Space and Power* (Bible and Postcolonialism 7, 2002). **P. Duke,** *Irony in the Fourth Gospel* (1985). **J. du Rand,** *Johannine Perspectives* (1991). **Erasmus,** *Paraphrase on John* (Collected Works of Erasmus 46, tr. J. E. Philips, 1991). **E. Evanson,** *The*

Dissonance of the Four Generally Received Evangelists, and the Evidence of Their Respective Authenticity Examined (1792, 1805[2]). **C. Farmer,** *The Gospel of John in the Sixteenth Century: The Johannine Exegesis of W. Musculus* (Oxford Studies in Historical Theology, 1997). **A. Fehribach,** *The Women in the Life of the Bridegroom: A Feminist Historical-Literary Analysis of the Female Characters in the Fourth Gospel* (1998). **R. Fortna,** *The Gospel of Signs* (SNTSMS 11, 1970); *The Fourth Gospel and Its Predecessor: From Narrative Source to Present Gospel* (1989). **R. T. Fortna and T. Thatcher** (eds.), *Jesus in Johannine Tradition* (2001). **K. Frommann,** *Der Johanneische Lehrbegriff in seinem Verhältnisse zur gesammten biblisch-christlichen Lehre* (1839). **P. Gardner-Smith,** *Saint John and the Synoptic Gospels* (1938). **M. Gourgues,** "Conquante ans de recherche johannique: De Bultmann à la narratologie," and "De Bien des manières," *La recherche biblique aux abords du xxie siècle* (LD 163, 1995) 229-306. **H. Grotius,** *Annotationes in libros Evangeliorum* (1641). **H. Gunkel,** *Zum religionsgeschichtlichen Verständnis des Neuen Testaments* (1903). **J. J. Gunther,** "Early Identification of Authorship of the Johannine Writings," *JEH* 31 (1980) 407-27. **N. C. Habel,** "An Ecojustice Challenge: Is Earth Valued in John 1?" *The Earth Story in the New Testament* (ed. N. C. Habel and V. Balabansky, Earth Bible 5, 2002) 76-82. **E. Haenchen,** "Aus der Literatur zum Johannesevangelium, 1929-56," *TRu* 23 (1955) 295-335; *John: A Commentary on the Gospel of John* (Hermenia, 1984). **A. von Harnack,** *Die Entstehung der christlichen Theologie und des kirchlichen Dogmas* (1927). **R. Harris,** *The Odes and Psalms of Solomon* (1909). **S. Harstine,** *Moses as a Character in the Fourth Gospel: A Study of Ancient Reading Techniques* (JSNTSup 229, 2002). **R. E. Heine,** "The Role of the Gospel of John in the Montanist Controversy," *SecCent* 6 (1987-88) 1-19. **J. Heise,** *Auslegen durch Nachdenken : Exegese johanneischer Texte und hermeneutische Äœberlegungen* (Theologie 33, 2001). **M. Hengel,** *The Johannine Question* (tr. J. Bowden, 1989). **E. Hirsch,** *Studien zum vierten Evangelium* (BHT 4, 1936a); *Das vierte Evangelium in seiner ursprünglichen Gestalt verdeutscht und erklärt* (1936b). **M. Hoffmann,** "Rhetoric and Dialogue in Erasmus's and Melanchthon's Interpretation of John's Gospel," *P. Melanchthon (1497-1560) and the Commentary* (ed. T. J. Wengert and M. P. Graham, 1997) 48-78. **P. L. Hofrichter,** *Modell und Vorlage der Synoptiker: Das vorredaktionelle "Johannesevangelium"* (Theologische Texte und Studien 6, 2002[2]a); ed., *Für und wider die Priorität des Johannesevangeliums* (Theologische Texte und Studien 9, 2002b). **W. F. Howard,** *The Fourth Gospel in Recent Criticism and Interpretation* (1931; rev. C. K. Barrett, 1955). **D. A. Ihenacho,** *The Community of Eternal Life: The Study of the Meaning of Life for the Johannine Community* (2001). **M. de Jonge** (ed.), *L'Évangile de Jean: Sources, rédaction, théologie* (BETL 44, 1977). **A. Jülicher,** *Einleitung in das Neue Testament* (1894). **J.-D. Kaestli,** et al. (eds.), *La communaut johannique et son histoire: La trajectoire de l'évangile de Jean aux deux premiers siècles* (Monde de la Bible 20, 1990). **E. Käsemann,** *The Testament of Jesus: A Study of the Gospel of John in the Light of Chapter 17* (tr. G. Krodel, 1968). **S. P. Kealy,** *John's Gospel and the History of Biblical Interpretation* (Mellen Biblical Press Series 60a-b, 2002). **H. Klein,** "Die lukanisch-johanneische Passionstradition," *ZNW* 67 (1976) 155-86. **A. J. Köstenberger,** *Studies on John and Gender: A Decade of Scholarship* (Studies in Biblical Literature 38, 2001). **C. R. Koester,** *Symbolism in the Fourth Gospel: Meaning, Mystery, Community* (2003[2]). **T. Kriener,** *"Glauben an Jesus"—ein Verstoss gegen das zweite Gebot: die johanneische Christologie und der jüdische Vorwurf des Götzendienstes* (Neukirchener theologische Dissertationen und Habilitationen 29, 2001). **J. Kügler,** *Der andere König: religionsgeschichtliche Perspektiven auf die Christologie des Johannesevangeliums* (SBS 178, 1999). **R. Kysar,** *The Fourth Evangelist and His Gospel: An Examination of Contemporary Scholarship* (1975); "The Fourth Gospel: A Report on Recent Research," *ANRW* II.25.3 (1984) 2389-480; "Community and Gospel: Vectors in Fourth Gospel Criticism," *Interpreting the Gospels* (ed. J. Mays, 1981).

M. Labahn, *Jesus als Lebensspender: Untersuchungen zu einer Geschichte der johanneischen Tradition anhand ihrer Wundergeschichten* (BZNW 98, 1999). **T. Larsson,** *God in the Fourth Gospel: A Hermeneutical Study of the History of Interpretations* (ConBNT 35, 2001). **D. Lee,** *Flesh and Glory: Symbol, Gender, and Theology in the Gospel of John* (2002). **G. Lessing,** *Neue Hypothese über die Evangelisten als blosse menschliche Geschichtsschreiber betrachtet* (*1777-78; ET Lessing's Theological Writings,* ed. and tr. H. Chadwick, 1956) 65-81. **A.-J. Levine with M. Blickenstaff** (eds.), *A Feminist Companion to John* (Feminist Companion to the New Testament and Early Christian Writings 4-5, 2003). **M. Lidzbarski,** *Das Johannesbuch der Mandäer* (1915); *Ginza: Der Schatz oder das grosse Buch der Mandäer* (QR 4, 1925). **A. T. Lincoln,** *Truth on Trial: The Lawsuit Motif in the Fourth Gospel* (2000). **B. Lindars,** *The Gospel of John* (1972). **C. G. Lingad, Jr.,** *The Problems of Jewish Christians in the Johannine Community* (Tesi Gregoriana, Serie Teologia 73, 2001). **W. von Loewenich,** *Das Johannes-Verständnis im zweiten Jahrhundert* (BZNW 13, 1932). **A. Loisy,** *Le quatrième évangile* (1903, 1921[2]). **E. Lützelberger,** *Die kirchliche Tradition über den Apostel Johannes und seine Schriften in ihrer Grundlosigkeit nachgewiesen* (1840). **E. Malatesta,** *St. John's Gospel, 1920-65: A Cumulative and Classified Bibliography of Books and Periodical Literature on the Fourth Gospel* (AnBib 32, 1967). **B. J. Malina and R. L. Rohrbaugh,** *Social-science Commentary on the Gospel of John* (1998). **J. L. Martyn,** *History and Theology in the Fourth Gospel* (1979[2]; NTL, 2003[3]); *The Gospel of John in Christian History: Essays for Interpreters* (1978). **C. Maurer,** *Ignatius von Antiochien und das Johannesevangelium* (ATANT 18, 1949). **J. D. Michaelis,** *Einleitung in die göttlichen Schriften des Neuen Bundes 2* (1788[4]). **W. Meeks,** "The Man from Heaven in Johannine Sectarianism," *JBL* 91 (1972) 44-72. **R. Metzner,** *Das Verständnis der Sünde im Johannesevangelium* (WUNT 2/122, 2000). **W. E. Mills,** *The Gospel of John* (Bibliographies for Biblical Research, Periodical Literature for the Study of the New Testament 4, 2002). **F. J. Moloney,** *Belief in the Word: Reading John 1-4* (1993); *Signs and Shadows: Reading John 5-12* (1996); *The Gospel of John* (SP 4, 1998). **V. Naegeli,** *Wo rührt das hin?: Wort und Leiblichkeit bei Sigmund Freud und im Johannesevangelium* (2000). **W.-Y. Ng,** *Water Symbolism in John: An Eschatological Interpretation* (Studies in Biblical Literature 15, 2001). **T. Nicklas,** *Ablösung und Verstrickung: "Juden" und Jungergestalten als Charaktere der erzahlten Welt des Johannesevangeliums und ihre Wirkung auf den impliziten Leser* (Regensburger Studien zur Theologie 60, 2001). **J. Nissen and S. Pedersen** (eds.), *New Readings in John: Literary and Theological Perspectives* (JSNTSup 182, 1999). **F. Neirynck,** "John and the Synoptics: 1975-90," *John and the Synoptics* (ed. A. Denaux, BETL, 1992) 3-62. **J. Neyrey,** *An Ideology of Revolt: John's Christology in Social Science Perspective* (1988). **W. Nicol,** *The Semeia in the Fourth Gospel: Tradition and Redaction* (NovTSup 32, 1972). **G. O'Day,** "The Gospel of John," *NIB* (1995) 9:491-865; "John," *The Women's Bible Commentary* (ed. C. A. Newsom and S. H. Ringe, 1992); *Revelation in the Fourth Gospel: Narrative Mode and Theological Claim* (1986); "The Gospel According to John," *NISB* (2003) 1905-51. **O. Olajubu,** "Reconnecting with the Waters: John 9.1-11" *The Earth Story in the New Testament* (ed. N. C. Habel and V. Balabansky, Earth Bible 5, 2002) 108-21. **J. C. O'Neill,** "The Study of the NT," *NCRTW* 3 (ed. N. Smart, J. Elaytm, 1985) 143-78. **D. E. Orton** (ed.), *The Composition of John's Gospel* (Brill's readers in biblical studies 2, 1999). **J. Painter, R. A. Culpepper, and F. F. Segovia** (eds.), *Word, Theology, and Community in John* (2002). **S. Pancaro,** *The Law in the Fourth Gospel* (NovTSup 42, 1975). **N. Perrin,** *The NT, An Introduction: Proclamation and Paranesis, Myth and History* (1974). **N. Peterson,** *The Gospel of John and the Sociology of Light: Language and Characterization in the Fourth Gospel* (1993). **T. E. Pollard,** *Johannine Christology and the Early Church* (SNTSMS 13, 1970). **T. Popp,** *Grammatik des Geistes: literarische Kunst und theologische Konzeption in Johannes 3 und 6* (Arbeiten zur Bibel und ihrer Geschichte 3, 2001). **G. Reim,** *Studien zum alttestamentlichen*

Hintergrund des Johannesevangelium (SNTSMS 22, 1974). **H. S. Reimarus,** *Apologie oder Schutzschrift für die vernünftigen Verehrer* Gottes (ed. G. Alexander, 1972). **A. Reinhartz,** "The Gospel of John," *Searching the Scriptures,* vol. 2, *A Feminist Commentary* (ed. E. Schüssler Fiorenza, 1994); *Befriending the Beloved Disciple: A Jewish reading of the Gospel of John* (2001) **R. Reitzenstein,** *Das mandäische Buch des Herrn der Grösse und die Evangelien Uberlieferung* (SHAW.PH 12, 1919). **D. Rensberger,** *Johannine Faith and Liberating Community* (1988). **J. L. Resseguie,** *The Strange Gospel: Narrative Design and Point of View in John* (Biblical interpretation series 56, 2001). **J. Reuss,** *Johannes Kommentare aus der griechischen Kirche* (TU 89, 1966). **R. Riesner,** *Bethanien jenseits des Jordan: Topographie und Theologie im Johannes-Evangelium* (Biblische Archäologie und Zeitgeschichte 12, 2002). **S. H. Ringe,** *Wisdom's Friends: Community and Christology in the Fourth Gospel* (1999). **J. Robinson,** *The Priority of John* (1985). **E. Ruckstuhl,** *Die literarische Einheit des Johannesevangeliums* (NTOA 5, 1987). **S. Ruschmann,** *Maria von Magdala im Johannesevangelium: Jüngerin-Zeugin-Lebensbotin* (NTAbh n.s. 40, 2002). **M. Sabbe,** "The Footwashing in Jn 13 and Its Relationship to the Synoptic Gospels," *ETL* 58 (1982) 279-308. **H.-K., Saeed,** *Revelation and Concealment of Christ: A Theological Inquiry into the Elusive Language of the Fourth Gospel* (WUNT 2/120, 2000). **J. N. Sanders,** *The Fourth Gospel in the Early Church: Its Origin and Influence on Christian Theology up to Irenaeus* (1943). **M. Sasse,** *Der Menschensohn im Evangelium nach Johannes* (Texte und Arbeiten zum neutestamentlichen Zeitalter 35, 2000). **L. Schenke,** *Johannes: Kommentar* (1998). **A. Schlatter,** *Der Evangelist Johannes; Wie er spricht, denkt und glaubt: Ein Kommentar zum vierten Evangelium* (1930). **F. Schleiermacher,** *Homilien über das Evangelium des Johannes in den Jahren 1823 und 1824* (1837). **W. Schmidt,** *Der brennende Dornbusch: eine Darlegung des Evangeliums nach Johannes* (Kontexte, 2000). **R. Schnackenburg,** *The Gospel According to St. John* (HTC, 3 vols. tr. K. Smyth, 1968, 1980, 1982). **S. M. Schneiders,** *Written that You May Believe: Encountering Jesus in the Fourth Gospel* (1999). **U. Schnelle,** *Antidocetic Christology in the Gospel of John: An Investigation of the Place of the Fourth Gospel in the Johannine School* (1992); *Das Evangelium nach Johannes* (THKNT 4, 1998). **J. Schniewind,** *Die Parallelperikopen bei Lukas und Johannes* (1958). **K. Scholtissek,** *In ihm sein und bleiben: Die Sprache der Immanenz in den johanneischen Schriften* (Herders biblische Studien, Herder's Biblical studies 21, 2000). **L. Schottroff,** *Der Glaubende und die feindliche Welt: Beobachtungen zum gnostischen Dualismus und seiner Bedeutung für Paulus und das Johannesevangelium* (WMANT 37, 1970). **J.-M. Schräder,** *Das eschatologische Israel im Johannesevangelium: eine Untersuchung der johanneischen Israel-Konzeption in Joh 2-4 und Joh 6* (Neutestamentliche Entwürfe zur Theologie 3, 2003). **S. Schreiber and A. Stimpfle** (eds.), *Johannes aenigmaticus: Studien zum Johannesevangelium für Herbert Leroy* (Biblische Untersuchungen 29, 2000). **B. Schwank,** Evangelium nach Johannes (1998²). **E. Schwartz,** "Aporien im vierten Evangelium," *NGWG* (1907) 1:342-72; NGWG (1908) 2:115-48, 3:149-88, 4:497-560. **F. Segovia,** *The Farewell of the Word: The Johannine Call to Abide* (1991); *Love Relationships in the Johannine Tradition* (SBLDS 58, 1982); "What Is John?" Readers and Reading of the Fourth Gospel (SBL Symposium 3, ed. F. Segovia, 1996). **J. Semler,** *Paraphrasis Evangelii Johannis 2* (1771, 1772). **R. Simon,** *Histoire critique du texte du Nouveau Testament* (1689). **M. Simonetti,** *Biblical Interpretation in the Early Church: An Historical Introduction to Patristic Exegesis* (1996). **D. M. Smith,** *The Composition and Order of the Fourth Gospel: Bultmann's Literary Theory* (YPR 10, 1965); *Johannine Christianity: Essays on Its Setting, Sources, and Theology* (1987); *John Among the Gospels: The Relationship in Twentieth-century Research* (1992); *John* (ANTC, 1999); *John Among the Gospels* (2001²). **B. de Solages,** *Jean et les synoptiques* (1979). **J. Staley,** *The Print's First Kiss: A Rhetorical Investigation of the Implied Reader in the Fourth Gospel* (SBLDS 82, 1988).

M. Stibbe, *John's Gospel* (NT Readings, 1994). **H. Strathmann,** *Das Evangelium nach Johannes* (NTD 4, 1968). **D. F. Strauss,** *Das Leben Jesu, kritisch bearbeitet* (2 vols. 1835). **G. Strecker,** "Die Anfänge der Johanneischen Schule," *NTS* 32 (1986) 31-47; *Die Johannesbriefe* (KEK 14, 1989). **J. Tayler,** *An Attempt to Ascertain the Character of the Fourth Gospel, Especially in Its Relationship to the Three First* (1867). **T. Thatcher,** *The Riddles of Jesus in John: A Study in Tradition and Folklore* (SBLMS 53, 2000). **M. Theobald,** *Herrenworte im Johannesevangelium* (Herders biblische Studien 34, 2002). **A. Therath,** *Jerusalem in the Gospel of John: An Exegetical and Theological Inquiry into Johannine Geography* (1999). **M. M. Thompson,** *The God of the Gospel of John* (2001). **H. Thyen,** "Aus der Literatur zum Johannesevangelium," *TRu* 39 (1974) 1-69, 222-53; 40 (1975) 289-330; 42 (1977) 211-70; 43 (1978) 328-59; 44 (1979) 97-134; "Johannesevangelium," TRE 17 (1988) 200-225. **C. Urban,** *Das Menschenbild nach dem Johannesevangelium: Grundlagen johan-neischer Anthropologie* (WUNT 2/137, 2001). **E. Wainright,** "Which Intertext? A Response to An Ecojustice Challenge: Is Earth Valued in John 1?" *The Earth Story in the New Testament* (ed. N. C. Habel and V. Balabansky, Earth Bible 5, 2002) 83-88. **J. G. van der Watt,** *Family of the King: Dynamics of Metaphor in the Gospel According to John* (Biblical interpretation series 47, 2000). **D. Wead,** The *Literary Devices in John's Gospel* (TheoDis 4, 1970). **J. S. Webster,** *Ingesting Jesus: Eating and Drinking in the Gospel of John* (SBL Academia Biblica 6, 2003). **J. A. Weisheipl,** "The Johannine Commentary of Friar Thomas," *CH* 45 (1976) 185-95. **C. Weisse,** *Die evangelische Geschichte, kritisch und philosophisch bearbeitet* (2 vols. 1838). **J. Wellhausen,** *Erweiterungen und Änderungen im vierten Evangelium (1907); Das Evangelium Johannis* (1908). **T. J. Wengert,** *P. Melanchthon's "Annotationes in Johannem" in Relation to Its Predecessors and Contemporaries* (THR 220, 1987). **K. Wengst,** *Das Johannesevangelium* (Theologischer Kommentar zum Neuen Testament, 4, 2000-2001). **R. Whitacre,** *Johannine Polemic: The Role of Tradition and Theology* (SBLDS 67, 1980). **C. Wiezsäcker,** *Das apostolische Zeitalter der christlichen Kirche* (1902³). **M. F. Wiles,** *The Spiritual Gospel: The Interpretation of the Fourth Gospel in the Early Church* (1960). **H. Windisch** "Der johanneische Erzählungsstil," [ΕΥΧΑΡΙΣΤΗΡΙΟΝ] (1923) 174-213. **W. Wrede,** *Charakter und Tendenz des Johannesevangeliums* (SGV 37, 1903, 1933²).

R. D. KYSAR

Acts of the Apostles, Book of the

Although the name Luke occurs nowhere in the book, the early patristic tradition, including Irenaeus[§] (*Adv. Haer.* 3.1.1; see 3.14.1), Eusebius (*Hist. eccl.* 3.4), and the Muratorian canon (Canon of the Bible[§]), was unanimous in associating the book of Acts with the Third Gospel and in attributing both volumes to Luke. Almost nothing of commentary on or quotation of Acts from that time period has survived. Exceptions include Ephraem's[§] devotional writings (fourth century) and Chrysostom's[§] homilies (late fourth, early fifth century). Four noteworthy works have survived from the second half of the first millennium: (1) Arator's poetic paraphrase (c. 544), a symbolic, sacramental interpretation, used extensively throughout the medieval period. (2) Bede's[§] verse by verse commentaries (early eighth century) which appears to have drawn upon distinctive Greek and OL textual readings. (3) A commentary by the Syriac Nestorian bishop, Isho'dad of Merv (ninth century) which preserves quotations from earlier Syriac writers. (4) Rabanus Maurus's[§] commentary (early tenth century), which is still available only in manuscript and has been virtually unstudied. Hugh of St. Cher[§] and Nicholas of Lyra[§] wrote important commentaries during the High Middle Ages that have not yet been analyzed in detail (Stuehrenberg 1988, 111-58; see also Stuehrenberg 1987, 118-25).

The text of the book has been transmitted in two different recensions. That contained in the great uncial manuscripts (Sinaiticus, Vaticanus, and Alexandrinus), the so-called Egyptian or Alexandrian tradition, is shorter than the so-called Western tradition. The latter is not widely represented but appears in OL and in some Syriac manuscripts as well as in the bilingual (Latin and Greek) Codex Bezae, which contains the text of the Gospels and Acts (on the textual differences, see C. Barrett 1994–98, 1:2-29).

There is no evidence that the Gospel of Luke and the book of Acts circulated in the early church as a single work. Papyrus P[75] (Bodmer, 14-15), from the early third century, indicates that the two were detached from each other. In early canonical lists and in the great fourth- and fifth-century codices, Acts is variously placed: Eusebius[§] placed it after the four Gospels (*Hist. eccl.* 3.25), as did Athanasius[§] (Epistle 39), and Codex Alexandrinus. Other placements vary: after the Pauline epistles (Codex Sinaiticus and Mommsen Canon), after the book of Revelation (sixth cent., Codex Claromontanus), and before the book of Revelation (Augustine *On Christian Doctrine* 2.8.13). Cassiodorus[§] noted that the Bible was generally in nine volumes, with Acts and Revelation constituting the ninth volume (*Institutiones* 1.11.3).

Critical analysis of Acts began with L. Valla's[§] and Erasmus's[§] text critical work (Textual Criticism*[§]) on the Latin text of Acts. A portion of Valla's *Collatio Novi Testamenti* (not printed until 1970) concerns Acts, and folios 23-26 in his *In Latin am Novi Testamenti interpretationem,* published by Erasmus in 1505, are also on Acts. Erasmus included notes on Acts in the annotations to his *Novum instrumentum omne* (1516), the first published version of the Greek New Testament. The notes of both scholars were included in volume seven of the Critici Sacri[§] (1660). Erasmus also published a paraphrase of Acts (1524), the last of his paraphrases on the New Testament. (His paraphrases were translated into English through the influence of Catherine Parr, the sixth wife of Henry VIII; and Edward VI ordered the translation to be placed in all church parishes.)

Luther[§] did not write a commentary on Acts, but he applied his distinctive perspective in his preface to the book in the 1533 German edition of the Bible: "This book might well be called a commentary on the epistles of St. Paul. For what Paul teaches and insists upon with words and passages of scripture, St. Luke here points out and proves with instances and examples . . . namely, that no law, no work justifies men, but only faith in Christ" (ET 1960, 35:364). Some of the radical elements in the Reformation drew on the book of Acts in support of a theory of communitarianism or biblical communism in which property was to be held in common in imitation of the early church (see Acts 2:44-45; 4:32-37; G. Williams 1992[3], index under communitarianism). Luther apparently sought to defuse this use, noting in his preface that "this practice did not last long and in time had to stop."

Calvin[§] published his commentary on Acts in two installments, chapters 1–12 in 1552 and on the entire book in 1554 (ET, 2 vols., 1965–66). Here as elsewhere Calvin concentrated on the grammatical-historical dimensions of the text but with a homiletical and spiritualizing application. For him the book's theme fits the genre of sacred history, with a concern to show how God cared and still cares for the church and directed its life through the Spirit.

H. Grotius's[§] commentary on Acts in his *Annotationes in Novum Testamentum* (1646) was the first commentary on the book to suspend theological and homiletical concerns and to focus strictly on philological and historical matters. Standing in the Erasmian/humanistic tradition, Grotius drew upon a broad range of classical and Hellenistic texts to elucidate the background and context of the biblical narratives. His work was highly influential in England, especially among persons associated with the so-called Great Tew Circle, whose members included Grotius's great English defender H. Hammond[§] (see F. Beiser 1996, 84-133). Hammond treated Acts in his *A Paraphrase and Annotations upon All the Books of the New Testament* (1653), a widely read but only mildly critical work that was nonetheless pioneering in English biblical criticism.

The Semiticist J. Lightfoot[§] produced two works on Acts, a commentary on chaps. 1–12 (1645) and *Horae hebraicae et Talmudicae in Acta Apostolorum* (date uncertain [ET in his *Works* 8 1825, 353-501]), drawing heavily upon both rabbinic/Talmudic and Hellenistic writings (especially Josephus) to elucidate the text's background. J. Pearson (1613–86) lectured on Acts at Cambridge, but the lectures plus his *Annales Paulini* were published posthumously (Latin in 1688 [ET 1851]).

Within English Deism[§], several radical thinkers raised issues that would later set the agenda for interpretation of the book. J. Toland[§] and T. Morgan[§] argued that early church life was not characterized by theological harmony, as one finds in Acts, but by party strife (see W. Baird 1992, 1:39-41, 52-54). Morgan, who took a positive attitude toward Paul, argued that alongside the gentile, Pauline, anti-Jewish, anti-ceremonial, and universalistic form of Christianity stood a narrow, exclusivistic, legally oriented, Judaistic, Petrine version whose gospels were "as opposite and inconsistent as Light and Darkness, Truth and Falsehood" (1969, 1:377; Morgan, of course, saw Paul as a forerunner of the deistic thinkers and Peter as representative of the traditional, clergy-controlled and ceremonially bound religious establishment of his day). These two parties in the early church eventually combined during the time of persecution to produce what became Roman Catholic Christianity. The implication of this position was the necessity to study New Testament documents in light of early church history.

In his *History and Character of St. Paul,* P. Annet[§], the most radical of the English Deists, raised the issue of the relationship between Paul's epistles and the narratives in Acts and the discrepancies he found between the two, e.g., Paul's association with the church in Jerusalem. Although generally trusting the book of Acts, Annet printed the three accounts of Paul's conversion in parallel columns to highlight their inconsistencies. Annet denied common authorship of the Gospel of Luke and Acts, denied that Luke wrote Acts, and suggested that the "we" sections in Acts may have been written by Silas (see Baird, 49-52).

In 1792 E. Evanson[§], an Anglican turned Unitarian, declared Luke to be the only authentic Gospel and affirmed Luke–Acts (with some excisions) to be historically accurate. He considered most of the letters of Paul to be inauthentic. His work, like Annet's, raised the issue of the relationship of the Paul of the epistles to the Paul pictured in Acts.

The traditional view that Acts was written "to recount the achievements of the apostles, or the history of the early church" came under scrutiny with the dominance of the historical-critical approach to the Bible. "It was evident at once to the critical eye that the book fulfilled in a very imperfect way the historical purpose which had been ascribed to it by tradition. Instead of recording the acts of the apostles it confined itself almost exclusively to Peter and Paul, and even Peter received but scant attention. Moreover, the fragmentary nature of the account, the many omissions evident to any one acquainted with Paul's Epistles, the frequent repetitions, the extreme sketchiness of some parts and the minute detail of others, the marked emphasis upon certain matters, and the brief and casual reference to others of equal importance all seemed to demand some explanation. If the author was familiar with the period he was writing about, as had been commonly taken for granted, he must have had some other than a purely historical motive, or if not, then his knowledge of the period must have been very limited and fragmentary" (A. McGiffert 1922, 363-64).

In 1721 the German Lutheran theologian E. Heumann published a short article that was a harbinger of matters to come ("Dissertation ed Theophilo, cui Lucas Historiam Sacram Inscripsit," *BHPT*, class 4 [1721] 483-505). He argued that Luke–Acts was written, not as a straightforward historical account, but as an apology for the Christian religion addressed to a pagan official, thus raising questions about the work's intended purpose and historical reliability.

In England N. Lardner[§] was aware of the rising historical issues in biblical interpretation. But in his *Credibility of the Gospel History* (14 vols. 1727–57) he merely collected the traditions testifying to the work's Lukan origins and to its historical value and reliability (see his Works 6 1838, 388-98).

In his 1750 introduction to the New Testament (ET 1780), J. D. Michaelis[§] argued that Luke had more reasons for his work than merely "to write a church-history." Michaelis noted two: "to give an authentic relation of the effusion of the Holy Ghost, and the first miracles, by which the truth of the Christian religion was established" and "to impart those accounts, which evince the claim of the Gentiles to the church of Christ" (ET, 216). In his fourth edition (1788 [ET, 4 vols. 1793–1801]), Michaelis added another reason: "to record only those facts, which he had either seen himself, or heard from eye-witnesses," which explained Luke's silence about so much of early church history (ET, 3.1 1802[2], 331).

J. Semler[§], "directly dependent for the questions . . . as well as for many of the answers . . . on the writings of the English Deists" (W. Kümmel 1970, 62), described the early church as possessing a "dissimilarity and disunity" in which "the aversion of the supporters of Peter for the followers of Paul is undeniable" (from preface to vol. 4, *Abhandlung von freier Untersuchung des Canon* 1771–75 [ET in W. Kümmel 1973[2], 67]).

The author of *A View of the Evidences of Christianity,* W. Paley[§], wrote a work on Paul (*Horae Paulinae* 1790) that typified mainline British scholarship of the time, based as it was on an anti-deistic methodology initially given widespread circulation by C. Leslie[§]. Carrying out a comparison of the Paul of the epistles with the Paul of Acts under the assumption that the epistles and the book were written independently of each other, Paley argued that, considering their "undesignedness," the number of coincidental agreements between the two versions indicates that they are based on events whose historicity cannot be doubted (on Paley, see J. Cadbury 1955, 123-27).

The idea that the early church was composed of diverse groups often in theological conflict was given wide circulation by W. De Wette[§]. In his *Lehrbuch der christlichen Dogmatik in ihrer historischen Entwicklung* (1813), he argued that the New Testament books could be divided into three categories: "(1) Jewish Christian, to which belong the first three Gospels, the Book of Acts, the Letters of Peter, James, and Jude, and the Apocalypse. . . . (2) Alexandrian or Hellenistic, to which the Gospel and the Letters of John and the Letter to the Hebrews are to be reckoned. . . . (3) Pauline, including the Letters of Paul and, in part, the Book of Acts" (ET in Kümmel, 106-7).

F. C. Baur[§], primarily a church historian, was the most influential and controversial New Testament scholar of the nineteenth century (Baird, 258-69; W. Gasque 1975, 1989, 26-54; Kümmel, 127-43, with extracts from Baur's writings). Basic to his attempt to produce a history of early Christianity and to associate the New Testament writings with this history was his view that two parties, the Petrine (Jewish) and the Pauline (Hellenistic), were in open opposition, even conflict, in the early church (first propounded in 1831). Various New Testament writings, he argued, reflect the interests and theologies of these parties. Other later New Testament writings (produced in the late first and early second cents.) reflect attempts to reconcile these factions. Among the latter, "the Acts of the Apostles . . . is the apologetic attempt of a Paulinist to facilitate and bring about the *rapprochement* and union of the two opposing parties by representing Paul as Petrine as possible and, on the other hand, Peter as Pauline as possible" (1838 [ET in Kümmel, 133]). Because of its *tendenz* the book of Acts cannot be accepted as a reliable source for the history of the apostolic age or for the work and thought of Paul, which, Baur argued, must be based on the four genuine Pauline letters (Romans, Galatians, 1 and 2 Corinthians). Baur's positions were summarized and developed in his *Paul the Apostle of Jesus Christ: His Life, His Work, His Epistles and His Doctrine. A Contribution to the Critical History of Primitive Christianity* (1845; 1866[2] ed. E. Zeller [ET, 2 vols. 1876]).

The followers and students of Baur, the so-called Tübingen School, further developed his main ideas on Acts—namely, that the work was tendentious and therefore generally unhistorical and that it was produced in the post-apostolic church of the second century (see Baird, 269-78; Gasque, 21-54). Among these were M. Schneckenberger[§], A. Schwegler, and E. Zeller. Zeller's work, *The Contents and Origin of the Acts of the Apostles, Critically Investigated* (1854 [ET, 2 vols. 1875–76]), based on earlier articles, contained an examination of much of the book's content, only to reach negative conclusions with regard to its historicity. Zeller concluded that Acts originated in Rome about 110–130 C.E., during a time of persecution, and was produced with an apologetic purpose: to demonstrate to the Romans that Christianity was not a politically dangerous religion but a religious development within Judaism.

The critics of the Tübingen School in Germany were numerous: H. Meyer[§], J. Neander, F. Tholuck[§], and others (see Baird, 278-94; Gasque, 55-72). Several of the critics were church historians who challenged Baur's reconstruction of early church history. Some of Baur's followers were Hegelians, although Baur himself reached most of his conclusions before becoming acquainted with G. W. F. Hegel (see Kümmel, 427, no. 177); this allowed critics to argue that the presumed conflict and then consolidation of parties in the early church was based on the Hegelian concept of thesis-antithesis-synthesis. Critics also argued that just because a work was written for a special purpose did not automatically mean that its contents were primarily nonhistorical.

In contrast, some contemporary scholars felt that Baur and the Tübingen School had not gone far enough (see Gasque, 72-94). This element in scholarship reached its apogee in the so-called Radical Dutch School, which had early roots that drew on the work of E. Evanson. The most significant member of this circle was W. van Manen (for his views on Paul, see *EncBib* 3 1902, 3603-38). The Tübingen approach was advocated in England by S. Davidson[§] in the second edition of his New Testament introduction (2 vols. 1868, 2:196-290) and by W. Cassels. In his widely read book *Supernatural Religion: An Inquiry into the Reality of Divine Revelation* (2 vols. 1874, pub. anonymously), Cassels argued for a natural explanation of church origins and that much of the New Testament, including Acts, was fictitious.

As a rule, British scholarship adhered to the more traditional interpretation of Acts. Two popular works widely circulated the views that Acts was historical and that Luke was its author:

The Voyage and Shipwreck of St. Paul (1848), by J. Smith, drew on travel experience and literature to argue for the historicity of Acts 27:1–28:16; and *The Medical Language of St. Luke* (1882), by W. Hobart, examined the medical terminology in Luke–Acts to demonstrate that the work had to have been written by someone trained in medicine, i.e., by Luke the physician. However, two British scholars, J. B. Lightfoot[§] and W. Ramsay[§], the staunchest and most effective proponents of the historical value of the New Testament writings and especially of Acts, undergirded their works with pragmatic realism and an appeal to archaeological (Archaeology and New Testament Interpretation[†§]) and geographical evidence. This British line of scholarship has been continued by F. F. Bruce[§] (1951, 1990[3]), I. H. Marshall (1970, 1992), B. Winter (1993–97), and others.

In Germany, T. von Zahn[§] and A. von Harnack[§] strongly defended the historical value of Acts. The latter argued, in more scholarly fashion than did Hobart, that the writer of Luke–Acts was a physician (a view generally assumed to have been subsequently laid to rest by Cadbury in his dissertation [1919–20]).

By the early twentieth century radical approaches to Acts had almost disappeared from mainline scholarship, although one should note the work of J. O'Neill (1961, 1970[2]), who dates Acts to about 115–130 C.E. and views it as reflective of early Catholicism. The massive five-volume work edited by F. Foakes Jackson and K. Lake[§] (1920–33) sought to summarize and assess all Acts research but was weak on such issues as Lukan theology.

Throughout the nineteenth and early twentieth centuries, investigations also focused on two subsidiary elements in Acts research: the issue of possible sources and the two textual traditions that had circulated in the early church. Various theories were proposed about possible sources used by the author but produced no general consensus (see below). Renewed interest in this topic was stimulated by C. C. Torrey[§] (1916), who proposed that Acts 1–15 was a translation of an Aramaic or Hebrew source made by the author of chaps. 16–28. Explanations for the two textual traditions also led to no majority opinions. F. Blass revised an old theory that the author of Acts had produced two editions of his own work. M. Boismard and A. Lamouille (1984) have explored the issues involved and decided in favor of the historical priority of the longer Western text (see J. Taylor 1990).

The work of M. Dibelius[§] (see Gasque, 201-50), partially anticipated by Cadbury, focused on the literary quality of the author, what Dibelius called style criticism *(Stilkritik)*. He compared the work to ancient historiography, examining closely the role of the book's speeches; and this Literary*[§] analysis has produced a trajectory running through much recent scholarship (R. Pervo 1987; C. Talbert 1974; R. Tannehill 1986–90, and others).

H. Conzelmann's 1954 monograph proved to be a major stimulus to the study of Lukan theology. He argued that Luke–Acts was written as a response to the delay of the parousia so as to emphasize the importance of the life of the church in the unfolding history of redemption.

Later interpretation of Acts takes as one of its principal points of departure the generally recognized fact that the book, together with the Gospel of Luke, forms the second part of an extensive historical monograph that was conceived as a unity (L. T. Johnson 1992; cf. M. Parsons and R. Pervo 1993). The unity of these two books is concealed, however, by the association of Luke with the three Synoptic Gospels*[§] and its placement before John in the New Testament Canon.[§] Because of stylistic, compositional, and thematic features that Luke and Acts share, there is little doubt in modern scholarship that a single person wrote them. All indications favor the view that from the beginning the author of Acts planned a two-part work and composed both parts in close temporal succession. Accordingly, the literary program set forth in Luke's prologue (Luke 1:1-4) refers to Acts, whose introductory sentence (Acts 1:1-2) can be understood as a recurring reference to the Gospel's prologue. Similar cross-referenced forewords are attested in multivolume works of Hellenistic antiquity (e.g., Josephus *Contra Apionem*). The double ascension story forms another skillfully created link between both parts. Luke 24:50-53 forms the conclusion to the earthly deeds of Jesus, the subject to which the first volume is dedicated; thus the continuing history plays no role in this initial work. In Acts 1:1-14, however, the ascension story forms the narrative core of a preface (Acts 1:1-8) that introduces the continuing history—the subject of the second part of the work, which also required a sequential presentation (Luke 1:3). A thematic arch is recognizable stretching from the beginning of the Gospel to the end of Acts. The rejection of the message of salvation by great parts of the Jewish people, anticipated in Luke 4:16-30, and the Gentiles' acceptance of it through the ministry of Paul are expressly confirmed as having been accomplished in the final scene of Acts (28:17-28).

The superscription *Praxeis [ton] apostolon,* "Deeds of the Apostles" (Irenaeus *Adv. Haer.* 3.133; Clement of Alexandria *Strom.* 5.82.4), or *actus omnium apostolorum,* "Deeds of all Apostles" (Canon Muratori), is secondary and in no way fits the book's contents. The deeds of the apostles do not form the focus of the work, nor is Paul, the central figure of the book's second half, veiwed as an apostle. In order to appreciate the book's content, one must start with the statement of purpose in 1:8, which has been put into the mouth of the resurrected Jesus. Accordingly, the subject is the continuation of the salvation event that began with Jesus, who was led by the Holy Spirit. Under the guidance of this Spirit the witnesses spread the gospel over the entire earth, extending from Jerusalem into the way stations of Judea and Samaria to the ends of the earth—i.e., to Rome and beyond. The central theme is the Holy Spirit's diffusion of the church. Reports about individual apostles and witnesses, their deeds and words, should be understood solely in terms of their contribution to this subject. Thus Acts' failure to sketch out thoroughgoing biographical notices is understandable: Figures like Philip (6:5; 8:5-40; 21:8) and Barnabas (4:36; 9:27; 11:22, 30; 12:25; 13:1–15:39), found here and there in the history, disappear abruptly from the scene. Even Peter and Paul appear only in the course of the story when the macro-topic requires or tolerates them.

In searching for Acts' intended organization it seems best not to focus on the persons described. Certainly, Acts has frequently been divided into a Peter section (chaps. 1–12) and a Paul section (chaps. 13–28), but this division proves to be inadequate since Peter is by no means the focus of chaps. 1–12. Instead, he shares his protagonist role with many others (Stephen, 6:8–7:60; Philip, 8:4-40; Paul, 9:1-30). In contrast, the programmatic sentence in 1:8 suggests an organization based on geography: the spread of the gospel in Jerusalem (2:1–8:3), in Samaria and the coastal regions of Judea (8:4–11:18), in the Gentile world and "to the ends of the earth" (11:19–28:31). Of course, even this arrangement is unsatisfying because its third major section is much too long and thematically diverse. For this reason most of the more recent exegetes who maintain a geographical organization (E. Haenchen 1956 [ET 1971]; G. Schneider 1980–82; A. Weiser 1982–85) indicate an additional break after the report about the apostolic council (15:35) and begin a fourth major section at 15:36, describing the path to Rome of the witness to Christ.

A satisfying organization can be attained only if the diverse thematic references found in the book's individual sections are considered along with the geographical aspects in 1:8. The summarizing remarks at the end of the book, which retrospectively describe the significance of the reported events for the development of the church, allude to the individual thematic references (5:42; 9:31; 15:35; 19:20). Accordingly, five major parts can be found after the preface (1:1-12, the instruction of the apostles by the risen Christ). Part 1 (2:1–5:42) depicts the early period of the church in Jerusalem. Part 2 (6:1–9:31) portrays the first stage of the church's diffusion, clearly beginning a new narrative context even though at 6:1 the stage at Jerusalem has not yet been abandoned. The persecution in Jerusalem results in the mission that spreads into Samaria and the coastal regions. The topic of part 3 (9:32–15:35) is the controversy surrounding the beginnings of the mission to the Gentiles. The climax and at the same time the compositional center of the book is the report about the apostolic council (15:1-35). From this point, the way is open for Paul's mission to Asia Minor and Greece in part 4 (15:36–19:20). The subject of part 5 (19:21–28:31) is introduced by Paul's solemn announcement that he intends to travel to Rome (19:21-22); thus Paul is the gospel's witness in Jerusalem and Rome.

Modern scholarship still widely questions authorship of Acts by Luke, a companion of Paul. This ancient identification seems to follow the general tendency to identify unknown figures with known ones. Its purpose was to derive Acts, which could not immediately be attributed to an apostolic author, from an apostolic circle. The only indications that might suggest that Paul's assistant was the author of Acts are the "we" sections (16:10-17; 20:5-15; 21:1-18; 27:1–28:16).

There are several counterarguments suggesting the improbability that Acts originated within Paul's closest circles: (1) From the specific motifs of Paul's theology (overcoming the law as a path to salvation, justification of the sinner by faith alone, the atoning death of Jesus as a salvation event), Luke–Acts has hardly appropriated anything. That is striking even if one takes into account the possibility of shifts in the theological emphasis of the more recent followers of Paul and if one recognizes additionally that Acts' chief interest was less Paul the theologian than Paul the missionary and founder of the church. (2) Acts does not include Paul in the circle of apostles (in spite of 14:4, 14). Instead, Luke–Acts limits apostleship to the circle of twelve established in the pre-Easter period (Luke 6:13; Acts 1:22). In doing so it contradicts the central perspective of Paul's own self-understanding, i.e., that he was an apostle of Jesus Christ (e.g., Gal 1:1). (3) Acts' history of Paul contradicts Paul's letters at important points. Acts has Paul traveling to Jerusalem twice between his call and the apostolic council (9:26-30; 11:30), whereas Paul emphasizes that he had been there only once (Gal 1:17-18). Acts reports the minimal requirements in regard to Jewish ritual law that the Jerusalem Christians at the apostolic council imposed on the Gentile Christians (the so-called apostolic decree in 15:20, 29). Paul denies any such impositions (Gal 2:6). (4) Acts preserves hardly any biographical information, especially for Paul's early years, that would go beyond the legendary enhanced tradition about the great apostle that was alive in the Pauline communities (7:58–8:1; 9:1-19a; 22:3).

Scholars have often wanted to conclude that Acts came into being even in the lifetime of Paul, c. 60 C.E. (J. Munck 1967), based on its open-ended conclusion, which neither reports the end of Paul's life nor mentions the persecution of Christians under Nero (62 C.E.). Since it is necessary to date the Gospel of Luke after 70 C.E., the second part of the two-volume work must have come into existence at a significantly later period. The author of the Gospel of Luke writes as a Christian of the third generation. The conflicts and the theological difficulties of the incipient mission to the Gentiles are at some distance from him, even though his own background may have been in Jewish Christianity. The central question for him concerns the historical changes that he as a historian recognizes in the identity of the church. He expects the Roman Empire to grant Christians who behave as loyal citizens their own possibilities of development. Accordingly, the anti-Christian sanctions under Domitian, and particularly under Trajan, still lie in the future. Therefore, Acts was probably written around 90 C.E.

Dependable references are lacking that would help to answer the question about the place where Acts was composed. Its origin in Palestine cannot even be considered because of its slight geographical knowledge of this area, although, in contrast, its statements about local conditions in Jerusalem are surprisingly exact. Its intense use of local Antiochian traditions might suggest Antioch as the place of composition; however, the arguments favoring Ephesus are even stronger: (1) the concern with the origin and history of the Ephesian community; (2) the distinctive veneration of Paul; and (3) the similarity of the presupposed communal conditions in Acts to those in the Pastoral Letters[§], which likewise probably derive from Ephesian circles. However, one might just as seriously consider Rome, for there lies the narrative goal of Acts, whose final and most extensive section (19:21–28:31) reveals that Paul's arrival in Rome was an act carried out by God in the face of all forms of opposition. The parallels between Acts 28 and *1 Clem* 5:1-7 as well as Phil 1:12-17 regarding the situation prevailing within the Roman community are conspicuous (if a Roman origin is assumed).

In contrast to the Gospel of Luke, Acts is not dependent on extensive written sources for its composition. The numerous source hypotheses of older scholarship, which were concerned with the reconstruction of written *Vorlagen,* have proved to be failures. The widespread consensus maintains that Acts' author wanted to base his presentation on material that he as a historian judged to be more or less authentic. Nevertheless, this material was diverse in form, origin, structure, and content. Probably only a very small portion of it was available to him in written form. Two factors indicate that most of the material came from oral tradition. (1) Relatively convincing traces of written *Vorlagen* can be demonstrated for only five passages: (a) The presentation of the so-called first missionary trip (chaps. 13–14) probably had as its source a missonary report of the Antiochian community that preserved the important stations of the trip and briefly reviewed the course of the mission (13:1, 4-5, 13-14a, 43-45a, 49-52; 14:1-2, 4-7, 21-22a, 24-27). (b) A short itinerary (Dibelius) proves to be the basic framework for the presentation of Paul's great mission to the Aegean (the so-called second and third missionary journeys). Deriving from the circles of Paul's fellow travelers, this itinerary preserves a list of routes and way stations (16:6-8, 10b, 11-15; 17:1-4, 10-11a, 15a, 17, 34; 18:1-5a, 7-8, 11) that deals with travel routes, places visited, and special difficulties. (c) Lying behind the story about the collection trip was possibly an official protocol concerning this collection (20:2b-6, 14-16; 21:1-17). (d) Similarly, the story about the imprisoned Paul might depend on a prison report transmitted in the Pauline communities (21:27-36; 22:24-29; 23:12–24:23, 26-27; 25:1-12). (e) The source of the story about the sea voyage and the shipwreck possibly was the report of a traveling companion, perhaps the Macedonian Aristarchus (27:1-9a, 12-20, 27-30, 32, 38-44; 28:1, 11-13, 14b, 16b). (2) The multiform oral tradition preserved stories about notable events that occurred in the early years of the Jerusalem community (e.g., 4:46-47; 5:1-11; 6:1-6), legends about the founding of communities (8:4-13; 13:6-12), lists of names (1:13; 6:5), and legends about persons, principally concerning Peter (3:1-10; 9:36-42; 12:3-17) and Paul (9:1-19a) as well as legendary depictions of Paul's activities in individual communities (14:8-18; 16:16-24, 35-40; 19:1-7, 11-20).

The author of the Gospel of Luke and Acts was the first Christian to write a far-reaching piece of literature. This intention becomes clear in the prefaces to his two works, both of which, following a common practice in the Hellenistic period, are dedicated to an influential person. Even more so than the Gospel of Luke, Acts conforms to established norms in terms of composition and style (Thucydides, Polybius, Lucian, Josephus). That conformity, however, does not preclude his theological intention to present history as a medium for divine activity. In doing so he follows the Hebrew Bible's style of history writing. In contrast, the influence of Hellenistic and Roman biography and novel writing are of subordinate significance.

Like other ancient historians, Acts' author forgoes the use of all the facts and developments relevant to an extensive presentation of his subject—the initial history of Christianity. Instead, he restricts himself to central events and typical situations. Persons, places, and communities appear suddenly and disappear just as abruptly. Especially marked is his use of the "style of the dramatic episode" (Dibelius). He develops individual events (e.g., 10:1-48; 15:1-29; 17:16-21) in such a narrative fashion that these occurrences become transparent for prominent constellations (e.g., the confrontation between the gospel and Gentile philosophy, 17:16-21) and typical developments (e.g., the transition to the Gentile mission without the law, 15:1-29).

Of special weight are the numerous speeches, which, as is typical of ancient historians, are not the reproduction of speeches that were actually delivered but are, rather, a stylistic tool used to bring characters and situations to life (M. Soards 1994). The composition of these speeches proves that Acts was written by a thoughtful historian who attempted to reconstruct how the individual speakers might have dealt with historical circumstances and audiences. He also appropriates valuable old traditions to accomplish this: For Peter's speeches (2:14-36; 3:12-26; 4:9-12; 5:29-32; 10:23-43), he appeals to elements of an ancient Jewish-Christian christology; for Paul's orations (13:17-41; 14:15-17; 17:22-31), he depends on an old rudimentary model of the gentile missionary—*kerygma* (cf. 1 Thess 1:8-9).

Acts' language is an elevated *Koinē* Greek, which is controlled to extremely varying degrees. Peter's speeches are written in a Hebraizing tone that attempts to echo the sound of the Septuagint[§], whereas the speech of Paul on the Areopagus (17:22-31) represents an attempt to imitate an elevated Greek style. On a middle level between these two extremes are those sections that report on deeds and miraculous occurrences involving the gospel's messengers. They employ a broadly informative and popular narrative tone (e.g., 12:6-17; 13:6-12; 19:24-40). Moreover, characteristic of Acts' style is the considerable change in the narrative's rhythm. Chapters 2–5 arouse a feeling of non-movement by constantly repeating similar material, whereas the forward-driving rhythm of chaps. 6–15, which is created by constantly changing scenes, reflects the dynamics of the early mission. In contrast, in 15:36–19:20 the narrator gives the impression of a continuing development by sketching out Paul's course. The concluding section (19:21–28:31) is conditioned by the connection of individual scenes that are parallel in content and in which a central, major motif is varied with growing intensification to make an impression on the reader. Paul's path from Jerusalem to Rome is depicted as the final break with Judaism.

The central concern of Acts, which has been hotly debated (see the surveys in Marshall 1998), is closely coupled with the identification of the book's intended readership. The opinion, based on the mundane literary form of Acts and on its purposefully positive depiction of Roman courts and authorities, that his reading audience consisted of non-Christian circles may lead to the assumption of an apologetic intention vis-à-vis the gentile public. Thus the intention of Acts has been thought to be either (based on an early dating) to defend Paul in his trial (A. Mattill 1970) or, more generally, to argue that Christianity deserves the privileges of a *religio licita*.

However, it has become increasingly certain that Acts was primarily directed to Christian readers. Although a bit of truth can be found in the view that Acts' intention regarding its Christian readership was simply evangelization (Bruce 1990) or confirmation of the gospel (W. van Unnik 1973), this does not do justice to the work's complex structure. In opposition to this view a greater number of scholars have seen Acts' primary intention as inner-Christian polemics or apologetics; however, no agreement has been reached as to the exact goal of such a purpose. According to some scholars (e.g., Talbert 1966; G. Klein 1961), Acts is defending the developing early catholic church against Gnosticism (Gnostic Interpretation*[§]). They cite (1) the obvious concern with demonstrating personally and institutionally secure tradition; (2) the leveling out of the profile of Paul's theology; and (3) the closeness to the pastoral letters, which overtly share the same intentions. Other scholars, following Conzelmann's influential interpretation, regard the overcoming of a crisis of faith caused by the delay of the Parousia as Acts' main concern. They maintain that a sequel was annexed to the Gospel of Luke in order to demonstrate that the epoch of the church, which had dawned instead of the expected Parousia, was a new period of salvation history anchored in the divine plan. In contrast, the theory that Acts was written to combat a radical Jewish Christianity (J. Jervell 1972) makes a point of noting that Acts is concerned with proving Paul's devotion to the law and with legitimating the inclusion of the Gentile Christians among the holy people of Israel.

In spite of their elements of truth, these attempts at interpretation have captured only partial aspects of Acts. One cannot be fair to Acts unless it is understood as an attempt to overcome the basic problem faced by the church in its third generation: securing its own identity. How can the church, which lived in transformed social, ethnic, and geographical circumstances, be certain of its legitimate connection with its historical Christian origins, which were totally different? Acts answers this question by presenting the deeds of the risen Christ as established in God's plan. It is the Spirit who guides the church on its way through history. In choosing narrative history as his mode of presentation, the writer of Acts acknowledges that God's salvation works through the medium of history, a view consciously based on the Hebrew Bible. From this salvation-historical perspective the relationship between the dominant Gentile church in the third generation and Israel is of special significance. Therefore, the fulfillment of the promise to Israel is accented first in the Gospel and then in Acts 1–5. Created by the activity of Jesus, the church is the people of God gathered in the final days. Acts shows that the Gentiles whom Paul has won for the faith become members of this people, which thereby attains its eschatological fullness. The church is God's eschatological people made up of Jews and Gentiles. Moreover, the nature of God's people is not changed by the parallel development of opposition on the part of unfaithful Jews, a development that leads externally to their manifest separation from the eschatological people of salvation (Acts 28:17-28). While Jerusalem, the old place of the divine presence and of the gathering of God's people, turns into a place of hostile opposition, God grants the community new space for living and growing in the spaciousness of the inhabited world. God leads Paul, the missionary bearer of the gospel, from Jerusalem to Rome.

As previously noted, the text of Acts has been transmitted in two versions that diverge significantly: (1) the Egyptian text type represented by most of the textual witnesses, which prevailed canonically both in the East and in the West; and (2) the Western text, above all the text of Codex Bezae Cantabrigiensis (D), the OL, and part of the Syriac tradition. The second version, which is approximately 8.5 percent longer than the first, deviates significantly at points from the first in substance, e.g., 15:20, 29; 16:10-11; and 28:29. The increasing criticism of Israel is especially obvious (E. Epp 1966). There is no doubt that this version must have already emerged in the second century C.E.; nevertheless, it is also clear that this version can be neither the original nor a variant from the hand of Luke. It must be considered a free reworking from a very early period, which was only possible for a writing that was not yet considered canonical and was not imbued with an aura of sacred awe.

Recent commentaries on Acts include Eckey (2000), Gaventa (2003), Johnson (1992), and Reid (2003). Grässer (2001), Green and McKeever (1994), (Mbachu 1995) and Mills (2002) are recent reviews of research. Hengel and Schwemer (1998), Marguerat (1999), Nicklas and Tilly (2003), Reiser (1998), and Sánchez (2002) discuss various aspects of Acts' historicity and historiography, chronology, and relationship to the historical Paul. Talbert (2003) is a recent collection of essays on various aspects of interpreting Acts. Smith (2002) studies Acts from the perspective of CANONICAL CRITICISM. Boismard (2000), Read-Heimerdinger (2002), Tavardon (1999), and Taylor (1999) investigate the text critical issues underlying the interpretation of Acts. Johnson (2002), Martín-Asensio (2000), and Okoronkwo (2001) study the nature of the language in Acts from various perspectives. Investigations of the ancient literary and cultural context of Acts include Bonz's analysis (2000) of the relationship between Acts and ancient epic, the studies of Klauck (2000) and Reimer (2002) on magic in Acts, and Omerqu's study (2002) of Paul's imprisonment in Acts. Various literary approaches to Acts include Darr (2002), Heil (1999), and Wasserberg (1998). Tyson (1999) investigates the troubled waters of New Testament scholarship, anti-Semitism, and Luke-Acts exegesis. Trainor (2002) uses an environmental ethic to interpret Acts. Recent discussions of the various theological issues in Acts include Avemarie (2002), Cifrak (2003), Hagene (2001), Hintermaier (2003), Janzen (2002), K.-J. Kim (1998), LaVerdiere (1998), Mineshige (2003), Moessner (1999), Mount (2002), Nave (2002), Poklorný (1999), Porter (1999), Rusam (2003), Stenschke (1999), Verheyden (1999), and Wenk (2000).

Bibliography: F. **Avemarie,** *Die Tauferzählungen der Apostelgeschichte: Theologie und Geschichte* (WUNT 139, 2002). W. **Baird,** *History of NT Research* (1992). C. K. **Barrett,** *Luke the Historian in Recent Study* (A. S. Peake Memorial Lecture 6, 1961); *A Critical and Exegetical Commentary on the Acts of the Apostles* (2 vols., ICC 30, 1994–98). W. **Beider,** *Die Apostelgeschichte in der Historie* (ThSt 61, 1960). F. C. **Beiser,** *The Sovereignty of Reason* (1996). M. **Black,** *An Aramaic Approach to the Gospels and Acts* (1988[3]). M.-E. **Boismard,** *Le texte occidental des actes des apôtres* (Etudes bibliques, n.s. 40, 2000). M. E. **Boismard and A. Lamouille,** *Le texte Occidental des Actes des Apôtres: Reconstitution et réhabilitation* (2 vols. Synthèse 17, 1984). M. P. **Bonz,** *The Past as Legacy: Luke-Acts and Ancient Epic* (2000). F. **Bovon,** *De Vocatione Gentium: Histoire de l'interprétation d'Act. 10, 1-11, 18 dans les six premiers siècles* (BGBE 8, 1967); *Luke the Theologian: Thirty-three Years of Research (1950–83)* (1978; ET 1987); *L'oeuvre de Luc* (LD 130, 1987). F. F. **Bruce,** *The Acts of the Apostles: The Greek Text with Introduction and Commentary* (1951, 1990); "The Acts of the Apostles: Historical Record or Theological Reconstruction?" *ANRW* II.25.3 (1985) 2569-2603. C. **Burchard,** *Der Dreizehnte Zeuge: Traditions—und kompositionsgeschichtliche Untersuchungen zu Lukas' Darstellung der Frühzeit des Paulus* (FRLANT 103, 1970). H. J. **Cadbury,** *The Style and Literary Method of Luke* (2 vols. HTS 6, 1919–20); *The Making of Luke–Acts* (1927); *The Book of Acts in History* (1955). J. **Calvin,** *The Acts of the Apostles* (tr. J. W. Fraser and W. J. G. McDonald; ed. D. W. Torrance and T. F. Torrance; Calvin's New Testament commentaries 6-7, c1965-66). M. **Cifrak,** *Die Beziehung zwischen Jesus und Gott nach den Petrusreden der Apostelgeschichte: ein exegetischer Beitrag zur Christologie der Apostelgeschichte* (FB 101, 2003). H. **Conzelmann,** *Die Mitte der Zeit* (BHT 17, 1954; ET 1961); *Apostelgeschichte* (HNT 7, 1963; ET Hermeneia, 1987). J. A. **Darr,** *Herod the Fox: Audience Criticism and Lukan Characterization* (JSNTSup 163, 1998). M. **Dibelius,** *Aufsätze fur Apostelgeschichte* (ed. H. Greeven, FRLANT 60, 1951; ET 1956). M. **Dömer,** *Das Heil Gottes: Studien zur Theologie des lukan-ischen Doppelwerkes* (BBB 51, 1978). J. **Dupont,** *Les sources du livre des Actes* (1960; ET 1964); *The Salvation of the Gentiles: Esssays on the Acts of the Apostles* (1979). W. **Eckey,** *Die Apostelgeschichte: Der Weg des Evangeliums von Jerusalem nach Rom* (2000). E. J. **Epp,** *The Theological Tendency of Codex Bezae Cantabrigiensis in Acts* (SNTSMS 3, 1966). P. F. **Esler,** *Community and Gospel in Luke–Acts* (SNTSMS 57, 1987). E. **Evanson,** *The Dissonance of the Four Generally Received Evangelists* (1792). J. A. **Fitzmyer,** *The Acts of the Apostles* (AB 31, 1998). H. **Flender,** *Heil und Geschichte in der Theologie des Lukas* (BEvT 41, 1965). F. J. **Foakes Jackson and K. Lake (eds.),** *The Beginnings of Christianity,* vol. 1, *The Acts of the Apostles* (5 vols. 1920–33, 1979). W. W. **Gasque,** *A History of the Criticism of the Acts of the Apostles* (BGBE 17, 1975; with addendum, 1989). B. R. **Gaventa,** "Towards a Theology of Acts: Reading and Rereading," *Int 42* (1988) 146-57; *Acts* (ANTC, 2003). E. **Grässer,** "Die Apostelgeschichte in der Forschung der Gegenwart," *TRU* 26 (1960) 93-167; 41 (1976) 141-94, 259-90; 42 (1977) 1-68; *Forschungen zur Apostelgeschichte* (WUNT 137, 2001). J. B. **Green and M. C. McKeever,** *Luke-Acts and New Testament Historiography* (IBR Bibliographies 8, 1994). E. **Haenchen,** *Acts of the Apostles: A Commentary* (1965[14]; ET 1971). S. **Hagene,** *Zeiten der Wiederherstellung: Studien zur lukanischen Geschichtstheologie als Soteriologie* (NTAbh n.s. 42, 2001). H. **Hammond,** *A Paraphrase, and Annotations upon all the Books of the NT* (1653). A. **von Harnack,** *Luke the Physician* (1906; ET 1907); *The Acts of the Apostles* (1908; ET 1909). J. P. **Heil,** *The Meal Scenes in Luke-Acts: An Audience-Oriented Approach* (SBLMS 52, 1999). C. J. **Hemer,** *The Book of Acts in the Setting of Hellenistic History* (WUNT 49, 1989). M. **Hengel,** *Zur urchristlichen Geschichtsschreibung* (1979; ET 1980). M. **Hengel and A. M. Schwemer,** *Paulus zwischen Damaskus und Antiochien: Die unbekannten Jahre des Apostels* (WUNT 108, 1998). R. **Hillier,** *Arator on the Acts of the Apostles: A Baptismal Commentary* (Oxford Early Christian Studies, 1993). J. **Hintermaier,**

Die Befreiungswunder in der Apolstelgeschichte: Motiv- und formkritische Aspekte sowie liter-arische Funktion der wunderbaren Befreiungen in Apg 5,17-42; 12,1-23; 16,11-40 (BBB 143, 2003). **A. Janzen,** *Der Friede im lukanischen Doppelwerk vor dem Hintergrund der Pax Romana* (2002). **J. Jervell,** *Luke and the People of God: A New Look at Luke–Acts* (1972); *The Theology of the Acts of the Apostles* (NT Theology, 1996); *Die Apostelgeschichte* (KEK, 1998). **L. T. Johnson,** "Luke–Acts, Book of," *ABD* (1992) 4:403-20; *The Acts of the Apostles* (SP 5, 1992); *Septuagintal Midrash in the Speeches of Acts* (The Père Marquette Lecture in Theology 2002, 2002). **L. E. Keck and J. L. Martyn (eds.),** *Studies in Luke–Acts* (1966). **K.-J. Kim,** *Stewardship and Almsgiving in Luke's Theology* (JSNTSup 155, 1998). **H. J. Klauck,** *Magic and Paganism in Early Christianity: The World of the Acts of the Apostles* (trans. B. McNeil, 2000). **G. Klein,** *Die zwölf Apostel: Ursprung und Gehalt einer Idee* (FRLANT 77, 1961). **W. L. Knox,** *St. Paul and the Church of Jerusalem* (1925); *The Acts of the Apostles* (1948). **J. Kremer** (ed.), *Les Actes des Apôtres: Traditions, rédaction, théologie* (BETL 48, 1979). **G. Krodel,** *Acts* (ACNT, 1986). **W. Kümmel,** *NTHIP* (ET 19732). **E. LaVerdiere** *The Breaking of the Bread: The Development of the Eucharist According to the Acts of the Apostles* (1998). **J. C. Lentz, Jr.,** *Luke's Portrait of Paul* (SNTSMS 77, 1993). **G. Lüdemann,** *Early Christianity According to the Tradition in Acts: A Commentary* (1987; ET, ACNT, 1989). **M. Luther,** *Luther's Works* (ed. E. Bachman; v. 30, 1960). **A. C. McGiffert,** "The Historical Criticism of Acts in Germany," *The Beginnings of Christianity* (5 vols. ed. F. J. Foakes Jackson and K. Lake, 1922) 2:363-95. **R. L. Maddox,** *The Purpose of Luke–Acts* (FRLANT 126, 1982). **D. Marguerat,** *La première histoire du christianisme: les Actes des apôtres* (Lectio divina 180, 1999). **I. H. Marshall,** *Luke: Historian and Theologian* (1970, 1988³); *The Acts of the Apostles* (NTGu, 1992). **I. H. Marshall and D. Peterson (eds.),** *Witness to the Gospel: The Theology of Acts* (1998). **G. Martín-Asensio,** *Transitivity-based Foregrounding in the Acts of the Apostles: A Functional-Grammatical Approach to the Lukan Perspective* (JSNTSup 202, Studies in New Testament Greek 8, 2000). **A. J. Mattill, Jr.,** "Luke as a Historian in Criticism Since 1840" (diss., Vanderbilt, 1959); "The Purpose of Acts," *Apostolic History and Gospel* (ed. W. W. Gasque and R. P. Martin, 1970) 108-22; "The Jesus-Paul Parallels and the Purpose of Luke–Acts," *NovT* 17 (1975) 15-46; "The Date and Purpose of Acts," *CBQ* 40 (1978) 335-50. **A. J. Mattill, Jr. and M. B. Mattill,** *A Classified Bibliography of Literature on the Acts of the Apostles* (NTTS 7, 1966). **H. Mbachu,** *Survey and Method of Acts research from 1826 to 1995* (1995). **W. E. Mills,** *A Bibliography of the Periodical Literature on the Acts of the Apostles* (NovTSup 58, 1986); *The Acts of the Apostles* (Bibliographies for Biblical Research, Periodical Literature for the Study of the New Testament 5, 2002). **K. Mineshige,** *Besitzverzicht und Almosen bei Lukas: Wesen und Forderung des lukanischen Vermögensethos* (WUNT 2/163, 2003). **D. P. Moessner, ed.,** *Jesus and the Heritage of Israel: Luke's Narrative Claim upon Israel's Legacy* (Luke the interpreter of Israel 1, 1999). **T. Morgan,** *The Moral Philosopher* (repr. 1969). **C. Mount,** *Pauline Christianity: Luke-Acts and the Legacy of Paul* (NovTSup 104, 2002). **J. Munck,** *The Acts of the Apostles* (AB 31, 1967). **G. D. Nave, Jr.,** *The Role and Function of Repentance in Luke-Acts* (Academia Biblica 4, 2002). **T. Nicklas and M. Tilly (eds.),** *The Book of Acts as Church History: Text, Textual Traditions and Ancient Interpretations* (BZNW 120, 2003). **M. E. Okoronkwo,** *The Jerusalem Compromise as a Conflict-Resolution Model: A Rhetoric-Communicative Analysis of Acts 15 in the Light of Modern Linguistics* (Arbeiten zur Interkulturalität 1, 2001). **H. Omerzu,** *Der Prozess des Paulus: eine exegetische und rechtshistorische Untersuchung der Apostelgeschichte* (BZNW 115, 2002). **J. C. O'Neill,** *The Theology of Acts in Its Historical Setting* (1961, 19702). **M. C. Parsons and R. I. Pervo,** *Rethinking the Unity of Luke and Acts* (1993). **R. I. Pervo,** *Profit with Delight: The Literary Genre of the Acts of the Apostles* (1987); *Luke's Story of Paul* (1990). **R. Pesch,** *Die Apostelgeschichte* (EKKNT 5:1-2, 1986). **E. Plümacher,** *TRE 3* (1978) 483-528; "Luke as

Historian," *ABD* 4 (1992) 398-402. **P. Pokorný,** *Theologie der lukanischen Schriften* (FRLANT 174, 1998). **S. E. Porter,** *The Paul of Acts: Essays in Literary Criticism, Rhetoric, and Theology* (WUNT 115, 1999). **J. Read-Heimerdinger,** *The Bezan Text of Acts: A Contribution of Discourse Analysis to Textual Criticism* (JSNTSup 236, 2002). **B. Reid,** "The Acts of the Apostles," *NISB* (2003) 1953-2006. **A. M. Reimer,** *Miracle and Magic: A Study in the Acts of the Apostles and the Life of Apollonius of Tyanna* (JSTNSup 235, 2002). **I. R. Reimer,** *Frauen in der Apostelgeschichte des Lukas* (1993; ET 1995). **R. Riesner,** *Paul's Early Period: Chronology, Mission Strategy, Theology* (trans. D. Stott, 1998). **J. Roloff,** *Die Apostelgeschichte* (NTD 5, 1981). **M. E. Rosenblatt,** *Paul the Accused: His Portrait in the Acts of the Apostles* (Zacchaeus Studies NT, 1995). **D. Rusam,** *Das Alte Testament bei Lukas* (BZNW 112, 2003). **H. Sánchez,** *Das lukanische Geschichtswerk im Spiegel heilsgeschichtlicher Übergänge* (Paderborner theologische Studien 29, 2002). **G. Schneider,** *Die Apostelgeschichte* (HTHK 5, 1-2, 1980–82). **R. J. Schrader** (ed.), Arator's "On the Acts of the Apostles" *(De Actibus Apostolorum)* (Classics in Religious Studies 6, 1987). **D. E. Smith,** *The Canonical Function of Acts: A Comparative Analysis* (2002). **M. L. Soards,** *The Speeches in Acts: Their Content, Context, and Concerns* (1994). **C. W. Stenschke,** *Luke's Portrait of Gentiles Prior to Their Coming to Faith* (WUNT 2/108, 1999). **P. F. Stuehrenberg,** "The Study of Acts Before the Reformation," *NovT* 29 (1987) 100-136; "Cornelius and the Jews: A Study of the Interpretation of Acts before the Reformation" (diss., University of Minnesota, 1988). **C. H. Talbert,** *Luke and the Gnostics* (1966); *Literary Patterns, Theological Themes, and the Genre of Luke–Acts* (SBLMS 20, 1974); (ed.) *Perspectives on Luke–Acts* (PerspRelStud Special Studies Series 5, 1978); (ed.) *Luke–Acts: New Perspectives from the SBL Seminar* (1984); *Reading Luke-Acts in its Mediterranean Milieu* (NovTSup 107, 2003). **R. C. Tannehill,** *The Narrative Unity of Luke–Acts: A Literary Interpretation* (2 vols. 1986–90). **P. Tavardon,** *Sens et enjeux d'un conflit textuel: Le texte occidental et le texte alexandrin des Actes des Apôtres* (CahRB 44, 1999). **D. G. K. Taylor** (ed.), *Studies in the Early Text of the Gospels and Acts* (Text-critical studies 1, 1999). **J. Taylor,** "The Making of Acts: A New Account," *RB* 97 (1990) 504-24. **C. C. Torrey,** *The Composition and Date of Acts* (HTS 1, 1916). **M. Trainor,** "A Footstool or a Throne? Luke's Attitude to Earth *(ge)* in Acts 7," *The Earth Story in the New Testament* (ed. N. Habel and V. Balabanski, The Earth Bible 5, 2002). **C. M. Tuckett (ed.),** *Luke's Literary Achievement: Collected Essays* (JSNTSup 116, 1995). **J. B. Tyson,** *Luke, Judaism, and the Scholars: Critical Approaches to Luke-Acts* (1999). **L. Valla,** *Collatio Novi Testamenti* (ed. A. Perosa, 1970). **W. C. van Unnik,** *Sparsa Collecta* (NovTSup 29-31, 1973). **J. Verheyden** (ed.), *The Unity of Luke-Acts* (BETL 142, 1999). **G. Wasserberg,** *Aus Israels Mitte—Heil für die Welt: eine narrativ-exegetische Studie zur Theologie des Lukas* (BZNW 92, 1998). **A. Weiser,** *Die Apostelgeschichte* (ÖTK 5, 1-2, 1982–85). **M, Wenk,** *Community-Forming Power : The Socio-Ethical Role of the Spirit in Luke-Acts* (Journal of Pentecostal Theology Supplement Series 19, 2000). **U. Wilckens,** *Die Missionsrede der Apostelgeschichte* (WMANT 5, 1961, 1974). **M. E. Wilcox,** *The Semitisms of Acts* (1965). **G. H. Williams,** *The Radical Reformation* (SCES 15, 1992). **S. G. Wilson,** *The Gentiles and the Gentile Mission in Luke–Acts* (SNTSMS 23, 1973). **B. W. Winter** et al. (eds.), *The Book of Acts in Its First-century Setting* (6 vols. 1993–98). **B. Witherington** (ed.), *History, Literature, and Society in the Book of Acts* (1996); *The Acts of the Apostles: A Socio-rhetorical Commentary* (1997).

J. H. Hayes and J. Roloff

THE NEW TESTAMENT CANON

Romans, Letter to the

This epistle was apparently written around 56 C.E. as Paul[†§] and representatives of his Gentile congregations were about to bring their offerings to Jerusalem (15:25). It was intended (1) to prepare the way for Paul's projected visit and mission in the West (1:5-6; 15:17-29), (2) (presumably) to ensure some wider understanding of his gospel and law-free Gentile mission at that critical moment (15:25-31), and (3) to help foster good relations between Jewish and Gentile believers in Rome (14:1-15:12, esp. 15:7). Copies of the epistle may possibly have been sent elsewhere (e.g., Ephesus), accounting for the occasional absence of "in Rome" (present at 1:7, 15) late in the manuscript tradition, and the varying position of the final doxology (16:25-27). The absence of chaps. 15 and 16 from some manuscripts probably stems from Marcion's[§] having omitted them.

In Romans, even more than elsewhere, Paul's practical aims led him to articulate his understanding of the gospel; and from the end of the first century, when the epistle began to be treated as Christian Scripture, its influence has been incalculable. In the second century Paul was already, for most Gentile Christians, the apostle *par excellence;* and in the Western church, since Augustine[§], Rom has been the most important single source of the Christian tradition's theological vocabulary. Even earlier its scriptural status and evident theological depth made it a prime quarry for doctrinal construction; its use in liturgy, preaching, apologetics, and polemic was supported by a rich exegetical tradition, most of which is now lost, although some fragments have been preserved in the surviving catenae.

To Western eyes focused on the themes of law, sin, and grace, or faith and works, the Greek fathers' understandings of the epistle have generally seemed inadequate. Despite some fine exegetical observations, Paul's statements have been read into very different theological contexts and so have been misread. But even the more appropriate Western interpretative models now appear remote from the historical Paul. The relativization of all theological interpretations opens a door to more positive assessments of Romans's reception by the fathers and by heretics alike. Every age has read the epistle from its own perspective, relating this classic to contemporary understandings of the gospel or to other cultural preoccupations, such as the historical and Social-Scientific*[§] study of religions or the wider study of literature. Paul's historical intentions are rightly prominent in Western interpretation today, but larger and more personal questions also influence how this literary text from the Christian Canon*[§] of Scripture is read.

1. *Antiquity.* The early history of the epistles is uncertain, but Rom was apparently familiar to the authors of Eph and 1 Pet, arguably (the minority view) to Luke-Acts, possibly even to Heb and James, and certainly to Clement of Rome[§], Ignatius[§], and Polycarp. But apart from Eph (a thematic presentation of Paul's concern for the unity of Jews and Gentiles in the church) and despite Ignatius (whose devotion to Paul was not matched by much theological affinity), the influence of the apostle's thought on early "orthodox" writers is surprisingly slight. Since Paul's missionary policy on the Mosaic law prevailed and since some of his Jewish presuppositions were no longer shared, his arguments were no longer necessary or fully intelligible. His apocalyptic dualism (Apocalypticism*[§]) and dialectical relating of law and gospel caused problems for early Roman Catholic writers when seized on by theologians they judged to be heretical.

Various Gnostic groups found support in Paul's language for their ascetic, metaphysical dualism. But the greatest and most notorious early Christian interpreter of Paul was Marcion, who excised those parts of Romans (1:3; 1:19-2:1; 3:31-4:25; 9; 10:5-11:32; 12:1; 15-16) that were positive about Judaism and central to Paul's conciliatory aim. Marcion appealed to his expurgated version of Gal and Rom when he defined the gospel as the antithesis of the Jewish law.

As deeply as he misunderstood the historical Jew Paul, he took the apostle's most crucial argument more seriously than anyone before Luther[§] and was a catalyst, perhaps even the pioneer, in the formation of the New Testament canon. Paul's popularity among the so-called heretics (2 Pet 3:16), the hostility to him among some Jewish Christians (see the Pseudo-Clementine literature), and the slow emergence of a New Testament canon account for the limited appeal to Paul in the second century. The task facing emergent Roman Catholicism was to reclaim Paul from under the Gnostic cloud by building the anti-Gnostic elements in his writings into its own doctrinal structure. Irenaeus[§] decisively achieved this goal, finding support in Rom as he reaffirmed the unity of creation and redemption against Gnostic dualism and the unity of Hebrew Bible and New Testament in a salvation-history theology. Most other early apologists, such as Tertullian[§], Cyprian, and Hippolytus made little use of Paul beyond Tertullian's use of Paul against Marcion. Clement of Alexandria[§] and Origen[§] were both enthusiastic admirers of Paul and interpreted him in the framework of their Christian Platonism. By asserting the unity of Hebrew Bible and New Testament against Gnostic dualism, they minimized Paul's ambivalence about the Jewish law; in defending free will they weakened Paul's teaching on predestination (Rom 9) to divine foreknowledge. Writers from the Eastern Mediterranean (e.g., Origen, Cyril[§], Methodius, Theodore of Mopsuestia[§], and Chrysostom[§]) concerned themselves primarily with the doctrine of God and Christology, and noticed little of the anthropology, psychology, and soteriology in Romans that so preoccupied the West, instead relying upon individual texts rather than the epistle's theological themes. "Ambrosiaster," mid to late fourth century, and Augustine[§] represent Western exegesis of Romans.The former's practical historical sense and understanding of Judaism anticipate modern scholarship, and he deeply influenced Augustine, who quoted his comment on Rom 5:12 *(in quo omnes peccaverunt)* that everyone has sinned in Adam. This exegesis of what became the key text for the doctrine of original sin highlights the role of Translation*[§] in biblical interpretation. The OL rendering that suggested the mistaken exegesis was adopted by the Vulgate*[§] and held sway in both Roman Catholic and Protestant exegesis long after being challenged by Erasmus[§] in 1516.

This passage also exemplifies how Augustine's theological engagement with Paul, and especially with Rom, has had an incalculable influence on Western culture. A passage from Rom (13:13-14) was instrumental in his conversion (*Conf.* 8). After defending free will in 394 in his short anti-Manichean *Expositio quarundam Propositionum ex Epistula ad Romanos,* he accepted that God's election precedes justification in 396 in his longer treatment of Rom 9:10-29, thus making predestination a problem for Christian doctrine for the first time. By later (412) focusing on human incapacity, based on Rom 7 and explained by a doctrine of original sin drawn from Rom 5 (v. 19, if not v. 12), Augustine supplied a profound reading of the epistle and informed subsequent theological anthropology. Although tangential to Paul's intentions, Augustine's interpretation echoes much that is central to the apostle's religion: Righteousness and faith are God's gift; the law, which gives knowledge of sin, contributes nothing to this saving act. Ethics flow from the new life in the Spirit. Guided by his study of Paul, Augustine refocused Western theology on the human subject and through his exegesis of Rom 7:7-25 foreshadowed Luther's view of the Christian as *simul iustus et peccator* (simultaneously justified yet sinful).

2. *Middle Ages.* Early medieval exegetes added nothing to the understanding of Rom, but preserved the patristic tradition. With Berengar[§], Lanfranc[§], Bruno of Chartreaux, and especially Anselm of Laon[§] (who was responsible for the *Glossa Ordinaria*[§] on Paul) a new and independent exegesis began to emerge.

The exegetical debates given powerful impetus by Augustine remain unabated. They no longer carry the same theological weight, but for centuries Augustine's interpretation of chap. 7 nourished "the introspective conscience of the West" (K. Stendahl 1976) even as his reading of chaps. 9-11 informed its bleak view of human history. The human condition as interpreted by Augustine's pessimistic Paulinism was offered healing in the Middle Ages and beyond by a sacramental system that mediated grace and gradually made believers righteous. Paul's discussion of baptism and ethics in Rom 6 provided a foundation for this sacramental theology, but it was another phrase from Rom that under Augustine's influence became central to both medieval and Reformation theology, and so to most of Western Christianity. The phrase "the righteousness of God" is scarcely found outside this epistle, but it is presupposed throughout the most intensively read book in Scripture, the psalter. The monastic conjunction of Paul with the psalter at this point, represented brilliantly (if one-sidedly) by the Augustinian monk Luther, arguably penetrated to the religious roots of what Paul intended; and did so more successfully than could a critical exegesis that limited itself to literary and historical issues.

Augustine's predestinarianism was less influential and, despite Rom 9, perhaps less true to Paul. It later became central in much Protestant theology, but was never accepted by the Roman Catholic Church. The renewal of theology in the late eleventh century was able to build on an exegetical tradition in which the Vulgate of Rom, filtered through Augustine's doctrine of grace, was shaping the Western theological vocabulary. The more strongly legal flavor of the Latin phrase *iustitia Dei* had been apparent as early as Tertullian, and the question of its relationship to God's mercy became urgent when Anselm of Canterbury[§] shifted the discussion of human salvation from mythological to moral and legal categories *(Proslogion 9)*. This medieval attempt to root God's saving act (justifying grace) in philosophical reflection on God's nature is foreign to Paul; but by rejecting any idea of God's justice as rendering to all people their due, Anselm was true to the main thrust of Paul's statements in Rom. Abelard[§] appealed to Rom 3:21 in his "subjective" theory of the atonement, in his understanding that God's love revealed in Christ evokes human faith and love, drawing believers into a loving relationship with God. That this theory is unfolded directly through an exposition of Romans is evidence of the epistle's centrality in medieval theology. Second only to Origen, Augustine's Pauline theology of grace also rings through the monastic meditation on Scripture. Again, the close association of Paul and the psalter arguably echoed chords in Romans that modern exegesis has been slow to recover.

Early medieval commentaries on Paul's epistles helped shape the theological language of the productive period that followed; but a new development is evident in the more analytic exegesis of the scholastics, who worked through entire texts posing *quaestiones,* discussions of grammatical and philological points. The scientific exactitude of Thomas Aquinas's[§] commentary on Paul represents a high point and feeds into his *Summa.* Romans 1:19-20 provided Aquinas and subsequent Roman Catholic theologians with clear support for their teaching that God can be known through the light of reason, and Romans 4 provided material for their salvation-history framework of Christian belief.

3. *Renaissance and Reformation.* In the opinion of Aquinas, God acts rationally, i.e., in accordance with wisdom, in saving humanity. Other scholars, like Eriugena[§] and later G. Biel[§], stressed the sovereignty of the divine will. The combination of this voluntarism with Cicero's understanding of *iustitia* as rendering to each what is due led to the position of the *via moderna,* which Luther inherited from his teachers and still accepted in his *Dictata super Psalterium* (1513-15), but then (in 1515) rejected, as he explained in his autobiographical preface to his Latin writings (1545).

In his *Lectures on Romans* (1515-16), Luther the Roman Catholic monk still understood grace as healing, similar to Augustine. His understanding of Romans, reached independently but confirmed by reading Augustine, caused his break with his teachers, although not the break with Rome. Even his new and distinctive understanding of justification, already emerging here in his claim that the Christian is *simul iustus et peccator,* i.e., extrinsically (in God's reckoning) justified but intrinsically (as we are in ourselves and in our own estimation) sinners, might have remained within the limits of legitimate theological argument within Roman Catholicism had not other factors contributed to the rupture. Luther's interpretation of Romans contributed massively to the development of doctrine and to the reform in the church, but cannot be held responsible for the divisions of Western Christianity. It is conveniently summarized in his 1522 preface to the epistle. The sermons, "Two Kinds of Righteousness" (1519) and "On Good Works" (1520), also reflect it and show how the early chapters of 1 Corinthians informed Luther's reading of Romans and (historically and exegetically, if not theologically) distorted it. The notion of Christ's righteousness becoming the believer's, for example, derives from 1 Cor 1:30, not from Romans.

Luther's insistence that justification is on the basis of faith alone "without the works of the law" (Rom 3:28) is as old as Origen, whereas his understanding of faith and his polemical application of the doctrine of justification against "the law" mark an epoch. Paul was generally thinking of Torah observance, especially the circumcision of gentile converts; but Luther's generalization of this to include morality and all human achievement radicalized Augustine's anti-Pelagian stance and made it the heart of the gospel for a large part of Western Christianity.

In his response to Erasmus in *De Servo Arbitrio* (1525), Luther drew heavily on Romans 9 to support his insistence on the doctrine of predestination. This controversy again reveals Luther as the radical Augustinian breaking with his late medieval teachers. The Renaissance was simultaneously breaking with scholastic exegesis in other ways. J. Colet's§ Oxford lectures on Romans in the 1490s had offered a plain running exegesis of the Vulgate text, influenced not only by Augustine but also by M. Ficino's (1433-99) Neoplatonic commentary on this epistle. Faber Stapulensis§ made a fresh Latin translation and exegesis of Paul's epistles (1512), which was used by Luther; but it did not advance philological research as L. Valla's§ notes had done. Erasmus published Valla's *Adnotationes* in 1505 before himself carrying through the exegetical achievements of Renaissance humanism, especially in his own lengthy *Annotations*. These notes accompanied the successive editions of his Greek New Testament from 1516 to 1535, justifying his editorial decisions and both citing and criticizing much patristic and medieval exegesis and even his humanist predecessors. They include Textual Criticism*§, exegesis, corrections of inaccurate Latin translations, and comparison of Septuagint*§ citations with the Hebrew. His corrections of the Vulgate at Rom 5:12 *(quatenus for in quo)* followed the Greek fathers and withdrew one support from the doctrine of original sin, while his introduction at Rom 4:5 of the verb *imputare* with its forensic implications apparently contributed to P. Melanchthon's§ forensic doctrine of justification. Erasmus never wrote his promised commentary on Rom, but his *Paraphrases* (1518) were a form of commentary with a future. They owe much to Origen, something to Ambrosiaster, Chrysostom, and Theophylact, and they contradict Augustine.

The controversies excited by Erasmus's notes (e.g., on Rom 5:12 and 9:5) account for a proportion of the intense exegetical activity of this period. Although the invention of printing was a stimulus, the main factor behind the activity was the centrality of Rom for the new religious movements, movements that hinged on their interpretation of Scripture and that made Scripture available in the vernacular.

Luther the Augustinian monk remains the fountainhead of Reformation exegesis of Paul, but he left his *Roman Catholic Lectures on Romans* unprinted and undiscussed. They were rarely read and not published until 1908. His dialectic of law and gospel and his correlation of the Word and faith, however, placed Rom at the heart of Protestant theology and was closely followed, e.g., by W. Tyndale§. The other reformers were deeply indebted to humanism as well as to Luther, and of these Melanchthon had the most direct influence on Protestant readings of Rom. His widely used *Loci Communes* of 1521, the first Protestant dogmatics, draws much of its form and content from this epistle; his lecture notes *(Annotationes)* on Romans were published in 1522. His 1529 commentary reveals more of the humanist and friend of Erasmus in its use of classical rhetoric. The climax of Melanchthon's work on the epistle, however, is the commentary of 1532 (revised 1540). *His Apology to the Augsburg Confession* (1530) made his forensic understanding of justification the standard Protestant view, introducing the idea of imputation on account of the alien merit of Christ (Art. 21, par. 19). Instead of the Roman Catholic (Augustinian) "making righteous," we have here the Protestant "pronouncing righteous" (Art. 4, par. 252).

The centrality of this doctrine and the importance of predestination for some Reformers led to intensive exegeses of Rom by Roman Catholic as well as by Protestant humanists during this period. All used the Greek text and Erasmus's *Annotationes,* whether producing their own translations into Latin and the vernacular or retaining the Vulgate. The leading scholastic theologian of the day, T. Cajetan[§], undertook to rescue the Bible from the heretics and published a major commentary on Paul's epistles in 1529. In the same year the Louvain friar F. Titelmann followed up his *Elucidatio* of all the New Testament epistles (1528) with his *Collatio* on Romans (1529); and in 1533 J. Gagny of Paris published his paraphrase *(Epitome Paraphrastica),* to be followed by his *Scholia* on Paul's epistles in 1539. Although the humanist bishop J. Sadoleto's *Tres Libri Commentariorum* (1535) were suspected of Pelagianism and of affinities with M. Bucer[§], the denominational divisions were not yet hardened. Many scholars on both sides were looking for reconciliation through open-minded study of Scripture (e.g., M. Grimani's 1542 commentary, which maintains the medieval emphasis on "grace alone").

Of those who became Protestants, J. Bullinger[§] had lectured on Rom in 1525 while in the Cistercian monastery at Kappel. In writing his commentary (1533), he used Origen, Ambrosiaster, and Theophylact and was deeply influenced by Melanchthon and Erasmus. The largest and most learned Romans commentary was that of Bucer (1536), which was then much used by lesser figures like the Hebraist C. Pellican[§] (1539) and the Roman Catholic C. Guilliaud (1542). But the greatest Romans commentary of the whole period is the taut work of Calvin[§] (1540). In this, his first biblical commentary, Calvin was still strongly influenced by Erasmus's Latin text and notes. Like Melanchthon for Lutheranism, Calvin made Romans central for subsequent Reformed Christianity through both his commentary and his complementary systematic theology. The theology of *Institutes* (1536) and especially of the greatly enlarged edition of 1539 and its French translation (1541; which included a chapter on justification by faith and one on predestination), owed much to Romans. Where Melanchthon was critical of the law, Calvin defended it. He was, like Luther, more true to Augustine than the other Reformers were, but he was also indebted to other fathers and to scholasticism. Unlike Luther, whose lectures retained the medieval format of gloss and *scholia,* and Melanchthon, who self-consciously pursued Renaissance "method," Calvin used humanist grammatical and rhetorical insights in the service of a profound yet concise theological exposition that sought to clarify the intention of the author.

This short period of astonishing creativity in the interpretation of Rom, when humanist scholarship combined with the Augustinian revival in a Reformation theology centered on Paul's most doctrinal epistle, was followed by three centuries and more in which its interpretation reflected rather than propelled the history of doctrine. Justification remained characteristic of Lutheranism; Rom was read for its doctrinal content, with the emphasis on chaps. 1-8, understood with reference to the individual. There were disagreements among Lutherans—e.g., A. Osiander's rejection of the forensic character of justification—and marked differences of emphasis between Lutherans and Reformed within a shared Protestant framework. As in the Middle Ages, Rom was central but variously interpreted.

Luther had transferred Christian political responsibility to the state, and Rom 13:1-7 reinforced a more conservative political stance. The Calvinist doctrine of predestination (see Rom 8:28-30; 9:15, 18; 11:7) was challenged by J. Arminius[§] as a result of his study of Rom (1612);

this disagreement has persisted, with H. Grotius[§], the Laudians, and later J. Wesley[§] also reject-ing the deterministic Calvinism of the Puritans. That use of Rom 9 had sustained both Reformers and Puritans under siege, as it had Augustine; but in England their revolution was defeated, with the later Caroline divines preferring the more conservative political thought of Augustine to that of the radical Reformers. G. Bull's reconciliation of Paul and James indicates an unwillingness to let the apostle rock the boat. In Europe the scholasticism of German and Swiss Protestant orthodoxy multiplied but did not advance the study of this epistle. Neither did the "biblical theology" that first bolstered this orthodoxy and then, through Pietism[*§], chal-lenged it. The modern critical study of the Bible had different roots.

The religious potential of Paul's doctrine, evident in the Reformation, was discovered by both Lutherans and Reformed in Pietism and by the Anglican Wesley, whose heart was "strangely warmed" in 1738 at the reading of Luther's preface to Rom. All these revivalists set such store by holiness or perfection as to be accused by Calvinists of relapsing into "works righteousness." But their moral seriousness was true to Paul, even if their separation of sanctification from jus-tification and consequent division of Rom between chaps. 1-5 and 6-8 was a misreading of the epistle. Wesley's recovery of justification by faith for English Christianity was true to Rom as understood by T. Cranmer[§], whose homilies he abridged and used as a summary of doctrine.

In Roman Catholicism, the decree on justification at the Council of Trent (1546-47) marked the end of compromise with Protestantism and of convergence in both sides' understanding of Romans. The Augustinian revival in Jansenism brought some Roman Catholic interpretation on Romans closer to Protestantism, but Jansenism's defeat contributed to the decline of this Pauline language within Roman Catholicism.

4. *Modern Period.* Modern historical interpretation of Rom grew out of Renaissance human-ism. Grotius's posthumous *Annotationes* (vol. 2, 1646) took the decisive step of clarifying the New Testament by drawing on classical and Hellenistic Jewish materials. Grotius influenced H. Hammond[§] (1653), the father of English biblical criticism, who studied Paul's language closely and also set the epistles in their historical contexts. Both men stand behind J. Locke[§], whose brilliant preface, paraphrase, and notes (1705-7) on the epistles are unsurpassed. These hermeneutical principles (Hermeneutics[*§]) were later introduced into Germany by J. Ernesti[§], whose *Institutio* appeared in 1761 (rev. 1765). The tradition made popular by Erasmus of inter-preting Rom by paraphrasing it into Latin was continued in Germany by J. Semler[§] (1769).

More important, Semler was a conduit introducing English Deism[§] into Germany, including T. Morgan's[§] theory about the difference between Pauline and Petrine Christianity, as developed in Morgan's *The Moral Philosopher* (1738-40). This theory proved decisive for the historical study of early Christianity. In 1831 F. C. Baur[§] made the theory pivotal for his understanding of Christianity's development and, in 1836, applied it to the interpretation of Rom. By then the Enlightenment scholarship of Semler and J. D. Michaelis[§], joined by the new historical biblical theology of J. P. Gabler[§] and G. Bauer[§], had inaugurated the great surge of modern German scholarship accumulating in textbooks of New Testament introduction and theology as well as in commentaries; scholarship soon to explode in historical monographs, articles, and reviews.

The application of Baur's historical method to Rom is best seen in his early essay on the epis-tle's "purpose and occasion" (1836), which broke with the "doctrinal" interpretation that had guided Protestant theology since Melanchthon (1521). W. De Wette[§] (1835) had already recog-nized an argument going on in Rom; but he had identified the opposition in general terms as Judaism, making the epistle a battle of ideas and subordinating its polemical aspect to the tra-ditional doctrinal perspective. Baur saw Paul's argumentative intention in relation to the inner-Christian dispute about the inclusion of Gentiles in the church. He was possibly mistaken about the composition of the Roman church, which he thought predominantly Jewish-Christian; but he achieved a much sharper historical profile. His interpretation made sense of chaps. 9-11 as the climax of the apostle's argument, not merely as an appendix to its doctrinal heart in chaps. 1-8, as most Protestant exegesis has done. This new historical perspective signaled an interpretative shift away from the Augustinian and Protestant emphasis on the individual's sin and salvation, with chaps. 1-8 becoming doctrinal prologue rather than doctrinal center. But Baur still read Rom in anthropological and doctrinal terms, even though the doctrine now reflected more of Enlightenment and idealism than of Augustine and Luther. Baur's Paul asserted salvation for all believers—i.e., Jews and Gentiles—on a basis of faith ("universalism") as opposed to Jewish "particularism." The theory we call justification by faith was hammered out in the forge of social conflict and answered a practical question; but it was still a doctrine, one the theologian Baur thought true about God and the world and the historian Baur thought true to Paul. The epistle's arguments are a principled exploration of "the truth of the gospel" (Gal 2:5, 14) occasioned by disputes about the admission of Gentiles without requiring conformity to the law, not merely a pragmatic justification of Paul's missionary policy.

In his early essay and thereafter Baur disputed the authenticity of Rom 15 and 16. Some scholars, like the eighteenth-century vicar of Tewkesbury E. Evanson[§], would go further. B. Bauer[§] (1851) denied the authenticity of the whole epistle and was followed by the Dutch school: e.g., A. Loman, S. Naber, A. Pierson, and W. van Manen. Others, from C. Weisse[§] and F. Spitta[§] to J. O'Neill[§] (1975), have thought it extensively interpolated; and a few, e.g., W. Schmithals (1975, 1988), have thought it composite. Chapter 16 is now generally agreed to be Pauline, but many scholars, e.g., T. Manson[§] (1948), have doubted whether it was directed to Rome. The doxology of 16:25-27 is still widely thought inauthentic; but of R. Bultmann's[§] (1947) eight proposed glosses, only 7:25b has found many supporters.

These literary questions have been marginal to the history of exegesis; although attempts to relate Rom to other Greek literature (J. Weiss 1897; P. Wendland 1907; Bultmann 1910) have become more central in modern times, the interpretation of Rom has always been mainly the study of its ideas. Baur's classic monograph on Paul (1845) analyzes them brilliantly in terms of the Christian's spiritual self-consciousness. Bultmann later (1929) saw in Baur's analysis an anticipation of his own existential interpretation, but the decline of Hegelianism allowed the metaphysics of spirit only a weak echo in the contrast liberal interpreters drew between the spiritual and the material ("flesh") in Paul's thought (cf. the NEB translation of *sarx* as "lower nature"). Baur's analysis of Paul's terms nevertheless contributed significantly to the biblical theology of German liberal Protestantism, where Paulinism remained central and Rom the main quarry for that doctrinal type. Baur's admirer C. Holsten introduced the dichotomy found in many subsequent accounts of Paul's theology by contrasting his negative view of "flesh" in Rom 7 and 8, based on Greek dualism, with his more neutral Hebraic usage elsewhere. H. Lüdemann's classic study of Paul's anthropology (1872) extended this distinction to two different doctrines of human nature and so of redemption: the Jewish juridical subjective idea found in Rom 1-4 and the Greek dualistic ethical and "physical" concepts present in chaps. 5-8. This dichotomy within Rom was widely explained in terms of Paul's double background in Jewish Hellenism, with more weight being given to the Greek influence, e.g., by O. Pfleiderer[§] (1873). Lüdemann and E. Reuss[§] (1864[4]) before him also thought the ethical/physical strand more characteristic of Paul than the juridical and so prepared for the denial by W. Wrede[§] (1904) and later A. Schweitzer[§] (1930) that justification was central to Paul's theology. Most Protestant exegesis and theology remained more traditional, however; and the Reformation interpretation of Rom was defended and updated by more conservative scholars and by systematic theologians (e.g., in A. Ritschl's[§] *Die christliche Lehre der Rechtfertigung und Versöhnung 2* 1872).

The main stimulus to new understandings of Rom in this period came from history-of-religion research (Religionsgeschichtliche Schule*[§]) on Judaism and on the wider Hellenistic milieu. Like Grotius, Baur had recognized the importance of the religious context; but

J. Droysen's discovery of the Hellenistic age and advances in the understanding of first-century Judaism rendered some of his conclusions obsolete. In 1888, H. Gunkel's[§] monograph on Paul's understanding of the Spirit undercut modern idealist assumptions and placed Paul more accurately in his religious environment. Also in 1888, O. Everling clarified Paul's apocalyptic cosmology (Rom 8) by reference to Jewish apocalyptic (Apocalypticism*[§]), showing that redemption meant liberation from demonic powers. R. Kabisch's[§] monograph on Paul's eschatology (1893) credited him with a "physical" view of redemption, as had Lüdemann, but derived this from Jewish apocalyptic, adumbrating Schweitzer's theory of Paul's "eschatological mysticism" (1911, 1930). H. Holtzmann's[§] preference, shared by E. Teichmann, for the non-Jewish elements in Paul was reinforced in the 1890s and 1900s by the debate about the influence of the mystery religions on Paul's baptismal ideas in Rom 6:3-5 (W. Heitmüller 1903, 1911; R. Reitzenstein 1910; and many others). Reitzenstein[§] (1904) dated the Poimandres myth to the first century, and W. Bousset[§] (1913) followed him in looking there for the religious milieu of Hellenistic gentile Christianity and (granted the apostle's modifications) Paul's Christ mysticism, his talk of spirit, his idea of dying and rising with Christ (Rom 6), and the Adam myth he offers in Rom 5. Bultmann and his pupils followed this derivation of Paul's ecclesiology and Christology from the supposed Gnostic milieu of early Hellenistic Christianity; but they found his distinctive contribution, most clearly visible in Romans, elsewhere.

All these representative studies of Paul's "system" have affected how Paul's most systematic letter has been read within New Testament scholarship. They are reflected in critical commentaries, histories of Christianity, accounts of "Paulinism," and New Testament theologies. Biographical studies (e.g., Deissmann 1911, 1925[2]) were also popular among liberals, for whom Paul's religion was more interesting and admirable than his theology. Rom 7 was sometimes interpreted as Pauline autobiography, and Paul's divided mind was understood to explain his conversion in psychological terms until W. Kümmel[§] (1929) provided a more convincing account of the passage. The focus of history-of-religion research shifted from intertestamental Judaism to the mystery religions and Gnosticism before drawing the interpretation of Rom back to Paul's religious heritage and locating him more firmly on the map of first-century Judaism, now illuminated by Qumran (Dead Sea Scrolls[§]) as well as by the Apocrypha, Pseudepigrapha[†§], Philo[§], and later rabbinic sources. C. H. Dodd[§], among others, clarified the importance of the Septuagint for understanding Rom (1932, 1935); and Schweitzer's insistence on the centrality of apocalyptic has, with modifications, been maintained for Rom by E. Käsemann[§] (1973) and Beker (1980). Yet other factors revolutionized the German study of Rom in the 1920s. The Luther renaissance was fueled by the rediscovery of Luther's early lectures on Rom, and the "dialectical theology" of K. Barth[§] and F. Gogarten began with the study of Romans and the reformers. Both these and A. Schlatter's[§] New Testament interpretation contributed to the new Romans-based syntheses of Paul's theology forged by Bultmann and Käsemann and still echoing in the writings of J. Dunn, H. Hübner, and P. Stühlmacher, among many others.

Barth's contribution (1919, 1921-22[2]) was to sharpen the hermeneutical question of how to interpret Paul's talk of God. His Pauline and Reformation understanding of revelation, taking place in and through proclamation, encouraged him to "speak with" Paul and articulate in his own modern way what the text of Rom is saying. This approach went beyond historical exegesis and gained little support in biblical scholarship apart from Bultmann's appreciative review article (1922); however, its contribution to conservative biblical theology makes it part of the larger story of the impact of Romans on Christian history. Barth's aim was carried through in New Testament scholarship by Bultmann's account (1948) of the human being prior to faith (see Romans 1-3) and the human being under faith (see Rom 3:21-8:39 and 10).

This distillation of Paul's (mainly Rom's) anthropological ideas corresponded to Bultmann's theory that God-talk is, at the same time, talk of human existence, and it formed one of the two planks of his existential interpretation of the New Testament. The process was continued by his pupils, notably H. Conzelmann (1967), G. Bornkamm[§] (1969), and G. Klein (1969). But another pupil, Käsemann (1969), was critical of Bultmann's idealistic and individualistic account of Paul's theology. To do justice to the physicality of human beings, to Paul's futurist and cosmic eschatology, and to the lordship of Christ, the sacraments, and the salvation-historical element in Rom, Käsemann insisted on the realism of Paul's *sōma* language and the primacy of Christology, giving more weight to the mythological language of Rom 5-8 and to the historical and ecclesiological dimensions of Rom 9-11. Some of Käsemann's exegesis, notably his apocalyptic interpretation of the righteousness of God, has been challenged (e.g., E. Lohse 1973; Klein 1976), and some has been developed (C. Müller 1964; Stühlmacher 1965). But this synthesis integrates the history-of-religion school's research with a Luther-inspired *(iustificatio impii,* "justification of the ungodly") interpretation of Rom and illuminates many aspects of Paul's theology, worship, and ethics.

The discussion of Rom within twentieth-century German exegesis, notably in the Bultmann school (but, since O. Kuss [1957-78], also in ecumenical Roman Catholic scholarship), has thus combined historical exegesis with strong theological interests, again reflecting the centrality of Rom to Christian (especially Lutheran) theology and proclamation. Elsewhere, a larger space between the interpretation of Paul and theologians' own understanding of Christianity has permitted a less directly theological engagement with Rom. In Christian practice, the themes of the epistle have usually been read in the light of traditional belief: e.g., 1:3-4 in terms of Chalcedon and 3:24-26 as related to atonement doctrine. That interaction survives in German New Testament theology, even though historical exegesis provides controls and stimulates new reflection. However, historical research in a pluralist society has relativized that tradition of Christian theological exegesis. While it can be defended as a legitimate set of options for reading Rom, persuasive to some persons whose religion is largely shaped by Paul and Luther, it is scarcely the only historically responsible way of interpreting the epistle today.

More sympathetic and better-informed studies of early Judaism, sometimes motivated by a laudable desire to improve Jewish-Christian relations (e.g., W. D. Davies 1948, 1978; K. Stendahl 1976), have reoriented research on Rom in North America, Great Britain, and Scandinavia. In 1963 and 1976 Stendahl[§] again set Rom firmly in the context of Paul's Gentile mission. He agreed with Baur that chaps. 9-11 form the climax of the epistle and echoed Wrede and Schweitzer in rejecting Luther's preoccupation with justification; but he followed J. Munck[§] (1954) against all three in denying that Rom was primarily a polemic against Jewish Christianity. Instead, Stendahl maintained that it was apologetic in function: Rom defended Paul's Gentile mission by showing how the mission fitted into God's plan. The apostle was not attacking other people or positions, as Luther later attacked the Roman Catholic system by means of the Pauline antithesis of faith and works.

Whether Luther's reading of the epistle was legitimate in his time or is defensible now are further questions that involve more than Paul's authorial intentions; but these intentions are usually agreed to be at least relevant to, and perhaps decisive for, theological interpretation. Modern critical advocates of traditional readings of Rom assumed that the readings were broadly true to the apostle's intentions. Stendahl's persuasive historical contextualization of Rom in Paul's mission was therefore provocative. It initiated the conflict of interpretations that has surrounded Rom since the 1970s.

Historical understanding of the circumstances in which any ancient document, but especially a letter, was written solves some problems and improves a modern reader's understanding of the text. Stendahl's suggestions received strong independent support from E. P. Sanders's account of Palestinian Judaism (1977). Sanders demonstrated that Judaism is not about merit and earning salvation through good works and that, therefore, Paul could not have been opposing such a system. A significant portion of traditional Pauline interpretation was thus rendered implausible. Still, Sanders was more willing than Stendahl to admit that Paul was critical of his former pharisaic Judaism for its failure to recognize Jesus as Messiah. Christology and soteriology (i.e., salvation in Christ) was Paul's ultimate concern, even though this salvation comes from membership in the people of God. The faith/works antithesis concerns "getting in" rather than describing different ways of relating to God. Justification by faith, according to Sanders, was neither Paul's Christology (as Bultmann thought) nor his central idea. But it was connected with salvation in Christ, and was not simply a missionary tactic, as F. Watson (1986) later argued. Sanders thus stands closer to the traditional view than Stendahl or Watson because he takes Paul's antithesis seriously. The phrase "not by works," however, is not about what Luther had thought. Sanders (1983) made sense of Paul's conflicting statements about the law (aside from Rom 2) by seeing them in context. H. Räisänen (1983) reached broadly similar conclusions but expressed them more negatively. Watson, through a fresh reconstruction of the situation in Rome (1986, 94-105), was able to incorporate Rom 2 into the new perception of Rom's theology initiated by Baur and revived by Stendahl. This "Romans debate" (K. Donfried 1977, 1991[2]) about the character and purpose of the epistle and the situation addressed (see also P. Minear 1971) is evidence of Baur's methods and mapwork being followed and his conclusions being modified (see, e.g., Hübner 1978; Dunn 1988a, 1988b; Wedderburn 1988). The variety of possible conclusions shows how much is uncertain at the historical level, as also in the exegetical debates, on account of the epistle's many grammatical and syntactical ambiguities.

The interpretation of Romans at the beginning of the twenty-first century, however, is more complicated than that "Romans debate" suggests because both historical and exegetical enquiries are a means to an interpretive end, not the goal of most attempts to make sense of the epistle. Knowledge of the language is a necessary but not a sufficient condition of genuine understanding; knowledge of the literary conventions prevalent at the time of writing and of other historical information also provides aids to understanding and supports arguments in favor of one interpretation and against another. A more important issue still is the kind of understanding that is being sought. Diversity is evident in the various ways the subject matter is defined. Different interpretative aims and different assessments of Paul's subject matter may well affect how the epistle is read. Such diversity reveals another dimension of the interpretation of Romans, one arising from secularism and religious pluralism: Biblical scholars disagree about Paul's subject matter and its possible truth or bearing on their lives. In this situation interpreters can be questioned regarding the theological stances (if any) that inform their respective proposals, not only about their historical understanding of some first-century ideas and conflicts. Stendahl and Käsemann have contemporary interests at heart in their conflicting interpretations of the Pauline antithesis of faith and works: the one in fostering better relations between Christians and Jews, the other in maintaining a particular understanding of the gospel of salvation. Käsemann sees the world, rather than the church, as the stage of God's saving activity: God justifies the ungodly (Rom 4:5). Thus the authentic response to this gospel proclaimed is personal existential faith in Christ rather than membership in a pious club. Käsemann's Pauline theology of the cross subjects the necessary corporate, ecclesial, "horizontal" dimension of Christian commitment to a christological criterion. Both he and Stendahl include historical and exegetical components in their proposals that might be falsified or lose plausibility in the course of argument. But theological insights can survive the destruction of some historical and exegetical supports. The validity of Luther's criticism of late medieval theology and practice, for example, is not wholly dependent on the historical accuracy of his understanding of Paul. Luther applied the text with its powerful antithesis to a new situation and in doing so changed the point at issue. That application is not history, but it may be truer in some sense to Paul than would be a more historically correct interpretation that fails to echo the religious power of the text.

Similar observations may be made regarding attempts by Liberation*§ theologians to achieve a socially relevant interpretation of the text (e.g., J. Miranda 1974). Such attempts, along with the use of psychological categories to clarify the transformation of self-understanding intended by Paul's soteriological language (R. Scroggs 1977; G. Theissen 1983), raise again the question, posed most challengingly by Baur and Bultmann, of what conceptualities are appropriate to interpret Romans in one's own day. The answers will depend on what kind of interpretation is wanted. Theological interpretations are no longer the only options, and what counts as a theological interpretation today is itself disputed. Political and psychological readings of Romans may be deeply theological.

The majority of readers of Romans are Christian believers who share some of Paul's assumptions. But other readers are not believers, and some believers choose to cultivate the ground they share with their non-Christian contemporaries rather than to explore what they share with Paul. The various approaches have led to new insights. New Testament scholars' specialization directs them back to the first-century context of the epistle in order to make their particular contributions to how it is appropriately read both within Christianity and in the broader culture. The epistle's historical context includes ancient literature and rhetoric. The debate about Paul's use of the "Cynic-Stoic diatribe" in Romans continues (S. Stowers 1981), and RHETORICAL Criticism*§ promises further illumination of Paul's literary activity. The historical aspect of history-of-traditions research has been most fruitful for the exegesis of Romans, identifying liturgical traditions quoted or echoed and commented on by Paul. Identifying these traditions, especially in Rom 3:24-25, has allowed some interpreters (Bultmann 1948; Käsemann 1960) to deny that Jewish-Christian atonement theology is characteristic of Paul, whereas others (Stühlmacher 1981) have given special weight to what Paul takes over from early Christian tradition. However, the literary aspects of Paul's use of earlier traditions are proving most fascinating. Scholars agree on the importance of Scripture for Paul, and the extent of his scriptural quotation in Romans 3-4; 9-11; 15 has attracted increasing attention (F. Umbreit 1856; O. Michel 1929; L. Goppelt 1939; Dodd 1952; E. Ellis 1957; R. Hays 1989). Among the methods and approaches of modern Literary Theory*§, debates about Intertextuality*§ (Hays) and Reader-Response*§ (A. Thiselton 1992) have seemed more illuminating than has structuralist exegesis (D. Via 1975; D. Patte 1983; Structuralism and Deconstruction*§).

These brief indications confirm how the interpretation of Romans has exploded in several new directions at the close of the twentieth century, while historical exegesis continues to wrestle with central ideas and key phrases such as "in Christ" (A. Deissmann 1892; F. Neugebauer 1961; C. F. D. Moule 1977). A dramatic new interpretation of a small ambiguous phrase "the faith of Jesus (Christ)" at Rom 3:22, 26, etc., still has the capacity to stimulate contrary understandings of Paul's theology and therefore conflicting readings of Romans. The translation of a single word, *hilastērion* (3:25), has similarly caused or reflected conflicting interpretations in the past. Historical and linguistic study exercises some control over the diversity of interpretations but less than most theologians could wish. Religious interests have always been present in theological interpretation, and this no longer appears disreputable. They are sometimes present in historical exegesis too, and anti-religious interests are also sometimes present in biblical scholarship. Modern historical and other newer approaches continue to stimulate a conversation that has always included diverse and conflicting interpretations of this powerfully ambiguous text.

Recent commentaries include Edwards (2003), Haacker (1999), Johnson (1997), Lohse (2003), Talbert (2002), Wilckens (1997), and Wright (2002). There is a thorough bibliography through 2000 in Miller (2001). Güting and Mealand (1998) offer a recent linguistic investigation of Rom. Bryan (2000) and Reasoner (1999) investigate the ancient cultural and literary setting of Rom. Chae (1997), Cosgrove (1997), Gathercole (2002), Grenhom and Patte (2000), Keller (1998), and Neubrand (1997) all study the thorny issue of Paul's understanding of

Judaism in Rom. Berkley (2000), Keesmaat (1999), Shum (2002), Wagner (2002), and Wilk (1998) all analyze Paul's use of the Hebrew Bible. Blumenfeld (2001) analyzes political thought in Rom in his study of Paul's relationship to ancient politics. Collections of essays on Rom include Bergmeier (2000), Cranfield (1998), Soderlund and Wright (1999), and Theobald (2001). Studies of Paul's rhetorical and narrative techniques in Rom include Anderson (1999), Burton (2001), Kim (2000), and Longenecker (2002). Byrne (2000) interprets Romans using an environmental perspective. Treatments of miscellaneous theological issues in Rom include Bell (1998), Dabourne (1999), Grieb (2002), Middendorf (1997), Miller (2000), Reichert (2001), and Westerholm (1997).

Bibliography: P. Abelard, *PL* 178:783-978; ET, LCC 10 (1956) 276-87. W. Affeldt, "Verzeichnis de Römerbriefkommentare bis zu Nikolaus v. Lyra," *Traditio* 13 (1957) 369-407. E. Aleith, *Das Paulusverständnis in der alten Kirche* (BZNW 18, 1937); "Das Paulusverständnis des J. Chrystostomus," *ZNW* 38 (1939) 181-88. B. Altaner, *Patrologie* (1963[6]; ET 1960[5]). P. Althaus, *Paulus und Luther über den Menschen* (1938, 1963[4]). **Ambrosiaster,** CSEL 81.1, 224-38. R. D. Anderson, Jr., *Ancient Rhetorical Theory and Paul* (Contributions to Biblical Exegesis and Theology 18, 1999[2]). **Anselm of Laon,** *PL* 114:469-520. **Atto of Vercelli,** *PL* 134:125-288. J. Auer, *Die Entwicklung der Gnadenlehre in der Hochscholastic* (2 vols. 1942-51). **Augustine,** *Expositio quarundam Propositionum ex Epistula ad Romanos, PL* 35:2063-87, CSEL 84:3-52, cf. 183-85 *(Retractiones); Inchoata expositio, PL* 35:2088-106, CSEL 84:145-81 and 186 *(Retractiones); De div. Quaestiones Ad Simplicianum* (ET, LCC 6, 1953) 376-406; *De Spiritu et Littera,* CSEL 60:155-229; ET, LCC 8 (1955) 182-250; *De peccato originalis,* CSEL 42:167-206. W. S. Babcock, "Augustine's Interpretation of Romans (AD 394-396)," *Augustinian Studies* 10 (1979) 55-74; (ed.), *Paul and the Legacies of Paul* (1990). R. Badenas, *Christ the End of the Law* (1985). C. K. Barrett, *From First Adam to Last* (1952). K. Barth, *Der Römerbrief* (1919, 1921[2]; ET 1933); *Kurze Erklärung des Römerbriefes* (1956). J. Bassler, *Divine Impartiality: Paul and a Theological Axiom* (SBLDS 59, 1982). B. Bauer, *Kritik der paulinischen Briefe* (3 vols. 1851). F. C. Baur, Die Christuspartei in der korinthischen Gemeinde, *Tübinger Zeitschrift für Theologie* 4 (1831) 61-206; "Über Zweck und Veranlassung des Römerbriefes," *TZT* (1836, repr. 1963); *Paulus, der Apostel Jesu Christi* (2 vols. 1845; 1866-67[2]; ET 1875-76). R. Baxter, *Paraphrase* (1685). J. C. Beker, *Paul the Apostle: The Triumph of God in Life and Thought* (1980). R. H. Bell, *No One Seeks for God: An Exegetical and Theological Study of Romans 1.18-3.20* (WUNT 106, 1998). J. A. Bengel, *Gnomon New Testament* (1742; ET 1855). J. H. Bentley, *Humanists and Holy Writ* (1983). R. Bergmeier, *Das Gesetz im Römerbrief und andere Studien zum Neuen Testament* (WUNT 121, 2000). T. W. Berkley, *From a Broken Covenant to Circumcision of the Heart: Pauline Intertextual Exegesis in Romans 2:17-29* (SBLDS 175, 2000). T. Beza, *Annotationes 2:3-152* (1556). B. Blumenfeld, *The Political Paul: Justice, Democracy, and Kingship in a Hellenistic Framework* (JSNTSup 210, 2001). H. Boers, *The Justification of the Gentiles* (1994). G. Bornkamm, *Early Christian Experience* (1969); *Paulus* (1969; ET 1971). W. Bousset, *Kyrios Christos* (1913; ET 1970). E. Brandenburger, *Adam und Christus* (1962). F. F. Bruce, *The Epistle of Paul to the Romans* (1963). C. Bryan, A *Preface to Romans: Notes on the Epistle in its Literary and Cultural Setting* (2000). **Bruno of Chartreaux,** PL 153:15-122. J. Bugenhagen, *Interpretatio* (1527). G. Bull, *Harmonia Apostolica* (1669-70). H. Bullinger, *De gratia Dei justicante* (1554). R. Bultmann, *Der Stil der paulinischen Predigt und die kynisch-stoische Diatribe* (1910); "K. Barths Römerbrief in seiner 2. Ausgabe," *Die Christliche Welt* 36 (1922) 320-23, 330-34, 358-61, 369-73; "Zur Geschichte der Paulus-Forschung," *TRu* n.f. 1 (1929) 26-59; "Glossen im Römerbrief," *TLZ* 72 (1947) 197-202; *Theologie des NTs* 1 (1948; ET 1952). K. A. Burton, *Rhetoric, Law, and the Mystery of Salvation in Romans 7:1-6*

(Studies in the Bible and Early Christianity 44, 2001). **B. Byrne**, "Creation Groaning: An Earth Bible Reading of Romans 8:18-22," *Readings from the Perspective of the Earth* (ed. N. Habel, The Earth Bible 1, 2000) 193-203. **J. Cambier**, *L'Évangile de Dieu selon L'Épître aux Romains* (1967). **C. P. Carlson, Jr.**, *Justification in Earlier Medieval Theology* (1974). **D. J.-S. Chae**, *Paul as Apostle to the Gentiles: His Apostolic Self-Awareness and Its Influence on the Soteriological Argument in Romans* (Paternoster Biblical and Theological Monographs, 1997). **Chrysostom**, *PG* 60:391-682. **J. Colet**, *Enarratio in Ep. S. Pauli ad Rom* (c. 1497; ET, ed. J. Lupton, 1873; repr. 1965). **H. Conzelmann**, *Grundriss der Theologie des NTs* (1967; ET 1968). **C. H. Cosgrove**, *Elusive Israel: The Puzzle of Election in Romans* (1997). **J. A. Cramer**, *Catenae Graecorum Patrum in New Testament* (3 vols. 1838-44, repr. 1967). **C. E. B. Cranfield**, *On Romans: and Other New Testament Essays* (1998). **Cyril of Alexandria**, PG 74:773-856. **W. Dabourne**, *Purpose and Cause in Pauline Exegesis: Romans 1:16-4:25 and a New Approach to the Letters* (SNTSMS 104, 1999). **N. A. Dahl**, *Studies in Paul* (1977). **W. D. Davies**, *Paul and Rabbinic Judaism* (1948); "Paul and the People of Israel," *NTS* 24 (1978) 4-39. **A. Deissmann**, *Die neutestamentliche Formel "in Christo Jesu"* (1892); *Paulus: Eine kultur- und religionsgeschichtliche Skizze* (1911; 1925[2]). **D. Demmer**, *Lutherus interpres, der theol. Neuansatz in den Römerbriefexegese* (1958). **H. Denifle**, *Die abendländischen Schriftausleger bei Luther über Iustitia Dei* (Rom 1.17) *und Iustificatio* (1905). **W. M. L De Wette**, *Kurze Erklärung des Briefes an die Römer* (1835; 1847[4]). **C. H. Dodd**, *The Epistle of Paul to the Romans* (1932, rev. ed. 1959); *The Bible and the Greeks* (1935); *According to the Scriptures: The Sub-structure of New Testament Theology* (1952). **K. P. Donfried**, *The Romans Debate* (1977, 1991[2]). **R. M. Douglas, J. Sadoleto**, *1477-1547, Humanist and Reformer* (1958). **J. D. G. Dunn**, *Romans 1-8* (WBC 38A, 1988a); *Romans 9-16* (WBC 38B, 1988b). **G. Ebeling**, *Lutherstudien* 3 (1985). **G. Eichholz**, *Die Theologie des Paulus im Umriss* (1972, rev. ed. 1975). **J. R. Edwards**, "The Letter of Paul to the Romans," *NISB* (2003) 2007-34. **N. Elliott**, *The Rhetoric of Romans* (1990). **E. E. Ellis**, *Paul's Use of the OT* (1957). **Erasmus**, *Annotationes* (1516, 1527) 318-92 (ET, ed. A. Reeve and M. A. Screech, 1990); *Paraphrasis New Testament* (1622; ET, ed. R. D. Sider, 1984). **O. Everling**, *Die paulinische Angelologie und Damonologie* (1888). **O. Fatio and P. Fraenkel (ed.)**, *Histoire de l'exégèse au XIVe siècle* (1978). **M. Ficino**, *Opera Omnia 1:425-91* (1561, repr. 1959). **J. A. Fitzmyer**, *Romans* (AB 33, 1993). **Florus of Lyons**, *PL* 119:279-318. **K. Froehlich**, "Romans 8.1-11: Pauline Theology in Medieval Interpretation," *Faith and History* (ed. J. T. Carroll et al., 1991) 239-60. **K. Froehlich and M. Gibson (eds.)**, *Biblical Latina cum Glossa Ordinaria* (1480 fac., 1992). **J. Gagny**, *Epitome Paraphrastica* (1533); *Scholia* (1539). **H. Gamble**, *The Textual History of the Letter to the Romans* (SD 42, 1977). **L. Gaston**, *Paul and the Torah* (1987). **S. J. Gathercole**, *Where is Boasting? Early Jewish Soteriology and Paul's Response in Romans 1-5* (2002). **B. Girardin**, *Rhétorique et théologique: Calvin, le commentaire de l'épître aux Romains* (1979). **L. Goppelt**, *Typos: The Typological Interpretation of the OT in the New* (1939; ET 1982). **P. Gorday**, *Principles of Patristic Exegesis* (1983). **L. Grane**, *Modus loquendi theologicus* (1975). **C. Grenholm and D. Patte (eds.)**, *Reading Israel in Romans: Legitimacy and Plausibility of Divergent Interpretations* (Romans Through History and Culture Series, 2000). **A. K. Grieb**, *The Story of Romans: A Narrative Defense of God's Righteousness* (2002). **H. Grotius**, *Annotationes* (3 vols. 1641-50). **W. Grundmann**, *Der Römerbriefauslegung zu Gum. und Ref.: Eine Studie zu H. Bullingers Römerbrief von 1525* (1970). **A. J. Guerra**, *Romans and the Apologetic Tradition* (1995). **C. Guillaud**, *Collatio* (1542). **H. Gunkel**, *The Influence of the Holy Spirit* (1888; ET 1979). **W. Gutbrod**, *Paulinische Anthropologie* (1934). **E. W. Güting and D. L. Mealand**, *Asyndeton in Paul: A Text-Critical and Statistical Enquiry into Pauline Style* (Studies in the Bible and Early Christianity 39, 1998). **K. Haacker**, *Der Brief des Paulus an die Römer* (THKNT 6, 1999). **H. Hammond**, *A Paraphrase with Annotations* (1653, repr. 1845). **A. von Harnack**,

Marcion (1921). **V. E. Hasler,** *Gesetz und Evangelium in der alten Kirche bis Origines* (1953). **R. B. Hays,** *Echoes of Scripture* (1989). **W. Heitmüller,** *Taufe und Abendmahl bei Paulus* (1903); *Taufe und Abendmahl im Urchristentum* (1911). **A. Hilgenfeld,** "Der Römerbrief," *ZWT* 35-36 (5 articles, 1892-93). **R. J. Hoffmann,** *Marcion* (1984). **H. H. Holfelder,** *Solus Christus* (1981). **K. Holl,** *Gesammelte Aufsätze zur Kirchengeschichte* (vols. 1 and 3, 1923-28). **H. Hübner,** *Rechtfertigung und Heiligung in Luthers Römerbriefvorlesung* (1965); *Das Gesetz bei Paulus* (1978; ET 1984); *Int* 34 (1980) 1; "Paulusforschung seit 1945," *ANRW* II. 25.4 (1987) 2699-2840. **R. Jewett,** *Paul's Anthropological Terms* (1971). **L. T. Johnson,** *Reading Romans: A Literary and Theological Commentary* (1997). **R. Kabisch,** *Die Eschatologie des Paulus* (1893). **E. Käsemann,** Exegetische *Versuche und Besinnungen 1-2* (1960; ET 1964, 1969); *Paulinische Perspektiven* (1969; ET 1971); *An die Römer* (HNT 8a, 1973, 1980[4]; ET 1980). **L. Keck,** *Paul and His Letters* (1979). **S. C. Keesmaat,** *Paul and His Story: (Re)interpreting the Exodus Tradition* (JSNTSup 181, 1999). **W. Keller,** *Gottes Treue, Israels Heil: Röm 11, 25-27: die These vom "Sonderweg" in der Diskussion* (SBB 40, 1998). **K. Kertelge,** *"Rechtfertigung" bei Paulus* (1969). **W. Keuck,** "Sünder und Gerechter: Rom 7.14-25 in der Auslegung der grieschischen Väter" (diss., Tübingen, 1955). **J. Kim,** *God, Israel, and the Gentiles: Rhetoric and Situation in Romans 9-11* (SBLDS 176, 2000). **G. Klein,** *Rekonstruktion und Interpretation* (1969); "Righteousness in the New Testament," *IDBSup,* 750-52; "Romans, Letter to the," *IDBSup,* 752-54. **W. G. Kümmel,** *Römer 7 und die Bekehrung des Paulus* (1929, repr. 1974). **O. Kuss,** *Der Römerbrief* (3 vols. 1957-78). **P. F. Landes,** *Augustine on Romans* (Texts and Translations 23, 1982). **A. M. Landgraf,** *Einfrühscholastik* (1948). **Lanfranc of Bec,** *PL* 150:105-56. **Lefèvre d'Étaples,** *S. Pauli ep xiv ex vulgata ed.* (1512). **A. Lekkerkerker,** "Römer 7 und Römer 9 bei Augstin" (diss., Amsterdam, 1942). **J. B. Lightfoot,** *Biblical Essays* (1895). **A. Lindemann,** *Paulus in ältesten Christentum* (1979). **R. A. Lipsius,** *Die paulinische Rechtfertigungslehre* (1853). **J. Locke,** *A Paraphrase and Notes on the Epistle of St. Paul to the Galatians, I and II Corinthians, Romans, Ephesians* (1707, repr. 1987; GT 1768-69), preface by Michaelis, including "An Essay for the Understanding of Paul's Epistles, by Consulting St. Paul Himself." **W. von Loewenich,** *Von Augustin zu Luther* (1959). **E. Lohmeyer,** *Grundlagen paulinische Theologie* (1929). **E. Lohse,** "Die Gerechtigkeit Gottes in der paulinischen Theologie," *Die Einheit des Neuen Testaments* (1973) 209-27; *Der Brief an die Römer* (KEK 6, 2003). **A. D. Loman,** "Quaestiones paulinae," *ThT* 16 (1882) 141-85, *ThT* 20 (1886) 42-113; "Paulus en de kanon," *ThT* 20 (1886) 387-406. **B. W. Longenecker** (ed.), *Narrative Dynamics in Paul: A Critical Assessment* (2002). **H. Lüdemann,** *Die Anthropologie des Apostels Paulus* (1872). **W. Lütgert,** *Der Röm. als hist. Problem* (1913). **M. Luther,** *Lectures on Romans* (1515/16; LT, ed. J. Ficker, 1960); WA 56 (ET, ed. W. Pauck, LCC 15, 1961); *Der Servo Arbitrio,* WA 18, 600-787 (ET, P. S. Watson, LCC 17, 1969). **S. Lyonnett,** *Questiones in Ep. ad Rom.* (2 vols. 1962-75). **A. E. McGrath,** *Iustitia Dei* (2 vols. 1986). **W. C. van Manen,** *Paulus,* vol. 2, *De Brief aan de Romeinen* (1891). **T. W. Manson,** "St. Paul's Letter to the Romans—and Others," *BJRL* 31 (1948) 224-40. **F.-W. Marquardt,** *Die Juden im Römerbrief* (1971). **R. M. Martin,** *La controverse sur le péch, originel au debut du XIVe siècle* (1930). **C. Martini,** *Ambrosiaster* (1944). **W. Maurer,** *Melanchthon-Studien* (1964). **W. Meeks,** *The First Urban Christians* (1983). **P. Melanchthon,** *Loci Communes* (1521, 1535[2], 1559); *Annotationes* (1522); Dispositio orationes, CR 15:441-92; *Commentarii in Epistolam Pauli ad Romanos* (1540); Enarratio, CR 15:797-1052; *Studienausgabe* (ed. H. Engelland, 1952; ET, ed. W. Pauck, LCC 19, 1969). **B. Metzger,** *Index to Periodical Literature on the Apostle Paul* (1960). **O. Michel,** *Paulus und seine Bibel* (1929, 1972[2]). **J. D. Michaelis,** *Einleitung* (1750; ET 1790). **M. P. Middendorf,** *The "I" in the Storm: A Study of Romans 7* (1997). **J. C. Miller,** *The Obedience of Faith, the Eschatological People of God, and the Purpose of Romans* (SBLDS 177, 2000); "The Romans Debate: 1991-2001," *CurBS* 9 (2001) 306-49. **P. Minear,** *The Obedience of Faith* (1971).

J. P. Miranda, *Marx and the Bible: A Critique of the Philosophy of Oppression* (1974).
E. Molland, *The Conception of the Gospel in Alexandrian Theology* (1938). **D. Moo,** *The Epistle to the Romans* (NICNT, 1996). **J. D. Moores,** *Wrestling with Rationality in Paul* (1995).
C. F. D. Moule, *The Origin of Christology* (1977). **C. Müller,** *Gottes Gerechigkeit und Gottes Volk* (1964). **J. Müller,** *M. Bucers Hermeneutik* (1965). **J. Munck,** *Paulus und die Heilsgeschichte* (1954; ET 1959); *Christus und Israel* (1956; ET 1967). **W. Mundle,** "Die Exegese der paulinischen Briefe im Kommentar des Ambrosiaster" (diss., Marburg, 1919).
M. Neubrand, *Abraham, Vater von Juden und Nichtjuden: eine exegetische Studie zu Röm 4* (FB 85, 1997). **F. Neugebauer,** *In Christus: "En Christo." Eine Untersuchung zum paulinischen Glaubensverständnis* (1961). **A. Nygren,** *Commentary on Romans* (1949). **G. Nygren,** *Das Prädestinationproblem in der Theologie Augustins* (1956). **Oecolampadius,** *Adnotationes* (1525). **J. C. O'Neill,** *Paul's Letter to the Romans* (PNTC, 1975). **Origen,** *Origenis opera omnia* (ed. E. Lommatzsch, 1831-48) vols. 6-7; PG 14:837-1291. **E. Pagels,** *The Gnostic Paul* (1975).
W. Paley, *Horae Paulinae* (1790). **T. H. L. Parker,** *Calvin's New Testament Commentaries (1971); Commentaries on the Epistle to the Romans, 1532-42* (1986). **P. M. Parvis,** "Theodoret's Commentary on the Epistles of St. Paul" (diss., University of Oxford, 1975). **D. Patte,** *Paul's Faith and the Power of the Gospel: A Structural Introduction to the Pauline Letters* (1983).
J. B. Payne, "Erasmus: Interpreter of Romans," *Sixteenth-century Essays and Studies 2* (1971) 1-35; "Erasmus and Lefèvre d'Étaples as Interpreters of Paul," *ARG* 65 (1974) 54-82.
O. Pfleiderer, *Der Paulinismus* (1873; ET 1877). **A. Pierson and S. A. Naber,** *Verisimilia laceram conditionem Novi Testamenti* (1886). **P. Platz,** "Der Römerbrief in der Gnadenlehre Augustins," *Cassiciacum* 5 (1938). **J. F. Quasten,** *Patrology* (3 vols. 1950-60). **H. Räisänen,** *Paul and the Law* (1983); *The Torah and Christ* (1986); "Römer 9-11: Analyse eines geistigen Ringens," *ANRW* II.25.4 (1987) 2891-939. **M. Reasoner,** *The Strong and the Weak: Romans 14.1-15.13 in Context* (SNTSMS 103, 1999). **A. Reichert,** *Der Römerbrief als Gratwanderung: eine Untersuchung zur Abfassungsproblematik* (FRLANT 194, 2001). **R. Reitzenstein,** *Poimandres* (1904); *Die hellenistischen Mysterienreligionen* (1910). **K. H. Rengstorf,** *Das Paulusbild in der neueren Deutschen Forschung* (1964). **E. Reuss,** *Die Geschichte der Heiligen Schriften Neuen Testaments* (1864[4]); *Les Épîtres pauliniennes* (1878). **H. Ridderbos,** *Paulus* (1970; ET 1975). **B. Rigaux,** *The Letters of St Paul: The State of Research* (1962; GT 1964; ET 1968). **H. Rückert,** *Die Rechtfertigungslehre auf die Tridentischen Konzil* (1925). **E. Rummel,** *Erasmus' "Annotations" on the New Testament* (1986). **E. P. Sanders,** *Paul and Palestinian Judaism* (1977); *Paul, the Law, and the Jewish People* (1983). **A. Scaino,** *Paraphrasis* (1589).
M. Schar, *Das Machleben des Origenes im Zeitalter des Humanismus* (1979). **C. Schäublin,** *Untersuchungen zu Methode und Herkunft des antiochenischen Exegese* (1974). **K. H. Schelkle,** *Paulus, Lehrer der Väter* (1959[2]). **A. Schirmer,** *Das Paulusverständnis Melanchthons, 1518-22* (1944). **A. Schlatter,** *Luthers Deutung des Röm.* (1917). **W. Schmithals,** *Der Römerbrief als historische Problem* (SNT 9, 1975); *Der Römerbrief: Ein Kommentar* (1988). **P. Schoeps,** *Paulus* (1959). **J. Schupp,** *Die Gnadenlehre des Petrus Lombardus* (1952). **R. Scroggs,** *Paul for a New Day* (1977). **A. Schweitzer,** *Geschichte der paulinischen Forschung* (1911; ET 1912); *Die Mystik des Apostels Paulus* (1930; ET 1931). **H. Seesemann,** "Das Paulusverständnis des Clemens Alexandrinus," *TSK* 107 (1936) 312-46. **J. S. Semler,** *Paraphrasis* (1769).
S.-L. Shum, *Paul's Use of Isaiah in Romans* (WUNT 2/156, 2002). **F. Siegert,** *Argumentation bei Paulus* (1985). **R. Simon,** *Histoire critique des principaux commentateurs du New Testament* (1693). **B. Smalley,** *The Study of the Bible in the Middle Ages* (1952, rev. ed. 1964).
S. K. Soderlund and N. T. Wright (eds.), *Romans and the People of God* (1999). **A. Souter,** *Pelagius' Expositions of Thirteen Epistles of St Paul* (TS 9, 3 vols. 1922-31); *The Earliest Latin Commentaries on the Epistles of St Paul: A Study* (1927). **C. Spicq,** *Esquisse d'une histoire de l'exégèse latine au moyen âge* (1944). **K. Staab,** *Die Pauluskatenen, nach den handschriftlichen*

Quellen untersucht (1926); *Pauluskommentare aus der griechischen Kirche, aus Katenenhandschriften* (NTAbh 15, 1933), includes Didymus (1-6), Acacius (53-56), Apollinaris (57-82), Diodore (83-112), Theodore of Mopsuestia (113-172), Severian (213-225), Gennadius (352-418), Photius (457-570). **F. Stegmüller,** *Repertorium Biblicum Medii Aevi* (11 vols. 1950-80). **D. C. Steinmetz** (ed.), *The Bible in the Sixteenth Century* (1990). **K. Stendahl,** *Paul Among Jews and Gentiles* (1976), includes 1963 essay. **S. K. Stowers,** *The Diatribe and Paul's Letter to the Romans* (1981); *A Rereading of Romans: Justice, Jews, and Gentiles* (1994). **P. Stühlmacher,** *Gerechtigkeit Gottes bei Paulus* (1965); *Das paulinische Evangelium* (1968); *Der Brief an die Römer* (1989; ET 1994). **C. H. Talbert,** *Romans* (Smyth and Helwys Bible Commentary, 2002). **J. Taylor,** *Paraphrase* (1745). **E. Teichmann,** *Die paulinischen Vorstellungen von Auferstehung und Gericht und ihre Beziehung zur jüdischen Apokalyptik* (1896). **G. Theissen,** *Psychological Aspects of Pauline Theology* (1983; ET 1987). **M. Theobald,** *Römerbrief* (2 vols. 1992); *Studien zum Römerbrief* (WUNT 136, 2001). **Theodoret,** *PG* 82:43-226. **Theophylact,** *PG* 124:335-560. **A. C. Thiselton,** *New Horizons in Hermeneutics* (1992). **Thomas Aquinas,** *Expositio in ep. omnes Divi Pauli Apostol* (1593, repr. 1948-50). **T. Titelmann,** *Collatio* (1529); *Elucidatio* (1532, repr. 1540). **K. J. Torjesen,** *Hermeneutical Procedure and Theological Method in Origen's Exegesis* (1986). **J. W. Trigg,** *Biblical Interpretation: Message of the Fathers of the Church* (1986). **C. H. Turner,** "Greek Patristic Commentaries on the Pauline Epistles," *DBSup* (1904) 484-531. **W. Tyndale,** *Prologue on Romans* (1526; ed. G. E. Duffield, 1964). **F. W. C. Umbreit,** *Der Brief an die Römerauf dem Grunde des Alten Testamentes ausgelegt* (1856). **L. Usteri,** *Entwicklung des paulinischen Lehrbegriffs* (1824, 1851⁶). **L. Valla,** *Collatio New Testament* (1444; ed. A. Perosa, 1970); "In ep. ad Rom," *Opera Omnia* (1540, repr. 1962). **C. Verfaillie,** "La doctrine de la justification dans Originème d'après son commentaire de l'Épître aux Romains" (diss., Strasbourg, 1926). **D. O. Via,** *Kerygma and Comedy in the New Testament: A Structuralist Approach to Hermeneutic* (1975). **W. Völker,** "Paulus bei Origines," *TSK* 102 (1930) 258-79. **J. R. Wagner,** *Heralds of the Good News: Isaiah and Paul 'In Concert' in the Letter to the Romans* (NovTSup 101, 2002). **F. Watson,** *Paul, Judaism, and the Gentiles: A Sociological Approach* (SNTSMS 56, 1986). **V. Weber,** *Kritische Geschichte der Exegeses des 9 Kapitels, resp. der Verse 14-23 des Römerbriefs bis auf Chrysostomus und Augustinus einschliesslich* (1899). **A. G. M. Wedderburn,** *The Reasons for Romans* (1988). **J. Weiss,** "Beiträge zur paulinischen Rhetorik," *Theologishe Studien* (FS, B. Weiss, 1897). **C. H. Weisse,** *Beiträge zur Kritik der paulinischen Briefe an die Galater, Römer, Philipper, und Kolosser* (1867). **H. D. Wendland,** *Die Mitte der paulinischen Botschaft* (1935). **P. Wendland,** *Die hellenistisch-romische Kultur in ihren Beziehungen zu Judentum und Christentum* (HNT Bd. 1, T. 2, 1907). **J. Werner,** *Der Paulinismus des Irenaeus* (TU 6.2, 1889). **S. Westerholm,** *Israel's Law and the Church's Faith: Paul and His Recent Interpreters* (1988); *Preface to the Study of Paul* (1997). **U. Wilckens,** *Rechtfertigung als Freiheit (1974); Der Brief an die Römer* (3 vols. 1978-82); *Der Brief an die Römer* (EKKNT 6, 1997-3). **F. Wilk,** *Die Bedeutung des Jesajabuches für Paulus* (FRLANT 179, 1998). **W. F. Wiles,** *The Divine Apostle* (1967). **W. Wrede,** *Paulus* (1904, repr. 1964; ET 1907). **N. T. Wright,** "The Letter to the Romans," *NIB* 10 (2002) 393-770. **K. Zickendraht,** *Der Streit zwischen Erasmus und Luther über die Willensfreiheit* (1909). **J. A. Ziesler,** *The Meaning of Righteousness in Paul* (1972); *Paul's Letter to the Romans* (TPINTC, 1989).

R. MORGAN

THE NEW TESTAMENT CANON

Corinthians, First Letter to the

1. *The Early Period. a. The original interpreters.* This letter is the only Pauline writing with an undisputed sequel. Originally it was part of a series of exchanges between Paul[†§] and the Corinthians: (i) Paul's previous letter to Corinth (see 5:9-11); (ii) the Corinthians' written response to Paul (see 7:1); (iii) Paul's response to that letter and to oral news from Corinth (1 Cor); (iv) Paul's "severe" letter (now lost; see 2 Cor 2:3-4; 7:8); (v) 2 Cor 1-9; and (vi) 2 Cor 10-13 (probably separate and later).

Paul's converts in Corinth, as the recipients of the letter, were its first interpreters. As far as we can tell from the later letters, the Corinthians understood 1 Cor to Paul's satisfaction. In contrast to his claim in 5:9-11 that they had misinterpreted his previous letter (5:9-11), Paul does not complain in subsequent correspondence that they had misunderstood 1 Cor. Paul's discussion of the topics in chaps. 7–14 is convoluted, but he makes no further reference to these subjects. Some scholars have argued that 2 Cor 5:1-10 is a clarification of 1 Cor 15 in response to Corinthian misunderstanding, but it is more probable that Paul had simply learned new ways to express his eschatological beliefs. In fact, there are only two topics that continue: the "incestuous" man whom Paul orders to be excommunicated (5:1-5) and the collection of money for the relief of the poor among the Jerusalem Christians (16:1-4).

The case of the incestuous man may have been the occasion for the severe letter, and he may be the one who has (finally) been punished "by the majority" (2 Cor 1:23–2:11, specifically 2:6).

The collection and general concerns about money are the subject of 2 Cor 8–9; 11:7-10; and 12:13-18. On these topics Paul complains, not that they have misunderstood him, but that they have not carried out his wishes quickly enough.

b. Text history as interpretation. The letter was preserved privately by the Corinthian congregation and seems to have remained in relative obscurity until near the end of the first century. Then Paul's letters were collected and "published" as a corpus. In this new format, the historical situation of Paul and the Corinthians was no longer the focus of interpretation; instead, Christian readers applied the material to their own situations, personally and corporately. Some of their concerns can be identified by tracing the variations that occurred in the letter as it was copied and recopied.

Three examples illustrate this type of interpretation: First, Paul expected that he and a portion of his converts would live to see the return of Christ (the Parousia), at which time the whole community would receive spiritual bodies. Thus, he wrote, "We shall not all sleep, but we shall all be changed" (15:51, author's translation).

Later, as the hope of an immediate Parousia faded, some copyists "corrected" the first half to read, "We shall all sleep." Similarly, when the church became conscious of itself as a mixed community (see Matt 13:24-30, 36-43, 47-50), other copyists altered the second half: "We shall not all be changed." Early manuscripts exist with either or both of these adaptations. Second, in 11:23-26 Paul gives us the earliest account of the Lord's Supper, a description of its celebration in Corinth at the time he founded the congregation. Numerous variant readings to the text indicate that Paul's account was made to conform to such later eucharistic practices as those found in Matt 26:26-29 and Luke 22:14-20. Conversely, some of Paul's words found their way into the canon of the mass. Third, Paul seems to have thought that sexual distinctions, which would be eliminated in the kingdom (Mark 12:25), should already be discarded in his eschatological communities. Thus he allowed women to preach and lead prayer in the church's worship (11:5).

It appears that a protesting note ("Let the women keep silence," 14:34-35) was later added near or at the end of Paul's long discussion of worship (chaps. 11–14).

c. *Patristic interpretation.* The first full-scale commentary on 1 Cor was Origen's[§], now, unfortunately, known only through fragmentary quotations. His commentaries established the Alexandrian School[§] of interpretation whereby the text was considered in three senses—literal, moral, and allegorical—with the latter (in the style of Philo of Alexandria) being the most important. His exegetical work continued to be quoted in the *catena,* or "chain" commentaries, into the Middle Ages. Chrysostom[§], (P. Schaff 1956) whose forty-four homilies with exegetical notes, opposed allegory beyond that already found in Scripture (e.g., 1 Cor 10:1-10), emphasized the literal grammatical meaning of the text, a hallmark of the Antiochene School[§]. Theodoret's[§] commentary is philological and remarkably critical.

2. *Middle Ages.* The Antiochene tradition continued in the Byzantine East, influenced by Chrysostom. In the West, allegorical interpretation flourished by adding a fourth "analogical" meaning to Origen's three senses of Scripture. Commentaries generally became collections of quotations (*catenae*) from ancient authorities: Augustine[§], Jerome[§], Ambrose[§], and Gregory of Nyssa[§]. Peter Lombard[§] compiled a long commentary on the Pauline letters, and there are a number of others. In general, commentary was a matter of collecting quotations from authorities of the past. In addition, however, there was a "dialectical" tradition that was more actively concerned with the theological meaning of the text. Thomas Aquinas[§] stuck closely to the literal meaning of the text, which he illumined with quotations from the fathers (including some Greek authors), theological reflection, and moral application. He was systematic, logical, interested in the definition of words, and actively concerned with the theological meaning of the text. This tradition was continued in T. Cajetan[§], whose exegetical interests were unexpectedly modern, and in J. Colet[§] (B. O'Kelly and C. Jarrott 1985), who was more discursive, less systematic, and more aware of Paul as a historical person than was Thomas.

3. *Renaissance-Reformation.* Cajetan and Colet, while theological in their interests, were already part of the Renaissance revival of classical learning. Cajetan wrote to reclaim Scripture from the humanists, and Colet was a friend and supporter of Erasmus[§], another commentator on the letter. With the Reformation the interpretation of Scripture underwent a profound change. The view that Scripture should be interpreted by and within tradition was rejected in favor of the conviction that Scripture is the sole judge of the church and Christian conduct. ZWINGLI, also indebted to humanism, commented on 1 Cor, using Erasmus's new Greek text. But the most influential Reformation exegete was Calvin[§] (1960), who wrote a commentary on 1 Cor and attempted, in his *Institutes,* to summarize biblical theology*[§]. On the Roman Catholic side, Estius continued the Antiochene tradition at Douai, and C. Lapide[§], a Jesuit, favored a mystical and allegorical exegesis.

4. *Enlightenment.* The rationalism of the eighteenth century caused a reaction to the traditional, "supernaturalist" reading of Scripture. The English Deist J. Locke[§] (Deism*[§]) pointed out (1695) the extent to which 1 Cor and the rest of Paul's letters were historically conditioned and thus occasional. M. Tindal[§] (1730) cited the texts in 1 Cor about Paul's expectation to live to see the Parousia as evidence that, like all human documents, Scripture contained mistakes. T. Morgan[§] (1738-40), using the letter to affirm a radical opposition between Peter and Paul, concluded that both could not have been infallibly inspired (Inspiration of the Bible*[§]).

Such observations were not based on a concern for history, however, but had theological and philosophical motives. J. Bengel[§], who published a critical edition of the Greek text, also produced the notably pithy commentary, *Gnomon of the New Testament* (1742).

5. *Modern Period.* While the patristic and medieval commentators tended to attach traditional theological ideas to the text, and the Reformation authors sought Paul as an ally in their theological controversies, the nineteenth-century scholars introduced a disinterested, historical

approach to the New Testament and the investigation of a wide range of literary, historical, theological, and exegetical problems. Although considerable attention continues to be devoted to Paul's theology, the modern period has increasingly appreciated the historical and psychological factors (Psychology and Biblical Studies*[§]) that motivated Paul and has valued immensely the literary forms and structures through which he expressed himself. Instead of harmonizing the letters into a theological system, the modern interpreter tends increasingly (and rightly) to treat the letters individually.

   a. *Authenticity*. Historical criticism addressed first the question of authorship. Although 1 Cor does not contain the characteristic Pauline doctrine of justification by faith, F. C. Baur[§] accepted the letter as genuine because of what it revealed about tensions in the early church. Using the letter as the key for understanding the evolution of early Christianity, he concluded that the groups Paul mentioned—"I am of Paul . . . I am of Cephas, I am of Christ" (1:12, author's translation)—corresponded to the thesis-antithesis-synthesis pattern of G. W. F. Hegel's dialectical analysis of history: (i) Cephas (Peter), the proponent of original, Jewish Christianity; (ii) Paul, the innovating apostle to the Greeks; and (iii) the "Christ party," representing the resulting catholic Christianity as found, e.g., in the Fourth Gospel (1831).

   His model has had great influence on New Testament historians (see the strictures of J. Munck 1959, 69-86), although his time scale has been greatly compressed; John's Gospel is now usually dated about 100 C.E., a century earlier than Baur's dating.

   Baur's heirs, the so-called Tübingen school, made the criteria for genuineness increasingly more stringent, reaching its extreme expression in the "Dutch radical school," which rejected 1 Cor along with the rest of the canonical letters and believed that the Acts traditions about Paul were the only surviving traces of the early missionary hero. However, the mainstream of later scholarship, which is no less critical but has a fuller understanding of the historical evidence, has no doubts about the authenticity of this letter.

   b. *Integrity*. In 1 Cor the abrupt changes of subject, the repetitions, and the apparent inconsistencies on some points made this letter a natural candidate for theories of editorial compilation. The first theory with lasting influence appeared in the 1910 commentary of J. Weiss[§] (see also C. Clemen 1894, 19-57).

   He took 2 Cor 6:14-7:1 as part of the letter to which Paul referred in 1 Cor 5:9-11. To this vigorous letter he also assigned 1 Cor 10:1-23 (which he believed to be at variance with chaps. 8-9), as well as 6:12-20 and 11:2-34 (which he took to have a similar tone).

   He next suggested that when Paul received the Corinthians' letter, mentioned in 7:1, he responded with 1 Cor 7-9; 10:24-11:1; 12:1-16:6; 16:15-19. Shortly thereafter, when "those of Chloe" arrived (1 Cor 1:11, author's translation), he wrote 1:1-6:11 and 16:10-14 in some distress.

   Although other arrangements have been suggested, a number of important scholars have followed Weiss, albeit with individual variations (J. Hurd 1965, 1994).

   Theories that involve smaller units or multiple interpolations are inherently improbable and have not found a following. Weiss's analysis does follow the subject matter of the letter in a reasonable fashion and provides a single letter for each occasion for writing. Nevertheless, it is probably better to do as most scholars do and take the letter as a unity and understand its disjointed nature as the result of the circumstances that occasioned it.

   c. *Cultural background*. O. Pfleiderer[§] (1906-10), one of Baur's pupils, was the first to interpret Paul consistently against the religious background of his day. He understood Paul as the combination of Pharisaic and Hellenistic Judaism transformed by Christian faith. This approach informed the two commentaries on 1 Cor by C. Heinrici[§] (1881), who was the first to use Hellenistic parallels extensively to explain Paul's thought. In 1895 A. Deissmann[§] began to publish his large collection of material illustrative of the New Testament drawn from the non-literary papyri, the first editions of which were just beginning to appear. R. Reitzenstein[§] (1904, 1910) and W. Bousset[§] (1895, 1913) as well as others presented deeper parallels between Paul and Greco-Roman religion and Mythology*[§] and especially illuminated Paul's ideas about sacraments and food in 1 Cor. A. Schweitzer[§] objected, as did P. Billerbeck[§] (1922–28), G. Kittel[§] (1926), and W. D. Davies[§] (1948), who all emphasized the rabbinic parallels.

d. The date of writing. Traditionally, scholars have used Acts to provide the biographical background for Paul's letters. First Cor is assigned to Paul's stay in Ephesus (1 Cor 16:8-10; Acts 19:22) following his founding visit to Corinth, a visit dated by the reference to the proconsul Gallio (Acts 18:12-17).

J. Knox[§] (1950), however, has challenged the use of Acts to date Paul's travels and has, instead, reconstructed Paul's life primarily on the basis of his letters. A number of scholars (see G. Lüdemann 1980, 1-43) have adopted this procedure, and its influence on Pauline studies is growing. This approach allows the letters to find their natural place in relationship to each other. The early eschatology of 1 Cor (Lüdemann 1980, 201-61) may indicate an earlier dating for the letter than is usually supposed. Further, the later biography of Paul can be organized around the collection for the saints first described in 1 Cor 16:1-4 (see 2 Cor 8-9; Rom 15:25-32).

e. Epistolary conventions. Deissmann called attention to the importance of the nonliterary papyri, especially the letters, for the study of Paul (1908, 1925). Building on Deissmann's view of letters as conversation, Hurd (1965) attempted to reconstruct the exchanges between Paul and the Corinthians prior to 1 Cor. From a more functional/structural point of view (Structuralism and Deconstruction[§]) P. Schubert made a pioneering study (1939) of the initial thanksgiving sections of the letters. Then in 1971 the Society of Biblical Literature[§], at R. Funk's[§] initiative, established a seminar to study Paul's writings specifically as letters. A letter (as Deissmann maintained) is part of an actual conversation between two parties. An epistle, on the other hand, is an essay in epistolary form intended for a general audience. A letter does not include information the author knows that readers know. By contrast, an epistle must include all the information needed by its readers. The seminar, however, went further by noting many structural and traditional aspects of Paul's letters. Schubert had shown how the thanksgiving section of 1 Cor (1:4-9) anticipates the major themes of the letter (ecstatic speech, knowledge, spiritual gifts, the Parousia, and fellowship).

The seminar discussed, among many other things, how Paul in 1 Cor followed the usual custom by beginning with a reminder to his readers of their past relationship, then by dealing with present concerns, and finally by anticipating their future contact. Notable, too, in 1 Cor are the large ABÁ structures (chaps. 8, 9, 10; and 12, 13, 14), and a number of chiastic passages (e.g., 1:18-25; 9:19-23).

f. Rhetorical criticism. In contrast to the study of Paul's letters as "letters," other scholars have analyzed the extent to which Paul reflected the literary, philosophical, and rhetorical conventions of his day (Rhetorical Criticism*[§]). In 1910 R. Bultmann[§] wrote on "Paul's preaching and the Cynic-Stoic diatribe." More recently the ancient handbooks of rhetoric have been used to illuminate the structure of Paul's arguments. Although 1 Cor lacks the sustained theological argument of, e.g., Galatians (see H. Betz 1979), M. Mitchell (1991), H. Probst (1991), A. Wire (1990), and B. Witherington (1995) have made fruitful use of this approach in the interpretation of the letter.

g. Social-scientific criticism. As early as 1880 C. Heinrici specifically examined the sociological background of 1 Cor (Sociology and New Testament Studies*[§] and Social-Scientific Criticism*[§]). In the 1930s a school of criticism flourished at Chicago that emphasized the sociological component of history. More recently, this emphasis has reemerged through the work of G. Thiessen (1979), W. Meeks (1983), and others. First Cor is an especially rich source of data of which we can ask questions like, "From what social levels did the Corinthian converts come?" "What kind of education did they have?" "What sort of organization did this house church have?" "What was the nature of family relationships?" and "What was the relationship between men and women?" There is a growing consensus, e.g., that Deissmann underestimated their social level and that the congregation included a number of tradesmen, small business owners, and perhaps some persons of greater economic means.

h. Feminist interpretation. Recent studies have also focused on the role of women in the Corinthian church (Feminist Interpretation*§), in particular, Paul's instructions about women's prayer and Prophecy‡†§ (11:2-16) and his command for women's silence in the church (14:33*b*-36).

J. Bassler (1992) summarizes and evaluates several possible interpretations: (1) 11:2-16 is directed toward women's prophesying and praying at home, whereas 14:33*b*-36 is directed toward women's speaking in worship; (2) Paul approves of inspired speech but not of uninspired speaking; (3) Paul allows holy unmarried women to speak but not married women (see E. Schüssler Fiorenza 1983, 231); (4) the critical circumstances at the Corinthian church led Paul to silence the women; (5) Paul is quoting the Corinthian position in 14:34-35 in order to correct the church members in 14:36; and (6) 14:34-35 originally was a marginal gloss that a scribe placed in the body of the letter (see also Wire 1990, 1994).

Recent commentaries on 1 Cor include Collins (1999), Hays (1997), Horsley (1998), Lindemann (2000), Wolff (1996), and Sampley (2002, 2003). Considerable recent scholarship is devoted to the historical and socio-cultural setting of the Corinthian church and Paul's advice and admonitions to it: Horrell (1996), Lanci (1997), Martin (1995), Robertson (2001), and Winter (2001). Dunn (1995) is a basic introduction to the issues in interpreting the letter. Recent text-critical work includes Hannah (1997). Eriksson uses ancient rhetorical theory to analyze Paul's arguments in 1 Cor. Brown (1995), Furnish (1999), and Voss (2002) each address various theological issues in the letter.

Bibliography: F. Altermath, *Du corps psychique au corps spirituel: Interpretation de 1 Cor. 15, 35-49* (BGBE 18, 1977). **W. S. Babcock** (ed.), *Paul and the Legacies of Paul* (1990). **J. M. Bassler,** "1 Corinthians," *The Women's Bible Commentary* (ed. C. A. Newsom and S. H. Ringe, 1992) 321-29. **F. C. Baur,** "Die Christuspartie in der korinthischen Gemeinde," *TZT* 4, 4 (1831) 61-136. **J. A. Bengel,** *Gnomon of the NT* (1742; ET 1860-62). **J. H. Bentley,** *Humanists and Holy Writ: NT Scholarship in the Renaissance* (1983). **H. D. Betz,** *Der Apostel Paulus und die sokratische Tradition* (BHT 45, 1972); *Galatians* (Hermeneia, 1979). **P. Billerbeck,** *Kommentar zum Neuen Testament aus Talmud und Midrash* (6 vols. 1922-28) vols. 1-4. **W. Bousset,** *Der Antichrist in der überlieferung des Judentums, des Neuen Testaments, und der alten Kirche* (1895); *Kryios Christos: Geschichte des Christos glabens* (1913; ET 1970). **A. R. Brown,** *The Cross and Human Transformation: Paul's Apocalyptic Word in 1 Corinthians* (1995). **R. Bultmann,** *Der Stil der paulinischen Predigt und die kynischstoische Diatribe* (1910). **J. Calvin,** *The First Epistle of Paul the Apostle to the Corinthians* (tr. J. W. Fraser, Calvin Commentaries, 1960). **C. Clemen,** *Die Einheitlichkeit der paulinischen Briefe* (1894). **J. Colet,** *J. Colet's Commentary on First Corinthians* (tr. B. O'Kelly and C. A. L. Jarrot, 1985). **R. F. Collins,** *First Corinthians* (SP 7, 1999). **J. A. Cramer,** *Catenae graecorum patrum 5* (1844). **W. D. Davies,** *Paul and Rabbinic Judaism: Some Rabbinic Elements in Pauline Theology* (1948). **A. Deissmann,** *Light from the Ancient East* (1908; ET 1910); *Paul: A Study in Social and Religious History* (1925; ET 1926). **W. G. Doty,** *Letters in Primitive Christianity* (1973). **J. D. G. Dunn,** *1 Corinthians* (New Testament Guides, 1995). A. **Eriksson,** *Traditions as Rhetorical Proof: Pauline Argumentation in 1 Corinthians* (ConBNT 29, 1998). **V. P. Furnish,** *The Theology of the First Letter to the Corinthians* (New Testament Theology, 1999). **D. D. Hannah,** *The Text of I Corinthians in the Writings of Origen* (SBLNTGF 4, 1997). **R. B. Hays,** *First Corinthians* (IBC, 1997). **P. Henry,** *New Directions in NT Study* (1979). **C. Heinrici,** *Der erste Brief an die*

Korinther (KEK[5] 6, 1881). **R. A. Horsley,** *1 Corinthians* (ANTC, 1998). **D. G. Horrell,** *The Social Ethos of The Corinthians Correspondence: Interests and Ideology from 1 Corinthians To 1 Clement* (Studies of the New Testament and Its World, 1996). **J. C. Hurd,** *The Origin of 1 Corinthians* (1965); "Good News and the Integrity of 1 Corinthians," *Gospel in Paul: Studies on Corinthians, Galatians, and Romans for R. N. Longenecker* (JSNT Sup 108, 1994). **C. Jenkins,** "Origen on 1 Corinthians," *JTS* 9 (1908) 231-47, 353-72, 500-514; 10 (1909) 29-51. **G. Kittel,** *Die Probleme des palästinischen Spätjudentums und das Urchristentum* (BWANT 3, 1926). **J. Knox,** *Chapters in a Life of Paul* (1950). **W. G. Kümmel,** *The NT: The History of the Investigation of Its Problems* (1958; ET 1972). **J. R. Lanci,** *A New Temple for Corinth: Rhetorical and Archaeological Approaches to Pauline Imagery* (Studies in Biblical Literature 1, 1997). **A. Lindemann,** *Der Erste Korintherbrief* (HNT 9.1, 2000). **J. Locke,** *Vindications* (1695). **G. Lüdemann,** *Paul, the Apostle to the Gentiles* (FRLANT 123, 1980; ET 1984). **D. B. Martin,** *The Corinthian Body* (1995). **W. A. Meeks,** *The First Urban Christians: The Social World of the Apostle Paul* (1983). **M. M. Mitchell,** *Paul and the Rhetoric of Reconciliation: An Exegetical Investigation of the Language and Composition of 1 Corinthians* (1991). **T. Morgan,** *The Moral Philosopher* (3 vols. 1738-40; repr. 1969). **J. Munck,** *Paul and the Salvation of Mankind* (1959). **S. Neill,** *The Interpretation of the NT, 1861-1961* (1964). **E. H. Pagels,** *The Gnostic Paul* (1975). **O. Pfleiderer,** *Primitive Christianity* (1906-1909). **H. Probst,** *Paulus und der Brief: Die Rhetorik des antiken Briefes als Form der paulinischen Korintherkorrespondenz (1 Kor 8-10)* (WUNT 2, 45, 1991). **R. Reitzenstein,** *Poimandres: Studien zur griechisch-ägyptischen und frühchristlicher Literatur* (1904); *Hellenistic Mystery-Religions: Their Basic Ideas and Significance* (1910; ET 1978). **C. K. Robertson,** *Conflict in Corinth: Redefining the System* (Studies in Biblical Literature 42, 2001). **J. P. Sampley,** "The First Letter to the Corinthians," *NIB* (2002) 10:771-1003; "The First Letter of Paul to the Corinthians," *NISB* (2003) 2035-60. **P. Schaff** (ed.), *Saint Chrysostom: Homilies on the Epistles to the Corinthians* (NPNF 12, 1956). **E. Schendel,** *Herrschaft und Unterwerfung Christi: 1 Kor. 15,24-28 in Exegese und Theologie der Väter biz zum Ausgang des 4. Jahrhunderts* (BGBE 12, 1971). **P. Schubert,** *The Form and Function of the Pauline Thanksgiving* (BZNW 20, 1939). **E. Schüssler Fiorenza,** *In Memory of Her: A Feminist Theological Reconstruction of Christian Origins* (1983). **J. H. Schütz,** *Paul and the Anatomy of Apostolic Authority* (1975). **A. Schweitzer,** *Paul and His Interpreters* (1911; ET 1912). **G. Sellin,** "Hauptprobleme des ersten Korintherbriefes," *ANRW* II.25.4 (1987) 2940-3044. **K. Staab,** *Pauluskommentare aus der griechischen Kirche* (1933). **G. Theissen,** *The Social Setting of Pauline Christianity: Essays on Corinth* (1979; ET 1982). **M. Tindal,** *Christianity as Old as the Creation* (1730). **L. Vischer,** *Die Auslegungsgeschichte von I. Kor. 6,1-11* (BGBE 1, 1955). **F. Voss,** *Das Wort vom Kreuz und die menschliche Vernunft: eine Untersuchung zur Soteriologie des 1. Korintherbriefes* (FRLANT 199, 2002). **J. Weiss,** *Der erste Korintherbrief* (KEK, 1910). **J. L. White,** *The Body of the Greek Letter* (SBLDS 2, 1972); *Light from Ancient Letters* (1986). **A. N. Wilder,** *Early Christian Rhetoric: The Language of the Gospel* (1971). **M. F. Wiles,** *The Divine Apostle* (1967). **A. C. Wire,** *The Corinthian Women Prophets: A Reconstruction Through Paul's Rhetoric* (1990); "1 Corinthians," *Searching the Scriptures: A Feminist Commentary* (ed. E. Schüssler Fiorenza, 1994) 2:153-95. **B. Witherington,** *Conflict and Community in Corinth: A Socio-Rhetorical Commentary on 1 and 2 Corinthians* (1995). **B. W. Winter,** *After Paul Left Corinth: The Influence of Secular Ethics and Social Change* (2001). **C. Wolff,** *Der erste Brief des Paulus an die Korinther* (THKNT 7, 1996). **G. Zuntz,** *The Text of the Epistles* (Schweich Lectures, 1946, 1953).

J. C. HURD

Corinthians, Second Letter to the

1. *The Early Period. a. First to third centuries.* There are no clear traces of the use or influence of Paul's[†§] so-called second letter to the Corinthians before the middle of the second century. The first certain use of 2 Cor is by Marcion[§], who included it in his Canon[§] (see Tertullian *Adv. Marc.* 5.11-12). Both Tertullian[§] (*Adv. Marc.* 5.11, 17; *De praescr haeret* 24.56) and Irenaeus[§] (*Adv. Haer.* 2.30.7-8) cited 2 Cor in their arguments against Marcion and the Valentinian Gnostics (Gnostic Interpretation[§]). The Alexandrian[§] exegete, Origen[§] cited 3:6-18 (esp. 3:6, "the letter kills, but the Spirit gives life") to support his allegorical method of biblical interpretation (*De Prin.* 1.1.2; *Con. Cel.* 5.60; 6.70; 7.20).

b. Fourth and fifth centuries. During this period, Chrysostom[§] infrequently commented on the historical setting of Paul's letters in his homilies, addressing such questions when he deemed them important (*Hom.* 1.12, 26.2, 8.2; texts in Schaff 1956). Ambrosiaster[§], more than most others of this period, paid close attention to the apostle's words and intentions.

2. *Middle Ages.* Neither 2 Cor as such nor specific passages within it played a prominent role in theology during the medieval period. Commentaries on the letter, as on scriptural books in general, usually took the form of homiletical glosses that were often little more than collections of citations from the church fathers. The theologian Thomas Aquinas[§], although not primarily an exegete, had a special concern for the literal sense of Scripture, as distinguished from its spiritual sensess.

3. *Renaissance and Reformation.* Along with the other writings of the New Testament, 2 Cor was subjected for the first time to careful Textual*[§] and philological analysis by the Renaissance humanist Erasmus[§]. Not content simply to compile quotations from the fathers, he was quite deliberate about investigating the New Testament texts and discerning their original meaning. The first edition of his Greek New Testament, accompanied by annotations, appeared in 1516; and Erasmus lived to see a fifth edition published, with the annotations significantly expanded, in 1535. Although he wrote admiringly of Origen, Erasmus did not resort to excessive allegorizing but aimed at a strictly grammatical and literal reading of Scripture.

Allegorical exegesis was emphatically rejected by Luther[§] and Calvin[§]. In particular, both Reformers took issue with the Origenist reading of chap. 3. Luther, who often preached on 2 Cor 3:4-11, found in the contrast between "letter" and "spirit" (v. 6) a succinct summary of the opposition between law and gospel, works and grace. While the letter can only say what one should and should not do, the gospel declares what Christ has done; and with this word the Holy Spirit penetrates to the heart with saving power. Calvin offered similar comments on this passage. In his commentary on 2 Cor 3:6, he specifically charged Origen and other allegorists with profoundly distorting the meaning of Paul's contrast between letter and spirit, with the result that "any mad idea, however absurd or monstrous, could be introduced under the pretext of an allegory" (1964, 43).

4. *Seventeenth and Eighteenth Centuries.* The textual and philological investigations of Paul's letters begun by Erasmus and others continued into the seventeenth and eighteenth centuries. These studies, coupled with the reformers' conviction that Paul must be understood on his own terms, prompted interpreters to pay increasingly close attention to the argument in each letter and thus also to the occasion and purpose of each. On the continent these concerns are especially evident in the prefaces to the Pauline letters that H. Grotius[§] included in his *Annotationes in Novum Testamentum* (1641-50). In England Grotius's work found an echo in that of H. Hammond[§] and M. Poole[§].

Regarding 2 Cor specifically, the annotations that J. Collinges contributed to Poole's *Annotations upon the Holy Bible* (1688) exhibit the author's interest in both the purpose of the letter ("partly Apologetical or Excusatory . . . partly Hortatory," and "Partly Minatory or Threatening") and its argumentative structure (each chapter is introduced with a synopsis of the argument). The same interests are even more apparent in J. Locke's[§] remarkable *Paraphrase and Notes on the Epistles of St. Paul to the Galatians, 1 and 2 Corinthians, Romans, Ephesians* (1707).

In Europe this historical reading of Paul's letters is also seen in the work of such eighteenth-century scholars as J. Bengel[§], J. Wettstein[§], and S. Baumgarten[§]. Indeed, credit must go to one of Baumgarten's students, J. Semler[§], for inaugurating a thoroughly historical-critical study (see H. Betz 1985, 3-7). While some earlier interpreters had noted that chaps. 10-13 were much more severe in tone than chaps. 1–9, the usual explanation was that in the last four chapters Paul has some small group of antagonists in view. Thus Collinges (1688), commenting on 2 Cor 10:1, had postulated "another (though possibly the lesser) Party who had much vilified him." But Semler departed from that kind of explanation, arguing that 2 Cor must be a composite of at least two originally distinct letters. The earlier, he held, was composed of chaps. 1–9, 13:11-13[14] and Romans 16, and the later of 10:1–13:10. He thought it possible, however, that Paul had not intended both of the collection chaps. (8, 9) for Corinth, but that chap. 9 had been directed to churches elsewhere in Achaia. Although Semler's partitioning of 2 Corinthians was not widely accepted at the time, he had succeeded in placing the question of the letter's literary unity on the scholarly agenda, where it has remained a major item for more than two hundred years.

5. *Nineteenth and Twentieth Centuries.* Semler's views about 2 Cor prompted others to examine more closely both the argument of the letter and the course of Paul's Corinthian ministry and correspondence. As a result, while the significance of the letter for an understanding of Paul's thought has not gone unnoticed (see esp., R. Bultmann[§] 1976), most of the important studies in the last two centuries have been devoted to Literary*[§] and historical matters.

a. *Literary Integrity.* Many, perhaps even a majority of, interpreters have come to agree with Semler's separation of chaps. 10-13 from the rest of 2 Cor (notable exceptions include P. Hughes 1962; N. Hyldahl 1973; C. Wolff 1989; also F. Young and D. Ford 1987, 28-36). Yet in contrast to Semler, certain advocates of this partitioning found indications that the last four chapters had been written prior to some, if not all, of chaps. 1–9 and that they constituted at least part of the "tearful" letter to which Paul refers in 2 Cor 2:3-4 and 7:8 (first A. Hausrath 1870 and J. Kennedy 1900; later J. Weiss 1917, A. Plummer 1915, Bultmann). Although subsequent studies have shown that an association with the tearful letter is unlikely, the earlier dating of chaps. 10–13 is not thereby precluded and is often proposed (G. Bornkamm 1971; D. Georgi 1964, 1965; H. Betz 1985; G. Dautzenberg 1987; otherwise, H. Windisch 1924; C. K. Barrett 1973; V. Furnish 1984; R. Martin 1986; M. Thrall 1994-2000).

Questions have also been raised about the literary integrity even of chaps. 1–9. There is general agreement that 6:14–7:1 to some extent interrupts the appeal of 6:11-13 (which is, in fact, continued only in 7:2). A number of interpreters believe that Paul is responsible for the interruption (E. Allo 1956; Barrett; Hughes; Thrall), while others have argued that 6:14–7:1 is a fragment from the letter to Corinth mentioned in 1 Cor 5:9 that has been inserted after 2 Cor 6:13 by some later redactor (A. Hilgenfeld 1875; W. Schmithals 1973, 282-86). Still others, citing the style and content as well as the inappropriateness of the paragraph in this context, have argued that it is a later, non-Pauline interpolation (first proposed by K. Schrader 1835; see also Bornkamm; Betz 1973 calls it anti-Pauline). A few have described the passage as non-Pauline material incorporated (with certain adaptations) by the apostle himself (Martin; Wolff; tentatively, N. Dahl 1977, 62-69).

Numerous scholars (following a suggestion by Weiss 1917, 348-49) believe that 2:14–7:4 (excluding 6:14–7:1) is also separable from chaps. 1–9. The argument in general is that the section interrupts a travel narrative that begins in 2:12-13 and is completed only in 7:5-16; and that in 2:14–7:4 Paul is concerned to legitimate his apostleship in the face of challenges to it, while in the remainder of chaps. 1-9 he writes as if his position with the Corinthians is relatively secure. Some scholars have suggested that this unit originally went with chaps. 10–13 as part of the tearful letter (Weiss, Bultmann). The more usual conclusion has been that it is (or belongs to) a letter written after 1 Cor and at some point before the tearful letter (Betz 1985; Bornkamm; Georgi 1964, 1965; Schmithals 1973). Among those who remain unconvinced by the evidence adduced for 2:14-7:4 as a separate letter are Barrett, Dautzenberg, Furnish (1984), Martin, and Thrall.

Semler's suggestion that the two collection chapters (8, 9) might not have belonged to the same letter has found favor with many investigators, but specific proposals about their original locations vary. Weiss (1917, 353-55) identified chap. 8 as an independent letter written earlier than the tearful letter and kept chap. 9 with 1:1–2:13; 7:5-16. Others have proposed that chap. 9 was part of the tearful letter and thus earlier than chap. 8 (e.g., Bultmann). In the most extensive and important study of the matter so far, Betz (1985; followed by Carrez 1986) has argued that the chapters represent two independent letters written at the same time (chap. 8 to the church in Corinth, chap. 9 to other Achaian churches), and later than any other part of 2 Cor. Thrall affirms the integrity of chaps. 1–8 but suggests that chap. 9 may have been dispatched a bit later.

Advocates of partition theories have usually dated 2 Cor in its present form to about the end of the first century, but relatively little attention has been given to what may have prompted and guided the redactor's work (see Furnish 1984, 38-41; F. Zeilinger 1992, 24-25; Thrall 1994–2000, 45-47). The two principal suggestions have been a need to invoke Paul's authority in the fight against Gnosticism (Schmithals 1971, 239-74; elaborated by Jewett) and a concern to enhance Paul's image and to give the redacted letters a testamentary character (Bornkamm 1971, 179-90). D. Trobisch has advanced the highly original, but also highly speculative, theory that Paul himself edited Romans, his letters to Corinth (originally seven in number), and Galatians for the instruction of the Ephesian church and, in case of his death, to stand as his literary testament (1989, esp. 119-31; 1994, esp. 55-96).

b. Paul's Visits and Letters to Corinth. Until the nineteenth century it was usual to identify the tearful letter with 1 Cor, the painful visit (2 Cor 2:1) with Paul's first, evangelizing visit, and the wrongdoer mentioned in 2 Cor 2:5-11; 7:12 with the man Paul had earlier wanted to expel from the congregation (1 Cor 5:1-13). The difficulties with the first of these identifications were originally pointed out by F. Bleek§ (1830), who postulated that the tearful letter had been written in the interim between the two canonical letters (Canon of the Bible*§) and does not survive. Subsequently, H. Ewald§ (1857) proposed that the painful visit had occurred during the same interim, that it had been unsuccessful because of Paul's difficulties with the wrongdoer, and that the lost tearful letter had been written in response to the whole unpleasant affair.

After more than 150 years of further research and discussion, most scholars concur that the tearful letter cannot be identified with 1 Cor and that an interim visit must be hypothesized (exceptions, P. Hughes 1962, N. Hyldahl 1973). Thus the currently prevailing view is that references in 2 Cor 2:1, 3-4, 5-11; 7:8, 12 (and, to an impending third visit, in 12:14; 13:1- 2) presume two prior visits and at least three prior letters to Corinth: the first, evangelizing visit, the letter referred to in 1 Cor 5:9, 1 Cor itself, a subsequent painful visit, and a tearful letter written in the wake of the painful visit.

Moreover, consequent upon conclusions reached about the literary integrity of 2 Cor, various interpreters have hypothesized as many as three additional letters to Corinth: one sent in the interim between 1 Cor and the tearful letter (2:14–7:4, excluding 6:14–7:1) and two separate letters about the collection for Jerusalem (chaps. 8, 9). Betz, for example, has derived five separate letters from 2 Cor and arranged them in the following sequence: (1) 2:14–6:13 and

7:24; (2) 10:1–13:10, two "apologies" sent in response to challenges of Paul's apostolic legitimacy; (3) 1:1–2:13, 7:5-16, and 13:11-13, a "letter of reconciliation" sent following Titus's successful resolution of the crisis; (4) chapter 8; and (5) chapter 9, two "administrative letters" sent to the Corinthians and other Achaians, respectively, on behalf of the collection for Jerusalem (1985, 142-43; cf. Bornkamm; Georgi 1964, 1965).

c. The opposition to Paul. No clear consensus has emerged about the opponents with whom Paul had to reckon during the period represented by 2 Cor (surveys of research: Georgi 1964, 1-9; J. Sumney 1990, 15-73). On the one hand, F. C. Baur[§] (1831) argued that in both 1 and 2 Cor Paul was contending with Judaizers, representatives of Peter who were intent on imposing certain requirements of the Mosaic law on Gentile converts. This view was dominant throughout most of the nineteenth century and has been newly argued, with modifications, in the twentieth (D. Oostendorp 1967; G. Lüdemann 1989). On the other hand, with W. Lütgert's (1908) contention that it was the Spirit, not the law, that was at issue, the way was opened for identifying the opponents as Gnostic[§] enthusiasts (Bultmann; Schmithals 1971).

Advocates of both of these views have ordinarily believed that Paul was contending with essentially the same kind of opposition in 1 and 2 Cor. Others, however, have insisted that one must distinguish between the resident opposition evident in 1 Cor and an intrusion by outsiders, for which 2 Cor 11:4 provides evidence. Some have identified the intruders as Jewish-Christian emissaries sent out from, or who claimed to have been sent out from, the Jerusalem apostles (E. Käsemann 1942; Barrett). Others have identified them as itinerant Christian propagandists with a Hellenistic-Jewish background, which does not, however, preclude their Palestinian connections (esp. Georgi 1964). Most proponents of these two views have defined the main point of dispute as neither the law nor the Spirit but the legitimacy of Paul's apostleship.

d. Newer Areas of Research. In the last half of the twentieth century several special areas of research were developed that show promise of shedding new light on 2 Cor. Studies devoted to the genre and Rhetorical*[§] characteristics of particular sections (Betz 1972, 1985, 129-40; J. Zmijewski 1978; J. Fitzgerald 1990; F. Hughes in D. Watson 1991), or of the whole (G. Kennedy 1984, 86-96; Young and Ford 1987, 27-59; F. Danker in Watson 1991) are contributing not only to a better understanding of Paul's style but also to a better understanding of his dealings with the Corinthians and his self-understanding as an apostle. The same can be said about investigations of the social setting of Paul's ministry in important urban centers like Corinth (e.g., W. Meeks 1983) and of the particular Greco-Roman social conventions that influenced the apostle (e.g., P. Marshall 1987).

Few of the scholars who have been responsible for new understandings of the compositional history, genre(s), rhetorical character, or social setting of 2 Cor have considered the possible consequences of their work for the interpretation of Paul's theology. Although several short theological studies of 2 Cor have taken account of recent developments in these areas (e.g., essays by D. Hay; S. Kraftchick; and B. Gaventa in Hay 1993), a major theological reassessment of the letter(s) has yet to appear.

Recent commentaries on 2 Cor include Barnett (1997), Belleville (1996), Lambrecht (1999), Osiek (2003), Sampley (2000), and Thrall (2000). Kreitzer (1996) is a basic introduction to the issues in interpreting the letter. Recent discussions of theology in the letter include Brendle (1995), Harvey (1996), Savage (1996), and Wan (2000).

Bibliography: E.-B. Allo, *Saint Paul: Seconde Épître aux Corinthiens* (1956). **W. S. Babcock** (ed.), *Paul and the Legacies of Paul* (1990). **P. Barnett,** *The Second Epistle to the Corinthians* (NICNT, 1997). **C. K. Barrett,** *A Commentary on the Second Epistle to the Corinthians* (HNTC, 1973). **J. M. Bassler,** "2 Corinthians," *The Women's Bible Commentary* (ed. C. A. Newsom and S. H. Ringe, 1992) 330-32. **F. C. Baur,** "Die Christus partei in der korinthischen

Gemeinde" (1831; repr. in Ausgewählte Werke in Einzelausgaben 1 1963) 1-164. **L. L. Belleville,** *2 Corinthians* (IVP New Testament Commentary 8, 1996). **J. H. Bentley,** *Humanists and Holy Writ: NT Scholarship in the Renaissance* (1983). **H. D. Betz,** *Der Apostel Paulus und die sokratische Tradition* (BHT 45, 1972); "2 Cor 6:14-7:1: An Anti-Pauline Fragment?" *JBL* 92 (1973) 88-108; *2 Corinthians 8 and 9* (Hermenia, 1985). **R. Bieringer and J. Lambrecht,** *Studies on 2 Corinthians* (BETL, 1994). **F. Bleek,** "Erörterungen in Beziehung auf die Briefe Pauli an die Korinther," *TSK* 3 (1830) 614-32. **G. Bornkamm,** "Die Vorgeschichte des sogenannten Zweiten Korintherbriefes," *Geschichte und Glaube* 2 (1971) 162-94. **A. Brendle,** *Im Prozess der Konfliktüberwindung: Eine exegetische Studie zur Kommunikationssituation zwischen Paulus und den Korinthern in 2 Kor 1,1-2; 13; 7,4-16* (1995). **R. Bultmann,** *The Second Letter to the Corinthians* (ed. E. Dinkler 1976; ET 1985). **J. Calvin,** *The Second Epistle of Paul to the Corinthians* (1547; tr. T. A. Smail, 1964). **M. Carrez,** *La deuxième Épître de Saint Paul aux Corinthiens* (1986). **W. Chau,** *The Letter and the Spirit: A History of Interpretation from Origen to Luther* (1995). **N. Dahl,** *Studies in Paul: Theology for the Early Christian Mission* (1977). **E. Dassmann,** *Der Stachel im Fleisch* (1979). **G. Dautzenberg,** "Der zweite Korintherbrief als Briefsammlung: Zur Frage der literarischen Einheitlichkeit und des theologischen Gefüges von 2 Kor 1-8," *ANRW* II.25.4 (1987) 3045-66. **H. G. A. Ewald,** *Die Sendschreiben des Apostels Paulus* (1857). **J. T. Fitzgerald,** "Paul, the Ancient Epistolary Theorists, and 2 Corinthians 10-13," *Greeks, Romans, and Christians: Essays in Honor of A. J. Malherbe* (1990) 190-200. **V. P. Furnish,** *II Corinthians* (AB 32A, 1984); "2 Corinthians," *1 and 2 Corinthians* (ed. D. Hay, 1993). **D. Georgi,** *The Opponents of Paul in Second Corinthians: A Study of Religious Propaganda in Late Antiquity* (1964; ET 1986); *Remembering the Poor: The History of Paul's Collection for Jerusalem* (1965; ET 1992). **A. E. Harvey,** *Renewal Through Suffering: A Study of 2 Corinthians* (Studies of the New Testament and Its World, 1996). **A. Hausrath,** *Der Vier-Capitel-Brief des Paulus an die Korinther* (1870). **D. Hay** (ed.), *Pauline Theology,* vol. 2, *1 and 2 Corinthians* (1993). **M. A. G. Haykin,** *The Spirit of God: The Exegesis of 1 and 2 Corinthians in the Pneumatomachian Controversy of the Fourth Century* (1994). **A. Hilgenfeld,** *Historisch-kritische Einleitung in das Neue Testament* (1875). **P. E. Hughes,** *Paul's Second Epistle to the Corinthians* (NICNT, 1962). **N. Hyldahl,** "Die Frage nach der literarischen Einheit des Zweiten Korintherbriefes," *ZNW* 64 (1973) 289-306. **R. Jewett,** "The Redaction of I Corinthians and the Trajectory of the Pauline School," *JAAR* 44 (supp. B, 1978) 389-444. **E. Käsemann,** "Die Legitimität des Apostels," *ZNW* 41 (1942) 33-71. **G. Kennedy,** *NT Interpretation Through Rhetorical Criticism* (1984). **J. H. Kennedy,** *The Second and Third Epistles of St. Paul to the Corinthians* (1900). **L. Kreitzer,** *2 Corinthians* (New Testament Guides, 1996). **J. Lambrecht,** *Second Corinthians* (SP 8, 1999). **A. Lindemann,** *Paulus im ältesten Christentum* (BHT 58, 1979). **G. Lüdemann,** *Opposition to Paul in Jewish Christianity* (1989). **W. Lütgert,** *Freiheitspredigt und Schwärmgeister in Korinth* (1908). **M. Luther,** *Luther's Works* (ed. **J. Pelikan,** 1955-76). **P. Marshall,** *Enmity in Corinth* (1987). **R. P. Martin,** *2 Corinthians* (WBC 40, 1986). **S. Matthews,** "2 Corinthians," *Searching the Scriptures: A Feminist Commentary* (ed. E. Schüssler Fiorenza, 1994) 196-217. **W. A. Meeks,** *The First Urban Christians: The Social World of the Apostle Paul* (1983). **J. Murphy-O'Connor,** *The Theology of the Second Letter to the Corinthians* (1991). **R. Noormann,** *Irenäus als Paulusinterpret: Zur Rezeption und Wirkung der paulinischen und deuteropaulinischen Briefe im Werk des Irenäus von Lyon* (WUNT 66, 1994). **D. W. Oostendorp,** *Another Jesus: A Gospel* (1967). **C. Osiek,** "The Second Letter of Paul to the Corinthians," *NISB* 2061-77. **A. Plummer,** *A Critical and Exegetical Commentary on the Second Epistle of St. Paul to the Corinthians* (CGTC 8, 1915). **J. P. Sampley,** "The Second Letter to the Corinthians," *NIB* (2000) 1-180. **T. B. Savage,** *Power Through Weakness: Paul's Understanding of the Christian Ministry in 2 Corinthians* (SNTSMS 86, 1996). **P. Schaff** (ed.), *Saint Chrysostom: Homilies on the Epistles* *to the Corinthians* (NPNF 12, 1956). **W. Schmithals,** *Paul and the Gnostics* (1965; ET 1972); *Gnosticism in Corinth* (1969; ET 1971); "Die Korintherbriefe als Briefsammlung," *ZNW* 64 (1973) 263-88. **W. Schneemelcher,** "Paulus in der griechischen Kirche des zweiten Jahrhunderts," *ZKG* 75 (1964) 120. **K. Schrader,** *Der Apostel Paulus 4* (1835). **J. S. Semler,** *Paraphrasis II: Epistolae ad Corinthios* (1776). **B. Smalley,** *The Study of the Bible in the Middle Ages* (1983³). **L. Staab,** *Pauluskommentare aus der griechischen Kirche* (1933). **C. L. Stockhausen,** "Early Interpretations of II Corinthians 3: An Exegetical Perspective," *Studia Patristica* 19 (1989) 392-99. **J. Sumney,** *Identifying Paul's Opponents* (1990). **M. E. Thrall,** *A Critical and Exegetical Commentary on the Second Epistle to the Corinthians,* vol. 1, *Introduction and Commentary on II Corinthians I-VII* (2 vols. ICC, 1994-2000). **D. Trobisch,** *Die Entstehung der Paulusbriefsammlung: Studien zu den Anfängen christlicher Publizistik* (NTOA 10, 1989); *Paul's Letter Collection: Tracing the Origins* (1994). **S.-K. Wan,** *Power in Weakness: Conflict and Rhetoric in Paul's Second Letter to the Corinthians* (New Testament in Context, 2000). **D. Watson** (ed.), *Persuasive Artistry: Studies in NT Rhetoric in Honor of G. A. Kennedy* (1991). **J. Weiss,** *The History of Primitive Christianity* (1917; ET 1937). **M. F. Wiles,** *The Divine Apostle* (1967). **H. Windisch,** *Der zweite Korintherbrief* (1924). **C. Wolff,** *Der zweite Brief des Paulus an die Korinther* (1989). **F. Young and D. Ford**, *Meaning and Truth in 2 Corinthians* (1987). **F. Zeilinger,** *Krieg und Friede in Korinth: Kommentar zum 2 Korintherbrief des Apostels Paulus,* vol. 1, *Der Kampfbrief; Der Versöhnungsbrief; Der Bettelbrief* (1992). **J. Zmijewski,** *Der Stil der paulinischen "Narrenrede"* (1978).

V. P. FURNISH

THE NEW TESTAMENT CANON

Galatians, Letter to the

The epistle of Paul[†§] to the Galatians has come down to us as part of the corpus of Pauline letters. These letters belong to a class of Jewish and Christian epistles, sacred books written by prophets (Prophecy and Prophets[*§]) or apostles with Authority[*§] from God, the archetype being the epistle Jeremiah wrote to the exiles in Babylon (Jer 29), which was assumed by tradition to have been dictated to Baruch (Bar 6:1; see Jer 36:4). Epistles were treasured in religious communities as holy documents to be read in worship and studied for further meaning. (So Jeremiah's reference to seventy years [Jer 29:10] became a key apocalyptic text that was interpreted and reinterpreted in later writings.)

1. *Galatians as Evidence of Paul's Gospel.* The epistle to the Galatians first became a scholarly problem when Marcion[§] published a version he claimed was freed from the Jewish-Christian additions that had obscured Paul's original message about a God of mercy who was superior to the Jewish God of judgment. Tertullian[§] attacked Marcion's hypothesis on the grounds that even Marcion's shorter version showed a Paul who believed in the one God, the Creator, who was both merciful and just. Perhaps as a result of Marcion's two-part Canon[*§], consisting of the Gospel (a shorter version of Luke) and the apostolic corpus (shorter versions of Gal, 1-2 Cor, Rom, 1-2 Thess, Laodiceans [Eph], Col, Phil, Phlm), the corpus of Paul's letters began to attain full canonical status in all provinces of the church. The main problem about Gal as part of the canon was its reference to the rebuke Paul administered to Peter in Antioch. The Eastern church interpreted Peter's silence under Paul's rebuke as a sign of the tacit agreement of both apostles in holding the same gospel; the Western church interpreted Peter's silence as his morally praiseworthy submission to a well-earned censure (F. Overbeck 1877). The Western tradition was continued by Luther[§], who drew comfort in his own struggle against the papacy, with its cry "the church, the church," from the fact that Paul withstood false apostles and that he even reproved Peter when the article of justification was at issue—though Peter's lapse was only temporary, since Peter defended this article at Jerusalem (Acts 15).

In the eighteenth century Dutch and English scholars began to deploy Gal as evidence that "the Jewish and Gentile Christianity, or Peter's Religion and Paul's, were as opposite and inconsistent as Light and Darkness, Truth and Falsehood" (T. Morgan 1737). J. SEMLER took over this theory, opposing Paul's inner spiritual religion to Peter's Jewish external religion on the basis of his reading of 1 Cor and Gal. Semler believed that the early church was divided between Paul's disciples and the admirers of Peter and the Palestinians. The latter fabricated a history of Peter in Rome to match the history of Paul in Rome, remnants of which are extant in the Pseudo-Clementine literature (Semler 1779, 5, 6). F. C. Baur[§] took over and elaborated this theory (1831). According to Baur's hypothesis about the deep split in the early church, many other letters in the Pauline corpus reflected catholic Christianity and could not, therefore, be regarded as genuine. Baur summed up the critical consensus of his day by dividing the Pauline corpus into three parts: the four genuine epistles (Gal, 1-2 Cor, and Rom), the questionably genuine (1-2 Thess, Eph, Col, Philemon, and Philippians), and the inauthentic (1-2 Tim and Titus). Baur regarded the Acts of the Apostles, with its attempt to make the histories of Peter and Paul run parallel to each other and to make the two men agree in doctrine, as tendentious.

In 1850 B. Bauer[§] published two books, one on Acts and the other on Gal, to show that both Acts and Gal belonged to the same stage in the history of the church and that they were equally tendentious. He argued that Gal presupposed the split between Judaism and Christianity that had not occurred during Paul's lifetime and that the epistle was clumsily derived from Romans and the Corinthian epistles. He thought Rom, 1 Cor, and perhaps 2 Cor were written before

Acts; Gal, in full knowledge of Acts; then 1 Thess, Eph, Col, Phil, 1-2 Tim, and Titus. He held all of the Pauline corpus to be pseudonymous.

C. Weisse[§] (1855) took up Bauer's challenge, which was otherwise ignored for thirty years, and proposed that 1 Cor, 1 Thess, and Phlm were genuine and that 2 Cor was compiled from three genuine letters. Rom and Phil were compiled from more than one genuine letter, but they were also interpolated with other material. Gal and Col were each based on a genuine letter but interpolated by the same hand. Weisse distinguished the work of Paul from the work of the interpolator by the criterion of style, "the defraction a beam of thought undergoes when it passes through the prism of a personality." Thus he omitted from the genuine Gal such remarks as the asides that the other gospel is not really different (1:7) and "if really in vain" (3:4*b*) as well as such a notoriously complicated passage as 3:16*b*-20, 21*b*. (J. O'Neill [1972, 1982] has argued that Weisse's approach should be taken seriously. If the text of Gal as part of the New Testament canon was glossed [e.g. 3:1 + "that you not obey the truth," Textus Receptus; "crucified" + "among you," Textus Receptus], it is more likely that it was glossed before the Pauline corpus became part of the canon and more likely that it was glossed before Gal became part of the Pauline corpus; Gal was always a sacred writing and, therefore, likely to be glossed.)

This whole approach flourished in the Netherlands from about 1879 to 1890, culminating in a commentary by J. Cramer (1890). The revival of Bauer's theory (by R. Steck 1888 and J. Friedrich 1891) that the entire epistle was spurious probably helped to discredit the school; Steck converted W. van Manen from an earlier belief that Gal was interpolated. R. Lipsius noted the suggested excisions of the school in his commentary (1891, 1892[2]).

Since the time of the Reformation exegetes have tried to identify the center of Paul's thought. Luther said Paul taught the law and works for the "old man" and taught passive righteousness, the righteousness received from heaven, and the promise of forgiveness of sins for the "new man." Luther was answered by those who cited Gal 5:6-Paul taught faith working through love (H. Schlier 1949). Many scholars couple Paul's defense of his apostolic office with his defense of the gospel as the double theme of the epistle (e.g., J. B. Lightfoot 1865). Others see the center in Gal 4:4-6: God sent the Son, born under the law, to redeem those under the law, in order that we might receive adoption and the gift of the Spirit. H. Betz (1979) has argued that the center is liberty: Paul presents his defense of the gospel as a defense of the Spirit. H. Räisänen (1983) maintains that Paul's thought in Gal is full of unresolved contradictions concerning the law.

2. *Style and Arrangement of Galatians.* The style and arrangement of Gal are on the small scale disjointed, although on the large scale clear, consisting of three parts: after greetings and introduction (1:1-10), first, a defense of the apostle and his gospel (1:11-2:21); second, a theological part (3:1-4:31); and third, a hortatory part (5:1-6:18). Betz (1974-75, 1979) contends that the epistle belongs to the genre of apologetic autobiography in an epistolary framework and that every division in the apologetic autobiography is governed by the conventions of rhetoric (epistolary prescript 1:1-5; *exordium* 1:6-11; *narratio* 1:12-2:14; *propositio* 2:15-21; *probatio* 3:1-4:31; *exhortatio* 5:1-6:10; epistolary postscript = conclusio 6:11-18). P. Kern (1998) argues that there is little evidence that Paul reflects the advice of the handbooks on rhetoric and notes that the church fathers did not think Paul's writing was like Greco-Roman oratory.

3. *Date of Galatians and Its Recipients.* The contention that Gal borrowed from Romans was one of Bauer's main arguments against its authenticity. C. Clemen (1894), who wrote a decisive refutation of Bauer and Steck, regarded the dating of Gal after Rom as the grain of truth in his opponents' case. Marcion probably placed Gal first in his canon, and Chrysostom[§] said Gal seemed to him prior to Rom ("Preface to Romans"). L. Cappel[§] was probably the first to suggest the order 1-2 Thess, Gal, 1 Cor (*Historia apostolica illustrata* 1634). He dated Gal to 51 C.E., the twelfth year of Claudius. Most scholars date the writing of the book soon after (see

Gal 1:6, "so quickly") Paul's visit to the Galatians, mentioned in Acts 18:23, and settle on anything from 51 C.E. to 58 C.E.; e.g., J. MILL (Novum Testamentum 1707), J. G. Eichhorn[§] (*Einleitung in das Neue Testament* 2 vols., 1804-12). J. D. Michaelis[§] (*Introductory Lectures to the Sacred Books of the New Testament* 1761) put the writing of Gal before Paul left Thessalonica on his second journey (Acts 17:10) and dated it to 49 C.E. on the grounds that it was written while all those who had accompanied him in Galatia were still with him.

The discrepancy between Acts, which says Paul made three visits to Jerusalem before his last visit to that city (Acts 9; 11; 15), and Gal, which says Paul made only two visits to Jerusalem up to the date of writing the epistle, did not much trouble scholars, who put the discrepancy down to Acts' hearsay information. However, the suggestion that the Galatians had been evangelized by Paul and Barnabas on their first missionary journey when they fled Iconium to the Lycaonian cities of Lystra and Derbe and the surrounding parts (Acts 16:6) opened up other possibilities. The opinion that the Galatians were inhabitants of Lycaonia seems to have been offered first by J. Schmidt (1748, 1754), who argued that as Derbe and Lystra were part of the Roman province of Galatia, the Christians there could have been addressed as "Galatians." H. Paulus (1831) and T. von Zahn[§] (1905), among others, followed this same line, which became popular in the English-speaking world through the writings of W. Ramsay[§], professor of humanities at Aberdeen (1890, 1899), and which has been revived by J. Dunn (1993). The issues are fully treated in Encyclopaedia Biblica (1899-1903). J. Koppe[§] (1778) argued the earlier date for the Galatian mission without the supposition that the citizens of Derbe and Lystra were addressed as "Galatians." He based his case on the grounds that the visit to Galatia mentioned in Acts 16:6 was to strengthen the brethren (Acts 15:36, 41), not to found new churches. If the Galatians had been evangelized on Paul's first missionary journey it becomes possible to suppose that the events recorded in Gal 2:1-10 were not the same as the events recorded in Acts 15 but took place before that meeting. This view was assumed in the Chronology[§] of the seventh-century *Chronicon Paschale* and was adopted by Calvin[§]. The most common of the possible identifications of Gal 2:1-10 (if not with Acts 15) is with the visit to Jerusalem recorded in Acts 11:30 (F. F. Bruce 1982; R. Longenecker 1990).

4. *Paul's Opponents.* The Marcionite prologue to Galatians said that the Galatians were tempted by false apostles to turn to the law and circumcision, and this is the usual view to this day. These false apostles are usually thought of as incomers, though some think they were local; and they are most often regarded as Jewish Christians (Dunn 1993), although J. Munck[§] (1954) thought they were Gentiles and N. Walter (1986) has revived the possibility that they were simply Jews engaged in a countermission. W. Lütgert (1919) argued that Paul was fighting on two fronts: (1) Heathen influence of a pneumatic kind had begun to penetrate the Galatian churches, and the representatives of this party accused Paul of still being a half-Jew; (2) Jews began to persecute the churches, and Jewish Christians in defense preached circumcision for all Gentile Christians. This theory was taken over and adapted by J. Ropes (1929). W. Schmithals (1965) has argued that Paul's opponents combined the characteristics of both of Lütgert's imagined parties and were Jewish Christian Gnostics (Gnostic Interpretation[§]).

Recent commentaries on Gal include Becker and Luz (1998), Esler (1998), Hays (2000), Matera (2003), Vouga (1998), and Witherington (1998). Bachman (1999), Nanos (2001), and Perkins (2001) study the difficult issue of Paul's understanding of Judaism in Galatians. Braxton (2002) offers a contemporary African-American reader-response analysis of the letter. Wilder (2001) and Wisdom (2001) investigate Paul's use of the Hebrew Bible in Gal. Various other recent approaches (rhetoric, narrative, theology, etc.) to Gal include Bryant (2001), Cummins (2001), Davis (2002), Hays (2002), Jürgens (1999), Kern (1998), Mitternacht (1999), Rapa (2001), and Witulski (1998).

Bibliography: M. Bachmann, *Antijudaismus im Galaterbrief?: Exegetische Studien zu einem polemischen Schreiben und zur Theologie des Apostels Paulus* (NTOA 40, 1999). **B. Bauer,** *Die Apostelgeschichte, eine Ausgleichung des Paulinismus und des Judenthums innerhalb der christlichen Kirche* (1850); *Kritik der paulinischen Briefe, pt. 1, Der Ursprung des Galaterbriefs* (1850, repr. 1972). **F. C. Baur,** *TübingerZeitschrift fürTheologie 4 (1831)* 61-206, repr. in *Ausgewählte Werke in Einzelausgabe* (ed. K. Scholder, vol. 1, *Historisch-kritische Untersuchungen zum Neuen Testament* 1963). **J. Becker and U. Luz,** *Die Briefe an die Galater, Epheser und Kolosser* (NTD 8/1, 1998). **H. D. Betz,** "The Literary Composition and Function of Paul's Letter to the Galatians," NTS 21 (1974-75) 353-79; *Galatians: A Commentary on Paul's Letter to the Churches in Galatia* (Hermeneia, 1979). **B. R. Braxton,** *No Longer Slaves: Galatians and African American Experience* (2002) **R. A. Bryant,** *The Risen Crucified Christ in Galatians* (SBLDS 185, 2001). **F. F. Bruce,** *The Epistle to the Galatians: A Commentary on the Greek Text* (1982). **E. D. Burton,** *The Epistle to the Galatians* (ICC, 1921). **R. E. Ciampa,** *The Presence and Function of Scripture in Galatians 1 and 2* (WUNT 2/102, 1998). **C. Clemen,** *Die Einheitlichkeit der paulinischen Briefe an der Hand der bisher mit bezug auf sie aufgestellten Interpolations- und Compilationshypothesen geprüft* (1894). **J. Cramer,** *De Brief van Paulus aan de Galatiërs in zijn oorsprokelijken Vorm hersteld, en verklaard* (1890). **S. A. Cummins,** *Paul and the Crucified Christ in Antioch: Maccabean Martyrdom and Galatians 1 and 2* (SNTSMS 114, 2001). **B. S. Davis,** *Christ as Devotio: The Argument of Galatians 3:1-14* (2002). **J. D. G. Dunn,** *The Epistle to the Galatians* (BNTC, 1993). **P. F. Esler,** *Galatians* (New Testament Readings, 1998). **J. Friedrich,** *Die Unechtheit des Galaterbriefes: Ein Beitrag zu einer kritischen Geschichte des Urchristentums* (1891). **R. B. Hays,** "The Letter to the Galatians," *NIB* (2000) 11:181-348; *The Faith of Jesus Christ: The Narrative Substructure of Galatians 3:1-4:11* (2002²). **B. Jürgens,** *Zweierlei Anfang: Kommunikative Konstruktionen heidenchristlicher Identität in Gal 2 und Apg 15* (BBB 120, 1999). **P. H. Kern,** *Rhetoric and Galatians: Assessing an Approach to Paul's Epistle* (SNTSMS 101, 1998). **J. B. Koppe,** *Novum Testamentum Graece perpetua annotatione illustratum* (1778³; rev. and ed. T. C. Tychsen, 1823). **D. Kremendahl,** *Die Botschaft der Form: Zum Verhältnis von antiker Epistolographie und Rhetorik im Galaterbrief* (NTOA 46, 2000). **J. B. Lightfoot,** *Saint Paul's Epistle to the Galatians: A Revised Text with Introduction, Notes, and Dissertations* (1865). **R. A. Lipsius,** *Briefe an die Galater, Römer, Philipper* (HCNT II.ii, 1891, 1892²). **B. W. Longenecker,** *The Triumph of Abraham's God: The Transformation of Identity in Galatians* (1998). **R. N. Longenecker,** *Galatians* (WBC 41, 1990). **W. Lütgert,** *Gesetz und Geist: Eine Untersuchung zur Vorgeschichte des Galaterbriefes* (BFCT 22, 6, 1919). **J. L. Martyn,** *Galatians* (AB 33A, 1997). **F. J. Matera,** *Galatians* (SP 9, 1992); "The Letter of Paul to the Galatians," *NISB* (2003) 2079-88. **D. Mitternacht,** *Forum für Sprachlose: Eine kommunikationspsychologische und epistolär-rhetorische Untersuchung des Galaterbriefs* (ConBNT 30, 1999). **T. D. Morgan,** *The Moral Philosopher: In a Dialogue Between Philalethes, a Christian Deist, and Theophanes, a Christian Jew* (1737). **J. Munck,** *Paulus und die Heilsgeschichte* (1954; ET *Paul and the Salvation of Mankind* 1959). **M. D. Nanos,** *The Irony of Galatians: Paul's Letter in First-Century Context* (2001). **J. C. O'Neill,** *The Recovery of Paul's Letter to the Galatians* (1972); "Glosses and Interpolations in the Letters of St. Paul," *StEv* 7 (TU 126, 1982) 379-86; "The Holy Spirit and the Human Spirit in Galatians: Gal 5:17," *ETL 71* (1995) 107-20. **F. Overbeck,** *Über die Auffassung des Streits des Paulus mit Petrus in Antiochien (Gal. 2,11ff.) bei den Kirchenvätern* (Programm zur Rectoratsfeier der Universität Basel, 1877; repr. 1968). **H. E. G. Paulus,** *Des Apostels Lehr-briefe an die Galater und Romer Christen* (1831). **P. Perkins,** *Abraham's Divided Children: Galatians and the Politics of Faith* (New Testament in Context, 2001). **Heikki Räisänen,** *Paul and the Law* (WUNT 29, 1983). **W. M. Ramsay,** *Historical Geography of Asia Minor* (1890, repr. 1962); *A Historical Commentary on St. Paul's*

Epistle to the Galatians (1899, repr. 1965). **R. K. Rapa,** *The Meaning of "Works of the Law" in Galatians and Romans* (Studies in Biblical Literature 31, 2001). **J. H. Ropes,** *The Singular Problem of the Epistle to the Galatians* (HTS 14, 1929) 28-42. **H. Schlier,** *Der Brief an die Galater* (Meyer, 1949, 19654). **J. J. Schmidt,** *Prolusio de Galatis, ad quos Paulus literas misit* (1748); *Prolusionem suam de Galatis-ab objectionibus doctissimorum virorum vindicare conatur* (1754). **W. Schmithals,** *Paul and the Gnostics* (1965; ET 1972). **J. S. Semler,** *Paraphrasis epistolae ad Galatas cum Prolegomenis, Notis, et varietate Lectionis Latinae* (1779). **V. M. Smiles,** *The Gospel and the Law in Galatia: Paul's Response to Jewish-Christian Separatism and the Threat of Galatian Apostasy* (1998). **R. Steck,** *Der Galaterbrief nach seiner Echtheit untersucht nebst kritischen Bemerkungen zu den paulinischen Hauptbriefen* (1888). **A. Suhl,** "Der Galaterbrief-Situation und Argumentation," *ANRW* II. 25.4 (1987) 3067-134. **F. Vouga,** *An die Galater* (HNT 10, 1998). **N. Walter,** "Paulus und die Gegner des Christus-evangeliums in Galatien," *L'Apôtre Paul: personnalité, style et conception du ministère* (ed. A. Vanhoye, 1986) 351-56. **C. H. Weisse,** *Philosophische Dogmatik oder Philosophie des Christenthums* (3 vols. 1855-62); *Beiträge zur Kritik der paulinischen Briefe an die Galater, Römer, Philipper, und Kolosser* (ed. E. Sulze, 1867). **W. N. Wilder,** *Echoes of the Exodus Narrative in the Context and Background of Galatians 5:18* (Studies in Biblical Literature 2, 2001). **S. K. Williams,** *Galatians* (ANTC, 1997). **J. R. Wisdom,** *Blessing for the Nations and the Curse of the Law: Paul's Citation of Genesis and Deuteronomy in Gal 3.8-10* (WUNT 2/133, 2001). **B. Witherington,** III, *Grace in Galatia: A Commentary on St. Paul's Letter to the Galatians* (1998). **T. Witulski,** *Die Adressaten des Galaterbriefes: Untersuchungen zur Gemeinde von Antiochia ad Pisidiam* (FRLANT 193, 1998). **T. Zahn,** *Der Brief des Paulus an der Galater* (1905, 19223)

J. C. O'NEILL

THE NEW TESTAMENT CANON

Ephesians, Letter to the

1. *Early and Medieval.* Second-century Gnostics (Gnostic Interpretation[§]), especially Valentinians, adopted Eph as a favorite text. They considered the Paul[†§] of Eph the first Gnostic because of his language about *gnōsis, plērōma,* the heavenly *anthrōpos,* and the latter's partner, the *ekklēsia.* The anti-Gnostic bishop Irenaeus[§] used Eph against them as had Ignatius[§] before him. Irenaeus emphasized the oneness motifs of the letter: one God, who is both Creator and Redeemer; one Christ; and one church, the unity of which was guaranteed by apostolic tradition and succession.

The next period of major study occurred during the Arian dispute (Arius[§]). Marius Victorinus wrote a commentary on Eph shortly after 360 in which he answered objections to Christ's divinity. Ambrosiaster and Jerome[§] also wrote commentaries. Jerome was among the first to register surprise that Paul, who knew the Ephesians so well, could write as though he did not know them. In his early fifth-century commentary, Theodore of Mopsuestia[§] also wondered whether the Ephesians were the proper addressees of the letter.

Thomas Aquinas[§] gave lectures on Eph either between 1261 and 1263, or in 1266. The theme of ecclesiological unity in Eph contributed to the construction of his doctrinal system.

2. *Renaissance and Reformation.* In 1519 Erasmus[§] identified stylistic peculiarities in Eph that separated it from other letters of Paul, although he ultimately decided on the basis of spiritual content that Paul wrote it. Luther[§] penned many scattered comments and preached a number of sermons on Eph (E. Ellwein 1973, 11-174). He thought the letter was theologically one of Paul's most important letters. Calvin[§] wrote a detailed commentary and forty-eight sermons on Eph and cited Eph 277 times in his Institutes of the Christian Religion.

3. *Rise of Historical Scholarship.* The earliest historical questions focused on the letter's recipients. In 1598 Beza[§] wrote that the letter was written for the Ephesians but that it was also a circular letter for other churches in Asia Minor. J. Ussher[§] moved one step further (1654), maintaining that Paul had left a space after the words *tois ousin* in 1:1 so that each church could insert its own name when reading the letter. Grotius, going back to the opinion of Marcion[§], decided that the letter was written to both Laodicea and Ephesus (1646), while J. Mill[§] thought that the Laodiceans alone were the original recipients (1710).

The first person to maintain in print that someone other than Paul was the author was E. Evanson[§], for whom the contradiction between the address and the content was too great to reconcile (1792). The first European to take that step was Usteri, for whom the relationship with Colossians was crucial (1824). The earliest major work to investigate thoroughly the authenticity of Eph was that of W. De Wette[§] (1843). His reasons have remained fundamental to those who identify an author other than Paul: (1) the literary dependence on Colossians; (2) the complex and overloaded Greek style; and (3) the large number of phrases atypical of Paul's time (e.g., 2:20 and 3:5)

F. C. Baur[§] and his followers understood Eph as an example of an attempt by followers of Pauline Christianity to effect a synthesis with the followers of Petrine Christianity (1845). The combination of Gnostic ideas and an approach typical of early Catholicism caused Baur to place Eph in the second century. H. Holtzmann[§] also argued for non-Pauline authorship (1872), identifying an original, shortened letter to the Colossians written by Paul that in the second century was used as the model for a pseudonymous letter to the Ephesians. This letter, in turn, became the basis of an expanded Colossians.

4. *Twentieth-Century Interpretation. a. History of religions and place in the early church.* H. Schlier (1971) and E. Käsemann[§], both students of R. Bultmann[§], first applied to Eph insights

from newly discovered manuscripts, especially from Gnostic texts that seemed to evidence a pre-Christian Gnosticism. Schlier detected a meditation on the mystery of the church's unity with Christ (1930). The Gnostic myth (Mythology and Biblical Studies[§]) is applied to Christ, the heavenly Man. As the Man, Christ is simultaneously in heaven (as the head) and on earth (as the body). Other concepts like knowledge, the worldview, *pleroma,* the church as the wisdom of God, and the marital tie between Christ and the church all confirmed for Schlier the Gnostic background, hence he argued for non-Pauline authorship.

In his commentary, first published in 1957, Schlier continued to hold that Gnosticism had strongly influenced the letter, especially in its cosmology and ecclesiology. In the intervening decades, however, he had decided that Paul did in fact write the letter, and he traced the roots of the Ephesian (New Testament Theology*[§]) to the undisputed letters, explaining that the latter deal with the kerygma, while Eph develops the *sophia,* or wisdom, of Paul's thought (1 Cor 2:6ff.) Thus he styled the letter a wisdom speech written by Paul while a prisoner in Rome.

Käsemann distinguished between the body of Christ as represented in the undisputed letters of Paul and in Ephesians-Colossians (1933). In the undisputed letters the cosmic aspect of the body of Christ is not a primary motif and is modified by the concept of the body as organism. In contrast, in Ephesians-Colossians the body of Christ is much more central, and the background of its usage is Gnostic. In Col the dominant perspective is that of image and members because the emphasis is on the relationship of the individual Christian to Christ, while in Eph the chief schema is that of body and head because the meaning of the church is most important. Similarly to Schlier, Käsemann viewed Christ as the heavenly Man and the eschatology as Gnostic.

Käsemann also had definite views of the place of Eph within early Christianity. The emphasis on the church in Eph led him to identify it, pejoratively, as early Roman Catholic. He also linked the letter with Acts because of their common use of church tradition, which he saw as another sign of the centrality of the church. In tandem with the weight placed on the church were the new importance in Eph of the apostles and the clear movement toward bishops despite the absence of explicit references to them.

The themes of church order and Gnosticism have continued in scholarly discussion. For F. Mussner (1982) the ecclesiological developments in Eph are a natural development of the early confession of the church and are unrelated to any supposed Gnostic influence. K. Fischer (1973) has also moved in a direction quite different from Käsemann. Since bishops are not mentioned in 4:7-16, even though the letter was written at a time when the role of bishop was elsewhere being adopted, Fischer concludes that Eph was a post-Pauline utopian attempt both to rescue the charismatic organization of Paul's missionary congregations and to unify the church. Thus Eph is the opposite of early Catholic. H. Merklein, however, agrees with Käsemann on the early Roman Catholic label, although for him that designation is positive and establishes the legitimacy of the development from the undisputed letters through Eph to the Pastoral Letters*[§].

Gnosticism has been the key to other studies. According to E. Schweizer (1963), Eph attempts to combat a type of cosmic Christology that viewed Christ as a macro-anthropos. P. Pokorný (1965) pushes further the theme of opposition to Gnosticism, seeing in Eph a homily against the Gnostic danger and dating it to the 80s or 90s. He significantly softens that position in his commentary (1992), stating that Eph was not written as a direct defense against Gnosticism. R. Martin (1968), who also sees Eph as anti-Gnostic, argues that the author, the same Luke as the author of Acts, wrote to combat antinomian tendencies in the Gentile church. For E. Best (1993), the author of Eph was refuting no heresy, including Gnosticism. The use of any Gnostic terminology resulted from the fact that such terms were familiar to the letter's recipients. A. Lindemann (1975) does not understand Eph as anti-Gnostic at all. For him the past, present, and future have been collapsed together in such a way that the church is a timeless entity that does not exist within history. The idea that Christians are already resurrected

(2:5-6) indicates an ethics based on a past salvation event rather than on the future. The proper background for both ideas is Gnostic. Not only is the language similar to Gnosticism, it is thoroughly Gnostic.

Less widely debated has been the apparent influence on Eph of the type of Jewish apocalyptic thinking (Apocalypticism*§) and formulation evident in the Dead Sea Scrolls§. Election, predestination, mystery, conflicting spirits of light and darkness, spiritual warfare, the community as a holy house or temple, and the revealing of the divine plan of salvation are all paralleled at Qumran. The Greek of Eph shows strong Semitic coloring quite close to the Hebrew of the Dead Sea Scrolls, especially the hymns. K. Kuhn§ (1968) has argued that both the author of Eph and the Dead Sea community drew on a common tradition.

b. Authorship and purpose. Many scholars have continued to argue for Pauline authorship. T. Abbott (1897) introduced the argument that a development in Paul's theology, in part spurred by the delay of the Parousia, accounts for the differences in Eph. E. Percy (1946) wrote a most thorough defense of Pauline authorship, dealing one-by-one with the peculiarities of thought and style and illustrating how each is rooted in Paul's earlier writings. G. Schille (1957) suggested another line of approach based on Form Criticism*§, explaining the unusual writing style by isolating Paul's heavy quotation of pre-Pauline hymnic and paraenetic material. M. Barth (1974) built on his predecessors, placing heavy weight on the liturgical background, especially as it related to the Qumran literature, but consistently discounted theories of Gnostic influence. A. van Roon (1974) has also surveyed the literature and defended Paul as author; for him the content of Eph is typically Pauline and, indeed, quite close to Rom. He places Paul in Caesarea, thus accounting for Semitic influences by the bilingual milieu, but identifies no traces of Gnosticism. The relationship between Eph and Col is explained by a common draft completed in different ways by different scribes.

Other scholars have developed a variety of positions on pseudonymous authorship. E. Goodspeed§ (1933) proposed that Paul's letters were soon forgotten. Near the end of the first century the former slave Onesimus received a copy of Luke-Acts; he then gathered Pauline letters and decided to publish them. To update the letters he wrote Eph as an introduction to the collection, using Col as his basic source. The theory (except for Onesimus as the author) has continued to exert a great deal of influence, as is seen in the work of C. Mitton (1951). Identifying a more gradual process of letter collection, Mitton views the publication of Acts as the final factor that caused the author to summarize Paul's message. F. W. Beare§ (1953) found no evidence that Paul was ever forgotten, although he did think that the purpose of Eph was to commend Paul's teaching to a later generation.

Other directions have been set by N. Dahl§, who understood Eph as an appeal to gentile Christians to be united with their Jewish(-Christian) predecessors and contemporaries. He styled Eph as a letter of reminder and congratulation in which baptism is the basic teaching and serves as the foundation for both unity and ethical action. The letter is further meant to establish a relationship between the Asian recipients and the author, who in his earlier writings Dahl held to be the historical Paul; his later work, however, identified a post-Pauline author. At the same time Dahl saw a quiet polemic against heresy, particularly in the author's statements about ministry and marriage, although he refused to identify the heresy as Gnostic, here agreeing with G. Johnston (1962), who found the supposed Gnostic material to be amply paralleled outside Gnostic texts.

Providing another theory of authorship, J. Kirby (1968) argued that an elder of the church in Ephesus was asked to furnish a collector of Paul's letters with a copy of Paul's correspondence with Ephesus. Since such a letter did not exist, the elder composed one based on his memory of Paul's preaching but structured around the Pentecost liturgy followed by the early church. J. Gnilka (1971) rejects Kirby's theory and views Eph as a reworking of Col and the authors of both books as heavily dependent on pre-existent traditions.

R. Schnackenburg's commentary (1991) summarizes the non-Pauline authorship position. The deciding factor for him is the distinctive theology of Eph in which Paul's theology of the cross has become a theology of the resurrection, exaltation, and heavenly enthronement of JESUS Christ. That view inevitably moved toward a position in which the church is at the center of human existence. Determinative for P. Pokorný in opting for pseudonymous authorship was the great care exercised by the author in preserving and applying the tradition of Paul to a new situation in which the peculiar features and unity of the church were being threatened.

W. Taylor (1985), building on Dahl, calls Eph a congratulatory communication written in letter format. He argues that the genre of Eph is epideictic, a type of literature usually devoted to praising a person, an object, or an event, and is particularly concerned to show nascent Gnosticism as the opponent against whom the letter was written sometime between 75 and 90. V. Furnish (1992) disputes Taylor's classification of Eph as epideictic but agrees with him and others that Eph is pseudonymous (see also J. Sampley 1993). Especially important for Furnish are two arguments for authorship by Paul: The non-Pauline vocabulary and style are partly due to the author's use of traditions; Paul's imprisonment and his more fully developed thought explain the differences between Eph and the undisputed letters. According to Furnish, the first argument provides another reason to question authorship by Paul, since nowhere in the undisputed letters does Paul make similar wholesale use of traditional material. The second argument falls because scholars who argue for Pauline authorship for Eph usually place it during the same imprisonment mentioned in Phil. The latter epistle, however, exhibits neither the marked stylistic peculiarities nor the same kind of "developed" theology as Eph.

Sampley posits identity formation as the chief purpose of the letter. That formation begins in baptism and instructs the readers concerning who they are and how they are to live the Christian life. A. Lincoln has a parallel understanding, although without the more exclusive emphasis on baptism. Chaps. 1-3 remind Gentile Christians of their privileges and status as believers in Christ and members of the church; chaps. 4-6 appeal to them to demonstrate that identity in their lives. Lincoln understands Eph, therefore, as a combination of the epideictic (chaps. 1-3) and deliberative (chaps. 4-6) rhetorical genres. In his commentary (1990) he moves from his earlier position that Paul wrote Eph to the assertion that the author belonged to a Pauline "school." The usual arguments and the dependence of Eph on Col and other Pauline letters convinced Lincoln that Paul did not write Eph. He explains various concerns of the letter (e.g., lack of unity and communal identity) by referring to the serious shift caused by Paul's death. He thinks that the letter may have been written for the churches of Hierapolis and Laodicea in the Lycus Valley.

Scholars who have studied the household code in Eph 5:2-6:9 have also rejected Pauline authorship. C. Martin (1991), who classifies Eph as a deutero-Pauline letter, argues for a study of the household code that advocates black women's as well as black men's liberation. S. Tanzer (1994) thinks that a disciple of Paul wrote Eph and another writer later added 5:22-6:9 to teach Christians how to fulfill their calling (4:1). Tanzer notices that the household code interrupts the instructions in chaps. 4-6 about how Christians can put into practice the equality of the Jews and Gentiles in the church that chaps. 1-3 claim Christ has accomplished. Both Martin's and Tanzer's studies draw from E. Schüssler Fiorenza's hermeneutics of suspicion. Schüssler Fiorenza (1983) argues that the author's concern for the unity of the church might account for the instructions about the proper social behavior of women.

Recent commentaries on Eph include Aletti (2001), Boismard (1999), Hoehner (2002), Luz (1998), MacDonald (2000), Muddiman (2001), Perkins (2000), and Thurston (2003). Recent collections of essays include Best (1997) and Hellholm, Blomkvist, and Fornberg (2000). Recent investigations of the theology of Eph include Gese (1997), Jeal (2000), Kittredge (1998), Mayer (2002), Mouton (2002), and Schwindt (2002).

Bibliography: T. K. Abbott, *A Critical and Exegetical Commentary on the Epistles to the Ephesians and to the Colossians* (ICC, 1897). **J.-N. Aletti,** *Saint Paul Epître aux Éphésiens* (EBib n.s. 42, 2001). **C. E. Arnold,** *Ephesians: Power and Magic: The Concept of Power in Ephesians in Light of Its Historical Setting* (SNTSMS 63, 1993). **M. Barth,** *Ephesians* (AB 34 and 34a, 1974). **F. C. Baur,** *Paulus der Apostel Jesus Christi* (1845). **F. W. Beare,** "The Epistle to the Ephesians: Introduction and Exegesis," *IB* (1953) 10:597-749. **E. Best,** *Ephesians* (NTGu, 1993); "Recipients and Title of the Letter to the Ephesians: Why and When the Designation 'Ephesians'?" *ANRW* 2.25.4 (1987) 3247-79; *Essays on Ephesians* (1997). **M.-É. Boismard,** *L'Énigme de la lettre aux Éphésiens* (Ebib n.s. 39, 1999). **N. A. Dahl,** "Adresse und Proömium des Epheserbriefes," *TZ* 7 (1951) 241-64; "Anamnesis," *StTh* 1 (1947 [1948]) 69-95; *IDBSup* (1962) 268-69; "Gentiles, Christians, and Israelites in the Epistle to the Ephesians," *HTR* 79 (1986) 31-39; "Interpreting Ephesians Then and Now," *CurTM* 5 (1978) 133-43; *TD* 25 (1977) 305-15. **E. Ellwein** (ed.), *D. Martin Luthers Epistel-Auslegung, vol. 3: Die Briefe an die Epheser, Philipper, und Kolosser* (1973). **K. M. Fischer,** *Tendenz und Absicht des Epheserbriefes* (FRLANT 111, 1973). **V. P. Furnish,** "Ephesians, Epistle to the," ABD (1992) 2:535-42. **M. Gese,** *Das Vermächtnis des Apostels: Die Rezeption der paulinischen Theologie im Epheserbrief* (WUNT 2/99, 1997). **M. A. Getty,** *Ephesians, Philippians, Colossians* (Read and Pray Series, 1980). **J. Gnilka,** *Der Epheserbrief* (HTKNT, 1971). **E. J. Goodspeed,** *The Meaning of Ephesians* (1933); *The Key to Ephesians* (1956). **D. Hellholm, V. Blomkvist, and T. Fornberg** (eds.), *Studies in Ephesians: Introductory Questions, Text- and Edition-Critical Issues, Interpretation of Texts And Themes* (WUNT 131, 2000). **H. W. Hoehner,** *Ephesians: An Exegetical Commentary* (2002). **R. R. Jeal,** *Integrating Theology and Ethics in Ephesians: The Ethos of Communication* (Studies in the Bible and Early Christianity 43, 2000). **G. Johnston,** "Ephesians, Letter to the," *IDB* (1962) 2:108-14. **E. Käsemann,** "Epheserbrief," RGG3 2:517-20; "Ephesians and Acts," *Studies in Luke-Acts* (ed. L. E. Keck and J. L. Martyn, 1966) 288-97; "Das Interpretationsproblem des Epheserbriefes," *Exegetische Versuche und Besinnungen* (1965²) 2:253-61; *Leib und Leib Christi: Eine Untersuchung zur paulinischen Begrifflichkeft* (BHT 9, 1933); "Paul and Early Catholicism," *NT Questions of Today* (NTLi, 1969) 236-51; "The Theological Problem Presented by the Motif of the Body of Christ," *Perspectives on Paul* (1971) 102-21. **J. C. Kirby,** *Ephesians: Baptism and Pentecost* (1968). **C. B. Kittredge,** *Community and Authority: The Rhetoric of Obedience in the Pauline Tradition* (HTS 45, 1998). **W. W. Klein,** *The Book of Ephesians: An Annotated Bibliography* (Books of the Bible 8, 1996). **K. G. Kuhn,** "The Epistle to the Ephesians in the Light of the Qumran Texts," *Paul and Qumran* (ed. J. Murphy-O'Connor, 1968) 115-31. **A. T. Lincoln,** *Ephesians* (WBC 42, 1990); "The Theology of Ephesians," *The Theology of the Later Pauline Letters* (NT Theology, A. T. Lincoln and A. J. M. Wedderburn, 1993) 75-166. **A. Lindemann,** *Die Aufhebung der Zeit: Geschichtsverständnis und Eschatologie im Epheserbrief* (SNT 12, 1975). **U. Luz,** "Epheser," *Die Briefe an die Galater, Epheser und Kolosser* (J. Becker und U. Luz, NTD 8/1, 1998¹⁸). **M. Y. MacDonald,** *Colossians and Ephesians* (SP 17, 2000). **C. J. Martin,** "The Haustafeln (Household Code) in African American Biblical Interpretation: 'Free Slaves' and 'Subordinate Women,'" *Stony the Road We Trod: African American Biblical Interpretation* (ed. C. H. Felder, 1991). **R. P. Martin,** "An Epistle in Search of a Life-Setting," *ExpTim* 79 (1968) 296-302. **A. C. Mayer,** *Sprache der Einheit im Epheserbrief und in der Ökumene* (WUNT 2/150, 2002). **H. Merklein,** *Christus und die Kirche: Die theologische Grundstruktur des Epheserbriefes nach Eph. 2.11-18* (SBS 66, 1973); "Der Epheserbrief in der neueren exegetischen Diskussion," *ANRW* 2.25.4 (1987) 3156-246; *Das kirchliche Amt nach dem Epheserbrief* (SANT 33, 1973). **C. L. Mitton,** *Ephesians* (NCB, 1976); *The Epistle to the Ephesians* (1951). **E. Mouton,** *Reading a New Testament Document Ethically* (Academia Biblica, 2002). **J. Muddiman,** *A Commentary on the Epistle to the Ephesians* (BNTC, 2001). **F. Mussner,** *Der Brief an die*

Epheser (ÖTBK/NT 10, 1982); *Christus, das All und die Kirche* (TTS 5, 1968²); "Contributions made by Qumran to the Understanding of the Epistle to the Ephesians," *Paul and Qumran* (ed. J. Murphy-O'Connor, 1968) 159-78. **E. Pagels,** *The Gnostic Paul: Gnostic Exegesis of the Pauline Letters* (1975) 115-33. **P. Perkins,** "The Letter to the Ephesians," *NIB* (2000) 9:349-466. **E. Percy,** *Die Probleme der Kolosser- und Epheserbriefe* (1946). **P. Pokorny,** *Der Brief des Paulus an die Epheser* (THKNT 10, 2, 1992); *Der Epheserbrief und die Gnosis: Die Bedeutung des Haupt-Glieder-Gedankens in der entstehenden Kirche* (1965). **P. Perkins,** *Ephesians* (ANTC, 1997). **J. H. P. Reumann,** *Colossians* (ACNT, 1985). **L. M. Russell,** *Imitators of God: A Study Book on Ephesians* (1984). **J. P. Sampley,** *The Deutero-Pauline Letters* (Proclamation Commentaries, ed. Gerhard Krodel, 1993) 1-23. **G. Schille,** "Der Autor des Epheserbriefes," *TLZ* 82 (1957) 325-34. **H. Schlier,** *Der Brief an die Epheser: Ein Kommentar* (1971⁷). **R. Schnackenburg,** *Ephesians: A Commentary* (1991). **E. Schüssler Fiorenza,** *In Memory of Her: A Feminist Theological Reconstruction of Christian Origins* (1983). **E. Schweizer,** "Die Kirche als Leib Christi in den paulinischen Antilegomena," *Neotestamentica* (1963) 293-316. **R. Schwindt,** *Das Weltbild des Epheserbriefes: Eine religionsgeschichtlich-exegetische Studie* (WUNT 148, 2002). **C. L. Stockhausen,** *Letters in the Pauline Tradition* (1989). **S. J. Tanzer,** *Searching the Scriptures,* vol. 2, *A Feminist Commentary* (ed. E. Schüssler Fiorenza, 1994) 323-48. **W. F. Taylor,** Jr., *Ephesians* (ACNT, 1985). **B. Thurston,** "The Letter of Paul to the Ephesiasn," *NISB* (2003) 2089-98. **A. van Roon,** *The Authenticity of Ephesians* (1974).

W. F. TAYLOR

Philippians, Letter to the

Populated by significant numbers of Macedonians, Greeks, and a Jewish minority as well as by Roman settlers, Philippi was a truly cosmopolitan city and an important gateway to Europe from Asia. Although it was "a leading city of the district of Macedonia and a Roman colony" (Acts 16:12), it was the tiny Pauline church established there that secured Philippi's place in Western history. That church played an important role in the apostle's mission to Greece and perhaps to Ephesus, and the association with Paul[†§] later gave Philippi a certain status and even authority in the Western world. Crossing over from Asia Minor via Neapolis to Philippi sometime between 49 and 52 C.E. (if one follows Acts 16:6-40), Paul launched a mission to Europe whose horizon ultimately was to embrace Spain.

Certainly the letter Paul later wrote to the church he founded at Philippi helped to shape the theological language of the post-apostolic church: *1 Clem.* 21 echoes 1:27, *1 Clem.* 16 echoes 2:6-11, *1 Clem.* 47 echoes 4:15. Ign. *Rom.* 2 quotes 2:17 and Ign. *Phld.* 1.1 and 2.2 seem to allude to 2:3. Polycarp (*Phil.* 2.1-2) borrows his language from Phil 2:9-10. Additional quotations and allusions are in *Testament of the Twelve Patriarchs, Acts of Thomas,* Irenaeus[§], Tertullian[§], Clement of Alexandria[§], and Marcion[§]. Laodiceans, the mid-second-century pseudepigraph attributed to Paul, contains a string of sentences and phrases taken from Philippians (J. B. Lightfoot 1896).

For centuries theologians regularly appealed to Phil 2:6-11 to support the two natures Christology of the Nicene Creed (Calvin[§] 1948, 56-58). But the nineteenth century witnessed a change with the genesis of kenotic (from the Gr. *kenō,* "to empty," used in Phil 2:7) Christology. Drawing on Phil 2:7, German theologians were joined by English scholars in arguing that the preexistent Christ surrendered his divinity to become completely human. The only way to affirm the full humanity of Jesus[†§], it was believed, was to insist on the abandonment of the Christ's divine nature during his earthly sojourn. However, kenotic Christology was widely assailed, if not refuted, and its influence waned (D. Dawe 1962, 337-49). That issue left behind, modern research on Phil focused on four related issues: (1) the place and date of composition, (2) the occasion and purpose of the letter, (3) the unity of the letter, and (4) the provenance of the Christ hymn in 2:6-11.

1. *Place and Date of Composition.* Although the Acts account (16:6–17:14) of Paul's crossing over from Asia Minor to Europe, thence to Philippi, and thence south to Thessalonica and Beroea is reliable, the question of the place from which Paul wrote to the Philippian church is much disputed. From the second to the eighteenth centuries, the view that Paul wrote Phil from Rome went unchallenged. In Paul's own words he wrote the letter during an imprisonment known to the whole *praetorium* (1:13); and he concluded the letter with greetings from "those of Caesar's household" (4:22). These passages convinced Marcion that the apostle was "writing to them from Rome in prison" (J. Knox 1942, 170). The *praetorium* of 1:13 was taken to mean the Praetorian Guard in Rome, and "those of Caesar's household" was believed to refer to believers from within the imperial household. Paul anticipated a trial, with death as a possible outcome (1:20-26), which fits well into the Roman context.

Since 1799, however, when H. Paulus first argued against the prevailing position, the Roman hypothesis has lost the support of the majority of Pauline scholars. The difficulties with the Roman hypothesis are manifold. The distance between Rome and Philippi (some 730 miles by land) rules out the frequent exchanges the letter assumes have already taken place (five) or are anticipated (four). Even as Paul writes, Timothy has come to join him (1:1), word of his imprisonment has reached Philippi (4:14), Epaphroditus has been dispatched by the church to offer assistance to Paul (2:25; 4:18), news of Epaphroditus's critical illness has filtered back to Philippi (2:26), and word of the church's grave concern for Epaphroditus has now reached Paul (2:26). In the imminent future Paul plans to dispatch Epaphroditus to Philippi with a letter (2:25, 28); he expects soon after to send Timothy to Philippi (2:19); he looks forward to Timothy's return with news from the congregation (2:19); and he hopes to journey to Philippi himself for a reunion (2:24). Such a number of exchanges over a distance requiring two months to traverse makes a Roman provenance for the letter highly improbable.

Moreover, the references to the *praetorium* (1:13) and to "Caesar's household" (4:22) do not require a Roman setting. The Praetorian Guard was present in many provincial capitals throughout the empire, including Ephesus and Caesarea; and imperial servants in the Roman bureaucracy qualify as members of Caesar's household. With the weight of probability against Roman authorship, what conceivable provenance for the letter is left? Although a location at Corinth or Caesarea Maritima would overcome some of the objections, other reservations arise. Paul nowhere mentions a Corinthian imprisonment, and Acts reports no such physical danger as Paul faces in the prison from which he writes. Furthermore, the great distance between Caesarea and Philippi weighs almost as heavily against that location as against Rome. In the absence of any other compelling alternative, most scholars prefer Ephesus as the locus of the imprisonment from which Paul wrote Phil. Inscriptional evidence supports Ephesus as the location for a proconsular headquarters with a *praetorium*. "Caesar's household" then could refer to imperial bureaucrats of some type associated with the Roman administration. Moreover, a round trip from Ephesus to Philippi could be covered in less than ten days, allowing for the frequent exchanges anticipated in the letter.

The primary weakness of the Ephesian hypothesis is that neither Paul's letters nor Acts refer to an imprisonment there. Paul himself tells us, however, that he was in prison many times (2 Cor 11:23); he emphasizes that he was the victim of great "affliction . . . in Asia," being so "unbearably crushed" that he despaired of life (2 Cor 1:8). Clement of Rome reported that Paul "wore chains seven times" *(1 Clement)*, and the *Acts of Paul* refers to an Ephesian imprisonment (E. Hennecke 1963, 2:338). Although these late traditions cannot bear the weight of primary proof, they do offer cumulative evidence that an Ephesian imprisonment is not pure conjecture.

In support of the Ephesian over the Roman provenance one might appeal to Acts and Rom as well. Paul expresses his hopes to return to Philippi for a second visit, which would be possible from Ephesus. However, a visit from Rome does not seem a possibility; for if the Acts Chronology[§] is correct, by the time Paul was incarcerated in Rome he had already been in Philippi twice and could only anticipate a third visit. Moreover, as Rom tells us, even before he reached Rome his attention had already turned westward toward Spain. In light of that preoccupation, the hope to visit the Phil would be strange if he wrote from Rome; such a visit would have required Paul to backtrack to Philippi before launching the Spanish mission. Thus, while the Ephesian provenance of the letter is conjectural, for good reason most Pauline scholars prefer it to the alternatives.

The decision on this question inevitably influences the dating of the letter. A Roman origin would require a date late in the decade (58-60), whereas an Ephesian origin would argue for a date in the mid-fifties (55-56). The decision on the provenance of the letter affects where one places it in relation to Paul's other epistles and has importance for any discussion of development in Paul's theology.

2. *The Unity of the Letter.* Since J. Weiss[§] noticed the dramatic eruption "Look out for the dogs . . . " in Phil 3:2 in the early part of this century, scholars have disputed the letter's unity. Weiss concluded from his study that 3:2–4:1 "suits the context so badly . . . that one is again led to the hypothesis that this part did not originally belong with the rest of the letter" (1917; ET

1959, 387). E. Goodenough[§] later argued that the break between the first part of the letter and 3:2–4:1 is so jarring that it defies explanation on hypothetical grounds (1990, 90). The disjuncture is made more severe by the conclusion begun in 3:1: "Finally, my brethren, rejoice in the Lord." The explicitly final admonition appears to cross over from the body of the letter to its termination, yet its genial admonition is interrupted with an acrimonious warning beginning in 3:2 and extending through 4:1. This warning is so at odds with the rest of the letter that in the view of many scholars it indicates an originally separate letter.

Several proposals have arisen to account for the disjuncture. Among the more common reconstructions are those found in W. Schmithals (1972; A: 4:10-23 [a letter of thanksgiving]; B: 1:1–3:1, 4:4-7 [a prison letter]; C: 3:2–4:3, 4:8-9 [a warning letter]); G. Bornkamm[§] (1962; A: 1:1–3:1, 4:4-7, 4:21-23; B: 3:2–4:3; C: 4:10-20); B. Rahtjen (1959–60; A: 4:10-20; B: 1:1–2:30, 4:21-23; C: 3:1–4:9); and W. Marxsen (1964; A: 4:10-20; B: 1:1–3:1, 4:4-7, 4:21-23; C: 3:2–4:3, 4:8-9). J. Gnilka (1968), H. Koester (1962), and J. Müller-Bardorf (1957–58) have suggested other variations. Because of the widespread disagreement over how chapter 4 is to be divided, the multiple-letter hypothesis has enjoyed less acceptance for Phil than it has for 2 Corinthians. Moreover, the "finally" in 3:1 followed by a chapter of warning and admonition, is not without parallel; e.g., the "Finally . . . " of 1 Thess 4:1 is followed by a lengthy exhortation before the letter crosses over irrevocably into its ending.

V. Furnish (1963-64), R. Jewett (1970), and T. Pollard (1966–67), all on different grounds, have accepted the letter as a unity. Furnish argues that 3:1 is a crucial link verse—3:1a reaches back to chap. 2, and 3:1b stretches forward to chap. 3 and the special warning carried by Epaphroditus and Timothy to the church at Philippi. Pollard and Jewett find sufficient verbal correspondence between chapter 3 and the remainder of the letter to convince them that Phil was written and delivered as a single unit. But if the letter is a unity, then one must explain the rupture between 3:1 and 3:2. Had Paul suddenly received the unwelcome report of trouble in Philippi? And what caused him to wait until the end of the letter to express his thanksgiving for the help Epaphroditus brought from the church in Philippi?

The pseudepigraph *Laodiceans* may offer external evidence for the resolution of this dilemma. Although the author of *Laodiceans* closely follows Phil in his compilation, he shows no knowledge of Phil 3:2–4:3, suggesting that he was working from a copy of Phil different from our canonical version (P. Sellew 1994, 20-28). That multiple letters of Paul to the Phil were known in antiquity is proven by Polycarp's statement in his letter to the Philippians that when Paul was absent, he wrote "letters *(epistolas)* to you. . . . " (3:2; A. Lindemann, [1990] 41). Phil 3:2–4:3 may have been one of those letters; perhaps 4:10-20 was another. In the second century these letters probably were combined to form our canonical version of Phil.

3. *The Identity of Paul's Opposition.* Some scholars have sought to resolve the question of the letter's unity by identifying Paul's opposition. In 1:28 Paul warns his readers not to fear their "opponents." But who were these "opponents"? What was their quarrel with Paul? And what were they doing? In 1:17 we learn that they were preaching a partisan gospel intended to nettle the apostle. They urged Gentile Christians to accept circumcision (3:2); they rejected the importance of the cross in favor of the glory of the resurrected life (3:18); and they made a fetish of self-indulgence: "their god is their belly" (3:19). In the absence of any sustained discussion of the law, it is unlikely that the opponents were Judaizers like those in Gal; and in light of their proclamation of Christ (1:17), they could hardly have been from the synagogue. If the opposition was unified, then it may well have been a form of Jewish-Christian syncretism. Circumcision was retained as a sign of the covenant, and certain Hellenistic enthusiastic tendencies were embraced, allowing the initiates to pass over directly from death to the glory of the resurrected life. To these were added the emphasis of the gospel on grace and freedom, which allowed a form of indulgence that sounds proto-Gnostic in character. Schmithals has

argued that Paul was slow to recognize the character of the opposition and that this tardiness accounts for his confused response. But given the range of Paul's opposition elsewhere it is unlikely that he would have been confused about its nature in Philippi.

An alternative to this view is that Paul faced different groups of opponents in Philippi: Jews intent on reclaiming Gentile God-fearers attracted to the church, pagan converts who had relapsed into their morally lax ways, and Hellenistic enthusiasts who were critical of Paul's gospel. R. Martin (1980) argues that the attempt to avoid persecution may best explain the dual emphases in Phil, i.e., Jewish and Hellenistic. Jewish Christian missionaries, he claims, encouraged Philippian Christians to accept circumcision to avert persecution from Jewish revolutionaries inspired by a surging Jewish nationalism in Palestine. A Christian eschatology of glory sparked by Hellenistic enthusiasm provided the impulse for eluding persecution and suffering. While religious enthusiasm did exist in some of Paul's churches and would explain the libertine tendencies in Philippi, we have no evidence that a feverish "nationalism" penetrated the Diaspora in the way Martin suggests. And if Paul faced different groups, why are the lines between them so indistinct?

It would be a mistake to allow the competing claims, internal strife, and external threats to eclipse the genuine warmth and human tenderness in Phil, especially when these are compared to the acrimonious exchanges in Gal and Cor. We see here that Paul was not always the divine warrior. He was a pastoral figure so confident of the truth of his apocalyptic gospel (Apocalypticism[§]) that he could look past the immediate disturbances with confidence.

4. *The Provenance of 2:6-11.* Since the late nineteenth century, scholars have recognized the poetic or hymnic form of Phil 2:6-11 (Weiss 263); but both the character and the provenance of the hymn have been disputed (Martin 1983; J. T. Sanders 1971). The rhythm, parallelism, clearly defined strophes, poetic expression, and non-Pauline language confirm the pre-Pauline quality of this hymn; but whether its provenance was Jewish or Hellenistic has been vigorously debated. The opening verses of the hymn usher the worshiper into the celestial abode to witness Jesus' humble descent and glorious ascent to assume his cosmic lordship as the glorified Christ to whom all powers "in heaven and on earth and under the earth" (2:10) will do obeisance. These opening verses display unmistakable Hellenistic features. The closing doxology, however, echoes Isa 45:23: "To me every knee shall bow, /every tongue shall swear" (NRSV). Possibly the hymn's allusion to Jesus as a slave also draws on Isaiah. With these two emphases established, the hymn's origin cannot be found in either the Jewish or the Hellenistic milieu alone. What the hymn displays instead is a synthesis of both Jewish and Hellenistic elements. Traces of a Jewish background remain, but they have coalesced with a Hellenistic cosmology and soteriology (Sanders). Therefore, the hymn most likely came from a Hellenistic Jewish Christian mission of which we catch a glimpse in Stephen's vision of Christ's cosmic victory at his martyrdom (Martin 1983 113).

Recent commentaries on Phil include Bassler (2003), Bockmuehl (1998), Fee (1995), Hooker (2000), Osiek (2000), Walter, Reinmuth, and Lampe (1998), and Witherington (1994). Bormann (1995), Oakes (2001), Peterman (1997), and Pilhofer (1995) investigate the ancient cultural, social, and historical setting of the city of Philippi in relationship to Phil. Recent discussions of the Christ hymn in Phil 2:6-11 include Brucker (1997), Kennel (1995), Martin (1997), and Martin and Dodd (1998). Koperski (1996) analyzes the letter's Christology in 3:7-11. Rhetorical analyses of the letter include Davis (1999), Edart (2002), Holloway (2001), Reed (1997), Wansink (1996), and Williams (2002). Treatments of miscellaneous theological issues include Kittredge (1998) and Peterlin (1995).

Bibliography: J. Bassler, "The Letter of Paul to the Philippians," *NISB* (2003) 2099-2107. **F. W. Beare,** *Commentary on the Epistle to the Philippians* (HNTC, 1959). **M. Bockmuehl,**

The Epistle to the Philippians (BNTC 11, 1998). **L. Bormann,** *Philippi: Stadt und Christengemeinde zur Zeit des Paulus* (NovTSup 78, 1995). **G. Bornkamm,** "Der Philipperbrief als paulinische Briefsammlung," *Neotestamentica et Patristica* (NovTSup 6, 1962) 192-202. **R. Brucker,** *'Christushymnen' oder 'epideiktische Passagen'?: Studien zum Stilwechsel im Neuen Testament und seiner Umwelt* (FRLANT 176, 1997). **J. Calvin,** *Commentary on the Epistle of Paul to the Philippians* (1948) 56-58. **J.-F. Collange,** *L'Épître de Saint Paul aux Philippiens* (CNT 10a, 1973). **C. W. Davis,** *Oral Biblical Criticism: The Influence of the Principles of Orality on the Literary Structure of Paul's Epistle to the Philippians* (JSNTSup 172, 1999). **D. G. Dawe,** "A Fresh Look at the Kenotic Christologies," *SJT* 15 (1962) 337-49. **J.-B. Edart,** *L'Épître aux Philippiens: Rhétorique et composition stylistique* (Ebib n.s. 45, 2002.) **G. D. Fee,** *Paul's Letter to the Philippians* (NICNT, 1995). **V. P. Furnish,** "The Place and Purpose of Philippians III," *NTS* 10 (1963) 80-88. **J. Gnilka,** *Der Philipperbrief: Auslegung* (HTKNT 10, 1968). **E. Goodenough,** *Goodenough on the Beginnings of Christianity* (BJS 212, ed. A. T. Kraabel, 1990). **P. N. Harrison,** *Polycarp's Two Epistles to the Philippians* (1936). **E. Hennecke,** *NT Apocrypha* (2 vols., ed. W. Schneemelcher; ET, ed. R. M. Wilson, 1963). **P. A. Holloway,** *Consolation in Philippians: Philosophical Sources and Rhetorical Strategy* (SNTSMS 112, 2001). **M. Hooker,** "The Letter to the Philippians," *NIB* (2000) 11:467-550. **R. Jewett,** "The Epistolary Thanksgiving and the Integrity of Philippians," *NovT* 12 (1970) 40-53. **G. Kennel,** *Frühchristliche Hymnen?: Gattungskritische Studien zur Frage nach den Liedern der frühen Christenheit* (WMANT 71, 1995). **C. B. Kittredge,** *Community and Authority: The Rhetoric of Obedience in the Pauline Tradition* (HTS 45, 1998). **J. Knox,** *Marcion and the NT: An Essay in the Early History of the Canon* (1942). **H. Koester,** "The Purpose of the Polemic of a Pauline Fragment (Phil. III)," *NTS* 8 (1962) 317-32. **V. Koperski,** *The Knowledge of Christ Jesus My Lord: The High Christology of Philippians 3:7-11* (Contributions to Biblical Exegesis and Theology 16, 1996). **J. B. Lightfoot,** *Saint Paul's Epistle to the Philippians* (1896). **A. Lindemann,** "Paul in the Writings of the Apostolic Fathers," *Paul and the Legacies of Paul* (1990) 25-45. **T. W. Manson,** "St. Paul in Ephesus," *BJRL* 23 (1939) 182-200. **R. P. Martin,** *Philippians* (NCB, 1980); *Carmen Christi, Philippians 2:5-11 in Recent Interpretation and in the Setting of Early Christian Worship* (SNTSMS 4, 1983); *A Hymn of Christ: Philippians 2:5-11 in Recent Interpretation and in the Setting of Early Christian Worship* (1997). **R. P. Martin and B. J. Dodd,** eds., *Where Christology Began: Essays on Philippians 2* (1998). **W. Marxsen,** *Introduction to the NT* (ET 1964) 59-68. **J. Müller-Bardorff,** "Zur Frage der literarischen Einheit des Philipperbriefes," *WZ(J)* 7 (1957-58) 591-604. **P. Oakes,** *Philippians: From People to Letter* (SNTSMS 110, 2001). **C. Osiek,** *Philippians, Philemon* (ANTC, 2000). **D. Peterlin,** *Paul's Letter to the Philippians in the Light of Disunity in the Church* (NovTSup 79, 1995). **G. W. Peterman,** *Paul's Gift from Philippi: Conventions of Gift-Exchange and Christian Giving* (SNTSMS 92, 1997). **P. Pilhofer,** *Philippi* (2 vols., WUNT 87, 119, 1995). **T. E. Pollard,** "The Integrity of Philippians," *NTS* 13 (1966-67) 57-66. **B. D. Rahtjen,** "The Three Letters of Paul to the Philippians," *NTS* 6 (1959-60) 167-73. **J. T. Reed,** *A Discourse Analysis of Philippians: Method and Rhetoric in the Debate over Literary Integrity* (JSNTSup 136, 1997). **J. T. Sanders,** *The NT Christological Hymns: Their Historical Religious Background* (SNTSMS 15, 1971). **W. Schenk,** "Der Philipperbrief in der neueren Forschung (1945-85)," *ANRW* II.25.4 (1987) 3280-313. **W. Schmithals,** "The False Teachers of the Epistle to the Philippians," *Paul and the Gnostics* (1972) 65-122. **P. Sellew,** "Laodiceans and the Philippians Fragments Hypothesis," *HTR* 87 (1994) 17-28. **N. Walter, E. Reinmuth und P. Lampe,** *Die Briefe an die Philipper, Thessalonicher und an Philemon* (NTD, 1998[18]). **C. S. Wansink,** *Chained in Christ: The Experience and Rhetoric of Paul's Imprisonments* (JSNTSup 130, 1996). **J. Weiss,** *Earliest Christianity: A History of the Period AD 30-150* (2 vols., 1917; ET 1959).

D. K. Williams, *Enemies of the Cross of Christ: The Terminology of the Cross and Conflict in Philippians* (JSTNSup 45, 2002). **B. Witherington, III,** *Friendship and Finances in Philippi: The Letter of Paul to the Philippians* (New Testament in Context, 1994).

C. J. ROETZEL

Colossians, Letter to the

1. *The Early Church.* The earliest interpretations of Col stem from Marcion[§] and the Valentinian Gnostics (Gnostic Interpretation[§]). Marcion characteristically omitted Col 1:15-16 from his text, although he did find support in 2:16-17, 21 for rejecting the Mosaic law. The Valentinians saw in 1:15-17 and 2:13-15 proof of the Savior's spiritual origin and his triumph over the rulers (*Irenaeus Haer.* 1.3.4; Clement of Alexandria Exc. *Theod.* 69-74.1). Reinterpreting many of the same verses, Irenaeus[§] and Tertullian[§] denied any fundamental opposition between God and the material world or between the Christian gospel and the Jewish law (e.g., Adv. Marc. 5.19). Both Ambrosiaster and Theodore foreshadow contemporary exegetical methodology by interpreting each verse in the light of the epistle's overall argument. Ambrosiaster's insistence that all humans are created free and that slavery results from sin is striking, as is Theodore's singularly contorted argument that "of his love" (1:13, AT) indicates Christ's adoption. Similarly several historical issues, much debated in contemporary scholarhsip, were also contested by these early exegetes. Whether Archippus (Marcionite prologue) or Epaphras (Theodore) had first preached to the Colossians and whether Paul[†§] was personally acquainted with them (Chrysostom, Severian, Theodoret; Marcionite prologue, Theodore) seem to have hinged on the variant readings of 1:7. The location of Paul's imprisonment was alternatively noted as Ephesus (Marcionite prologue) or Rome (Chrysostom). While the Marcionite prologue simply stated that the Colossian community was attacked by false prophets (Prophecy and Prophets, New Testament[†§]), Chrysostom described the false teachings as the Jewish and Greek practices of approaching God through angels (so also Severian and Theodoret, who stated that this practice was still prevalent in Phrygia). Theodore identified the opponents as Jewish legalists who feared (but did not worship) angels. Ambrosiaster asserted that astrological beliefs and Jewish festivals lay behind 2:16-17 and 2:18-19 respectively.

The interpretation of 1:15-17 was highly disputed during the Arian (Arius[§]) and christological controversies. The primary issue dividing exegetes was whether the term "image" referred to Christ's divine or human nature. Origen interpreted it as proof of Christ's unity with God, despite his subordinate status (*De Prin.* 1.2.2-5). The Arian reading of "image" held that it demonstrated Christ's status as a created being. The orthodox response took two forms: Chrysostom adopted the more common understanding of "image" as a reference to Christ's invisible divine nature and its absolute equality with God. Theodore devoted one-third of his commentary to 1:13-20, arguing that in 1:15 "image" applied to Christ's human nature and thus that this passage concerned redemption and not the creation of the world. Other points of debate included: whether "first-born" implies temporal priority (Severian) or preeminence (Theodore, Pelagius); whether baptism removes sin (Chrysostom, Severian) or mortality (Theodore); and whether according to 2:15 Christ stripped off the body (the Latin fathers) or the powers of evil (Chrysostom, Severian, Theodore, Theodoret).

2. *The Medieval Period.* Until the advent of scholasticism, most medieval exegesis was conservative and largely preserved ancient commentaries, paraphrased the text, and quoted the fathers. Scholasticism brought a new interest in clarifying Paul's Theology (New Testament Theology[†§]). Peter Lombard[§] and Thomas Aquinas[§], both of whom wrote commentaries or lectured on Col, noted the fathers' often divergent interpretations and weighed their relative authority. Because of the philosophical basis of scholasticism, Col 2:8 became the subject of intense debate. Lombard echoed Paul's warning against deceptive philosophy in his response to P. Abelard's[§] reduction of the Trinity to a philosophical problem. According to Aquinas, however,

Paul did not condemn philosophy in its entirety; the scholastic use of philosophy was vindicated by philosophy's proper application and subordination to Christ.

3. *Sixteenth to Eighteenth Centuries.* Renaissance and Reformation commentaries reflect the renewed interest in classical antiquity, the development of Textual Criticism*§, a commitment to Antiochene over Alexandrian exegesis, and a critical approach to the fathers. Erasmus's§ annotations (1516; final ed. 1535) began by addressing the location of Colossae and refuting the popular opinion that the Colossians were inhabitants of Rhodes (where the Colossus stands). Erasmus's citation of classical authors (1:1), examination of textual variants (1:1, 7), appeal to philology (1:1; 2:18), and attention to idiomatic phrases (1:13) and figures of speech (1:23) demonstrate his humanistic approach to biblical interpretation. He engaged in patristic exegesis but rarely quoted the scholastics; of his contemporaries, he drew upon Lefèvre d'Etaples, the classical scholar and Pauline commentator (1512). Erasmus's comments on 1:15 were brief, although unlike his scholastic predecessors his christological opinions developed through the commentary's successive editions. While nearly one-third of his commentary is devoted to 2:8-23, his notes on 2:8 are surprisingly brief and do not address the scholastic debate on philosophy.

Of the Protestant reformers, the most important Colossian commentators were P. Melanchthon§ and Calvin§; Luther's§ interpretation of Col must be sought in occasional comments and in his sermons. In his *scholia* on Col (1527), Melanchthon used classical rhetorical categories to analyze the letter's structure and meaning. Contemporary theological and social issues also guided his exegesis. His lengthy comment on 2:8 was sparked by the debate between Luther and Erasmus on the freedom of the will. While maintaining the sovereignty of God (1:15; 3:3), Melanchthon, as both Reformer and humanist, vindicated humanistic scriptural interpretation and the philosophical analysis of reality and social morals. Philosophy errs when it goes beyond its divinely given propaedeutic function and formulates opinions about God's will or claims to impart virtue. In response to T. Müntzer's§ rebellion (1525), Melanchthon justified a conservative approach to social and religious change and a separation of ecclesiastical and spiritual authority in his extensive comment on 2:23. He argued that since secular laws are divinely given, civil officials do not require ecclesiastical guidance. Civil ordinances, unless enjoining sin, must always be obeyed; only those ecclesiastical traditions that blaspheme the gospel or endanger the weak may be disobeyed.

Although conversant with the fathers, Calvin wrote his commentary (1548) with different theological issues in mind (see his discussion on 1:15); and not surprisingly, in the context of the Protestant break with Rome, Col was often read by the Reformers as a polemic against medieval Catholicism. Calvin declared that Papists, ignoring the Christology of 1:12, based the system of indulgences on the mistaken notion of the insufficiency of Christ's suffering (1:24). Following Luther, Calvin argued that the "worship of angels" (2:18) referred to papal religion—i.e., the worship of the saints—and that 2:23 was a graphic description of monasticism. According to Calvin, Paul condemned papal theology because it erroneously sought knowledge of things unseen and unrevealed (2:8, 18; commenting on 2:8, Luther had condemned scholasticism because it neglected an eschatological analysis of reality in favor of an Aristotelian one). With the exception of the Eucharist, Calvin condemned religious ceremonies as "shadows" abolished by Christ (2:14, 17).

In contrast, many commentaries of the seventeenth and eighteenth centuries lapse into an unimaginative orthodoxy. Some contain no more than footnotes (as by the proverbial J. Fell) or do little more than enumerate doctrines found within each verse (as by J. Fergusson and P. Bayne). The most substantial treatment of Col from this period was produced by J. Davenant, bishop of Salisbury, whose two-volume work went through several editions and was hailed as extraordinary through the nineteenth century. Davenant's exposition contained numerous polemics against papal teachings on apostolic succession (1:1), justification by works (1:12), and Christ (1:12); he was conversant with authors from the classical period up to his contemporaries, and he continued the Rhetorical*§ analysis begun by Melanchthon. Other influential commentators on Col from this period include H. Grotius§, G. Estius, and J. Bengel§.

4. *Nineteenth to Twentieth Centuries.* Modern investigations of Col have concentrated on a limited number of issues, primarily its authenticity and the identification of the Colossian opponents; some attention has also been given to its use of traditional materials and its theological emphases.

a. Authenticity and dating. The Pauline authorship of Col had been generally accepted until 1839, when E. Mayerhoff argued that the letter contained lexical, stylistic, and theological differences from Paul, was dependent upon Eph, and could be traced to a conflict with Cerinthus. Although other nineteenth-century critics cast further doubt on the authorship of Col (most notably F. C. Baur§ 1845, who placed it in the context of second-century Gnosticism, and H. Holtzmann§, who thought the author of Eph had revised Col), its authenticity was still generally affirmed through the middle of the twentieth century (so M. Dibelius and H. Greeven 1953; P. O'Brien 1982). Since the 1960s, however, an increasing defense of Colossians's pseudonymity (E. Lohse 1971; W. Bujard 1973; E. Schweizer 1982) has occurred. Col lacks certain connective words and inferential particles characteristic of Paul (Lohse 1971, 84-91); the length and complexity of the letter's sentences and its lack of logical argument (Bujard 1973, 72-75, 129) are clear indications of non-Pauline authorship.

The dating of Col is primarily dependent on one's judgment of its authenticity. Those who hold it to be genuine have been guided by conventional theories of Paul's theological development and his place of imprisonment (4:3, 10, 18). A Roman or Caesarean (E. Lohmeyer 1930) imprisonment would place Colossians's developed theology at the end of Paul's career (c. 57-61), although there are significant objections to both theories. Based on Paul's hints of trouble in Ephesus (c. 55; Rom 16:3-4; 2 Cor 1:8) and its proximity to Colossae, some scholars have suggested this location (G. Duncan 1930). If Col is held to be pseudonymous, the presumed author's imprisonment contributes to the image of the suffering apostle perpetuated by his followers. In this case dating must be based on Ephesians's generally accepted dependence on Col (cf. E. Best 1997); the composition of Ephesians (prior to c. 100; Ignatius Pol. 5.1; Smyrn. 1.1) would provide the latest date and Paul's death the earliest. In light of the destruction of Colossae c. 60 (Tacitus Ann. 14.27), the intended audience must be sought elsewhere, perhaps in southwest Asia Minor.

b. Identity and theology of Colossian opponents. The precise identification of the Colossian opponents has proved to be elusive. In addition to the difficulties of determining whether the language of the opponents has been adopted (e.g., whether "philosophy" or "mystery" was a self-designation) or of distinguishing polemic from independently formulated arguments, this project has been beset by recurring exegetical difficulties: (1) whether angels (2:18) were understood as malevolent or beneficial; (2) whether the *stoicheia* (2:8, 20; cf. Gal 4:3, 9) referred to these angels or to the four primal elements, the Jewish law, or religious regulations; (3) whether *thrēskeia tōn angelōn* (2:18) consisted in worshiping angels or in the angelic worship of God; (4) whether *embateuō* (2:18) referred to initiation into a mystery cult or to entering heaven; (5) whether ritual and ascetic practices (2:16, 20-23) were necessary prerequisites for salvation or required acts of subservience. This constellation of disputed issues has further resulted in conflicting descriptions of the opponents' theology. Most scholars concur that it was a synthesis of several religious traditions (including Gnosticism, Phrygian religious practices, Hellenistic philosophy, and Jewish apocalyptic and mysticism), although no consensus exists on the role Judaism played in their theology.

J. B. Lightfoot[§] (1875) understood the Colossian theology as a mixture of heterodox Jewish sabbath observance and dietary laws with a Gnostic interest in wisdom, cosmology, intermediary beings, and asceticism. Dibelius[§] similarly argued (F. Francis and W. Meeks 1975, 61-121; followed by Lohse) that angels and the *stoicheia* were enslaving deities and that *embateuō* was a technical term for initiation into a mystery cult; he concluded that the opponents proclaimed a gnostic mystery religion that required preparatory ascetic practices and lacked any significant Jewish elements. G. Bornkamm[§] (Francis and Meeks, 123-45) understood the angels as positive forces who imposed ritual and ascetic practices; in contrast to Dibelius, he balanced pagan and Persian influences with the Jewish origin of these practices and cosmology. Recently parallels between the Colossian philosophy and the Nag Hammadi Gnostic texts *Hypostasis of the Archons, Eugnostos of the Blessed, Sophia of Jesus Christ, Apocryphon of John*, and *Zostrianos* have been cited. Rejecting this widely held theory of Gnostic origins, Lyonnet explained the Colossian philosophy purely on the basis of the Essene interest in purity, wisdom, angelology, and the law found in the Dead Sea Scrolls*[§] (Francis and Meeks, 147-61).

A more convincing theory of Jewish origins argues for parallels with Jewish apocalyptic (Apocalypticism*[§]) and mystical literature: Francis (Francis and Meeks, 163-207) argued that *thrēskeia tōn angelōn* should be understood as the angelic worship of God glimpsed during a mystical ascent; this foretaste of heaven assured the adherent of salvation. A third line of interpretation (most recently C. Arnold 1995) draws significantly on archaeological evidence (Archaeology and the Hebrew Bible*[§], Archaeology and New Testament Interpretation*[§], Archaeology and Biblical Studies*[§]) and argues that the Colossian theology was a synthesis of Judaism (of varying degrees) with local Phrygian religious expression, including asceticism, interest in intermediary beings, and folk belief. A final line of interpretation understands the Hellenistic philosophical schools as the key to the Colossian philosophy. Schweizer links the Colossian interest in ritual laws, asceticism, and the four primal elements *(stoicheia)* to Pythagoreanism. R. DeMaris (1994) argues for a blend of Middle Platonism with Jewish and Christian elements, while T. Martin (1996) identifies the opponents as Cynics. In view of such diverse results, further investigations should refine a reliable methodology for analyzing polemical literature and must contain a historically grounded explanation of the origin of the particular syncretism observed.

c. Use of traditional materials. On the basis of stylistic and linguistic criteria 1:15-20 have been identified as a christological hymn that presents Christ as a preexistent being (v. 15) whose supremacy extends over both creation (vv. 16-17) and redemption (vv. 18-20). Numerous structural analyses have been proposed, and there is debate over the extent to which the original hymn has been altered and whether those alterations were done by the author of Col. The history-of-religions background (Religionsgeschichtliche Schule*[§]) of the hymn is variously identified as philosophically influenced Judaism, pre-Christian Gnosis, the Jewish Day of Atonement, rabbinic biblical interpretation, Hellenistic Jewish wisdom speculation, the heavenly Anthropos, and Jewish monotheistic confessions. Despite the failure to achieve consensus on these issues, most scholars acknowledge the presence of a pre-Pauline hymn in these verses; some, however, have suggested that they are better understood as the author's own composition from fragments of traditional materials (Dibelius and Greeven, 10-12; O'Brien, 36). Form-critical studies (New Testament Form Criticism*) have also identified two other liturgical fragments: Col 1:12-14 and 2:13c-15 (some scholars include as much as vv. 9-15). Both portray the work of Christ as a victory over the forces of evil and may stem from a baptismal liturgy (see G. Cannon 1983, 37-49). Earlier exegetes followed the patristic understanding of the *cheirographon* ("record," v. 14) as the pact made between humanity and the devil; more appropriate is the meaning "note of indebtedness," although its exact meaning and relationship to dogma are still debated. But again the lack of consensus on the extent, structure, and setting of these fragments has led some to reject their identification as traditional material.

The virtue and vice catalogues in 3:5-12 contain prohibitions and encouragement to a conventional morality. Discussion has centered on the precise form and source of this type of exhortation (Hellenistic, Jewish, or Iranian); whether the elements of the catalogues were chosen to fit the precise situation addressed, e.g., baptism in Col (Cannon, 51-94), remains an open question. Of recent interest are the household codes (*Haustafeln;* 3:18-4:1), which detail the duties and responsibilities of the members of the ancient household. The majority of research has again addressed the issues of form and source (Stoicism, Hellenistic Judaism, Aristotle); more pertinent to Col in particular is the observation that in the letter the household codes have been only marginally christianized (so also 1 Pet 2:18-3:7; cf. Eph 5:22-6:9) and that despite their restriction of women's behavior for the sake of the church's social acceptance (E. Johnson 1992; see also C. Martin 1991), they do contain a critique of the slave system (D. Balch 1981; for a different view, see M. D'Angelo 1994).

d. Theological emphases and Pauline response. Comparatively less emphasis has been given to analyzing the author's response to the Colossian teaching. His aim is clearly to ensure that the Col continue to obey the gospel as it had been delivered to them (1:23). Previously hidden, this newly manifest gospel (2:2; 4:3), which consists in Christ's presence among the Gentiles (1:27), is now reaching the entire world (1:6, 23). The angelic beings with whom the Colossians have become obsessed are not relevant to Christian experience. Preeminent in all spheres (1:12-20; 3:11) and embodying the divine (2:9), Christ rescued them from oppression and offers forgiveness through baptism (1:12-14); their allegiance to him alone must be vigilantly maintained (1:23). Further analysis of the author's theological construction in response to the Colossian teaching is necessary. The polemical response to a syncretistic religious movement rooted in Judaism may later have been understood as an attack on Judaism (e.g., by Marcion). The author of Ephesians may have sought to reinterpret this seeming contradiction in the Pauline writings in his appropriation of Col and its traditional materials (J. Maclean 1995). In addition, the role of moral instruction in community formation (W. Meeks 1993) is a fruitful new line of approach.

Recent commentaries on Col include Bullard (2003), Hay (2000), Hübner (1997), Lincoln (2000), Luz (1998), MacDonald (2000), and Schweizer (1997). Barclay (1997) provides an introduction to the letter. Stettler analyzes the Christ hymn of Col 1:15-20. Discussions of various other issues in the epistle include Bevere (2003), Stanhartinger (1999), and Wilson (1997).

Bibliography: C. E. **Arnold,** *The Colossian Syncretism: The Interface Between Christianity and Folk Belief at Colossae* (WUNT 77, 1995). D. L. **Balch,** *Let Wives Be Submissive: The Domestic Code in 1 Peter* (SLBMS 26, 1981). J. M. G. **Barclay,** *Colossians and Philemon* (New Testament Guides, 1997). F. C. **Baur,** *Paulus, der Apostel Jesu Christi* (1845; ET 1873-75). E. **Best,** "Who Used Whom? The Relationship of Ephesians and Colossians," *NTS* 43 (1997) 72-96. A. R. **Bevere,** *Sharing in the Inheritance: Identity and the Moral Life in Colossians* (JSNTSup 226, 2003). W. **Bujard,** *Stilanalytische Untersuchungen zum Kolosserbrief als Beitrag zur Methodik von Sprachvergleichen* (SUNT 11, 1973). R. **Bullard,** "The Letter of Paul to the Colossians," *NISB* (2003) 2107-14. J. **Calvin,** *Commentarii in Pauli Epistolas* (ed. H. Feld, Ioannis Calvini Opera Exegetica 16, 1992). G. E. **Cannon,** *The Use of Traditional Materials in Colossians* (1983). L. **Cope,** "On Rethinking the Philemon-Colossians Connection," *BR* 30 (1985) 45-50. J. **Chrysostom,** *Homilies on the Epistle of St. Paul the Apostle to the Colossians* (NPNF 1.13; 1983). M. R. **D'Angelo,** "Colossians," *Searching the Scriptures,* vol. 2, *A Feminist Commentary* (ed. E. Schüssler Fiorenza, 1994) 313-24. J. **Davenant,** *An Exposition of the Epistle of St. Paul to the Colossians* (1831-32). M. **Dibelius and**

H. Greeven, *An die Kolosser, Epheser, an Philemon, erklärt von M. Dibelius* (HNT 12, 1953[3]).
R. E. DeMaris, *The Colossian Controversy: Wisdom in Dispute at Colossae* (JSNTSup 96, 1994). **G. S. Duncan,** *St. Paul's Ephesian Ministry* (1930). **F. O. Francis and W. A. Meeks** (eds.), *Conflict at Colossae: A Problem in the Interpretation of Early Christianity* (SBLSBS 4, 1975). **M. Goulder,** "Colossians and Barbelo," *NTS* 41 (1995) 601-19. **D. M. Hay,** *Colossians* (ANTC, 2000). **A. Hockel,** *Christus, Der Ertsgeborene: Zur Geschichte der Exegese von Kol 1,15* (1965). **H. Hübner,** *An Philemon, an die Kolosser, an die Epheser* (HNT 12, 1997). **E. E. Johnson,** "Colossians," *Women's Bible Commentary* (ed. C. A. Newsom and S. H. Ringe, 1992) 346-48. **J. B. Lightfoot,** *Saint Paul's Epistles to the Colossians and to Philemon* (18793). **A. T. Lincoln,** "The Letter to the Colossians," *NIB* (2000) 11: 551-670. **E. Lohmeyer,** *Die Briefe an die Philipper, an die Kolosser, und an Philemon* (1930). **E. Lohse,** *Colossians and Philemon* (Hermeneia, 1971). **U. Luz,** "Kolosser," *Die Briefe an die Galater, Epheser und Kolosser* (J. Becker und U. Luz, NTD 8.1, 1998[18]). **M. Y. MacDonald,** *Colossians and Ephesians* (SP 17, 2000). **J. K. B. Maclean,** "Ephesians and the Problem of Colossians: Interpretation of Text and Tradition in Eph 1:1-2:10" (diss., Harvard University, 1995). **C. J. Martin,** "The *Haustafeln* (Household Code) in African American Biblical Interpretation: 'Free Slaves' and Subordinate Women," *Stony the Road We Trod: African American Biblical Interpretation* (ed. C. H. Felder, 1991) 206-31. **T. W. Martin,** *By Philosophy and Empty Deceit: Colossians as Response to a Cynic Critique* (JSNTSup 118, 1996). **E. T. Mayerhoff,** *Der Brief an die Colosser mit vornehmlicher Berücksichtigung der drei Pastoralbriefe* (1838). **W. A. Meeks,** " 'To Walk Worthily of the Lord': Moral Formation in the Pauline School Exemplified by the Letter to Colossians," *Hermes and Athena: Biblical Exegesis and Philosophical Theology* (ed. E. Stump and T. P. Flint, 1993) 71-74. **P. Melanchthon,** *Paul's Letter to the Colossians* (HTIBS, 1989). **P. T. O'Brien,** *Colossians, Philemon* (WBC 44, 1982). **A. Reeves** (ed.), *Erasmus' Annotations on the NT: Galatians to the Apocalypse* (SHCT 52, 1993). **J. A. Robinson,** *Pelagius's Expositions of Thirteen Epistles of St. Paul* (TS 9.2, 1926). **W. Schenk,** "Der Kolosserbrief in der neueren Forschung (1945-85)," *ANRW* II.25.4 (1987) 3327-64. **E. Schweizer,** *The Letter to the Colossians: A Commentary* (1982); *Der Brief an die Kolosser* (EKKNT 12, 1997[4]). **K. Staab,** *Pauluskommentare aus der griechischen Kirche* (NTAbh 15, 1933). **A. Standhartinger,** *Studien zur Entstehungsgeschichte und Intention des Kolosserbriefs* (NovTSup 94, 1999). **C. Stettler,** *Der Kolosserhymnus: Untersuchungen zu Form, traditionsgeschtlichem Hintergrund und Aussage von Kol 1, 15-20* (WUNT 2/131, 2000). **H. B. Swete,** *Theodori Episcopi Mopsuesteni in Epistolas b. Pauli Commentarii* (1880-82). **H. J. Vogels,** *Ambrosiastri Qui Dicitur Commentarius in Epistulas Paulinas* (CSEL 81, 1966-69). **M. F. Wiles,** *The Divine Apostle: The Interpretation of St Paul's Epistles in the Early Church* (1967). **W. T. Wilson,** *The Hope of Glory: Education and Exhortation in the Epistle to the Colossians* (NovTSup 88, 1997). **N. T. Wright,** "Poetry and Theology in Colossians 1:15-20," *NTS* 36 (1990) 444-68.

J. B. Maclean

Thessalonians, First and Second Letters to the

1. *Place in Early Christian Literature.* The epistolary prescripts of these works claim authorship by the apostle Paul[†§]. The letters were alluded to and quoted by various early Christian writers and documents in the late first century to early second century C.E. (Ignatius of Antioch, the *Didache*, Polycarp of Smyrna, and the *Shepherd of Hermas*). Parts of 1 Thess (but not 2 Thess) are found in P[46], the earliest manuscript of the Pauline corpus, which dates from about 200 C.E. Second Thess is also discussed along with other biblical apocalyptic literature (Apocalypticism*[§]) in Hippolytus of Rome's *De antichristo*. Dozens of patristic and medieval commentaries exist for both Thessalonian letters, including those by Chrysostom[§], Theodore of Mopsuestia[§], Theodoret of Cyrrhus[§], in the East, along with those of Jerome[§], Rabanus Maurus[§], Peter Lombard[§], Thomas Aquinas[§], and L. Valla[§] in the West.

2. *The Renaissance and the Reformation.* Although Luther[§] wrote no commentary on the Thessalonian letters, several other Reformers did, including Calvin[§] and T. Beza[§]. Calvin's interpretation is notable for his descriptions of present sufferings as evidence of the Thessalonians being made worthy of the kingdom of God (2 Thess 1:5) as well as for his discussion of attacks from the enemies of Christians as indicating the seal of the Christians' adoption by God.

3. *Modern Interpretation.* The central problems dealt with by modern interpretation of the Thessalonian letters are their relation to each other and their authorship. Modern scholarship on 2 Thess began with H. Grotius[§] in the seventeenth century. Grotius examined both letters and argued that Paul could not have written 1 Thess with no mention of the "sign" referred to in 2 Thess 3:17, then shortly thereafter have referred to such a sign in 2 Thess (2 Thess 2:2) and warned against a forged Pauline letter that lacked it. Since Grotius believed Paul wrote both letters, he concluded that 2 Thess was written first. Grotius also recognized the strongly inflammatory character of the rhetoric of 2 Thess, which he believed made it likely that the early church would not have made the letter public until it became politically safer (during the reign of Vespasian). Thus the conventional position of 2 Thess in the Canon[§] relates to when it was published rather than to when it was written.

J. Schmidt was the first to argue against Pauline authorship for 2 Thess (1801), showing inconsistencies between the two letters if taken at face value as Pauline. Schmidt reasoned that 2 Thess 2:1-2 presupposed an earlier letter purporting to be by Paul that taught a speedy arrival of Christ's second coming, which letter 2 Thess attacks as a forgery. However, the most plausible candidate for such a letter bearing Paul's name was, in Schmidt's view, 1 Thess (assuming that it had been written first). He held that there were insuperable problems associated with the maintenance of Pauline authorship for both of the Thessalonian epistles because the conflict of the eschatologies espoused in the two letters mitigated against their having the same author—especially given the warnings against forged Pauline letters in 2 Thess 2:1-2 and the "authentication" in 3:17. Hence, Schmidt concluded against Pauline authorship of 2 Thess.

F. Kern (1839) made a detailed analysis of 2 Thess 2:1-2, sketching the history of interpretation of that passage as organized around possible interpretations of the Parousia of Christ. He stressed that the man of lawlessness was a real person, an insight that led Kern to look for the man's identity among the Roman emperors of the first century C.E. The most likely candidate, Kern thought, was Nero; hence the prophecy of the man of lawlessness belongs to a time (68-70 C.E.) that would make Pauline authorship of 2 Thess impossible.

F. C. Baur[§] (1845) argued against the authenticity of 1 Thess primarily by showing the similarities between 1 Thess and the material about Paul's Thessalonian ministry in Acts 17; he also believed that the similarities between 1 Thess and 1 Cor were too great. Baur likewise attacked the Pauline authorship of 2 Thess, noting that the theology of the apocalyptic section in chap. 2 is too Jewish-Christian and in his view not classically Pauline enough for Paul to have written the letter. For the true Pauline view of the second coming of Christ, Baur turned exclusively to 1 Cor 15, finding the differences between that chapter and 2 Thess 2 simply too great for 2 Thess to be genuinely Pauline.

R. Lipsius (1830-92) held that Baur's objections to Pauline authorship of 1 Thess were groundless, since the audience to which 1 Thess was addressed included "enthusiastic, eccentric prophets" (1854). Therefore, because the situation in Thessalonika was in some ways similar to that in Corinth, similarities between 1 Thess and 1 Cor are not surprising. Responding in 1855 with an article in which he attempted to identify the situation that evoked both of the letters to the Thessalonians, Baur concluded not only that Paul did not write either letter but also that 1 Thess was literarily dependent on 2 Thess; thus the latter must have been written first.

A. Hilgenfeld[§] (1862) was very critical of Baur for his treatment of 1 Thess but agreed with him in opposing Pauline authorship of 2 Thess. Regarding Baur's statement that in 1 Thess "there is so little for criticism to lay hold of," Hilgenfeld found the information about the Thessalonian community in the letter to be essentially consistent with that in Acts 17. The reason that 1 Thess is so different from other genuinely Pauline letters is that "the relationship of the apostle to the Christians in Thessalonika was in no way strained." Hence Hilgenfeld held that "Paul appears here, in fact, not yet at the height of his dialectic and his apostolic consciousness, as we see that his struggle against a Christian Judaism, which was forced into the Churches he had planted, made him; but Paul appears in this letter in the total kindness of his affectionate care for a young community of Christians, in their depression requiring fatherly words of encouragement" (1862, 242). Thus the reason for the great differences between 1 Thess and the *Hauptbriefe* ("chief letters," i.e., Rom, 1-2 Cor, Gal) is that Paul had not yet risen to the occasions that produced the lofty and powerful letters to the Romans, the Corinthians, and the Galatians. However, 1 Thess is appropriate to the earlier occasion.

The fine commentary by W. Bornemann (1894) includes an exhaustive history of scholarship on and interpretation of both epistles, especially as regards the eschatology of 2 Thess 2:1-12, from the early patristic period to 1894. Bornemann accepted Pauline authorship for both epistles, arguing that their similarities, along with the lack of personal and local information in 2 Thess, are due to the fact that Paul had practically nothing new to say to the Thessalonians. Bornemann noted an impersonal and objective character in 2 Thess due to its being not a personal letter, but a hortatory, official letter to the community. The two letters are similar in their common eschatological orientation as well as in form. They differ in that several sections in 2 Thess are not found in 1 Thess: the mention of punitive judgment at the Parousia of Christ in 1:8-12; the eschatological section of 2:1-12 with the request for prayer by the writer for the spread of the gospel despite those who are opposed to the faith; the discipline of work commanded in 3:13-16; and finally, the remark about the peculiar attestation of letters truly by Paul. Bornemann admitted that these peculiarities raise a number of questions about the authenticity of 2 Thess; but he offered a psychological explanation (Psychology and Biblical Studies*[§]) to account for the differences, rather than appealing to a misunderstanding of Paul's earlier letter or to Paul's own unclarity or lack of certainty.

H. Holtzmann[§] (1901), writing in favor of Pauline authorship of 2 Thess, pointed out the difference in tone between "we thank God" and "we are obliged to thank God" in the two letters. He concluded that 2 Thess 2:1-12 is a new section (without parallel in 1 Thess) but that the rest of the letter consists of paraphrases and variations of 1 Thess. Holtzmann agreed with

Bornemann that the author of the second letter had known the first letter and was somehow dependent on it. However, he argued that one can understand 2 Thess only in light of Paul's intention to replace the first, longer letter, which accounts for what Holtzmann termed the *Ersatzcharakter* (replacement character) of 2 Thess.

W. Wrede's[§] 1903 monograph marks a watershed in interpretation of 2 Thess. Wrede explored several issues, most notably that of the literary dependency of 2 Thess on 1 Thess. Comparing the texts of the two letters in parallel columns, he found that there were major parallels to 1 Thess 1:2-12 in 2 Thess 1:3-12. Other parallels were found at 2 Thess 2:13-14 (parallel to 1 Thess 2:12-13) and 2 Thess 3:6-15 (parallel to 1 Thess 4:1-5:23). Most notably, parallels to 1 Thess were lacking at 2 Thess 2:1-12, the much-debated eschatological section. The similarities between 1 and 2 Thess were striking to Wrede, particularly if Paul was the author of both epistles and if they were supposed to have been written within about three months of each other, especially since whole phrases seem to have been taken over from 1 Thess to 2 Thess without change. Wrede concluded that the parallels between the letters were simply too close for Paul to have been the author of both. Also, he held the eschatological differences between the two letters to be quite sharp, since 1 Thess 5:1-4 advises that the day of the Lord is coming at an unknown time, as a "thief in the night," whereas 2 Thess 2:1-12 gives detailed instructions as to when the day of the Lord is to come. Wrede also held that 2 Thess presupposed Paul having become a figure of unquestioned authority; thus 2 Thess could not have been written by Paul.

The reaction to Wrede was sharp. J. Wrzol (1916) attacked Wrede and other scholars by arguing in favor of the truly Pauline character of 2 Thess eschatology and against the alleged impersonal character of the epistle. He maintained that the developing situation in the Thessalonian church could account for the differences in the letters. In his commentary E. von Dobschütz[§] (1909) expressed strong doubts about the reliability of material from Acts concerning Paul's activity and rejected as impossibly short the account of Paul's stay in Thessalonika (Acts 17), a conclusion more recent Pauline chronologists have also reached. Dobschütz did not accept the reversal of the canonical order of 1 and 2 Thess, nor was it clear to him whether 2 Thess 2:2 opposed a misunderstanding of Pauline theology or a forged Pauline letter. Analyzing vocabulary in the two letters, he concluded that word frequencies did not point away from Pauline authorship, although he admitted that many parts of 2 Thess read like rewritings of 1 Thess. Nonetheless, he decided in favor of Pauline authorship.

A. von Harnack[§] also responded (1910), stating that 2 Thess was written to a different, Jewish-Christian group within the Thessalonian church rather than to the group to which 1 Thess was written. This explanation accounts for the fact that the language in 2 Thess is not as personal as that in 1 Thess, since Paul usually identified with the Gentile Christians. The apocalyptic was especially designed to appeal to the Jewish-Christian minority in Thessalonika, as were the strong words about endurance under persecution in chap. 1. Thus, von Harnack argued, Paul identified the real addressees of 2 Thess in 2:13, where the Jewish-Christians are described as the "firstfruits unto salvation (AT)." Von Harnack's conclusion that 2 Thess was written by Paul but to a different group in the same Thessalonian church from the one for whom 1 Thess was intended was followed by M. Dibelius[§] in his commentary (1911, 1925[2], 1937[3]).

J. Frame's substantial commentary (1912) on the letters included, along with a detailed philological analysis, a thorough sifting of issues and of the previous secondary literature. Frame made correlations to extra-biblical historical documents and especially to Acts. Accepting Pauline authorship for both epistles, he read 1 Thess as Paul's response to serious problems within the Thessalonian community. Like other commentators, Frame identified the "disorderly" persons of 1 Thess 5:14 with those acting "in a disorderly way" in 2 Thess 3:6, which then allowed him to understand the *ataktoi* in 1 Thess as "idle brethren" whose enthusiastic activities and rebelliousness caused the trouble that evoked the two letters. According to Frame, the disorderly ones stirred up the church in Thessalonika by misinterpreting 1 Thess, teaching that the day of the Lord had already arrived, which caused the fainthearted to think that their salvation was no longer possible. Hence Frame found the differences between 1 and 2 Thess to be, on the one hand, not very great and, on the other hand, well accounted for by rapid changes in the community.

In 1945 E. Schweizer pointed out that the earliest patristic quotation of or allusion to 2 Thess, Polycarp's letter to the Philippians (3.12 and 11.3), mentions "letters" that Paul had written to the Philippians. Schweizer argued that Polycarp understood the letter he quoted (2 Thess) as having been originally written by Paul to the church at Philippi, a plausible possibility since Philippi and Thessalonika are relatively near to each other in Macedonia. Further, Schweizer reasoned, 1 and 2 Thess are so similar to each other because Paul wrote them within a short time span. And, deducing no motive for a supposed forger to have written 2 Thess, Schweizer contended that the mention of the same addressees in 1 and 2 Thess was from force of habit.

The most complete commentary on 1–2 Thess from the second half of the twentieth century is that of B. Rigaux (1956). This learned but cautious work is filled with philological and theological notes drawing many parallels between Pauline language and Jewish literature.

According to R. Jewett (1971), the Thessalonian church was being overrun by a libertinistic, enthusiastic group; the congregation was also shocked by the deaths of some of its members. Jewett also believed that the Thessalonians radically misinterpreted the apocalyptic of 1 Thess, making it necessary for Paul to write a second letter, much cooler in tone. In a later monograph (1986) Jewett has attempted to correlate the letters with a rapidly changing social situation within the city of Thessalonika, supporting his interpretation by drawing parallels from the practices of various millenarian communities.

Several more recent scholars have interpreted 2 Thess as a pseudo-Pauline letter. W. Trilling (1972, 1980) has put together various form-critical (Form Criticism*§) and linguistic arguments against Pauline authorship. W. Marxsen (1982) maintained that 2 Thess argues against a kind of Pauline Gnosticism (Gnostic Interpretation§) that held that the day of the Lord has already come (2:2). F. Hughes (1989) has made a Rhetorical*§ analysis of 2 Thess and argues that the letter's theological rhetoric opposed the theology spread by a letter or letters claiming to be by Paul that advanced a particular form of fulfilled eschatology. Hughes maintains that the theology 2 Thess attacks is the same as that underlying Eph and particularly Col. A. Malherbe (1987) has interpreted both letters in terms of Greek philosophical tradition, and B. Johanson (1987) has analyzed 1 Thess using the text-linguistic method popular in Scandinavia.

Most contemporary interpreters believe that 1 Thess is the earliest of the extant Pauline letters, written before the Jerusalem conference and before Gal. The chronological placement of 1 Thess before Gal is historically and theologically crucial because 1 Thess then displays Paul acting as a pastor and theologian to a congregation evidently untroubled by Judaizers. One sees clearly in 1 Thess the roots of Pauline theology in early Christian traditions about the imminently expected second coming of Jesus. Therefore, in 1 Thess at least, Pauline theology is centered on faith in Jesus as a returning heavenly redeemer, "Jesus who saves us from the coming wrath" (1:10). The Pauline categories of flesh vs. spirit and the opposition to the imposition of Torah observance in Gentile congregations, so well attested in Galatians, do not appear in 1 Thess, leading Jewett (1971) to argue that these categories were developed as part of Paul's conflict with Jewish-Christian agitators. If it is desirable to posit a "center" of Pauline theology, 1 Thess raises the question of whether justification by faith can be that center, since it seems to several interpreters to be absent from the letter.

Drawing on the chronologies of G. Lüdemann (1984) and Jewett (1986), K. Donfried (1993) has suggested that the whole issue of the early Paul needs to be revisited, arguing that much of the tradition in Acts 17 about Paul's founding visit to the church in Thessalonika may be correct. Donfried contends that the reference to three sabbaths in Acts 17:2 may not include the total length of time of Paul's ministry in Thessalonika. He also gives an excellent summary of historical and theological issues, along with cogent proposals for the contemporary relevance of 1–2 Thess.

4. *Literary Integrity of 1–2 Thessalonians.* Some scholars have argued against the literary integrity of 1–2 Thess either in favor of understanding 1 Thess 2:14-16 as an interpolation (B. Pearson 1971) or positing the existence of several Thessalonian letters that were subsequently edited into the present collection (W. Schmithals 1984; R. Pesch 1984). A strong consensus is that 1 Thess is an integral letter (Donfried, Hughes, Jewett, Johanson, Lüdemann, among others).

Recent commentaries on the Thessalonians correspondence include Collins (2003*a*, 2003*b*), Gaventa (1998), Haufe (1999), Holtz (1998), Malherbe (2000), Reinmuth (1998*a*, 1998*b*), and Smith (2000*a*, 2000*b*). Weima and Porter (1998) provide bibliography. Collected essays on various topics of the interpretation of the Thessalonian epistles are in Donfried (2002) and Donfried and Beutler (2000). Börschel (2001) and Still (1999) both use sociological methods to analyze 1–2 Thess in their ancient cultural, social, and historical setting. Smith (1995) analyzes the rhetoric and audience of 1 Thess. Riesner (1998) attempts to correlate the chronological data from 1 Thess, the rest of the Pauline letters, and Acts to reconstruct Paul's early career.

Bibliography: J. A. Bailey, "Who Wrote II Thessalonians?" *NTS* 25 (1978-79) 131-45. F. C. Baur, *Paul, the Apostle of Jesus Christ* (1845, 1866-67²; ET 1876); "Die beiden Briefe an die Thessalonicher, ihre Unechtheit und Bedeutung für die Lehre der Parusie Christi," *ThJb(T)* 14 (1855) 141-68. W. Bornemann, *Die Thessalonicherbriefe* (KEK 10, 1894). R. Börschel, *Die Konstruktion einer christlichen Identität: Paulus und die Gemeinde von Thessalonich in ihrer hellenistisch-römischen Umwelt* (BBB 128, 2001). R. F. Collins, *Studies on the First Letter to the Thessalonians* (BETL 66, 1984); (ed.), *The Thessalonian Correspondence* (BETL 87, 1990); "The First Letter of Paul to the Thessalonians," *NISB* (2003*a*) 2115-22; "The Second Letter of Paul to the Thessalonians," *NISB* (2003*b*) 2123-28. M. Dibelius, *An die Thessalonicher I-II, An die Philipper* (HNT, 1911, 1925², 1937³). E. von Dobschütz, *Die Thessalonicher-Briefe* (KEK 10, 1909). K. P. Donfried, "Paul and Judaism: 1 Thess 2:13-16 as a Test Case," *Int* 38 (1984) 242-53; "The Cults of Thessalonica and the Thessalonian Correspondence," *NTS* 31 (1985) 335-56; *Paul, Thessalonica, and Early Christianity* (2002). K. P. Donfried and J. Beutler (eds.), *The Thessalonians Debate: Methodological Discord or Methodological Synthesis?* (2000). K. P. Donfried and I. H. Marshall, *The Theology of the Shorter Pauline Letters* (NT Theology, 1993). J. E. Frame, *A Critical and Exegetical Commentary on the Epistles of St. Paul to the Thessalonians* (ICC, 1912). B. R. Gaventa, *First and Second Thessalonians* (IBC, 1998). C. H. Giblin, *The Threat to Faith: An Exegetical and Theological Re-examination of 2 Thessalonians 2* (AnBib 31, 1967). C. L. W. Grimm, "Die Echtheit der Briefe und die Thessalonicher," *TSK* 23 (1850) 753-813. H. Grotius, *Annotationes in Novum Testamentum* (1641-50). A. von Harnack, "Das Problem des 2. Thessalonicherbriefes," *Sitzungsberichte der Preussischen Akademie der Wissenschaften zu Berlin* (1910) 560-78. G. Haufe, *Der erste Brief des Paulus an die Thessalonicher* (THKNT 12.1, 1999). A. Hilgenfeld, "Die beiden Briefe an die Thessalonicher nach Inhalt und Ursprung," *ZWT* 5 (1862) 225-64. T. Holtz, *Der erste Brief an die Thessalonicher* (EKKNT 13, 1986, 1998³). H. J. Holtzmann, "Zum zweiten Thessalonicherbrief," *ZNW* 2 (1901) 97-108. F. W. Hughes, *Early Christian Rhetoric and 2 Thessalonians* (JSNTSup 30, 1989). R. Jewett, *Paul's Anthropological Terms: A Study of Their Use in Conflict Settings* (AGJU 10, 1971); *The Thessalonian Correspondence: Pauline Rhetoric and Millenarian Piety* (FFNT, 1986). B. C. Johanson, *To All*

the Brethren: A Text-linguistic and Rhetorical Approach to I Thessalonians (ConBNT 16, 1987).
F. H. Kern, "Über 2. Thess 2,1-12: Nebst Andeutungen über den Ursprung des zweiten Briefs an
die Thessalonicher," *TZT* 2 (1839) 145-214. **W. G. Kümmel**, "Das literarische und geschichtliche
Problem des ersten Thessalonicherbriefes," *Neotestamentica et Patristica* (NovTSup 6, 1962) 213-
27. **A. Lindemann**, "Zum Abfassungszweck des zweiten Thessalonicherbriefes," *ZNW* 68 (1977)
35-47. **R. A. Lipsius**, "Über Zweck und Veranlassung des ersten Thessalonicherbrief," *TSK* 27
(1854) 905-34. **G. Lüdemann**, *Paul, Apostle to the Gentiles: Studies in Chronology* (1984).
A. J. Malherbe, " 'Gentle as a Nurse': The Cynic Background to 1 Thess ii," *NovT* 12 (1970)
203-17; "Exhortation in First Thessalonians," *NovT* 25 (1983) 238-56; *Paul and the
Thessalonians: The Philosophic Tradition of Pastoral Care* (1987); *The Letters to the
Thessalonians: A New Translation with Introduction and Commentary* (AB 32B, 2000).
I. H. Marshall, *1 and 2 Thessalonians* (NCB, 1983). **W. Marxsen**, *Der erste Brief an die
Thessalonicher* (ZBNT 11.1, 1979); *Der zweite Thessalonicherbrief* (ZBNT 11.2, 1982).
B. Pearson, "1 Thessalonians 2:13-16: A Deutero-Pauline Interpolation," *HTR* 64 (1971) 79-
94. **R. Pesch**, *Die Entdeckung des ältesten Paules-Briefes* (Herderbücherei 1167, 1984).
E. Reinmuth, "Der erste Brief an die Thessalonicher," *Die Briefe an die Philipper,
Thessalonicher und an Philemon* (N. Walter, E. Reinmuth and P. Lampe, NTD 8.2, 1998[18]a);
"Der zweite Brief an die Thessalonicher," *Die Briefe an die Philipper, Thessalonicher und an
Philemon* (N. Walter, E. Reinmuth and P. Lampe, NTD 8.2, 1998[18]b). **R. Riesner**, *Paul's Early
Period: Chronology, Mission Strategy, Theology* (trans. D. Stott, 1998). **E. J. Richard**, *First
and Second Thessalonians* (SP 11, ed. D. J. Harrington, 1995). **B. Rigaux**, *Saint Paul: Les
Épîtres aux Thessaloniciens* (Ebib, 1956). **J. E. C. Schmidt**, "Vermuthungen über die beyden
Briefe an die Thessalonicher," *Bibliothek für Kritik und Exegese des Neuen Testaments und
ältesten Christengeschichte 2, 3* (J. E. C. Schmidt, 1801) 380-86. **W. Schmithals**, *Paul and the
Gnostics* (1972); *Die Briefe des Paulus in ihrer ursprünglichen Form* (Zürcher Werkkomentare
zur Bibel, 1984). **E. Schweizer**, "Der zweite Thessalonicher ein Philipperbrief?" *TZ* 1 (1945)
90-105. **A. Smith**, *Comfort One Another: Reconstructing the Rhetoric and Audience of
1 Thessalonians* (Literary Currents in Biblical Interpretation, 1995); "The First Letter to the
Thessalonians," *NIB* (2000*a*) 11:671-738; "The Second Letter to the Thessalonians," *NIB*
(2000*b*) 11:739-772. **T. D. Still**, *Conflict at Thessalonica: A Pauline Church and Its Neighbours*
(JSNTSup 183, 1999). **W. Trilling**, *Untersuchungen zum zweiten Thessalonicherbrief* (ETS 27,
1972); *Der zweite Brief an die Thessalonicher* (EKKNT 14, 1980); "Die beiden Briefe des
Apostels Paulus an die Thessalonicher: Eine Forschungsbericht," *ANRW* 2.25.4 (1987) 3365-
403. **J. A. D. Weima and S. E. Porter**, *An Annotated Bibliography of 1 and 2 Thessalonians*
(NTTS 26, 1998). **W. Wrede**, *Die Echtheit des zweiten Thessalonicherbriefs* (TU NF 9, 2,
1903). **J. Wrzol**, *Die Echtheit des zweiten Thessalonicherbrief* (BibS(F) 19, 1916).

F. W. HUGHES

THE NEW TESTAMENT CANON

Pastoral Letters

This designation for 1–2 Tim and Titus is generally accepted as due to P. Anton (1726), although he did not restrict it to these letters alone (see P. Harrison 1921, 13-16).

1. *Early Period*. These three letters formed a recognized group from the beginning and as letters to individuals were usually followed by Philemon in canonical lists (in the Muratorian canon they follow Philemon) and in manuscripts. They also usually follow the order 1–2 Tim, Titus, although in both Muratori and Ambrosiaster, Titus precedes 1–2 Tim; in the latter, Col is inserted between them. Found neither in Marcion's[§] Canon[§] nor in P[46], they are first quoted as Pauline by Irenaeus[§] (*Adv. Haer.* 1.16.3, 2.14.7, 3.14.1). Clement of Alexandria[§] wrote that some heretics rejected 1–2 Tim (*Strom.* 2.11). Tertullian[§] maintained that Marcion accepted Phlm but rejected the Pastorals (*Adv. Marc.* 5.21), although it may be that he was unaware of their existence. In the prologue to his commentary on Titus, Jerome[§] alleged that Tatian[§] rejected 1–2 Tim and that Origen[§] provided a commentary on Titus but none on 1–2 Tim.

From the beginning of the third century the letters were accepted as canonical. The patristic commentaries rarely went further than a simple expansion of the text, and the letters exercised little influence except in the liturgies and church orders (C. Spiq 1969, 1:11-14; W. Lock 1924, xxxviii-xli).

2. *Reformation*. During this period no doubts were expressed about the authenticity of the letters. Calvin[§] viewed them as useful for setting in order the many failings of the church (preface to 1 Tim). Since many Protestant scholars had begun to regard Scripture as providing the essential basis for their own church order, the letters were examined closely, especially in relation to whether they distinguish between bishops and presbyters (elders). Most denominations used them in their ordinals, although they understood them differently.

3. *Modern Period*. Although J. Schmidt (1804) had earlier voiced doubts, F. Schleiermacher[§] (1807) was the first to question directly the authenticity of the letters, though only of 1 Tim, basing his argument on linguistic considerations. J. G. Eichhorn[§] (1812) was the first to impugn the authenticity of all three letters; he regarded their content as Pauline, but written by a disciple. F. C. Baur[§] (1835, 8-39) provided the first systematic challenge, arguing that they could be understood only against the background of the second-century Gnostic movement, which they were written to rebut. Since Marcion did not know them they must have been written after his time and were probably directed against him. Many scholars supported Baur in his rejection of Pauline authorship, although they did not always date them as late as he did or accept their anti-Marcionite nature.

a. Holtzmann's interpretation and influence. The classical nineteenth-century treatment opposing Pauline authorship is that of H. Holtzmann[§] (1880). He not only provided a history of earlier interpretation during that century (1880, 7-15) but set out in great detail the areas on which discussion has centered ever since. Negatively he pointed to: (1) the difficulty of finding a place for the Pastorals in Paul's known lifetime; (2) difficulties in relation to Timothy and Titus; and (3) the un-Pauline nature of their language and style. In his positive development of the thought of the letters he pointed to: (4) the heresy they attack, which fits a period later than Paul's lifetime; (5) their doctrinal teaching; (6) the ecclesiastical organization they depict; and (7) the external evidence.

i. Relation to Paul's lifetime. The letters indicate that Paul was imprisoned when writing 2 Tim but free at the time of 1 Tim and Titus. Since in 2 Tim 4:6 he is about to die and the three letters form a unit, all three must have been written toward the end of his life and during his final imprisonment in Rome. Since prior to that imprisonment he is envisaged as making a journey to Macedonia (1 Tim 1:3), leaving Titus in Crete and spending a winter in Nicopolis (Titus 3:12), and since there is no place in Acts into which these and other data can be fitted, some scholars have concluded that after the imprisonment of Acts 28 Paul was set free, traveled in the East, and was imprisoned again in Rome. During this imprisonment he wrote 2 Tim and shortly thereafter was executed. Those who defend this view differ as to the date of execution, choosing either 64 or 67 C.E. The suggestion of a second Roman imprisonment can be traced back as far as Eusebius§ (*Hist. eccl.* 2.22.2). However, all this entails a reconstruction of Paul's life for which there is no support in Acts; moreover, Acts 20:25 suggests that Paul did not travel again to the East (on possible journeys by Paul see W. Metzger 1976). Increasing doubts as to the reliability of Acts have not served to soften this attack since those who defend the authenticity of the Pastorals usually also defend the reliability of Acts (on the question of whether all, some, or none of the historical data are fictitious see A. Hanson 1982, 14-23).

ii. Difficulties regarding Timothy. Holtzmann argued that if we assume a second imprisonment for Paul, Timothy by that time must have been no longer a youth; yet he is bidden to flee youthful lusts (2 Tim 2:22) and to allow no one to despise his youth (1 Tim 4:12). Paul advises him as a catechumen rather than as the mature Christian he must then have been. It is also surprising that Paul should write to him in such detail after just having left him.

iii. Un-Pauline language and style. Holtzmann devoted considerable space to this argument. Harrison (1921, 18-86) extended his line of approach, providing an exhaustive analysis and pointing out that (a) there is a high number of *hapax legomena*; (b) words appearing in both the Pastorals and in the genuine Paulines are often used differently; (c) the same thing is said with different words; (d) favorite Pauline particles and many words characteristic of Pauline theology are absent; (e) un-Pauline grammatical constructions are used; (f) the letters are generally less vivid, intense, and dynamic than the genuine Paulines; (g) the letters, being similar in these various points, form a distinct group; (h) the language of the letters approximates more closely that of the apostolic fathers and of the apologists than that of Paul. Since Harrison's arguments are based on statistics, statistical experts have refined them and provided a sounder basis than simple enumeration (P. Trummer 1978, 28-34; see K. Grayston and G. Herdan 1959 and the more detailed work of S. Michaelson and A. Morton 1973 with various associates). Ignoring many of the above points, Morton turned the discussion into new areas by examining features characteristic of a writer (sentence length, use of simple words like "and," etc.), which he claims are unaffected by an author's age or subject matter. Defenders of Pauline authenticity (e.g., Spicq 1969, 1:179-200) have concentrated their attention on showing errors in Harrison's work (e.g., the fact that words are first found in the apostolic fathers apart from the Pastorals is no proof that they were unknown in Paul's day and that more evidence has turned up since Harrison wrote; see D. Guthrie 1957, 212-28). More positively, it is argued that changes in subject matter ensure the introduction of new words, that writers develop, and that increasing age (Paul would have been an old man when writing the Pastorals) affects vigor of style.

iv. Attack on heresy. The Pastorals reject false teaching, and Holtzmann indicated that scholars had taken its source to lie in one or more of four areas: Gnosticism, Judaism or Judaizers, Samaritan Gnosis (Simon), or Essenism. The last two are no longer taken seriously as direct sources for the alleged heresy, although the teachings of Qumran (Dead Sea Scrolls§) may be seen as part of Judaism and as influencing the growth of Gnosticism. The first two views were held by various church fathers (see sec. 1 above). Some scholars have identified the heresy as that of particular Gnostic sects (Baur, 8-39; thought of Marcion). Such identifications would be difficult if the letters are dated in the earlier part of the second century and impossible if regarded as Pauline. Continuing discussion of the nature and origin of Gnosticism has not completely clarified the issues, nor have the discoveries at Nag Hammadi led to a more precise identification, although J. Sell (1982) sees a connection with *Thomas the Contender* (CG II 138.1-145.23).

Meanwhile, many scholars, especially those wishing to defend Pauline authorship, have seen the heretics as Jewish Christians (e.g., Spicq, 91); this permits their placement in Paul's lifetime, although it is not claimed that the heresy is the same as that encountered by Paul in Galatia. Most scholars, however, appear to view the heresy as linked to the beginning of Gnosticism but as also including strong Jewish elements (e.g., G. Haufe 1973; see also W. Lütgert 1909; N. Brox 1969, 31-42). It is generally agreed that the heresy was ascetic rather than christological. There is also a growing tendency to use a more neutral term than heresy and speak of a faction within the church that the writer opposes.

v. Doctrinal teaching. Holtzmann's conclusions on the teaching of the letters, although not directly addressing the question of authenticity, entailed an author much later than Paul. In particular he found teaching on the law, Christology, justification, and faith that differed from Paul's and an un-Pauline emphasis on piety, together with a stress on good works, to be signs of a growing orthodoxy. Although Holtzmann did not use the term, later critics would describe these emphases, when allied with the stress on church order (see below), as indicating early Catholicism. Since A. Deissmann[§] the absence of Christ-mysticism has been emphasized. Those who defend Pauline authorship explain these differences by arguing that genuine Pauline theology is not entirely absent, that his theology was never stereotyped, that a changed situation would lead to new elements, and that an imitator would never omit key Pauline doctrines.

vi. Ecclesiastical organization. In his discussion of the nature of the order of the community envisaged in the Pastorals (he surveyed such matters as bishops, elders, deacons, widows, worship, church discipline), Holtzmann concluded that the form of ministry belongs to the second century rather than to the first. A hardening has taken place; there is an established church; and the spontaneity of the authentic Paulines seen in charismatic activity has almost disappeared. Defenders of Pauline authorship (see, e.g., Guthrie, 24-32) point to Paul's appointment of elders in Acts (14:23; 20:17; these references are taken as historical). As his death approached, Paul necessarily became more interested in arranging the continuance of the church; no actual position is spelled out for him in the church; and the language used of the actual offices is imprecise (Spicq, 70, 73-74). As in earlier years some writers still adopt confessional positions in discussing organization, emphasizing the distinction between laity and hierarchy or the equivalence or non-equivalence of bishops and elders. However, because of the ecumenical movement most commentators no longer attempt to draw from the Pastorals models for church organization today.

The letters themselves do not suggest that the ministerial pattern they set out was intended to be adhered to forever. In comparison with the authentic Pauline letters, the charismatic nature of ministry is minimized in the Pastorals, and its institutional nature is emphasized. This emphasis is in line with a changed view of the nature of the church. The phrases with which Paul linked the church to Christ—body of Christ, bride of Christ—have disappeared, and the church is likened instead to a great household whose head is God. Consequently, much of the instruction on behavior in the church is modeled on the household, and proper conduct is what would be appropriate in a household. This led to the use of the *haustafel* form of Eph 5:22–6:9 and Col 3:18–4:6. H. Hübner (1990, 1:378) can therefore justly characterize the Pastorals as the domestication of early Christianity.

vii. External evidence. Holtzmann (257-75) argued that Clement of Rome[§] was not acquainted with the Pastorals but that Polycarp was. Although the letters were not expressly quoted until the last third of the second century, their content was known by its middle. Since Holtzmann's time the realization of their use of common catechetical, liturgical, and creedal material (see below) has made estimations of their dependence on others or of others on them much more difficult.

b. Following Holtzmann. Holtzmann indeed set the agenda for the succeeding discussion, although, of course, as new techniques have developed through the application of modern social theory (M. MacDonald 1983; D. Verner 1983) and culture changes, e.g., the rise of the feminist movement, new questions have arisen and have been addressed. In consequence, the delay in the Parousia is no longer seen as the main factor controlling the thought of the letters. Insofar as attention has been given to the place of widows in the letters, their position and evaluation appear different from that in the genuine letters of Paul (J. Bassler 1984; J. Dewey 1992; L. Maloney 1994). No consensus has yet appeared as to whether 1 Tim 3:11 refers to Roman officials or to wives of male deacons.

Closely linked to the issue of the dependence of the Pastoral letters on catechetical and liturgical material is that of date. Upholders of Pauline authorship adhere to a period just prior to his death. Others vary considerably. Baur's original claim that the Pastorals were anti-Marcionite is still upheld (e.g., W. Bauer, 226; H. von Campenhausen 1963, 205-6, 243-45), necessitating a date near the middle of the second century. Most scholars prefer to place them closer to its beginning because of their similarity of thought to that of other writings from that period, but all recognize that they are particularly difficult to date precisely. Those who do not accept as genuine their historical and geographical data generally agree that their provenance is Asia Minor.

If the letters are not by Paul, then who was their actual author? Many suggestions have been made. Luke's influence has regularly been seen, but not many scholars have gone as far as J. Quinn (1990, 19) in suggesting that Luke intended the Pastorals as a third and concluding volume to his Gospel and Acts. Since Holtzmann's time and in agreement with him, those who reject Pauline authorship customarily take the letters to have been written in the order 2 Tim, Titus, 1 Tim (the traditional order accords with length) on the basis of development of ministry, literary standpoint, and lessening of personal references (E. Scott 1936, 17-19).

Apart from their response to the arguments of those attacking Pauline authorship, its defenders say that it is improbable that a devout Christian would compose a forgery in Paul's name (e.g., J. Kelly 1963, 33), that there were better ways of passing on Paul's teaching than writing letters in his name, and that the multitude of personalia make the letters read like genuine letters rather than like fictions. Apart from the simple suggestion that the letters are pseudonymous because Paul did not write them, there is a kind of double pseudonymity, for the letters are not directed to the real Timothy and Titus but to the groups that support them. Their real purpose is to instruct these groups on how the church is to be continued.

The cricitism of Holtzmann and others led to Roman Catholic scholars' being forced by a decision of the Pontifical Biblical Commission of 1913 to defend the authenticity of the letters (Trummer, 25-26). They were, however, freed from this decision by Divino Afflante Spiritu[§] (1962); and many now no longer accept Pauline authorship.

It cannot be said that since Holtzmann's time the discussion of authenticity has been much advanced. No substantially new arguments have been produced; however, fresh avenues of study have been opened up, mostly, though not entirely, pioneered by those who view the letters as coming from a time later than Paul. Rejection of Pauline authorship allows the letters to be treated as deriving from a single author who wrote for his own community and not another, and whose thinking should be studied in its own right. This has raised the question of whether the letters' author is merely a compiler of traditional material and views or a consistent theologian (see Trummer, 161-226; L. Donelson 1986, 129-54; H. von Lips 1979 for attempts to set out his thinking), even if one who is not as profound as Paul or the Fourth Evangelist. Much study of the letters in the past was dominated by the quest to show how they repeated, modified, and misunderstood the genuine Paulines. It was always, however, accepted that the Pastorals stood a stage farther away from Paul than Eph and Col. Before turning to new attempts to understand the Pastorals, it is necessary to point to two approaches that have attempted to find a middle ground for those who wish to retain a connection with Paul while accounting for evidence that suggests he did not write the letters.

First, the letters have been held to contain genuine Pauline fragments. Initially proposed by Credner (1836) and Hitzig (1843; see Harrison, 94), this became a widespread theory after Holtzmann (see J. Moffatt 1918, 402-6). Harrison (86-135), who provided the most detailed presentation of the theory, discovered clusters of Pauline terms and thought that enabled him to separate five fragments, place them in Paul's own lifetime as revealed in Acts, and account for the existence of the personalia. Different scholars identify fragments differently (Harrison later decided that there were only three); this lack of unanimity has led to skepticism about the attempt, as has also the letters' supposed nature and the way the author of the Pastorals is alleged to have dismembered them. As a variation of this theory R. Falconer (1937, 5-19; cf. P. Dornier 1965, 25) held that a disciple of Timothy worked over a number of brief genuine letters to adapt them for his own period.

Second, it is claimed that the use of a secretary would account for linguistic differences from the accepted Paulines (on secretaries in the ancient world see O. Roller 1933, 18-22 and notes 120-40; see also E. Richards 1991). H. Schott (1830) first suggested this, proposing Luke as the secretary (Silvanus and Tychicus have also been suggested). If Paul was manacled (2 Tim 1:16; 2:9), a secretary would have been essential. (Roller suggested a secretary only for 2 Tim, but the unitary style and thought of the three letters would necessitate the same secretary for all.) The linguistic differences from Paul, however, require some freedom on the part of the secretary; and linguistic freedom entails a degree of theological freedom. The thought of the letters cannot then be purely Pauline.

Work on the Pastorals as well as on other New Testament letters has led to a renewed examination of the attitude of the ancient world to pseudonymity. (For the discussion with its particular reference to the Pastorals see Brox, 60-61; Donelson, 1-66; Guthrie 1965; D. Meade 1986, 118-60.) If the letters are pseudonymous, then the mass of personalia suggests that the writer was consciously aware of what he was doing and that the letters of Paul were well known.

If Paul was not the author, either directly or indirectly, who was? Luke has been regularly suggested (see F. Strobel 1969), although others have also been proposed (Polycarp, by Campenhausen). Lukan authorship, argued on linguistic, theological, and historical grounds, is attractive to some scholars as preserving a link with Paul, although this attractiveness is lost if the author of Luke-Acts was not Paul's medical companion (so S. Wilson 1979). Other scholars have followed Morton, using different parameters and methods in applying statistics (e.g., A. Kenny 1986; K. Neumann 1990; D. Mealand 1995), facilitated through the use of computers, although it cannot be said that they have significantly modified his results.

Are they, however, genuine letters? They lack the personal and emotional tone one would expect if writer and recipient knew each other, although it was not uncommon in the ancient world to use letters for the purpose of instruction. The genre of Titus has thus been taken by many to be testamentary (A. Hultgren 1984, 27) rather than epistolary. Without naming an author, attempts have been made to characterize him: not a first-generation Christian, probably Jewish, the holder of a clerical office (Brox, 57); a child of Christian parents, a monarchical bishop, a conventional Gentile Christian (Campenhausen, 207-10); influenced by Stoic and Cynic teaching (B. Fiore 1986); governed by the logic of ancient rhetorical argumentation (Donelson, 67-113).

With the rise of Form Criticism*[§], increasing attention has been paid to the traditional material (see A. Hanson 1982, 42-47 for listing) within the letters. The "faithful sayings" (G. Knight 1968), the creed or hymn of 1 Tim 3:16 (W. Stenger 1977; W. Metzger 1979), the vice and virtue lists (N. McEleny 1974), and the *Haustafeln* (Verner) have all been examined in detail, as has the genre of the letters (Spicq 34-46; Donelson 67-113). As new tools have come into use in New Testament criticism, they have been applied to the Pastorals, e.g., concepts of ancient rhetoric (Donelson 67-113; Fiore) and sociological techniques (Verner; Sociology and New Testament Studies*[§]). The rise of feminism (Feminist Interpretation*[§]) has led to a clearer delineation of their male-dominated nature. The use of the Hebrew Bible in the letters has also drawn attention (Hanson 1968). The ethical teaching of the Pastorals is now regularly distinguished from that of Paul as more bourgeois, closer to Hellenistic moral teaching, directed toward *eusebeia* (piety) and dependent on traditional material (Trummer, 227-40; R. Schwarz 1983, 99-121; Donelson, 171-97).

Freed from denominational influence and the need to make a direct connection with Paul, discussion of the nature of the church and its ministry has not lost its impetus (Lips 1979, 94-288; Schwarz, 19-98, 123-71; A. Sand 1976; A. Lemaire 1971, 123-38). However, it is now more clearly recognized that the emphasis lies more on the selection of correct candidates than on the correctness of church order.

Those accepting Pauline authorship or authorship directly influenced by him have seen the purpose of the letters in much the same way as did the fathers. All others are forced to ask why they were written in Paul's name; thus the view taken of Paul after his death (A. Lindemann 1979) becomes important. If we include the quotations of and allusions to the Hebrew Bible among the traditional material, then there is proportionally more of this material in the Pastorals than in any other New Testament writings. It is generally recognized that the Pastorals represent a stage in the development of Pauline thought beyond that of Eph and Col and less faithful to the original Paul. Some of Paul's letters must have been known (opinions differ as to which, but certainly Rom and 1 Cor; see Lindemann, 136-47), as also his reputation as a letter writer. If different groups were claiming to be his true disciples, was the author putting in his own claim? (D. MacDonald 1983, 57, 76-77, 96, sees the letters as having been written to oppose a conception of Paul as a social radical.) Was Paul being enlisted against or rescued from the heretics (W. Bauer 1971, 228; this idea goes back as far as Baur, 57-58)? If the collection of Paul's letters was the first step in his actualization for a post-Pauline generation, are the Pastorals a further step (Trummer, 100-105)? Are they intended to guard the Pauline legacy against false interpretation (Lindemann, 147) or to ensure its continued effectiveness (E. Scott 1936, xxv)? Is Paul being presented as a paradigm either for church leaders or for all Christians (Donelson, 105-6)?

The Pastorals present a picture of Paul (Trummer, 116-32) as he appeared to some group at a period after his death. Paul was known to have persecuted the church yet to have been in prison and died a martyr; and both his pre-Christian failures, excused as having been done in ignorance (1 Tim 1:12-16), and his Christian greatness are emphasized: He is the sole apostle; he prophesies (1 Tim 4:1-5; 2 Tim 3:15-16), is a traveling missionary, is concerned with the life of the church, and courageously faces death.

What value do the letters have? Those who adhere to Pauline authorship see them as providing some information about what happened to Paul after the events of Acts 28. Those not accepting the letters as Pauline see them as throwing light on the church at some point in the post-Pauline period. Since their author chose to issue them in Paul's name there must have been an area of the church where his memory was revered; thus the once commonly held view that with his death Paul passed for a time into oblivion must be revised. A living Pauline tradition must have continued. All in all these letters throw light on the belief, ministry, and heresies of at least one part of the church.

Recent commentaries on the Pastoral Epistles include Collins (2002), Dunn (2000), Johnson (2001), Marshall (1999), Mounce (2000), and Smith (2003*a*, 2003*b*, 2003*c*). Davies (1996) and Harding (2001) provide introductions to the epistles and recent study of them. Läger (1996),

Lau (1996), and Stettler (1998) investigate the Christology of the Pastorals. Häfner studies the use of the Hebrew Scriptures in the Pastorals. Holmes (2000) analyzes four methods of analyzing 1 Timothy's perspective on women. Miller (1997) investigates the compositional history of the letters. Harding (1998) studies the use of tradition and rhetoric in the letters.

Bibliography: **J. Bassler**, "The Widow's Tale: A Fresh Look at 1 Tim. 5:3-16," *JBL* 103 (1984) 23-41; *1 Timothy, 2 Timothy, Titus* (ANTC, 1996). **W. Bauer**, *Orthodoxy and Heresy in Earliest Christianity* (1971). **F. C. Baur**, *Die sogenannten Pastoralbriefe des Apostels Paulus aufs neue kritisch untersucht* (1835). **L. A. Brown**, "Asceticism and Ideology: The Language of Power in the Pastoral Epistles," *Discursive Formations, Ascetic Piety, and the Interpretation of Early Christian Literature, pt. 1* (ed. V. L. Wimbush, Semeia 57, 1992) 77-94. **N. Brox**, *Die Pastoralbriefe übersetzt und erklärt* (1969). **H. von Campenhausen**, "Polykarp von Smyrna und die Pastoralbriefe," and "Bearbeitungen und Interpolationen des Polykarpmartyriums," *Aus der Frühzeit des Christentums: Studien zur Kirchengeschichte des ersten und zweiten Jahrhunderts* (1963) 197-252. **R. F. Collins**, *Letters That Paul Did Not Write* (1988); *1 and 2 Timothy and Titus: A Commentary* (New Testament Library, 2002). **M. Davies**, *The Pastoral Epistles* (New Testament Guides, 1996). **J. Dewey**, "1 Timothy," "2 Timothy," and "Titus," *Women's Bible Commentary* (ed. C. A. Newsom and S. H. Ringe, 1992) 353-58, 359-60, 361. **L. R. Donelson**, *Pseudepigraphy and Ethical Argument in the Pastoral Epistles* (1986). **P. Dornier**, *Les Épîtres pastorales* (1969). **J. D. G. Dunn**, "The First and Second Letters to Timothy and the Letter to Titus," *NIB* (2000) 11:773-880. **R. A. Falconer**, *The Pastoral Epistles: Introduction, Translation, and Notes* (1937). **B. Fiore**, *The Function of Personal Example in the Socratic and Pastoral Epistles* (1986). **K. Grayston and G. Herdan**, "The Authorship of the Pastorals in the Light of Statistical Linguistics," *NTS* 6 (1959) 1-15. **D. Guthrie**, *The Pastoral Epistles: An Introduction and Commentary* (1957); "The Development of the Idea of Canonical Pseudepigrapha in NT Criticism," *The Authorship and Integrity of the NT: Some Recent Studies* (SPCK Theological Collections 4, 1965) 14-39. **G. Häfner** *"Nützlich zur Belehrung" (2 Tim 3,16): Die Rolle der Schrift in den Pastoralbriefen im Rahmen der Paulusrezeption* (Herders biblische Studien 25, 2000). **A. T. Hanson**, *Studies in the Pastoral Epistles* (1968); *The Pastoral Epistles, Based on the RSV* (1982). **M. Harding**, *Tradition and Rhetoric in the Pastoral Epistles* (Studies in Biblical Literature 3, 1998); *What are They Saying About the Pastoral Epistles?* (WATSA, 2001). **P. N. Harrison**, *The Problem of the Pastoral Epistles* (1921). **G. Haufe**, "Gnostische Irrlehre und ihre Abwehr in den Pastoralbriefen," *Gnosis und Neues Testament* (ed. K.-W. Tröger, 1973) 325-39. **J. M. Holmes**, *Text in a Whirlwind: A Critique of Four Exegetical Devices at 1 Timothy* 2.9-15 (JSNTSup 196, Studies in New Testament Greek 7, 2000). **H. J. Holtzmann**, *Die Pastoralbriefe kritisch und exegetisch behandelt* (1880). **H. Hübner**, *Biblische Theologie des Neuen Testaments* (3 vols. 1990-). **A. J. Hultgren**, *1–2 Timothy, Titus* (1984). **L. T. Johnson**, *The First and Second Letters to Timothy: A New Translation with Introduction and Commentary* (AB 35A, 2001). **R. J. Karris**, "The Background and Significance of the Polemic of the Pastoral Epistles," *JBL* 92 (1973) 549-64. **J. N. D. Kelly**, *A Commentary on the Pastoral Epistles: I Timothy, II Timothy, Titus* (1963). **A. Kenny**, *A Stylometric Study of the NT* (1986). **G. W. Knight**, *The Faithful Sayings in the Pastoral Epistles* (1968). **K. Läger**, *Die Christologie der Pastoralbriefe* (Hamburger theologische Studien 12, 1996). **A. Y. Lau**, *Manifest in Flesh: The Epiphany Christology of the Pastoral Epistles* (WUNT 2/86, 1996). **A. Lemaire**, *Les ministères aux origines de l'Église: Naissance de la triple hierarchie ieveques, presbytres, diacres* (1971). **A. Lindemann**, *Paulus im ältesten Christentum: Das Bild des Apostels und die Rezeption der paulinischen Theologie in der frühchristlichen Literatur bis Marcion* (1979). **H. von Lips**, *Glaube, Geimeinde, Amt: Zum Verständnis der Ordination in den Pastoralbriefen* (1979). **W. Lock**, *A Critical and*

Exegetical Commentary on the Pastoral Epistles (1924). **E. Lohse**, *Theological Ethics of the NT* (1988). **W. Lütgert**, *Die Irrlehrer der Pastoralbriefe* (1909). **D. R. MacDonald**, *The Legend and the Apostle: The Battle for Paul in Story and Canon* (1983). **M. Y. MacDonald**, *The Pauline Churches: A Socio-historical Study of Institutionalization in the Pauline and Deutero-Pauline Writings* (SNTSMS 60, 1988). **N. J. McEleney**, "The Vice Lists of the Pastoral Epistles" *CBQ* 36 (1974) 203-19. **L. M. Maloney**, "The Pastoral Epistles," *Searching the Scriptures*, vol. 2, *A Feminist Commentary* (ed. E. Schüssler Fiorenza, 1994) 361-80. **I. H. Marshall**, *A Critical and Exegetical Commentary on the Pastoral Epistles* (ICC, 1999). **D. G. Meade**, *Pseudonymity and Canon: An Investigation into the Relationship of Authorship and Authority in Jewish and Early Christian Tradition* (1986). **D. L. Mealand**, "The Extent of the Pauline Corpus: A Multivariate Approach" *JSNT* 59 (1995) 61-92. **W. Metzger**, *Die letzte Reise des Apostels Paulus: Beobachtungen und Erwagungen zu seinem Itinerar nach den Pastoralbriefen* (1976); *Der Christushymnus 1. Timotheus 3,16: Fragment einer Homologie der paulinischen Gemeinden* (1979). **S. Michaelson and A. Q. Morton**, "Positional Stylometry," *The Computer and Literary Studies* (ed. A. J. Aitken, 1973). **J. D. Miller**, *The Pastoral Letters as Composite Documents* (SNTSMS 93, 1997). **J. Moffatt**, *An Introduction to the Literature of the NT* (1918). **W. D. Mounce**, *Pastoral Epistles* (WBC 46, 2000). **K. J. Neumann**, *The Authenticity of the Pauline Epistles in the Light of Stylostatistical Analysis* (SBLDS 120, 1990). **L. Oberlinner**, *Der Pastoralbrief, 1. Folge, Kommentar zum ersten Timotheusbrief: Auslegung* (1994); *Der Pastoralbrief, 2. Folge, Kommentar zum zweiten Timotheusbrief: Auslegung* (1995); *Der Pastoral briefe, 3 Folge, Kommentar zum Titusbrief* (1996). **J. D. Quinn**, *The Letter to Titus: A New Translation with Notes and Commentary and an Introduction to Titus, I and II Timothy, the Pastoral Epistles* (AB 35, 1990). **E. Richards**, *The Secretary and the Letters of Paul* (WUNT, 2. Reihe, 1991). **O. Roller**, *Das Formular der paulinischen Briefe: Ein Beitrag zur Lehre vom antike Briefe* (1933). **J. Roloff**, *Der erste Brief an Timotheus* (EKKNT 15, 1988); *Die Kirche im Neuen Testament* (1993) 250-57. **A. Sand**, "Anfänge einer Koordinierung verschiedener Gemeindeordnungen nach den Pastoralbriefen," *Kirchen im Werden* (ed. J. Hainz, 1976) 215-37. **W. Schenk**, "Die Briefe an Timotheus I und II und an Titus (Pastoralbriefe) in der neueren Forschung (1945-85)," *ANRW* 2.25.4 (1987) 3404-38. **F. Schleiermacher**, *Sendschreiben an J. C. Gass: Über den sogenannten ersten Brief des Paulos an den Timotheos* (1807). **R. Schnackenburg**, *Die sittliche Botschaft des Neuen Testaments* (HTKSup, 2 vols. 1986-88) 1:95-109. **R. Schwarz**, *Burgerliches Christentum im Neuen Testament? Eine Studie zu Ethik, Amt, und Recht in den Pastoralbriefen* (1983). **E. F. Scott**, *The Pastoral Epistles* (1936). **J. Sell**, *The Knowledge of the Truth—Two Doctrines: The Book of Thomas the Contender* (1982). **A. Smith**, "The First Letter of Paul to Timothy," *NISB* (2003a) 2129-36; "The Second Letter of Paul to Timothy," *NISB* (2003b) 2137-42; "The Letter of Paul to Titus," *NISB* (2003c) 2143-46. **C. Spicq**, *Les Épîtres pastorales* (2 vols. 1969). **W. Stenger**, *Der Christushymnus 1 Tim 3,16: Eine strukturanalytische Untersuchung* (1977). **H. Stettler**, *Die Christologie der Pastoralbriefe* (WUNT 2/105, 1998). **F. A. Strobel**, "Schreiben des Lukas? Zum sprachlichen Problem der Pastoralbriefe," *NTS* 15 (1969) 191-210. **P. Trummer**, *Die Paulustradition der Pastoralbriefe* (1978). **D. C. Verner**, *The Household of God: The Social World of the Pastoral Epistles* (1983). **S. G. Wilson**, *Luke and the Pastoral Epistles* (1979). **M. Wolter**, *Die Pastoralbriefe als Paulustradition* (1988).

E. Best

Philemon, Letter to

1. *The Fathers*. Some scholars believe that the first references to the epistle are in Ignatius[§] (*Eph.* 2; *Magn.* 12; *Pol.* 6). On three occasions (*Eph.* 1.3, *PG* 5.645; 2.1; 6.2) Ignatius cited a tradition identifying Onesimus as a bishop of Ephesus, but it is not altogether certain that the bishop is the same person as the runaway slave. If Bishop Onesimus were indeed the same person as the former slave, this would explain why the letter was so readily accepted into the Pauline corpus. Ignatius also indicated that Christians had to defend themselves against the accusation that conversion to Christianity required that slaves be freed (*Pol.* 4.3), but Phlm is of dubious utility in the discussion because it does not indicate what happened to Onesimus after the letter was sent.

Phlm does not appear to have been widely read during patristic times, but was universally attributed to Paul and most valued for the elements of wisdom and virtue it contained. The letter apparently belonged to the earliest collections of Pauline writings, perhaps dating back to the end of the first century. In the Muratorian Canon[§] it appears alongside the Pastoral Letters[†§], a placement apparently due to the fact that all four epistles were considered to have been addressed to individuals.

During the fourth century problems arose because of the paucity of edifying material contained in the letter. As a result some doubted its Inspiration[*§] or even its Pauline authorship, even to the point of making a claim that it had been rejected by ancient authorities. Jerome[§], among others, replied that Paul treats of similarly mundane matters in all of his epistles and that Phlm would not have been received by all the churches in the world had it not been by Paul (PL 26.599-601).

2. *The Medieval Period and the Reformation*. Because of its brevity, subject matter, and inability of its contents to easily lend themselves to allegorical interpretation, Phlm was not widely read in medieval times. Thomas Aquinas[§], for example, does not cite Phlm at all in his *Summa Theologica*, not even in those passages that treat slavery (II-II, q.104, a.5, ad 2; II-II, q.122, a.4, ad 3). The early Reformers, however, valued the brief text. Luther[§] saw reflected in the letter "a masterful and tender example of Christian love," noting that all of us are Onesimus in some way. Calvin[§] praised Paul's willingness to treat a mean subject and extolled the compassion of the apostle who pleaded for one of the lowest of men.

3. *Critical Scholarship*. The first real attack against the authenticity of Phlm was launched by F. C. Baur[§] in *Paulus*, his 1845 classic. Baur had to admit that no serious questions as to the Pauline origin of the letter had been previously raised; nonetheless, its linguistic peculiarities prompted him to reject it, just as he had rejected Eph, Phil, and Col. Baur believed that the tale of Onesimus's flight and his meeting with the venerable Paul (v. 9) smacked of a romance. "The letter," he wrote, "is the embryo of a Christian romance like the *Clementine Recognitions*, intended to illustrate the idea that what man loses in time in this world he regains forever in Christianity."

A few other nineteenth-century critics also rejected Phlm as a genuine Pauline writing. K. von Weizsäcker and O. Pfleiderer[§] believed that a pun on the name "Onesimus" (v. 11) indicated that the epistle was an allegorical composition. According to R. Steck (1888), the basis of the letter is to be found in a letter addressed by the younger Pliny to his friend Sabinianus in a similar set of circumstances (Ep. 9.21). H. Holtzmann[§] accepted the letter's basic authenticity but held that the present text is the work of a redactor who added vv. 4-6 to the original Pauline work. On the other hand, such nineteenth-century critics as J. Bengel[§], J. Renan[§], and Sabatier praised the work despite its brevity. It was, said Renan, a "chef d'oeuvre of the art of letter-writing," words echoed some years later by M. Goguel[§], who extolled Phlm as "a chef d'oeuvre of tact and cordiality."

The major critical issues in the study of Phlm have focused on its place and date of composition and on its destination. The similarities between Phlm and Col have led most scholars (e.g., J. B. Lightfoot 1890; K. Staab 1959; C. F. D. Moule 1957; and H. Gülzow 1969) to consider that Paul wrote the letter from Rome during his imprisonment there; supporting arguments could be found in Luke's description of Paul's circumstances in Acts 28. Other scholars (e.g., Holtzmann 1873 and H. Meyer 1855-61; in the twentieth century E. Lohmeyer 1953 and H. Greeven 1954) have opted for Caesarea as the locale of the letter's composition. Arguments for this position are to be found in Caesarea's geographical proximity to Colossae (facilitating Onesimus's access to the city [v. 10] and making it feasible for Paul to realize his desire to visit [v. 22]) and the letter's silence about the earthquake that probably occurred in Colossae in 60-61 C.E. Many commentators (e.g., E. Lohse 1971; G. Friedrich 1981; L. Jang 1964; P. Stulhmacher 1975) have opted for Ephesus (see 1 Cor 15:32; 2 Cor 1:8-9; 11:23-24) as the most likely site. Paul's long stay in Ephesus (Acts 19) and the relative proximity of Ephesus to Colossae are the principal reasons cited in favor of this option.

The location of the recipients of the letter is not explicitly identified in the salutation. The view that the letter was sent to a Colossian household is based on the similarities between Phlm and Col and the apparent identification of Colossae as the city of Onesimus (Col 4:9) and Archippus (Col 4:17). Some scholars (e.g., K. Wieseler 1813-83; E. Goodspeed 1871-1962; J. Knox 1935), however, believed that the letter was directed to a community at Laodicea.

Knox[§] proposed that Phlm was the letter from Laodicea mentioned in Col 4:16 and argued that it was written at approximately the same time as Colossians; that it was really directed to a church community (v. 1) and was intended to be read aloud within the community; that two distinct letters are involved; and that it is highly unlikely that the letter from Laodicea would have been lost. Knox added the suggestion that one of the reasons why Phlm was preserved was that Onesimus was the compiler of the early Pauline corpus. He also held that the letter was addressed to Philemon at Laodicea, urging him to bring the moral weight of his authority to bear upon Archippus, a resident of Colossae, to free his slave Onesimus.

Knox's theory has been strongly criticized (e.g., by Greeven, Moule 1957, and H.-M. Schenke 1978 who attacked its shaky grounds; e.g., Marcion cites both a letter to the Laodiceans [= Eph] and a letter to Philemon); but its principal features have been reiterated by L. Cope (1985), who proposed that Archippus was Onesimus's master and that Paul used the entire weight of his moral authority on Onesimus's behalf, not only sending Phlm along with Col but also intending that it be read to church leaders in Laodicea.

In 1961 U. Wickert suggested that despite its brevity Phlm should not be considered to be merely a personal letter; it is an apostolic writing of the same genus as that of the other genuine Pauline letters. As an apostolic text, the letter offers an illustration of apostolic freedom (see 1 Cor 9:19-23). Paul pleads for Onesimus, not on the basis of friendship, but on the basis of the gospel. In 1978 Schenke argued that Phlm, an authentic letter of the apostle, was published as a witness to the authenticity of Col (which is considered by many scholars to be inauthentic).

4. *Late Twentieth-Century Trends.* Of specific interest in exegesis in the last decades of the twentieth century, with its emphasis on sociological factors (Sociology and New Testament Studies*[§]), is Onesimus's situation as a runaway slave. Under Roman law, escape from slavery was forbidden and recaptured slaves were severely punished (e.g., by branding, fetters, etc.).

Runaway slaves were returned to their masters, while those who harbored runaways were subject to fines. If, however, a slave had run away to avoid maltreatment (legal appeals involved a time-consuming process), he or she was not considered a fugitive. In 1985 P. Lampe argued that the legal category of *fugitivus* did not apply to Onesimus. Whether Roman law was applicable to the case depends on Philemon's citizenship (Roman or not). On this matter the letter offers insufficient evidence.

Another sociological factor to be considered is the role of the household. Philemon appears to be a leader and patron of the assembly that gathered in his house. Apphia is also a church leader and perhaps the wife of Philemon as well. Philemon's social and ecclesial status are such that Onesimus's situation involves the life as well as the moral and social standards of the entire community (i.e., Philemon's household and the church that gathers in his house).

Following on J. White's earlier work (1971), F. Church's Rhetorical*§ analysis of Phlm (1978) led him to conclude that the letter was much more than a private plea by Paul on behalf of Onesimus. Onesimus may have been the subject of Paul's plea, but the object of his public letter is love and brotherhood.

An important step forward in research on Phlm was taken by N. Petersen (1985), who used a variety of Literary*§-critical and sociological methods, including the sociology of knowledge, to examine the symbolic forms and social arrangements of the letter's narrative world. For Petersen, the way in which Paul wrote (as an ambassador, v. 9) placed Philemon under an apostolic mandate to receive Onesimus as the brother he had become. Their relationship in the Lord governed their relationship in the secular world, thereby requiring Philemon to release his former slave. Were he not to do so, the church that met in his house would have had no available course of action other than to reject him as a leader and member of the church.

In a doctoral dissertation and related articles, S. Winter argues that Phlm is a letter to a church rather than a private letter and holds that Onesimus is not a runaway. She opines that the contents of the letter are primarily a matter of concern for Archippus insofar as he had sent Onesimus to Paul on behalf of the church at Colossae. The letter to the church meeting in Philemon's house, delivered by a person other than Onesimus, requests that Onesimus be allowed to stay and work with Paul, thereby implying that he is no longer to be considered a slave, a situation that would require his manumission by Archippus. From quite a different vantage point, J. Burtchaell (1973, 1998) argues that Phlm constitutes a radical demand for the Christian to revolutionize institutions from within.

Recent commentaries on Phlm include Barth and Blanke (2000), Callahan (2003), Felder (2000), Fitzmyer (2000), Lampe (1998), and Osiek (2000). Barclay (1997) provides an introduction to interpreting the letter. Mills (2002) provides a research bibliography. Cotrozzi (1998) is an introductory guide to interpreting and translating Paul's letter. Reuter (2003) is a detailed comparative study of Col and Phlm.

Bibliography: **J. M. G. Barclay,** *Colossians and Philemon* (New Testament Guides, 1997). **M. Barth and H. Blanke,** *The Letter to Philemon: A New Translation with Notes and Commentary* (Eerdmans Critical Commentary, 2000). J. M. Bassler, *Pauline Theology* (1991). **J. T. Burtchaell,** *Philemon's Problem; The Daily Dilemma of the Christian* (1973); rev. and expanded Jubilee edition published as *Philemon's Problem: A Theology of Grace* (Jubilee ed. 1998). **A. D. Callahan,** *Embassy of Onesimus: The Letter of Paul to Philemon* (1997); "The Letter of Paul to Philemon, *NISB* (2003) 2147-50. **F. F. Church**, "Rhetorical Structure and Design in Paul's Letter to Philemon," *HTR* 71 (1978) 17-33. **L. Cope**, "On Rethinking the Philemon and Colossians Connection," *BR* 30 (1985) 45-50. **S. Cotrozzi**, *Exegetischer Führer zum Titus- und Philemonbrief: Ein Wort-für-Wort-Überblick über sämtliche Auslegungs- und Übersetzungsvarianten* (Theologisches Lehr- und Studienmateriall, Biblia et symbiotica 16, 1998). **J. D. G. Dunn,** *The Epistle to the Colossians and to Philemon: A Commentary on the Greek Text* (1996). **C. H. Felder,** "Letter to Philemon," *NIB* (2000) 11:881-906. **J. A. Fitzmyer,** *The Letter to Philemon: A New Translation with Introduction and Commentary* (AB 34C, 2000). **G. Friedrich**, "Der Brief an Philemon," *Die Briefe an die Galater, Epheser, Philipper,*

Kolosser, Thessalonischer, und Philemon (1981). **M. A. Getty**, "The Letter to Philemon," *TBT* 22 (1984) 137-44. **H. Greeven**, "Prüfung der Thesen von J. Knox zum Philemonbrief," *TLZ* 79 (1954) 373-78. **H. Gülzow**, *Christentum und Sklaverei in den ersten drei Jahrhunderten* (1969). **H. J. Holtzmann**, "Der Brief an den Philemon, kritisch untersucht," *ZWT* 16 (1873) 428-41. **H. Hübner**, *An Philemon; An die Kolosser; An die Epheser* (1997). **L. Jang**, *Der Philemonbrief im zusammenhang mit dem theologischen Denken des Apostels Paulus* (1964). **J. Knox**, *Philemon Among the Letters of Paul: A New View of Its Place and Importance* (1935, rev. ed. 1959). **P. Lampe**, "Keine 'Sklavenflucht' des Onesimus," *ZNW* 76 (1985) 135-37; "Philemon," *Die Briefe an die Philipper, Thessalonicher und an Philemon* (N. Walter, E. Reinmuth, and P. Lampe, NTD 8.2, 1998[18]). **J. B. Lightfoot**, *Saint Paul's Epistles to the Colossians and to Philemon: Revised Text with Introduction, Notes, and Dissertations* (1890). **E. Lohmeyer**, *Die Brief und die Kolosser und an Philemon* (KEK 9, 2, 1953). **E. Lohse**, *Colossians and Philemon* (Hermeneia, 1971). **H. Meyer**, *Kritisch exegetischer Kommentar über das NT* (1855-61). **W. E. Mills**, *Philemon* (Bibliographies for Biblical Research, New Testament 15, 2002). **C. F. D. Moule**, *Christ's Messengers: Studies in the Acts of the Apostles* (World Christian Books 19, 1957). **C. Osiek**, *Philippians, Philemon* (ANTC, 2000). **P. Perkins**, "Philemon," *Women's Bible Commentary* (ed. C. A. Newsom and S. H. Ringe, 1992). **N. R. Petersen**, *Rediscovering Paul: Philemon and the Sociology of Paul's Narrative World* (1985). **T. Preiss**, *Life in Christ* (SBT 13, 1954) 32-42. **R. Reuter**, *Textvergleichende und synoptische Arbeit an den Briefen des Neuen Testaments: Geschichte - Methodik - Praxis; Textvergleich Kolosser- und Philemonbrief* (Studies in the Religion and History of Early Christianity 13, 2003). **W. Schenk**, "Der Brief des Paulus an Philemon in der neueren Forschung (1945-87)," *ANRW* II.25.4 (1987) 3439-95. **K. Staab**, *Die Thessalonicherbriefe, die Gefangenschaftsbriefe* (RNT 7, 1959). **R. Steck**, *Der Galaterbrief: Microform, nach seiner Echtheit untersucht, nebst Kritischen Bemerkungen zu den Paulinsichen Hauptbriefen* (1888). **P. Stuhlmacher**, *Der Brief an Philemon* (EKKNT 18, 1975). **J. White**, "The Structural Analysis of Philemon: A Point of Departure in the Formal Analysis of the Pauline Letter," *SBLSP* (1971) 1-47. **U. Wickert**, "Der Philemonbrief: Privatbrief oder apostoliches Schreiben?" *ZNW* 52 (1961) 230-38. **S. C. Winter**, "Paul's Letter to Philemon," *NTS* 33 (1987) 1-15; "Philemon," *Searching the Scriptures: A Feminist Commentary* (ed. E. Schüssler Fiorenza, 1994) 301-12.

R. F. COLLINS

Hebrews, Letter to the

1. *Authorship and Background*. The Epistle to the Hebrews has always confronted interpreters with difficulties, the first of which is its authorship. Origen[§] recognized that its style differed from that of Paul[†§], although he deemed its thought as Pauline and in casual reference usually quoted the epistle as Paul's words. Clement of Alexandria[§] claimed that Paul had written in Hebrew and then Luke had translated his words into Greek. According to Jerome[§], Tertullian[§] attributed the epistle to Barnabas, while others attributed it to Luke the Evangelist or to Clement of Rome[§].

Although Pauline authorship came to be assumed as the epistle established itself in the Canon[§] of Scripture, Luther[§] reopened the question. Aware of the early discussion, he concluded that Paul could not be the author. He noticed that the refusal to permit repentance after baptism in Heb (6:4-6) differed from the acceptance of repentance after baptism in the Gospels and in Paul's epistles. Instead, he suggested that Apollos (Acts 18:24) was the author. The rejection of Pauline authorship led him and others to question the epistle's canonicity.

Modern critical scholarship has universally rejected Pauline authorship. Various candidates have been suggested as author, including Priscilla (A. von Harnack 1900; R. Hoppin 1969); but the most plausible suggestion is undeniably Apollos, because his characterization in Acts 18:24 fits very well with the contents of Heb. Furthermore, he came from Alexandria, and many links have been traced with the works of Philo[§], the Jewish philosopher and scriptural exegete who lived during the rise of Christianity (C. Spicq 1952; H. Montefiore 1964). No solution can be regarded as proven, and many feel drawn to Origen's conclusion that only God knows the author of Heb.

Modern critical scholarship has also been engaged in the search for the true origin and background of Heb. The traditional idea that it was addressed to Jews has been questioned on the grounds that the addressees are exhorted as lapsing Christians, that Heb 13:4 implies readers who did not share basic Jewish moral standards, and that the treatment of sacrifice and temple ritual rests not on knowledge of contemporary practice but on theoretical assumptions based on the LXX (see Septuagint*[§]). Connections with the problems in the Pauline or deuteropauline epistles have also been made. T. Manson[§] (1949-50) suggested that the opening chapters imply a heresy similar to that at Colossae; and C. Montefiore[§] related various elements in the epistle with the problems in the Corinthian church. On the other hand, W. Manson[§] (1951) noted parallels with Stephen's speech in Acts and, therefore, connected the work with non-Pauline Gentile missions.

The discovery among the Dead Sea Scrolls[§] of 11Q Melchisedek has further complicated the question of background. Melchisedek is undeniably an important figure in the epistle. The etymological discussion can be paralleled in Philo; however, it is now claimed that the fragment from Qumran, which depicts Melchisedek as the eschatological agent who judges the world at the end, more adequately explains the speculations about the eternity of Melchisedek and Jesus's*[§] affiliation with Melchisedek's priesthood. If this position is further validated, then a closer relationship with Palestine and the Jewish mission might reassert itself. Meanwhile, the vexing question concerning the origins of Gnosticism (Gnostic Interpretation[§]) and its possible presence in the background to the New Testament continues to affect the discussion of Heb. The perception that Gnosticism may have its roots in Judaism, and particularly the dualism of Apocalypticism*[§], compounds the question about the thoughtworld of this epistle.

2. *Platonism and Eschatology*. Platonism and eschatology are closely related to the complex exegetical difficulties in Heb. Origen, for instance, assumed that the epistle was about the relation-

ship between the old and the new covenants. Although his homilies on Heb are unavailable, certain statements from Heb recur in his writings: "for the law made nothing perfect" (Heb 7:19); "they serve a copy and a shadow of the heavenly sanctuary" (Heb 8:5); "the law has a shadow of the good things to come and not the very image of the things" (Heb 10:1). Heb gave Origen scriptural warrant for his view that Christ is the key to the Hebrew Bible and justified his typological interpretation. Yet Origen also looked forward to a further fulfillment when what we see in shadow we shall see face to face; and for him the heavenly realities belong to a transcendent, rather platonically conceived realm. The same texts from Heb supported this double typology.

The "Platonism" of Heb has also figured in modern discussion, in particular its relationship with the epistle's eschatology. Those who assign to Heb an Alexandrian and Philonic background take Heb 8 and 10 as Platonic and speak of the eschatological perceptions of the earliest church as modified in these terms; the city of God is no longer future but transcendent. However, Heb 11–12 point forward, and the tension between "realized" and "future" eschatology is present in Heb as much as elsewhere in the New Testament. There is no unresolved conflict here and no need to call in Platonic influence, since apocalypticism already contained ideas about heaven that could explain the thought of the author (A. Lincoln 1981). Both Heb 8:5 and the rabbinic literature treat the Exodus text about Moses' revelation of the pattern of the tabernacle in a similar way. Therefore, Platonism is not necessarily helpful for explaining features of this epistle, although the question of Platonic influence remains intriguing, since verbal parallels with Philo cannot be denied.

3. *Interpretation of the Hebrew Bible.* Origen appreciated Heb's typological method of treating the Hebrew Bible and used it to justify his own procedures. Modern commentators, however, find it embarrassing. Responsible critics carefully explain how the author uses the Hebrew Bible because the method is foreign to modern readers. Critical studies have shown that the argument of Heb 10:5-10 depends on a scribal error that could have occurred only in Greek and does not work if the Hebrew text is followed; that the argument of Heb 2:5-10 depends on a misunderstanding of the Hebrew of Psalm 8 if proper attention is paid to context; that unrelated texts are conflated by catchword; and that the arbitrary methods of typology and allegory recur throughout the epistle. Such features can be paralleled in scriptural interpretation in this period and sometimes seem to have been deliberate techniques of exegesis. Although a study of ancient interpretive methods can account for the Hermeneutics*[§] of Heb, this study has the effect of distancing the epistle from the modern reader. The hermeneutical style of Heb is a subject at the center of any modern interpretative endeavor but one that tends to rest purely at the descriptive and explanatory level (S. Sowers 1965 and G. Hughes 1979 have tried to go further).

4. *Christology.* The Christology of Hebrews has been a perennial topic of interest. R. Greer (1973) has suggested that the Arian and Nestorian christological controversies of the fourth and fifth centuries significantly affected the interpretation of the epistle (Origen[§], Arius[§], Theodore[§], Cyril[§], Antiochene School[§]).

Consciously or unconsciously informed by this ancient debate, modern commentators have often spoken of the paradoxical nature of Heb's Christology. From a modern historical perspective the terms of the patristic discussion appear anachronistic; yet critics continue to note that Heb has both the highest Christology in the New Testament, except perhaps that of John's Gospel, and the most realistic portrayal of Christ's genuine human experiences of temptation, weakness, suffering, and death.

Modern discussion has focused on the background to Heb 1:3 in the figure of personified Wisdom found in Prov 8, Eccl 24, and especially Wis 7:25-26. It has also noted the way in which the scriptural quotation in Heb 1:8-9 implies that the Son is addressed as "God." Such comment tries to avoid anachronistic dogmatic interpretation, yet the questions it raises in relation to the humanness of Jesus perhaps distract from a proper perception of the integration of the author's thought. The "two natures" problem still lurks in the background. If the author simply regarded Jesus as the final embodiment of God's Word and Wisdom, which had been visible before in many and various ways, the apparent tension may be somewhat resolved. Wisdom may be described as the "image" of God; but then humans were created in the "image" of God. There is undoubtedly some "Adam-typology" in the thought of the epistle. The problems of interpreting Heb's Christology may lie in the heritage of dogmatic interpretation rather than in the text itself.

5. *Paraenesis.* The dominant theme in the epistle's overall argument is the pioneering and exemplary character of the Jesus story. Some modern commentators have tried to distinguish the paraenetic passages from the exegetical and theological passages, but in fact they are closely integrated and reinforce one another. Modern critical discussion has taken the paraenesis seriously and deduced that the epistle may have originated as a homily, especially since there is no epistolary introduction. It has also deduced that the epistle was written to a Christian community that was in danger of giving up, probably in the face of persecution. Some scholars have suggested on these grounds that Heb must be a second-generation document.

Patristic interest in the epistle also focused on the paraenesis. Origen found much material that related to his ideas of the spiritual journey and the parental discipline of God's fundamental purpose (esp. Heb 12). Modern studies have also turned to the pilgrimage theme of the epistle, and it is perhaps here that the unity of its Christology with every other aspect of its thrust is to be perceived.

Recent commentaries on Heb include DeSilva (2000), Gordon (2000), Hagner (2003), Karrer (2002), and Koester (2001). Social-scientific approaches to Heb include Isaak (2002), Johnson (2001), and Salevao (2002). Cadwallader (2002) approaches Heb 11 using environmental theology. Miscellaneous treatments of literary and theological issues include Anderson (2001), Croy (1998), Kurianal (2000), Rhee (2001), and Wray (1998).

Bibliography: D. R. Anderson, *The King-Priest of Psalm 110 in Hebrews* (Studies in Biblical Literature 21, 2001). **H. W. Attridge,** *The Epistle to the Hebrews* (Hermeneia 1989). **I. Backus et al.,** "Text, Translation and Exegesis of Heb. 9 (1516-99)," *JMRS* 14 (1984) 77-119. **F. F. Bruce,** *The Epistle to the Hebrews* (NICNT, 1964); " 'To the Hebrews': A Document of Roman Christianity?" *ANRW* II.25 (1987) 3496-3521. **A. H. Cadwallader,** "Earth as Host or Stranger? Reading Hebrews 11 from Diasporan Experience," *The Earth Story in the New Testament* (ed. N. C. Habel and V. Balabanski, Earth Bible 5, 2002). **J. Casey,** *Hebrews* (1980). **F. B. Craddock,** "Hebrews," *NIB* (1998) 12:1-173. **N. C. Croy,** *Endurance in Suffering: Hebrews 12:1-13 in its Rhetorical, Religious, And Philosophical Context* (SNTSMS 98, 1998). **M. R. D'Angelo,** "Hebrews," *The Women's Bible Commentary* (ed. C. A. Newsom and S. H. Ringe, 1992) 364-67. **B. A. Demarest,** *A History of Interpretation of Hebrews 7, 1-10 from the Reformation to the Present* (BGBE 19, 1976). **D. A. deSilva,** *Perseverance in Gratitude: A Socio-Rhetorical Commentary on the Epistle "to the Hebrews"* (2000). **H. Feld,** *M. Luthers und W. Steinbachs Vorlesungen über den Hebräerbrief: Eine Studie zur Geschichte der neutestamentlichen Exegese und Theologie* (1971); "Der Hebräerbrief: Literarische Form, religionsgeschichtlicher Hintergrunde, theologische Fragen," *ANRW* II.25.4 (ed. W. Haase, Principat 25, 4, 1987) 3522-3601. **R. P. Gordon,** *Hebrews* (Readings, 2000). **R. A. Greer,** *The Captain of Our Salvation: A Study in the Patristic Exegesis of Hebrews* (BGBE 15, 1973). **K. Hagen,** *Hebrews Commenting from Erasmus to Bèze, 1516-1598* (BGBE 23, 1981). **D. A. Hagner,** "The Letter to the Hebrews," *NISB* 2151-70. **K. G. A. von Harnack,** "Probabilia über die Addresse und den Verfasser der Hebräer-briefs," *ZNW* 1 (1900) 16-41. **R. Hoppin,** *Priscilla: Author of Epistle to the Hebrews and Other Essays* (1969). **F. L. Horton,** *The Melchizedek Tradition* (SNTSMS 30, 1976). **G. Hughes,** *Hebrews and Hermeneutics* (SNTSMS 36, 1979).

J. M. Isaak, *Situating the Letter to the Hebrews in Early Christian History* (Studies in the Bible and Early Christianity 53, 2002). **R. W. Johnson,** *Going Outside The Camp: The Sociological Function of the Levitical Critique in the Epistle to the Hebrews* (JSNTSup 209, 2001). **M. de Jonge and A. S. van der Woude,** "11Q Melchisedek and the NT," *NTS* 12 (1965-66) 318-26. **M. Karrer,** *Der Brief an die Hebräer* (ÖTK 20, 2002-). **E. Käsemann,** *The Wandering People of God: An Investigation of the Letter to the Hebrews* (1938; ET 1984). **C. B. Kittredge,** *Searching the Scriptures: A Feminist Commentary* (ed. E. Schüssler Fiorenza, 1994) 428-52. **C. R. Koester,** *Hebrews: A New Translation with Introduction and Commentary* (AB 36, 2001). **James Kurianal,** *Jesus, Our High Priest: Ps. 110,4 as the Substructure of Heb. 5,1-7,28* (2000). **W. L. Lane,** *Hebrews 1-8* (WBC 47A, 1991); *Hebrews 9-13* (WBC 47B, 1991). **S. Lehne,** *The New Covenant in Hebrews* (JSNTSup 44, 1990). **A. T. Lincoln,** *Paradise Now and Not Yet: Studies in the Role of the Heavenly Dimension in Paul's Thought with Special Reference to His Eschatology* (SNTSMS 43, 1981). **T. G. Long,** *Hebrews* (Interpretation, 1997). **T. W. Manson,** "The Problem of the Epistle to the Hebrews," *BJRL* 32 (1949/50) 1-17; *Studies in the Gospels and Epistles* (1962) 242-58. **W. Manson,** *The Epistle to the Hebrews* (The 1949 Baird Lecture, 1951). **H. W. Montefiore,** *A Commentary on the Epistle to the Hebrews* (HNTC, 1964). **D. Peterson,** *Hebrews and Perfection* (SNTSMS 47, 1982). **V. C. Pfitzner,** *Hebrews* (ANTC, 1997). **V. Rhee,** *Faith in Hebrews: Analysis Within the Context of Christology, Eschatology, and Ethics* (Studies in Biblical Literature 19, 2001). **I. Salevao,** *Legitimation in the Letter to the Hebrews: The Construction and Maintenance of a Symbolic Universe* (JSNTSup 219, 2002). **S. G. Sowers,** *The Hermeneutics of Philo and Hebrews* (1965). **C. Spicq,** *L'Épitre aux Hébreux* (Ébibss, 1952). **J. H. Wray,** *Rest as a Theological Metaphor in the Epistle to the Hebrews and the Gospel of Truth: Early Christian Homiletics of Rest* (SBLDS 166, 1998). **F. M. Young,** "Christological Ideas in the Greek Commentaries on the Epistle to the Hebrews," *JTS* 20 (1969) 150-62.

F. M. YOUNG

THE NEW TESTAMENT CANON

James, Letter of

Just as the origins of the Letter of James are obscure, so also is the history of its early reception. Was the author an apostle and identified as the "brother of the Lord" (Gal 1:19)? Did he write for Jewish Christians? Was the "diaspora" of 1:1 literal or symbolic? Did he write early or late? These questions puzzle us as much as they may have puzzled James's first readers.

How and when the church first appropriated Jas is, in fact, unclear. No official canonical list (such as the Muratorian canon) contained the letter until the late fourth century. Eusebius§ listed Jas among the "disputed books," although it was "recognized by most" (*Hist. eccl.* 25.3). Substantive objections to Jas were not made, and its neglect—if such it was—seems to have been benign. The Alexandrian School§ under Clement§ and Origen§ gave the letter its first explicit literary attention. Origen called James an apostle and explicitly quoted from and designated the letter as Scripture (see, e.g., *Commentary on John* 19.6, *PG* 14:569; *Homilies on Leviticus* 2.4, *PG* 12:41; and the *Commentary on Romans* iv, 8, *PG* 14:989). After Origen, the letter came into wider use and gained Authority*§, as Jerome§ put it, "little by little" (*De Viris Illustribus* 2, *PL* 23:639).

The precritical commentary tradition is sparse and is resolutely non-allegorical, treating Jas very much as moral exhortation. Particular concern was shown for harmonizing Jas and Paul[†§] in the matter of faith and works (Jas 2:14-26), either by distinguishing the condition of the believer before and after baptism (so *Oecumenius and Bar Salibi* twelfth cent.) or by distinguishing kinds of faith (so Theophylact c. 1150-1225). One also finds acute linguistic observations, as when Chrysostom noted the apposite use of *makrothymia* in Jas 5:10 rather than the expected *hypomonē* (PG 64:1049) or when Bar Salibi commented on the various kinds of "zeal" (*zēlos*) in Jas 3:14.

The patristic and medieval commentary tradition is sparse, interdependent, and remarkably uniform. It is also uninformative concerning the role the letter of James may have played in liturgical, homiletical, or didactic settings. Research into such usage has scarcely begun (L. T. Johnson 1995), so our knowledge of the letter's pre-critical reception remains partial.

In the fourteenth through the sixteenth centuries, first the Renaissance, then the Reformation stimulated a transition to a more critical reading of Jas. Three figures established lines of interpretation that have continued to the present: Erasmus§, Luther§, and Calvin§.

Erasmus provided short comments on the verses of Jas in his *Annotationes* of 1516. In contrast to earlier commentators, he treated Jas as he would any other ancient author, raising questions concerning attribution, providing alternative manuscript readings, clarifying linguistic obscurities on the basis of parallel usage, and even suggesting textual emendations (e.g. reading *phthoneite* for the difficult *phoneuete* in Jas 4:2). The letter's moral or religious teaching was scarcely dealt with.

Luther wrote no commentary on Jas but exercised considerable influence over subsequent scholarly interpretation. In the preface to his 1522 German Bible, he dismissed the letter as an "epistle of straw" compared to the writings that "show thee Christ." Luther would therefore not include Jas among the "chief books" of the Canon§, although he admired "the otherwise many fine sayings in him." What was the reason for Luther's rejection? Jas "does nothing more than drive to the law and its works," which Luther found "flatly against St. Paul and all the rest of Scripture." This is the clearest application of Luther's *sachkritik* (content criticism) within the canon; the disagreement between Jas and Paul on one point removes Jas from further consideration. The fact that Jas 5:14 was cited in support of the sacrament of extreme unction did not soften Luther's hostility. In this light, the commentary by the Roman Catholic T. Cajetan§ in

1532 is all the more fascinating. Cajetan also questioned the apostolicity of Jas and denied that 5:14 could be used as a proof text for extreme unction. But concerning Paul and James on faith, he diplomatically concluded, "They both taught truly."

In contrast to Luther, Calvin wrote a sympathetic commentary on Jas in 1551. He found the reasons for rejecting the letter unconvincing and saw nothing in its teaching unworthy of an apostle. Although ready to accept Erasmus's emendation at 4:2, he scoffed at those who found a fundamental conflict between Paul and Jas on faith and works. As in all of his commentaries Calvin brought great exegetical skill to the text, anticipating contemporary sensitivity to the rhetorical skill of Jas as well as a systematic reflection over its religious significance.

With the obvious modifications caused by the ever-growing knowledge of the first-century world and the cumulative weight of scholarship itself, the basic approaches established by the Reformation continued to dominate scholarship on the letter. The legacy of Calvin continued in those commentaries that, however learned, focused primarily on James as teacher of the church. An outstanding example is the 1640 commentary by the Puritan divine T. Manton. Fully conversant with past and contemporary scholarship (much of it no longer available to us), Manton's approach remains essentially pious and edifying. The German commentary of A. Gebser (1828) is similar in character. He cited many ancient sources to illuminate the text, but above all he gave such extensive citations from patristic commentaries and discussions that his commentary virtually provided a history of interpretation. This tradition can be said to have continued in the commentaries of J. Mayor (1910[3]) and F. Vouga (1984). In a real sense these commentaries continued the patristic tradition; the meaningful context for understanding James is the Bible. The strength of this approach is its accommodation to the writing's religious purposes. The weakness is its narrowness and scholastic tendency.

The heritage of Luther continued in the historical approach associated with the Tübingen School, in which Jas was studied primarily as a witness to conflict and development in the early Christian movement. When such scholars as F. Kern (1838) viewed Jas as written by Paul's contemporary, they saw it as representing a Jewish-Christian outlook in tension with Paul's teaching. When such scholars as F. C. Baur[§] (1853-62, 1875) regarded Jas as a pseudonymous composition, they understood it as a second-century mediation of the conflict between Peter and Paul. In either case James's discussion of faith in 2:14-26 and its apparent disagreement with Paul became the central point for interpretation. L. Massebieau (1895) and F. Spitta[§] (1896), however, maintained that Jas represented an entirely Jewish outlook; they considered the Christian elements in the letter the result of interpolation into a pre-Christian writing. This approach continued in those (often "rehabilitating") studies that used Paul as the essential key to understanding Jas (J. Jeremias 1955; D. Via 1969; J. Lodge 1981). The strength of this approach is its historical sensibility. The weakness is its tendency to reduce Jas to a few verses and earliest Christianity to the figure of Paul.

The Erasmian tradition sought to place Jas explicitly within the language and literature of the Hellenistic world. The pioneering monument was the two-volume *Novum Testamentum Graecum* (1752) of J. Wettstein[§], who brought together a storehouse of parallel illustrative material from both Greek and Jewish sources, a collection all the more tempting because it is unsorted. The Jewish side of this approach was developed in the commentary of A. Schlatter[§] (1900), who especially emphasized rabbinic parallels. Mayor (1910[3]) also brought together a rich collection of Hellenistic and Christian material. The commentary by J. Ropes (1916) paid particular attention to the letter's diatribal element and singled out the striking resemblances between it and the Testaments of the Twelve Patriarchs[†§]. The Erasmian approach found its greatest modern exemplar in the commentary by M. Dibelius[§] (1976). Dibelius combined the best of previous scholarship and brought to the text an acute sense of the appropriate illustrative material, bringing to bear pagan, Jewish, and Christian parallels that placed Jas squarely in the tradition of paraenetic literature. Most late twentieth-century scholarship on the letter either derives from or reacts to this magisterial study (cf. L. Perdue 1981; Johnson 1995), although studies have also used more Semiotic*§ (see T. Cargal 1993) and Rhetorical*§ approaches (see D. Watson 1993). The strength of the Erasmian approach is its textual focus and comparative scope. Its weakness is its ability to miss James's religious dimension entirely.

These assertions would meet with fairly general consent among scholars: Jas is a moral exhortation (*protrepsis*) of rare passion whose instructions have general applicability more than specific reference. Although not tightly organized, the letter is more than a loose collection of sayings; the aphorisms in chap. 1 establish themes that are developed in the essays in chaps. 2-5. James's Christianity is neither Pauline nor anti-Pauline but another version altogether. It appropriates Torah as the "law of liberty" as mediated through the words of Jesus*§. James opposes empty posturing and advocates active faith and love. He contrasts "friendship with the world" (living by a measure contrary to God's) and "friendship with God" (living by faith's measure). He wants Christians to live by the measure they profess, and his persuasion has a prophet's power.

Recent commentaries on Jas include Burchard (2000), Popkes (2001), Perkins (2003), Sleeper (d1998), and Wall (1997). Bauckham (1999) and Edgar (2001) situate Jas within its ancient literary and socio-cultural setting. Forster (2002), Jackson-McCabe(2001), and Konradt (1998) study various theological issues in the letter.

Bibliography: E. Baasland, "Literarische Form, Thematik, und geschichtliche Einordung des Jakobsbriefes," *ANRW* II 25 (1987) 3646-62. R. Bauckham, *James: Wisdom of James, Disciple of Jesus the Sage* (New Testament Readings, 1999). F. C. Baur, *The Church History of the First Three Centuries* (1853-62); *Paul, the Apostle of Jesus Christ* (1875[2]). C. Burchard, *Der Jakobusbrief* (HNT 15.1, 2000). T. B. Cargal, *Restoring the Diaspora: Discursive Structure and Purpose in the Epistle of James* (SBLDS 144, 1993). J. A. Cramer, *Catena Graecorum Patrum* (1840). P. H. Davids, "The Epistle of James in Modern Discussion," *ANRW* II 25.5 (1987) 36-45. M. Dibelius, *A Commentary on the Epistle of James* (rev. H. Greeven, Hermeneia; ET 1976). D. H. Edgar *Has God not Chosen the Poor?: The Social Setting of the Epistle of James* (JSNTSup 206, 2001). G. Forster, *The Ethics of the Letter of James* (Grove Ethics E124, 2002). A. R. Gebser, *Der Brief des Jakobus* (1828). M. D. Gibson (ed. and tr.), *Horae Semiticae X: The Commentaries of Isho'dad of Merv, vol. 4, Acts of the Apostles and Three Catholic Epistles* (1913). F. Hahn and P. Müller, "Der Jakobusbrief," *TRu* 63 (1998) 1-73. M. A. Jackson-McCabe, *Logos and Law in the Letter of James: The Law of Nature, the Law of Moses, and the Law of Freedom* (NovTSup 100, 2001). J. Jeremias, "Paul and James," *ExpTim* 66 (1955) 368-71. L. T. Johnson, *The Letter of James* (AB 37A, 1995); "The Letter of James," *NIB* (1998) 12:175-225. F. H. Kern, *Der Brief Jakobi* (1838). M. Konradt, *Christliche Existenz nach dem Jakobusbrief: Eine Studie zu seiner soteriologischen und ethischen Konzeption* (SUNT 22, 1998). S. Laws, *A Commentary on the Epistle of James* (HNT, 1980). J. G. Lodge, "James and Paul at Cross-purposes: James 2:22," *Bib* 62 (1981) 195-213. L. Massebieau, "L'Épître de Jacques: Est-elle l'oeuvre d'un Chrétien?" *RHR* 31-32 (1895) 249-83. T. Manton, *A Practical Commentary or an Exposition with Notes on the Epistle of James* (1640). J. B. Mayor, *The Epistle of St. James* (1910[3]). L. G. Perdue, "Paraenesis and the Epistle of James," *ZNW* 72 (1981) 241-56. P. Perkins, "The Letter of James," *NISB* (2003) 2171-80. W. Popkes, *Der Brief des Jakobus* (THK 14, 2001). J. H. Ropes, *A Critical and Exegetical Commentary on the Epistle of St. James* (ICC, 1916); "The Greek Catena to the Catholic Epistles," *HTR* 19 (1926) 383-88. A. Schlatter, *Des Briefe des Petrus, Judas, Jakobus, der Brief an die Hebraer* (1900). I. Sedlacek (ed.), *Dionysius bar Salibi in Apocalypsim Actus et Epistulas Catholicas* (CSCO 60, Scriptores Syri 20, 1910). C. F. Sleeper,

James (ANTC, 1998). **F. Spitta**, *Zur Geschichte und Literatur des Urchristentums 2: Der Brief des Jakobus* (1896). **D. O. Via**, "The Right Strawy Epistle Reconsidered: A Study in Biblical Ethics and Hermeneutics," *JR* 49 (1969) 253-67. **F. Vouga**, *L'Épître de Saint Jacques* (CNT, 2nd ser., 13a, 1984). **R. W. Wall**, *Community of the Wise: The Letter of James* (New Testament in Context, 1997). **D. F. Watson**, "James 2 in the Light of Greco-Roman Schemes of Argumentation," *NTS* 39 (1993) 94-121.

L. T. JOHNSON

THE NEW TESTAMENT CANON

Peter, First Letter of

1. *Early Interpretations.* The history of the interpretation of 1 Pet probably begins within the New Testament Canon[§]. The author of 2 Pet, writing as the apostle Peter, claims, "This is now, beloved, the second letter I am writing to you; in them I am trying to arouse your sincere intention by reminding you that you should remember the words spoken in the past by the holy prophets, and the commandment of the Lord and Savior spoken through your apostles" (2 Pet 3:1-2). "Second letter" implies a first, and there is wide agreement that the letter now known as 1 Pet is in the writer's mind. Yet the reference shows little awareness of the actual content of 1 Pet. Second Pet is more interested in describing its own intentions than those of its predecessor (the same is true of the brief reference to the letters of Paul[†§] in 2 Pet 3:15-16). At most it is possible that "the words spoken in the past by the holy prophets" may refer vaguely to 1 Pet 1:10-12. Yet the slender link forged by the reference in 2 Pet 3:1, strengthened by the pairing of the two letters under Peter's name in the New Testament canon, inevitably affected the interpretation of this letter in the church. In the eighteenth century J. Bengel[§] outlined 1 Peter and entitled the body of the letter (1 Pet 1:3-5:11), "The stirring up of a pure feeling," on the ground that this is the purpose of both letters according to 2 Pet 3:1 (1877, 5:43).

During the early period, very little formal interpretation of 1 Pet seems to have taken place. However, the church fathers (Clement of Alexandria[§], Cassiodorus[§], Clement[§], Irenaeus[§], Tertullian[§] , Jerome[§], and many others) frequently quote the letter and sometimes briefly summarize it.

2. *Author and Audience.* Eusebius in the fourth century, taking 1 Pet 1:1 at face value, concluded that the epistle is "indisputably Peter's, in which he writes to those of the Hebrews in the Dispersion of Pontus and Galatia, Cappadocia, Asia, and Bithynia" because he had preached "the Gospel of Christ to those of the circumcision" in those provinces (*Hist. eccl.* 3.4.2; this is in contrast to "Paul, in his preaching to the Gentiles," 3.4.1; cf. 3.1). This characterization of 1 Pet as a letter to Jewish Christians (probably based as much on Gal 2:7-8 as on 1 Pet) was enormously influential in later centuries—e.g., on 1 Pet 1:1: Calvin[§] ("This can apply only to the Jews" 1948, 26) and J. Wesley[§] ("Christians, chiefly those of Jewish extraction" 1755, 872). J. Bengel's[§] comment was more nuanced ("He addresses the dispersed Jews...although he afterwards addresses believers of the Gentiles, who are mixed with them, ch. ii.10, note, iv.3" 1877, 5:45). Luther[§] took a different, also nuanced, approach: "It is surprising that while St. Peter was an apostle to the Jews, he is nevertheless writing to the heathen.... Accordingly, he is writing to those who had formerly been heathen but had now been converted to the faith and had joined the believing Jews" (LW 30 1967, 6; cf. W. Tyndale's comment in his *Prologue upon the First Epistle of St. Peter* that Peter wrote "to the heathen that were converted" 1965, 163).

For the most part the judgment of Eusebius prevailed well into the nineteenth century. A stark contrast between the "Gentile-oriented" Paul and the "Jewish-oriented" Peter is evident in Christian history at least back to the third-century Pseudo-Clementine literature. The historical reconstructions of F. C. Baur[§] and the Tübingen school in the nineteenth century were built on that assumption; yet at the same time Baur found in 1 Pet "striking points of agreement in language and ideas with the Pauline letters." Consequently he gave up apostolic authorship of the letter, proposing that both 1 and 2 Pet were second-century documents mediating and harmonizing the conflicting views of Peter and Paul (cited in W. Kümmel 1972, 130-31).

Whatever one may think of Baur's reconstruction, it is true that Christian interpreters, both critical and pre-critical, have seen a considerable measure of agreement between Paul's letters and 1 Pet. Luther stated that Peter in this letter "does the same thing that St. Paul and all the evangelists do; he teaches the true faith and tells us that Christ was given to us to take away our sins and to save us" (30 1967, 4). Because thirteen canonical letters are attributed to Paul and only two to Peter and because the self-designation in 1 Pet 1:1 seems to echo those of Paul, it seems that 1 Pet was assimilated to Paul and not the other way around.

The full history of the interpretation of 1 Pet up to the nineteenth century remains to be written. In the bibliography to his commentary (1996, 359-61), P. Achtemeier provides some tools for such an undertaking, and T. Martin (1992, 3-39, 277-84) has made a beginning with respect to the compositional analysis of the letter's structure. For the most part, however, scholars have concentrated instead on tracing the interpretation of specific passages, above all passages that became the focus of doctrinal controversies in or between Christian churches.

3. *Christ and the Disobedient Spirits.* The classic case study by which to illustrate the latter point is the reference in 1 Pet 3:19 to Christ's journey to preach to imprisoned spirits from the time of Noah (see W. Dalton's thorough summary 1989, 27-50). The notion of Christ's "descent into hell" for the redemption of lost souls was a topic of interest in early Christianity almost from the beginning, but not until Clement of Alexandria (*Strom.* 6.6.38-39) was this teaching linked in any way to 3:19. This line of interpretation was followed in the Greek church by Origen, Cyril[§], and others; and in the Syriac tradition, by the Peshitta[§] version ("And he preached to those souls detained in Sheol who had once been disobedient in the days of Noah," J. Murdock 1858, 424). Augustine[§], by contrast, saw in the passage a reference to the preexistent Christ preaching through Noah to the wicked of his generation (PL 33.708-16). Because it avoided the doctrinal problem of conversion after death, Augustine's view became popular in the West among both Catholics and Protestants. Although it had little basis in the text or context, this view could appeal to 1:11 for a preexisting "spirit of Christ" and to 2 Pet 2:5 for Noah as a "preacher of righteousness." More influential among Roman Catholics since the Counter Reformation was the view of R. Bellarmine[§], who linked the passage with Christ's descent but argued that Christ preached to souls from Noah's time who had already repented and, in effect, delivered them from purgatory. He did this by identifying the "spirits" of 3:19 with "the dead" to whom "the gospel was preached" according to 4:6 (see Dalton, 40, 44).

With modern historical criticism came a new awareness of Jewish apocalyptic literature (Apocalypticism*[§]), especially 1 Enoch[†§], and consequently new interpretations of 3:19. Christ was seen, not as offering salvation to lost souls, but as pronouncing judgment either on the fallen angels of the flood story and their offspring (Gen 6:1-4), or on the wicked who died in the flood, or both. This judicial act was linked either to Christ's "descent into hell" between death and resurrection (E. Selwyn 1946; B. Reicke 1946) or, more recently, to his ascension after the resurrection (K. Gschwind 1911; Dalton; J. Kelly 1969; N. Brox 1979; J. Michaels 1988; Achtemeier). The latter interpretation afforded a link between this controversial passage and the letter's general theme of the vindication of Christians against their "disobedient" oppressors in the Roman Empire (2:8; 3:1; 4:17). Other modern scholars, however, still view the passage as some kind of an offer of salvation, whether to humans or to angels (see K. Schelkle 1970; F. Beare 1970[3]; L. Goppelt 1978 [ET 1993]).

4. *Modern Interpretations of 1 Peter.* The rise of historical criticism affected the interpretation of 1 Pet in other ways as well. Doubts about the Petrine authorship of 2 Pet (and to a lesser extent 1 Pet) severed the traditional connection between the two canonical letters. First Pet was seen as a self-contained early Christian document in its own right and not as the first of two reminders of "the words spoken in the past by the holy prophets, and the commandment of the Lord and Savior spoken through your apostles" (2 Pet 3:2). Yet this did not exclude the recognition that the letter does contain traditional material. For decades the modern discussion centered on assessing the relationship between 2 Pet and the traditions of 1 Pet. On the matter of authorship, an increasing number of scholars suggested that the work was pseudonymous (that

is, written by someone other than Peter in the apostle's name). Still, the traditional view continued to find defenders, at least in the sense of a connection (direct or indirect) with the historical Peter. So far as the letter's readers were concerned, however, the older view that they were Jewish Christians gave way to the theory that they were largely or even exclusively Gentile Christians (as Luther and Tyndale had thought and as the language of 1:14, 18, and 4:3-4 suggests).

The years 1946-47 marked a turning point in the study of the letter. In 1946 B. Reicke[§] made extensive use of comparative Jewish and Hellenistic material to shed light on 3:18-22 and 4:6 and at the same time to call attention to the significance of Christian baptism in the letter as a whole. In the same year Selwyn (in an appendix to his commentary, 314-64) independently reached some of the same conclusions about the same two texts. More important, he applied the methods of Form Criticism*[§] (previously used only in the study of the Gospels) to argue for 1 Pet's dependence on a common early Christian catechism known to Paul and to other Christian writers and based on the Holiness Code of Leviticus 17-26 (365-466). In 1947 F. W. Beare[§] (in the first edition of his commentary) raised acutely in the English-speaking world the doubts already current in Germany (going back to Baur, A. von Harnack, and others) about the letter's traditional Petrine authorship and first-century date.

In the decade or so that followed, more attention was given to the traditions behind 1 Pet than to the letter in its present form. First Pet 1:3–4:11 was seen as originally not a letter at all but as a baptismal homily or liturgy. Beare regarded this section as a homily on baptism later placed in an epistolary framework consisting of 1:1-2 and 4:12–5:14. H. Preisker, in his revision of H. Windisch's[§] commentary (1951), constructed an elaborate liturgy in which the baptism of candidates was said to have taken place between 1:21 and 1:22. Even 4:12–5:11 was no longer viewed as a letter but as a concluding liturgy for the whole congregation. F. Cross (1954) proposed on the basis of second-century sources (Melito's *On the Passover and the Apostolic Tradition of Hippolytus*) a wordplay between the Greek verb *paschein* (to suffer) in 1 Pet (twelve occurrences) and the Hebrew noun *pascha* (Passover). Consequently he interpreted the letter in its entirety as a Passover/Easter liturgy centering on baptism (again with the baptism of candidates taking place after 1:21). In contrast, E. Lohse in 1954 maintained the epistolary character of 1 Pet and saw it as an example of early Christian paraenesis—that is, as an actual letter using traditional forms of expression in order to encourage its readers in the face of impending persecution (1986). C. F. D. Moule[§] (1956-57), impressed by the change of tone and apparent break between 4:11 and 4:12, proposed two forms of the letter sent to two different audiences: one (consisting of 1:1–4:11 and 5:12-14) for churches not yet suffering actual persecution, and the other (1:1–2:10 and 4:12–5:14) for those already facing the "fiery trial" signaled in 4:12.

Since the early 1960s the unity and epistolary character of 1 Pet have been strongly reasserted (e.g., in the commentaries of Schelkle; Kelly; E. Best 1971; Goppelt; Brox; Michaels; and Achtemeier), even though its use of traditional materials continued to be recognized and ever more carefully charted (see, e.g., D. Balch 1981 on the "household code" of 2:13–3:9). This trend followed in the wake of a corresponding shift in the study of the Gospels from form to Redaction Criticism*[§]. Just as the Gospel writers had come to be regarded not as mere compilers of tradition but as authors and theologians in their own right, so also 1 Pet (whether written by the apostle Peter or not) was being more and more appreciated for its distinctive contributions to early Christian theology and ethics. It was no longer possible to view the letter as just another deuteropauline writing, as if its author were trying to imitate Paul but was not quite succeeding.

In one area at least—the sociological interpretation of New Testament texts (Sociology and New Testament Studies*[§])—studies in 1 Pet showed the way, beginning with W. van Unnik's

1954 article on good works and civic virtue and coming to fruition in L. Goppelt's[§] commentary and the monographs of J. Elliott (1981) and Balch. In the 1980s the letter's accent on "honor" and "shame" and the contrast between the two captured the attention of those who advocated a sociological approach. Elliott's emphasis was on "boundary maintenance" (that is, on the attempt to preserve Christian distinctives in a hostile Roman culture), while Balch found more significant the interest in "acculturation" (i.e., in conforming as far as possible to dominant Roman values so as to minimize social conflict). Their debate is concisely documented in a volume edited by C. Talbert, who in conclusion recognizes both social goals in the letter: "(1) the social cohesion of the Christian groups, and (2) the social adaptation of the Christian groups to their cultural setting. Without the first, Christian identity would have been lost. Without the second, Christians would have had no social acceptability, which is also necessary for survival and outreach" (1986, 148).

Another factor introduced into the discussion (see Michaels; T. Martin 1992) is the analogy between the social self-consciousness of these early Gentile Christians and that of the Jews in the diaspora. The evidence that misled Eusebius long ago into supposing a Jewish Christian audience (e.g., the language of 1:1) could suggest that 1 Pet, like James, was intended as a Christian "diaspora letter" based on just such an analogy. Comparative studies are needed on the place of Judaism and of Gentile Christianity respectively in the Roman Empire of the late first century. Such studies could enrich and be enriched by the continuing investigation of 1 Pet in its historical and social setting.

At least two other tasks remain in connection with the letter. The first task is theological. Despite an ever-widening recognition of 1 Pet's significant place in early Christianity, no major work of New Testament theology has yet tried to do justice to its distinctive witness to Christ and to the Christian life. The second task has to do with Literary*[§] and/or Rhetorical Criticism*[§]. Aside from questions of genre (i.e., liturgy, homily, or genuine letter), the only major foray into these areas has been the Semiotic*[§] analysis of J. Calloud and F. Genuyt (1982). Part of the reason is that the newer methodologies in literary criticism have been applied more frequently to New Testament narratives than to New Testament letters; yet rhetorical criticism has been applied to the letters of Paul, Jas, 2 Pet, Jude, and Heb. At this writing, 1 Pet needs more attention from this perspective. Still, a growing number of commentaries and monographs testify that the letter, if never quite "the storm centre of New Testament studies" that S. Neill claimed it was (1964, 343), is no longer the "exegetical step-child" that Elliott (with some justification) called it in 1976 (Talbert, 3-16). Slowly but surely this "minor" New Testament voice distinct from Paul and distinct from the Gospels is making itself heard both in the academy and in the church.

Recent commentaries on 1 Pet include Boring (ANTC, 1999), Elliott (2000), and Senior (2003). Shimada (1998) is a recent set of collected essays on 1 Pet. Bechtler (1998) and Campbell (1998) use anthropological and sociological approaches to interpret 1 Pet. Dubis (2002), Herzer (1998), Ostmeyer (2000), Pearson (2001), and Prasad (2000) study various theological elements in the letter.

Bibliography: P. J. Achtemeier, *1 Peter: A Commentary on First Peter* (Hermeneia, 1996). **D. Balch**, *Let Wives Be Submissive: The Domestic Code in 1 Peter* (SBLMS 26, 1981). **D. L. Bartlett**, "The First Letter of Peter," *NIB* (1997) 12:227-319. **F. W. Beare**, *The First Epistle of Peter* (1947, 1970[3]). **S. R. Bechtler,** *Following in His Steps: Suffering, Community, and Christology in 1 Peter* (SBLDS 162, 1998). **J. A. Bengel**, *Gnomon of the New Testament* (ed. A. R. Fausset, 1877). **E. Best**, *1 Peter* (NCB, 1971). **M. E. Boring,** *1 Peter* (ANTC, 1999). **N. Brox**, "Der erste Petrusbrief in der literarischen Tradition des Urchristentums," *Kairos 20* (1978) 182-92; *Der erste Petrusbrief* (EKKNT, 1979). **J. Calloud and F. Genuyt,** *La première* *épître de Pierre: Analyse semiotique* (LD 109, 1982). **J. Calvin**, *Catholic Epistles: Calvin's Commentaries* (ed. J. Owen, 1948). **B. L. Campbell,** *Honor, Shame, and the Rhetoric of 1 Peter* (SBLDS 160, 1998). **F. L. Cross**, *1 Peter: A Paschal Liturgy* (1954). **W. J. Dalton**, *Christ's Proclamation to the Spirits* (AnBib 23, 1989[2]). **M. Dubis,** *Messianic Woes in First Peter: Suffering and Eschatology in 1 Peter 4:12-19* (Studies in Biblical Literature 33, 2002). **J. H. Elliott**, "The Rehabilitation of an Exegetical Step-child: 1 Peter in Recent Research," *JBL* 95 (1976) 243-54; *Perspectives on First Peter* (ed. C. H. Talbert, NABPR.SS 9, 1986) 3-16; *A Home for the Homeless: A Sociological Exegesis of 1 Peter, Its Situation and Strategy* (1981); "Peter, First Epistle of," *ABD* (1992) 5:269-78; *1 Peter: A New Translation with Introduction and Commentary* (AB 37B, 2000). **L. Goppelt**, *Der erste Petrusbrief* (MeyerK, 1978; ET 1993). **K. Gschwind**, *Die Niederfahrt Christi in die Unterwelt: Ein Beitrag zur Exegese des Neuen Testamentes und zur Geschichte des Taufsymbols* (1911). **A. von Harnack**, *Die Chronologie der altchristlichen Literatur bis Eusebius* (1897). **J. Herzer**, *Petrus oder Paulus? Studien über das Verhältnis des Ersten Petrusbriefes zur paulinischen Tradition* (WUNT 103, 1998). **U. Holzmeister**, *Commentarius in Epistulas SS. Petri et Judae Apostolorum* (1937). **J. N. D. Kelly**, *A Commentary on the Epistles of Peter and Jude* (HNTC, 1969). **W. G. Kümmel**, *The New Testament: The History of the Investigation of Its Problems* (1972). **E. Lohse**, "Parenesis and Kerygma in 1 Peter," *Perspectives on First Peter* (ed. C. H. Talbert, NABPR.SS 9, 1986) 37-59. **M. Luther**, *The Catholic Epistles* (LW 30, 1967). **R. P. Martin**, "The Composition of 1 Peter in Recent Study," *VE* 1 (1962) 29-42. **T. W. Martin**, *Metaphor and Composition in 1 Peter* (1992). **J. R. Michaels**, *1 Peter* (WBC 49, 1988). **C. F. D. Moule**, "The Nature and Purpose of 1 Peter," *NTS* 3 (1956/57) 1-11. **J. Murdock**, *The New Testament: A Literal Translation from the Syriac Peshito Version* (1858). **S. Neill**, *The Interpretation of the New Testament, 1861-1961* (1964). **K.-H. Ostmeyer**, *Taufe und Typos: Elemente und Theologie der Tauftypologien in 1. Korinther 10 und 1. Petrus 3* (WUNT 2/118, 2000). **S. C. Pearson**, *The Christological and Rhetorical Properties of 1 Peter* (Studies in the Bible and Early Christianity 45, 2001). **J. Prasad,** *Foundations of the Christian Way of Life According to 1 Peter 1, 13-25: An Exegetico-Theological Study* (AnBib, 146, 2000). **B. Reicke**, *The Disobedient Spirits and Christian Baptism: A Study of 1 Pet 3:19 and Its Context* (1946). **K. H. Schelkle**, *Die Petrusbriefe, der Judasbrief* (HKNT 13, 1970). **E. G. Selwyn**, *The First Epistle of St. Peter* (1946). **K. Shimada,** *Studies on First Peter: With a Concordance to the Epistle* (1998). **C. H. Talbert**, "Once Again: The Plan of First Peter," *Perspectives on First Peter* (ed. C. H. Talbert, NABPR.SS 9, 1986) 141-51. **W. Tyndale**, *Doctrinal Treatises and Introductions to Different Portions of the Holy Scriptures* (1848); *The Work of W. Tyndale* (ed. G. E. Duffield, 1965). **W. C. van Unnik**, "The Teaching of Good Works in 1 Peter," *NTS* 1 (1954/55) 92-100. **J. Wesley**, *Explanatory Notes upon the New Testament* (1755). **H. Windisch and H. Preisker**, *Die katholische Briefe* (HNT, 1951[3]).

J. R. MICHAELS

Peter, Second Letter of

This epistle embodies many typical features of a formal letter: introduction (1:1-2); episto-lary thanksgiving (1:3-11); letter occasion (1:12-15); first defense: Prophecy[†‡§] of the Parousia (1:16-21); polemic against heretics (2:1-22); second defense: end of the world (3:1-7); third defense: delay of judgment (3:8-16); conclusion (3:17-18). Simultaneously, it is also cast in the genre of a farewell address of a dying leader/patriarch in which references to the writer's past are drawn upon and exhortations are made about the future (Gen 49; Deut 33; John 13-17; Acts 20; and numerous non-biblical texts; see also A. Kolenkow 1975). As the leader is about to die the texts generally mention (a) a prediction of death (1:12-15); (b) appointment of a successor (the possessor of this very document); (c) prediction of future troubles and trials (heretics attacking the group, 2:1-22; 3:3-10); and (d) exhortation to virtue (faithfulness to the tradition). The letter is addressed from "Simon Peter, a servant and apostle of Jesus Christ" (1:1); refers to his eyewitness presence at Jesus' transfiguration (1:16-18); and mentions a previous letter written to the same audience (3:1).

No New Testament writing is less attested to in the early church than 2 Peter. Specific refer-ences to the work or use of it do not appear in the first two centuries. The third-century papyrus Bodmer P[72] shows that the work was being copied in Egypt at the time, although the Syriac Peshitta[§] contains only three of the Catholic Epistles (Jas, 1 Pet, and 1 John) but not 2 Pet. According to Eusebius[§] (*Hist. eccl.* 6.25.11), Origen[§] was familiar with the work and was also aware of doubts about its genuineness. Eusebius placed it among the antilegomena, or works that were "disputed" (*Hist. eccl.* 3.25.3-4) although "generally recognized." Jerome[§] noted that Peter "wrote two epistles which are called Catholic, the second of which, on account of its dif-ference from the first in style, is considered by many not to be by him" (*Lives of Illustrious Men* 1). Jerome also suggested that the difference in style between 1 and 2 Pet might have been due to Peter's use of two different secretaries. Augustine[§] apparently had no problem with the work and lists two epistles of Peter as canonical (*On Christian Doctrine* 1.8.13). Second Peter appears in Athanasius's[§] list of biblical books in his Easter letter of 367 C.E.

In the medieval period acknowledgment of seven Catholic Epistles became standard. A basic commentary on these works was that by Bede[§], *In epistolas VII catholicas* (1983).

During the Renaissance and the Reformation the old suspicions about 2 Peter resurfaced, as they did with all the antilegomena. D. Erasmus[§], A. von Karlstadt[§], and T. Cajetan[§] all raised doubts about the book. Interestingly, Luther[§] was complimentary of this work, "written against those who think that Christian faith can be without works" (35 [1960] 391). H. Grotius[§] in his *Annotationes* (1650) gave widespread circulation to the objections against the book and to the issues of relating 1 and 2 Pet to each other and 2 Pet to Jude. He argued that 2 Pet was proba-bly written by Simeon, who succeeded James as the head of the church in Jerusalem, and that the opponents mentioned in the book were the second-century heretical group called the Carpocratians. Material like the name "Peter" and 1:16-18 he considered interpolations added to the text.

Defenses of the apostolic origin and authenticity of the epistle were published throughout the seventeenth to the nineteenth centuries. The renowned anti-Deist T. Sherlock (Deism[§]) argued (1) that Jude and 2 Pet were based on the use of a no longer extant ancient Jewish writing (not *1 Enoch*) and (2) that both epistles were based on an earlier communiqué, circulated in the church (see 2 Pet 3:2; Jude 5) warning about false teachers (1725). Their similar depiction of heretics was not based on mutual dependence but on the warning circulated to various churches.

Similar arguments were made by others defending the authenticity of the work (*CBTEL* 8 1879, 21-27 for a survey of publications in the eighteenth-nineteenth cents.).

At the end of the nineteenth and the beginning of the twentieth century, two views on the book came to dominate (see E. Abbot 1882; F. Chase 1900; and J. Mayer 1907): (1) Jude and 2 Pet are literarily related, with 2 Pet dependent on Jude, which is not an apostolic work. Second Pet thus came to be considered the latest book of the New Testament to have been written. (Few followed F. C. Baur and the Tübingen school, who placed 2 Pet along with the Pastoral Epistles and the Gospel of John in the middle of the second cent.) (2) Second Pet is a pseudonymous work written in Peter's name and reflective of conditions in the early post-apostolic church. (For arguments against both views see B. B. Warfield 1882; E. Green 1962.)

The lateness of the epistle is indicated by concern with the delay of the Parousia (3:3-10), awareness of a collection of Paul's[§] letters (3:16), and utilization of a rich collection of biblical and Christian traditions (e.g., 1:16-19). The work has affinities with *1* and *2 Clement* and the *Shepherd of Hermas* (R. Bauckham 1983, 145-51, 158-62); it shares in the fascination with Peter reflected in the apocryphal *Apocalypse of Peter*, *Gospel of Peter*, *Preaching of Peter*, and *Acts of Peter* (Apocrypha[†§], New Testament), which some scholars have seen as indicative of a Petrine group or school in the early church (see F. Chase 1900; M. Soards 1987); and it reflects some of the characteristics of a pluralistic Hellenistic-Jewish context (see T. Fornberg 1977) in which Epicureanism was a significant factor (see J. Elliott 1992).

A major impetus to contemporary discussion of 2 Pet was a 1952 article by the Lutheran E. Käsemann[§] arguing that the epistle is representative of "early Catholicism" in which the church is "so concerned to defend herself against heretics, that she no longer distinguishes between Spirit and letter; that she identifies the Gospel with her own tradition and further, with a particular world-view; that she regulates exegesis according to her system of teaching authority and makes faith into a mere assent to the dogmas of orthodoxy" (1964, 195). Clearly, Käsemann's views reflect a Protestant/Lutheran approach informed by Reformation perspectives opposed to identifying faith with believing truths, to placing confidence in authoritative tradition, and to playing down private interpretation. Many of these issues, however, are reflected in other New Testament writings. Reactions to Käsemann have called into question whether he has properly understood the epistle (Bauckham 1983, 151-54; C. Talbert 1966); nonetheless, his article renewed interest in the writing.

M. Rosenblatt (1994), examining female imagery and the absence of women in the letter, has attempted to reconstruct the role of women in the congregation of 2 Pet. According to Rosenblatt, reconstruction of women's roles in 2 Pet indicates that women taught and interpreted the Scriptures in the Christian churches in the first century and that ecclesial authority attempted to suppress women's leadership.

Recent scholarly work on 2 Pet includes commentaries (Kraftchick 2002, Senior 2003), a text-critical study of the Coptic manuscript tradition (Schmitz 2003), and the Hellenistic backgrounds of "divine nature" in 2 Pet 1:4 (Starr 2000).

Bibliography: E. A. Abbott, "The Second Epistle of St. Peter," *Expositor* 2nd ser. 3 (1882) 49-63, 139-53, 204-19. **R. J. Bauckham**, "2 Peter: A Supplementary Bibliography," *JETS* 25 (1982) 91-93; *Jude, 2 Peter* (WBC 50, 1983); "2 Peter: An Account of Research," *ANRW* II.25.5 (1987) 3713-52. **Bede**, *In epistolas VII catholicas* (ed. M. L. W. Laistner, CCSL 121, 1983). **K. Berger**, "Streit um Gottes Vorsehung: Zur Position der Gegner in 2 Petrusbrief," *Tradition and Re-interpretation in Jewish and Christian Literature: Essays in Honor of J. C. H. Lebram* (ed. J. W. van Henten et al., 1986) 121-35. **G. H. Boobyer**, "The Indebtedness of 2 Peter to 1 Peter," *NT Essays: Studies in Memory of T. W. Manson* (ed. A. J. B. Higgins, 1959) 34-53. **F. H. Chase**, *HDB* 3 (1900) 796-818. **J. Crehan**, "New Light on 2 Peter from the

Bodmer Papyrus," *SE* 7 (1982) 145-49. **F. W. Danker**, "2 Peter 1: A Solemn Decree," *CBQ* 40 (1978) 64-82. **S. Dowd**, "2 Peter," *Women's Bible Commentary* (ed. C. A. Newsom and S. H. Ringe, 1992) 373. **J. H. Elliott**, *ABD* (1992) 5:282-87. **D. Farkasfalvy**, "The Ecclesial Setting and Pseudepigraphy in Second Peter and Its Role in the Formation of the Canon," *SecCent* 5 (1985-86) 3-29. **T. Fornberg**, *An Early Church in a Pluralistic Society: A Study of 2 Peter* (ConBNT 9, 1977). **E. M. B. Green**, *2 Peter Reconsidered* (1960 Tyndale NT Lecture, 1962). **D. E. Hiebert**, "Selected Studies from 2 Peter," *BSac* 141 (1984) 43-54, 158-68, 255-65, 330-40. **W. G. Hupper**, "Additions to 'A 2 Peter Bibliography,'" *JETS* 23 (1980) 65-66. **J. Kahmann**, "The Second Letter of Peter and the Letter of Jude: Their Mutual Relationship," *The NT in Early Christianity* (ed. J. M. Sevrin, BETL 86, 1989) 105-21. **E. Käsemann**, "An Apology for Primitive Eschatology," Essays on NT Themes (SBT 41, 1964) 169-95. **J. N. D. Kelly**, *A Commentary on the Epistles of Peter and Jude* (HNTC, 1969). **G. Klein**, "Der zweite Petrusbrief und der neutestamentliche Kanon, Argernisse," *Konfrontation mit dem Neuen Testament* (1971) 109-14. **J. Klinger**, "The Second Epistle of Peter: An Essay in Understanding," *SVTQ* 17 (1973) 152-69. **J. Knight**, *2 Peter and Jude* (NTG, 1995). **S. J. Kraftchick**, *Jude, 2 Peter* (ANTC, 2002). **A. B. Kolenkow**, "The Genre Testament and Forecasts of the Future in the Hellenistic Jewish Milieu," *JSJ* 6 (1975) 57-71. **M. Luther**, *LW* 35 (ed. E. T. Bachmann, 1960). **J. B. Mayor**, *The Epistle of St. Jude and the Second Epistle of St. Peter* (1907). **J. H. Neyrey**, "The Form and Background of the Polemic in 2 Peter" (diss., Yale University, 1977); "The Apologetic Use of the Transfiguration in 2 Peter 1:16-21," *CBQ* 42 (1980) 504-19; "The Form and Background of the Polemic in 2 Peter," *JBL* 99 (1980) 407-31; *2 Peter, Jude* (AB 37C, 1993). **M.-E. Rosenblatt**, "2 Peter," *Searching the Scriptures*, vol. 2, *A Feminist Commentary* (ed. E. Schüssler Fiorenza, 1994), 399-405. **J. Schmitt**, *DBSup* 7 (1966) 1455-63. **F.–J. Schmitz, ed.**, *Das Verhältnis der koptischen zur griechischen Überlieferung des Neuen Testaments:* Dokumentation und Auswertung der Gesamtmaterialien beider *Traditionen zum Jakobusbrief und den beiden Petrusbriefen* (ANTF 33, 2003). **D. Senior**, "2 Peter," *NISB* (2003) 2189-93. **T. Sherlock**, *The Authority of the Second Epistle of Saint Peter* (1725; repr. in his *Works* 5 vols. ed. T. Hughs, 1830) 4:137-52. **T. V. Smith**, *Petrine Contoversies in Early Christianity: Attitudes Toward Peter in Christian Writings of the First Two Centuries* (WUNT 2, 15, 1985). **J. Snyder**, "A 2 Peter Bibliography," *JETS* 22 (1979) 265-67. **M. L. Soards**, "1 Peter, 2 Peter, and Jude as Evidence for a Petrine School," *ANRW* II.25.5 (1987) 3827-49. **C. Spicq**, *Les Epîtres de Saint Pierre* (SB, 1966). **F. Spitta**, *Der zweite Brief des Petrus und der Brief des Judas* (1895). **J. M. Starr**, *Sharers in Divine Nature: 2 Peter 1:4 in its Hellenistic Context* (ConBNT 33, 2000). **C. H. Talbert**, "II Peter and the Delay of the Parousia," *VC* 20 (1966) 137-45. **B. B. Warfield**, "The Canonicity of Second Peter," *Southern Presbyterian Review* 33 (1882) 45-75. **D. F. Watson**, *Invention, Arrangement, and Style: Rhetorical Criticism of Jude and 2 Peter* (SBLDS 104, 1988); "The Second Letter of Peter," *NIB* (1997) 12:321-361. **H. Windisch**, *Die Katholischen Briefe* (1951[3]).

J. NEYREY

THE NEW TESTAMENT CANON

Johannine Letters

1. *The Early Church and the Middle Ages.* Polycarp of Smyrna clearly alluded to 1 John 4:2-3 in his second century *Letter to the Philippians* (7:1). Justin Martyr[§] (*Dial.* 123:9; 1 John 3:1-2) confirmed that 1 John was used in the churches no later than the middle of the second century. Papias[§] of Hierapolis also attested to this same fact (Eusebius *Hist. eccl.* 3.39.17) and may have known of 3 John as well (cf. *Hist. eccl.* 3.39.3 with 3 John 12). The second-century Muratorian Canon[§] (though some date it to the fourth century) attested to all three Johannine letters, but the significance of the relevant lines (68-69) is controversial. Eusebius listed 1 John among the "recognized" and 2 and 3 John among the "disputed" writings of the New Testament canon (*Hist. eccl.* 3. 25), which was also Origen's position (cf. *Hist. eccl.* 6.25.9-10). Clement of Alexandria[§] cited only 1 and 2 John as authoritative (Authority of the Bible*[§]) but had examined all "catholic" epistles in his *Hypotyposeis* (*Hist. eccl.* 6.14.1). The testimony of a secure place for all three Johannine epistles in the New Testament Canon[§] was not attested until the beginning of the fourth century. Along with the other Catholic Epistles they are found in the Codex Claromontanus, in the canon of Cyril of Jerusalem, in the appendix to the fifty-ninth canon of the Synod of Laodicea (held c. 360), in Athanasius's Easter letter of 367, and in the great biblical manuscripts of the fourth and fifth centuries.

2. *The Reformation.* Luther[§] preached frequently on 1 John. In addition to a collection of sermons that carries the characteristic title "Concerning Love" (WA 36.416-77), there is the lecture on 1 John given during the outbreak of the plague in Wittenberg in 1527 (WA 20.599-801; 48.314-23). Luther connected 1 John with the Gospel of John, which demands faith, and claimed that 1 John contains the call to the reciprocal love that comes from this faith, which is grounded in the love of God. Luther's exegesis railed against the Roman Catholic Church and the tendency to enthusiasm, to which there is a double correspondence from the pronouncements of 1 John: Faith without love is just as untenable as love (works) without faith (WA 7.326-27). Similarly Zwingli[§] and Calvin[§] commented on 1 John; the latter stressed the (unordered) succession from doctrine and exhortation. Some sermons from J. Brenz on 1 John have also been handed down, while a complete commentary from H. Bullinger[§] on John has been preserved (see Bullinger 1972, 37, 91). Roman Catholic exegesis in this period is represented by T. Cajetan[§] and A. Salmeron.

3. *The Seventeenth through Nineteenth Centuries.* Critical exegesis took its point of departure from the saying of J. Scaliger[§]: *Tres Epistolae Joannis non sunt Apostoli Joannis* ("The three Johannine Epistles are not from the apostle John" [*Scaligerana ou Bons Mots, rencontres agreables, et remarques judicieuses et scavantes de J. Scaliger. Avec des notes de Mr. Le Fevre et Mr. de Colomies,* nouvelle edition 1695, 138]). H. Grotius[§] (1650), a student of Scaliger, rejected John the disciple of Jesus*[§] as the author of 2 and 3 John and proposed the elder John as author. Renewed doubt concerning apostolic authorship was expressed in 1797 by S. Lange, who nonetheless acquiesced to the received witness of tradition. Even J. Augusti held firmly to the authenticity of 1 John and interpreted it as an "introductory writing" to the Gospel (1808, 184); there was an interpolation in 1 John 5:14-21—namely, an addendum by a foreign hand, which may possibly have been introduced by the author of chapter 21 of the Gospel of John.

A new phase of criticism began with the doubts regarding the apostolic origin of the Gospel of John, raised by K. Bretschneider: *Si evangelium non esse potest Joannis apostoli scriptum sequitur, nec epistolas Joannem habuisse auctorem* ("If the Gospel is not from John the apostle, it follows that the letters do not have John as their author either" 1820, 162). The Elder is the author of 2 and 3 John and 1 John as well, not the apostle, since the doctrine of the Logos in 1 John, which is directed against docetic opponents, points to a Gentile Christian as the author. Even H. Paulus (1829) doubted that the son of Zebedee wrote the Johannine epistles.

The Tübingen school especially developed the critical study of the Johannine correspondence. F. C. Baur[§] viewed the author as an imitator of the Evangelist who was deeply under the influence of the Gospel and borrowed ideas from it, but who did not "develop these in a thorough-going connection in an independent way" (1848, 297). According to Baur, the letter's distinction between sins of neglect and mortal sins points to the world of Montanist ideas. A. Hilgenfeld[§], influenced by the portrait of the apostle John in the Synoptic[†§] Gospels and Paul[†§] (Gal 2), considered the Apocalypse to have been the work of the son of Zebedee and consequently declared both the Gospel and letters of John to be inauthentic. In contrast to the Apocalypse, he understood 1 John as the argument of the orthodox establishment against false teachers of a docetic-Gnostic[§] persuasion, a theory that highlighted the differences between the Johannine letters and the Gospel (1849, 322ff.; 1855). On the basis of the Tübingen school's developmental history premise the Johannine epistles indicate "the transition of early Johannine prophecy to the Gnosis of the Fourth Gospel" (1849, 526).

Baur (1857), however, disagreed with Hilgenfeld, asserting on the basis of an analysis of the letter's structure that the Fourth Gospel provided the foundation for 1 John. F. Lücke (1856[3]) in turn opposed Baur and traced both the Gospel and 1 John back to the apostle John; he argued that the author of 2–3 John was, not the son of Zebedee, but rather John the Elder. H. Ewald[§] (1861), W. De Wette[§] (1863), and particularly P. Haupt[§] (1870) disagreed with those who disputed the identity of the disciple John as the author of the Gospel and of the letters; R. Rothe (1878) and J. Huther (1880[4]) took similar stances. The latter supposed (as previously had Hilgenfeld and others) a temporal precedence of 1 John over the Gospel, since 1 John nowhere makes direct reference to the Gospel, and especially since 1 John 1:1-4 in comparison with John 1:1ff. supports the earlier character of the letter (similarly Hilgenfeld 1855). This reasoning was represented by B. Weiss[§] (1899[6]) as well, who defended the common authorship of the three letters of John, the Gospel, and the Apocalypse, with the latter being the oldest writing of John the son of Zebedee. This idea was developed by H. Holtzmann[§], who maintained the priority of the Gospel (1881; see also 1908[3]) since a thoroughgoing analysis highlights linguistic and conceptual differences that demonstrate that the Fourth Evangelist could not be identical with the author of 1 John (1882; see also 1908[3]).

4. *Twentieth Century.* Although the Johannine epistles are to be reckoned among the lesser writings of the New Testament, they have not led a shadow existence in New Testament scholarship of the twentieth century. The primary focus of the discussion has been the relationship of 1 John to 2–3 John, wherein the differences in form and content emerge. In contrast to 2–3 John, which are to be understood as actual letters (see R. Funk 1967), 1 John lacks the essential features of a letter. Previously M. Dibelius[§] (1929) had tentatively concluded that 2–3 John could be artificial letters; E. Hirsch (1936) thought them a fiction that served to introduce the Gospel and 1 John; similarly R. Bultmann[§] (1967), J. Heise (1967), and G. Schunack (1982) sought to prove that 2 John was a fictional letter imitating 3 John (in opposition see R. Brown 1982; K. Wengst 1976, 1978; G. Strecker 1989a).

The order and authorship of the Johannine epistles are as controversial as before. Even if a great number of exegetes reckon with a common authorship of all Johannine letters (R. Brown 1982; C. H. Dodd 1946, 1953[3]; E. Ruckstuhl 1985; R. Schnackenburg 1984[7]; H. Windisch 1911, 1951[2]; S. Smalley 1984; and W. Langbrandtner 1977 also consider this possibility), this position is increasingly called into question. To be sure, Schnackenburg (1967) considered inadequate R. Bergmeier's attempt (1966) on the basis of the term "truth" to prove a different authorship for 1 John than for 2–3 John. Nevertheless, it appears necessary on the basis of further considerations to ascribe different authors to 1 John and 2-3 John (H. Balz 1973, 1980[2];

U. Schnelle 1987; K. Wengst 1976, 1978; Strecker 1989*a*). Schunack and, finally, B. Bonsack (1988) assume different authors for each letter, though not very persuasively.

Besides these suggestions there are different hypotheses regarding the relative order of the Johannine epistles. Bultmann (1967), Schunack, and W. Loader (1992) affirm the order 1-3-2 John on the basis of their reconstruction of the relationships between 2 and 3 John. F.-M.Braun (1973[3]) and R. Edwards (1996), however, affirm the order 3-2-1 John. H. Wendt argued for 2-3-1 John (1925; cf. Langbrandtner; further Schnelle, Strecker 1989*a*, sec. 5) and Balz for 1-2/3 John (cf. Ruckstuhl 1976, Wengst 1978). Smalley (1984) clearly distinguishes 3 John as the endpoint for 2 John.

The thesis that 1 John is a "Johannine pastoral epistle" has greatly influenced the discussion concerning the relationship of 1 John to the Gospel of John (H. Conzelmann 1954, 1974; see also O. Baumgarten 1918[3]; previously A. Neander 1862[5], 490; E. Reuss 1887,1:254). The sub-ordination of 1 John to the Gospel, which is linked to the above view, at least as it is generally represented (A. Brooke 1912; G. Klein 1971; Wengst 1976, 1978; etc.), is in no way compelling (Strecker 1989*a*; see also F. Büchsel 1933). Numerous studies have investigated the commonal-ities between the Gospel of John and 1 John. While Dodd emphasized the linguistic differences (cf. already Holtzmann 1908[3] above) and from there moved on to posit a different audience, W. Howard[§] (1947), W. Wilson (1948), A. Salom (1955), and others stressed the similarity of language. Substantive commonalities can be established just as easily as substantive differences, with the result that the question of authorship has remained controversial in the twentieth century. D. Rensberger (1997) and D. M. Smith (1991), for instance, argue that the three Johannine let-ters have the same author, although the Gospel of John was written by someone else. The thesis of a common authorship (Brooke; Büchsel 1933; I. Marshall 1979[2]; see also W. Schmithals 1992, 219; M. Hengel 1989) has increased in contrast to the thesis of a divergent authorship (Dodd; J. Houlden 1973; Klein; Schnackenburg [clearly since 1975[5]]; Schnelle; Strecker 1989*a*; and others). The latter position, however, becomes more probable as the assumption of a Johannine school out of which the commonalities arose receives validation (see sec. 5 on this topic).

Even though the question of the authorship of the Johannine epistles by the son of Zebedee may be considered almost thoroughly obsolete, the question remains whether the author of any of these letters can be identified with any certainty. Here the designation of the addressant as *ho presbyteros* (2 John 1; 3 John 1) is the starting point for the discussion. If earlier scholarship took as its reference the presbyter designated as John, following the testimony of Papias in Eusebius (*Hist. eccl.* 3.39.3-4), more recent study has confirmed this position (see Strecker 1989*a*). Nor is the authorship of all of the Johannine epistles by the elder John to be excluded (see R. Brown 1982, who assumes that the author belonged to the school of the "beloved dis-ciple"). Whereas Bultmann (1967) considered a connection to one of the presbyters named by Papias possible (see also the more reserved reference by G. Bornkamm 1959; further, Schunack), others (e.g., Wengst 1976, 1978) exclude an identification of the presbyter of the Papias reference with the author of 2 and 3 John. With less certainty Schnackenburg (1984[7]) proposes that the author is a prominent personality, perhaps a disciple of the apostle.

In view of a number of ostensible breaks in the body of the letter, Bultmann contested the lit-erary unity of 1 John and reconstructed a source document that the author of 1 John may have used as a *Vorlage,* (1927; cf. 1959, and in agreement, Heise, Windisch; H. Preikser [in Windisch] reckons with a further *Vorlage*, described as an eschatological text; against this view E. Lohmeyer[§] 1928 and Büchsel 1929). For Bultmann this *Vorlage*, which is supposed to have comprised twenty-six distichs, is similar to the "revelation source" he postulated for the Gospel of John; its ostensible origin was "a group whose world view was one of cosmological and reli-gious dualism" (1927, 157). J. O'Neill (1966) went his own way on the source question, marking off twelve poetic subsections, which supposedly the author took to expand a source of sectarian Jewish exhortations. Conversely, W. Nauck (1957) thought that the Vorlage reconstructed on form-critical grounds (Form Criticism, New Testament*[§]) also stems from the writer of 1 John. These attempts at source criticism are, however, generally rejected in the present discussion (Schnackenburg 1984[7]; Wengst 1988; Strecker 1989a). Analogous to his work on the Gospel of John, Bultmann brought the idea of a church redaction into his work (1951; cf. 1959; also Hirsch). The claim of a secondary redaction for the concluding section (1 John 5:14-21) has found some agreement. The conclusory nature of 5:13 as well as the plethora of *hapax legomena* and an apparently non-Johannine character were especially cited (Wengst 1978, 1988; Schunack). These considerations have been rejected as inconclusive by Balz, F. Francis (1970), M. de Jonge (1973[2]), E. Stegemann (1985), and Strecker (1989a), among others. Regarding the hypothesis of unity, questions were raised about the rhetorical structure of the sermon in 1 John (e.g., F. Vouga 1990; critically, H.-J. Klauck 1990, 213; regarding literary character, Strecker 1992, 67-68) and the letters of the Elder (D. Watson 1989; H.-J. Klauck 1990, 216-24).

While the state of research during the twentieth century at first showed a far-reaching consensus concerning the identification of the opponents in 1 John by means of the catchwords docetic and Gnostic[§], this unity was also shown to be fragile in the face of incisive critical observation. Indeed, whether a polemic against an opposing group governs the letter in its totality is still a topic of controversy. Bultmann (1967), Schnackenburg (1984[7]), J. Painter (1986), and W. Loader think that such a polemic shaped the letter, whereas Büchsel (1929, 1933) and J. Lieu (1981, 1991) do not.

The definition by Bultmann is classic: "Thus it is obviously a question of Gnostics who want to differentiate between Jesus and the Christ and who do not want to see in the human Jesus the incarnation of the heavenly pre-existent Christ, and who therefore represent a type of docetism, related to the docetism of Cerinth" (1959, 837). These opponents have been pushed into the vicinity of libertinism (so W. Lutgert 1911; Wengst 1988; Dodd; J. Bogart 1977; and Smalley). Despite points of contact with Gnostic thought, K. Weiss (1973) seeks to locate the opponents less in the realm of Gnosis than in the neighborhood of Jews addressed by Paul in 1 Cor 1 alongside the Greeks, i.e., in Hellenistic Judaism. J. Blank (1984), in turn, reckons with a Jewish-Christian misinterpretation of the Johannine Shekinah-Christology, which he connects to the Gnostic Kerinth. The opponents are placed in the realm of Judaism, though not very persuasively, by A. Wurm (1903), J. O'Neill (1966), J. Robinson[§] ("gnosticizing Movement within Greek-speaking Diaspora Judaism" 1960/61, 65), and H. Thyen (1988). P. Bonnard (1983) and Painter refer to the Hellenistic environment of the New Testament.

Holtzmann, U. Müller (1975), Langbrandtner, Schunack, F. Segovia (1982), and U. Schnelle (1992), among others, more specifically identify the opponents as "docetists." On the basis of the prejudiced sequence of reading 1 John after the Gospel of John, the opposing position was considered to be either a radical (Müller) or faulty interpretation (Schunack) of the Fourth Gospel. Disagreeing with the Gnostic-docetic interpretation of the opponents, F. Vouga seeks to highlight elements of Gnostic thought in 1 John and evaluates the Johannine letters as "precursors of the Gnostic polemic against the proto-Catholic church" (1988, 380). A distinction between docetism and Gnosis is, however, necessary (N. Brox 1984; G. Strecker 1989a). Even if the docetic false teachers possess a "Gnostic" self-awareness, this perspective is still not to be put on the same level as a mythological Gnosis, as inferred from the Christian systems of the second century.

Concerning the question of the opposition between the Elder and Diotrephes, W. Bauer[§] (1964[2]), in his epoch-making work on orthodoxy and heresy, maintained that the position later called orthodoxy first emerged in the struggle with heresy. According to this view, Diotrephes is a leader of heretics (see Wengst 1976, 1988: Diotrephes has the "orientation of the gnostic innovators" condemned in 2 John 7, 27). E. Käsemann[§], who succeeded Bauer in his chair at Göttingen, contested this claim. In Käsemann's view, the Elder, "a Christian gnostic who possesses the unimaginable audacity...to write a gospel (i.e., the Gospel of John)," acutely disagreed with the monarchical bishop Diotrephes (1970[6], 178). Along with a dogmatic interpretation of the conflict but without allowing this conflict to acquire exclusive significance (cf. Strecker 1989*a*; Schunack), the dissent is understood as a practical-ecclesiastical matter (A. von Harnack 1897; R. Schnackenburg 1984[7]), as a private affair (A. Malherbe 1977: the refusal of hospitality to opponents), or as an internal community dispute (J. Taeger 1987).

Recent scholarship has examined the familial concerns and imagery in the three letters, especially the address in 2 John, "to an elect lady and her children." E. Schüssler Fiorenza (1984, 1; 1983, 248-49) maintains that 2 John is "the only writing in the New Testament addressed to a woman." M. Hutaff suggests that the terms "elect lady" (2 John 1, 5) and "elect sister" (2 John 13) more plausibly refer to "sister" churches whose members are God's children. G. O'Day comments that the use of female imagery for the church may reflect either high regard for women in the early church or the initiation of patriarchal structures of leadership into the church. R. Edwards, providing several interpretations of "an elect lady," claims that the term may actually refer to a real woman who hosted or led a congregation but that the letter nevertheless is written to that congregation.

5. *The Johannine School.* The close relationship of the Johannine writings in language and thought has occasioned speculation about a "Johannine circle" (O. Cullmann 1975). It is more precise, however, to speak of a "Johannine school" (see W. Bousset 1915; W. Heitmüller 1914). New Testament schools have also been postulated alongside the religious and philosophical schools of Hellenism and Judaism (Gospel of Matthew: K. Stendahl 1954; Pauline school: H. Conzelmann 1979). The derivation of a school from a founder is its primary characteristic and guarantees its autonomy, which is expressed via stereotypical forms of language and thought. That this is true of the Johannine writings has been demonstrated with convincing arguments (see R. Culpepper 1975; Schnelle), even though in individual cases many questions may remain open.

Although the starting point for the school is mostly sought in the Gospel, in accordance with the canonical subordination of the letters (Culpepper identifies the "beloved disciple" as the founder of the school; see also Barrett 1989; Smalley), the author of 2–3 John is understood as the head of the school and identified with the Elder mentioned in Eusebius's citation of Papias (*Hist. eccl.* 3.39.4; cf. Strecker 1989*a*; Schnelle). As early as 1914 Heitmüller designated the Elder John, whom he identified with the "beloved disciple," but whom he also distinguished from the son of Zebedee, as the standard authority. Thyen, on the other hand, sees evidence of the author of 2–3 John in the "beloved disciple" (1977).

The association of the Apocalypse with the Johannine corpus is disputed. Even if this work is to be understood as a pseudepigraphon (Strecker 1990; cf. Heitmüller; see Pseudepigrapha[†§]), a relatively close connection to this circle of writings is nonetheless probable.

6. *The "Johannine Comma" (comma Johanneum).* The so-called Johannine Comma designates an addendum to 1 John 5:7-8 in the text-critical tradition (see Textual Criticism, New Testament*[§]), which has found its way almost exclusively into Latin biblical manuscripts. There are no Greek exemplars prior to 1400. In 1592 in the official Catholic Vulgate*[§], the Sixto-Clementine, the following reading was included (here printed in italic):

(7) Quoniam tres sunt, qui testimonium dant *in caelo: Pater, Verbum, et Spiritus Sanctus et hi tres unum sunt.*
(8) Et tres sunt, qui testimonium dant in terra: Spiritus et aqua et sanguis, et hi tres unum sunt.

(7) For there are three that bear record *in heaven, the Father, the Word, and the Holy Spirit, and these three are one.*
(8) *And there are three that bear witness in earth*: The Spirit, and the Water, and the Blood, and these three agree in one (KJV).

The oldest indubitable citation of this Johannine Comma is found in Priscillian (d. 385), up to whose time there is, aside from possible allusions (Tertullian, Cyprian), no certain documentary evidence. The authenticity of this text, which is frequently attested after Priscillian and which Erasmus[§] only reluctantly took up in the third edition of his New Testament, received a critical judgment from Luther (WA 20.780, 21ff.; WADB 7.628-29). Although Calvin accepted it with some hesitation (cf. CR 83.364-65), Zwingli rejected it (Opera, ed. Schulero and Schulthessio, 6.2.338). Ever since J. Semler[§] contested its originality in 1764, the Johannine Comma has been regarded in most of Protestantism as secondary (cf. G. Hornig 1988). This view became accepted in Roman Catholic exegesis only in this century by academic prohibition of the Congregatio S. Inquisitionis on Jan. 13, 1897, and with subsequent confirmation limited by Pope Leo XIII.

Recent commentaries on the Johannine epistles include Kysar (2003*a*, 2003*b*, 2003*c*), Painter (2002), and Rensberger (2001). Culpepper (1998) and Lindars, Edwards, and Court (2000) are introductory guides to interpretative issues in the Johannine literature. Collected exegetical essays on the Johannine epistles are in Beutler (1998) and Wilckens (2003). Schmid (2002) and Uebele (2001) both study the opponents mentioned in the epistles. Heinze (1998) and North (2001) investigate the relationship between the Johannine epistles and the wider Johannine literature including Revelation. Forster (2003), Griffith (2002), and Scholtissek (2000) study various theological issues in the letters.

Bibliography: J. C. W. Augusti, *Die katholischen Briefe* (1808). **H. Balz**, "Die Johannesbriefe," Die "Katholischen" *Briefe* (H. Balz and W. Schrage, NTD 10[11], 1973) 150-216; (1980[2]) 156-222. **C. K. Barrett**, "School, Conventicle, and Church in the NT," *Wissenschaft und Kirche* (FS E. Lohse, ed. K. Aland and S. Meurer, TAzB 4, 1989) 96-110. **W. Bauer**, *Rechtglaubigkeit und Ketzerei im ältesten Christentum* (ed. G. Strecker, BHT 10 1964[2]). **O. Baumgarten**, "Die Johannes-Briefe," *SNT* 4 (1918[3]) 185-228. **F. C. Baur**, "Die johannischen Briefe: Ein Beitrag zur Geschichte des Kanons," *ThJb* 7 (1848) 293-337; "Das Verhältnis des ersten johanneischen Briefes zum johanneischen Evangelium," *ThJb* 16 (1857) 315-31. **R. Bergmeier**, "Zum Verfasserproblem des II. und III. Johannesbriefes," *ZNW* 57 (1966) 93-100. **J. Beutler**, *Studien zu den johanneischen Schriften* (Stuttgarter biblische Aufsatzbände 25, 1998). **C. Black**, "The First, Second, and Third Letters of John" *NIB* (1998) 12:363-469. **J. Blank**, "Die Irrlehrer des ersten Johannesbriefes," *Kairos NF* 26 (1984) 166-93. **J. Bogart**, *Orthodox and Heretical Perfectionism in the Johannine Community as Evident in the First Epistle of John* (SBLDS 33, 1977). **P. Bonnard**, *Les Épîtres Johanniques* (CNT(G) 2, 13c, 1983). **B. Bonsack**, "Der Presbyteros des dritten Briefs und der geliebte Jünger des Evangeliums nach Johannes," *ZNW* 79 (1988) 45-62. **G. Bornkamm**, "πρεσβυς, κτλ." *TDNT* 6 (1959) 651-83. **W. Bousset**, *Jüdisch-Christlicher Schulbetrieb in Alexandria und Rom* (FRLANT 23, 1915). **F.-M. Braun**, "Les Épîtres de Saint Jean," *L'Évangile de Saint Jean* (F.-M. Braun and D. Mollat, SB(J), 1973[3]) 231-77. **H. Braun**, "Literar-Analyse und theologische Schichtung im ersten Johannesbrief," *ZTK* 48 (1951) 262-92; *repr., idem, Gesammelte Studien zum Neuen Testament und seiner Umwelt* (1971[3]) 210-42. **K. G. Bretschneider**, *Probabilia de evangelii et epistolarum Joannis, apostoli, indole et origine eruditorum judiciis modeste subjecit* (1820). **A. E. Brooke**, *A Critical and Exegetical Commentary on the Johannine Epistles* (ICC, 1912). **R. E. Brown**, *The Community of the Beloved Disciple* (1979); *The Epistles of*

John (AB 30, 1982). **N. Brox**, " 'Doketismus'—eine Problemanzeige," *ZKG* 95 (1984) 301-14. **F. Büchsel**, "Zu den Johannesbriefen," *ZNW* 28 (1929) 235-41; *Die Johannesbriefe* (THKNT 17, 1933). **H. Bullinger**, *Werke, I/1: Beschreibendes Verzeichnis der gedruckten Werke von Bullinger* (ed. J. Staedtke, 1972). **R. Bultmann**, "Analyse des ersten Johannesbriefes," *Festgabe für A. Jülicher zum 70. Geburtstag* (ed. R. Bultmann and H. von Soden, 1927) 138-58; *his Exegetica* (1967) 105-23; "Die kirchliche Redaktion des ersten Johannesbriefes," *In memoriam E. Lohmeyer* (ed. W. Schmauch, 1951) 189-201; Exegetica (1967) 381-93; "Johannesbriefe," *RGG*[3] 3 (1959) 836-39; *The Johannine Epistles* (KEK 14[8], 1967, 1969[2]; ET *Hermeneia*, 1973). **H. Conzelmann**, "Die Schule des Paulus," *Theologia Crucis-Sigmum Crucis* (FS E. Dinkler, ed. C. Andresen and G. Klein, 1979) 85-96; " 'Was von Anfang war,' " *Neutestamentliche Studien für R. Bultmann* (BZNW 21, 1954) 194-201; *his Theologie als Schriftauslegung: Aufsätze zum Neuen Testament* (BEvT 65, 1974) 207-14. **O. Cullmann**, *The Johannine Circle* (1975; ET 1976). **R. A. Culpepper**, *The Johannine School: An Evaluation of the Johannine School Hypothesis Based on an Investigation of the Nature of Ancient Schools* (SBLDS 26, 1975); *The Gospel and Letters of John* (Interpreting Biblical Texts, 1998). **W. M. L. de Wette**, *Kurze Erklärung des Evangeliums und der Briefe Johannis* (ed. B. Brückner, KEH/NT 1, 3, 1863). **M. Dibelius**, "Johannesbriefe," *RGG*[2] 3 (1929) 346-94. **E. von Dobschütz**, "Johanneische Studien I," *ZNW* 8 (1907) 1-8. **C. H. Dodd**, *The Johannine Epistles* (MNTC, 1946, 1953[3]). **R. B. Edwards**, The Johannine Epistles (NTGu, 1996). **H. Ewald**, *Die johanneischen Schriften, erster Band, Des Apostels Johannes Evangelium und drei Sendschreiben* (1861). **F. O. Francis**, "The Form and Function of the Opening and Closing Paragraphs of James and I John," *ZNW* 61 (1970) 110-26. **R. W. Funk**, "The Form and the Structure of II and III John," *JBL* 86 (1967) 424-30. **G. Forster,** *The Ethics of the Johannine Epistles* (Grove ethics Series E129, 2003). **T. Griffith**. *Keep Yourselves from Idols: A New Look at 1 John* (JSNTSup 233, 2002). **H. Grotius**, *Annotationum in Novum Testamentum pars tertia ac ultima* (1650). **E. Haenchen**, "Neuere Literatur zu den Johannesbriefen," *TRu* 26 (1960) 1-43; 267-91 his Die Bibel und wir: Gesammelte Aufsätze 2 (1968) 235-311. **A. von Harnack**, *Über den dritten Johannesbrief* (TU XV 3b, 1897). **E. Haupt**, *Der erste Brief des Johannes: Ein Beitrag zur biblischen Theologie* (1870). **A. Heinze,** *Johannesapokalypse und johanneische Schriften: Forschungs- und traditionsgeschichtliche Untersuchungen* (BWANT 8/2, 1998). **J. Heise**, *Bleiben: Menein in den johanneischen Schriften* (HUT 8, 1967). **W. Heitmüller**, "Zur Johannes-Tradition," *ZNW* 15 (1914) 189-209. **M. Hengel**, *The Johannine Question* (1989). **A. Hilgenfeld**, *Das Evangelium und die Briefe Johannis, nach ihrem Lehrbegriff* (1849); "Die johanneischen Briefe," *ThJb* 14 (1855) 471-526. **E. Hirsch**, *Studien zum vierten Evangelium (Text-Literarkritik-Entstehungsgeschichte)* (BHT 11, 1936). **H. J. Holtzmann**, "Das Problem des ersten johanneischen Briefes in seinem Verhältnis zum Evangelium," *JPT* 1, 7 (1881) 690-712; 2, 8 (1882) 128-52; 3, 316-42; 4, 460-85; *Evangelium, Briefe, und Offenbarung des Johannes* (HC 4, 1908[3]). **G. Hornig**, "Hermeneutik und Bibelkritik bei J. S. Semler," *Historische Kritik und biblischer Kanon in der deutschen Aufklärung* (Wolfenbütteler Forschungen 41, 1988) 219-36. **J. L. Houlden**, *A Commentary on the Johannine Epistles* (BNTC, 1973). **W. F. Howard**, "The Common Authorship of the Johannine Gospel and the Epistles," *JTS* 48 (1947) 12-25. **M. D. Hutaff**, "The Johannine Epistles," *Searching the Scriptures*, vol. 2, *A Feminist Commentary* (ed. E. Schüssler Fiorenza, 1994). **J. E. Huther**, *Kritisch exegetisches Handbuch über die Briefe des Apostels Johannes* (KEK 14, 1880[4]). **M. de Jonge**, *De brieven van Johannes* (1973[2]). **E. Käsemann**, "Ketzer und Zeuge: Zum johanneischen Verfasserproblem," *ZTK* 48 (1951) 292-311 = his *Exegetische Versuche und Besinnungen* 1 (1970[6]) 168-87. **H.-J. Klauck**, "Zur rhetorischen Analyse der Johannesbriefe," *ZNW* 81 (1990) 205-24; *Die Johannesbriefe* (EdF 276, 1991); *Der erste Johannesbrief* (EKKNT 13, 1 1991). **G. Klein**, " 'Das wahre Licht scheint schon': Beobachtungen zur Zeit-und

Geschichtserfahrung einer urchristlichen Schule," *ZTK* 68 (1971) 261-326. **R. Kysar**, *I, II, III John* (ACNT, 1986); "The First Letter of John," *NISB* (2003*a*) 2195-2202; "The Second Letter of John," *NISB* (2003*b*) 2203-4; "The Third Letter of John," *NISB* (2003*c*) 2205-6. **W. Langbrandtner**, *Weltferner Gott oder Gott der Liebe: Der Ketzerstreit in der johanneischen Kirche. Eine exegetisch religionsgeschichtliche Untersuchung mit Berücksichtigung der koptisch-gnostischen Texte aus Nag-Hammadi* (BBET 6, 1977). **S. G. Lange**, *Johannis drei Briefe nebst drei Abhandlungen* (Schriften Johannis Bd. 3, 1797). **J. M. Lieu**, " 'Authority to Become Children of God': A Study of I John," *NovT* 23 (1981) 210-28; *The Second and Third Epistles of John: History and Background* (ed. J. Riches, Studies of the NT and Its World, 1986); *The Theology of the Johannine Epistles* (NT Theology, 1991). **B. Lindars, R. B. Edwards, and J. M. Court,** *The Johannine Literature* (Biblical Guides 1, 2000). **W. Loader**, *The Johannine Epistles* (Epworth Commentaries, 1992). **E. Lohmeyer**, "Über Aufbau und Gliederung des ersten Johannesbriefes," *ZNW* 27 (1928) 225-63. **F. Lücke**, *Commentar über die Briefe des Evangelisten Johannes* (ed. E. Bertheau, 1856[3]). **W. Lütgert**, *Amt und Geist im Kampf: Studien zur Geschichte des Urchristentums* (BFCT 15.4/5, 1911). **A. J. Malherbe**, "The Inhospitality of Diotrephes," *God's Christ and His People: Studies in Honour of N. A. Dahl* (ed. J. Jervell and W. A. Meeks, 1977) 222-32. **I. H. Marshall**, *The Epistles of John* (NIC, 1979[2]). **U. B. Müller**, *Die Geschichte der Christologie in der johanneischen Gemeinde* (SBS 77, 1975). **W. Nauck**, *Die Tradition und der Charakter des ersten Johannesbriefes: Zugleich ein Beitrag zur Taufe im Urchristentum und in der alten Kirche* (WUNT 3, 1957). **A. Neander**, "Circular-Pastoralschreiben," *Geschichte der Pflanzung und Leitung der christlichen Kirche durch die Apostel* (1862[5]) 490. **W. E. S. North**, *The Lazarus Story Within the Johannine Tradition* (JSNTSup 212, 2001). **G. R. O'Day**, "1, 2, and 3 John," *The Women's Bible Commentary* (ed. C. A. Newsom and S. H. Ringe, 1992) 374-75. **J. C. O'Neill**, *The Puzzle of I John: A New Examination of Origins* (1966). **J. Painter**, "The 'Opponents' in 1 John," *NTS* 32 (1986) 48-71; *1, 2, and 3 John* (SP 18, 2002). **H. E. G. Paulus**, *Die drey Lehrbriefe des Johannes* (1829). **P. Perkins**, *The Johannine Epistles* (NT Message, 1984). **H. Preisker**, "Appendix," *Die katholischen Briefe* (H. Windisch, HNT 15, 1911, 1951[3]). **D. Rensberger**, *1 John, 2 John, 3 John* (ANTC, 1997); *The Epistles of John* (WBC, 2001). . Reuss, "Pastoralschreiben," *Die Geschichte der Heiligen Schriften des Neuen Testaments* (1887) 1:254. **J. A. T. Robinson**, "The Destination and Purpose of the Johannine Epistles," *NTS* 7 (1960/61) 56-65. **R. Rothe**, *Der erste Brief Johannis, Aus R. Rothe's Nachlass* (ed. K. Mülhäusser, 1878). **E. Ruckstuhl**, Jakobusbrief, 1.-3 Johannesbrief (Die Neue Echter Bibel 17-19, 1985). **A. P. Salom**, "Some Aspects of the Grammatical Style of I John," *JBL* 74 (1955) 96-102. **K. Scholtissek,** *In ihm sein und bleiben: Die Sprache der Immanenz in den johanneischen Schriften* (Herders biblische Studien 21, 2000). **H. Schmid,** *Gegner im 1. Johannesbrief?: Zu Konstruktion und Selbstreferenz im johanneischen Sinnsystem* (BWANT 8/19, 2002). **A. Schmidt**, "Erw"agungen zur Eschatologie des 2 Thessalonicher und des 2 Johannes," *NTS* 38 (1992) 477-80. **W. Schmithals**, *Johannesevangelium und Johannesbriefe* (BZNW 64, 1992). **R. Schnackenburg**, *Die Johannesbriefe* (HThK 13, 3, 1953, 1975[5], 1984[7]; ET *The Johannine Epistles* [tr. R. and I. Fuller, 1992]); "Zum Begriff der 'Wahrheit' in den beiden kleinen Johannesbriefen," *BZ* n.f. 11 (1967) 253-58. **U. Schnelle**, *Antidoketische Christologie im Johannesevangelium: Eine Untersuchung zur Stellung des vierten Evangeliums in der johanneischen Schule* (FRLANT 144, 1987; ET 1992). **G. Schunack**, *Die Briefe des Johannes* (ZBK NT 17, 1982). **E. Schüssler Fiorenza**, *Bread Not Stone: The Challenge of Feminist Biblical Interpretation* (1984); *In Memory of Her: A Feminist Theological Reconstruction of Christian Origins* (1983). **F. F. Segovia**, *Love Relationships in the Johannine Tradition: Agape/Agapan in I John and the Fourth Gospel* (SBLDS 58, 1982). **J. S. Semler**, *Paraphrasis in I. Epistolam Joannis, acc. de Jo. Sal. Semlero eiusque ingenio narratio Jo. Aug. Nässeli* (1792). **S. S. Smalley**, *1, 2, 3 John* (WBC 51, 1984).

D. M. Smith, *First, Second, and Third John* (Interpretation, 1991). **E. Stegemann**, " 'Kindlein, hütet euch vor den Götterbildern!' Erwägungen zum Schluss des 1. Johannesbriefes," *TZ* 41 (1985) 284-94. **K. Stendahl**, *The School of St. Matthew and Its Use of the OT* (ASNU 20, 1954). **G. Strecker**, "Die Anfänge der johanneischen Schule," *NTS* 32 (1986) 31-47; "Chiliasm and Docetism in the Johannine School," *ABR* 38 (1990) 45-61; *Die Johannesbriefe übersetzt und erklärat* (1989*a*; ET *The Johannine Letters* [Hermeneia, 1996]); *History of NT Literature* (1992; ET 1997); "Neues Testament," *Neues Testament-Antikes Judentum* (Strecker and J. Maier, GT 2, UTB 422, 1989*b*) 72-74; "Rez. F. Vouga, Die Johannesbriefe," *Bib* 73 (1992) 280-86. **J. W. Taeger**, "Der konservative Rebell: Zum Widerstand des Diotrephes gegen den Presbyter," *ZNW* 78 (1987) 267-87. **H. Thyen**, "Entwicklungen innerhalb der johanneischen Theologie und Kirche im Spiegel von Joh. 21 und der Lieblingsjüngertexte des Evangeliums," *L'Évangile de Jean: Sources, rédaction, théologie* (ed. M. de Jonge, BETL 44, 1977) 259-99); "Johannesbriefe," *TRE* 17 (1988) 186-200. **W. Uebele**, *"Viele Verführer sind in die Welt ausgegangen" : Die Gegner in den Briefen des Ignatius von Antiochien und in den Johannesbriefen* (BWANTS 8/11, 2001). **F. Vouga**, "The Johannine School: A Gnostic Tradition in Primitive Christianity?" *Bib* 69 (1988) 371-85; *Die Johannesbriefe* (HNT 15, 3, 1990). **D. F. Watson**, "A Rhetorical Analysis of 2 John According to Greco-Roman Convention," *NTS* 35 (1989) 104-30; "A Rhetorical Analysis of 3 John: A Study in Epistolary Rhetoric," *CBQ* 51 (1989) 479-501. **B. Weiss**, *Die drei Briefe des Apostels Johannes* (KEK 14, 1899[6]). **K. Weiss**, " 'Die Gnosis' im Hintergrund und im Spiegel der Johannesbriefe," *Gnosis und Neues Testament: Studien aus Religionswissenschaft und Theologie* (ed. K.-W. Träger, 1973) 341-56. **H. H. Wendt**, *Die Johannesbriefe und das johanneische Christentum* (1925). **K. Wengst**, *Häresie und Orthodoxie im Spiegel des ersten Johannesbriefes* (1976); *Der erste, zweite, und dritte Brief des Johannes* (ÖTK 16, 1978); "Probleme der Johannesbriefe," *ANRW* II 25.5 (1988) 3753-72. **U. Wilckens**, *Der Sohn Gottes und seine Gemeinde: Aufsätze zur Theologie der Johanneischen Schriften* (FRLANT 200, 2003). **W. G. Wilson**, "An Examination of the Linguistic Evidence Adduced Against the Unity of Authorship of the First Epistle of John and the Fourth Gospel," *JTS* 49 (1948) 147-56. **H. Windisch**, *Die katholischen Briefe* (with appendix by H. Preisker, HNT 15, 1911, 1951[3]). **A. Wurm**, *Die Irrlehrer im ersten Johannesbrief* (BibS(F) 8.1, 1903).

G. STRECKER

THE NEW TESTAMENT CANON

Jude, Letter of

Addressed to no specific audience but "to those who are called" (v. 1), Jude is one of the catholic, or general, epistles in the New Testament. Although the author is alarmed at the presence of scoffers (v. 18) who contest the foundations of authority (v. 4) and whose errors lead to immorality, Jude remains extremely general in polemic and perception, giving scant clues to the identity of those condemned but nonetheless expressing an acute discomfort with heresy in the church. The writer, Jude (= Judas), describes himself as "a servant of Jesus Christ and brother of James" (v. 1) and admonishes his readers "to contend for the faith, handed on once for all" (v. 3, author's translation).

The opinion of the early church was divided about the letter (L. Lardner 1788). It was quoted by Tertullian[§] and Clement of Alexandria[§] and appears in the list of biblical books in the Muratorian Canon (dated from late second to fourth cent.). Origen[§] quoted it on several occasions, but gave indications that there was some uncertainty about the work. Eusebius[§] listed Jude among the antilegomena, works of disputed canonicity (*Hist. eccl.* 3.25.3-4), although he classified it as "generally recognized." The epistle does not appear in the Peshitta[†§]. Jerome[§] and others were aware that the work was suspect to some since it contained quotes from the nonbiblical books of *1 Enoch* (Enoch, First Book of[†§]) and a no longer extant *Assumption of Moses* (R. Bauckham 1990, 137-44, 235-80).

The Greek and Latin churches were no longer troubled by the letter after the fourth century. It appears in the canonical list in Athanasius'[§] Easter letter of 367 C.E. The most prominent medieval commentary on Jude was Bede's *In epistolas VII catholicas.* During the Renaissance and the Reformation, uncertainties about the Authority*[§] and canonicity of Jude resurfaced. T. Cajetan[§] had doubts; and, in his two 1520 works on the Canon*[§], A. von Karlstadt[§] arranged the books of the Bible into three categories of authority, placing the antilegomena in the third, least authoritative, category. Luther[§] placed the books of Hebrews, James, Jude, and Revelation at the end of the New Testament and did not assign them consecutive numbers as he had the other twenty-three books he considered to be "the true and certain and chief books of the New Testament" (1960, 394). Of Jude he wrote: "No one can deny that it is an extract or copy of St. Peter's second epistle, so very like it are all the words. He also speaks of the apostles like a disciple who comes long after them and cites sayings and incidents that are found nowhere else in the Scriptures. This moved the ancient fathers to exclude this epistle from the main body of the Scriptures. . . . Therefore, although I value this book, it is an epistle that need not be counted among the chief books which are supposed to lay the foundations of faith" (1960, 397-98).

Danish theologian N. Hemmingsen, providing an enumeration of the New Testament writings, declared: "All these books of the New Testament are in the canon except Second Peter, Second and Third John, the Epistles of James and Jude along with the Apocalypse. Some also place the Epistle to the Hebrews outside the canon" (*De Methodis libro duo* 1555, 124). Jude could thus be in the Bible but not canonical. This radical position was not widespread in subsequent study, although H. Grotius[§] in his *Annotationes* (1650) doubted its attribution to an early church leader and suggested that it was written by a certain Jude who was the last bishop of Jerusalem during the reign of Hadrian (117–138 C.E.), as noted by Eusebius (*Hist. eccl.* 4.5.3).

N. Lardner[§] (1727-57) expounded a traditional view, but J. D. Michaelis[§] revived the radical position in his New Testament introduction: "We have very little reason for placing the Epistle of St. Jude among the sacred writings . . . which contains accounts apparently fabulous, and which was suspected by the ancient church. . . . I cannot therefore acknowledge that this Epistle is canonical. And I have really some doubt whether it be not even a forgery, made in the name of Jude, by some person, who borrowed the chief part of his material from the second Epistle of St. Peter, and added some few of his own" (1750 [ET 1802²] 4:394-95). Opposition to such a radical approach to Jude was widespread: J. G. Herder[§] (1775) defended the epistle's authorship by a brother of Jesus[†§], while A. Jessien (1821) defended authorship by distinguishing between the brother of Jesus named Jude (the author of the epistle) and the apostle Jude.

In the nineteenth–twenty-first centuries several issues have been much discussed: (1) The relationship between Jude and 2 Pet 2 has shifted from Jude's dependence on 2 Pet to the opposite (as Herder had already claimed in the eighteenth century), although some scholars argue for a common source or even common authorship (see Bauckham 1990, 144-47 for review and bibliography). (2) The question of authorship—whether the letter was written pseudonymously under the name of Jude, or by Jude ("Judas") the brother of Jesus (Matt 13:55; Mark 6:3), and/or by one of the early apostles (so the Council of Trent in 1546)—remains unsettled. The majority of scholars deny that the work was produced by a first-generation Christian because (a) v. 17 speaks of "the apostles of our Lord" as figures of the distant past; (b) reference to "the faith, handed on once for all" (v. 3, author's translation) is characteristic of late writings; and (c) the excellence of the Greek is unlikely for Galilean peasants. Bauckham (1990) defends possible authorship by a brother of Jesus and, on the basis of evidence about Jesus' family (especially that from Hegesippus reported by Eusebius in *Hist. eccl.* 3.19.1-3.20.7) and internal considerations, concludes that the book reflects early Palestinian Jewish Christianity. J. Gunther (1984) argues for an Alexandrian origin. (3) The evidence about the opponents is too generalized to allow for identification (F. Wisse 1972). (4) Proposed dates for the letter range from the middle of the first to the middle of the second century (see the listing in Bauckham 1990, 168-69). (5) Interest in Jude's use of nonbiblical traditions and exegetical techniques (Bauckham 1990, 179-280) and its relationship to ancient rhetoric (D. Watson 1988) as well as to general sociocultural factors (J. Neyrey 1993) illustrates the broader contexts within which the letter is presently studied.

Recent commentaries include Harrington (2003), Kraftchick (2002), Richard (2000), Senior (2003), and Turner, Deibler, and Turner (1996). Recent text-critical study includes Landon (1996). Mills has compiled a research bibliography (2000). Theological studies include Lyle (1998) and Reese (2000).

Bibliography: R. J. Bauckham, *Jude, 2 Peter* (WBC 50, 1983); *Jude and the Relatives of Jesus in the Early Church* (1990). **Bede,** *In epistolas VII catholicas* (ed. M. Laistner, CCSL 121, 1983). **C. Bigg,** *A Critical and Exegetical Commentary on the Epistles of St. Peter and St. Jude (ICC, 1902²).* **J D. Charles,** *Literary Strategy in the Epistle of Jude* (1993). **W. M. Dunnett,** "The Hermeneutics of Jude and 2 Peter: The Use of Ancient Jewish Tradition," *JETS* 31 (1988) 287-92. **E. E. Ellis,** "Prophecy and Hermeneutic in Jude," *Prophecy and Hermeneutic in Early Christianity* (WUNT 18, 1978) 221-36. **I. H. Eybers,** "Aspects of the Background of the Letter of Jude," *Essays on the General Epistles of the NT* (ed. W. Nicol et al., 1975) 113-23. **J. J. Gunther,** "The Alexandrian Epistle of Jude," *NTS* 30 (1984) 549-62. **D. J. Harrington,** *Jude and 2 Peter* (SP 15, 2003). **R. Heiligenthal,** "Der Judas Brief: Aspekte der Forschung in den letzten Jahrzehnten," *TRu* 51 (1986) 117-29. **J. G. Herder,** *Briefe zweener Brüder Jesu in unserm Kanon* (1775). **D. E. Hiebert,** "Selected Studies from Jude," *BSac* 142 (1985) 142-51, 238-49, 355-66. **A. Jessien,** *De authentia epistolae Judae* (1821). **S. J. Joubert,** "Language, Ideology, and the Social Context of the Letter of Jude," *Neot* 24 (1990) 335-49; "Persuasion in the Letter of Jude," *JSNT* 58 (1995) 75-87. **J. N. D. Kelly,** *A Commentary on the Epistles of Peter and of Jude* (HNTC, 1969). **J. Knight,** *2 Peter and Jude* (NTG, 1995). **S. J. Kraftchick,** *Jude, 2 Peter* (ANTC, 2002). **C. Landon,** *A Text-Critical Study of the Epistle of Jude* (JSNTSup 135, 1996). **L. Lardner,** "St. Jude and His Epistle," *Works* (ed. B. Coles, 11 vols. 1788) 6:298-317.

N. Lardner, *The Credibility of the Gospel History* (14 vols. 1727-57). **M. Luther,** *Luther's Works* 35 (ed. H. J. Grimm et al., 1960). **K. R. Lyle, Jr.,** *Ethical admonition in the Epistle of Jude* (Studies in Biblical Literature 4, 1998). **J. D. Michaelis,** *Introduction to the NT* (1750; ET 4 vols. 1802²). **W. E. Mills,** *2 Peter and Jude* (Bibliographies for Biblical Research, New Testament Series 19, 2000). **J. H. Neyrey,** *2 Peter, Jude* (AB 37C, 1993). **C. D. Osborn,** "The Christological Use of I Enoch I.9 in Jude 14-15," *NTS* 23 (1977) 334-41. **R. A. Reese,** *Writing Jude: The Reader, the Text, and the Author in Constructs of Power and Desire* (Biblical Interpretation Series, 2000). **E. J. Richard,** *Reading 1 Peter, Jude, and 2 Peter: A Literary and Theological Commentary* (Reading the New Testament, 2000). **D. J. Rowston,** "The Most Neglected Book in the NT," *NTS 21* (1975) 554-63. **D. Senior,** "Jude," *NISB* (2003) 2207-9. **J. D. Turner, E. Deibler, and J. L. Turner,** *Jude: A Structural Commentary* (Mellen Biblical Press Series 44, 1996). **D. F. Watson,** *Invention, Arrangement, and Style: Rhetorical Criticism of Jude and 2 Peter* (SBLDS 104, 1988); "The Letter of Jude," *NIB* (1998) 12:471-500. **R. L. Webb,** "The Eschatology of the Epistle of Jude and Its Rhetorical and Social Functions," *BBR 6* (1996) 139-51. **F. Wisse,** "The Epistle of Jude in the History of Heresiology," *Essays on the Nag Hammadi Texts in Honor of A. Böhling* (ed. M. Drause, NHS 3, 1972) 133-43. **T. R. Wolthuis,** "Jude and Jewish Traditions," *CTJ* 22 (1987) 21-45; "Jude and Rhetoricism," *CTJ* 24 (1989) 126-34.

J. NEYREY

THE NEW TESTAMENT CANON

Revelation, Book of

Also known as the Apocalypse, the last book of the Bible is one of the most controversial. From the time of the early church onward, its date, authorship, and meaning have been disputed; and for many years its right to a place in the New Testament Canon[§] was also debated. Apparently written when Christians feared persecution by Rome, Rev has exercised through its visions and prophecies an unceasing fascination both within and beyond the Christian church; its interpretation has been linked with that of other apocalyptic writings (Apocalypticism*[§]), especially Daniel.

1. *Early Interpretations to 300.* The prevailing early interpretation of Rev was Chiliasm, a position that regarded Rev 20:1-6 as a prediction of Christ's coming reign on earth for a millennium, i.e., a thousand years. Justin[§] and Irenaeus[§] both had chiliastic tendencies. A widespread expectation was that the fall of Rome, symbolized by Babylon, would precede the millennium; and the connection between Antichrist and the beasts mentioned in the Apocalypse was much discussed. However, writers such as Origen[§] (*De Prin.* 2.11) and Dionysius of Alexandria[§] (Eusebius *Hist. eccl.* 7.24-25) rejected the materialistic hopes characteristic of Chiliasm and advocated a spiritual interpretation of the book.

Most writers believed that John, the son of Zebedee, had written Rev; Irenaeus dated it in the reign of Domitian (c. 96). But Caius, an opponent of Chiliasm, refused to accept it as Scripture (Eusebius *Hist. eccl.* 3.28); Marcion[§] (Tertullian *Adv. Marc.* 4.5) and the Alogoi (Epiphanius *Haer.* 51.3) also rejected its canonical status.

2. *From 300 to 1100.* At the beginning of the fourth century, opinion was divided about the book's canonical status (Eusebius *Hist. eccl.* 3.25), and hesitation continued in the East. Cyril of Jerusalem did not include it in his canon. The Syrian church was reluctant to accept it; it was not included in the Peshitta[§], although it appeared in some later Syriac New Testaments. Athanasius[§] and several other Greek writers, however, accepted it. In the West there was less uncertainty, and in 397 the Synod of Carthage recognized Rev as canonical. With the end of pagan Rome and the absence of any visible return of Christ, the popularity of Chiliasm declined. Tyconius[§] appears to have thought that the millennium was Christ's reign in the church between the first and second advents, the latter of which he seems to have expected in the near future. Augustine[§], who had formerly accepted Chiliasm (*Serm.* 259), later rejected it and interpreted Rev in a manner similar to Tyconius. (*Civ. Dei* 20.7-9, 17). Their views dominated Western interpretation (e.g. Bede's[§] commentaries) well into the Middle Ages.

3. *From 1100 to 1500.* Joachim of Fiore[§], the most important writer on Rev in this period, laid the foundation for a renewal of millenarian teaching with his doctrine of the three ages of the Father, the Son, and the Spirit. The age of the Spirit was already dawning, and the millennium, which began with Christ's first advent, would come in its fullness after the destruction of the beast and the false prophet. He also explained the visions in Rev as allusions to the course of history from ancient Israel to his own day.

After Joachim many authors interpreted the course of history as being predicted in the book. Matthias of Janow, J. Wyclif[§], the Lollards, and J. Hus[§] interpreted Revelation antipapally.

4. *From 1500 to 1770. a. The Reformation.* Erasmus[§] (1527) expressed doubts about the authorship of the Apocalypse. Although Luther[§] questioned its divine Inspiration*[§] in his New Testament (1522), he withdrew the criticism in a later edition and was prepared to use the book as ammunition in his conflict with the papacy. Calvin[§] wrote no commentary on Rev, and Zwingli[§] (1982) had a negative opinion of it.

In spite of these hesitations, Rev became a rallying point for opponents of the papacy. Antipapal writings on the book during the sixteenth century include the sermons of J. Bullinger[§] and the commentaries of D. Chytraeus (1563), J. Bale (1548), J. Foxe (1587), and J. Napier (1593). Many of these writers saw references in the book to the Turks, especially in the vision of 200 million cavalry in Rev 9:16. The most spectacular treatment of the Apocalypse is to be seen in the Chiliasm of extremists like T. Müntzer[§] and John of Leyden, who tried to facilitate the fulfillment of prophecy by the use of force. The Augsburg Confession of the Lutherans and the Second Helvetic Confession of the Calvinists, however, denounced Chiliasm.

b. Roman Catholic reactions and Protestant replies. Eventually there was a Roman Catholic reaction to the antipapal interpretation of the book, led by the Jesuits R. Bellarmine[§], Ribera, and Alcazar. Ribera, a pioneer of futurist interpretation (1591), accepted the Augustinian idea of the millennium but rejected world- and church-historical approaches. Most of the book's prophecies, he contended, had not yet been fulfilled; and Rome, symbolized by Babylon, would eventually break away from the pope. Alcazar (1614), following J. Hentennius, gave a preterist interpretation (the prophecies of Rev had already been fulfilled), the beginning of a contemporary-historical approach. Most of the book, he claimed, referred to the judgment on Judaism and Rome in the first three centuries. The beast from the sea was pagan Rome, and the millennium was the life of the church ever since the time of Constantine.

Two Protestants, H. Grotius[§] (1644) and H. Hammond[§] (1653), produced modified versions of Alcazar's interpretation, dating the millennium from Constantine until about 1300 and explaining Gog and Magog (Rev 20:8) as the Turks and Syrians. They suggested that John received his revelations on several different occasions, beginning in the reign of Claudius. A preterist interpretation was also advocated by the Roman Catholic J.-B. Bossuet (1689). Further Protestant responses came from T. Brightman[§] (1609) and D. Pareus (1618), both of whom restated the antipapal interpretation. A distinctive feature of Pareus was his explanation of Rev as a drama, which led to J. Milton's[§] description of the book as "the majestick image of a high and stately Tragedy."

c. Millenarian interpretations. In the seventeenth century the chiliastic type of interpretation won great popularity. J. Alsted (1627) predicted that the millennium would begin in 1694. J. Mede[§] (1627, 1632) expected it in the near future but refused to give a precise date; according to his theory of synchronisms, different passages in the book referred to the same event. Both Alsted and Mede combined their expectations with a church-historical interpretation. Their works provided a scholarly justification for speculation about a future millennium and were very popular during the upheavals of the Thirty Years' War and the English Civil War.

During this period prophets appeared both in Great Britain and in Europe. In Great Britain, L. Muggleton and J. Reeve claimed to be the witnesses of Rev 11, and J. Robins wanted to lead the 144,000 of the Apocalypse to the Holy Land. In Europe, P. Felgenhauer, J. Warner, and C. Kotter were among the prophetic interpreters of Rev and of other apocalyptic books. Developments in France had their impact on the treatment of the book: The revocation of the Edict of Nantes in 1685 led the Protestant P. Jurieu (1687) to see in that event the death of the two witnesses; it also led to the rise of French prophets whose visions showed the influence of the Apocalypse.

The impact of scientific discoveries can be seen in the writings of T. Burnet[§] (1684-90) and W. Whiston[§] (1737), both of whom expected the fulfillment of the prophecies through such natural events as volcanic eruptions and the approach of comets. I. Newton[§], on the other hand, preferred to confine his attention to the ways in which he thought prophecy had already been fulfilled.

There was strong opposition to millenarian teaching in orthodox Lutheran and Calvinistic circles, but mediating views emerged. J. Cocceius[§] (1665) regarded the millennium as already past but expected an earthly New Jerusalem. According to P. J. Spener[§] (1693) there would be a future millennium on earth, but it would not be preceded by the visible return of Christ.

d. Eighteenth-century developments. Views similar to Spener's were developed by D. Whitby[§] (1702), who argued that the millennium would be a period of great prosperity for the church, followed by the visible return of Christ. This interpretation, known as postmillennial, was adopted by C. Vitringa[§] (1705), M. Lowman (1747), and J. Edwards[§] (1774). It was a form of interpretation congenial to the advocates of missionary expansion.

An unusual account of the book was given by J. Bengel[§] (1740), who claimed that there would be two millennia. The first would be a period of prosperity for the church, beginning with the fall of the papacy in 1836. During the second, a false sense of prosperity on earth would be followed by the glorious coming of Christ. Bengel's interpretation was influential in Germany and at one stage was given sympathetic consideration by J. Wesley[§].

The eighteenth century was conspicuous for the emergence of open criticism of the book. The Deist (Deism[§]) T. Morgan[§] (1738-40) accepted traditional authorship but regarded Rev as an example of Judaizing. Another Deist, H. St. John, Viscount Bolingbroke[§] (1754), dismissed it as "the reveries of a mad Judaizing Christian" and ascribed it to Cerinthus; and Voltaire[§] made some characteristically caustic remarks about it. At the same time the preterist contemporary-historical approach gained momentum, counting among its practitioners F. Abauzit (1770) and J. Wettstein[§] (1752). According to Abauzit, Rev was written during the reign of Nero and predicted the fall of the Jewish state, symbolized by the seven-headed beast. Wettstein thought that the beast stood for the emperors before Vespasian and that the millennium had lasted just over sixty years from 70 C.E. until the time of Bar Kochba.

e. Mystical interpretations. Mystical approaches to the book gained popularity in the seventeenth and eighteenth centuries. These writers referred to historical events, but they were primarily concerned with explaining the Apocalypse in terms of the inner life. J.-M. Guyon[§] (1713) wrote a commentary relating the book to stages of spiritual development. J. Lead[§] (1683), J. E. Petersen (1696), and J. W. Petersen (1706) gave accounts based on claims to special revelations. E. Swedenborg (1766) was one of the most famous interpreters in this tradition.

f. Russia. Although most of the writings on Rev were produced in the West, both sides in the controversy that split the Russian Church in the seventeenth century used its prophecies with those of other apocalyptic writings as weapons to argue their views. Patriarch Nikon described his monastery as the New Jerusalem, while his opponents, the Old Believers, regarded it as the kingdom of the Antichrist and used the number 666 (Rev 13:18) to calculate 1666 as the time of Antichrist's arrival. The use of apocalyptic imagery in Russian church conflict continued in the eighteenth century.

5. 1770 to the Present. a. The rise of modern criticism. At first the world- and church-historical method of interpretation continued to flourish. Among its advocates were J. Bicheno (1793) and J. Priestley (1803-4), both of whom saw the French Revolution as the earthquake of Rev 11:13. Often used in the nineteenth century, the detailed church-historical method ceased to exercise much influence in academic circles by the twentieth century.

During this period important developments took place in academic research on the Apocalypse. Questions about the nature of its theology and the accuracy of its prophecies led scholars to make adverse criticisms. J. Semler[§] (1771-76) thought it unfit for inclusion in the Bible, while J. D. Michaelis[§] (1788) questioned its authorship and inspiration. However, the most skeptical approach came from C. Dupuis (1795), who regarded it as a Phrygian cultic document based on an ancient solar myth.

Contemporary-historical interpretation was widely practiced. G. Herder (1779) followed Abauzit in explaining Revelation as a prediction of the downfall of Judaism. J. G. Eichhorn[§]

(1791) saw it as a prophecy of both the destruction of the Jewish state and the fall of the Roman Empire, and F. Lücke (1832) examined it in relation to other writings belonging to the genre of what he called "apocalyptic." In the 1840s C. Fritzsche, F. Benary, F. Hitzig[§], and E. Reuss[§] (see W. Bousset 1906, 105-6) argued that 666, the number of the beast, signified Nero Caesar. F. C. Baur[§] (1864) contended that Revelation was written in opposition to Pauline teaching (see Paul[†§]). In a modified form of the church-historical method, C. Auberlen (1854) argued that the book prophesied the great epochs in the development of the kingdom of God. E. Hengstenberg[§] (1849-50) combined that modified approach with preterism.

In the late nineteenth century, theories about sources and Redaction[*§] were developed. E. Vischer (1886) and F. Spitta[§] (1889) argued that Jewish sources lay behind Revelation, and even more complex theories were put forward by D. Völter (1886) and others. W. Bousset[§] (1896) claimed that the book was a unified work that had assimilated various apocalyptic fragments. According to R. Charles[§] (1920), it contains earlier sources but in its present form is mostly the work of one author, although a redactor has worked on the text. H. Swete[§] (1951) maintained that Rev is a unity, a viewpoint that became more fashionable later in the twentieth century.

There was growing interest in the book's relationship to myth, a theme developed earlier by Dupuis. Both Bousset and Charles were influenced by H. Gunkel[§] (1895), who stressed Rev's debt to Near Eastern, especially Babylonian, Mythology[*§] . Other scholars, including F. Boll (1914), related its visions to universal astral myths.

Most subsequent commentators have used a combination of critical methods, giving serious consideration to the mythological background, the possibility of sources and redaction, the influence of the first-century situation, and the relationship to Judaism and other apocalyptic literature (e.g., W. Hadorn 1928; E. Lohse 1960; G. Caird[§] 1966; G. Beasley-Murray 1974; H. Kraft 1974; R. Mounce 1977; J. Sweet 1979; and J. Roloff 1993). E. Allo (1921) and P. Prigent (1981) maintained both an Augustinian theory of the millennium and the principle of recapitulation. E. Lohmeyer[§] (1926) and J. Sickenberger (1940) rejected the notion that the book is related directly to Roman persecution. E. Corsini (1983) claims that it describes events from the creation to the fall of Jerusalem. P. Minear (1968) thinks that it alludes to opposition from false teachers. A. Farrer[§] (1949) and Prigent (1964) have given attention to its liturgical setting.

According to E. Schüssler Fiorenza (1998[2]), its author belonged to a Christian prophetic-apocalyptic school. R. Bauckham (1993b) made a detailed study of the book's theology, and T. Holtz (1971) and Slater (1999) investigated its Christology. M. Rissi (1965) interpreted it in relation to salvation history, while W. Ramsay[§] (1904), P. Touilleux (1935), and C. Hemer (1986) examined its background in Asia Minor. Among the many popular works that have taken serious account of modern scholarship are those by H. Lilje (1940) and W. Barclay[§] (1976). In addition to taking account of scholarship, A. Boesak (1987) in South Africa and R. Foulkes (1989), D. Ramírez (1989-90), and P. Richard (1995) in Latin America interpret the Apocalypse in light of the social injustices of their own times.

b. Literary criticism and the social sciences. The poetic and dramatic qualities of the book have been recognized for a long time. Herder emphasized its poetic excellence. M. Stuart[§] (1851) argued that it was an epic, and Lohmeyer attempted to divide it into strophes. Following in Pareus's footsteps, F. Hartwig (1780-83), Eichhorn, F. Palmer (1903), J. Bowman (1955), and J. Blevins (1984) have explained it as a drama. The second half of the twentieth century has seen an intensification of interest in its literary qualities. There have been discussions of the book's genre and function (J. Collins 1979; F. Mazzaferri 1989), while other scholars have combined the insights of the social sciences (Social-Scientific Criticism[*§]) with those of Literary[*§] criticism. Rhetorical Criticism[*§] has been applied to the book as well; its structure has been closely examined and attention has been paid in varying degrees to the insights of Sociology[*§], anthropology, Psychology*§ (J. Gager 1975; A. Y. Collins 1984; Schüssler Fiorenza), and the role of gender (T. Pippin 1992).

Writers from disciplines other than biblical criticism have reflected on issues connected with the Apocalypse. F. Engels (1964) compared the community depicted in the book with socialist movements of his day. N. Cohn (1957) and E. Tuveson (1964, 1968), studying the impact of millenarian thought on society, also included discussions of Revelation's impact. C. Jung§ (1954; also Edigner 1999) made observations from the viewpoint of psychology. Prominent in the writings of such literary critics as F. Kermode (1967) and N. Frye (1982), Rev has also given rise to reflections by the philosopher and critic J. Derrida (1983).

c. Authorship and date. Many scholars in the nineteenth century and most in the twentieth rejected traditional authorship. F. Hitzig§ (1843) argued for John Mark as the author, and Lohmeyer (1926) suggested John the Elder. According to J. Ford (1975), most of the book is a product of the John the Baptist circle, to which a Christian redactor has made additions; however, some scholars, including Allo and I. Beckwith (1919), have favored the traditional view. Although rejecting apostolic authorship, Lohmeyer argued that its author also wrote John's Gospel and the Johannine Letters†§. Most scholars have dated the work in the reign of Domitian, but others, especially in the nineteenth century, preferred 66-70, while A. Farrer (1964) assigned it to the reign of Trajan.

d. Other interpretations. The theosophist J. Pryse (1906) and the anthroposophist R. Steiner (1943) have given esoteric interpretations of Rev. The book has also played an important part in formulating the expectations of several popular religious movements. Reflected in the oracles of the visionaries R. Brothers and J. Southcott in the late eighteenth and early nineteenth centuries, it has figured prominently in the teaching of Mormons, Seventh-Day Adventists, Jehovah's Witnesses, and many popular interpreters who have affirmed the imminence of the second advent. Dispensationalism, which can be traced back to J. Darby in the mid-nineteenth century, has attracted an enormous number of supporters. Their position, stated in the Scofield§ Reference Bible (1909 and 1917) and in the work of H. Lindsey (1970), is that the redeemed will be snatched to heaven in the "rapture," escaping the seven-year tribulation that will precede the millennium. Millenarianism is also advocated by those who believe that Great Britain and the United States are the lost tribes of Israel (e.g., E. Hine 1874; H. Armstrong 1959) and appeared in a violent form in the activities of D. Koresh's Branch Davidians.

The impact of the Apocalypse has extended far beyond the sphere of organized religion. Its language and images have been adopted by the advocates of social change and have been enlisted in the service of nationalism. Not confined to traditional Western culture, it has influenced millenarian-type movements in other cultures as well.

Few books have generated such diverse interpretations or awakened the interest of as wide a variety of people as the Apocalypse. On many occasions the book seems to have been at the mercy of the personal concerns and expectations of its interpreters; nevertheless, its vivid and evocative imagery and the power and passion with which it gives expression to the hopes and fears of individuals have made their mark on the way people think and feel about their present predicaments and their ultimate destiny.

Recent commentaries on Rev include Aune (1997-98), Barr (1998), Beale (1999), Brighton (1999), Faley (1999), Knight (1999), Malina and Pilch (2000), Mounce (1998), Murphy (1998), Osborne (2002), and Thompson (1998). Collections of essays on Rev include Backhaus (2001) and Giesen (2000). Bøe (2001) and Mathewson (2003) study the use of the Hebrew Bible in Rev. Court (2000) and Lindars, Edwards, and Court (2000) study Rev as part of the wider Johannine literature. Jack (1999) performs a postmodern deconstructionist analysis of Rev. Briggs (1999) and Stevenson (2001) analyze the imagery of the Jerusalem Temple in Rev. Friesen (2001) and Riemer (1998) analyze Rev in relation to the Roman imperial cult.

Resseguie (1998) has done a narrative analysis of Rev. Howard-Brook and Gwyther (1999) use liberation theology to interpret Revin both the ancient and modern context. Lee (2001), McDonough (1999), Müller-Fieberg (2003), and Schimanowski, (2002) analyze the Jewish backgrounds to Rev. Miscellaneous studies of Rev include Barker (2000), Duff (2001), Glonner (1999), González (1999), Heinze (1998), Hirschberg (1999), Hirschberg (1999), Kalms (2001), Kerner (1998), Lioy (2003), Maier (2002), McKelvey (1999), Puthussery (2002), Roose (2000), Rossing (1999), and Royalty (1998).

Bibliography: **F. Abauzit**, *Oeuvres diverses* (1770). **L. de Alcazar**, *Vestigatio arcani sensus in Apocalypsi* (1614). **E. B. Allo**, *Saint Jean, L'Apocalypse* (1921). **J. H. Alsted**, *Diatribe de mille annis apocalypticis* (1627). **H. W. Armstrong**, *The Book of Revelation Unveiled at Last!* (1959). **C. A. Auberlen**, *Der Prophet Daniel und die Offenbarung Johannis* (1854). **Augustine**, *Sermones* (PL 38); *De civitate Dei* (PL 41; CSEL 40; CCSL 48). **D. E. Aune**, *Revelation* (three vols. WBC 52, 1997-98). **K. Backhaus** (ed.), *Theologie als Vision: Studien zur Johannes-Offenbarung* (SBS 191, 2001). **J. Bale**, *The Image of Bothe Churches After the Most Wonderfull and Heavenly Revelacion of Sainct John the Evangelist* (1548). **B. W. Ball,** *A Great Expectation: Eschatological Thought in English Protestantism to 1660* (1975). **W. Barclay,** *The Revelation of John* (2 vols. 1976). **M. Barker,** *The Revelation of Jesus Christ: Which God Gave to Him to Show to His Servants What Must Soon Take Place (Revelation I.I)* (2000). **D. L. Barr,** *Tales of the End: A Narrative Commentary on the Book of Revelation* (Storytellers Bible, 1998). **R. Bauckham,** *Tudor Apocalypse: Sixteenth-century Apocalypticism, Millenarianism, and the English Reformation* (1978); *The Climax of Prophecy: Studies on the Book of Revelation* (1993a); *The Theology of the Book of Revelation* (1993b). **F. C. Baur,** *Vorlesungen über neutes-tamentliche Theologie* (1864). **G. K. Beale,** *The Book of Revelation: A Commentary on the Greek Text* (NIGTC, 1999). **G. R. Beasley-Murray,** *The Book of Revelation* (1974). **I. Beckwith,** *The Apocalypse of John* (1919). **R. Bellarmine,** *Controversiae Generales 3.1* (Opera 2, 1870; repr. 1965) 5-75. **J. A. Bengel,** *Erklärte Offenbarung* (1740). **J. Bicheno,** *Signs of the Times* (1793). **J. H. Billington,** *The Icon and the Axe: An Interpretive History of Russian Culture* (1966). **J. L. Blevins,** *Revelation as Drama* (1984). **O. Böcher**, *Die Johannesapokalypse* (1975); "Die Johannes-Apokalypse in der neueren Forschung," *ANRW* II. 25.5 (1988) 3850-93. **S. Bøe,** *Gog and Magog: Ezekiel 38-39 as Pre-text for Revelation 19,17-21 and 20,7-10* (WUNT 2/135, 2001). **A. Boesak,** *Comfort and Protest: Reflections on the Apocalypse of John of Patmos* (1987). **Viscount Bolingbroke (Henry St. John),** *Philosophical Works 2* (1754, repr. 1977) 337. **F. Boll**, *Aus der Offenbarung Johannis: Hellenistische Studien zum Weltbild der Apokalypse* (1914). **J. B. Bossuet,** *L'Apocalypse avec une explication* (1689). **W. Bousset,** *Die Offenbarung Johannis* (1896, rev. ed. 1906). **J. W. Bowman,** *The Drama of the Book of Revelation: An Account of the Book, with a New Translation in the Language of Today* (1955). **R. A. Briggs,** *Jewish Temple Imagery in the Book of Revelation* (Studies in Biblical Literature 10, 1999). **T. Brightman,** *Apocalypsis Apocalypseos* (1609). **L. A. Brighton,** *Revelation* (Concordia Commentary, 1999). **T. Burnet,** *The Theory of the Earth* (2 vols. 1684-90). **G. B. Caird,** *A Commentary on the Revelation of St. John the Divine* (1966). **R. H. Charles,** *Studies in the Apocalypse: Being Lectures Delivered Before the University of London* (1913); *The Revelation of St. John* (2 vols. 1920). **D. Chytraeus,** *Commentarius in Apocalypsin* (1563). **J. Cocceius,** *Cogitationes de Apocalypsi Johannis* (1665). **N. Cohn,** *The Pursuit of the Millennium* (1957). **A. Y. Collins,** *Crisis and Catharsis: The Power of the Apocalypse* (1984). **J. J. Collins** (ed.), *Apocalypse: the Morphology of a Genre* (Semeia 14, 1979). **E. Corsini,** *The Apocalypse: The Perennial Revelation of Jesus Christ* (1983). **J. M. Court,** *The Book of Revelation and the Johannine Apocalyptic Tradition* (JSNTSup 190, 2000). **J. W. Davidson,** *The Logic of Millennial Thought: Eighteenth-century New England* (1977). **J. Derrida,** *D' un ton apocalyptique* *adopté naguère en philosophie* (1983). **C. Diobouniotis and A. von Harnack** (eds.), *Der Scholien-Kommentar des Origenes zur Apokalypse Johannis nebst einem Stuck aus Irenaeus, lib. V. Graece* (TU 38, 1911). **P. B. Duff,** *Who Rides the Beast? Prophetic Rivalry and the Rhetoric of Crisis in the Churches of the Apocalypse* (2001). **C. F. Dupuis,** *Origine de tous les cultes* (4 vols. 1795). **E. F. Edinger,** *Archetype of the Apocalypse: A Jungian Study of the Book of Revelation* (1999). **J. Edwards,** *History of the Work of Redemption* (1774). **J. G. Eichhorn,** *Commentarius in Apocalypsin Joannis* (1791). **E. B. Elliott,** *Horae Apocalypticae: Or a Commentary on the Apocalypse, Critical and Historical 4* (1862). **J. Ellul,** *Apocalypse: The Book of Revelation* (1977). **F. Engels,** *On Religion* (K. Marx and F. Engels, 1964) 205-12, 316-47. **D. Erasmus,** *Annotationes in Novum Testamentum* (1527). **M. J. Erickson,** *Contemporary Options in Eschatology: A Study of the Millennium* (1977). **R. J. Faley,** *Apocalypse Then and Now: A Companion to the Book of Revelation* (1999). **A. Farrer,** *A Rebirth of Images: The Making of St. John's Apocalypse* (1949); *The Revelation of St. John the Divine* (1964). **A. Feuillet,** *The Apocalypse* (1965). **K. R. Firth,** *The Apocalyptic Tradition in Reformation Britain, 1530-1645* (1979). **J. M. Ford,** *Revelation* (1975). **R. Foulkes,** *El Apocalipsis de San Juan: Una lectura desde America Latina* (1989). **J. Foxe,** *Eicasmi, seu meditationes in sacram Apocalypsin* (1587). **S. J. Friesen,** *Imperial Cults and the Apocalypse of John: Reading Revelation in the Ruins* (2001). **L. E. Froom,** *The Prophetic Faith of Our Fathers: The Historical Development of Prophetic Interpretation* (4 vols. 1950-54). **N. Frye,** *The Great Code: The Bible and Literature* (1982). **J. G. Gager,** *Kingdom and Community: The Early World of Early Christianity* (1975). **H. Giesen,** *Studien zur Johannesapokalypse* (SBAB 29, 2000). **G. Glonner,** *Zur Bildersprache des Johannes von Patmos: Untersuchung der Johannesapokalypse anhand einer um Elemente der Bildinterpretation erweiterten historisch-kritischen Methode* (NTAbh n.f. 34, 1999). **J. L. González,** *For the Healing of the Nations: The Book of Revelation in an Age of Cultural Conflict* (1999). **H. Grotius,** *Annotationes in Vetus Testamentum* (1644). **H. Gunkel,** *Schöpfung und Chaos in Urzeit und Endzeit: Eine Religionsgeschichtliche Untersuchung über Gen 1 und Ap Joh 12* (1895). **J.-M. Guyon,** *La sainte Bible ou le Vieux et le Nouveau Testament, avec des explications et réflexions qui regardent la vie intérieure 20* (20 vols. 1790). **W. Hadorn,** *Die Offenbarung des Johannes* (1928). **H. Hammond,** *Paraphrase and Annotations on the NT* (1653). **J. F. C. Harrison,** *The Second Coming: Popular Millenarianism, 1780-1850* (1979). **F. G. Hartwig,** *Apologie der Apokalypse* (4 pts. 1780-83). **A. Heinze,** *Johannesapokalypse und johanneische Schriften: Forschungs-und- traditionsgeschichtliche Untersuchungen* (BZANT 8/2, 1998). **C. J. Hemer,** *The Letters to the Seven Churches in Their Local Setting* (1986). **E. W. Hengstenberg,** *Die Offenbarung des heiligen Johannes* (2 vols. 1849-50). **G. F. Herder,** *Maranatha* (1779). **E. Hine,** *Forty-seven Identifications of the British Nation with the Lost Ten Tribes of Israel* (1874). **P. Hirschberg,** *Das eschatologische Israel: Untersuchungen zum Gottesvolkverständnis der Johannesoffenbarung* (1999). **F. Hitzig,** *Über Johannes Markus* (1843). **T. Holtz,** *Die Christologie der Apokalypse des Johannes und seine Schriften, oder: Welcher Johannes hat die Offenbarung verfasst?* (1971). **W. Howard-Brook and A. Gwyther,** *Unveiling Empire: Reading Revelation Then and Now* (Bible and Liberation, 1999). **A. M. Jack,** *Texts Reading Texts, Sacred and Secular* (JSNTSup 179, 1999). **James I,** *Works* (1616). **Joachim of Fiore,** *Concordia novi et veteris Testamenti* (1519, repr. 1964); *Expositio in Apocalypsim* (1527, repr. 1964). **C. G. Jung,** *Answer to Job* (1954). **P. Jurieu,** *The Accomplishment of the Scripture Prophecies or the Approaching Deliverance of the Church* (1687). **J. H. Kalms,** *Der Sturz des Gottesfeindes: Traditionsgeschichtliche Studien zu Apokalypse 12* (WMANT 93, 2001). **W. Kamlah,** *Apokalypse und Geschichtstheologie: Die mittelalterliche Auslegung der Apokalypse vor Joachim von Fiore* (1935). **F. Kermode,** *The Sense of an Ending: Studies in the Theory of Fiction* (1967). **J. Kerner,** *Die Ethik der Johannes-Apokalypse im Vergleich mit der des 4.*

Esra: Ein Beitrag zum Verhältnis von Apokalyptik und Ethik (BZNW 94, 1998). **J. Knight,** *Revelation* (Readings, 1999). **H. Kraft,** *Die Offenbarung des Johannes* (1974); *Die Bilder der Offenbarung des Johannes* (1994). **G. Kretschmar,** *Die Offenbarung des Johannes: Die Geschichte ihrer Auslegung im 1 Jahrtausend* (1985). **A. Kuyper,** *The Revelation of St. John* (1964). **J. Lead,** *A Revelation of the Revelations* (1683). **P. Lee,** *The New Jerusalem in the Book of Revelation: A Study of Revelation 21-22 in the Light of Its Background in Jewish Tradition* (WUNT 2/129, 2001). **H. Lilje,** *Das letzte Buch der Bibel* (1940). **B. Lindars, R. B. Edwards, and J. M. Court,** *The Johannine Literature* (2000). **H. Lindsey,** *The Late Great Planet Earth* (1970). **D. Lioy,** *The Book of Revelation in Christological Focus* (Studies in Biblical Literature 58, 2003). **E. Lohmeyer,** *Die Offenbarung des Johannes* (1926). **E. Lohse,** *Die Offenbarung des Johannes* (1960). **M. Lowman,** *A Paraphrase and Notes on the Revelation of St. John* (1747). **F. Lücke,** *Versuch einer vollständigen Einleitung in die Offenbarung Johannis und in die gesammelte apokalyptische Literatur* (1832). **M. Luther,** *Das Neue Testament Deutsch* (1522). **B. W. McGinn,** *Visions of the End: Apocalyptic Traditions in the Middle Ages* (1979). **B. W. McGinn et al.** (eds.), *The Encyclopedia of Apocalypticism* (3 vols. 1998). **H. O. Maier,** *Apocalypse Recalled: The Book of Revelation after Christendom* (2002). **B. J. Malina and J. J. Pilch,** *Social-science Commentary on the Book of Revelation* (2000). **D. Mathewson,** *A New Heaven and a New Earth : The Meaning and Function of the Old Testament in Revelation 21.1-22.5* (JSNTSup 238, 2003). **F. D. Mazzaferri,** *The Genre of the Book of Revelation from a Source-critical Perspective* (1989). **S. M. McDonough,** *YHWH at Patmos: Rev. 1:4 in its Hellenistic and Early Jewish Setting* (WUNT 2/107, 1999). **R. J. McKelvey,** *The Millennium and the Book of Revelation* (1999). **J. Mede,** *Clavis Apocalyptica* (1627, rev. ed. 1632). **F. van de Meer,** *Apocalypse: Visions from the Book of Revelation in Western Art* (1978). **J. D. Michaelis,** *Einleitung in die göttlichen Schriften des Neuen Bundes* (2 vols. 1788). **P. S. Minear,** *I Saw a New Earth: An Introduction to the Visions of the Apocalypse* (1968). **T. Morgan,** *The Moral Philosopher in a Dialogue Between Philalethes, a Christian Deist, and Theophanes, a Christian Jew* (1738-40) 1:364-82. **R. H. Mounce,** *The Book of Revelation* (NICNT, 1998²). **R. Müller-Fieberg,** *Das "neue Jerusalem" : Vision für alle Herzen und alle Zeiten?: Eine Auslegung von Offb 21,1-22,5 im Kontext von alttestamentlich-frühjüdischer Tradition und literarischer Rezeption* (BBB 144, 2003). **F. J. Murphy,** *Fallen is Babylon: The Revelation to John* (New Testament in Context, 1998). **J. Napier,** *A Plaine Discovery of the Whole Revelation of Saint John* (1593). **I. Newton,** *Observations upon the Prophecies* (1733). **G. R. Osborne,** *Revelation* (Baker Exegetical Commentary on the New Testament, 2002). **F. Palmer,** *The Drama of the Apocalypse in Relation to the Literary and Political Circumstances of Its Time* (1903). **D. Pareus,** *In divinam Apocalypsin S. Apostoli et evangelistae Johannis Commentarius* (1618). **C. A. Patrides and J. Wittreich** (eds.), *The Apocalypse in English Renaissance Thought and Literature: Patterns, Antecedents, and Repercussions* (1985). **J. E. Petersen,** *Anleitung zu gründlicher Verständnis der heiligen Offenbarung* (1696). **J. W. Petersen,** *Die Verklärte Offenbarung Jesu Christi: nach dem Zusammenhang ... des Geistes* (1706). **T. Pippin,** *Death and Desire: The Rhetoric of Gender in the Apocalypse of John* (1992). **J. Priestley,** *Notes on all the Books of Scripture for the Use of the Pulpit and Private Families* (4 vols. 1803-4). **P. Prigent,** *L'Apocalypse et Liturgie* (1964); *L'Apocalypse de Saint Jean* (1981). **J. M. Pryse,** *The Apocalypse Unsealed* (1906). **J. Puthussery,** *Days of Man and God's Day: An Exegetico-Theological Study of* ημερα *in the Book of Revelation* (Tesi gregoriana, Serie teologia 82, 2002). **D. Ramírez Fernández,** "La idolatría del poder," *Revista de Interpretacion Bíblica Latinoamericana* 4 (1989) 109-28; "El juicio de Dios a las transnacionales," *Revista de Interpretación Bíblica Latinoamericana* 5-6 (1990) 55-74. **W. M. Ramsay,** *Letters to the Seven Churches of Asia and Their Place in the Plan of the Apocalypse* (1904). **J. L. Resseguie,** *Revelation Unsealed: A Narrative Critical Approach to John's Apocalypse* (Biblical interpretation

Series 32, 1998). **F. Ribera**, *Commentarius in Apocalypsin* (1591). **P. Richard**, *Apocalypse: A People's Commentary on the Book of Revelation* (1995). **U. Riemer,** *Das Tier auf dem Kaiserthron?: Eine Untersuchung zur Offenbarung des Johannes als historischer Quelle* (Beiträge zur Altertumskunde 114, 1998). **M. Rissi**, *Was ist und was geschehen soll danach: Die Zeit- und Geschichtsauffassung der Offenbarung des Johannes* (1965); *Die Hure Babylon und die Verführung der Heiligen: Eine Studie zur Apokalypse des Johannes* (c. 1995). **J. Roloff**, *The Revelation of John* (1993). **H. Roose,** *"Das Zeugnis Jesu": Seine Bedeutung für die Christologie, Eschatologie und Prophetie in der Offenbarung des Johannes* (TANZ 32, 2000). **B. R. Rossing**, *The Choice Between Two Cities: Whore, Bride, and Empire in the Apocalypse.* (HTS 48, 1999). **C. Rowland**, "Revelation," *NIB* (1997) 12:501-736. **R. M. Royalty, Jr.,** *The Streets of Heaven: The Ideology of Wealth in the Apocalypse of John* (1998). **G. Schimanowski,** *Die himmlische Liturgie in der Apokalypse des Johannes: Die frühjüdischen Traditionen in Offenbarung 4-5 unter Einschluss der Hekhalotliteratur* (WUNT 2/154, 2002). **E. Schüssler Fiorenza**, *The Book of Revelation: Justice and Judgment* (1998[2]). **J. S. Semler,** *Abhandlung von freier Untersuchung des Canons* (4 pts. 1771-76). **J. Sickenberger,** *Erklärung der Johannesapokalypse* (1940). **T. B. Slater,** *Christ and Community: A Socio-Historical Study of the Christology of Revelation* (JSNTSup 178, 1999). **P. J. Spener,** *Behauptung der Hoffnung künftiger besserer Zeiten* (1693). **F. Spitta**, *Die Offenbarung des Johannes untersucht* (1889). **E. Stauffer**, *Christ and the Caesars* (1952). **R. Steiner**, *The Apocalypse* (1943). **G. Stevenson,** *Power and Place: Temple and Identity in the Book of Revelation* (BZNW 107, 2001). **M. Stuart,** *Commentary on the Apocalypse* (2 vols. 1851). **E. Swedenborg**, *Apocalypse Revealed* (1766). **J. P. M. Sweet**, *Revelation* (1979). **H. B. Swete**, *The Apocalypse of St. John* (1951). **L. L. Thompson,** *Revelation* (ANTC, 1998). **P. Toon** (ed.), *Puritans, the Millennium, and the Future of Israel: Puritan Eschatology, 1600-1660. A Collection of Essays* (1970). **P. Touilleux**, *L'Apocalypse et les cultes de Domitien et de Cybèle* (1935). **E. E. Tuveson**, *Millennium and Utopia: A Study in the Background of the Idea of Progress* (1964); *Redeemer Nation: The Idea of America's Millennial Role* (1968). **E. Vischer**, *Die Offenbarung Johannis: Eine jüdische Apokalypse in christlicher Bearbeitung* (1886). **C. Vitringa**, *ANAKRII apocalypsios Joannis Apostoli* (1705). **F. M. A. de Voltaire**, *Dictionnaire philosophique* (1765). **D. Völter**, *Die Entstehung der Apokalypse* (1882); *Die Offenbarung Johannis* (1904). **A. W. Wainwright,** *Mysterious Apocalypse: Interpreting the Book of Revelation* (1993). **J. J. Wettstein**, *Novum Testamentum Graecum* 2 (1752, repr. 1962). **W. Whiston**, *A New Theory of the Earth* (1737). **D. Whitby**, *Paraphrase and Commentary on the NT* (1702). **B. R. Wilson**, *Magic and the Millennium: A Sociological Study of Religious Movements of Protest Among Tribal and Third-world Peoples* (1973). **T. von Zahn**, *Die Offenbarung des Johannes* 1 (1924) 100-28. U. Zwingli, *Werke* 6, 1 (1982) 395.

A. W. WAINWRIGHT

GENERAL NEW TESTAMENT ARTICLES

Sermon on the Mount

The Sermon on the Mount, found in Matt 5-7 with parallels in Luke 6:17-49 (Sermon on the Plain), contains such well-known passages as the Beatitudes, the Lord's Prayer, and the Golden Rule. It has engendered a body of literature more vast than any other segment of the New Testament.

1. *Composition.* The relationship between the Sermon on the Mount in Matt and the Sermon on the Plain in Luke represents a problem that has been frequently addressed. Those who are skeptical of biblical criticism have suggested that Jesus*[§] preached the sermon on more than one occasion and that this accounts for the differences in the length, content, and setting of the respective sermons in Matt and Luke.

Critical scholarship, however, has attempted to explain the literary relationship between Matt and Luke and to analyze the sources of the respective sermons. The scholarly consensus is that the passages are not independent but bear a close relationship to each other. Except for minor discrepancies in order and phrasing, Luke's Sermon on the Plain is contained almost entirely in Matt's Sermon on the Mount. There are about twenty-eight verses in Matt with parallels in Luke 6, while forty-seven verses are peculiar to Matt.

One possible explanation for these similarities is that Matt's Sermon on the Mount represents Jesus' original discourse, which Luke shortened by omitting some material and dispersing other portions throughout his Gospel. A more widely held view, following the conclusions of the Four Document Hypothesis, Form Criticism*[§] , and Redaction Criticism*[§], is that both Matt and Luke drew on a common written source or sources. This source consisted of three major sections: It began with the Beatitudes, followed with a series of admonitions, and concluded with the parable of the two builders. The evangelists were redactors who compiled their sermons from traditional units that originally circulated orally and later were written down by the early Christian community. Moreover, the material was written for a specific purpose: the community's catechetical needs. According to this view, the sermons in Matt and Luke are not discourses of Jesus that they "remembered" but, rather, compilations of Jesus' sayings that were preserved separately, first in an oral and later in a written tradition. Thus the Sermon on the Mount and the Sermon on the Plain are not sermons preached by Jesus on one or even two occasions; rather, they represent the post-Easter modification of the evangelists' sources according to their respective purposes and those of the primitive Christian community. Critical scholars differ among themselves on the nuances of the process, and the rift between conservative and liberal biblical exegesis persists.

2. *Relevance and Application.* While there is widespread agreement that the Sermon on the Mount represents a compendium of Jesus' teachings and that it is one of the most lofty and powerful ethical expressions ever put forth, there is considerable disagreement as to its meaning and relevance. Did Jesus institute a new law that is as binding for Christians as the Torah is for Judaism? What are the implications of Jesus' eschatological outlook for our understanding of the sermon's application? How can we relate the sermon to problems and conditions strikingly different from those that prevailed in first-century Palestine? These are only a few of the problems that confront those who seek to interpret and apply the Sermon on the Mount.

3. *Ante-Nicene Period.* An examination of the ante-Nicene writers shows that references to Matt's Sermon on the Mount appear more frequently than those to any other segment of Scripture. These early writers often spoke of Jesus' relationship to the Mosaic law and concluded that his message is not contrary to past laws or an abrogation of them but a fulfillment and extension. There is ample evidence that such writers as Justin Martyr[§], Irenaeus[§],

Tertullian[§], and Chrysostom[§] employed the sermon for apologetic purposes; it defined Jesus' teaching and became a concise statement of Christian ethics. Jesus' respect for the Torah as expressed in the sermon served to counteract the Marcionite heresy (Marcion[§]) regarding the discontinuity between the Hebrew Bible and the New Testament. The early Christian writers, including Augustine[§], assumed that the Sermon on the Mount was a perfect rule and pattern for the Christian life and that it was relevant and applicable to their situation; they did not regard the sermon's counsel as reserved for some future application.

Augustine was probably the first to speak of Jesus' sermon as the "Sermon on the Mount." However, this designation was not generally used until after the Reformation.

4. *Medieval Period.* In the medieval period a new way of understanding the ethic of the Sermon on the Mount developed, which subsequently became basic for Roman Catholic moral theology. In his *Summa Theologica*, Thomas Aquinas[§] drew the distinction between "precepts" and "counsels of perfection." Evangelical counsels, as distinguished from moral precepts or commandments, are advisory directives of Christ, given as guides that lead to a closer approximation to perfection and an imitation of Christ himself. They have traditionally been associated with the virtues of poverty, chastity, and obedience. While obedience to precepts or commandments is necessary for salvation, adherence to the evangelical counsels is essential for perfection and to obtain greater merit and favor with God. C. Lapide[§], a late medieval exegete, suggested that Jesus' statement about fulfilling the law consisted of his adding evangelical counsels of perfection to matters of precept. Thus the medieval period introduced a new way of understanding the Sermon on the Mount: In it (and in the rest of the New Testament) one finds both precepts, or commandments, and evangelical counsels; and these in effect become two paths leading to salvation. This dialectical dichotomy between precepts and counsels helped pave the way for Reformation theology and much contemporary thought on the Sermon on the Mount.

5. *Reformation.* The Reformation produced three movements, related to Luther[§], Calvin[§], and the Anabaptists[§], respectively, that have influenced interpretation of the Sermon on the Mount to the present time. In a series of sermons on Matt 5–7, Luther set forth his doctrine of the two kingdoms, by which he sought to maintain the validity of the Sermon on the Mount for all Christians. One must, he argued, distinguish between the secular and the spiritual, between the kingdom of Christ and the kingdom of the world. Christians can participate in government—as soldiers, judges, lawyers, etc.—because there is a difference between the person and the office. They may engage in all sorts of secular business, not as Christians, but as secular persons. All the while, their hearts remain pure in their Christianity, as Christ demands.

The relationship between faith and works posed another problem for Luther's understanding of the Sermon on the Mount. The sermon appears to emphasize works, merit, and reward; but it is speaking about works and fruit that are manifestations of the state of grace. The passages on reward and merit are simply intended to comfort Christians. The insistence on grace alone must be preserved, Luther maintained, and then terms like merit and reward can be applied to the fruit that follows.

Calvin, with his insistence on the unity of the Bible, viewed Jesus not as a new legislator, but as the one who restored the law to its integrity and cleansed it from the falsehoods of the Pharisees. Jesus was a faithful expounder who showed us the law's nature, object, and extent. There is a sacred tie between the law and the gospel; the latter fulfills the former so that both declare God to be their author.

Like Luther and Zwingli[§], Calvin criticized the Anabaptists for their "misunderstanding" of Jesus' teaching about oaths, nonresistance, and lawsuits. They were misguided in their "ethical radicalism," just like the schoolmen, who perverted Jesus' teachings by turning them into evangelical counsels.

The Anabaptists are often referred to as the left wing of the Reformation, or the radical Reformation. Their radical stance was to a significant degree dependent on their understanding of the Sermon on the Mount. Taking the ethic of the sermon literally, they made it incumbent on all Christians, finding in it an ideal that led them to view the kingdom of God as being in radical opposition to all secular interests. The Anabaptists believed that the essence of the Christian life was discipleship—a following after Jesus (*Nachfolge Christi*)—and their directive or charter for such a lifestyle was best expressed in the sermon. Their rejection of infant baptism, their insistence on the strict separation of church and state, their commitment to nonresistance and to loving their enemies, their refusal to swear oaths—all these were grounded in the teachings and example of Jesus as found in the Sermon on the Mount.

6. *Protestant Scholasticism.* In contrast to the Anabaptists, the post-Reformation followers of Luther and Calvin (Protestant scholastics) viewed the Sermon on the Mount as an impossible ideal representing the uncompromising expression of God's righteousness which no human could attain. They believed that to make the sermon the essence of the gospel or of the Christian life is to embrace a new legalism, or works righteousness. In reality, the sermon serves to expose human sin and finitude and thus prepares the way for justification by faith alone. It throws believers upon the grace of God in Christ; its intent is to expose human failure and despair and to prepare persons for the message of salvation through the cross alone. Widely held by orthodox Protestants, this view has been restated by C. Stange and G. Kittel[§].

7. *Modern Period.* In the modern period, with the advent of biblical criticism, increasing diversity and complexity are discernible in the interpretation of the Sermon on the Mount. The literal or absolutistic understanding that the Anabaptists espoused was restated by L. Tolstoy, who summarized the sermon's central teaching in five rules: Be not angry; commit no adultery; swear not; go not to law; war not. For Tolstoy the central reality was Jesus' teaching about nonresistance in Matt 5:38-39. The Sermon on the Mount, and especially the command of nonviolence, is an ethical ideal that is possible for both individuals and society. If it is taken literally, one cannot go to court, take part in government, use violence against one's neighbor, or participate in military service.

Tolstoy's absolutism was set in a different context by L. Ragaz, the father of Christian socialism. Jesus' teachings apply, not merely to the personal realm, but to the social arena, where the struggle for freedom, justice, and peace takes place. While Ragaz did not equate the kingdom of God with socialism, he nevertheless viewed the Sermon on the Mount as the Magna Carta of Christian socialism and held that the whole of socialism is contained in the kingdom of God.

The predominant theological temper of the nineteenth and early twentieth centuries was characterized by Protestant liberalism or liberal theology. Among its later exponents were A. von Harnack[§] and W. Herrmann[§], who tended to view the kingdom of God as a present and inner reality. It was Herrmann who developed a widely influential understanding of the Sermon on the Mount, according to which the most serious and widespread mistake is to regard it as a set of laws to be fulfilled in every case. This is impossible, he argued. If Jesus had intended his teaching to be general rules, he would have been much worse than the teachers of the law he attacked. Rather, the meaning of his teaching lies in the fact that he wished to open the way for a right disposition (*Gesinnung*). The sermon is a *Gesinnungsethik* (an ethic of disposition); its teachings lead to a renewal of the mind and the will, directing us to freedom, moral power, and development grounded in Jesus. Consequently, the Sermon on the Mount relates more to what we should *be* than to what we should *do*.

A. Schweitzer[§], going beyond the proposals of J. Weiss[§], introduced the concept of "consistent eschatology" as the key to understanding Jesus' life and message. The nineteenth-century quest of the historical Jesus had produced a teacher of morality who sought to establish the spiritual reign of God in people's hearts, and thus induce the reign of the kingdom of God on earth.

But the Jesus presented in the Gospels is a quite different figure—mysterious, otherworldly, unknown—whose worldview is foreign to ours because it is steeped in the eschatology and Apocalypticism*§ of late Judaism. Jesus believed that the consummation of the Kingdom was imminent, that it would occur in his lifetime; and the urgency of the situation demanded a radical ethic, i.e., an ethic of repentance that would prepare and equip persons for the crisis confronting them. The ethics of the Sermon on the Mount are "interim ethics," relevant only for that brief interim before the eschaton. Those who adopted this radical ethic would be members of the coming Kingdom. Schweitzer believed that it is possible that later Christians can find meaning and relevance in the sermon, but this was not Jesus' intention. His entire horizon was permeated by eschatology, and it is only in this milieu that we can understand his teachings and his mission.

One of the most thorough twentieth-century studies of the Sermon on the Mount is that of H. Windisch§ (1929 [ET 1951]). Throughout his work, Windisch insisted on a strict differentiation between historical exegesis and theological interpretation. His purpose was to examine the sermon and to show what historical and critical exegesis has taught us to see. The biblical interpreter dares not jump to theological and philosophical conclusions without first doing the prerequisite historical exegesis. Thus Windisch criticized Herrmann, M. Dibelius§, and R. Bultmann§ for modernizing the teachings of Jesus, and Stange and Kittel for superimposing a Pauline, or dogmatic, framework on them. The Pauline dogmatic is absent from the Sermon on the Mount; from the standpoint of Paul†§, Luther, and Calvin, its soteriology is hopelessly heretical.

Windisch maintained that the Sermon on the Mount stands wholly within the framework of Jewish religion. Like the Torah, the sermon is essentially a collection of commandments that are to be obeyed. Its teaching is characterized by an ethic of obedience. The intent of the evangelist is to portray Jesus as a new lawgiver who intends to both fulfill the Mosaic law and improve on it. The sermon, however, has no political reference. It is individualistic in the sense that it deals with relationships between individuals; although political and social implications may derive from it, the sermon does not consider community, economic, and national organizations and their ethical ramifications. The entire social ethic of the sermon is couched in individual sayings that are to be understood literally and interpreted literally.

Dibelius, one of the original exponents of form criticism, produced an important study of the Sermon on the Mount (1940). Applying the form-critical method, he held that the sermon was not one that Jesus preached on a single occasion but, rather, a collection of individual sayings spoken by Jesus on a variety of occasions and brought together to form a kind of Christian law. For Dibelius, the Sermon on the Mount must be understood as the "pure will of God." It is not an interim ethic, valid only for the period before the end of the world; it is given for eternity because it represents the will of the eternal God. Jesus did not consider the circumstances of our life and the conditions of this world but looked only to the coming world, to the kingdom of heaven. Thus the Sermon on the Mount has a definite eschatological reference. Jesus' words are "signs of the kingdom of God" and consequently cannot be carried out in this life. He intended them to be signs of hope, but after Easter they became laws of conduct. Today Jesus' directives seem impractical because we have lost the eschatological outlook. According to Dibelius, the sermon should not be viewed as an ideal of religion or ethics. It has no validity for the workaday life, since it was not given as a body of instruction for this life or as a program of reform for this world. Rather, it is an "eschatological stimulus" intended to make persons well acquainted with the pure will of God. Although we cannot perform the sermon's demands fully, nevertheless, we can be transformed by it; the most important thing is that it become effective in our hearts. For the Christian, law does not demand that we do something, but that we be something.

174

Of twentieth-century interpretations, perhaps none is more impressive, provocative, and controversial than D. Bonhoeffer's[§] *Nachfolge* (*The Cost of Discipleship*, now reprinted as *Discipleship* [1940[2], ET 2000). Its popularity and significance stem to a great degree from the time in which it was written and from the subsequent martyrdom of its author. Bonhoeffer's chief interest was not in dealing with the usual philological and critical problems relating to the sermon but in confronting the church with the life of discipleship—with the imperative of uncompromising, unmitigated, single-minded obedience to Jesus Christ. More important than the critical questions are the ones that ask what Christ's will is for Christians today. The Sermon on the Mount calls believers to a life of surrender and obedience. Bonhoeffer observed that, humanly speaking, the sermon could be understood and interpreted in a thousand different ways. However, Jesus intended only one possibility: obedience.

An interpretation of the Sermon on the Mount that has been influential in certain conservative movements is that of the dispensationalists. The basic premise of dispensationalism is that sacred history is divided into a number of dispensations (usually seven), in each of which God deals with people on a different basis. Dispensationalists maintain that the sermon is pure law and does not contain the gospel; consequently, it does not apply to the church age, the dispensation of grace, but to the coming Kingdom age, the final dispensation. Thus the Sermon on the Mount is the code of laws of the kingdom of heaven.

Two noteworthy Jewish interpreters of the Sermon on the Mount are C. Montefiore[§] and G. Friedlander. Montefiore pointed out that the sermon is individualistic and ignores social questions due to Jesus' eschatological view that the old order was approaching a catastrophic end. One of Montefiore's major concerns was the relationship between the Sermon on the Mount and the Hebrew Bible, and he drew a parallel between Jesus on the "mount" and Moses on Mt. Sinai. Matthew wanted to contrast the two laws: the one old, imperfect, and transitory, and the other new, perfect, and definitive. Montefiore concluded that in spite of the sermon's antitheses, Jesus had no deliberate intention of teaching a new religion or a new righteousness. Comparing the sermon with rabbinic teaching, Montefiore stated that the sermon is more enthusiastic, while the rabbinic literature is more sober; and although it is not very extensive, the Sermon on the Mount contains some original materials not found in Judaism.

Montefiore believed the sermon could be a meeting ground for Jew and Christian because of its lack of Christology. It contains no article of faith concerning the person of Jesus; thus the Jew can live in its spirit without acknowledging anyone as lord and/or savior. Furthermore, the sermon makes a rapprochement between Jew and Christian possible because it contains nothing essentially antagonistic to Judaism. According to Montefiore, the sermon remains for all time a religious document of "immense importance and significance, and mostly of a high greatness and nobility."

While Montefiore was conciliatory in his evaluation of the Sermon on the Mount, Friedlander (1911) took a polemical and apologetic position, concluding that four-fifths of the sermon is exclusively Jewish. Those parts that are original are insignificant, and Judaism has nothing to learn from them. Indeed, the Pharisaic teaching is infinitely superior to that of the gospel. Friedlander was more outspoken than Montefiore on the "unfair" treatment of the Pharisees in the Sermon on the Mount, maintaining that the New Testament view of the Pharisees is one-sided, prejudiced, and neither charitable nor just. In Jesus' teaching about wealth, anxiety, and nonresistance, Friedlander discerned an un-Jewish asceticism. Jesus' views are world-denying, while the stance of Judaism is world-affirming.

Friedlander rejected Montefiore's suggestion that the Sermon on the Mount could be the ideal meeting ground and bond of union between Jews and Christians. He affirmed that Gentiles have been unwilling to accept the heavy yoke of the Torah and have instead taken up the easy yoke of the gospel. Nevertheless, he stated: "This is not to condemn the teaching of the Sermon. It has its part to play in the religious training of the world."

Allison's recent study (1999) places the sermon in the context of the whole of Matthew's Gospel and utilizes early Christian and patristic exegesis. Bonhoeffer's spiritual and theological classic has been freshly translated in a critical English edition (2000). Feldmeier (1998) has edited a collection of studies on the Sermon. Jeremias' classic short study (1959, ET 1963) has been reissued (ET 2002). Wierzbicka (2001) has analyzed the sermon using linguistics and Zager (2001) in light of the Jewish wisdom tradition.

Bibliography: **D. C. Allison, Jr.,** *The Sermon on the Mount: Inspiring the Moral Imagination* (Companions to the New Testament, 1999). **C. Bauman**, *The Sermon on the Mount: The Modern Quest for Its Meaning* (1985). **U. Berner**, *Die Bergpredigt: Rezeption und Auslegung im 20. Jahrhundert* (1979). **H. D. Betz**, "Sermon on the Mount/Plain," *ABD*, 5:1106-12; *The Sermon on the Mount* (Hermeneia, 1995). **T. D. Bonham**, *The Demands of Discipleship: The Relevance of the Sermon on the Mount* (1967). **D. Bonhoeffer**, *Discipleship* (1940[2]; ed. M. Kuske and I. Tödt; ET ed. G. B. Kelly and J. D. Godsey, trans. B. Green and R. Krauss, Dietrich Bonhoeffer Works, 2000).). **W. D. Davies**, *The Setting of the Sermon on the Mount* (1966). **M. Dibelius**, *The Sermon on the Mount* (1940). **J. Dupont**, *Les béatitudes* (3 vols. 1954). **R. Feldmeier**(ed.), *"Salz der Erde" : Zugänge zur Bergpredigt* (Biblisch-theologische Schwerpunkte 14, 1998). **G. Friedlander**, *The Jewish Sources of the Sermon on the Mount* (1911, repr. 1969). **R. Grant**, "The Sermon on the Mount in Early Christianity," *Semeia* 12 (1978) 215-31. **J. Jeremias**, "The Sermon on the Mount," *Jesus and the Message of the New Testament* (Calwer Hefte 32; ET, FBBS, 1963; Fortress Classics in Biblical Studies, 2002) 1-17. **J. Lambrecht**, *The Sermon on the Mount* (OBO 26, 1985). **W. S. Kissinger**, *The Sermon on the Mount: A History of Interpretation and Bibliography* (1975). **H. K. McArthur**, *Understanding the Sermon on the Mount* (1960). **I. A. Massey**, *Interpreting the Sermon on the Mount in the Light of Jewish Tradition as Evidenced in the Palestinian Targums of the Pentateuch* (SBEC 25, 1991). **C. Montefiore**, *The Synoptic Gospels* (2 vols. 1909, 1927[2]); *Some Elements of the Religious Teaching of Jesus* (1910). **D. Patte**, *Discipleship According to the Sermon on the Mount* (1996). **L. Ragaz**, *Die Bergpredigt Jesu* (1945). **A. Schweitzer**, *The Quest of the Historical Jesus: A Critical Study of Its Progress from Reimarus to Wrede* (1906, 1913[2]; ET 1910, 1966, 1998). **T. Soiron**, *Die Bergpredigt Jesu: Formgeschichtliche exegetische und theologische Erklärung* (1941). **G. Strecker**, *The Sermon on the Mount: An Exegetical Commentary* (1984;ET 1988). **A. Wierzbicka**, *What did Jesus Mean? Explaining the Sermon on the Mount and the Parables in Simple and Universal Human Concepts* (2001). **H. Windisch**, *The Meaning of the Sermon on the Mount* (UNT 16, 1929, 1937[2]; ET 1951). **R. H. Worth**, *The Sermon on the Mount: Its OT Roots* (1997). **W. Zager**, "Weisheitliche Aspekte in der Bergpredigt," *Weisheit, Ethos und Gebot: Weisheits- und Dekalogtraditionen in der Bibel und im frühen Judentum* (ed. H. G. Reventlow, Biblisch-theologische Studien 43, 2001) 1-28.

W. S. KISSINGER

Parables of Jesus

Among the literary genres of the Bible, the parables of Jesus*[§] occupy a unique place. While they have antecedents in the Hebrew Bible and in rabbinic literature, they are virtually a new and highly original form in reference to both purpose and content.

The parables of Jesus are confined to the Synoptic[†§] Gospels, and they occur in different forms and lengths. Some are brief similes or metaphors, while others, like the parables of the Good Samaritan (Luke 10:30-35) and the Prodigal Son (Luke 15:11-32), are expanded into larger stories. As for the number of parables found in the Gospels, the figure varies depending on how many of Jesus' short, figurative sayings are included: The count has ranged from a low of about thirty to a high of sixty or more.

Historically, allegorization has occupied a central role in parable interpretation. In distinction from the comparative or analogous form of the similitude, an allegory substitutes one thing for another and must be interpreted symbolically; single comparisons are not what they appear to be but must be probed for their deeper meaning. The allegorical method of parable interpretation largely prevailed from the patristic period to the end of the nineteenth century.

1. *Ante-Nicene Period.* Irenaeus[§] and Tertullian[§] used modest, restrained forms of the allegorical method to interpret the parables.

Both Clement of Alexandria[§] and Origen[§], members of the Alexandrian school of interpretation, most fully developed the allegorical method of parable interpretation through their attempts to harmonize Christian theology and the Scriptures with Hellenistic philosophy. Clement believed that the style of the Scriptures is parabolic, i.e., its mysteries are veiled and preserved for certain chosen persons endowed with knowledge and faith. Thus the parables have hidden meanings that lie behind what appears to be the principal subject and that are evident only to those who are chosen to comprehend them.

Origen, the supreme articulator of the allegorical method, believed that the Scriptures were an inspired (Inspiration of the Bible*[§]) and infallible repository of truth. However, this truth was not readily evident to the average reader, because it required spiritual discernment to understand the text's hidden and mystical import. With Origen the allegorical method of parable interpretation attained perhaps its supreme articulation. For example, in his exposition of the parable of the Good Samaritan, the man going down from Jerusalem to Jericho represents Adam, or the doctrine of man, and the fall caused by his disobedience. Jerusalem signifies paradise or heaven; Jericho is the world. The robbers are the powerful adversaries or demons or the false prophets who lived before Christ. And so on.

Members of the Antiochene School[§], such as Theodore of Mopsuestia[§] and Chrysostom[§], sought to set forth the literal sense intended by the author, concerning themselves more with the historical and grammatical than with the spiritual and mystical. For example, Chrysostom appears to have been far more interested in the parables' moral emphases than in discerning their hidden spiritual or mystical significance.

Augustine[§] embraced the exegetical tradition of Alexandria but seldom offered extended discussions of the parables. While he believed that the literal and historical meaning was fundamental, he employed allegory when the literal sense of a passage appeared incoherent or obscure and relied heavily upon number symbolism. For example, in his exposition of the parable of the ten virgins, he asked why the virgins are "five and five" and concluded that it is because the number five denotes the five senses.

2. *Medieval Period.* Gregory the Great[§] added the moral sense of meaning to parable interpretation. The parables are never only bearers of hidden and esoteric meanings; their intention

is to call people to repentance and to a lifestyle becoming to citizens of the kingdom of God. In such parables as those of the laborers in the vineyard (Matt 20:1-15) and the rich man and Lazarus (Luke 16:19-31), Gregory emphasized the moral virtues of discipline, charity, simplicity, poverty, and mercy.

The allegorical method and contemporary theological motifs were central in medieval parable interpretation. Peter Lombard[§] suggested that the Good Samaritan used the bands of the sacraments against the wounds of original and actual sin.

Thomas Aquinas[§] gave a new turn to biblical exegesis by minimizing the allegorical and emphasizing the literal sense of the Scriptures. With him, allegorization neared its end as a viable and meaningful method of biblical interpretation.

3. *Reformation.* The reformers, particularly Luther[§] and Calvin[§], centered upon the historical and literal approach to the Bible. Castigating allegorization as "pure jugglery" and "tomfoolery," Luther advocated pursuing the plain and literal sense as far as possible before resorting to hidden or symbolic meanings. His exegesis was also marked by a christological centrality: Everything must be understood and evaluated in relation to Jesus Christ.

The primary emphases of the Reformation can be discerned in Luther's interpretation of the parables. Thus Abraham's words to the rich man in Luke 16 represent Christ's underscoring of the Authority[*§] of the Bible. In opposition to this "true and godly teaching," certain "learned scholars" have devised other ways to learn the truth, including innumerable laws, statutes, and articles like canon law and rules for religious orders.

In expounding the parable of the great banquet (Matt 22:2-14; Luke 14:16-24), Luther commented on the incident of the one who took a place of honor and was later demoted (Luke 14:7-11). He applied this parable to the canon of the mass, which occupied a place of honor; but "it should now get up with shame and give place to Christ, its master, and sit in the lowest place, as it should properly have done in the beginning."

The central Lutheran concept of grace and faith alone is likewise reflected in Luther's parable interpretation. The foolish virgins had "served without oil," which implied for Luther that they had done good works on their own resources and not by virtue of grace. In the parable of the good Samaritan the priest and the Levite were "ministers of the Law." The dichotomy between the actions of the priest and the Levite and those of the Samaritan shows that "the Law makes sin known, but Christ heals through faith and restores man to the grace of God."

With Calvin even more than with Luther there is an absence of allegorizing and a directness that seeks to go immediately to the central point of the parable. In the parables of the Good Samaritan and the laborers in the vineyard, which were frequently allegorized, Calvin manifested a marked restraint. He maintained that Jesus' primary purpose in giving the parable of the Good Samaritan was to show that neighborliness obliges us to do our duty to each other, duty that is not restricted to friends and relations but is open to the whole human race.

In his analysis of the laborers in the vineyard, Calvin criticized those who would examine the parable's details or who would find the Jews and the Gentiles in it. According to him, such efforts represent "empty curiosity" and a "cleverness that is out of place." There is no hidden symbolism in the denarius or in the various hours when the laborers were hired. Christ's one aim in this parable was to encourage perseverance. However, like Luther, Calvin found theological and doctrinal motifs in the parables. The story of the laborers in the vineyard points to divine sovereignty: God is under obligation to no one and calls whom God wills. Furthermore, God pays those who have been called the reward that seems good to God. The parable of the Pharisee and the publican (Luke 18:9-14) reflects divine sovereignty and grace and human depravity. Jesus condemns human pretention, pride, and a depraved self-trust in the Pharisee, who denies God's grace and places his trust in the merit of his own works.

Although Luther's and Calvin's interpretations are not entirely free of allegorization, the two nevertheless centered their attention on the historical and literal sense of the parables. Their exegesis grounded the sayings in a focused and meaningful theological and ethical framework.

4. *Modern Period.* The so-called modern period in biblical interpretation can be dated from the advent and development of biblical criticism, from the latter part of the eighteenth century to the present. During this period the Bible has been subjected to the same scrutiny and rigorous analysis as has any other literature. In parable interpretation a number of new methodologies appeared.

An exception to this trend must be noted first, however: R. Trench, whose *Notes on the Parables of Our Lord* was for many years the standard English work on the parables. Published in 1841 and appearing in many subsequent editions, Trench's work set forth a number of principles or guidelines for parable interpretation: e.g., one should distinguish the parable's central truth from all cognate truths that border on it; one must pay careful attention to the introduction and the application of a parable; one should not use the parables as primary sources and bases of theological doctrine. A man of immense learning and erudition, Trench nevertheless was reluctant to employ the new critical methods being developed in his time. He looked back to the church fathers; and in spite of principles seemingly to the contrary, he found allegorization a congenial method of parable interpretation.

Perhaps the first English-language interpreter of the parables to employ higher criticism was A. Bruce[§]. He rejected allegorization in favor of the historical and linguistic senses of the parables, and he was among the first to propose a scheme of parable classification.

The most influential modern interpreter of the parables was A. Jülicher[§], whose two-volume *Die Gleichnisreden Jesu* (2 vols., 1888, 1899[2]) set a new direction in interpretation, one that had a widespread impact on subsequent scholarship. Jülicher maintained that although the parabolic speech of Jesus may vary in form, the basic unit is always the simile. Unlike metaphor and allegory, simile needs no interpretation; it is clear and self-explanatory. Because the function of simile is to teach, there is no need for questions regarding its meaning and intention. Jülicher's rejection of allegorization was nearly total. He attributed the instances of allegorization in the parables, not to Jesus, but to the early church, maintaining that the parables are characterized by literal speech and are self-explanatory. Parables are related to real life; their intention is to convey a point or moral, and their function is to compel the reader to form a judgment. Jülicher concluded that parables are intended to illuminate one point: a rule, an idea, or an experience that is as valid on the spiritual as on the secular level.

The relationship between Jesus' parables and those in rabbinical writings was explored especially by C. Bugge and P. Fiebig . Both Bugge (1895) and Fiebig (1904) criticized Jülicher for his non-acquaintance with rabbinical literature and his bias toward Greek and particularly Aristotelian thought. Jesus was a Jew and an Oriental, they argued; consequently, he thought concretely and intuitively rather than abstractly. They maintained that Jülicher should have turned to rabbinical writings because these, rather than the Greek, represent the closest approximation to Jesus' parables.

One of the central themes of the parables is the kingdom of God. Protestant liberalism tended to emphasize the imminent, evolutionary, spiritual, and moral aspects of the kingdom. Contrary to this viewpoint, J. Weiss[§] and A. Schweitzer[§] emphasized its transcendent and apocalyptic dimensions (Apocalypticism*[§]). Jesus' view of the kingdom of God was radically otherworldly, rather than evolutionary and ethical. This recovery of the eschatological understanding had a marked impact on subsequent parable scholarship.

Emphasizing the eschatological element in Jesus' teaching, C. H. Dodd[§] began a new era in parable study (1935). He set forth a twofold purpose: to explore the eschatological dimensions of the parables and to determine the original intention of a given parable in its historical setting.

Dodd followed Jülicher in rejecting allegorization. However, Dodd was not convinced that in the parables Jesus simply intended to teach great and enduring moral and religious truths. While Jülicher laid the foundation for the right understanding of the parables, his method must be supplemented by an attempt to relate them to their particular setting in the eschatological crisis created by Jesus' ministry; that setting should determine their original meaning and application. The parables were given in the context of "realized eschatology" in which the eschaton had moved from the future to the present, from the sphere of expectation into that of realized experience. While parables are works of art and have significance and application beyond their original occasion, one must nevertheless understand them in terms of the realized eschatology in the life and ministry of Jesus.

Acknowledging his indebtedness to Dodd and Jülicher, J. Jeremias[§] (1947, 1954[2]) thought that an additional approach was needed. The main task that remained was to recover the original meaning of the parables.

Jeremias noted that each of the parables was given in an actual situation of Jesus' life. They were chiefly apologetic in nature, primarily weapons of conflict, and had an existential dimension in that each of them called for immediate response. The task of the interpreter is to recover their distinct historical settings. However, following Form Criticism*[§], Jeremias pointed out that our return to Jesus via the parables must of necessity be from the primitive church. Thus the parables have a double historical location—an original setting in some particular moment of Jesus' activity and another grounded in the life of the primitive church. Before they assumed a written form they "lived" in the early Christian community, which employed them for purposes of preaching and teaching. Jeremias maintained that as we attempt to reconstruct the original setting of the parables we meet with certain "definite principles of transformation," which he grouped under ten headings.

In addition to the ten principles of transformation, Jeremias suggested that the parables and similes fall naturally into ten groups and that the major reference of these ten themes is eschatological. Nonetheless, they also have an existential dimension because it is clear that all of Jesus' parables compel his hearers to come to a decision about his person and mission.

Later parable interpreters have acknowledged their indebtedness to Jeremias, Dodd, and Jülicher but have introduced new motifs. The eschatological setting of the parables that Dodd and Jeremias emphasized became the central focus in the so-called new Hermeneutic*[§]. Coupled with this has been a new understanding of the nature of language and of the existential aspect of the parables.

The new hermeneutic developed through dialogue between theologians in Germany and the United States and centered primarily on the writings of E. Fuchs[§] and G. Ebeling , who had been students of R. Bultmann[§]. It began with the publication of Fuchs's *Hermeneutik* in 1954. Drawing on motifs found in Bultmann and especially in Heidegger's later works, Fuchs wrote about Jesus' understanding of his own existence and situation, maintaining that the best, though not exclusive, sources for apprehending this understanding are the parables. Fuchs called the parables "language-events," for in them Jesus expressed his understanding of his situation in the world and before God, thus creating the possibility of the hearer's sharing that situation. The pictorial language of parable has the potential to change the hearer's existence and his relationship to reality, e.g., to Jesus, to God, and to the kingdom of God.

Another trend, which developed in the United States, views the parables in their literary and aesthetic dimensions. This approach was especially influenced by the writings of A. Wilder[§]. Among those identified with this movement are N. Perrin[§], R. Funk[§], D. Via, and J. D. Crossan. Perrin's (1976) basic concern was to bring to the forefront of contemporary discussion the hermeneutical interaction between author, text, and reader. The "hermeneutical moment" is realized when a text is read and interpreted by an individual and a dynamic relationship ensues between person and text.

The central theme of Funk's analysis (1966; 1982) is the distinction between simile and metaphor, particularly the literary study of the nature of metaphor. While a simile is illustrative, metaphorical language creates meaning. However, the parable or metaphor also has an existential character because it is incomplete until the hearer is drawn into it as a participant.

Perhaps the most significant study of the parables since Jeremias is Via's *The Parables: Their Literary and Existential Dimension* (1967). Via begins at the literary level and maintains that the parables must be seen as works of art, genuine aesthetic objects that are carefully organized, self-contained, and coherent literary compositions. He emphasizes the non-referential character of the parables: Their revelatory character cannot be traced to their author's biography or environment, for as works of literary art the only important consideration is their internal meaning. By approaching the parables as aesthetic objects, one gains fresh insight into their existential and theological dimensions.

Crossan, like Funk and Via, is interested in the literary and linguistic aspects of the parables. In a succinct definition he states that a parable is a metaphor of normalcy that is intended to create participation in its referent. Unlike Via, Crossan is much concerned about the relationship between the parables and the historical Jesus (1973). The parables provide an avenue to the historical Jesus: They express and contain the temporality of Jesus' experience of God, and they proclaim and establish the historicity of his response to the kingdom.

Crossan uses three terms or categories that he regards as basic for an understanding of all the parables as well as the whole message of Jesus: advent, reversal, and action. He views these categories as "three modes of the Kingdom's temporality." Its advent is a gift of God, which in turn can bring a reversal of the recipient's world; but it also empowers for life and action.

B. Scott's commentary (1989) analyzes Jesus' parables in their literary context within the Gospels (and within the Gospel of Thomas), in their development within the oral tradition of the early church, and in their situation within the life and ministry of Jesus. Informed by the work of several modern interpreters, Scott endeavors to reconstruct an originating structure for each parable and to determine how that structure affects the parable's meaning. He sees a "parabolic effect" in the interaction between the story told and the kingdom referred to. Of particular interest is Scott's use of methods from the social sciences (Social-Scientific Criticism*§) to clarify the social world in which Jesus' parables arose.

It appears evident that developing trends in parable interpretation reflect a decreasing emphasis on historical, moralistic, and theological concerns and an increasing emphasis on the Literary*§-critical, existential, and social aspects of the parabolic speech of Jesus.

Recent commentaries on the parables include Hultgren (2000) and Jones (1995). Giowler (2000) is a basic introduction to recent parables scholarship. Recent collections of essays on the parables include Beavis (2002), Harnisch (1999), Longenecker (2000), Mell (1999), and Shillington (1997). Wierzbicka (2001) analyzes the parables using contemporary linguistic theory. Ford (1997), Kähler (1995), and Winterhalter and Fisk (1993) have utilized contemporary psychological theory (especially Jung) to interpret Jesus' parables. Herzog (1994) interprets the parables from a liberation perspective. Hezser (1990), McArthur and Johnston (1990), and Westermann (1990) analyze the parables in light of their Jewish and Hebrew Bible backgrounds. Carter and Heil (1998) use literary theory to study the parables of Matthew. Miscellaneous studies on the parables include Aerts (1990), Culbertson (1995), Cuvillier (1993), Fisher (1990²), Forbes (2000), Green (1997), Lambrecht (1992), Liebenberg (2001), Meurer (1997), Parker (1996), Rau (1990), Reiser (1990), Sider (1995), and Tucker (1998).

Bibliography: L. Aerts, *Gottesherrschaft als Gleichnis? Eine Untersuchung zur Auslegung der Gleichnisse Jesu nach Eberhard Jüngel* (1990). **L. Agisi,** *Gesu et le sue parabole* (1963). **M. Beavis** (ed.), *The Lost Coin: Parables of Women, Work, and Wisdom* (Biblical seminar 86, 2002). **M. Boucher,** *The Mysterious Parable* (CBQMS 6, 1977). **C. A. Bugge,** *Jesu Hoved Parabler: ud lagate* (1895). **W. Carter and J. P. Heil,** *Matthew's Parables: Audience-Oriented Perspectives* (CBQMS 30, 1998). **J. D. Crossan,** *In Parables: The Challenge of the Historical Jesus* (1973); *Finding Is the First Act: Trove Folktales and Jesus' Treasure Parable* (1979); *Cliffs of Fall: Paradox and Polyvalence in the Parables of Jesus* (1980). **P. L. Culbertson,** *A Word Fitly Spoken: Context, Transmission, and Adoption of the Parables of Jesus* (SUNY Series in Religious Studies, 1995). **E. Cuvillier,** *Le concept de parabole dans le second évangile : son arrière-plan littéraire, sa signification dans le cadre de la rédaction marcienne, son utilisation dans la tradition de Jésus* (Ebib, n.s., 19, 1993). **C. H. Dodd,** *The Parables of the Kingdom* (1935; rev. ed. 1948, 1958[3]). **P. Fiebig,** *Altjudische Gleichnisse und die Gleichnisse Jesu* (1904). **N. F. Fisher,** *The Parables of Jesus: Glimpses of God's Reign* (1990[2]). **D. Flusser,** *Die rabbinischen Gleichnisse und der Gliechniserzähler Jesus I* (1981). **G. W. Forbes,** *The God of Old: The Role of the Lukan Parables in the Purpose of Luke's Gospel* (JSTNSup 198, 2000). **R. Q. Ford,** *The Parables of Jesus: Recovering the Art of Listening* (1997). **E. Fuchs,** *Hermeneutik* (1954; 1958[2], with Ergänzungsheft; 1970[4]); "L'évangile et l'argent: Le parabole de l'intendant intelligent," *BCPE* 20 (1978) 1-14. **R. W. Funk,** *Language, Hermeneutics, and the Word of God* (1966); *Parables and Presence* (1982). **D. B. Gowler,** *What are They Saying About the Parables?* (WATSA, 2000). **D. M. Granskou,** *Preaching on the Parables* (1972). **B. Green,** *Like a Tree Planted: An Exploration of Psalms and Parables Through Metaphor* (1997). **W. Harnisch,** *Die Zumutung der Liebe: Gesammelte Aufsätze* (ed., U. Schoenborn, FRLANT 187, 1999). **W. R. Herzog,** *Parables as Subversive Speech: Jesus as Pedagogue of the Oppressed* (1994). **C. Hezser,** *Lohnmetaphorik und Arbeitswelt in Mt 20, 1-16: Das Gleichnis von den Arbeitern im Weinberg im Rahmen rabbinischer Lohngleichnisse* (NTOA 15, 1990). **A. J. Hultgren,** *The Parables of Jesus: A Commentary* (Bible in Its World, 2000). **A. M. Hunter,** *Interpreting the Parables* (1960). **I. H. Jones,** *The Matthean Parables: A Literary and Historical Commentary* (NovTSup 80, 1995). **J. Jeremias,** *The Parables of Jesus* (1947, 1952[2]; ET rev. ed. 1963). **G. V. Jones,** *The Art and Truth of the Parables: A Study in Their Literary Form and Modern Interpretation* (1964). **A. Jülicher,** *Die Gleichnisreden Jesu,* pt. 1, *Die Gleichnisreden Jesu im Allgemeinen;* pt. 2, *Auslegung der Gleichnisreden der drei ersten Evangelien* (1889, 1899[2]; repr. of both vols. 1910). **C. Kähler,** *Jesu Gleichnisse als Poesie und Therapie: Versuch eines integrativen Zugangs zum kommunikativen Aspekt von Gleichnissen Jesu* (WUNT 78, 1995). **J. D. Kingsbury,** "Major Trends in Parable Interpretation," *CTM* 42 (1971) 579-96; "The Parables of Jesus in Current Research," *Dialog* 11 (1972) 101-7. **W. S. Kissinger,** *The Parables of Jesus: A History of Interpretation and Bibliography* (1979). **J. Lambrecht,** *Out of the Treasure: The Parables in the Gospel of Matthew* (Louvain Theological and Pastoral Monographs 10,1992). **J. Liebenberg,** *The Language of the Kingdom and Jesus: Parable, Aphorism, and Metaphor in the Sayings Material Common to the Synoptic Tradition and the Gospel of Thomas* (BZNW 102, 2001). **R. N. Longenecker** (ed.), *The Challenge of Jesus' Parables* (McMaster New Testament Studies, 2000). **H. K. McArthur and R. M. Johnston,** *They also Taught in Parables: Rabbinic Parables from the First Centuries of the Christian Era* (1990). **U. Mell** (ed.), *Die Gleichnisreden Jesu 1899-1999: Beiträge zum Dialog mit Adolf Jülicher* (BZNW 103, 1999). **H.–J. Meurer,** *Die Gleichnisse Jesu als Metaphern: Paul Ricoeurs Hermeneutik der Gleichniserzählung Jesu im Horizont des Symbols "Gottesherrschaft/Reich Gottes"* (BBB 111, 1997). **A. Parker,** *Painfully Clear: The Parables of Jesus* (Biblical Seminar 37, 1996). **N. Perrin,** *Jesus and the Language of the Kingdom* (1976). **E. Rau,** *Reden in Vollmacht: Hintergrund, Form und Anliegen der Gleichnisse Jesu*

(FRLANT 149, 1990). **M. Reiser,** *Die Gerichtspredigt Jesu: eine Untersuchung zur eschatologischen Verkündigung Jesu und ihrem frühjüdischen Hintergrund* (NTAbh, n.f., 23, 1990). **B. B. Scott,** *Hear Then the Parables: A Commentary on the Parables of Jesus* (1989). **V. G. Shillington** (ed.), *Jesus and His Parables: Interpreting the Parables of Jesus Today* (1997). **J. W. Sider,** *Interpreting the Parables: A Hermeneutical Guide to Their Meaning* (Studies in Contemporary Interpretation, 1995). **C. Thoma and M. Wyschogrod** (eds.), *Parable and Story in Judaism and Christianity* (1989). **M. A. Tolbert,** *Perspectives on the Parables: An Approach to Multiple Interpretations* (1979). **J. T. Tucker,** *Example stories: Perspectives on Four Parables in the Gospel of Luke* (JSNTSup 162, 1998). **D. O. Via,** *The Parables: Their Literary and Existential Dimension* (1967); "The Relation of Form to Content in the Parables of the Wedding Feast," *Int* 25 (1971) 171-85; "Kingdom and Parable: The Search for a New Grasp of Symbol, Metaphor, and Myth," *Int* 31 (1978) 181-83. **S. L. Wailes,** *Medieval Allegories of Jesus' Parables* (1987). **C. Westermann,** *The Parables of Jesus in the light of the Old Testament* (trans. and ed. F. W. Golka and A. H.B. Logan, 1990). **A. Wierzbicka,** *What did Jesus Mean?: Explaining the Sermon on the Mount and the Parables in Simple and Universal Human Concepts* (2001). **A. N. Wilder,** *Early Christian Rhetoric: The Language of the Gospel* (1971). **R. Winterhalter with G. W. Fisk,** *Jesus' Parables: Finding Our God Within* (Jung and Spirituality, 1993).

W. S. KISSINGER

GENERAL NEW TESTAMENT ARTICLES

Prophecy and Prophets, New Testament

Many of the references to early Christian prophets and prophecy in the New Testament have been interpreted in a variety of apologetic, exegetical, homiletical, and theological contexts throughout the history of Christian thought, although they are often overshadowed by more numerous and substantive references to Hebrew Bible prophets and prophecy, including commentaries on many of the prophetic books. The New Testament passages that deal most extensively with early Christian prophetic phenomena include 1 Cor 12-14 on the gifts of the Spirit and their place in worship, the early Christian prophetic work called the Revelation of John, the extensive warning against false prophets in Matt 7:15-23, and the prophetic gift of glossolalia on the day of Pentecost narrated in Acts 2. There are also many shorter passages in which prophets are mentioned, including references to Jesus[†§] as a prophet (Matt 21:10-11, 46; Mark 6:14-15; 8:28; Luke 7:16; 24:19; John 6:14; 7:40, 52; Acts 3:22; 7:37); early Christian prophets and their oracles (Acts 11:28; 15:32; 21:9-10); prophecy and glossolalia as gifts of the Spirit (Rom 12:6; 1 Cor 12:10; 14:6; Eph 4:11; 1 Pet 4:10-11); and the problem of discerning the spirits (1 John 4:1-3).

The problem of evaluating prophets and their oracles and discerning true from false prophets and prophecies was a subject that continued to exercise Christian churches during the second century and later (*Did.* 11; *Hermas Mand.* 11; *Acts of Thomas* 79). The primary criterion for recognizing false prophecy according to Matt 7:15-23, an important passage referred to frequently in attempts to deal with heresy, was moral rather than doctrinal: False prophets are "wolves in sheep's clothing" (i.e., they are charlatans who say one thing and do another), and they are known by their "fruit" (i.e., by behavior inconsistent with their teaching). Like the Gospel of Matthew, the *Didache*, which originated early in the second century in northern Syria, also used the criterion of behavior to determine whether itinerant apostles, teachers, and prophets were true or false (*Did.* 11-13); but it also added other criteria (e.g., staying more than two or three days and asking for food and money; *Did.* 11:5). The criteria of "wolves in sheep's clothing" and "fruit" of Matt 7:15-23, vague as they are, continued to be important in identifying false prophets. For Roman Catholic theological writers before and after the Reformation, "fruit" was generally understood as immoral behavior. However, with Calvin[§] and post-Reformation Protestant interpretation generally, the "fruit" was primarily interpreted as doctrine, although later Pietistic writers (Pietism*[§]) reverted to interpreting it as works (e.g., J. Bengel, H. Grotius).

Through the middle of the second century, Christian writers (including Justin Martyr[§] [*Dial.* 82.1, 88.1] and Irenaeus[§], who also knew of demonically possessed false prophets [*Adv. Haer.* 1.13.3-4].) reflected an awareness that the gifts of the Spirit, including glossolalia and prophecy, continued to be exercised in the church. However, in the early second century Origen[§] had already expressed the belief that the signs of the Spirit (including prophecy and speaking in tongues) so frequent in the time of Jesus and the apostles had become comparatively rare (*Con. Cel.* 7.8). Thus, prophecy and other gifts of the Spirit were understood as restricted to the apostolic period, in part because of the definition of the biblical Canon*[§] by the fourth century. All such activity in later periods manifested heretical teaching and behavior. One prophetic movement that was labeled heretical was Montanism or Cataphrygianism, which was inspired by the book of Revelation and began in Asia Minor in the mid to late third century and survived until the sixth century (Eusebius *Hist. eccl.* 5.16.6-9; 6.20.3; Hippolytus *Pan.* 7.19.1; some preserved Montanist oracles are available in R. Heine 1989). Tertullian[§] was a convert to this movement, which was extremely rigorist and ascetic in opposition to the moral laxity perceived in the larger institutionalized and secularized church. The Montanists and their opponents debated whether or not Montanism was false prophecy (Eusebius *Hist. eccl.* 5.17.3, 5.16.8, 5.16.17; also Heine 1989, 3).

Some early interpreters (*Barn.* 15; Irenaeus *Adv. Haer.* 5.28-29; with nearly similar calculations by Hippolytus *On Daniel* 2.4-5), under the influence of Hebrew Bible and New Testament prophecy, used predictive Apocalypticism*[§] with its periodization of history to predict the coming of Christ in the year 6000. Augustine's[§] refutation of millenarianism was extremely influential, for predictions of the end of the world were generally avoided from 400 to 1000. During the medieval period, Joachim of Fiore[§], relying on Dan 9 and Jer 25:11-12, 29:10, predicted that the millennium would start c. 1260, when new religious orders would convert the whole world, including Jews, Muslims, and other "heathen," who would unite in prayer, mystical contemplation, and voluntary poverty.

From the late Middle Ages to the rise of biblical criticism in the early eighteenth century, the subject of New Testament prophets and prophecy continued to be eclipsed by the study of Hebrew Bible prophets and prophecy and by the continued influence of the exegesis of the Revelation of John. New impetus was given to the subject of New Testament prophecy by the discovery of the ancient church order called the *Didache*, or *Teaching of the Twelve Apostles*, by Archbishop Bryennios in 1873 and its subsequent publication in 1883. The final form of the compilation of this work probably occurred by the mid-second century C.E., suggesting that its constituent traditions reach back into the late first century. Since it is an early non-canonical document, the ensuing discussion exhibited a historical rather than a theological character, extending the interest in early Christian prophetic phenomena beyond the New Testament into the late first and early second centuries. *Didache* 11-13 contains instructions regarding itinerant apostles, teachers, and prophets, which encouraged a variety of hypotheses regarding the relationship between those who claimed to possess gifts of the Spirit, particularly Christian prophets, and the regular non-charismatic offices like bishop and presbyter. The rediscovery of the *Didache* was a major factor that, before and after the turn of the twentieth century, provoked the inner-Lutheran Sohm-Harnack debate on the essential nature of the church, in which the alternatives were spirit or law. R. Sohm, author of *The Nature and Origin of Catholicism* (1909), argued that the later development of ecclesiastical law stood in contradiction to the earlier, essentially spiritual and charismatic nature of the church. A. von Harnack[§] (1910), on the other hand, argued that complementary spiritual and institutional tendencies existed in the church from the very beginning since the church is both the invisible, spiritual people of God and an actual visible, empirical institution.

During the late nineteenth century, a renewed interest in the gifts of the Spirit began to permeate some of the more conservative wings of Protestant denominations in the United States and Great Britain, completely uninfluenced by the interest in early Christian prophecy sparked by the *Didache*. This interest remains to this day. Pentecostalism, a Protestant renewal movement that began in the United States in the late nineteenth century, emphasizes the possibility of experiencing the baptism of the Holy Spirit (Acts 1:5) and receiving the same spiritual gifts as those described in Acts 2 and 1 Cor 12-14, including glossolalia (or speaking in tongues), the interpretation of tongues, prophecy, healing, and exorcism. Spirit baptism, distinguished from conversion or sacramental baptism, is a postconversion experience signaled by speaking in unknown languages, or glossolalia. The charismatic movement, related to Pentecostalism, is a transdenominational movement that gained significance in the 1960s and has found general acceptance in some portions of mainline Protestant denominations, Roman Catholicism, and Orthodoxy.

With the development of Form Criticism* by German New Testament scholars early in the twentieth century came the recognition on the part of many critics that not all of the sayings attributed to Jesus in the gospel tradition could, in fact, be traced back to the historical Jesus. R. Bultmann[§] (1963, 163) and others proposed that many of the "I" sayings originated as oracles of early Christian prophets who spoke in the name of the risen Lord. "I" sayings of the risen Jesus found in Revelation provided examples of this phenomenon (Rev 1:17-20; 3:20; 16:15). This view has been defended in great detail by M. E. Boring (1991), although others have not been convinced (D. Hill 1974; D. Aune 1983, 233-45). New Testament prophets and prophecy were assigned a significant role in the creation of sayings of Jesus, which were then thought to have become assimilated to existing collections of such sayings.

Bultmann was not only a leading form critic but also one of a circle of German biblical scholars (including H. Gunkel, W. Bousset, W. Heitmüller, R. Reitzenstein, and J. Weiss, among others) called the Religionsgeschichtliche Schule*[§] (history-of-religions school), who were interested in the influences the Hellenistic environment exerted on early Christianity. H. Gunkel[§], in a short book on the Holy Spirit (1979) originally published in 1888, demonstrated that the "Spirit" is not simply the principle of the moral-religious life but that which is irrational and inexplicable, i.e., supernatural; and he related the Pauline concept of the Spirit to that of late Judaism. Influenced by Gunkel, M. Dibelius[§] combined an interest in Hellenistic ideas with those of early Judaism as the background for examining the world of spirits in the faith of Paul[†§] (1909). R. Reitzenstein[§] focused almost exclusively on the Hellenistic world in his attempt to illuminate the phenomenon of early Christian prophecy and Paul's role as a pneumatic (1978). A renewed interest in the phenomenon of early Christian prophecy, influenced in part by the rise of form criticism, began to manifest itself in E. Fascher's influential book *Prophêtês* (1927), in which the author (who had already written a critique of form criticism) focused on a philological investigation of the Greek word *prophêtês* (prophet) and its history-of-religions background.

Following World War II, a renewed interest in New Testament prophets and prophecy arose within the context of the biblical Theology*[§] movement, which tended to focus on the legitimacy of influences from the Hebrew Bible and early Judaism. The first detailed study of New Testament prophecy was produced by H. Guy in 1947, in which the prophecy of Jesus is presented as the culmination of biblical prophecy. This was followed in 1959 by the influential article by G. Friedrich on early Christian prophecy in the *Theological Dictionary of the New Testament*, which was the standard treatment on the subject for several years. Friedrich emphasized the similarities between the Hebrew Bible prophets and John the apocalyptist, but regarded the type of prophecy practiced by the Corinthian prophets as inferior to that of John. Friedrich was later followed in this view by W. Grudem (1982). By the 1970s and 1980s a number of important studies treated all aspects of early Christian prophetic phenomena, many recognizing the importance and influence of Hellenistic prophetic phenomena alongside that of Judaism. Studies surveying the subject include works by É. Cothenet (1972), T. Crone (1973), Hill (1979), and Aune (1983), while several scholars focus more exclusively on one of the central New Testament passages on the subject, 1 Cor 12-14, including G. Dautzenberg (1975), Grudem (1982), and C. Forbes (1995). An important and neglected feminist perspective is brought to bear in A. Wire's work on the Corinthian women prophets (1990). An attempt to provide a form-critical analysis of the relatively scarce example of early Christian prophetic speech was proposed by B. Müller (1975) and Aune (1983, 317-38).

Recent studies of early Christian prophecy include an analysis of Jesus as a prophetic figure (Witherington 1999) and studies of prophecy and prophets in the early church (Bonneau 1998, Gillespie 1994, *Wünsche 1997*).

Bibliography: D. E. Aune, *Prophecy in Early Christianity and the Ancient Mediterranean World* (1983). **G. Bonneau** *Prophétisme et institution dans le christianisme primitif* (Sciences bibliques, Collection Sciences bibliques 4, 1998). **M. E. Boring,** *The Continuing Voice of Jesus: Christian Prophecy and the Gospel Tradition* (1991). **R. Bultmann,** *The History of the Synoptic Tradition* (1931[2]; ET 1963). **S. M. Burgess and G. B. McGee,** *Dictionary of Pentecostal and Charismatic Movements* (1988). **H. von Campenhausen,** *Ecclesiastical Authority and Spiritual Power in the Church of the First Three Centuries* (ET 1969). **É. Cothenet,** "Prophétisme dans le Nouveau Testament," *DBSup* 8 (1972) 1222-337. **T. M. Crone,** *Early Christian Prophecy: A Study of Its Origin and Function* (1973). **G. Dautzenberg,** *Urchristliche Prophetie: Ihre Erforschung, ihre Voraussetzungen im Judentum, und ihre Struktur im ersten Korintherbrief* (BWANT 6, 4; 1975). **M. Dibelius,** *Die Geisterwelt im Glauben des Paulus* (1909). **E. Fascher,** *Prophêtês: Eine sprach- und religionsgeschichtliche Untersuchung* (1927). **C. Forbes,** *Prophecy and Inspired Speech in Early Christianity and Its Hellenistic Environment* (WUNT 75, 1995). **G. Friedrich,** *TDNT* 6 (1959; ET 1968) 781-861. **T. W. Gillespie,** *The First Theologians: A Study in Early Christian Prophecy* (1994). **W. Grudem,** *The Gift of Prophecy in 1 Corinthians* (1982). **H. Gunkel,** *The Influence of the Holy Spirit* (1888; ET 1979). **H. A. Guy,** *NT Prophecy: Its Origins and Influence* (1947). **A. von Harnack,** *The Constitution and Law of the Church in the First Two Centuries* (1910). **R. E. Heine,** "The Role of the Gospel of John in the Montanist Controversy," *SecCent* 6 (1987-88) 1-19; *The Montanist Oracles and Testimonia* (PatMS 14, 1989). **D. Hill,** "On the Evidence for the Creative Role of Christian Prophets," *NTS* 20 (1974) 262-74; NT Prophecy (New Foundations Theological Library, 1979). **U. B. Müller,** *Prophetie und Predigt im Neuen Testament* (Studien zum Neuen Testament 10, 1975). **J. Reiling,** *Hermas and Christian Prophecy: A Study of the Eleventh Mandate* (NovTSup 37, 1973). **R. Reitzenstein,** *Hellenistic Mystery-religions: Their Basic Ideas and Significance* (PThMS 15, 1978). **A. C. Wire,** *The Corinthian Women Prophets: A Reconstruction Through Paul's Rhetoric* (1990). **B. Witherington III,** *Jesus the Seer: The Progress of Prophecy* (1999). **M. Wünsche,** *Der Ausgang der urchristlichen Prophetie in der frühkatholischen Kirche: Untersuchungen zu den Apostolischen Vätern, den Apologeten, Irenäus von Lyon und dem anti-montanistischen Anonymus* (Calwer theologische Monographien Reihe B, Systematische Theologie und Kirchengeschichte ; Bd. 14 1997).

D. E. AUNE

GENERAL NEW TESTAMENT ARTICLES

Synoptic Problem

The Gospels of Matthew, Mark, and Luke are called synoptic because their similarities and differences make it possible and desirable to study them in a synopsis (from a Greek word meaning "seen together"), an instrument that presents the texts of these Gospels in parallel columns and eventually even on parallel lines. The first adequate synopsis was created by J. J. Griesbach[§] in 1774 as part of his critical edition of the Greek New Testament and was published in 1776 as a separate book entitled *Synopsis evangeliorum Matthaei, Marci, et Lucae*. These publications became the starting point for all modern studies of the synoptic problem, which have included investigations of the historical, literary, and theological relationships between and among these Gospels.

1. *The Synoptic Problem in Antiquity.* The synoptic problem was already being discussed by scholars in antiquity who were first concerned that the four canonical Gospels (Canon of the Bible[§]) did not always narrate the sayings and deeds of Jesus*[§] in the same order.

Irenaeus[§], bishop of Lyons after 178 C.E. stressed the divine revelation that he believed was imparted to each of the authors of the four canonical Gospels (Eusebius *Hist. eccl.* 3.39.1-17). Also during the second century C.E., Tatian[§], a Syrian theologian, constructed a harmonized and combined text of the canonical Gospels, which he called the *Diatessaron* ([One Gospel] Through Four). Eusebius, writing between 300 and 325 and relying upon the work of the Alexandrian scholar Ammonius (*c.* 250) numbered the various parallel pericopes from the Gospels and collected these numbers into tables of various canons, with which one could cross-reference sections of the Gospels according to the categories of agreements among and between them. Eusebius's canons included tables for agreements among all four canonical Gospels, among any three, and between any two except Mark and John, as well as tables displaying sections that are unique to each Gospel. These Eusebian canons were often added to the texts of the Gospels, and the numbers of the sections in the tables were copied into the margins. The canons remained important for centuries as aids for comparative study of the Gospels. (See NA[27], 84-89 for the canon tables, and the inner margins of the canonical Gospels for the corresponding numbers of the Ammonian/Eusebian sections.)

The oldest explicit reference to the sequence in which the Gospels were composed is attributed to Clement of Alexandria[§], "those gospels were first written which include the genealogies [i. e., Matthew and Luke and perhaps others with genealogies]" (*Hypotyposeis* 6, as quoted in Eusebius, *Hist. eccl.* 6.14.5-7).

The first detailed and explicitly literary attempt to explain the agreements and differences among the canonical Gospels is found in Augustine's[§] *De consensu evangelistarum*, written around 400 C.E. In book 1 of this work, Augustine asserted that Mark had followed and epitomized Matthew, but in book 4 he declared it more probable that Mark had been influenced by both Matthew and Luke. Augustine's first, but implicitly less probable, source theory about the Gospels, implying the order Matt, Mark, Luke as the order of composition was adopted by many later scholars and eventually became known as the Augustinian hypothesis.

2. *Middle Ages, Reformation, and Enlightenment.* J. Gerson[§] made a remarkable endeavor to harmonize the four Gospels in his *Harmonia evangelica* (c. 1420), and during the Reformation A. Osiander offered a very detailed exposition of this kind in his *Harmonia evangelica* (1537). During the Enlightenment, scholars gradually replaced apologetic harmonies of the Gospels with critical presentations that simply juxtaposed the texts more or less in their own sequence. J. Le Clerc prepared the way for a transition to a new era in synoptic study with his *Harmonia evangelica* (1699), which contained Greek and Latin texts of the canonical Gospels in four parallel

columns. However, the decisive step into this new era of synoptic presentation, as distinct from harmonization of the Gospels, was taken by Griesbach, whose critical edition of the Greek New Testament (1774) arranged the entire Gospels of Matthew, Mark, and Luke and selected sections of John in parallel columns. Griesbach intended to facilitate comparative analysis of the Gospels, not their harmonization, which he rejected as impossible. His synoptic arrangement, published as a separate volume in 1776, became the model for all later multi-columned synopses.

3. *1780-1820.* Griesbach's synopsis inspired him and other Protestant theologians in Germany to intensified studies of the synoptic problem. Prior to 1800 Griesbach and his competitors had developed four main source theories about the Gospels, descendants of which can be found in all later contributions to the problem. These four classical theories have been described, particularly in the German literature, as: (a) the utilization hypothesis; (b) the proto-gospel theory; (c) the multiple source theory; and (d) the oral tradition hypothesis.

a. The utilization hypothesis. This hypothesis implies that one canonical Gospel was a source for one or more of the others, although their interrelationships and order of composition have been understood in different, sometimes even opposite, ways by different scholars.

At least between the time of Thomas Aquinas[§] and the second half of the eighteenth century, most scholars accepted the generally received canonical sequence—Matt, Mark, Luke—as the order of composition. In antiquity this sequence was affirmed by Origen[§] (Eusebius *Hist. eccl.* 6.25.3-6); by Jerome[§] (*Prologus quattuor evangeliorum* [*praefatio in comm. in Mattheum*]); and, at one stage of his work, by Augustine (*De consensu evangelistarum* 1.2.4, 1.3.6). This Augustinian hypothesis was later advocated by the Dutch jurist and theologian H. Grotius[§] (1641), among many others.

This hypothesis, however, included the view that Mark was the abbreviator of Matt (*De consensu* 1.3.6), a view called into question at least since the time of Calvin[§]. Calvin and some other scholars argued that there was no literary relationship among the canonical Gospels at all; but others, e.g., J. Mill[§] and J. Wettstein[§], accepted the generally received canonical order as the order of composition while denying that the relevant literary evidence supported the view that Mark was an abbreviator of Matt.

Then in 1764 an English scholar, H. Owen, advocated that the sequence of composition was Matt, Luke, and Mark. Owen argued that Mark was a conflation of Matt and Luke rather than an abbreviation of Matt.

Somewhat later, at Jena in Germany, F. Stroth, in an anonymously published article (1781), came to similar conclusions. Griesbach, Stroth's colleague at Jena, then advocated this source theory in three speeches delivered at the university at Easter 1783 and at Whitsunday 1789 and 1790. Inspired by the intermediary function of Mark presented in his synopsis, Griesbach first argued that Luke had made use of Matt, and then demonstrated in more detail that Mark alternately depended on Matt or Luke or both. Known as the Griesbach hypothesis, this form of the utilization hypothesis became the most popular source theory about the Gospels from his time into the middle decades of the nineteenth century. A brilliant discussion of a modified form of Griesbach's theory was published in 1826 by his former student, W. De Wette[§].

No decisive evidence has yet been presented by modern scholars that Stroth or Griesbach knew of Owen's earlier work on the synoptic problem, but it is a fact that Griesbach's extended visit to London (September 1769 to June 1770) overlapped the three-year period (1769-71) when Owen was Boyle lecturer. In deference to this possible connection and for other reasons, some scholars today refer to the Owen-Griesbach hypothesis. A few scholars on both sides of the English Channel during this same period, e.g., A. F. Büsching and E. Evanson[§], agreed that Mark was a conflation of Matthew and Luke but gave priority to Luke rather than to Matthew.

The view opposing the Augustinian hypothesis, that Mark had been a source of Matthew and Luke, was advocated in 1786 by G. Storr of Tübingen. Storr's theory does not seem to have influenced his contemporaries, and although the priority of Mark was suggested again in the years 1836-38 (see sec. 4), its advocates did not base their arguments on Storr's. Nevertheless, this founder of the so-called first Tübingen school anticipated the Markan form of the utilization hypothesis that rose to popularity from the middle decades of the nineteenth century.

Thus already in the eighteenth century the utilization hypothesis included advocates of the priority of Matt (Mill, Wettstein, Owen, Stroth, Griesbach), the priority of Luke (Büsching, Evans), and the priority of Mark (Storr).

b. The proto-gospel theory. This theory is characterized by the view that the extant Gospels derive from an earlier source rather than from one or more of the other canonical Gospels. This idea had its origins in Papias's statement that Matthew had "composed the Logia in *hebraidi dialekt?*," understood to mean "in the Hebrew language" or "in the Hebrew dialect," i. e., Aramaic. In the fourth century, Epiphanius and Jerome referred these Logia to an older Hebrew Gospel assumed to lie behind the Jewish-Christian Gospel of the Nazarenes. In 1689 R. Simon§, a pioneer of Textual Criticism*§, described this presumed older Gospel as an Aramaic proto-Gospel, a hypothesis popularized in 1778 by G. Lessing§, whose brilliant little study was published posthumously in 1784. Lessing regarded the Aramaic Gospel of the Nazarenes as the common source of all canonical and apocryphal gospels (Apocrypha, New Testament†§). His thesis was accepted in 1794 by J. G. Eichhorn§; but since this polyhistor combined it with the assumption of multiple sources (see sec. 3c), it seemed much too complicated in the eyes of his contemporaries. In 1832 F. Schleiermacher§ suggested much that the sayings of Jesus as quoted in Matt derived from Papias's proto-Matthew, which contained Logia (sec. 4 below). Since Schleiermacher believed Logia included only sayings, this suggestion developed into a reduced form of Lessing's proto-Gospel theory.

c. The multiple-source theory. This theory was initiated by J. Koppe§ in 1782. Drawing attention to the many authors mentioned in Luke 1:1, he assumed that Matt, Mark, and Luke had collected a number of circulating units structured in oral and written form as narratives, speeches, parables, sayings, etc. A similar fragment theory assuming short written notes was developed by Schleiermacher in a book on Luke (1817). This monograph had no great influence on later scholars, but Koppe's suggestion that the Gospels developed from earlier and smaller literary units containing differing literary forms anticipated the form-critical approach (see Form Criticism*§) that developed in the twentieth century (see sec. 5).

d. The oral tradition hypothesis. This hypothesis was created by J. G. Herder§ and made public in 1796-97. Repudiating the utilization and the proto-gospel theories, Herder called a common oral tradition the "protoplasm" from which the later written Gospels grew. He presumed that on this basis an oral, Aramaic proto-Mark was developed in the period 34-40 C.E., and that some years after 60 C.E. it became the source of the written Nazarean proto-Matthew, which, supported by proto-Mark, gave rise to the Greek Synoptic Gospels. Herder's enthusiastic occupation with Folklore*§ made him emphasize living traditions instead of fixed documents, and he found all ideas about redactional manipulations in the composition of the Gospels to be anachronistic. The Gospel writers, in Herder's view, should look more like first-century composers and less like eighteenth-century authors, publishers, and bookmen. Arguments in favor of living oral traditions and against literary traditions were also adduced in a monograph by J. Gieseler§ (1818).

4. *1830-70.* Synoptic Gospel studies during this period were dominated by contributions from German Protestant scholars, and their opinions influenced later scholars of different nationalities and confessions throughout the world. As Germany forged a unified political identity, middle-class standards, liberalism, and nationalism rose in popularity. German professors

were held in high esteem and thus were able to advance even radical suggestions about the development of earliest Christian history without restraint. In general, Protestant theologians in Germany during this period showed a preference either for bourgeois realism or for philosophical idealism, two views characteristic of the time.

a. The influence of realism. Around the year 1830 Griesbach's and Herder's synoptic theories were dominant among German divines. Soon, however, interest in realism prompted reactions against the more elaborate theology believed to be found in Matt and Luke and against the uncontrolled development that was supposed to characterize the growth of oral traditions. These reactions were intensified when D. F. Strauss[§] published his provocative two-volume work on Jesus in 1835-36. Influenced by G. W. F. Hegel's idealist philosophy, Strauss replaced history with Mythology*[§] in his interpretation of the Gospels, while presupposing Griesbach's and Herder's theories.

Other German scholars who preferred middle-class empiricism sought to reconstruct the life and teachings of Jesus based on documents that seemed the most primitive. They claimed to possess two such witnesses: Mark, whose narrative was neglected by Strauss even though it had been positively reevaluated by the well-known philologist K. Lachmann[§] in 1835; and the Logia of Matt, about which Papias had commented but which Schleiermacher in an 1832 article understood in the limited sense of "sayings."

Impressed by Lachmann and Schleiermacher, although not yet by Strauss, in 1836 K. Credner of Giessen proposed a source theory based on the priority of Mark and a Logia source. More detailed than Credner and in explicit opposition to Strauss, the empirical philosopher C. Weisse[§] also developed a two document hypothesis (1838). Weisse praised the simplicity of Mark and extended the influence of the presumed Logia source to Luke. In the same year, but without any knowledge of the works by Strauss and Weisse, a pastor in Saxony, C. Wilke[§], also argued for the priority of Mark. Credner's and Weisse's attempts to prove the historical nature of Mark's account were not immediately successful, but some of their arguments were taken up again ten years later.

b. The influence of Hegel's dialectic. Until the revolution of 1848 the idealism of the Prussian philosopher Hegel inspired several German theologians. They also found Griesbach's contention that Matt and Luke had provided source material for Mark most in harmony with Hegel's dialectic pattern of thesis, antithesis, and synthesis. This perspective especially characterized work by F. C. Baur[§], leader of the second Tübingen school. He and his followers understood the evangelists to represent dialectic principles and tendencies, which they characterized as Judaism, Hellenism, and Syncretism (early Roman Catholicism). To accommodate his schematic view of the development of earliest Christianity, Baur and other members of this school dated Luke and Mark sometime in the second century. This philosophical overlay on the synoptic theory of Griesbach and the results to which the second Tübingen school came in reconstructing early Christian origins did not enhance the popularity of Griesbach's source theory.

c. The resurgence of realism. After the revolution of 1848, liberal realism took command again in Germany, and Hegel's idealism became less popular. This led to another advancement of the Mark-and-Logia theory by the Göttingen professor H. Ewald[§] . In articles published between 1848 and 1850 and in an 1850 commentary, Ewald expressed the conviction that his revision of the theory would restore true religion and unify Germany; he was, in fact, followed by several of his countrymen in the 1850s.

In 1863 Heidelberg professor H. Holtzmann[§] summarized earlier proposals about the sources of the Gospels and commented on the Synoptic Gospels on the basis of his own distinctive two document theory. Major critiques of Holtzmann's work were offered by the German advocate of the Augustinian hypothesis, A. Hilgenfeld[§] of Jena (1863), and by a Dutch advocate of the Griesbach hypothesis, H. Meyboom, in his doctoral dissertation (1866). A distinctive contribution of Meyboom's dissertation was to call attention to the work done on the synoptic problem by members of the Strasbourg school, including T. Colani , M. Nicolas, E. Reuss[§], A. Réville, and E. Scherer. Although each of these scholars advocated some form of the Markan hypothesis, none affirmed the priority of canonical Mark. Reuss, Réville, and Nicolas advocated a proto-Mark hypothesis (Meyboom claimed that Réville coined the term proto-Mark). Because of the singular literary style Scherer found in canonical Mark, he published his doubts about the Markan hypothesis, particularly about Reuss's view that the canonical text of Mark had developed through several earlier stages at the hands of several authors and editors.

In spite of the cautious work of these French scholars, shortly after its appearance the 1863 work by Holtzmann came to be regarded by most European scholars as the definitive answer to the synoptic question. However, Holtzmann's names for the two oldest sources, Alpha and Lambda, did not replace the terms Ur-Marcus and Logia, which later developed into canonical Mark and Q. (Following the Franco-Prussian War of 1870-71 and the subsequent annexation of Alsace-Lorraine into a newly unified German nation, Holtzmann was appointed professor in Strasbourg to represent German New Testament scholarship there.)

5. *1870-1950.* Holtzmann's two source theory influenced scholars in all countries and denominations during the subsequent period of synoptic research. A former student and one time colleague on the Strasbourg faculty, A. Schweitzer[§], wrote that the two source hypothesis "is carried by Holtzmann to such a degree of demonstration that it can no longer be called a mere hypothesis, but it does not succeed in winning an assured position in the critical study of the Life of Jesus" (1906).

a. The spread of the Mark and Q hypothesis. The respect other scholars had for Holtzmann's detailed work during this period accelerated the spread of the Mark-and-Q version of the utilization hypothesis to Great Britain. A. Abbott discussed the Gospels in accord with Holtzmann's views in the 1879 EncBrit. At Oxford a group of scholars under the leadership of W. Sanday[§] met for years to study the importance of Mark and Q, publishing their results in 1911. One of the participants in Sanday's seminar was B. Streeter[§], whose 1924 monograph became a standard treatise on the synoptic problem throughout the English-speaking world.

The transmission of the work of Holtzmann and of other German Protestant biblical scholars to French, English, German, and Italian Roman Catholic circles, particularly among modernists, was often expedited through the efforts of the wealthy, scholarly, and influential Roman Catholic layman F. von Hügel. After delivering a paper on Luke to the Society for Biblical Studies in Rome in 1896, von Hügel corresponded for several months with the young E. Pacelli, the future Pope Pius XII, about historical-critical biblical interpretation as practiced by such Roman Catholic modernists as G. Tyrrell and by German Protestants, like J. Wellhausen[§] and Holtzmann. After the promulgation of the Roman Catholic encyclical Divino Afflante Spiritu[§] by Pope Pius XII in 1943, Roman Catholic theologians were no longer expected to suppress modernism; they developed a biblical scholarship in parallel with Protestants, which has mostly included a preference for the Mark-and-Q hypothesis, although other suggestions have also been made (see sec. 6*b*).

b. The rise of form criticism. Within the period 1870-1950 an important complement to the dominating Literary*[§] criticism of the Synoptic Gospels, based as it was on Mark and Q, emerged in 1919, when M. Dibelius[§] developed a method called Form Criticism*[§]. His leading idea was to study the synoptic pericopes as preliterary units of tradition, like tales and sayings occurring as oral traditions in folklore. Historically, this method shared features of Koppe's and Schleiermacher's fragment theory combined with Herder's and Gieseler's oral gospel theory, although Dibelius presupposed neither written fragments nor a comprehensive tradition. Essential for him was the distinction of forms like "paradigm" (short narrative ending in a point), "novel story" (longer narrative with concrete details), "paraenesis" (quotation of Jesus implying admonition), and "myth" (revelation of Christ's Messiahship). The common "life set-ting" of these various forms was "preaching," by which Dibelius meant both sermons and teaching.

Following WWI, German theologians found this approach stimulating; and Dibelius was fol-lowed by several young scholars, among whom R. Bultmann[§] was the most influential through his 1921 book. These and many later contributors to form criticism, however, presupposed the two-source theory. Accordingly, they concentrated form criticism on Mark and on the presumed Logia while exposing Matt and Luke to literary criticism in order to highlight alleged redactional changes of Mark and Q by the later Gospel writers. Such exclusion of other source-critical pos-sibilities was not compatible with the significant declaration of Luke that he, like other persons who had also undertaken to report on Jesus, had access to the oral traditions of eye-witnesses (Luke 1:2). The routine combination of form criticism with literary criticism based on Mark and Q implied a change to a different method and prevented the fresh approach of form criticism from becoming as fruitful as it might have been. Yet scholars generally accepted the source-crit-ical presuppositions of Dibelius and Bultmann along with the form-critical method.

6. *1950-84. a. Redaction criticism and structuralism.* Two of the new trends that developed during this period posited new understandings of the theology of the synoptic evangelists while presupposing the inherited two source theory or ignoring source criticism altogether. Redaction Criticism*[§], which started in western Germany just after WWII, was intended to explain in detail what message the redactors of each Gospel wanted to communicate. Early German pioneers of this method included H. Conzelmann on Luke, W. Marxsen on Mark, and G. Bornkamm[§], G. Barth, and H. Held on Matt. The application of this method produced a rich literature on the Gospels by scholars in many countries, and new theological insights have been gained. However, redaction criticism as it is often practiced is flawed because most redaction critics of Matt and Luke draw conclusions about the theology of these evangelists only from evidence provided by the alleged supplements and changes these authors are assumed to have made to the texts of Mark and Q, rather than from evidence provided in the complete texts of these Gospels.

The synoptic texts have also been interpreted on the basis of Structuralism*[§], a system of lin-guistic principles developed in Geneva and Paris. Its aim is the logical and structural analysis of texts without primary concern for whether they reveal something historical. A synchronic instead of a diachronic view is taken. Source criticism of the Gospels has scarcely interested the structuralists, but their skepticism contributed to the discussion of the synoptic problem after WWII.

b. Source theories. The years after 1950 have also included some positive contributions to the question of gospel origins, and they have led to a useful revival of the discussion of the syn-optic problem. Most source theories currently advocated had counterparts or precursors among the classical theories created in Germany before 1800, although the new theories also comprise modifications, elaborations, and sometimes combinations of the earlier theories, often due to new discoveries of relevant material. Thus one will find contemporary forms or combinations of (i) the utilization hypothesis, ascribing priority to Matt, Mark, or Luke; (ii) the proto-gospel hypothesis, usually in the form of a proto-Mark; (iii) multiple source hypotheses; and (iv) oral tradition hypotheses.

i. The utilization hypothesis. A scholarly attack on the Mark-and-Q form of the utilization hypothesis, which had been most popular since the time of Holtzmann, was delivered in 1951 by a Roman Catholic theologian in London, B. Butler, who wanted to revive the Augustinian hypothesis. He found a receptive following among a few scholars in the United States (J. Ludlum, Jr.) and England (B. Orchard, prior to 1970, and J. Wenham).

More attention, however, was paid to W. Farmer[§], who recommended Griesbach's hypothesis (1964). A group of scholars has continued to work together with this hypothesis, and since 1964 Farmer has coauthored works advocating the two gospel hypothesis with L. Cope, D. Dungan, T. Longstaff, A. McNicol, Orchard, D. Peabody, and P. Shuler. Other contemporary scholars who have come to advocate the neo-Griesbach (two gospel) hypothesis include G. Buchanan, N. Elliott, H. Hoehner, L. Maluf, C. Mann, and D. Tevis in the United States; A. Leske in Canada; H. Riley in England; D. Neville (1994) and B. Powers in Australia; H.-H. Stoldt in Germany; F. Collison and S. Samuel in India; G. Gamba in Italy; Y. Kim and J. Lee in Korea; and S. Abogunrin in Nigeria.

Adherents of the two-source theory have generally found no reason to give up their position or, in some cases, even to discuss the synoptic problem. Two exceptional advocates who have played major roles in the contemporary discussion are C. Tuckett (1983), formerly at Manchester but now at Oxford; and F. Neirynck of Louvain, who contributed to the defense of Markan priority with major publications in 1972 and 1974. Neirynck later summarized his defense of the two-source hypothesis in the IDBSup (1976) and in the NJBC (1990). Tuckett's major critique of the Griesbach hypothesis and defense of the two document hypothesis appeared in the published version of his doctoral dissertation in 1983. In 1995 he also provided his own summary of the current state of Gospel study in volume 8 of the *NIB*.

ii. The proto-gospel hypothesis. The University of Louvain was once a center of attempts to revive Lessing's proto-gospel theory, beginning in 1952 with lectures by L. Vaganay and L. Cerfaux[§], who started again from Papias's reference to a Hebrew or Aramaic proto-Matthew. However, since intermediary sources and stages were also included, these Roman Catholic scholars and their supporters have partly approached the multiple source theory.

iii. Multiple source hypotheses. Koppe's and Eichhorn's multiple source theories have found modern analogies in work by scholars connected with the Ecole Biblique in Jerusalem. In a synopsis published in 1972, M.-E. Boismard gave up the assumption of a common proto-gospel and preferred to regard multiple earlier stages of Matt, Mark, and Luke as the more original sources of the Gospels. His former student P. Rolland (1982, 1983*a*, 1983*b*, 1984) has reconstructed more sources and placed them in a complicated sequence on the basis of minute observations concerning double expressions in Mark, now interpreted as combinations of single expressions in Matt and Luke.

iv. The oral tradition hypothesis. Contemporary synoptic discussions have also resulted in a renascence of Herder's and Gieseler's oral tradition hypothesis. Its advocates have collected supporting arguments partly from Judaism, partly from folklore.

Jewish analogies have especially occupied Swedish scholars inspired by the Uppsala orientalist H. S. Nyberg's[§] *Studien zum Hoseabuche* (1935), in which he attacked literary criticism and pointed out the importance of the living traditions behind oriental texts. Similar approaches were taken in gospel studies by H. Riesenfeld in 1957 and by B. Gerhardsson, who in a 1964 work emphasized the use of memorization within the apostles' Jewish environment.

Folklore analogies have interested American theologians in recent years, especially under the influence of Harvard philologists who have studied the memorization technique of village minstrels in Bosnia and in parts of Yugoslavia. In addition, a symposium on the Gospels was held in San Antonio, Texas, in 1977, at which A. Lord (1978) of Harvard delivered the first lecture. Oral traditions behind the Gospels have been strongly emphasized also by W. Kelber (1983); and B. Reicke[§] (1986) attempted to find reflections of living oral traditions in the extant texts of all three synoptic Gospels.

7. *1984-98.* The classical synoptic theories of the years before 1800 are still represented in modified or combined forms; and exchanges of views among the advocates of these theories have taken place, especially at meetings of international societies like the Studiorum Novi

Testamenti Societas and the Society of Biblical Literature[§]. Another forum for such discussions was a symposium in Jerusalem at Easter 1984, at which leading representatives of three source hypotheses had rich opportunities for discussion and debate over a two-week period. Although the assembled scholars did not reach much agreement, one of the points of consensus has helped to shape some of the most recent publications. That consensus affirmed that "a literary, historical and theological explanation of the evangelists' compositional activity, giving a coherent and reasonable picture of the whole of each Gospel, is the most important method of argumentation in defense of a source hypothesis."

The classical utilization hypothesis was represented in Jerusalem by advocates of the two-source hypothesis and the two gospel (neo-Griesbach) hypotheses. Several multiple source hypotheses were also represented, and at least one representative of the oral tradition hypothesis was present. After the Jerusalem conference the discussion of the importance of oral traditions for a complete understanding of the development of the Synoptic Gospels continued at conferences in Dublin, Ireland (1989), and Varese, Italy (1990).

Experts in the synoptic problem gathered again in 1991 at the Georg-August Universität in Göttingen to discuss the significance of the "minor agreements" for a variety of competing source theories. Advocates of two other contemporary source theories not represented in Jerusalem engaged in the debate: Supporters for the Deutero-Markus theory (Matthew and Luke independently used a form of Mark later than canonical Mark as well as Q in composing their Gospels) included A. Fuchs, U. Luz, C. Niemand, and G. Strecker (1993), the conference host; and M. Goulder ably advocated and defended A. Farrer's[§] source theory (Matthew and Luke independently used canonical Mark, but Luke also made direct use of Matthew for material not found in Mark. There was no Q source). Other modern defenders of the J. H. Ropes-A. Farrer-M. Goulder hypothesis include Goulder's student M. Goodacre as well as J. Drury, E. Franklin, H. Green, E. Hobbs, E. P. Sanders, and D. Schmidt. The few contemporary advocates of the Augustinian hypothesis (Ludlum and Wenham) and of a form of the utilization hypothesis that gives priority to Luke (R. Lindsey) did not share in this particular international discussion.

A volume of essays, *Biblical Studies and the Shifting of Paradigms*, 1850-1914 (H. G. Reventlow and W. Farmer 1995), that came out of conferences held in Latrobe, Pa., in 1990 and at the University of the Ruhr in Bochum, Germany, in 1992, has also helped to advance contemporary understanding of the history of the discussion of the synoptic problem.

Public awareness and understanding of the synoptic problem has increased recently through the appearance of several related sites on the World Wide Web. The most comprehensive of these is "The Synoptic Problem" maintained by S. Carlson, http://www.mindspring.com/~scarlson/synopt/, who also provides links to several other sites.

In 1994 Farmer provided his answer to every clergy and layperson's fundamental question about the synoptic problem: Does one solution or another really make a difference? Farmer maintained that it makes a great deal of difference and illustrated his answer with comparative discussions, one presupposing the two source hypothesis and another presupposing the two gospel hypothesis, for understanding the Lord's Prayer, the Lord's Supper, justification by faith, the faithful witness of women, God's special commitment to the poor, and the keys to the Kingdom.

Recent studies on the synoptic problem include Blair (2003), Brandenburger and Hieke (1998), Hall (1998), Hultgren (2002), Krämer (1997), Neville (2002), and Paffenroth (1997). Recent collections of essays on the synoptic problem include Laban and Schmidt (2001), Orton (1999), and Thomas (2002). Dungan (1999) recounts the history of scholarship on the synoptic problem. Goodacre (2001, 2002) argues for Markan priority, for Luke's dependence upon Matt, and against the existence of Q. McNicol (2002) argues for the Griesbach hypothesis as the solution to the synoptic problem. Hofricheter (2002a, 2002b) studies the synoptic problem in relationship to the Gospel of John. Head (1997) studies the synoptic problem in light of Christology. Recent gospel synopses included Longstaff (2002, on CD-ROM). Hoffmann, Hieke, and Bauer have developed another synoptic concordance.

Bibliography: **F. C. Baur**, *Kritische Untersuchungen über die kanonischen Evangelien, ihr Verhältniss zu einander, ihren Charakter und Ursprung* (1847). **A. J. Bellinzoni, Jr. et al.** (eds.), *The Two-Source Hypothesis: A Critical Appraisal* (1985). **G. A. Blair,** *The Synoptic Gospels Compared* (Studies in the Bible and Early Christianity 55, 2003). **M.-E. Boismard et al.**, *Synopse des quatre Évangiles en français* 2 (1972) 15-59. **G. Bornkamm et al.**, *Tradition and Interpretation in Matthew* (1960, 1968[5]; ET, NTL, 1963). **S. H. Brandenburger and T. Hieke** (eds.), *Wenn drei das Gleiche Sagen: Studien zu den ersten drei Evangelien* (Theologie 14, 1998). **R. K. Bultmann**, *The History of the Synoptic Tradition* (FRLANT 29, 1921, 1931[2], 1961[5]; ET 1963, 1968[2], rev. 1994). **A. F. Busching**, *Die vier Evangelisten mit ihren eigenen Worten zusammengesetzt und mit Erklärungen versehen* (1766). **B. C. Butler**, *The Originality of Matthew: A Critique of the Two-Document Hypothesis* (1951). **L. Cerfaux**, *La mission de Galilée dans la tradition synoptique* (ALBO 2, 36, 1952). **H. Conzelmann**, *The Theology of St. Luke* (BHT 17, 1954, 1962[4]; ET 1960, 1982). **K. A. Credner**, *Einleitung in das Neue Testament* (2 vols. 1836) 1:201-5. **W. M. L. de Wette**, *An Historico-critical Introduction to the Canonical Books of the NT* (1826, 1848[5]; ET 1858) 129-86. **M. Dibelius**, *From Tradition to Gospel* (1919, 1933[2]; ET 1934). **D. L. Dungan** (ed.), *The Interrelations of the Gospels: A Symposium Led by M. E. Boismard, W. R. Farmer, and F. Neirynck; Jerusalem 1984* (BETL 95, 1990); *A History of The Synoptic Problem: The Canon, The Text, The Composition and the Interpretation of the Gospels* (ABRL, 1999). **J. G. Eichhorn**, "Über die drei ersten Evangelien," *ABBL* 5 (1794) 759-996. **E. Evanson**, *The Dissonance of the Four Generally Received Evangelists and the Evidence of Their Respective Authenticity Examined* (1792). **G. H. A. Ewald**, "Ursprung und Wesen der Evangelien," *JBW* 1 (1848) 113-54; 2 (1849) 180-224; 3 (1850) 140-77; *Die drei ersten Evangelien übersetzt und erklärt* (1850) xviii-xix. **W. R. Farmer**, *The Synoptic Problem: A Critical Analysis* (1964); *The Gospel of Jesus: The Pastoral Relevance of the Synoptic Problem* (1994). **B. Gerhardsson**, *Memory and Manuscript: Oral Tradition and Written Transmission in Rabbinic Judaism and Early Christianity* (tr. E. J. Sharpe, ASNU 22, 1961); *Tradition and Transmission in Early Christianity* (ConNT 20, 1964; repr. with *Memory and Manuscript*, 1997); *Origins of the Gospel Traditions* (1979). **J. K. L. Gieseler**, *Historisch-kritischer Versuch über die Entstehung und die frühesten Schicksale der schriftlichen Evangelien* (1818). **M. Goodacre**, *The Synoptic Problem: A Way Through the Maze* (Biblical Seminar 80, 2001); *The Case Against Q: Studies in Markan Priority and the Synoptic Problem* (2002). **J. J. Griesbach**, *Libri historici Novi Testamenti graece* 1 (1774); *Synopsis evangeliorum Matthaei, Marci, et Lucae* (1776); *Fontes unde evangelistae suas de resurrectione domini narrationes hauserint* (1783; repr. in his *Opuscula academica* 2, ed. J. P. Gabler, 1825); *Commentatio qua Marci evangelium totum e Matthaei et Lucae commentariis decerptum esse demonstratur* (1789-90; repr. in *Commentationes theologicae*, ed. J. K. Velthusen, C. T. Kuihnoel, and G. A. Ruperti, 1794; repr. in his *Opuscula academica* 2, ed. J. P. Gabler, 1825; ET, *J. J. Griesbach: Synoptic and Text Critical Studies*, SNTSMS 34, 1978 103-35). **H. Grotius**, *Annotationes in libros evangeliorum* (1641). **D. R. Hall,** *The Gospel Framework: Fiction or Fact?: A Critical Evaluation of Der Rahmen der Geschichte Jesu by Karl Ludwig Schmidt* (1998). **P. M. Head**, *Christology and the Synoptic Problem: An Argument for Markan Priority (SNTSMS 94, 1997).* **J. G. Herder**, *Vom Erlöser der Menschen, nach unsern drei ersten Evangelien* (CS 2, 1796) 149-233; *Von Gottes Sohn, der Welt Heiland, nach Johannes Evangelium: Nebst einer Regel der Zusammenstimmung unserer Evangelien aus ihrer Entstehung* *und Ordnung* (CS 3, 1797) 301-416. **A. Hilgenfeld**, "Die Evangelien und die geschichtliche Gestalt Jesu," *ZWT* 7 (1863) 311-40, esp. 311-27. **P. Hoffmann, T. Hieke, and U. Bauer,** *Synoptic Concordance: A Greek Concordance to the First Three Gospels in Synoptic Arrangement, Statistically Evaluated, Including Occurrences in Acts* (4 vols. 1999-2000). **P. L. Hofrichter,** *Modell und Vorlage der Synoptiker: Das vorredaktionelle "Johannesevangelium"* (Theologische Texte und Studien 6, 2002²a); *Für und wider die Priorität des Johannesevangeliums* (Theologische Texte und Studien, 9, 2002b). **H. J. Holtzmann**, *Die synoptischen Evangelien* (1863). **H. J. de Jonge**, "Augustine on the Interrelations of the Gospels," *The Four Gospels, 1992* (FS F. Neirynck, BETL 100, 3 vols. ed. F. Van Segbroeck et al., 1992) 3:2409-417. **S. Hultgren**, *Narrative Elements in the Double Tradition: A Study of Their Place Within the Framework of the Gospel Narrative* (BZNW 113, 2002). **W. H. Kelber**, *The Oral and the Written Gospel: The Hermeneutics of Speaking and Writing in Synoptic Tradition, Mark, Paul, and Q* (1983). **R. Kieffer**, "Die Bedeutung der modernen Linguistik für die Auslegung biblischer Texte" *TZ* 30 (1974) 223-33. **J. B. Koppe**, *Marcus non epitomator Matthaei* (1782; repr. in *Sylloge commentationum theologicarum* [ed. D. J. Pott and G. A. Ruperti, 1800] 1:35-69). **M. Krämer,** *Die Entstehungsgeschichte der synoptischen Evangelien: Das Matthäusevangelium* (1997). **M. Labahn and A. Schmidt (eds.),** *Jesus, Mark and Q: The Teaching of Jesus and Its Earliest Records* (JSNTSup 214, 2001). **K. Lachmann**, "De ordine narrationum in Evangeliis synopticis," *TSK* 8 (1835) 570-90 (partial ET in *The Two-Source Hypothesis: A Critical Appraisal* 1985, 123-39). **G. E. Lessing**, "New Hypothesis Concerning the Evangelists Regarded as Merely Human Historians" (1778; repr. in his *Theologischer Nachlass* 1784, 45-82; ET in *Lessing's Theological Writings,* ed. H. Chadwick, 1956, 65-81). **T. R. W. Longstaff**, *Synopsis of Mark, A CD: A Synopsis of the First Three Gospels Showing the Parallels to the Markan Text* (2002) **T. R. W. Longstaff and A. Thomas**, *The Synoptic Problem: A Bibliography, 1716-1988* (New Gospel Studies 4, 1988). **A. B. Lord**, "The Gospels as Oral Traditional Literature," *The Relationships Among the Gospels: An Interdisciplinary Dialogue* (TUMSR 5, 1978) 33-91. **A. J. McNicol, and edited by D. B Peabody**, *One Gospel From Two: Mark's Use of Matthew and Luke* (2002). **A. J. McNicol, D. L. Dungan, and D. B. Peabody** (eds.), *Beyond the Q Impasse: Luke's Use of Matthew. A Demonstration by the Research Team of the International Institute for Gospel Studies* (1996). **W. Marxsen**, *Mark the Evangelist* (FRLANT 67, 1956; ET 1969). **H. U. Meyboom**, *A History and Critique of the Origin of the Marcan Hypothesis* (1866; ET New Gospel Studies 8, ed. and tr. J. Kiwet, 1993). **P. Nautin**, *L'évangile retrouvé: Jésus et l'évangile primitif* (Christianisme Antique, 1998). **F. Neirynck**, *Duality in Mark* (BETL 31, 1972); *Minor Agreements of Matthew and Luke Against Mark with a Cumulative List* (BETL 37, 1974). **D. J. Neville**, *Arguments from Order in Synoptic Source Criticism: A History and Critique* (New Gospel Studies 7, 1994); *Mark's Gospel— Prior or Posterior?: A Reappraisal of the Phenomenon of Order* (JSNTSup 222, 2002). **K. F. Nickle**, *The Synoptic Gospels: An Introduction* (2001²). **H. H. Oliver**, "The Epistle of Eusebius to Carpianus: Textual Tradition and Translation," *NovT* 3 (1959) 138-145. **B. Orchard**, "The Historical Tradition," *The Order of the Synoptics: Why Three Synoptic Gospels?* (1987) 111-226. **B. Orchard and T. R. W. Longstaff** (eds.), *J. J. Griesbach: Synoptic and Text-critical Studies, 1776-1976* (SNTSMS 34, 1978). **D. E. Orton** (ed.), *The Synoptic Problem and Q: Selected Studies From Novum Testamentum* (Brill's Readers in Biblical Studies 4, 1999). **H. Owen**, *Observations on the Four Gospels Tending Chiefly to Ascertain the Times of the Publication and to Illustrate the Form and Manner of Their Composition* (1764); *The Intent and Propriety of the Scripture Miracles Considered and Explained, in a Series of Sermons Preached in the Parish Church of St. Mary Le-Bow in the Years 1769, 1770, and 1771* (Boyle Lectures, 2 vols. 1773). **K. Paffenroth**, *The Story of Jesus According to L* (JSNTSup 147, 1997). **N. H. Palmer**, "Lachmann's Argument," *NTS* 13 (1967) 368-78. **D. B. Peabody,**

"Augustine and the Augustinian Hypothesis: A Reexamination of Augustine's Thought in De consensu evangelistarum," *New Synoptic Studies* (ed. W. R. Farmer, 1983) 37-64; "Chapters in the History of the Linguistic Argument for Solving the Synoptic Problem: The Nineteenth Century in Context," *Jesus, the Gospels, and the Church: Essays in Honor of W. R. Farmer* (ed. E. P. Sanders, 1987) 47-68; "H. J. Holtzmann and His European Colleagues: Aspects of the Nineteenth-century European Discussion of Gospel Origins," *Biblical Studies and the Shifting of Paradigms, 1850-1914* (ed. H. G. Reventlow and W. R. Farmer, JSOTSup 192, 1995) 50-131. **B. Reicke**, *The Roots of the Synoptic Gospels* (1986); "From Strauss to Holtzmann and Meijboom," *NovT* 29 (1987) 1-21. **H. G. Reventlow and W. R. Farmer** (eds.), *Biblical Studies and the Shifting of Paradigms, 1850-1914* (JSOTSup 192, 1995). **H. Riesenfeld**, *The Gospel Tradition and Its Beginnings* (1957). **J. Rohde**, *Rediscovering the Teaching of the Evangelists* (1966; ET, NTL, 1968). **P. Rolland**, *Les premiers Évangiles: Un nouveau regard sur le probléme synoptique* (LD 116, 1984). **H. Rollmann**, "Baron F. von Hügel and the Conveyance of German Protestant Biblical Criticism in Roman Catholic Modernism," *Biblical Studies and the Shifting of Paradigms, 1850-1914* (1995) 197-222. **E. P. Sanders and M. Davies**, *Studying the Synoptic Gospels* (1989) 51-119. **W. Sanday** (ed.), *Oxford Studies in the Synoptic Problem* (1911). **F. Schleiermacher**, *A Critical Essay on the Gospel of Luke* (1817; ET 1825, repr. *as Luke: A Critical Study* [Schleiermacher Studies and Translations 13, 1993]); "Über die Zeugnisse des Papias von unsern ersten beiden Evangelien," *TSK* 5 (1832) 735-68. **A. Schweitzer**, *The Quest of the Historical Jesus* (1906; ET, 1910). **R. Simon**, *A Critical History of the Text of the NT* (1689; ET 1689) chaps. 7-9. **R. H. Stein**, *Studying the Synoptic Gospels: Origin and Interpretation* (2001[2]). **G. C. Storr**, *Ueber den Zweck der evangelischen Geschichte und der Briefe Johannis* (1786) 274-307. **D. F. Strauss**, *The Life of Jesus, Critically Examined* (2 vols. 1835-36; ET 3 vols. 1846, repr. with additional material, LJS, 1972). **G. Strecker (ed.)**, *Minor Agreements: Symposium Göttingen, 1991* (Göttinger theologische Arbeiten 50, 1993). **B. H. Streeter**, *The Four Gospels: A Study of Origins* (1924). **F. A. Stroth**, "Von Interpolationen im Evangelium Matthaei," *RBML* 9 (1781) 99-156. **R. L. Thomas** (ed.), *Three Views on the Origins of the Synoptic Gospels* (2002). **C. M. Tuckett**, *The Revival of the Griesbach Hypothesis: An Analysis and Appraisal* (SNTSMS 44, 1983). **L. Vaganay**, *La probléme synoptique: Une hypothèse de travail* (Bdt 3, 1, 1954); *Jesus and the Oral Gospel Tradition* (ed. H. Wansbrough, 1991). **C. H. Weisse**, *Die evangelische Geschichte kritisch und philosophisch bearbeitet* (2 vols. 1838) 56-87. **C. G. Wilke**, *Der Urevangelist, oder, exegetisch kritische Untersuchung über das Verwandtschaftsverhältniss der drei ersten Evangelien* (1838) 4-17, 656-91.

B. Reicke and D. B. Peabody

Q (The Sayings Gospel)

1. *Nature and Extent.* Q (from the German *Quelle*, "source") is a hypothetical source entailed in the two-document hypothesis, which holds that Mark is prior to Matt and Luke and that Matt and Luke independently used Mark. In order to account for the approximately 4,500 words of non-Markan (double tradition) material that Matt shares with Luke, it is necessary to posit a second common source consisting mainly of sayings of Jesus[†§]. The fact that there is high verbal agreement between Matt and Luke in much of the double tradition, coupled with the fact that more than one-third of the sayings occur in the same relative order in Matt and Luke (even though they are fused with different Markan contexts), makes the conclusion virtually inescapable that Q was a written document rather than simply a body of oral tradition (J. Kloppenborg 1987, 72-80). Matt and Luke independently combined Mark with Q and hence do not agree on the specific ways Q was attached to Markan contexts; but since they used a written document, both were influenced by Q's order and hence display significant agreements in the relative ordering of sayings.

The idea of a collection of sayings can be traced back as far as H. Marsh[§] (1801), who argued that the Synoptics derived from two sources: א, a Semitic proto-gospel and a sayings collection, and ב, containing both the material common to Matt and Luke and many of the parables and sayings used only by Matt or by Luke. F. Schleiermacher[§] (1832) later posited an Aramaic sayings collection used by Matt to compose his five discourses (Matt 5–7; 10; 13:1-52; 18; 23–25) and argued that this collection was the Hebrew *logia* (oracles) to which Papias[§] referred (Eusebius *Hist. eccl.* 3.39.16). The origins of the modern two-document hypothesis can be found in the work of K. Lachmann[§] (1835), who argued that, since it is easier to suggest reasons for Matt altering Mark's order of pericopae than vice versa, Mark probably stood closer to a now-lost primitive gospel narrative than did Matt or Luke. In 1838 C. Weisse[§] took the step of identifying canonical Mark (Canon of the Bible*[§]) with Lachmann's primitive gospel narrative, since Mark was the common denominator between Matt and Luke and appeared to be more primitive than the other two Gospels. In order to account for the shared non-Markan material, Weisse invoked Papias's logia as a common source that Matthew and Luke independently consulted. With this, the two-document hypothesis was born.

During the nineteenth century several variations of this hypothesis were proposed, each implying a different profile for the sayings source. Some scholars hypothesized a primitive version of Mark (Ur-Markus) that included some of the double tradition (e.g., Luke 3:7-9, 16-17; 4:1-13; 6:20-49; 7:1-10) and, therefore, a sayings source that was reduced in size (Weisse 1856; H. Holtzmann 1863); others posited a much expanded sayings source that contained Markan material (H. Wendt 1886; A. Resch 1898). The appeal of such speculative hypotheses declined significantly following P. Wernle's analysis of the Synoptic Problem*[§] (1899), which argued that an Ur-Markus was quite unnecessary to account for the form of Matt and Luke. This insight meant that the sayings source, by that time known simply as "Q" (J. Weiss 1890), became more or less coextensive with the double tradition and with the few instances where Matt and Luke have a longer version of a story that is also preserved in Mark (e.g., the preaching of John the Baptist, the temptation story, the Beelzebul accusation, and the parables of the mustard seed and leaven).

In the early part of the twentieth century several reconstructions of Q in Greek were published (A. von Harnack 1907; B. Weiss 1907; W. Haupt 1913), of which the most important and least idiosyncratic was von Harnack's[§]. Important discussions of the extent, order, style, and characteristics of Q followed (G. Castor 1918; C. Patton 1915; B. Streeter 1911, 1924); and in

1937 T. Manson[§] produced what would be the first commentary on Q. However, the rise of Form Criticism*[§] and its attention to oral tradition put Q as a document into eclipse, especially in Germany. The two-document hypothesis continued to be affirmed, but little attention was paid to Q's Literary*[§] and editorial features; there were even occasional, if ultimately unconvincing, suggestions that Q might have been oral (M. Dibelius 1935, 235; J. Jeremias 1930).

With the success of Redaction Criticism*[§] following World War II, efforts were rekindled to describe Q's literary organization and theology and to situate it on the landscape of primitive Christianity (D. Lührmann 1969; P. Hoffmann 1972; S. Schulz 1972; A. Polag 1977). Since the 1980s, a large number of studies have appeared examining the theology, genre, literary history, and social setting of the document (see D. Scholer 1989, with yearly supplements). Renewed interest in Q highlighted the need for a critical text to replace the sometimes ad hoc and idiosyncratic reconstructions previously used. The International Q Project (IQP), begun in 1989, is producing a critical edition of Q (J. Robinson et al. 1999) along with a multivolume database of reconstructions of Q from 1838 to the present (Robinson et al. 1996-).

The IQP text of Q contains 251 verses, some (unbracketed) assigned to Q with a high probability and others (bracketed) with less probability. Texts in braces {24-26} probably do not belong to Q. The resultant text, in Lukan versification, includes: 3:2*b*-3, 7-9, 16*b*-17, [21-22]; 4:1-13, 16; 6:20*b*-23, {24-26}, 27-28, 35*c*, 29, [Q/Matt 5:41], 30, 31, 32-33/34, {35*ab*}, 36, 37, {38*ab*}, 38*c*, 39-45, 46-49; 7:1*b*, 3, {4-6*a*}, 6*b*-10, 18-19, {20-21}, 22-23, 24-28, {29-30}, 31-35; 9:{1-2}, 57-60; 10:2-3, 4-6, [7*a*], 7*b*-[8], 9-11, 12-15, {Matt 11:23*b*-24}, 16, 21-22, {Matt 11:28-30}, 23-24, {25-28}; 11:2-4, {5-8}, 9-13, 14-15, 17-20, [21-22], 23, 24-26, [27-28], 16, 29-32, 33-35, [36], 39*a*, 42, 39*b*-41, 43-44, 46, 52, 47-51; 12:2-12, {Matt 10:23}, {12:13-14, 16-21}, 22-31, {32} 33-34, {35-38}, 39-40, 42b-46, [49], {50}, 51-53, [54-56], 58-59; 13:18-19, 20-21, 24, 25, 26-27, 28-29, [30], 34-35; 14:{1-4}, [5], {6}; 14:11/18:14; 14:[16-24], 26-27; 17:33; 14:34-35; 15:4-7, 8-10; 16:13, 16, 17, 18; 17:1*b*-2, 3*b*-4, 6*b*, {20-21}, 23-24, 37*b*, 26-27, {28-29}, 30, {31-32}, 34-35; 19:12-13, 15*b*-26; 22:28-30.

2. *History of the Interpretation of Q.* Although a sayings source approximating modern reconstructions of Q was posited as early as the 1830s, it had little impact on New Testament studies during the nineteenth century, being used instead as an algebraic variable for solving the problem of Mark's relation to Matt and Luke. Only at the beginning of the twentieth century did Q gain importance, first in relation to the quest of the historical Jesus and later for reconstructions of the history and theology of the Jesus movement. After W. Wrede[§] demolished confidence in the narrative framework and secrecy motif of Mark as reliable indexes of historical tradition, von Harnack turned to Q, declaring that it was uncontaminated by editorial bias and afforded access to the historical Jesus (1908, 171). The effort to base reconstructions of the historical Jesus on Q was short-lived, however. J. Wellhausen[§] (1905) attacked von Harnack's analysis, arguing that Q also displayed secondary editorial features and might be posterior to Mark.

With the rise of form criticism, attention quickly shifted from Jesus to the character of the early Jesus tradition, with R. Bultmann[§] appealing to Q as an instance of the intersection of two distinct streams of primitive Christian tradition, one heavily apocalyptic (Apocalypticism*[§]) and the other characterized by "thoroughly secular proverbial wisdom" (1913, 40). In the period between the world wars, Q was treated within the conceptual framework of form criticism. From a literary point of view, Q was paraenetic (Dibelius 1971[3], 233-65) or catechetical (Streeter 1924, 187-91; Manson 1949, 13-17); theologically it served as a supplement to the Easter kerygma. With the rise of redaction criticism, both the literary and the theological assessments of Q were revised. H. Tödt (1959) noted the distinctive lack of paraenetic and catechetical materials in Q and argued that Q's representation of Jesus' proclamation of the Kingdom amounted to a kerygma parallel to, but independent of, the Easter kerygma. J. Robinson (1964) advanced the thesis that Q represented an independent stream of theology focusing on the sapiential character of Q's Christology. As an instance of the genre *logoi sophon* ("words of the sages"), Q tended to associate the speaker of the wise sayings (Jesus) with heavenly Sophia (Wisdom) and ultimately displayed a Gnostic*§ proclivity that was neutralized only when Q was recast within the framework of Mark's Gospel. H. Koester (1965, 1971) likewise saw a Gnostic tendency in Q but located a decisive shift away from Gnosticism within the redaction history of Q itself: Q's original depiction of Jesus as a wisdom teacher was modified by the insertion of apocalyptic Son of Man sayings.

The studies of Robinson and Koester catalyzed a discussion of Q's genre. While a few scholars took the view that Q is *sui generis* (F. Neirynck 1976), the dominant stream of interpretation has taken seriously Q's significant component of wisdom sayings and their topical organization, the lack of a strong narrative framework, and the lack of a passion and resurrection narrative. Developing more casual suggestions by Streeter (1924), Robinson (1964) located Q on a trajectory of sapiential genres extending from Near Eastern wisdom collections to Gnostic dialogue collections (see also M. Küchler 1979). Kloppenborg (1987) combined a compositional and a generic analysis, suggesting that the earliest compositional stratum consisted of (in Lukan versification) 6:20b-49; 9:57-60, 61-62; 10:2-11, 16 (23-24?); 11:2-4, 9-13; 12:2-7, 11-12, (13-14, 15-20?), 22-31, 33-34; 13:18-19, 20-21, 24; 14:26-27; 17:33; 14:34-35. This stratum displayed strong affinities with the didactic genre of wisdom instruction, a common genre of Near Eastern wisdom (see also R. Piper 1989). It was later augmented by prophetic and other materials, most framed as *chriae* (a concise saying, applicable to daily life, often attributed to a well known person, or recounting their deeds) and eventually prefaced by the temptation story. Thus the shift toward a loose biographical presentation of Jesus' sayings is already evidenced within Q's compositional history.

M. Sato took a different view, also offering a compositional analysis of Q but suggesting that Q was composed as a prophetic book (similarly, C. Tuckett 1996). Sato included the baptism of Jesus in Q, treating it as a prophetic call story, but could find no place in this genre for most of the Q material in Luke 14-18 and so treated these as later accretions. Likewise, Sato considered Q 11:2-4, 9-13; 11:33-35; 12:2-12, 22-31, 33-34 as "unmotivated additions" to the original prophetic collection.

Other genres have been proposed. Based on an analysis of the use of verbs denoting speech, the allocation of space, topical organization, length, and general character, F. Downing (1994) has suggested that Q most closely resembles the philosophical "lives" (*bioi*), especially Cynic *bioi* like Lucian's Demonax.

In spite of differences in the assessment of Q's genre, there is wide agreement that the editing of Q has been strongly influenced by Deuteronomistic§ theology, which regarded the history of Israel as a repetitive cycle of sinfulness, prophetic calls to repentance, punishment by God, and renewed calls to repentance with threats of judgment (A. Jacobson 1992). In this schema the prophets are depicted as repentance preachers who are inevitably rejected, persecuted, and even killed. Q opens with an oracle of coming judgment (Q 3:7-9, 16-17); it privileges repentance as a central theological category (Q 3:8; 10:13; 11:32); and it views the rejection of Jesus (and John) through the lens of the deuteronomistic theology of the sorry fate of the prophets (Q 7:33-34; 11:47-51; 13:34-35). The story of Lot, invoked at several points (Q 3:2b-3, 7-9; 10:12; 17:28-29, 34-35), further dramatizes Q's announcement of an imminent fiery judgment (Kloppenborg 1991).

Q can be said to have a Christology; but it lacks the terms "Messiah" (*Christos*), "Son of David," and "King of Israel." The temptation account uses "Son of God" twice, but the main designation of Jesus is "Son of Man." This term occurs in reference to Jesus (Q 6:22; 7:34; 9:58; 11:30) and to a coming advocate or judge (Q 12:8, 10, 40; 17:24, 26, 30) but never in relation to Jesus as a suffering figure (contrast Mark). The Son of Man is treated in Q 7:33-35 as a child of heavenly Sophia along with John the Baptist. The depiction of Sophia as sending (Q 11:49-51; cf. 13:34-35) and vindicating prophetic figures, including John and Jesus, has led to suggestions that Q has a Sophia Christology or Sophialogy (cf. Wis 7:27). Q 10:21-22 comes close to depicting Jesus ("the Son") in the same exclusive relation to God that Sophia enjoyed in Second Temple wisdom literature. In this regard, Q anticipates the most vigorous development of wisdom Christology, evidenced in the Fourth Gospel.

A number of unresolved problems regarding Q's theology remain. Q's eschatology—whether it is fundamentally apocalyptic or not—is the topic of debate but turns largely on definitional issues rather than on the interpretation of individual sayings and is fueled by the agenda of historical Jesus scholarship. The lack of a passion account (and even direct references to Jesus' death) and a resurrection story raises the issue of Q's relationship to the Easter kerygma. Although it is obvious that Q presupposes Jesus' death, there is no evidence that his death is accorded specifically redemptive significance. Similarly, while Q assumes some form of vindication of Jesus by Sophia (Q 7:35; 13:35b), it does not employ the metaphor of resurrection to articulate that vindication.

Galilee is normally suggested as the provenance of Q (J. Reed 1995). The document is variously associated with a scribal (Kloppenborg 1991; Piper 1995), prophetic (Tuckett; R. Horsley 1991), or Cynic (L. Vaage 1994; B. Mack 1993) ethos. Q's attention to basic issues of subsistence, local violence and conflict, and debt and its negative representation of cities, judicial processes, rulers, and the priestly hierarchy suggest an origin in towns and villages of lower Galilee, probably before the first revolt but achieving its final form near the time of the revolt (Hoffmann 1995) or even slightly after it (M. Myllykoski 1996).

Since von Harnack, Q has been used in scholarship on Jesus and has in recent years become the focus of special attention. The stratigraphic analysis of Q proposed by Kloppenborg (1987) was employed in J. D. Crossan's book on Jesus (1991) in a larger effort to create a comprehensive stratigraphic analysis of the entire Jesus tradition. In contrast, J. Meier (1991) treats Q as an essentially unedited grab bag of sayings. Much remains to be done to clarify how the results of compositional analysis might be employed in the reconstruction of the historical Jesus. A naive understanding of literary stratigraphy has led to the misapplication of conclusions that pertain only to Q's documentary features, and to equally simplistic rejections of Q's significance for historical Jesus scholarship (Kosch 1992; Kloppenborg 1996).

Recent Q scholarship includes reconstructed editions of Q (Robinson 2002; Robinson, Hoffmann, Moreland, and Kloppenborg 2001). Neirynck, Verheyden, and Corstjens have compiled a bibliography of Q research from 1950-1995 (1998). Collected essays on Q include Asgeirsson, de Troyer, and Meyer (2000) and Hoppe and Busse (1998). Allison (2000) has studied Q's use of Scripture. Humphries studied a possible relationship between Mark and Q (1999). Kloppenborg Verbin (2000) has attempted to establish Q's social location. Various other Q studies on a variety of topics include Hultgren (2002), Loader (1997), Schröter (1997, 2001), and Zager (1996). McNicol (1996) is a substantial attempt to refute Q's very existence.

Bibliography: D. C. Allison, Jr., *The Intertextual Jesus: Scripture in Q* (2000). **J. M. Asgeirsson, K. de Troyer, and M. W. Meyer (eds.)**, *From Quest to Q: Festschrift James M. Robinson* (BETHL 146, 2000). **R. Bultmann,** "Was lässt die Spruchquelle über die Urgemeinde erkennen?" *Oldenburgisches Kirchenblatt* 19 (1913) 35-37, 41-44 (ET "What the Saying Source Reveals About the Early Church," *The Shape of Q: Signal Essays on the Sayings Gospel;* ed. J. S. Kloppenborg, 1994) 23-34. **G. D. Castor,** *Matthew's Sayings of Jesus* (1918). **J. D. Crossan,** *The Historical Jesus: The Life of a Mediterranean Peasant* (1991). **M. Dibelius,** *Die Formgeschichte des Evangeliums* (1919; ET *From Tradition to Gospel*, 1971³). **F. G. Downing,**

"A Genre for Q and a Socio-Cultural Context for Q," *JSNT* 55 (1994) 3-26. **A. von Harnack,** *Sprüche und Reden Jesu* (1907; ET *The Sayings of Jesus* 1908). **W. Haupt,** *Worte Jesu und Gemeindeüberlieferung* (UNT 3, 1913). **P. Hoffmann,** *Studien zur Theologie der Logienquelle* (NTAbh NF 8, 1972); "The Redaction of Q and the Son of Man: A Preliminary Sketch," *The Gospel Behind the Gospels: Current Studies on Q* (ed. R. A. Piper, NovTSup 75, 1995) 159-198. **H. J. Holtzmann,** *Die synoptischen Evangelien* (1863). **R. Hoppe and U. Busse,** *Von Jesus zum Christus: Christologische Studien: Festgabe für Paul Hoffmann zum 65. Geburtstag* (BZNW 93, 1998). **R. A. Horsley,** "The Q People: Renovation, not Radicalism," *Continuum* 1, 3 (1991) 49-63. **S. Hultgren,** *Narrative Elements in the Double Tradition: A Study of Their Place Within the Framework of the Gospel Narrative* (BZNW 113, 2002). **M. L. Humphries,** *Christian Origins and the Language of the Kingdom of God* (1999). **A. D. Jacobson,** *The First Gospel: An Introduction to Q* (Foundations and Facets, 1992). **J. Jeremias,** "Zur Hypothese einer schriftlichen Logienquelle Q," *ZNW* 29 (1930) 147-49. **J. S. Kloppenborg,** *The Formation of Q: Trajectories in Ancient Wisdom Literature* (Studies in Antiquity and Christianity, 1987); "City and Wasteland: Narrative World and the Beginning of the Sayings Gospel (Q)," *Semeia* 52 (1991) 145-60; "Literary Convention, Self-Evidence, and the Social History of the Q People," *Semeia* 55 (1991) 77-102; "The Sayings Gospel Q and the Quest of the Historical Jesus," *HTR* 89 (1996) 307-44. **H. Koester,** "ΓΝΩΜΑΙ ΔΙΑΦΟΡΟΙ: The Origin and Nature of Diversification in the History of Early Christianity," *HTR* 58 (1965) 279-318 (repr. *Trajectories Through Early Christianity;* ed. J. M. Robinson and H. Koester, 1971) 114-57. **D. Kosch,** "Q und Jesus," *BZ NF* 36 (1992) 30-58. **M. Küchler,** *Frühjüdische Weisheitstraditionen* (OBO 26, 1979). **K. Lachmann,** "De ordine narrationum in evangeliis synopticis," *TSK* 8 (1835) 570-90. **W. R. G. Loader,** *Jesus' Attitude Towards the Law: A Study of the Gospels* (WUNT 2/97, 1997). **D. Lührmann,** *Die Redaktion der Logienquelle* (WMANT 33, 1969). **B. L. Mack,** *The Lost Gospel: The Book of Q and Christian Origins* (1993). **T. W. Manson,** "The Sayings of Jesus," *The Mission and Message of Jesus* (1937) 299-639 (repr. *The Sayings of Jesus* 1949). **H. Marsh,** *A Dissertation on the Origin and Composition of Our Three First Canonical Gospels* (1801). **A. J. McNicol** (ed.), *Beyond the Q Impasse: Luke's Use of Matthew* (1996). **J. P. Meier,** *A Marginal Jew: Rethinking the Historical Jesus, vol. 2, Mentor, Message, and Miracles* (ABRL, 1991). **M. Myllykoski,** "The Social History of Q and the Jewish War," *Symbols and Strata: Essays on the Sayings Gospel Q* (ed. R. Uro, Publications of the Finnish Exegetical Society 65, 1996) 143-99. **F. Neirynck,** "Q," *IDBSup* (1962) 715-16. **F. Neirynck, J. Verheyden, and R. Corstjens,** *The Gospel of Matthew and the Sayings Source Q: A Cumulative Bibliography, 1950-1995* (BETHL 140, 1998). **C. S. Patton,** *Sources of the Synoptic Gospels* (University of Michigan Studies, Humanistic Series 5, 1915). **R. A. Piper,** *Wisdom in the Q-tradition: The Aphoristic Teaching of Jesus* (SNTSMS 61, 1989); "The Language of Violence and the Aphoristic Sayings in Q," *Conflict and Invention* (ed. J. S. Kloppenborg, 1995) 53-72. **A. Polag,** *Die Christologie der Logienquelle* (WMANT 45, 1977). **J. Reed,** "The Social Map of Q," *Conflict and Invention* (ed. J. S. Kloppenborg, 1995) 17-36. **A. Resch,** *Die Logia Jesu* (1898). **J. M. Robinson,** "ΛΟΓΟΙ ΣΟΦΩΝ]: Zur Gattung der Spruchquelle Q," *Zeit und Geschichte: Dankesgabe an R. Bultmann* (ed. E. Dinkler, 1964) 77-96 (ET "Logoi Sophōn: On the Gattung of Q," *In the Future of Our Religious Past* 1971) 84-130; (ed.), *The Sayings of Jesus: The Sayings Gospel Q in English* (Facets, 2002). **J. M. Robinson, P. Hoffmann, and J. S. Kloppenborg** (eds.), *The Critical Edition of Q* (1999). **J. M. Robinson, P. Hoffmann, J. S. Kloppenborg, and M. C. Moreland** (eds.), *The Sayings Gospel Q in Greek and English: with Parallels from the Gospels of Mark and Thomas* (2001). **J. M. Robinson, J. S. Kloppenborg, and P. Hoffmann** (eds.), *Documenta Q* (1996-). **M. Sato,** *Q und Prophetie* (WUNT 2, 29, 1988). **F. Schleiermacher,** "Über die Zeugnisse des Papias von unsern beiden ersten Evangelien," *TSK* 5 (1832) 735-68. **D. Scholer,** "Q Bibliography, 1981-89," *SBLSP* (ed.

D. J. Lull, 1989) 23-37. **J. Schröter,** *Erinnerung an Jesu Worte: Studien zur Rezeption der Logienüberlieferung in Markus, Q und Thomas* (WMANT 76, 1997); *Jesus und die Anfänge der Christologie: methodologische und exegetische Studien zu den Ursprüngen des christlichen Glaubens* (Biblisch-theologische Studien, 47, 2001). **S. Schulz,** *Q: Die Spruchquelle der Evangelisten* (1972). **B. H. Streeter,** "On the Original Order of Q," "St. Mark's Knowledge and Use of Q," and "The Original Extent of Q," *Oxford Studies in the Synoptic Problem* (ed. W. Sanday, 1911) 141-64, 165-83, 185-208; *The Four Gospels* (1924). **H. E. Tödt,** *Der Menschensohn in der synoptischen Überlieferung* (1959; ET *The Son of Man in the Synoptic Tradition* 1965). **C. M. Tuckett,** *Q and the History of Early Christianity* (1996). **L. E. Vaage,** *Galilean Upstarts: Jesus' First Followers According to Q* (1994). **J. S. Kloppenborg Verbin,** *Excavating Q: The History and Setting of the Sayings Gospel* (2000). **B. Weiss,** *Die Quellen des Lukasevangeliums* (1907). **J. Weiss,** "Die Verteidigung Jesu gegen den Vorwurf des Bündnisses mit Beelzebul," *TSK* 63 (1890) 555-69. **C. H. Weisse,** *Die evangelische Geschichte, kritisch und philosophisch bearbeitet* (1838); *Die Evangelienfrage in ihrem gegenwärtigen Stadium* (1856). **J. Wellhausen,** *Einleitung in die drei ersten Evangelien* (1905). **H. H. Wendt,** *Die Lehre Jesu* (1886). **P. Wernle,** *Die synoptische Frage* (1899). **W. Wrede,** *The Messianic Secret* (1901; ET 1971). **W. Zager,** *Gottesherrschaft und Endgericht in der Verkündigung Jesu: Eine Untersuchung zur markinischen Jesusüberlieferung einschliesslich der Q-Parallelen* (BZNW 82, 1996).

J. S. KLOPPENBORG

GENERAL NEW TESTAMENT ARTICLES

Paul

1. *The Precritical Era.* Paul[§] has never been easy to understand. From the start, his writings were open to quite different interpretations, even among those who were the most keen on preserving his legacy. In Paul's name Ephesians produced an account of divine mysteries in Gnostic[§] language while the Pastorals[†§] made Paul conform to the "sound doctrine" of the incipient ecclesiastical tradition. Focusing on the radical elements in Paul's writings, Marcion[§] produced a reading purified of anything that might suggest continuity with Judaism. Paul was venerated by Gnostics and hated by Jewish Christians for the same reason: He had done away with Hebrew Bible law. But just that view was denied by mainstream church fathers, who tried to reduce Paul's statements to a self-consistent system that would not contradict Hebrew Bible revelation (M. Wiles [1967]). These very issues—Paul's relation to the legacy of Israel and his consistency—still haunt Pauline interpretation.

Paul's importance to the church was enhanced when his ideas on grace were taken up and developed by Augustine[§]. Paul became a central support for Augustine's doctrines of original sin, human beings' lack of free will, and double predestination.

The Reformation was fought in his name. Holding Paul's teaching of justification by faith to be all-important, Luther[§] underlined, in the Augustinian vein, that persons can be saved only by divine grace through faith—not by works of the law. "Law" was taken in a very general sense. When Paul condemned "works," he had moral activity in general in mind (morality viewed as religious merit). The essence of sin consists in human self-reliance; therefore, those who keep the law are those most opposed to God's will. The purpose of the law is to teach human beings their helplessness and nothingness; it is used by God as "a large and powerful hammer" to crush human "presumption of righteousness" (F. Watson [1986,] 2-4; S. Westerholm [1988], 3-12).

While not ignoring Paul's positive statements on the law (it begins to be fulfilled in the believers with the aid of the Spirit), Luther put the main emphasis on Paul's negative assertions. In contrast, Calvin[§] emphasized Paul's continuity with the Hebrew Bible. Paul's criticisms were not aimed at the biblical revelation itself but rather at a misunderstood "bare law in a narrow sense" as seen "apart from Christ" (C. Cranfield [1975-79], 859). This inner-Protestant tension still exists in Pauline exegesis.

2. *From the Seventeenth to the Nineteenth Centuries.* Various Reformation commentators freely exploited Paul for their own purposes. Things began to change when such scholars as H. Grotius[§] and J. Locke[§] emphasized the importance of the literary and historical context of each passage (Kümmel [1970; ET 1973,] 33-38, 51-54).

Eighteenth-century scholars made a programmatic distinction between historical exegesis and dogmatic exposition. The result, however, was not yet disinterested historical study but rather a series of attempts to purify Christianity from elements that were temporally conditioned in order to turn it into a timeless ethical belief (J. Semler in A. Schweitzer [1911; ET 1912] 4-7). Slightly later and in the same vein, H. Paulus undertook to demonstrate "the agreement between the Gospel and a rational faith" by way of a purely moral interpretation (Schweitzer, [ET 1912], 10-11).

F. C. Baur's[§] analysis of Paul's relation to the primitive Christian community signaled a new era. An attempt to interpret Paul's thought historically had been made shortly before by L. Usteri (1799-1833; see Kümmel [ET 1973], 75-97), who had been anticipated by J. Toland[§] and T. Morgan[§]. However, Baur was the first to anchor Paul in place and time—actually, in the midst of fierce conflict.

While Usteri had still held that Paul's ideas were in full agreement with the rest of the New Testament, Baur claimed that Paul had developed his doctrine in complete opposition to that of the primitive community. Baur was assisted in his perception by G. W. F. Hegel's (1770-1831) dialectic of thesis, antithesis, and synthesis; but Hegel's importance to him has often been exaggerated. Baur described the conflicts in the early church somewhat schematically and was led to give too late a date to many texts that did not correspond to his idea of an early document. Nonetheless, that Paul was involved in conflicts is a fact quite independent of Baur's Hegelian perspective.

In Baur's view, Paul opposed Jewish exclusivism (held by the Jerusalem apostles), wishing to replace it with Christian universalism. If individuals could attain righteousness only by the works of the law, then it could only be attained by the Jews. Paul alone had understood the universal significance of Jesus*[§], and Pauline Christianity removed all that was particularist from the idea of God.

Baur's view conflicts with the standard Lutheran view. Luther and his followers made a bold generalization: Paul was attacking not just Judaism but also the universal human error of trying to earn salvation. Baur, in contrast, connected Paul's theology very closely with his concrete circumstances (Watson, 12-13). One looks in vain for a critique of religious hubris in his account of Paul Christianity is superior to Judaism just as the absolute and universal is superior to the particularist and local.

H. Lüdemann (1842-1933) discovered in Paul two different ideas of salvation (1872). Alongside a juridical/ethical Jewish doctrine of justification by faith there is a realistic or sacramental/mystical Hellenistic doctrine of redemption associated with baptism; the latter is more important to Paul. With Lüdemann the questions of the unity of Paul's thought and of its rootedness in either Jewish or gentile soil entered the agenda of scholarship and have remained there ever since.

H. Holtzmann's* textbook (1897, 1912[2]) is a classic monument of liberal theology. In it, too, Paul's "doctrine" appears as a combination of several independent, often contradictory, lines of thought, some of Jewish, others of Greek origin (with a preponderance of the latter). Paul was engaged in a mental struggle to combat his own past and also to come to terms with it. His thought is a secondary attempt to make sense of his conversion experience (understood as a breakdown under the burden of the law) in theoretical terms; its permanent value consists in the experience-based religious and moral insight that underlies the theory. However, in Paul's generalization of his personal experience lurks the danger of fanaticism. Liberal exegetes (Holtzmann; J. Weiss [1917; ET 1970]; W. Wrede [1904; ET 1907]) felt free to criticize those aspects of the apostle's thought that did not satisfy them intellectually or religiously.

3. *The History-of-Religions Perspective.* Liberal scholars recognized the existence of strange elements in Paul's thought but generally played them down, finding greater interest in those layers in which Paul seemed attuned to Jesus' (supposedly) simple religion of the heart. Yet from the ranks of the liberals arose some scholars who drew attention to the very oddities that made little sense to the modern mind and even claimed that such features lay at the center of Paul's thought.

H. Gunkel* (1888) argued that Paul did not conceive of the "Spirit" in a purely ethical sense but, realistically, as God's supernatural, miracle-working power. The early Christian thought world was thus made to appear strange and puzzling. O. Everling's book on angels in the same year had a similar effect, showing that Paul stood in the "late Jewish" angelological and demonological tradition; thus Paul's views were not to be modernized or spiritualized. In 1893 R. Kabisch[§] made a strong case that eschatological expectation lies at the center of Paul's thought. More problematic was his view that everything spiritual goes back to something corporeal, e.g., the Spirit is a super-earthly substance that must be found in one's body if one is to be resurrected.

Kabisch interpreted Paul in an extremely anti-modern way, paying no attention to the question of the apostle's contemporary relevance. Unlike H. Lüdemann, he traced Paul's doctrine of salvation back to Jewish eschatology rather than to Hellenistic influences. Kabisch's interpretation was enthusiastically taken over by A. Schweitzer[§], who regarded Paul as a thoroughly Jewish and very consistent thinker. However, Schweitzer was only able to publish his views in full in 1930 when Pauline scholarship already found itself in a quite new situation.

A splendid provisory synthesis was given by W. Wrede[§] (1904), who underlined the necessity of interpreting Paul in purely historical terms. Like Kabisch he recognized the importance of eschatology. He also called attention to Paul's fundamental pessimism, to his sense of relief at being released from the hostile angelic powers of this world, and to his understanding of salvation as an objective event mediated through baptism. Although Wrede was critical of Kabisch's "materialistic metaphysics," he held fast to a "physical" view of redemption. Paul's thoughts on justification by faith are, in contrast, a secondary theory arising from conflicts in which he became involved. Paul was not mainly concerned with the destiny of the individual but with that of humankind, i.e., with salvation history. His theology is based on rabbinic thought and Gnosticism; thus contradictions and problematic assertions are quite common. But Paul created a grand overall vision, so much so that he must be regarded as the second founder of Christianity. Wrede sharply posed the problem of "Jesus and Paul." Unlike Baur and most liberals, he denied that Paul was the authentic interpreter of Jesus and suggested the necessity of choosing between the two "founders."

Soon enough the issues were redefined. W. Heitmüller[§] (1912), followed by W. Bousset[§] (1921; ET 1970) and R. Bultmann[§] (1929, 1934), set out to uncover traces of a pre-Pauline Hellenistic Christianity that had existed between the time of the Jerusalem church and Paul and whose views Paul had adopted and developed further. The real problem was not "Jesus and Paul," but "Jesus and Hellenistic Christianity." It became important to ask how Paul had handled the inherited (Palestinian and Hellenistic) Christian traditions: What is their relation to the creative reinterpretation and new insights in Paul's letters?

Along with this reorientation went the discovery of analogies to Paul's (or the Hellenistic community's) ideas and sacramental practices from mystery religions, Gnosticism, and Mandaean texts. Taking his cue from 1 Corinthians, R. Reitzenstein[§] interpreted Paul consistently in terms of Hellenistic mysticism and Gnosticism. Nonetheless, because he failed to deal adequately with many crucial issues (e.g., the law and eschatology), his picture at best serves to underline the multifaceted nature of Paul's thought.

4. *The Epoch of Dialectical Theology.* At the beginning of the twentieth century, then, there were strong impulses toward a historical study of Paul's thought in the context of Hellenistic religion and culture. In part these leads were followed up in the next few decades. Bultmann elaborated Reitzenstein's view of a Gnostic myth supposed to underlie Paul's theology and interpreted Paul against that backdrop, as did his pupils, notably E. Käsemann[§]. In 1933 the latter interpreted "flesh" and "Spirit" as kinds of Gnostic *aeons* but did not deny the significance of eschatological expectation for Paul.

Religion-historical analysis was to stay in the background, however, due to the intervention of K. Barth[§] and dialectial theology. Even Bultmann and Käsemann pursued their radical history-of-religions work (Religionsgeschichtliche Schule[*§]) in the theologically charged framework of Barthian neo-orthodoxy. Barth held that contemporary human problems are identical to those Paul faced and that Paul's answers should be ours as well. An expositor should wrestle with the text of Romans until all but forgetting that he or she did not write it.

This approach was endorsed by Bultmann, who emphasized the importance of not remaining a detached observer. An interpreter has to clarify the significance of the texts for "me." To do so, one must distinguish between what Paul said and what he really meant. Although Bultmann criticized liberal and history-of-religions exegetes for an alleged disinterest in the existential message, his method was structurally similar to theirs. The liberals had found the New Testament's essential message in the preaching of (a modernized) Jesus and criticized aspects of Paul's theology in its light. Bultmann, by comparison, found the true subject matter of the New Testament in the human self-understanding manifest in the texts, most clearly in Paul's writing. Thus Bultmann often wrote about "eschatological existence"; but he really meant "authentic existence," as described by the existentialist philosopher M. Heidegger (1889-1976). Temporal eschatological elements in Paul were dismissed as mere illustrations of the real message.

For Bultmann, Paul was (along with John) a central figure in New Testament theology; all other formulations were to be gauged by Pauline standards. Yet Bultmann modernized Paul, and his approach was more intellectualist than that of the previous generation. Dialectical theology, turning against "religion" in the name of the kerygma, disliked the category of "experience" that had been central to liberal interpreters. Moreover, it had become easier to deemphasize experience in Pauline interpretation since W. Kümmel[§] had shown (1929) that Paul's conversion experience had been misconstrued and that Paul did not break down under the burden of the law.

Bultmann presented Paul's theology as a coherent system. Its center was anthropological: human existence "prior to the revelation of faith" and then "under faith." In sound Lutheran fashion the individual's relation to God became central again.

Bultmann elaborated Luther's generalized understanding of Paul's critique of the law: Paul was really attacking human self-assertion. In Judaism a specifically human striving had taken on a culturally distinct form, and Bultmann drew a desolate caricature of this Jewish legalism. Human effort to achieve salvation by keeping the law is an expression of human sin, of the need for recognition. Faith is the renunciation of such striving, a new self-understanding in acknowledgment of one's utter dependence on God.

Bultmann was aware of elements that did not rise to the level of Paul's real intentions as Bultmann saw them, e.g., the notion of an eschatological battle with spirit powers or of a "history of salvation" in general. His approach differed from that of his teacher, J. Weiss[§]. Weiss too had discerned different layers in Paul, maintaining that while the mythico-eschatological level is unimportant to us, Paul's talk of grace and love is seminal. But Weiss had made it clear that the two levels can only be separated in hindsight by modern scholars, and he did not let the separation guide his account of Paul's thought. Bultmann, on the contrary, programmatically refused to distinguish between historical reconstruction and contemporizing interpretation; many exegetes still adhere to this way of seeing the task.

Bultmann's interpretation was rejected by such scholars as O. Cullmann[§] (1965; ET 1967), J. Munck[§] (1954), U. Wilckens (1974), and Kümmel, who had a higher view of salvation history and wished to make God's act in Christ, rather than anthropology, the starting point of Paul's theology. Their historical criticism was well founded. However, they failed to see as clearly as Bultmann did how serious a problem it is to make sense of Paul's ancient message in modern times.

The fact that Bultmann's method results in historical distortion was in due course recognized by his own pupils as well. H. Conzelmann followed in Bultmann's footsteps, but he tried to do more justice to the historical component in Paul's thought. His work is beset with a formidable tension: If objectified, many of Paul's statements appear to be simply absurd; when, however, one penetrates through the salvation-historical surface to the underlying existential level, a profound revelation of the human plight emerges (Conzelmann [1967; ET 1969,] 225-28).

Käsemann criticized Bultmann for concentrating one-sidedly on the individualistic aspects in Paul's writings and neglecting their communality, concern for creation, and apocalyptic eschatology (see Apocalypticism*§). The main issue for Paul is seen not as the justification of the individual, but as the necessity that "Christ must reign." God's "righteousness" does not just denote God's gift to humans (so Bultmann); it bespeaks the Creator's right over creation (so also Paul Stuhlmacher [1965, 1966²]). An apocalyptic perspective was important for Paul in his battle against enthusiasts who held that everything Christians hoped for had already been realized with the resurrection of Christ and in the baptism of the believer. Käsemann combined his apocalyptic interpretation with a Lutheran-Bultmannian understanding of Paul's attitude to the law, using Paul's attack on legalism polemically "against every form of conservatism, especially theological or ecclesiastical" (Watson, 9).

5. Paul and Judaism. Pauline research has increasingly come to focus on the problem of Paul's relation to Judaism. In 1930 Schweitzer made a powerful, if rather forced, attempt to locate Paul's thought in apocalyptic Judaism. He focused on Paul's "Christ mysticism," contending that the believer's participation in the Lord and deliverance from bondage to hostile spirit powers are to be taken in a realistic sense. Schweitzer traced Paul's mysticism back to eschatology, regarding it as an intellectual attempt to account for the anomaly that although the Messiah had come, the times had not visibly changed.

The discussion was taken further in 1948 by W. D. Davies§, who interpreted Paul as a rabbi who believed that the Messiah had come. Davies' Paul is not diametrically opposed to Judaism; in fact there is great continuity, and Paul regards his new faith as a fulfillment of Judaism. Since Davies' article, attention to Paul's Jewish background has dominated the scene, and the issue of Hellenistic influences has faded (yet see the work of H.-D. Betz [1979]). The discovery of the Dead Sea Scrolls§ has strengthened this trend; scholars claim to have found precedents at Qumran for some of Paul's deviations from Hebrew Bible or rabbinic ideas. Another source that might seem to mediate between standard Jewish ideas and Paul's has been detected in wisdom traditions.

In painting the portrait of Paul in continuity with his Jewish past, Davies did not discuss the structural differences between Pauline and rabbinic religion. These were brought to light by Jewish scholars as early as 1914, when C. Montefiore§ pointed out that Paul paid no attention to the twin rabbinic ideas of repentance and forgiveness. Montefiore sought the reason for this strange omission in Paul's Hellenistic Jewish origins.

Like Davies, H.-J. Shoeps (1959) traced a number of individual Pauline concepts and notions back to rabbinic origins; but as for the essence of the two faiths, he found a crucial difference. Paul had severed the law from the context of the covenant to which it belonged in Palestinian Judaism. Like Montefiore, Schoeps found the reason in Paul's rootedness in Hellenistic Judaism, in which a legalistic development had supposedly taken place.

E. P. (1977) opened up a "new perspective on Paul." (J. Dunn [1983]). Sanders compared the "pattern" of rabbinic religion with that of Paul's, terming the former "covenantal nomism" (to avoid the somber overtones of "legalism"). A Jew wished to conform to the law, not because of self-assertion (Bultmann), but out of gratitude to God, who had made a covenant with Israel and obliged the people to obey the covenantal order. Paul displays a different pattern: "participationist eschatology." The mystical-sacramental union with Christ is the real center of his religion (in this, Schweitzer was right). Paul abandoned Judaism because in Christ he had found something better (not because of the supposed inferiority of nomistic piety). Humanity prior to faith (Bultmann) is not Paul's starting-point. Instead, he thinks backward from the solution to the plight. God has provided for universal salvation in Christ; it follows that all persons must be in need of this salvation (Sanders [1977] 474-75).

Paul abandoned Judaism because God had made salvation accessible in a new way. That is why Paul showed no interest in repentance, the classical Jewish way to salvation (Montefiore's problem). Paul's point was that commands of the Torah such as circumcision and the sabbath are not to be imposed on Gentiles who join the eschatological community (cf. also K. Stendahl [1976]; H. Räisänen [1983, 1987²]). Sanders thus breaks with the standard Lutheran understanding of Paul; in a sense, Baur with his emphasis on universalism might be taken as a precursor of this line of thought.

Recent studies by Jewish scholars argue along somewhat similar lines but from wider perspectives. A. Segal (1990) underlines the significance and the mystical nature of Paul's conversion experience, which he elucidates with sociological conversion studies (see Sociology and New Testament Studies[†§]). D. Boyarin (1994) points out that Paul's "universalizing drive" amounts, from a rabbinic perspective, to an eradication of the Jewish value system.

The view that connects Paul's break with Judaism intimately with the inclusion of gentile converts is strongly opposed by interpreters who cling to Bultmann's notion that the universal phenomenon of human pride is at stake (e.g., G. Klein [1973]; H. Hübner [1978, 1980²]). On the other hand, a number of scholars argue that Paul did not at all break with Judaism (e.g., Cranfield, Dunn); rather, he only rejected a false interpretation of the law. While the former group of scholars perpetuates Luther's concern, the latter can look to Calvin as their exegetical ancestor.

It was inevitable that at some point the Holocaust would cast its sinister shadow over Pauline studies. Some scholars (notably R. Ruether [1974]) ascribe to Paul a share in giving rise to the anti-Jewish sentiment that was to bear such horrendous fruit. Others (J. Gager [1983]; L. Gaston [1987]) try to whitewash Paul by claiming that he has nothing negative to say of Israel's covenantal privileges, neither of the law nor of its putative misinterpretation. In their judgment Paul did not even regard Jesus as the Messiah of Israel but only as the Savior of the Gentiles. These latter interpreters labor hard to do justice to Judaism, but they are forced to give many Pauline passages a twisted exegesis. In a less extreme vein, F. Mussner (1979) and others infer from Romans 11 that Paul reckoned with a special way to salvation for the Jews (in the parousia) independently of the failure of the Christian mission to them. In the eyes of still others even this reading makes Paul revoke most of his usual christological preaching, so they are not convinced.

U. Schnelle (1983, 1986²) takes up the concern of the history-of-religions school in his attempt to pinpoint the relation between justification and "being in Christ." Paul adopted and developed a Hellenistic theology that connected justification and new life with baptism, which is the experiential background of Paul's talk of justification. Being in Christ and possessing the Spirit are more central than justification by faith.

6. *Paul's Consistency.* At the turn of the twentieth century, liberal exegetes did not hesitate to assert that Paul is often inconsistent. With the upsurge of dialectical theology such criticisms receded, but they have begun began to reappear at the close of the century. While some scholars are content with speaking of a dialectic in Paul's thought, others believe that they can discern genuine discrepancies.

One way to account for such discrepancies is to posit that Paul's thought developed over time. H. Hübner argues that Paul's thinking on the law underwent a marked change between Galatians and Romans. In Galatians Paul distanced himself from Judaism and the law; in Romans he stressed his continuity with them. In Paul's view of Israel there is an analogous development from the negative statements in 1 Thessalonians and Galatians to the positive ones in Romans 11.

The development theory must face the problem that there are "radical" assertions also in Romans (Romans 9 is no less severe on Israel than is Galatians). Räisänen has revived the liberal approach: Paul is inconsistent on many points, for he is wrestling with problems that do not allow for neat solutions. Why should Christ have abolished a law given by God for life? Why is Paul's gospel being rejected by the chosen people? Räisänen sees Paul's theology as secondary to his experience, as did the liberals; but the experience in question includes Paul's social experience of conflict.

Other related attempts to account for the differences include J. Beker's (1984) distinction between the coherent theme of Paul's gospel (God's triumph) and its contingent application according to the circumstances; D. Patte's (1983) differentiation between a convictional and a theological level in Paul's discourse; and G. Klein's (1984) sharp separation, reminiscent of Conzelmann, between basic intentions and objectifications. More radical is Watson's proposal that what is coherent in Paul are his practical aims; to reach the same goal he can use quite different argumentative strategies. In all these cases the effect is the same, sometimes against the intention of the interpreter: Paul can be seen as consistent only if the interpreter is in possession of a key that enables him or her to tell the kernel from the husk.

In a pioneering synthesis, J. Becker (1989) brings many of the threads in scholarship together, taking pains to trace the movement of Paul's thought from one letter to another. Becker gives special attention to Paul's Antiochian roots (cf. Räisänen [1992] 191-97; E. Rau [1994]). Pre-Pauline Hellenistic Christianity (so termed since Heitmüller) is defined by Becker more precisely as Antiochian. In Antioch the ritual parts of the law were rejected as a consequence of charismatic experiences on the part of the uncircumcised. Baptism and new life in Christ, whose imminent return was eagerly expected, were all-important (cf. Schnelle). The legacy of Antioch is most palpable in 1 Thessalonians, but it constitutes the basis of Paul's argument in subsequent letters as well.

Paul's theology is wholly based on his experience of the gospel and of the Spirit that transforms people. In emphasizing this, Becker differs notably from Bultmann's intellectualist approach; nevertheless, Becker's Paul is an eminent thinker. Maintaining that tensions often arise due to Paul's use of blocks of previously shaped material, Becker also distinguishes between Paul's coherent basic decisions and his more situation-bound (often polemical) statements; the apostle developed his arguments with an amazing capacity for variation.

7. The Present Situation. The situation today, then, is somewhat confusing. On a number of key issues a wide range of interpretations is offered. Few of the basic problems that have arisen in the course of the history of interpretation have really been solved; most of them continue to engage modern scholars.

Regarding Paul's attitude toward Israel and the law, either continuity or discontinuity may be stressed. While many scholars take Paul's talk of eschatological expectation literally and regard this expectation as the central incentive for his work (Sanders, Käsemann, Beker), others understand the apocalyptic language in a more symbolical way and deny the importance of a concrete end expectation for Paul (most radically Klein).

The center of Paul's thought can be variously located, e.g., in the notion of justification (this concern tends to give the whole an individualistic flavor), in the baptismal union with Christ and the possession of the Spirit (with a preponderance of the corporate dimension in Paul's thought), or in the apocalyptic theme of God's triumph.

Such issues, furthermore, are affected by the problem of the nature of Paul's thought. Was he fundamentally consistent? Did his thought develop? Or did he just take different positions in different situations?

Still, some solutions seem to be advancing more than others. It will be difficult to maintain a thoroughly affirmative view of Paul's attitude toward Judaism and the law. It is hardly possible to explain all of Paul's critical statements in this regard in positive terms. But what is their real import? It would likewise be hard to deny any significance to the apocalyptic-eschatological expectation. But just how central was it to Paul? Moreover, what exactly is the relation between eschatology and being in Christ—between the Jewish and the more Hellenistic component (pace, Schweitzer) in Paul's thought? And one may wonder whether the question of Greek influences really has been settled. At least the impact of rhetorical conventions and popular philosophy (A. Malherbe [1989]) is obvious, and recently there have been efforts to reopen the question of Paul's relation to Greco-Roman religiosity but in a more nuanced way than in the time of Heitmüller and Reitzenstein (Betz; H.-J. Klauck [1986²]; A. Wedderburn [1987]).

Communication is rendered more difficult by the fact that different scholars are guided by different intentions in their interpretation of Paul. An increasing number of them advocate a separation between a historical and an actualizing interpretation (stressed early on by Wrede), and many would be content to concentrate on the former task alone. Other scholars, however, (in the vein of Barth and Bultmann) are strongly opposed to such a distinction and favor a self-consciously theological exegesis. Such an approach tries to avoid attributing to Paul self-contradictions or theologically problematic ideas.

Finally, new methodological perspectives have entered Pauline study, as they have other areas of New Testament research. Rhetorical Criticism*§ (Betz; S. Stowers [1981]) is used to elucidate the communication between Paul and his addressees. Paul's use of the Hebrew Bible can be viewed from the perspective of Literary Theory*§ (Intertexuality*§: R. Hays [1989]). If the danger of anachronism lurks in such readings, psychological interpretations (see Psychology and Biblical Studies*§) are even more exposed to it; yet the risk can be reduced by paying close attention to the history of traditions (G. Theissen [1983]; see Tradition History*§). Most promising from the point of view of historical understanding are sociological (G. Theissen [1979]; B. Holmberg [1978]; W. Meeks [1983]; Watson) and anthropological (B. Malina [1981]; J. Neyrey [1990]) approaches.

Recent basic introductions to Paul include Cousar (1996), Hooker (2003), Horrell (2000), Koperski (2001), Roetzel (1988⁴), Westerholm (1997), Witherup (2003), and Wright (1997). Recent studies on Paul's life and the chronology of his ministry and letters include Ashton (2000), Haacker (1997), Hengel and Schwemer (1997), den Heyer (2000), Horn (2001), Lohse (1996), McRay (2003), Murphy-O'Connor (1996), Riesner (1998), Roetzel (1998), Wuilson (1997), and Witherington (1998). Studies on the "Paul of Acts" include Bunine (2002), Dauer (1996), Mount (2002), Omerzu (2002), Pichler (1997), Porter (1999), Schreiber (1996), and Strelan (1996). Recent studies of Paul's theology and ethics include Alkier (2001), Barcley (1999), Beckheuer (1997), Bickmann (1998), Carter (2002), Chae (1997), Cosgrove (1997), Das (2001), Davis (2002), Donaldson (1997), Dunn (1998), Eastman (1999), Eskola (1998), Fatehi (2000), Finsterbusch (1996), Gorman, (2001), Gaukesbrink (1999), Hjort (2000), Gebauer (1997), Gräbe (2000), Gruber (1998), Hart (1999, 2000), Hays (2002²), Herzer (1998), Hillert (1999), Hotze (1997), Hovenden (2002), Hubbard (2002), Hunt (1996), Joubert (2000), Julius (1999), B.-M. Kim (2002), S. Kim (2002), Kraus (1996), Krug (2001), Kruse (1996), Macky (1998), Matand (1997), Middendorf (1997), Moore (2002), Olbricht and Sumney (2001), Pao (2002), Park (2003), Pate (2000), Pearson (2001), Powers (2001), Rapa (2001), Sandnes (2002), Savage (1996), Schrage (2002), Seifrid (2000), Simmons (1996), Smiles (1998), Smith (2002) Söding (1997), Son (2001), van Spanje (1999), Strom (2000), Stuhlmacher (2001), Thurén (2000), Umbach (1999), Walton (2000), Watson (2000), Wisdom (2001), Yeung (2002), and Yinger (1999).

Stirewalt (2003) and Müller (1997) provide studies of Paul's writings as letters. Walker (2001) discusses possible interpolations in the Pauline letters. Studies on the history of the interpretation of Paul include Gese (1997), Matlock (1996), and Wehr (1996). Recent studies of Paul in his Hellenistic context include Bakirtzis and Koeser (1998), Blumenfeld (2001), Cineira (1999), Downing (1998), Engberg-Pedersen (2000, 2001), Heininger (1996), Hollingshead (1998), McLean (1996), Meggitt (1998), Park (2000), Pickett (1997), Sumney (1999), Wallace and Williams (1998), and Wanskink (1996). Malina and Neyrey (1996) and Strecker (1999) use social science methods to study Paul Ascough (1998) and Kraus (1999) discuss the formation of the Pauline communities. Bachmann (1999), Gager (2000), Keller (1998), Lim (1997), Meissner (1996), Nanos (1996), Oegema (1998), and Wilk (1998) study various aspects of Paul's relationship to Judaism and the Hebrew Bible. Recent analyses of Paul's rhetoric and literary methods include Anderson (1999²), Dodd (1999), Given (2001), Vos (2002), and Winter (2001²). Dornisch (1999), Perriman (1998), and Polaski (1999) study Paul's views on gender and sexuality. Selected articles in Callahan, Horsley, and Smith (1998) discuss Paul's understanding of slavery. Studies of Pauline vocabulary, semantics, and linguistics include Adams (2000), Bash (1997), Baumert (2003), and Wong (1997). Reichardt (1999) is a historical overview of the psychological analysis of Paul's Damascus vision. Akenson (2000) uses Paul to reconstruct the historical Jesus. Maloney (1998) and Meier (1998) study Paul as a mystic. Jewett (1999) and Kreitzer (1999) relate Paul and his theology to modern film. Collections of essays on various aspects of Pauline studies include Bammel (1997), Barrett (2003), Baumert (2001), Capel Anderson, Sellew, and Setzer (2002), Carson, O'Brien, and Seifrid (2001), Donfried (2002), Dunn (1996), Hofius (2002), Horsley (1997, 2000), Hurd (1998), Lambrecht (2001), Longnecker (2002), Longenecker (1997), Lovering and Sumney (1996), Martyn (1997), Merklein (1998), Schnelle and Söding (2000), Scholtissek (2000), and Vollenweider (2002).

Bibliography: E. **Adams,** *Constructing the World: A Study in Paul's Cosmological Language* (Studies of the New Testament and Its World, 2000). S. **Alkier,** *Wunder und Wirklichkeit in den Briefen des Apostels Paulus: Ein Beitrag zu einem Wunderverständnis jenseits von Entmythologisierung und Rehistorisierung* (WUNT 134, 2001). R. D. **Anderson Jr.,** *Ancient Rhetorical Theory and Paul* (Contributions to Biblical Exegesis and Theology 18, 1999²). R. S. **Ascough,** *What are They Saying About the Formation of Pauline Churches?* (1998). J. **Ashton,** *The Religion of Paul the Apostle* (Wilde Lectures in Natural and Comparative Religion 1998, 2000). M. **Bachmann,** *Antijudaismus im Galaterbrief: Exegetische Studien zu einem polemischen Schreiben und zur Theologie des Apostels Paulus* (NTOA 40, 1999). C. **Bakirtzis and H. Koester, eds.** *Philippi at the Time of Paul and After His Death* (1998). E. **Bammel,** *Judaica et Paulina* (WUNT 91, 1997). W. B. **Barcley,** *"Christ in You": A Study in Paul's Theology and Ethics* (1999). C. K. **Barrett,** *Paul: An Introduction to His Thought* (1994); *On Paul: Aspects of His Life, Work, and Influence in the Early Church* (2003). K. **Barth,** *The Epistle to the Romans* (1919; ET 1933). A. **Bash,** *Ambassadors for Christ: An Exploration of Ambassadorial Language in the N T* (WUNT 2/92, 1997). N. **Baumert,** *Koinonein und metechein— synonym?: Eine umfassende semantische Untersuchung* (SBB 51, 2003); *Studien zu den Paulusbriefen* (SBAB 32, 2001). F. C. **Baur,** *Vorlesungen über neutestamenliche Theologie* (1864, repr. 1973). J. **Becker,** *Paul: Der Apostel der Völker* (1989). B. **Beckheuer,** *Paulus und Jerusalem : Kollekte und Mission im theologischen Denken des Heidenapostels* (1997). J. C. **Beker,** *Paul the Apostle* (1984). H.-D. **Betz,** *Galatians: A Commentary on Paul's Letter to the Churches in Galatia* (Hermeneia, 1979). J. **Bickmann,** *Kommunikation gegen den Tod: Studien zur paulinischen Briefpragmatik am Beispiel des Ersten Thessalonicherbriefes* (FB 86, 1998). B. **Blumenfeld,** *The Political Paul: Justice, Democracy, and Kingship in a Hellenistic* (JSNTSup 210, 2001). W. **Bousset,** *Kyrios Christos* (FRLANT 4, 1921; ET 1970). D. **Boyarin,** *A Radical Jew: Paul and the Politics of Identity* (1994). C. **Breytenbach,** *Versöhnung: Eine Studie zue paulinischen Soteriologie* (1989). R. **Bultmann,** *"Zur Geschichte der Paulus-Forschung," TRu* 1 (1929) 26-59; *"Neueste Paulusforschung," TRu* 6 (1934) 229-46;

8 (1936) 1-22; *Theology of the New Testament* (1948; ET 1951). **A. Bunine,** *Une légende tenace : Le retour de Paul à Antioche, après sa mission en Macédoine et en Grèce (Actes 18,18-19,1)* (CahRB 52, 2002). **A. D. Callahan, R. A. Horsley, and A. Smith,** eds. *Slavery in Text and Interpretation; Semeia* 83–84 (1998). **J. Capel Anderson, P. Sellew, and C. Setzer,** eds. *Pauline Conversations in Context: Essays in Honor of Calvin J. Roetzel* (JSNTSup 221, 2002). **D.A. Carson, P. T. O'Brien, and M. A. Seifrid,** eds., *Justification and Variegated Nomism* (WUNT 2/140, 2001). **T.L. Carter,** *Paul and the Power of Sin: Redefining 'Beyond the Pale'* (SNTSMS 115, 2002). **D. J.-S. Chae,** *Paul as Apostle to the Gentiles: His Apostolic Self-Awareness and Its Influence on the Soteriological Argument in Romans* (Paternoster Biblical and Theological Monographs, 1997). **D. A. Cineira,** *Die Religionspolitik des Kaisers Claudius und die Paulinische Mission* (Herders biblische Studien 19, 1999). **H. Conzelmann,** *An Outline of the Theology of the New Testament* (EET 2, 1967; ET 1969). **C. H. Cosgrove,** *Elusive Israel: The Puzzle of Election in Romans* (1997). **C. B. Cousar,** *The Letters of Paul* (Interpreting Biblical Texts, 1996). **C. E. B. Cranfield,** *The Epistle to the Romans* (2 vols., ICC, 1975-79). O. Cullmann, Savlation in History (1965; ET 1967). **Andrew Das,** *Paul, the Law, and the Covenant* (2001). **A. Dauer,** *Paulus und die christliche Gemeinde im syrischen Antiochia: Kritische Bestandsaufnahme der modernen Forschung mit einigen weiterführenden Überlegungen* (BBB 106, 1996). **W. D. Davies,** *Paul and Rabbinic Judaism: Some Rabbinic Elements in Pauline Theology* (1948). **S. K. Davis** *The Antithesis of the Ages: Paul's Reconfiguration of Torah* (CBQMS 33,, 2002). **B. Dodd.** *Paul's Paradigmatic "I" : Personal Example as Literary Strategy* (JSNTSup 177, 1999). **T. L. Donaldson,** *Paul and the Gentiles: Remapping the Apostle's Convictional World* (1997). **K. P. Donfried,** *Paul, Thessalonica, and Early Christianity* (2002). **L. Dornisch,** *Paul and Third World Women Theologians* (1999). **F. G. Downing,** *Cynics, Paul, and the Pauline Churches: Cynics and Christian origins II* 1998. **J. D. G. Dunn,** "The New Perspective on Paul," *BJRL* 65 (1983) 95-122; *Romans* (WBC 38, 1988); (ed.), *Paul and the Mosaic Law* (WUNT 89, 1996); *The Theology of Paul the Apostle* (1998). **B. Eastman,** *The Significance of Grace in the Letters of Paul* (Studies in Biblical Literature 11, 1999). **T. Engberg-Pedersen** (ed.), *Paul in His Hellenistic Context* (1995); *Paul and the Stoics* (2000); (ed.) *Paul Beyond the Judaism/Hellenism Divide* (2001). **T. Eskola,** *Theodicy and Predestination in Pauline Soteriology* (WUNT 2/100, 1998). **O. Everling,** *Die paulinische Angelologie und Dämonologie: Ein biblisch-theologischer Versuch* (1888). **M. Fatehi,** *The Spirit's Relation to the Risen Lord in Paul: An Examination of Its Christological implications* (WUNT 2/128, 2000). **K. Finsterbusch,** *Die Thora als Lebensweisung für Heidenchristen: Studien zur Bedeutung der Thora für die paulinische Ethik* (SUNT 29, 1996). **J. G. Gager,** *The Origins of Anti-Semitism: Attitudes Toward Judaism in Pagan and Christian Antiquity* (1983); *Reinventing Paul* (2000). **L. Gaston,** *Paul and the Torah* (1987). **M. Gaukesbrink,** *Die Sühnetradition bei Paulus: Rezeption und theologischer Stellenwert* (FB 82, 1999). **R. Gebauer,** *Paulus als Seelsorger: Ein exegetischer Beitrag zur praktischen Theologie (Calwer theologische Monographien A/18, 1997).* **M. Gese,** *Das Vermächtnis des Apostels: die Rezeption der paulinischen Theologie im Epheserbrief* (WUNT 2/99, 1997). **M. D. Given,** *Paul's True Rhetoric: Ambiguity, Cunning, and Deception in Greece and Rome* (Emory Studies in Early Christianity, 2001). **M. J. Gorman,** *Cruciformity: Paul's Narrative Spirituality of the Cross* (2001). **P. J. Gräbe,** *The Power of God in Paul's Letters* (WUNT 2/123, 2000). **M. M. Gruber** *Herrlichkeit in Schwachheit: eine Auslegung der Apologie des Zweiten Korintherbriefs 2 Kor 2,14-6,13.* (FB 89, 1998). **H. Gunkel,** *The Influence of the Holy Spirit According to the Popular View of the Apostolic Age and the Teaching of the Apostle Paul: A Biblical Theological Study* (1888; ET 1979). **K. Haacker,** *Paulus: Der Werdegang eines Apostels* (SBS 171, 1997). **D. Hagner,** "Paul in Modern Jewish Thought," *Pauline Studies: Essays Presented to F. F. Bruce on His 70th Birthday* (ed. D. A. Hagner and M. J. Harris, 1980) 143-65. **C. Hart,** *The*

Ethics of Paul (Grove Ethical Studies 115, 1999); *The Ethics of the Later Pauline Letters* (Grove Ethics Series, E119, 2000). **R. B. Hays**, *Echoes of Scripture in the Letters of Paul* (1989); *The Faith of Jesus Christ: The Narrative Substructure of Galatians 3:1-4:11* (Biblical Resource Series, 2002²). **B. Heininger**, *Paulus als Visionär: Eine religionsgeschichtliche Studie* (Herders biblische Studien 9, 1996). **W. Heitmüller**, "Zum Problem Paul und Jesus," *ZNW* 13 (1912) 320-37; *Das Paulusbild in der neueren deutschen Forschung* (WdF 24, ed. K. H. Rengstorf, 1964, 1969²) 124-43. **M. Hengel and A. M. Schwemer**, *Paul Between Damascus and Antioch: The Unknown Years* (1997). **J. Herzer**, *Petrus oder Paulus?: Studien über das Verhältnis des Ersten Petrusbriefes zur paulinischen Tradition* (WUNT 103, 1998). **C. J. den Heyer** *Paul: A Man of Two Worlds* (2000). **S. Hillert**, *Limited and Universal Salvation: A Text-oriented and Hermeneutical Study of Two Perspectives in Paul* (ConBNT 31, 1999). **B. G. Hjort**, *The Irreversible Sequence: Paul's Ethics: Their Foundation and Present Relevance* (2000). **O. Hofius**, *Paulusstudien II* (WUNT 143, 2002). **J. R. Hollingshead**, *The Household of Caesar and the Body of Christ: A Political Interpretation of the Letters from Paul* (1998). **B. Holmberg**, *Paul and Power: The Structure of Authority in the Primitive Church as Reflected in the Pauline Epistles* (1978). **H. J. Holtzmann**, *Lehrbuch der neutestamentlichen Theologie*, 2 (1897, 1912²). **M. D. Hooker**, *Paul: A Short Introduction* (2003). **F. W. Horn**, ed., *Das Ende des Paulus: Historische, theologische und literaturgeschichtliche Aspekte* (BZNW 106, 2001). **D. G. Horrell**, *An Introduction to the Study of Paul* (Continuum Biblical Studies, 2000). **R. A. Horsley, ed.** *Paul and Empire: Religion and Power in Roman Imperial Society* (1997); (ed.) *Paul and Politics: Ekklesia, Israel, Imperium, Interpretation: Essays in Honor of Krister Stendahl* (2000). **G. Hotze**, *Paradoxien bei Paulus: Untersuchungen zu einer elementaren Denkform in seiner Theologie* (NTAbh n. F. 33, 1997). **G. Hovenden**, *Speaking in Tongues: The New Testament Evidence in Context* (Journal of Pentecostal Theology Supplement Series 22, 2002). **M. V. Hubbard**, *New Creation of Paul's Letters and Thought* (SNTSMS 119, 2002). **H. Hübner**, *The Law in Paul's Thought* (1978, 1980²; ET 1984); "Paulusforschung seit 1945: Ein kritischer Literaturbericht," *ANRW* II.25.4 (1987) 2649-840; *Biblische Theologie des Neuen Testaments*, vol. 2, *Die Theologie des Paul und ihre neutestamentliche Wirkungsgeschichte* (1993). **A. R. Hunt**, *The Inspired Body: Paul, the Corinthians, and Divine Inspiration* (1996). **J. C. Hurd**, *The Earlier Letters of Paul—and Other Studies* (Arbeiten zur Religion und Geschichte des Urchristentums 8, 1998). **R. Jewett**, *Paul's Anthropological Terms: A Study of Their Use in Conflict Settings* (AGJU 10, 1971); *Saint Paul Returns to the Movies: Triumph over Shame* (1999). **S. Joubert**, *Paul as Benefactor: Reciprocity, Strategy, And Theological Reflection in Paul's Collection* (WUNT 2/124, 2000). **C.-B. Julius**, *Die ausgeführten Schrifttypologien bei Paulus* (1999). **R. Kabisch**, *Die Eschatologie des Paul in ihren Zusammenhängen mit dem Gesamtbegriff des Paulinismus* (1893). **E. Käsemann**, *Leib und Leib Christi: Eine Untersuchung zur paulinischen Begrifflichkeit* (BHT 9, 1933); *Perspectives on Paul* (1969; ET 1971); *Commentary on Romans* (1974³; ET 1980). **W. Keller.** *Gottes Treue, Israels Heil: Röm 11, 25-27: Die These vom "Sonderweg" in der Diskussion* (SBB 40, 1998). **S. Kim**, *Paul and the New Perspective: Second Thoughts on the Origin of Paul's Gospel* (WUNT 140, 2002). **B.-M. Kim**, *Die paulinische Kollekte* (TANZ 38, 2002). **H.-J. Klauck**, *Herrenmahl und hellenisticher Kult: Eine religionsgeschichtliche Untersuchung zum ersten Korintherbrief* (NTAbh 15, 1986²). **G. Klein**, "Apokalyptische Naherwartung bei Paul," *Neues Testament und christliche Existenz: Festschrift für H. Braun zum 70. Geburtstag am 4 Mai 1973* (1973) 241-652; "Gesetz III. Neues Testament," *TRE* 13 (1984) 58-75. **D.-A. Koch**, *Die Schrift als Zeuge des Evangeliums: Unterschungen zur Verwendung und zum Verständnis der Schrift bei Paul* (BHT 69, 1986). **V. Koperski** *What Are They Saying About Paul and the Law?* (WATSA, 2001). **W. Kraus**, *Zwischen Jerusalem und Antiochia: Die 'Hellenisten,' Paulus und die Aufnahme der Heiden in das endzeitliche Gottesvolk* (SBS 179, 1999). **W. Kraus**, *Das Volk*

Gottes: Zur Grundlegung der Ekklesiologie bei Paulus (WUNT 85, 1996). **L. J. Kreitzer,** *Pauline Images in Fiction and Film: On Reversing the Hermeneutical Flow* (Biblical Seminar 61, 1999). **J. Krug,** *Die Kraft des Schwachen: Ein Beitrag zur paulinischen Apostolatstheologie* (TANZ 37, 2001). **C. G. Kruse,** *Paul, the Law and Justification* (1996). **W. G. Kümmel,** *Römer 7 und die Bekehrung des Paul* (UNT 17, 1929); *Theology of the New Testament According to Its Major Witnesses: Jesus-Paul-John* (1969; ET 1974); *The New Testament: The History of the Investigations of Its Problems* (1970; ET 1973). **T. Laato,** *Paul und das Judentum: Anthropologische Erwagungen* (1991). **J. Lambrecht,** *Collected Studies on Pauline Literature and on the Book of Revelation* (AnBib 147, 2001). **T. H. Lim,** *Holy Scripture in the Qumran Commentaries and Pauline Letters* (1997). **E. Lohse,** *Paulus: Eine Biographie* (1996). **B. W. Longenecker,** ed. *Narrative Dynamics in Paul: A Critical Assessment* (2002). **R. N. Longenecker,** ed. *The Road from Damascus: The Impact of Paul's Conversion on his Life, Thought, and Ministry* (McMaster New Testament Studies, 1997). **E. H. Lovering, Jr. and J. L. Sumney,** eds. *Theology and Ethics in Paul and His Interpreters: Essays in Honor of Victor Paul Furnish* (1996). **G. Lüdemann,** *Paul und das Judentum* (TEH 215, 1983); *Paul, Apostle to the Gentiles: Studies in Chronology* (1984). **H. Lüdemann,** *Die Anthropologie des Apostels Paul und ihre Stellung innerhalb seiner Heilslehre nach den vier Hauptbriefen* (1872). **P. W. Macky,** *St. Paul's Cosmic War Myth: A Military Version of the Gospel* (Westminster College Library of Biblical Symbolism 2, 1998). **A. J. Malherbe,** *Paul and the Popular Philosophers* (1989). **B. J. Malina,** *The New Testament World: Insights from Cultural Anthropology* (1981). **B. J. Malina and J. H. Neyrey,** *Portraits of Paul: An Archaeology of Ancient Personality* (1996). **G. A. Maloney.** *The Mystery of Christ in You: The Mystical Vision of Saint Paul* (1998). **J. L. Martyn,** *Theological Issues in the Letters of Paul* (Studies of the New Testament and Its World, 1997). **J.-B. Matand,** *Bulembat Noyau et enjeux de l'eschatologie paulinienne: De l'apocalyptique juive et de l'eschatologie hellénistique dans quelques argumentations de l'apôtre Paul: Etude rhétorico-exégétique de 1 Co 15, 35-58; 2 Co 5, 1-10 et Rm 8,18-30* (BZNW 84, 1997). **R. B. Matlock,** *Unveiling the Apocalyptic Paul: Paul's Interpreters and the Rhetoric of Criticism* (JSTNSup 127, 1996). **B. H. McLean,** *The Cursed Christ: Mediterranean Expulsion Rituals and Pauline Soteriology* (JSNTSup 126, 1996). **J. McRay,** *Paul: His Life and Teaching* (2003). **W. A. Meeks,** *The First Urban Christians: The Social World of the Apostle Paul* (1983). **J. J. Meggitt,** *Paul, Poverty and Survival* (Studies of the New Testament and Its World, 1998). **H.-C. Meier,** *Mystik bei Paulus: Zur Phänomenologie religiöser Erfahrung im New Testament* (TANZ 26, 1998). **S. Meissner,** *Die Heimholung des Ketzers: Studien zur jüdischen Auseinandersetzung mit Paulus* (WUNT 2/87, 1996). **O. Merk,** "Paulus-Forschung, 1936-85," *TRu* 53 (1988) 1-81. **H. Merklein,** *Studien zu Jesus und Paulus. II* (WUNT 105, 1998). **M. P. Middendorf,** *The "I" in the Storm: A Study of Romans 7* (1997). **C. G. Montefiore,** *Judaism and St. Paul: Two Essays* (1914). **R. K. Moore,** *Rectification ('Justification') in Paul, in Historical Perspective, and in the English Bible: God's Gift of Right Relationship* (Studies in the Bible and early Christianity 50a, 2002). **C. Mount,** *Pauline Christianity: Luke-Acts and the Legacy of Paul* (NovTSup 104, 2002). **M. Müller,** *Vom Schluss zum Ganzen: Zur Bedeutung des paulinischen Briefkorpusabschlusses* (FRLANT 172, 1997). **J. Munck,** *Paul und die Heilsgeschichte* (AJut.T 26.1, 6, 1954). **J. Murphy-O'Connor,** *Paul: A Critical Life* (1996). **F. Mussner,** *Traktat über die Juden* (1979). **M. D. Nanos,** *The Mystery of Romans: The Jewish Context of Paul's Letter* (1996). **J. Neyrey,** *Paul, in Other Words: A Cultural Reading of His Letters* (1990). **G. S. Oegema,** *Für Israel und die Völker: Studien zum alttestamentlich-jüdischen Hintergrund der paulinischen Theologie* (NovTSup 95, 1998). **T. H. Olbricht and J. L. Sumney,** eds. *Paul and Pathos* (SBLSymS 16, 2001). **H. Omerzu,** *Der Prozess des Paulus: Eine exegetische und rechtshistorische Untersuchung der Apostelgeschichte* (BZNW 115, 2002). **D. W. Pao,** *Thanksgiving: An Investigation of a Pauline*

Theme (New Studies in Biblical Theology 13, 2002). **E. C. Park,** *Either Jew or Gentile: Paul's Unfolding Theology of Inclusivity* (2003). **J. S. Park,** *Conceptions of Afterlife in Jewish Inscriptions: With Special Reference to Pauline Literature* (WUNT 2/121, 2000). **C. M. Pate,** *The Reverse of the Curse: Paul, Wisdom, and the Law* (WUNT 2/114, 2000). **D. Patte,** *Paul's Faith and the Power of the Gospel: A Structural Introduction to the Pauline Letters* (1983). **B. W. R. Pearson,** *Corresponding Sense: Paul, Dialectic, and Gadamer* (Biblical Interpretation Series 58, 2001). **A. Perriman,** *Speaking of Women: Interpreting Paul* (1998). **J. Pichler,** *Paulusrezeption in der Apostelgeschichte: Untersuchungen zur Rede im pisidischen Antiochien* (Innsbrucker theologische Studien 50, 1997). **R. Pickett,** *The Cross in Corinth: The Social Significance of the Death of Jesus* (JSNTSup 143, 1997). **S. H. Polaski,** *Paul and the Discourse of Power* (Gender, Culture, Theory 8; Biblical Seminar 62, 1999). **S. E. Porter,** *The Paul of Acts: Essays in Literary Criticism, Rhetoric, and Theology* (WUNT 115, 1999). **D. G. Powers,** *Salvation Through Participation: An Examination of the Notion of the Believers' Corporate Unity with Christ in Early Christian Soteriology* (Contributions to Biblical Exegesis and Theology 29, 2001). **H. Räisänen,** *Paul and the Law* (WUNT 29, 1983, 1987[2]); *Beyond New Testament Theology: A Story and a Programme* (1990); *Jesus, Paul, and Torah: Collected Essays* (JSNTSup 43, 1992). **R. K. Rapa,** *The Meaning of "Works of the Law" in Galatians and Romans* (Studies in Biblical Literature 31, 2001). **E. Rau,** *Von Jesus zu Paul: Entwicklung und Rezeption der antiochenischen Theologie im Urchristentum* (1994). **W. Rebell,** *Gehorsam und Unabhängigkeit: Eine sozialpsychologische Studie zu Paulus* (1986). **M. Reichardt,** *Psychologische Erklärung der paulinischen Damaskusvision?: Ein Beitrag zum interdisziplinären Gespräch zwischen Exegese und Psychologie seit dem 18. Jahrhundert* (SBB 42, 1999). **R. Reitzenstein,** *Hellenistic Mystery-Religions: Their Basic Ideas and Significance* (1910; ET 1978). **K. H. Rengstorf** (ed.), *Das Paulusbild in der neueren deutschen Forschung* (1964, 1969[2]). **R. Riesner,** *Paul's Early Period: Chronology, Mission Strategy, Theology* (1998). **C. J. Roetzel,** *The Letters of Paul: Conversations in Context* (1998[4]); *Paul: The Man and the Myth* (Studies on Personalities of the NT, 1998). **R. Ruether,** *Faith and Fratricide: The Theological Roots of Anti-Semitism* (1974). **E. P. Sanders,** *Paul and Palestinian Judaism: A Comparison of Patterns of Religion* (1977); *Paul, the Law, and the Jewish People* (1983). **K. O. Sandnes,** *Belly and the Body in the Pauline Epistles* (SNTSMS 120, 2002). **T. B. Savage,** *Power Through Weakness: Paul's Understanding of the Christian Ministry in 2 Corinthians* (SNTSMS 86, 1996). **U. Schnelle,** *Gerechtigkeit und Christusgegenwart: Vorpaulinische und paulinische Tauftheologie* (1983, 1986[2]). **U. Schnelle and T. Söding, eds.** *Paulinische Christologie: Exegetische Beiträge; Hans Hübner zum 70. Geburtstag* (2000). **H.-J. Schoeps,** *Paulus: Die Theologie des Apostels im Lichte der jüdischen Religionsgeschichte* (1959). **K. Scholtissek, ed.,** *Christologie in der Paulus-Schule: Zur Rezeptionsgeschichte des paulinischen Evangeliums* (SBS 181, 2000). **W. Schrage,** *Unterwegs zur Einzigkeit und Einheit Gottes: Zum "Monotheismus" des Paulus und seiner alttestamentlich-frühjüdischen Tradition* (Biblisch-theologische Studien 48, 2002). **S. Schreiber,** *Paulus als Wundertäte: Redaktionsgeschichtliche Untersuchungen zur Apostelgeschichte und den authentischen Paulusbriefen* (BZNW 79, 1996). **A. Schweitzer,** *Paul and His Interpreters: A Critical History* (1911; ET 1912, repr. 1951); *Die Mystik des Apostels Paul* (1930, 1954[2]; ET 1998). **A. F. Segal,** *Paul the Convert: The Apostolate and Apostasy of Saul the Pharisee* (1990). **M. A. Seifrid,** *Christ, Our Righteousness: Paul's Theology of Justification* (New Studies in Biblical Theology 9, 2000). **W. A. Simmons,** *A Theology of Inclusion in Jesus and Paul: The God of Outcasts and Sinners* (Mellen Biblical Press Series 39, 1996). **V. M. Smiles,** *The Gospel and the Law in Galatia: Paul's Response to Jewish-Christian Separatism and the Threat of Galatian Apostasy* (1998). **B. D. Smith,** *Paul's Seven Explanations of the Suffering of the Righteous* (Studies in Biblical Literature 47, 2002). **T. Söding,** "Das Wort vom Kreuz: Studien zur paulinischen Theologie"

(WUNT 93, 1997). **S.-W. Son,** *Corporate Elements in Pauline Anthropology: A Study of the Selected Terms, Idioms, and Concepts in the Light of Paul's Usage and Background* (AnBib 148, 2001). **T.E. van Spanje,** *Inconsistency in Paul?: A Critique of the Work of Heikki Räisänen* (WUNT 2/110, 1999). **K. Stendahl,** *Paul Among Jews and Gentiles and Other Essays* (1976). **M. L. Stirewalt, Jr.,** *Paul, the Letter Writer* (2003). **S. K. Stowers,** *The Diatribe and Paul's Letters to the Romans* (SBLMS 57, 1981). **C. Strecker,** *Die liminale Theologie des Paulus: Zugänge zur paulinischen Theologie aus kulturanthropologischer Perspektive* (FRLANT 185, 1999). **R. Strelan,** *Paul, Artemis, and the Jews in Ephesus* (BZNW 80, 1996). **M. Strom,** *Reframing Paul: Conversations in Grace and Community* (2000). **P. Stuhlmacher,** *Gerechtigkeit Gottes bei Paul* (FRLANT 87, 1965, 1966²); *Biblische Theologie des Neuen Testaments,* vol. 1, *Grund-legung: Von Jesus zu Paul* (1992). **P. Stuhlmacher,** *Revisiting Paul's Doctrine of Justification: A Challenge to the New* (2001). **J. L. Sumney,** *'Servants of Satan', 'False Brothers' and Other Opponents of Paul* (JSNTSup 188, 1999). **G. Theissen,** *Studien zur Soziologie des Urchristentums* (WUNT 19, 1979; ET *The Social Setting of Pauline Christianity: Essays on Corinth* [1982]); *Psychologische Aspekte paulinischer Theologie* (FRLANT 131, 1983; ET *Psychological Aspects of Pauline Theology* [1987]). **F. Thielman,** *From Plight to Solution: A Jewish Framework for Understanding Paul's View of the Law in Galatians and Romans* (1989). **L. Thurén** *Derhetorizing Paul: A Dynamic Perspective on Pauline Theology and the Law* (WUNT 124, 2000). **H. Umbach,** *In Christus getauft, von der Sünde befreit: Die Gemeinde als sündenfreier Raum bei Paulus* (FRLANT 181, 1999). **S. Vollenweider,** *Horizonte neutestamentlicher Christologie: Studien zu Paulus und zur frühchristlichen Theologie* (WUNT 144, 2002). **J. S. Vos,** *Die Kunst der Argumentation bei Paulus: Studien zur antiken Rhetorik* (WUNT 149, 2002). **W. O. Walker, Jr.,** *Interpolations in the Pauline Letters* (JSNTSup 213, 2001). **R. Wallace and W. Williams,** *The Three Worlds of Paul of Tarsus* (1998). **S. Walton,** *Leadership and Lifestyle: The Portrait of Paul in the Miletus Speech and 1 Thessalonians* (SNTSMS 108, 2000). **C. S. Wansink,** *Chained in Christ: The Experience and Rhetoric of Paul's Imprisonments* (JSNTSup 130, 1996). **F. Watson,** *Paul, Judaism, and the Gentiles: A Sociological Approach* (SNTSMS 56, 1986). **F. Watson,** *Agape, Eros, Gender: Towards a Pauline Sexual Ethic* (2000). **A. J. M. Wedderburn,** *Baptism and Resurrection: Studies in Pauline Theology Against Its Graeco-Roman Background* (WUNT 44, 1987). **L. Wehr,** *Petrus und Paulus, Kontrahenten und Partner: Die Beiden Apostel im Spiegel des Neuen Testaments, der apostolischen Väter und früher Zeugnisse ihrer Verehrung* (NTAbh n.F. 30, 1996). **J. Weiss,** *Earliest Christianity: A History of the Period AD 30-150* (1917; ET 1970). **S. Westerholm,** *Israel's Law and the Church's Faith: Paul and His Recent Interpreters* (1988); *Preface to the Study of Paul* (1997). **U. Wilckens,** *Rechtfertigung als Freiheit: Paulusstudien* (1974); *Der Brief an die Römer* (EKKNT 6, 3 vols., 1978-82). **M. Wiles,** *The Divine Apostle: The Interpretation of St. Paul's Epistles in the Early Church* (1967). **F. Wilk,** *Die Bedeutung des Jesajabuches für Paulus* (FRLANT 179, 1998). **A.N. Wilson,** *Paul: The Mind of the Apostle* (1997). **B. W. Winter,** *Philo and Paul among the Sophists* (2001²) **J. R. Wisdom,** *Blessing for the Nations and the Curse of the Law: Paul's Citation of Genesis and Deuteronomy in Gal 3.8-10* (WUNT 2/133, 2001). **R. D. Witherup,** *101 Questions and Answers on Paul* (2003). **B. Witherington III,** *The Paul Quest: The Renewed Search for the Jew of Tarsus* (1998). **S. S. M. Wong,** *A Classification of Semantic Case-relations in the Pauline Epistles* (Studies in Biblical Greek 9, 1997). **W. Wrede,** *Paul* (1904; ET 1907). **N.T. Wright,** *What Saint Paul Really Said: Was Paul of Tarsus the Real Founder of Christianity?* (1997). **M. W. Yeung,** *Faith in Jesus and Paul: A Comparison with Special Reference to 'Faith that Can Remove Mountains' and 'Your Faith Has Healed/Saved You'* (WUNT 2/147, 2002). **K. L. Yinger,** *Paul, Judaism, and Judgment According to Deeds* (SNTSMS 105, 1999).

H. RÄISÄNE

APOCRYPHA

Tobit, Book of

Because the book of Tobit presents such a well-told story, it has been read and interpreted on many levels among Jews and Christians despite its disputed status in the Canon[§]. Its narrative presents an answer to the problem of how the God of Israel, who is merciful and righteous, rewards the righteous and kind Jew who suffers persecution in the Diaspora. Its characters, themes, and plot tell this message by using the everyday concerns of family, honor, sickness, money, death, and marriage along with the extraordinary elements of angels, demons, exorcism, healing, and prophecies (Prophecy and Prophets, Hebrew Bible[‡§]).

Although Tobit appears as an Israelite from the tribe of Naphtali in Assyrian exile, he; Anna, his wife; Tobias, his son; and Sarah, his daughter-in-law represent pious Jews caught in the problems of Diaspora life. A story of postexilic life for Jews, it seems to have been composed sometime between 250 and 170 B.C.E. (R. Doran 1986, 299; but see M. Rabenau 1994, 175-90). Its earliest use is indicated by four Aramaic fragments and one Hebrew fragment from Qumran (J. Milik 1966, 523, no. 3; G. Vermes 1986, 225; J. VanderKam 1994, 35; J. Fitzmyer 1994, 220-23; F. García-Martínez 1996, 293-99, 487-88). Its presence and likely use among these scrolls show also how Tob connects with other postexilic Jewish literature that "employed canonical novels for the final shaping of the book, with additional influences being exerted from other factors (sources, new beliefs, needs of the community for which the book was written)" (W. Soll 1989, 220, no. 38).

Tob was not recognized as canonical in rabbinic Judaism, yet manuscripts and references to it indicate its continued popularity into the medieval period. Although no commentaries were written on it, Jewish copiers and editors showed ongoing interest by making changes in the texts to conform to later Jewish practices (D. Simpson; R. Pfeiffer 1949, 266).

Early Christian authors also used Tob: Polycarp 10:2 and 2 Clem. 16:4 correspond to Tob 4:10 and 12:8-9 but do not cite Tob on the subject of almsgiving and love (J. Gamberoni 1969, 19-20). For the use and interpretation of Tob in the early church and in the West until 1600, see Gamberoni (1969).

The Christian humanistic scholarship of the Renaissance and Reformation aroused new interest in Tob. This led to the publication of two medieval Jewish manuscripts printed earlier in Constantinople, one by S. Münster[§] and one by P. Fagius[§], both in 1542 (Simpson, 178-80; Gamberoni, 250-52). These texts and a very shortened version of Tobit in the medieval homiletical Midrash*[§] *Tanhuma Yeladammedenu* show continuing Jewish use of the story.

The question of Tobit's canonicity quickly came to the forefront during this period. While Erasmus[§] was aware of the problems from Jerome and others, he did not take the step that A. von Karlstadt[§] did in viewing canonicity as something the church recognized, not established. Hence, for Karlstadt, books like Tob that were not in the Jewish canon were valuable but not on the same level and became apocryphal, not ecclesiastical or deuterocanonical (Gamberoni, 201-8).

Luther[§] gave his view in the 1534 German Bible: "Apocrypha: That is, books not equal to the Holy Scriptures but yet useful and good to read." His preface to Tob spoke highly of its value for Christian behavior, especially in marriage, and he considered it a pious comedy (*WA Bibel* 12, 108-11). During the sixteenth, seventeenth, and eighteenth centuries, interest in the book blossomed into numerous literary and musical works (C. Roth and B. Bayer 1971, 1186-87; Western Literature, the Bible and[§]; and Music, the Bible and[§]).

Following Luther, some commentators (C. Pellican, Flacius Illyricus, Osiander) adapted Tob to new theological and social views on such topics as alms and faith (vs. good works), abstention and marriage. A. Osiander raised questions about Tobit's genre, and C. Pellican[§] considered chaps. 13 and 14 secondary (Gamberoni, 257-73). All these commentaries assumed a basic historicity and probability for the story, whereas Zwingli[§] and other writers latched onto Jerome's doubts and began to talk of fables. The Reformed scholar F. Junius the elder went further: Since the book was non-canonical, it was human and open to error. Aware of other versions of Tob, he pondered its manuscript history, original language (Chaldean, i.e., Aramaic), author, and location, finding moral, theological, and historical errors. It was a bad Jewish sort of fable now safely outside the Bible (Gamberoni, 278-80). This view generally prevailed among Protestants, and scholarly interest in Tob declined. The wedding service in the 1549 *Book of Common Prayer* referred to Tobias and Sarah, following the older Sarum rite; and other Protestant groups, like the Old Order Amish, continued this mention of the book (B. Metzger 1957, 40). Roman Catholic writers, following Trent's favorable decision on Tobit's canonicity, used it in popular works and commentaries (Gamberoni, 281-93), but with a new sense of the problems in the book.

Attempts at dating Tob and attention to its literary structure began in the nineteenth century and have influenced all subsequent interpretations. Both of these aspects concerned Pentateuchal[‡§] source critic K. Ilgen[§] in 1800, who proposed several stages of composition (dating from the seventh to the first cents. B.C.E.), based partly on changes in style and on manuscript evidence (Pfeiffer, 276). German literary historian K. Simrock suggested on the basis of his work in folktales (Folklore*[§]) that Tobit's plot in part came from the folktale theme often called "The Grateful Dead," although this insight was developed only later (for biblical literature in general and for Tob specifically) by J. Renan[§] in 1879 (Pfeiffer, 269). Aside from scholarly interest, the story of Tob continued to engage such readers as S. Kierkegaard[§], who pondered it in *Fear and Trembling*, proposing Sarah as the real hero.

Despite the protests of some scholars defending Tobit's historicity or priority, by the end of the nineteenth century Tob was seen as a didactic tale drawing on at least three sources or influences: "The Grateful Dead," "The Dangerous Bride," and "The Story of Ahikar." Recognition of Tobit's connection to Ahikar came before access to the Ahikar text from Elephantine in 1911; in addition to earlier questions about written or oral dependence, interpretation has more recently looked at how the Ahikar material is used in the overall aims of Tob (P. Deselaers 1982, 424-48; J. Lindenberger 1985, 488-90; Soll, 221). Persian influence was also detected but was disputed (Pfeiffer, 271, no. 40; Soll, 225, no. 46). Egyptian influence (Simpson, 187-88) is now considered unlikely (Pfeiffer, 271).

Besides the Ahikar manuscript discovery, discovery of the Sinaiticus version of Tob (pub. 1862) and of Tob fragments from Qumran (Dead Sea Scrolls[§]) have given new directions to interpretation: Codex Sinaiticus with its Semiticisms (Thomas) and longer version seems favored now over Codices Alexandrinus and Vaticinus as the superior Greek version of the book (backed by the OL); and this in turn has been supported by study of the Qumran fragments, which largely agree with the longer version of Sinaiticus and also represent all fourteen chapters (VanderKam, 35). Aramaic may still be the likely original language (Vermes, 225; Doran, 296; VanderKam, 35; Rabenau, 7).

Work on source analysis (Simpson, 187-96) or the use of sources in Tob (M. Plath 1901, 404-14) continued in the early twentieth century alongside interest in the book as a source for historical reconstruction of early Judaism and Christianity—as can be seen in the early editions of E. Schürer[§] (*RGG*) and later in Pfeiffer's history and F. Zimmermann's commentary (1958).

Yet beside this more historical approach, literary study grew in new directions with the aid of work on folktales by G. Gerould (1908, 1973), S. Thompson (1933), and V. Propp (1968). S. Liljeblad (1927) proposed to move from the motif of "The Grateful Dead" to the story of "The Dangerous Bride" as the core of Tobit's plot; T. Glasson (1959) agreed but wished to connect the plot to the Admetus story in Apollodorus. Other literary research moved from listing biblical literary connections (Simpson, 192, nos. 6-7; Zimmermann, 12-13) to investigating how biblical themes or stories had been models for Tob. L. Ruppert (1972) looked to the Joseph story; A. Di Lella (1979) found connections to themes in Deut; Deselaers proposed the Isaac and Rebekah story in Genesis 24. J. Blenkinsopp (1981) drew these two directions closer in his 1981 work by comparing Tob as a sort of biography (along with the Jacob stories) with Propp's grid of folktale functions (actually fairytale functions, as P. Milne [1986] has pointed out). Blenkinsopp claimed to find enough similarities to Propp's functions to question the best genre description of Tob and also whether Tob has a pattern similar to other lives told in biblical narratives.

Tob has often carried the tag "didactic" or "paraenetic" story, or *Novelle*, with that sort of flavor (Deselaers, 271, no. 460; Vermes, 222); but like Blenkinsopp, Deselaer challenged this. His *Das Buch Tobit* impressively combined literary, historical, and theological research comparable to G. Nickelsburg's work. While Deselaers investigated the book's divisions, details, and development, giving some recognition to its totality, Nickelsburg invited the reader to consider it as a totality while appreciating its many constituent parts and complexities. Deselaers began with a Literary*§-critical investigation of the frame story (chaps. 1-3; 14) and of the internal story (chaps 4-14:1), which led him to propose that Tob originated in a basic didactic story, which was expanded three times (Deselaers, 48-56). After examining all its parts he concluded that the genre of *Novelle* fits for the internal story; but the fuller final shape is better described as a sort of novel (*Roman*) that has incorporated elements from some other genres (Deselaers, 273-79). Rabenau's studies on Tob enter into conversation with Deselaer's work by proposing a basic narrative focused on the theme of guidance involving various subthemes (Rabenau, 94-147), with expansions (Rabenau, 8-26; 148-74).

The briefer treatments of Tob by Nickelsburg (1984, 1988) emphasize the present shape of the book as "an integrated literary whole" that contains a complex, yet well-told story employing various literary forms, such as testaments, prayers, hymns, etc. (Nickelsburg 1984, 40; see also the index on Tobit). In his brief commentary he first analyzed the whole text as a "sophisticated and carefully crafted narrative," the plot (especially the parallels of Tobit and Sarah), and the complex forms and motifs woven into the total story (Nickelsburg 1988, 791-92).

On religious dimensions in Tobit, Deselaers and Nickelsburg are in general agreement. Nickelsburg shows a development from pious life to despair in sufferings, followed by God's actions, and finally doxology; he points to the theme that divine help is imperceptible to humans. Deselaers views the terms *hodos, eleēmosynē*, and *eulogein* (blessing) as important for Tobit's overall message. Nickelsburg speaks of the doxological and didactic tones and intention and points out social aspects of Tobit: concern with family, marriage, burial, Diaspora, etc. This Deselaers does in greater length and depth in his investigation of theological and sociological aspects, connecting family and kinship with mobility (*hodos*) and almsgiving (*eleēmosynē*) in Diaspora life (Deselaers, 309-73).

Both Deselaers and Rabenau propose stages for Tobit's development. Deselaers's three stages occur in 220, 195, and 185 B.C.E.; Tob was started in Alexandria and enlarged there and in Jerusalem (cf. Doran, 299). Rabenau argues for a Samaritan beginning in the third century B.C.E., with additions in the 140s and later in the last half of the second century among Jews, while recognizing interest in it in the Diaspora (Rabenau, 175-90).

J. Craghan's brief commentary on parts of Tob (1982) shows agreement with Di Lella's deuteronomic connections and attention to the story line (sTob 11:15). I. Nowell's commentary (1990) combines recent discussion on Tob with sensitivity to literary points and structure (the use of the inclusio, themes of journey, and healing) in its short scope. H. Gross's longer commentary (1987) tends to follow some of the directions set by Deselaers.

Soll's article has drawn together folktale research and refinements and biblical scholarship of the late twentieth century, developing an interesting analysis of one important function of fairy-tale plots (villainy or lack; Soll calls it misfortune). A brief introduction and overview of Tob incorporating an interest in the effect of the whole complex story line with attention to literary technique has appeared in N. Petersen's essay (1990). Nowell (1995) and D. McCracken (1995) point to humor in Tobit.

Interpretation of Tob (indeed of the Apocrypha and beyond) has again begun from interest in social and religious history (B. Bow and G. Nickelsburg 1991; A. J. Levine 1992; H. Engel 1993; M. Oeming 1994) and also for tracing literary and theological connections with canonical Jewish and early Christian writing (Nickelsburg 1984, 45-56; 1988, 792).

Recent commentaries on Tob include Fitzmyer (2003), Moore (1996, 2003), Schuller (1998), and H. Schüngel-Straumann (2000). Otzen (2002) has written a general introduction to Tob. Other recent studies include Jewish self-identification as seen in Tob (Ego 2002), the relationships between Tob and other ancient literature (MacDonald 2001, Nickelsburg 2001), magic in Tob (Stuckenbruck 2002), the environmental worldview of Tob (Urbrock 2000), and further study on Tobit's textual history (Skemp 2000).

Bibliography: K. Beyer, *Die aramäischen Texte vom Toten Meer: Ergänzungsband* (1994) 134-47. J. Blenkinsopp, "Biographical Patterns in Biblical Literature," *JSOT* 20 (1981) 27-46. B. Bow and G. W. E. Nickelsburg, "Patriarchy with a Twist: Men and Women in Tobit," *Women like This: New Perspectives on Jewish Women in the Greco-Roman World* (ed. A. J. Levine, 1991) 127-43. J. Cragan, *Esther, Judith, Tobit, Jonah, Ruth* (OT Message 16, 1982). P. Deselaers, *Das Buch Tobit: Studien zu seiner Entstehung, Komposition, und Theologie* (1982). A. A. Di Lella, "The Deuteronomic Background of the Farewell Discourse in Tob 14:3-11," *CBQ* 41 (1979) 380-89. R. Doran, "Narrative Literature," *Early Judaism and Its Modern Interpreters* (ed. R. A. Kraft and G. W. E. Nickelsburg, 1986) 287-310. B. Ego, "'Heimat in der Fremde': zur Konstituierung einer jüdischen Identität im Buch Tobit," *Jüdische Schriften in ihrem antik-jüdischen und urchristlichen Kontext* (ed. H. Lichtenberger and G. S. Oegema, Studien zu den Jüdischen Schriften aus hellenistisch-römischer Zeit 1, 2002) 270-83. E. E. Ellis, "The OT Canon in the Early Church," *Mikra* (ed. M. J. Mulder and H. Sysling, 1988) 653-90. H. Engel, "Auf zuverlässigen Wegen und in Gerechtigkeit: Religiöses Ethos in der Diaspora nach dem Buch Tobit," *Biblische Theologie und gesellschaftlicher Wandel* (ed. G. Braulik, 1993) 8-100. J. A. Fitzmyer, "Preliminary Publication of pap 4Qtob^a ar," *Bib* 75 (1994) 220-24; *Tobit* (Commentaries On Early Jewish Literature, 2003). J. Gamberoni, *Die Auslegung des Buches Tobias in der griechisch-lateinischen Kirche der Antike und der Christenheit des Westens bis um 1600* (1969). F. García Martínez, *The Dead Sea Scrolls Translated* (1996) 293-99, 487-88. G. H. Gerould, *The Grateful Dead* (1908, 1973). T. F. Glasson, "The Main Source of Tobit," *ZAW* 71 (1959) 275-77. H. Gross, *Tobit/Judit* (NEB.AT 19, 1987). K. Ilgen, *Das Buch Tobias: Die Geschichte Tobi's nach drey verschiedenen Originalen dem Griechischen dem Lateinischen des Hieronymus und einem Syrischen* (1800). A.-J. Levine, "Tobit: Teaching Jews how to Live in the Diaspora," *BRev* 8 (1992) 42-51, 64. S. Liljeblad, *Die Tobiasgeschichte und andere Märchen mit toten Helfern* (1927). J. M. Lindenberger, "Ahiqar," *OTP* 2 (1985) 479-93. D. R. MacDonald, "Tobit and the Odyssey," *Mimesis and Intertextuality in Antiquity and Christianity* (ed. D. R. MacDonald, SAC, 2001) 11-40. D. McCracken, "Narration and Comedy in the Book of Tobit," *JBL* 114 (1995) 401-18. B. M. Metzger, *An Introduction to the Apocrypha* (1957). J. T. Milik, "La Patrie de Tobie," *RB* 73 (1966) 522-30. P. J. Milne, "Folktales and Fairy Tales: An Evaluation of Two Proppian Analyses of Biblical Narratives," *JSOT* 34 (1986) 35-60; *V. Propp and the Study of Structure in Hebrew Biblical Narrative* (1988). C. A. Moore, *Tobit: A New Translation with Introduction and Commentary* (AB 40A,

1996); "Tobit," *NISB* (2003) 1357-77. **J. Müller**, *Beiträge zur Erklärung und Kritik des Buches Tobit* (BZAW 13, 1908). **G. W. E. Nickelsburg**, *Jewish Literature Between the Bible and the Mishnah: A Historical and Literary Introduction* (1981); "Tobit," *Jewish Writings of the Second Temple Period* (ed. M. E. Stone, CRINT 2/2, 1984) 40-46; "Tobit," *HBC* (1988) 791-803; "Tobit, Genesis, and the Odyssey: A Complex Web of Intertextuality *Mimesis and Intertextuality in Antiquity and Christianity* (ed. D. R. MacDonald, SAC, 2001) 41-55. **I. Nowell**, "Irony in the Book of Tobit," *TBT* 33 (1995) 79-83. **M. Oeming**, "Ethik in der Spätzeit des Alten Testaments am Beispiel von Hiob 31 und Tobit 4," *Altes Testament Forschung und Wirkung* (eds. P. Mommer and W. Thiel, 1994) 159-73. **B. Otzen**, *Tobit and Judith* (Guides to the Apocrypha and Pseudepigrapha 11, 2002). **N. R. Petersen**, "Tobit," *Books of the Bible* (ed. B. W. Anderson, 1990) 2, 35-42. **R. H. Pfeiffer**, *History of the NT Times with an Introduction to the Apocrypha* (1949). **M. Plath**, "Zum Buch Tobit," *TSK* 74 (1901) 377-414. **V. Propp**, *Morphology of the Folktale* (1968). **M. Rabenau**, *Studien zum Buch Tobit* (BZAW 220, 1994). **L. Réau**, Iconographie de l'art chrétien 2, 1 (1956). **C. Roth and B. Beyer**, "Book of Tobit: In the Arts," *EncJud* 15 (1971) 1186-87. **L. Ruppert**, "Das Buch Tobias: Ein Modelfall nachgestaltender Erzählung," *Wort, Lied, und Gottesspruch: Septuaginta* (ed. J. Schreiner, 1972) 109-19. **G. Schiller**, *Iconography of Christian Art* 1 (1971). **E. M. Schuller**, "Tobit," *Women's Bible Commentary* (ed. C. A. Newsom and S. H. Ringe, 1998²). **H. Schüngel-Straumann**, *Tobit* (HTKAT, 2000). **D. C. Simpson**, "The Book of Tobit," *APOT* 1 (1913a) 174-201; "The Chief Recensions of the Book of Tobit," *JTS* 14 (1913b) 516-30. **V. T. M. Skemp**, *The Vulgate of Tobit Compared with Other Ancient Witnesses* (SBLDS 180, 2000). **W. Soll**, "Misfortune and Exile in Tobit: The Juncture of a Fairy Tale Source and Deuteronomic Theology," *CBQ* 51 (1989) 209-31. **L. T. Stuckenbruck**, "The Book of Tobit and the Problem of 'Magic,'" *Jüdische Schriften in ihrem antik-jüdischen und urchristlichen Kontext* (H. Lichtenberger and G. S. Oegema, Studien zu den Jüdischen Schriften aus hellenistisch-römischer Zeit 1, 2002) 258-69. **J. D. Thomas**, "The Greek Text of Tobit," *JBL* 91 (1972) 463-71. **S. Thompson**, *Motif-index of Folk-literature* 2 (1933); *The Folktale* (1951). **W. J. Urbrock**, "Angels, Bird-Droppings and Fish Liver: The Earth Story in Tobit," *Readings from the Perspective of Earth* (ed. N. C. Habel, Earth Bible 1, 2000) 125-37. **J. C. VanderKam**, *The Dead Sea Scrolls Today* (1994). **G. Vermes**, "The Book of Tobit," *HJPAJC* 3, 1 (1986) 222-32. **H. Weskott**, "Tobias," *Lexikon der christlichen Ikonographie: Allgemeine Ikonographie* 4 (1972) 320-26. **F. Zimmermann**, *The Book of Tobit* (1958).

W. POEHLMANN

APOCRYPHA

Judith, Book of

One of the most masterfully composed narratives in the Hebrew Bible Apocrypha, indeed, in the entire Jewish literary corpus, the book of Judith meticulously develops the historical setting and crisis (chaps. 1–7) into which the character of Judith is introduced in chap. 8. Her story unfolds (chaps. 8–16) full of suspense and comes to full resolution with a horrifying climax and a victory song. The story's literary artistry, its enigmatic historical setting, the remarkable character of Judith, and the story's disturbing theological endorsement of her cold-blooded murder of Holofernes all have generated an intense fascination throughout the history of interpretation.

1. *Canonicity.* Despite some doubt to the contrary (A. Dubarle 1966; T. Craven 1983), most scholars posit an original but nonextant Hebrew text for the book, given the numerous Hebraisms in the earliest existing Greek texts. The text is extant in Greek, Latin, Syriac, and Ethiopic (Ethiopian Biblical Interpretation§). The Jewish tradition classified Jdt among the *hiconim* (the strange or foreign books in the holy writings), which were considered inspired but, nonetheless, inferior (Origen *Epist. ad Jul. Afric.* 13; Jerome§ *Praef. in lib. Jud.*). One wonders why the book did not gain Jewish canonical status as compared to the success of the book of Esther, which is patently less theological. The reasons may be both fortuitous and Ideological*§. C. Moore (1992) suggests that, given the early date for the canonization of the Hebrew Bible (2nd cent. B.C.E.), Judith's date of composition was too late for inclusion. P. Winter (1962) argues that Judith's exclusion from the Canon§ is due to the fact that the story is set in a small place, evidently in Samaritan territory, whereas Esther has a more prestigious setting in the center of Persia. Indeed, later Jewish traditions give Jdt more prominent locations and identities. Moreover, the book of Esther is intrinsically connected with the annual feast of Purim, whereas Jdt only gradually became associated with the festival of Hanukkah by the Middle Ages. Possibly the conversion of the Ammonite Achior, in whose lips even a declaration of Israel's faith history is found, was considered offensive by some Jews (see Deut 23:3). Also, the book's portrayal of male cowardice and impotence in the face of Judith's cunning courage may have been disturbing to the patriarchal society of the time it was written.

Within Christendom the book enjoyed a somewhat better, albeit ambiguous, status. It has been suggested that the New Testament consciously alludes several times to Judith: Matt 13:42, 50 = Jdt 16:17; Luke 1:42 = Jdt 14:7; Acts 4:24 = Jdt 9:12; 1 Cor 2:11 = Jdt 8:14. Indeed, if one can rely on the so-called *Decretum Gelasianum* (a sixth-century list of canonical Scriptures), Jdt (along with Tob, Wis, Sir, and 1 and 2 Macc) was considered canonical by the Roman Catholic Church by the beginning of the sixth century, but its eventual acceptance into the canon was not reached without controversy. It was initially considered authoritative (Authority of the Bible*§) as early as the end of the first century, as confirmed by the earliest reference to it made by Clement of Rome§ (1 Clem. 55.4-5). In the second and third centuries references to the book place it on the level of holy Scripture: Clement of Alexandria§ (*Strom.* 2.17 and 4.19); Tertullian§, *De monogamia* 17; *Adv. Marc.* 1.7), as well as Ambrose§ (De offi. minist. 3.13) and Augustine§ (*De doctrina Christiana* 2.8) a century later.

Voices of reservation and dissent were raised: Melito of Sardis§ (Eusebius Hist. eccl. 4.26); Origen§ (*Expos. in psalmum* 1); and Athanasius§ (*Ep. fest.* 39); Cyril of Jerusalem, and Gregory of Nazianzus§, among others. In the West, Hilary, Rufin, and Jerome§ opposed including Jdt in the canon. Jerome, who supported the boundaries of the Jewish canon, in his *Comment. in Agg.* 1.6 refers to Jdt 7:16 while giving the disclaimer: *si quis tamen vult recipere librum mulieris* (if one, however, wants to accept a woman's book). Indeed, Jerome's opinion was that the work was written by Judith herself. The favorable voices eventually won out, and its popularity in the

West forced Jerome to concede to including it in his Vulgate*§ translation (*acquievi postulatione vestrae, imo exactioni*, from his "Preface to Judith"). Jerome mentioned in his preface that it was included by the Council of Nicea among the Holy Scriptures. The approbations of the councils of Carthage, Florence, and Trent, as well as the book's inclusion in the lists of Codex Claramontanus and *Liber sacramentorum*, solidified its position among the books of the canonical Hebrew Bible.

2. *Interpretation. a. Early interpretation.* As noted above, the book of Judith came to be associated with the festival of Hanukkah in the medieval midrashim (see Midrash*§). Variant forms of the story appeared in medieval Jewish literature. Early Christian interpreters struggled to make sense of the confusing historical details in the book and emphasized Judith's character as either a model of resistance to persecution or as a model of chastity.

b. Reformation and Enlightenment interpretation. Luther§ was the first to popularize the notion that the book never intended to describe history, although the first major commentary on Jdt, by Rabanus Maurus§, treated the book as allegorical. For Luther the book was a "religious fiction or poem, written by a holy and ingenious man, who depicts therein the victory of the Jewish people over all their enemies" (*Vorrede aufs Buch Judith*). According to him the name "Judith" represents the Jewish people; Holofernes is the heathen lord of all ages, and the city of Bethulia denotes a virgin. Thus the Reformers interpreted the story in terms of the triumph of virtue over wickedness. H. Grotius§ pushed the approach further by regarding the book as an allegorical description of Antiochus IV Ephiphanes' attack on Judea: "Judith is the Jewish people; Bethulia is the temple; the sword which went out of it, the prayers of the saints; Nebuchadnezzar signifies the devil; Assyria is pride, the devil's kingdom; Holofernes is the devil's instrument." Grotius constructed etymologies out of the proper names in order to discover the allegorical allusions of the story, as with Holofernes and Joachim (God will arise). Once the allegorical approach became popular, commentators began to disparage the confusing historical details. Capellus's scathing appraisal in 1689 was representative of his day: Jdt is "a most silly fable invented by a most inept, injudicious, impudent and clownish Hellenist" (*Commentarii et notae criticae in Vet. Test.* 575).

c. Post-Enlightenment interpretation. The allegorical interpretation, however, did not win much approval. Other more daring interpreters, beginning with J. Ussher§, attempted to place the historical background of the text before the exile, specifically after Manasseh's return from Babylon. D. Calmet§, for instance, dated Judith's birth at 719 B.C.E., making her sixty-three years old at the time of Holofernes' expedition in 656 B.C.E. Her age, however, does not present a problem for Judith, "being then what we call a fine woman, and having an engaging air and person," according to Calmet.

This preexilic theory came into disfavor, despite such later proponents as O. Wolff (1881), when W. De Wette§ pointed out that the name "Holofernes" is attested with respect to Persian history in the works of the historians Appian and Polybius, thereby setting a new direction in scholarship and in part a return to the theories of the early church.

d. Modern scholarship. i. Historical issues. Much of modern scholarship has been devoted to cracking the enigmatic historical background of the story. It is widely recognized that the book is quasi-fictional, since it is replete with historical anachronisms and inaccuracies. For instance, the historically attested king of Neo-Babylonia, Nebuchadnezzar (605-562 B.C.E.), is introduced as king of the Assyrians (1:1), who declares war on Israel only after the Jews have returned from the exile and reconsecrated the Temple (4:3). However, the kingdoms of Assyria and Media no longer existed after the time of the Babylonian exile. This has led some commentators to treat Jdt 1:1 as intended fiction. C. C. Torrey§ claimed that the first verse intended to have the same effect on its ancient readers as the following statement would have on modern readers: "It happened at the time when Napoleon Bonaparte was king of England and Otto von Bismark was on the throne in Mexico" (89).

As noted above, Persian elements in the story have long been recognized. Vindicating the view of Sulpicius Severus, such modern scholars as T. Nöldeke[§], W. R. Smith[§], and J. Wellhausen[§] located the book in the time of Artaxerxes III Ochus (359/58-338/37). Variations of this theory include J. Grintz (1957), who favors a slightly earlier dating within the reign of Artaxerxes II during the "revolt of the satraps" in 362 B.C.E., and Dubarle (1966), who claims the book is based on a real but unidentifiable episode from the Persian age. The strongest evidence for the theory is that a general named Orophernes and a eunuch commander named Bagoas are recorded to have participated in Artaxerxes Ochus's campaigns against Phoenicia and Egypt (Diodorus 26.47.4; 27.5.3; 31.19.2-3). In addition, many scholars see the book's sociohistory as more reflective of the Persian than of the Hellenistic period.

Other commentators have pointed out, however, that the names "Holofernes" and "Bagoas" were common even in the Hellenistic age and that no Persian king ever demanded of the Jews to be worshiped as god. Indeed, the mention of Nebuchadnezzar proves that the author was drawing in part from past history rather than from the contemporary situation. Thus E. Schürer (1987), R. Pfeiffer[§] (1949), O. Eissfeldt[§] (1974), M. Enslin and S. Zeitlin (1972), and L. Alonso-Schökel (1974) suggest that the work is to be placed in the Maccabean era since the author portrays Israel's political and religious freedom to be externally threatened. As in the book of Daniel, Nebuchadnezzar in the book of Judith could be understood as representing Antiochus IV (175-164 B.C.E.). Zeitlin has pointed out striking parallels between Judas's defeat of Nicanor, general of Demetrius I (1 Macc 8:33-50) and that of Holofernes by Judith. Alonso-Schökel points out that the name of the protagonist is the feminine form of the Jewish national hero of the time, Judah.

Consensus and compromise suggest that the book of Judith drew from or was first redacted near the end of the Persian period with its final form realized in the Hasmonean period (so Eissfeldt, Schürer, and G. Nickelsburg 1984).

ii. Literary issues. A recent trend in modern scholarship has been to examine the work in terms of its Literary*[§] features. The traditional modern approach has been to view it as didactic literature (Zeitlin, Schürer), stressing its moral and religious message of encouragement to Jews in persecution. Others see the work as a novel (J. Dancy 1972; E. Zenger 1981). With regard to the characters and setting of the story, E. Haag (1963) and Zenger, recalling the allegorical approach popular during the Reformation, give the character of Nebuchadnezzar a suprahistorical quality. Zenger claims that Bethulia signifies Jerusalem, the "House of God." Indeed, Haag describes the book as a "parabolic presentation of history." Nickelsburg and others see Judith as a composite character building upon other Israelite heroines (Miriam, Jael, and Deborah) and heroes (Samson, David, Daniel, and Judas Maccabeus). P. Skehan[§] (1963) suggests that the story of Judith is modeled on the exodus story as a "haggadah for Passover."

Partly in response to A. Cowley's[§] widely accepted negative observation (1913) that the book is "out of proportion" due to its overly long introduction (chaps. 1–7), Alonso-Schökel and Craven (1983) have examined the work almost entirely in terms of its compositional structure. Craven argues on compositional grounds that it is a balanced, symmetrical work in which the first seven chapters constitute the "full half of the real story." Indeed, the first seven chapters describe men in leading roles, in contrast to the second half of the book. Furthermore, in each half is a threefold chiastic structure with a distinctive thematic repetition. Craven also recognizes comedy and satire as important dimensions that could help to explain the confusing historical setting. Similarly, C. Moore (1985) claims that irony is the key to the book's fictional character (85).

iii. Judith's example and theology. Another modern evaluation of the work has also experienced some slippage. Cowley and W. Oesterley§ (1935), representing most scholars of their day, described the work's theology as patently pharisaic, given the book's pietistic emphasis on prayer, devotion, and ritual and its orthodox adherence to the Mosaic law. H. Mantel (1976), however, has argued that the book represents a Sadducean orientation of life viewed from the perspective of the Jerusalem Temple. In contrast, Grintz argues that the *halakha* in Jdt is prepharisaic and reveals no trace of sectarianism. Craven points out that Judith's behavior, although meant to preserve the continuance of orthodox worship, involves some very unorthodox actions. She flatters (11:7-8), shamelessly lies (11:12-14, 18-19), and ruthlessly assassinates (13:7-8) with no respect for the dead (13:9-10, 15). "Judith is willing to break the law in order to maintain the greater principle for which it stands." Such an observance goes a long way from O. Zöckler's remark in his commentary on the Apocrypha (1891) that Jdt represents a degenerate and despicable standard of morality (186), or from that of E. C. Bissell (1886): "There are elements of moral turpitude in the character of Judith," who "would have been willing even to have yielded her body to this lascivious Assyrian for the sake of accomplishing her purpose" (163, italics added).

Last, the character of Judith has gained much attention from feminists. P. Montley (1978) describes her as the archetypal androgyny, a figure who is more than simply warrior woman and *femme fatale*. She "transcends the male/female dichotomy" (40). From more of a literary perspective S. White (1992) argues that Judith's character intentionally resembles the heroines Jael and Deborah in Judges 4-5.

The work of Gierlinger-Czerny (2000) and Stocker (1998) demonstrates the continued interest in feminist analyses of Jdt. Herrmann (1994) studies ancient Jewish self-understanding as seen in the book. Newman (1999) analyzes Judith's prayer in Jdt 9. Thompson (2002) has compiled a concordance for Jdt and Crawford (2003) has written a recent concise commentary on the book.

Bibliography: **L. Alonso-Schökel**, "Narrative Structures in the Book of Judith," *Protocol Series of the Colloquies of the Center for Hermeneutical Studies in Hellenistic and Modern Culture* 11 (ed. W. Wuellner, 1974) 1-20; "Judith," *HBC* (1988) 804-14. **M. Bal**, "Head Hunting: 'Judith' on the Cutting Edge of Knowledge," *A Feminist Companion to Esther, Judith, and Susanna* (ed. A. Brenner, 1995) 253-85. **B. Bayer**, "The Book of Judith in the Arts," *EncJud* 10 (1971) 459-61. **G. Brunner**, *Der Nabuchodonosor des Buches Judith* (1940, 1959²). **A. E. Cowley**, "Book of Judith," *APOT* (1913) 1:242-47. **T. Craven**, *Artistry and Faith in the Book of Judith* (1983). **S. W. Crawford**, "Judith," *NISB* (2003) 1379-1400. **J. C. Dancy**, *The Shorter Books of the Apocrypha: Tobit, Judith, Rest of Esther, Baruch, Letter of Jeremiah, Additions to Daniel, and Prayer of Manasseh* (CBC, 1972). **R. Doran**, "Judith," *Early Judaism and Its Modern Interpreters* (ed. R. A. Kraft and G. W. E. Nickelsburg, 1986) 302-5. **A. M. Dubarle**, *Judith: Formes et sens des diverses traditions* (AnBib 24, 2 vols., 1966). **O. Eissfeldt**, *The OT: An Introduction* (1974) 585-87. **M. S. Enslin and S. Zeitlin**, *The Book of Judith* (Jewish Apocryphal Literature 7, 1972). **M. Gaster**, "An Unknown Hebrew Version of the History of Judith," *PSBA* 16 (1893-94) 156-63. **E. Gierlinger-Czerny**, *Judits Tat: die Aufkündigung des Geschlechtervertrages* (2000). **J. M. Grintz**, *Sefer Yehudith* (1957, Hebrew); "Judith, Book of," *EncJud* 10 (1971) 451-59. **E. Haag**, *Studien zum Buch Judith* (1963). **R. Hanhart**, *Text und Textgeschichte des Buches Judith* (1979). **W. Herrmann**, *Jüdische Glaubensfundamente* (BEATAJ 36, 1994). **A. Lefèvre**, *DBSup* 4 (1949) 1315-319. **A. J. Levine**, "Sacrifice and Salvation: Otherness and Domestication in the Book of Judith," *"No One Spoke Ill of Her": Essays on Judith* (ed. J. C. VanderKam, 1992) 17-30. **K. Luke**, "The Book of Judith," *BiBh* 9 (1983) 17-37. **H. Mantel**, *Studies in Judaism* (1976) 60-80. **B. M. Metzger**, *An Introduction to* *the Apocrypha* (1957) 43-53. **C. Meyer**, "Zur Entstehungsgeschichte des Buches Judith," *Bib* 3 (1922) 193-203. **P. Montley**, "Judith in the Fine Arts: The Appeal of the Archetypal Androgyne," *Anima* 4 (1978) 37-42. **C. A. Moore**, *Judith* (AB 40, 1985); "Why Wasn't the Book of Judith Included in the HB?" *"No One Spoke Ill of Her": Essays on Judith* (ed. J. C. VanderKam, 1992) 61-72. **J. H. Newman**, *Praying by the Book: The Scripturalization of Prayer in Second Temple Judaism* (SLBEJL 14, 1999). **G. W. E. Nickelsburg**, "Judith," *Jewish Writings of the Second Temple Period* (ed. M. Stone, 1984) 46-52. **W. O. E. Oesterley**, *The Books of the Apocrypha: Their Origin, Teaching, and Contents* (1935). **R. H. Pfeiffer**, *History of NT Times, with an Introduction to the Apocrypha* (1949) 285-303. **E. Purdie,** *The Story of Judith in German and English Literature* (Bibliothèque de la Revue de Littérature Comparée 34, 1927). **D. A. Radavich**, "Judith and Her Interpreters" (diss., University of Kansas, 1979). **E. Schürer**, "The Book of Judith," *HJPAJC* 3.1 (1987) 216-22. **P. Skehan**, "The Hand of Judith," CBQ 25 (1963) 94-109. **L. Soubigou**, "Judith: Traduit et Commente," *La Sainte Bible* (ed. L. Pirot and A. Clamer, 1949). **M. Stocker**, *Judith: Sexual Warrior: Women and Power in Western Culture* (1998). **J. D. Thompson**, *A Critical Concordance to the Apocrypha. Judith* (The Computer Bible 105, 2002). **S. A. White**, "In the Steps of Jael and Deborah: Judith as Heroine," *"No One Spoke Ill of Her": Essays on Judith* (ed. J. C. VanderKam, 1992) 5-16. **P. Winter**, *IDB* (1962) 2:1023-26. **E. Zenger**, "Das Buch Judith," *JSHRZ* 1.6 (1981) 428-534. **F. Zimmermann**, "Aids for the Recovery of the Hebrew Original of Judith," *JBL* 57 (1938) 67-74.

W. P. Brown

APOCRYPHA

Additions to Esther

1. *Introduction.* No other biblical book has occasioned as much strong feeling and scholarly debate over its historicity, canonical status, textual integrity, and theological and moral stature as has the book of Esther[‡§]. Excluded by some Jews from their Canon[§] of the first century C.E. (and possibly from that of the second or even the third), Esther was gradually accepted as canonical by both Jews and Christians, only to be virtually ignored by the latter even as Jews increasingly venerated the Megilla (Scroll), as they called it. Judaism developed a rich talmudic and midrashic (Talmud*[§], Midrash*[§]) tradition about the book that was totally ignored by Christians, while the latter in turn were divided, first into Eastern and Western camps, and then later into sharply contrasting Protestant and Roman Catholic perspectives. All this becomes more understandable when one realizes that in the MT of Esther God is not mentioned (yet the Persian king is referred to 190 times in 167 verses!); nor are such key Jewish concepts as prayer, Temple, Jerusalem, or covenant (fasting is the only religious practice mentioned!). Moreover, the Greek version has two radically different texts (the Septuagint, or B-text; and the A-text), neither of which closely corresponds to the MT, plus six additions (Add Esth), which appreciably affect the book's purpose, dramatic appeal, appearance of authenticity, and religious and moral character. Jews and Protestants have regarded the Add Esth as noncanonical and "apocryphal," while Roman Catholics, since the decrees of the Council of Trent in 1546, have called them "deuterocanonical."

Esther's Add Esth (107 verses) differ from one another—and from the canonical sections—in purpose, content, and style. They consist of Add Esth A: Mordecai's dream (vv. 1-11) and a conspiracy uncovered by him (vv. 12-17); B: the royal edict composed by Haman for the destruction of the Jews (vv. 1-7); C: the prayers of Mordecai (vv. 1-11) and Esther (vv. 12-30); D: Esther's dramatic unannounced audience with the king (vv. 1-16); E: the royal edict dictated by Mordecai (vv. 1-24); and F: an explanation of Mordecai's dream (vv. 1-10) and the book's colophon (v. 11).

2. *Early Jewish Interpretations.* Although the earliest form of the Esther story may go back to the fourth century B.C.E, its Hebrew text probably took its final form in the early or middle Hellenistic period (331-168 B.C.E.). Nonetheless, Esther was one of the last books of the Hebrew Bible to be canonized. The Essene community at Qumran (c. 150 B.C.E.-68 C.E.) did not regard it as canonical, for not even a fragment of it has been found there (J. Milik 1992) nor was Purim part of their liturgical calendar. At least two rabbis in the third century (*b. Meg.* 7a) and two in the third/fourth (*b. Sanh.* 2) also regarded the book as noncanonical, and it is not found in the second-century Jewish Greek translations of Aquila[§], Symmachus[§], or Theodotion[§]. The Jewish historian Josephus[§] evidently accepted Esther's canonicity, however, for he paraphrased it and Add Esth B-E in his *Antiquities of the Jews* (c. 94 C.E.) and added additional material to it.

3. *The Early Christian Era.* Esther was not quoted by Jesus[§§] or alluded to by any New Testament writer. Even though included in the canonical lists of a few Eastern church fathers (notably, Origen[§], Epiphanius, Cyril of Jerusalem, the Laodicene Canons [343-381], the Apostolic Canons [380], the Synod of Trullo [692], John of Damascus and of most Western fathers, ranging from Hilary to Isidore of Seville[§] as well as the councils of Hippo (393) and Carthage (397), it was rarely alluded to, let alone quoted.

The fathers virtually ignored the book. Some exceptions include Clement of Rome[§] (1 *Clem.* 55), Clement of Alexandria[§] (*Strom.* 4:19), Athanasius[§] of Alexandria (*Fourth Festal Letter*), the author of the *Apostolic Constitutions* (5.3.20), Origen[§] (*peri euches* 13.2), Jerome[§] (*apologeticum ad Pammachius*), and Paulinus Nolanus (*Carmina* 26.95; 28.27). Augustine[§] commented on the book (*de divinis scripturis* 130), including Add Esth D 8 (*de Civitate Dei* 18.36, *de Gratia Christi et de peccato originali* 1.24)

4. *The Medieval Period*. a. *Jewish*. Traditional rabbinic exegesis continued during this period. A radically different type of scholarship that rejected this style of rabbinic exegesis and emphasized a literalistic interpretation of Scripture was that of Rashi[§], who emphasized lexical and grammatical analysis. Using much the same approach, the greatest of all Arabic-Jewish exegetes, A. ibn Ezra[§] also wrote a commentary on Esther. This literalistic approach to Scripture was productive, but short-lived, with the thirteenth-century rise of the esoteric, mystical Kabbalah[§] that emphasized allegorical and midrashic interpretations.

b. *Christian*. Rabanus Maurus's[§] *Expositio in librum Esther* (836) marked the appearance of the first full-length commentary on Esther (the canonical sections only) offering largely allegorical interpretations, e.g., the "linen and purple cords" in Esth 1:6 represent "mortification of the flesh" and "the blood of the martyrs," respectively.

Devotional and homiletical concerns prevailed over exegetical ones, e.g., the commentaries of Walafrid Strabo[§] and Hugh of St. Victor[§]. R. Tuitiensis (1135) regarded the book as essentially historical, but continued allegorical interpretations. Relying on the work of Rashi and Ibn Ezra, Nicholas of Lyra[§] made the major medieval contribution to the critical study of Esther with his *Postillae perpetuae*.

5. *The Renaissance-Reformation Period*. a. *Jewish*. Virtually unaffected by the intellectual revolution then going on among Christian scholars, Jewish commentators continued their midrashic approach to Scripture.

b. *Christian*. With the West's discovery of classical languages and literature, plus the Protestants' insistence on Scripture as the sole Authority*[§] for doctrines, the second half of the sixteenth century witnessed a strong emphasis on the study of the Bible in its original Hebrew and Greek, although most Roman Catholic scholars still used the Vulgate*[§]. Thus Roman Catholics continued to study the Add Esth[†§] while Protestants increasingly ignored them.

Following the earlier interpretations of the fathers, many Roman Catholics continued the allegorical approach (especially the idea that Queen Esther was a type of the Virgin Mary); but others showed a strong interest in textual and historical matters, notably, J. Menochius (1630), who also utilized Jewish and Protestant scholarship. J. de la Haye's *Biblia Maxima* (1660) was a compendium of Roman Catholic study for the previous 150 years.

Protestants, too, regarded Esther as essentially historical but employed allegory less, preferring to emphasize the book's literal, historical, and grammatical aspects. Neither Calvin[§] nor Luther[§] wrote a commentary on the book. The latter's attitude toward it is still sometimes quoted with approval: "I am so hostile to this book [2 Macc] and to Esther that I could wish that they did not exist at all; for they judaize too greatly and have much pagan impropriety" (*Table Talks*, 24).

S. Münster's[§] Latin translation of Esther (1546) was based on the Hebrew text. Critical studies were also made by scholars like H. Grotius[§] (1644), who cited such classical sources as Herodotus's *History of the Persian Wars* and Josephus, while S. Pagninus[§] (1556), the Westminster Assembly's *Annotations* (1657), and others continued along more devotional or homiletical lines. M. Poole's[§] *Synopsis criticorum aliorumque Sacrae Scripturae interpretum* (1669) included the critical insights of both Protestant and Roman Catholic scholarship for the past century and a half.

6. *The Post-Reformation Period*. The next 150 years was a period of retrenchment and theological narrowness for both churches during which little scholarly progress was made on Esther by either Roman Catholics or Protestants. Although B. Spinoza's[§] *Tractatus theologico-politicus*

(1670) demonstrated a genuinely critical spirit, it exerted little influence on his own compatriots, let alone on Christians.

7. *The Modern Period.* a. *Die Aufklärung, or the Enlightenment.* Under the influence of German rationalists and English Deists (Deism[§]), biblical books were scrutinized with a most critical eye. "Lower criticism" was advanced by J. H. Michaelis[§] (1720), B. Kennicott[§] (1776-80), and G. de Rossi (1784-88), all of whom collated variants of the Hebrew text, although most of the manuscripts were unfortunately of a late medieval date.

Considerable progress was also made in the area of higher criticism: the who, what, where, when, and why of a biblical book. When J. D. Michaelis[§] (Esther [1783]) conceded that one could be "a perfect [*vollkommener*] Lutheran" and yet have doubts about the historicity of the book, J. Semler[§] had already made an all-out attack on its historicity, characterizing the book as "a Jewish romance" or novel, a view to which a majority of scholars still subscribe.

The sustained attack on the book's historicity and its "unacceptable moral tone" by scholars like J. G. Eichhorn[§] (1780) and A. Niemeyer (1782), who first made the often-repeated observation that Queen Vashti was the only decent person in Esther, elicited conservative responses on the part of J. Vos (1775) and others. Increasingly, Christian scholars were divided into two camps: those contesting Esther's historicity and those defending it, the latter position more often taken by Roman Catholics.

b. *The nineteenth century. i. Jewish.* Jewish scholars began addressing some of the same problems as Christians, sometimes in the same journals, e.g., J. Bloch (1877, 1866), B. Hause (1879), and J. J. de Villiers (1893).

ii. Christian. Conservative treatments of Esther appeared in Jahn (1803), J. Scholz (1845), C. Keil[§] (1873, very scholarly and ultra-conservative), A. Scholz (1892, scholarly but allegory-laden), and E. Kaulen (1890).

Liberal treatments included W. de Wette[§] (1817), H. Ewald[§] (1843), T. Nöldeke (1868), E. Reuss[§] (1890); T. Cheyne[§] (1893), E. Kautzsch[§] (1896), and E. Schürer[§] (1898-1901), and V. Ryssel[§] (1887, the best of the liberal treatments).

As part of his efforts to reconstruct the Urtext of the LXX, P. Lagarde[§] (1883) "proved" that Esther's A-text was part of the Lucianic recension of the LXX, a view that universally prevailed among scholars until the discovery of the Dead Sea Scrolls[§], when various apocryphal and pseudepigraphical works (Pseudepigrapha[†§]) now appeared in Semitic form.

Protestants, too, exhaustively treated the Add Esth and regarded them as composed in Greek (so O. Fritzsche 1851, J. Fuller 1888, and Ryssel 1900, 1.193-212).

The nineteenth century's (and the twentieth's) decipherment of various cuneiform scripts and languages, as well as the excavation of various archaeological sites (Archaeology and the Hebrew Bible* = Archaeology and Biblical Studies[§]) and their artifacts, contributed much toward illuminating the book's Achaemenid setting but little toward confirming its historicity. During this same period scholars began looking for Purim's origins in pagan sources, in some Greek, Babylonian, or, especially, Persian festival—but without conspicuous success.

The critical work of the nineteenth century was actually best summarized in three works appearing in 1908: P. Haupt[§] L. Paton, (1908a, 1908b, the latter being the most comprehensive and detailed discussion in English thus far of the book's history of interpretation and its problems of higher and lower criticism).

c. *The twentieth century.* Especially after the works of Paton, Haupt, and H. Gunkel[§] (1916), the literary aspects of Esther became the primary concern of scholars, with some even arguing that the Joseph narrative in Genesis (A. Meinhold 1976, 72-93) or the Moses story in Exodus 1–12 (G. Gerleman 1970-73) provided the paradigm for Esther's plot and all its details of "fact."

While the dominant theory among liberal scholars at the turn of the century was that Esther was "pure" fiction, in the twentieth century (especially the second half), the "combination theory" gained ascendancy-that is, the book is a combination of fiction and "fact," the combining of a harem tale about Vashti, a Mordecai story, and an Esther/Hadassah story, the latter two stories being independent tales with a possible core of historicity to each. Thus Esther is a historical novel in which literary considerations determine the plot and details of fact (so H. Bardtke 1963, C. Moore 1971, 1992, S. Berg 1979, and D. Clines 1984). The book provides a lifestyle for Jews of the Diaspora (W. L. Humphreys 1973).

i. Jewish. In some respects, Jewish scholarship on Esther is more impressive than either Roman Catholic or Protestant studies, if only because of its marked increase in both quantity and scope. Some Jewish scholars were still concerned with the centuries-long Judaic approaches to Esther; e.g., L. Ginzberg (1939); H. Freedman and M. Simon (1939); J. Brown (1976); and B. Grossfeld (1983). But apart from J. Hoschander (1923), who was concerned with establishing the full historicity of the book, Jewish scholars became primarily interested in problems of higher criticism, especially those concerning the historical origins and theological meaning of Purim: N. Doniach (1933), S. Ben-Chorin (1938), J. Lewy[§] (1939), T. Gaster[§] (1950), S. Besser (1969), J. Lebram (1972), R. Herst (1973), and A. Cohen (1974). Their consensus is that although God is not mentioned in Esther and Purim may well be of pagan origin, the book has a genuinely religious meaning, veiled though it may be.

But Jewish scholars had other concerns as well; e. g., A. Yahuda, (1946); S. Talmon[§] (1963), which viewed Esther as a historicized wisdom tale; E. Bickerman[§] (1967); S. Zeitlin (1972); and R. Gordis[§] (1974, 1976, 1981), who hypothesized that the book was written by a gentile chronicler. S. Berg's study (1979) is, to date, the best Rhetorical*[§] analysis of Esther and clearly shows that the MT in its present form is an integrated and literary whole whose themes are those of power, loyalty to God and Israel, the inviolability of the Jewish people, and reversal.

In contrast to previous centuries, Jewish articles featured the Greek text, including the Add Esth; e.g., Bickerman, (1944, 1950) and E. Tov (1982),which argued that Esther's A-Text is a recension of the LXX corrected toward a Hebrew (or Aramaic) text quite different from the MT.

ii. Christian. Commentaries continuing the liberal tradition included those of A. Streane (1907); B. Anderson (1954); G. Knight (1955); H. Ringgren (1958), and H. Bardtke (1963), the most scientific and complete German commentary on Esther in the last two hundred years; Moore (1971); G. Gerleman (1970-73); W. Fuerst (1975); and J. Cragham (OTM, 1982). Roman Catholic commentaries, often more conservative and frequently containing Add Esth, included those of J. Schildenberger (1941), L. Soubigou (1952), A. Barucq (1959), and B. Girbau (1960).

Separate and detailed studies of the Add Esth were made by J. Gregg (1913, 665-84), and F. Roiron (1916), the latter arguing that Add Esth B and E are the actual Greek edicts of Haman and Mordecai respectively; and R. Pfeiffer[§] (1949). But thanks to the catalytic study of the problem by C. C. Torrey[§] (1944), scholars, while granting a Greek origin for Add Esth B and E, have increasingly argued for a Hebrew or Aramaic *Vorlage* for such interpolations as Add Esth A, C, D, and F (so E. Ehrlich 1955 69-74, Moore 1973, R. Martin 1975).

In contrast to the previous one hundred years, scholars increasingly maintained that the A-text is a separate and independent translation of another Semitic text, not a recension of the LXX (Torrey 1944, Moore 1967; and Clines 1984). In a foreshadowing of Vatican II, L. Soubigou (Esther 1952, 581-82, 597) noted that Roman Catholic scholars must accept as doctrinally true the inspirational character of Add Esth, but not that they were part of the original book.

Now, however, the legitimate, centuries-old distinctions between Jewish scholarship on Esther and that of Christians (including Catholic versus Protestant) are no longer useful. It is now much more the academic or methodological perspective rather than the theological or religious orientation that determines the nature and character of any particular study of Esther.

Redaction§* and Literary§* criticism (e.g., C. Dorothy 1989, M. Fox 1991, L. Day 1995, K. Craig 1995), Feminist§* scholarship (such as A. LaCoque 1990; K. Darr 1991; W. Phipps 1992; S. White 1992; A. Bellis 1994), and computer-generated studies (J. Miles 1985 and K. Jobes 1996) dominate the field of Esther studies—for now.

Recent commentaries on Esther (and the additions) include Berlin (2000) and Crawford (2003a, 2003b). Thompson has developed concordances for Esther (1999, 2002). Fountain (2002) studies the MT, LXX, and A versions of Esther from a reader-response perspective. Brenner (1999) is a collection of feminist analyses of Esther. Glickman (1999) studies the figure of Haman in Midrashic interpretation. Rottzoll (1999) translates and provides commentary on the medieval Jewish exegetes Ibn Ezra's§ Esther commentary. Harvey (2003) discusses morality within Esther's different textual recensions. Kossmann (2000) studies Esther from the perspectives of history of traditions and redactional history. Layzer (2001) compares the figure of Esther with figures in Irish folk tales to study the relationship of Celtic myth, Irish folktales, and biblical hero stories. Beal (Linafelt and Beal 1999) uses rhetorical criticism to investigate anti-Judaism in Esther and the contemporary questions raised by the text concerning sexism, ethnocentrism, and national identity.

Bibliography: B. W. Anderson, "The Book of Esther," *IB* (1954) 3:823-74. **H. Bardtke**, *Das Buch Esther* (KAT 17, 5, 1963); *Luther und das Buch Esther* (1964). **A. Barucq**, *Judith-Esther* (1959). **A. O. Bellis**, *Helpmates, Harlots, and Heroes: Women's Stories in the Hebrew Bible* (1994). **S. Ben-Chorin**, *Kritik des Estherbuches* (1938). **S. B. Berg**, *The Book of Esther: Motifs, Themes and Structure* (SBLDS 44, 1979). **A. Berlin,** *Esther: The Traditional Hebrew Text with the New JPS Translation* (JPS Bible commentary, 2001). **S. Besser**, "Esther and Purim—Chance and Play" *CCARJ 16* (1969) 36-42. **E. Bickerman**, *Four Strange Books of the Bible* (1967); "The Colophon of the Greek Book of Esther," *JBL* 63 (1944) 339-62; "Notes on the Greek Book of Esther," *PAAJR* 20 (1950) 101-33). **J. Bloch**, *Hellenistische Bestandtheile im biblischen Schriftthum, eine kritische Untersuchung über Abfassung, Charakter, und Tendenzen des Buches Esther* (1877); "Der historische Hintergund und die Abfassungszeit des Buch Esther," *MGWJ* (1886). **A. Brenner** (ed.), *Ruth and Esther* (Feminist Companion to the Bible, Second Series 3 1999). **J. M. Brown**, *Rabbinic Interpretations of the Characters and Plot of the Book of Esther: As Reflected in Midrash Esther Rabbah* (1976). **T. Cheyne**, *Founders of OT Criticism* (1893). **D. J. A. Clines**, *The Esther Scroll: The Story of the Story* (1984). **A. Cohen**, "'Hu Ha-goral': The Religious Significance of Esther," *Judaism 23* (1974) 87-94. **K. M. Craig, Jr.,** *Reading Esther: A Case for the Literary Carnivalesque* (Literary Currents in Biblical Interpretation, 1995). **S. W. Crawford**, "Esther," *NISB* (2003a) 689-701; "Esther (The Greek Version Containing the Additional Chapters)," *NISB* (2003b) 1401-1417. **K. P. Darr**, *Far More Precious Than Jewels: Perspectives on Biblical Women* (1991). **L. Day**, *Three Faces of a Queen: Characterization in the Books of Esther* (JSOTSup 186, 1995). **W. Dommershausen**, *Die Estherrolle* (SBM 6, 1968). **N. Doniach**, *Purim or the Feast of Esther: An Historical Study* (1933). **C. V. Dorothy**, *The Books of Esther: Structure, Genre, and Textual Integrity* (JSOTSup 187, 1989). **J. G. Eichhorn**, *Einleitung ins Alte Testament* (3 vols., 1780-83). **E. Ehrlich**, *ZRGG* 7 (1955) 69-74. **H. Ewald**, *Geschichte des Volkes Israel bis Christus* (1843). **A. K. Fountain**, *Literary and Empirical Readings of the Books of Esther* (Studies in Biblical Literature 43, 2002). **M. V. Fox**, *The Redaction of the Books of Esther* (SBLMS 40, 1991). **H. Freedman and M. Simon**, *Midrash Rabbah 9* (1939) 1-124. **O. Fritzsche**, *KEHA*(1851). **W. J. Fuerst**, *The Books of Ruth, Esther, Ecclesiastes, the Song of Songs, Lamentations* (CBC, 1975). **J. Fuller**, "Esther," *Apocrypha of the Speaker's Commentary*, vol. 1 (ed. H. Wace, 1888). **T. Gaster**, *Purim and Hanukkah in Custom and Tradition* (1950). **G. Gerleman**, *Esther* (BKAT 21, 1970-73). **L. Ginzberg**, *The Legends of the Jews 4* (1913) 365-448; *6* (1928) 451-81; *7* (1939).

B. Girbau, *La Biblia* (1960). **E. R. Glickman,** *Haman and the Jews: A Portrait from Rabbinic Literature* (1999). **R. Gordis,** *Megillat Esther: The Masoretic Hebrew Text with Introduction, New Translation and Commentary* (1974); "Studies in the Esther Narrative," *JBL 95* (1976) 43-58; "Religion, Wisdom and History in the Book of Esther—A New Solution to an Ancient Crux," *JBL 100* (1981) 359-88. **J. A. F. Gregg,** "The Additions to Esther," *APOT 1* (1913) 665-71. **H. Grossfeld,** *The First Targum to Esther* (1983). **H. Gunkel,** *Esther* (1916). **P. Haupt,** *Critical Notes on Esther* (1908). **B. Hause,** "Noch einmal das Buch Esther," *JBL 8* (1879). **C. D. Harvey,** *Finding Morality in the Diaspora?: Moral Ambiguity and Transformed Morality in the Books of Esther* (BZAW 328, 2003). **R. Herst,** "The Purim Connection," *USQR 28* (1973) 139-45). **J. Hoschander,** *The Book of Esther in the Light of History* (1923). **W. L. Humphreys,** *JBL 92* (1973) 211-23. **Jahn,** *Einleitung in die osttlichen Bücher des Alten Bundes* 2 (1803). **K. H. Jobes,** *The Alpha-Text of Esther: Its Character and Relationship to the Masoretic Text* (SBLDS 153, 1995). **E. Kaulen,** *Einleitung in die Heilige Schrift* (1890). **E. Kautzsch,** *HSAT* (1896). **C. Keil,** *Lehrbuch die historisch-kritischen Einleitung in die kanonischen Schriften des Alte Testament* (1873). **B. Kennicott,** *Vetus Testamentum Hebraicum* (1776-80). **G. F. Knight,** *Esther, Song of Songs, Lamentations: Introduction and Commentary* (TBC, 1955). **R. Kossmann,** *Die Esthernovelle: Vom Erzählten zur Erzählung: Studien zur Traditions- und Redaktionsgeschichte des Estherbuches* (VTSup 79, 2000). **A. LaCoque,** *The Feminine Unconventional: Four Subversive Figures in Israel* (1990). **P. Lagarde,** *Librorum Veteris Testamenti Canonicorum* (1883). **V. Layzer,** *Signs of Weakness: Juxtaposing Irish Tales and the Bible* (JSOTSup 321, 2001). **J. Lebram,** "Purimfest und Estherbuch," *VT 22* (1972) 208-22. **J. D. Levenson,** *Esther* (OTL, 1997). **J. Lewy,** "Old Assyrian puru'um and purum," *RHA 5* (1939) 117-24; "The Feast of the 14th Day of Adar," *HUCA 14* (1939) 127-51. **T. Linafelt and T. K. Beal,** *Ruth and Esther* (Berit Olam, 1999). **R. Martin,** *JBL 94* (1975) 65-72. **A. Meinhold,** *ZAW 88* (1976) 72-93. **J. D. Michaelis,** * *Esther* (1783). **J. H. Michaelis,** *Biblia hebraica* (1720). **J. R. Miles,** *Retroversion and Text Criticism: The Predicability of Syntax in an Ancient Translation from Greek to Ethiopic* (SBLSCS 17, 1985). **J. T. Milik,** "Les Modeles Araméens du Livre d'Esther dans La Grotte 4 de Qumran," *RdQ 15* (1992) 321-99. **C. A. Moore,** *ZAW 79* (1967) 351-58; *Esther* (AB 7B, 1971); *JBL 92* (1973) 382-93; *Daniel, Esther, and Jeremiah: The Additions* (AB 44, 1977); *ABD* (1992) 2:626-43. **A. Niemayer,** *Charakteristick der Bibel* (1782). **T. Nöldeke,** *Die Alttestamentliche Literatur* (1868). **L. B. Paton,** "A Text-critical Apparatus to the Book of Esther" (*Old Testament and Semitic studies in memory of William Rainey Harper,* vol. 2 (R. F. Harper, F. Brown, G. F. Moore, eds., 1908); *A Critical and Exegetical Commentary on the Book of Esther* (ICC, 1908). **R. Pfeiffer,** *History of New Testament Times* (1949). **W. E. Phipps,** *Assertive Biblical Women* (Contributions in Women's Studies 128, 1992). **E. Reuss,** *Geschichte der heiligen Schriften* (1890). **H. Ringgren,** *Das Buch Esther* (ATD 16, 1958). **F. Roiron,** *RSR* (1916). **G. de Rossi,** *Variae lectiones Veteris Testamenti* (1784-88). **D. U. Rottzoll,** *Abraham Ibn Esras Kommentare zu den Büchern Kohelet, Ester und Rut* (SJ 12, 1999). **V. Ryssel,** "Esther," *KEH* (1887); *APAT* (1900) 1.193-212. **J. Schildenberger,** *Das Buch Esther,* HSAT 4.3 (1941). **A. Scholz,** *Commentar über das Buch Esther mit seinen Zusätzen* (1892). **J. Scholz,** *Einleitung in Die heiligen Schriften des Alten und Neuen Testaments* 1 (1845). **E. Schürer,** *Geschichte des jüdischen Volkes im Zeitalter Jesu Christi* (1898-1901). **M. Simon,** "Megillah: Translated into English with Notes, Glossary, and Indices," *Babylonian Talmud* (1938). **L. Soubigou,** *Esther traduit et comment* (1952). **A. W. Streane,** *The Book of Esther, With Intro and Notes* (CBSC, 1907). **S. Talmon,** "'Wisdom' in the Book of Esther," *VT 13* (1963) 419-55). **J. D. Thompson,** *A Critical Concordance to the Septuagint Esther* (The Computer Bible 68, 1999); *A Critical Concordance to the Apocrypha. Esther* (The Computer Bible 104, 2002). **C. C. Torrey,** "The Older Book of Esther," *HTR 37* (1944) 1-40. **E. Tov,** "The Lucianic Text of the Canonical and the Apocryphal Sections of Esther," *Textus* 10 (1982) 1-25. **J. J. de Villiers,** "Modern Criticism and the Megilla," *Jus Canonicum* (1893). **W. Vischer**, *Esther* (TEH 48, 1937). **W. de Wette**, *Lehrbuch des historischen-kritischen Einleitung* (1817). **S. A. White**, "Esther: A Feminine Model for Jewish Diaspora," *Gender and Difference in Ancient Israel* (ed. P. Day, 1989) 161-77; *Women's Bible Commentary* (eds. C. A. Newsom and S. H. Ringe, 1992) 124-29. **A. Yahuda**, "The Meaning of the Name Esther," *JRAS* (1946) 174-78). **S. Zeitlin**, "The Books of Esther and Judith: A Parallel," *The Book of Judith* (ed. M. Enslin, 1972).

C. A. MOORE

APOCRYPHA

Wisdom of Solomon

This apocryphal book is a product of Jewish wisdom composed in Greek thought patterns and literary style. It is not included in Jewish and Protestant biblical canons (Canon of the Bible§), but it is retained among canonical books by the Roman Catholic Church. Scholarship in major commentaries has centered its critical approach principally around several issues— namely, division of contents, purpose, authorship, origin, original language, and date.

1. *Early Interest in the Book.* There are five uncial manuscripts: Codex Alexandrinus (A; fifth cent.); Codex Vaticanus (B; fourth cent.); Codex Ephraemi Syri Rescriptus (C; fifth cent.), containing only part of the text; Codex Sinaiticus (S, also known as א; fourth cent.); and Codex Venetus (V; eighth cent.), important for its witness to many Origenic readings (Origen§). *Sapientia Salomonis* in the *Göttingen Septuaginta* edited by J. Ziegler (1962) is the first critical edition of Wis based on all pertinent available recorded evidence. In Ziegler's view the original form of the text is best transmitted in the fourth-century codices Vaticanus and Sinaiticus and in the fifth-century Codex Alexandrinus. A more complete reading is achieved from the agreement among the manuscripts and the minuscules that depend on them. Ziegler also lists the secondary uncials Ephraemi and Venetus, which contain large gaps and scribal errors, and forty-five cursive minuscules of later age and inferior quality. There are also several papyrus fragments (third and fourth-fifth cents.), a fragment from Khirbet Mird, and two Greek commentaries. The earlier commentary of M. Monachus (fourteenth cent.) is important because of its use of Greek manuscripts no longer extant, while the work of M. Cantacuzenus (sixteenth cent.) has no special significance. Early documents have variations in the title of the book, all with principal emphasis on the theme of wisdom.

2. *Interpretations Before the Nineteenth Century.* Scholarship from early times through the eighteenth century includes the homilies of Ambrose§ and Augustine§ , which have been lost. The first extant commentary is that of Rabanus Maurus§ (856 C.E.), which shared the scene with the *Glossa Ordinaria§*, attributed to Walafrid Strabo§ , although now many doubt that the work was his. Anselm§, Hugo of St. Cher§ (1260), and Bonaventure§ wrote in the twelfth and thirteenth centuries; and the work of Nicholas of Lyra§ (1341) and R. Holcot appeared during the following century. Post-Reformation viewpoints come from both Roman Catholic and Protestant scholarship. P. Nannius and V. Strigel taught in the sixteenth century, followed by H. Grotius§ (in *Critici sacri,* 1660), Lorinus, and C. á Lapide§ in the seventeenth. Increased interest appeared in the eighteenth century with D. Calmet§ (1724), C. Houbigant's contributions of 1753 and 1777, and Klenker and Hasse in 1785. J. Nachtigal (1798) held that Wis is a mosaic to which seventy-nine sages contributed, a view termed bizarre by D. Winston (1979, 12). In the same work Winston gives detailed information on manuscripts and versions as well as on the book's status and influence (64-69).

3. *Scholarship from the Nineteenth Century.* In the critical study of Wis, the basic approach to understanding its structure is either in terms of subject matter or in terms of Literary*§ characteristics. The majority of commentators divide the text into two or three parts, with variations as to their composition. A few scholars have proposed a four-part division. Subject matter includes general and hortatory considerations (Wis 1–5); praise of wisdom and its role in human destiny (Wis 6–9); and wisdom in the history of God's people (Wis 10–19). Among literary characteristics are differences in style of the first part (Wis 1–9) and the second part (Wis 10–19) as well as the author's structuring of his work by using such rhetorical devices as *inclusio* or *kyklos* to mark off sections of the material.

a. Two-part division. W. Deane (1881), J. Harris (1929), and B. Metzger (1957) proposed a simple two-part division. The span of the dates of their works shows a continuing recurrence of this plan over a period of time. Interspersed with these works are others that agree substantially but incorporate variations on the basic two divisions and offer different subdivisions, e.g., W. Wright (1968) who followed J. Reese (1965 and 1970) in identifying the sections of Wis on the basis of literary genre but contributed his own intricate outline with two main parts and many subdivisions.

b. Three-part division. At the beginning of the nineteenth century, K. Bretschneider (1804) presented three distinct parts: 1:1–6:8; 6:9–10:21; 11–19. The landmark commentary of K. Grimm (1860) modified the arrangement to 1–5; 6–9; 10–19, and argued for the unity of the book. This position had continuing impact on subsequent scholars, who either accepted the views exactly or made minor modifications, from E. Bissell (1880) to R. Dentan (1971). W. Kohler (1906) laid out three independent parts of the book but disputed Grimm's conclusion on unity, while E. Stein (1936) proposed Wis as a compilation of three, or possibly four, books on the basis of sources. M. Hadas (1976) offers an interplay between a two-part and a three-part division by calling for two parts on the basis of theme and three parts on the basis of content. Winston (1979) retains the three-part division but marks the first part as 1:1–6:21 and the second as 6:22–10:21. For him the second part is the core of the book, where the author is at his best. While E. Clarke (1973) spoke of four subdivisions, each with a different theme but dependent on one another, his divisions basically followed Grimm.

c. Four-part division. Reese made a significant breakthrough by first presenting a true four-part division on the basis of the literary genre *logos protreptikos* (exhortation to follow one way of life over another), and he provided a scientific approach to unraveling the message of the sage. His methodology was followed by A. Wright (1965, 1990), who nevertheless reverted to a two-part structure. M. Gilbert (1984) shares interest in literary characteristics and patterns, but uses a three-part division of the book, which he sees as encomium.

d. Purpose of the book. The plan of the book is closely connected with its purpose and is a key factor in understanding it. There is substantial agreement as to the author's basic objective. Standing at one of the turning points in scholarship, Grimm described the purpose as hortatory-apologetic-polemic. In line with him was Deane, who emphasized the Greek influence. Although Bissell accepted this point, he did not follow Deane's positive view of the book's presentation of the Hebrew faith. E. Schürer[§] (1885) noted that Wis was directed as much to those outside Judaism as to those within it and aimed to offset the objections of heathen critics. Through the years other scholars have followed similar reasoning with one emphasis or another. Reese drew the sage's purpose into sharper focus by attributing a twofold purpose: (1) to glorify God's mercy in calling people to actively participate in his eternal reign (3:8 and 6:21) and (2) to urge all people to the righteousness that would provide an eternal inheritance among the saints (5:5). Reese's statement (1965) is at once specific and universal. The sage wished to enable future intellectual leaders of his people to view their situation positively, while he extended an orientation toward righteousness to all people who looked to eternity. Winston corroborates the prevailing view and adds that the sagacious author of Wis points a finger at pagan kings who have abandoned the principles of divine justice.

Some divergent views have had little following. C. Siegfried (1875) seemed to regard the reconciliation of Jewish and Greek philosophy as the book's main purpose. E. Plumptre thought it was a correction of the teaching of Qohelet or a current misrepresentation of it.

e. Authorship. Early critics hypothesized a wide range of authors including Zerubbabel, Aristobulus, Philo[§], and Apollos. Others have suggested a translator of the Septuagint*[§], one of the Therapeutae, a Christian, or a Samaritan patriot. Some church fathers, e.g., Clement of Alexandria[§], Tertullian[§], Cyprian, Hippolytus, and Lactantius, advanced Solomonic authorship and thus opened the issue of a Hebrew original. Augustine denied it, and Jerome[§] dropped the name of Solomon from the title. Solomonic authorship was also advanced by such medieval rabbis as Gedaliah ben Joseph Ibn Yahya (*Shalshelet ha Kabbalah*, 104) and Azariah dei Rossi (*Meor Ennayim*, 175). Whereas many scholars believe that the context makes use of Solomon only as a literary fiction, others allege that at least part of the book can be attributed to him. The discussion of Solomonic authorship continued into the twentieth century, but it receives little support.

i. Unity of authorship. Those who follow Grimm, reflected in F. Farrar[§] (1888), argue for unity of authorship and generally characterize the author as an Alexandrian Jew. D. Margoliouth (1890) differed in arguing for a Palestinian writer, but J. Freudenthal's (1891) response devastated this hypothesis. Such scholars as J. Reider (1957) basically argue for unity of authorship while suggesting that the various parts of the book may have been composed at different times in the author's life. Stein held a somewhat different view, proposing three or four parts redacted by one editor; however, his view does not have strong support. On the other hand, Reese's breakthrough represents careful scholarship and concludes that the book is a unified composition with a consistent theological outlook.

ii. Composite authorship. In the eighteenth century Houbigant (1777) and J. G. Eichhorn[§] (1795) argued for composite authorship, as did J. Nachtigal (1798) with his Mosaic theory. From the nineteenth century onward, scholarship was dotted with variations on the subject. R. Pfeiffer[§] (1949) and Winston (1979) cited the arguments of F. Focke (1913) as the most plausible, although they believed his reasons either unfounded or inconclusive. Reider placed in the same category theories that trace four hands in the work. Thus the stronger and more prevalent position is in favor of unity of authorship.

f. Origin of Wisdom. Discussion of authorship raises questions about the book's place of origin. A preponderance of scholarship has favored an Egyptian location, probably in the area of Alexandria. The writer's handling of Hebrew Bible doctrines shows contact with Western philosophy, which most plausibly would have occurred in Alexandria and could best have been expressed in Greek by an educated Jew who integrated his beliefs with those of the heathen culture. Grimm's influence is seen in a long line of scholars who advocated a totally Alexandrian-Jewish character for the book. This position was thus well established and remains so even into the twentieth century, although a few scholars advance a Palestinian locus of composition. The classic debate between Margoliouth and Freudenthal about original language turned in part on place of origin, with Margoliouth's Palestinian hypothesis (263-97) being refuted by Freudenthal (722-53). Focke attributed Wis 1–5 and 6–19 to different authors, with the first part being written in Hebrew by a Palestinian author and subsequently being translated into Greek and used as an introduction to the second part by a Greek writer. Focke's theory was refuted by Pfeiffer as based entirely on conjecture. Winston further dismantled Focke's arguments, showing that his position has no foundation. Stein called for a Hebrew and a Palestinian original for the first two of his divisions of the book and a Greek original for the third part; the book would then have been compiled by one hand outside of Israel (467-69). Opinions favoring Palestinian origin have a sparse following, however.

g. Original language. From the discussion of place of origin arise two possibilities about the work's original language: Greek or Hebrew. Scholars who followed Grimm's thought found the book abounding in Hebrew expressions, yet showing mastery of the Greek of the later epoch. Hebrew coloring is found chiefly in the earlier chapters and is due to the use of Hebrew Bible phrases that are heavily Septuagintal, whereas the later chapters reflect a mastery of the Greek language and style, and the use of unrestrained rhetoric. From Freudenthal to Reese, scholarship on original language generally took on the air of review. The notion of a Greek original is integral to Reese's analysis of the Hellenistic influence in Wis; he argues from detailed examination of vocabulary and style that the sage was trained in Greek rhetoric and was subject to a wide spectrum of Hellenistic influences (1970, 25-31). The preponderance of scholarship accepts Greek as the original language of the book.

The few scholars who favor a Hebrew original have also preferred a Palestinian locus of composition, e.g., Margoliouth, who argued against a Greek original on all points. Focke was refuted by Pfeiffer and Winston. Stein's theory of a final editor for three different sections, each with a different origin and language, has received little credence.

h. Dating of the book. The exact date of the book's composition cannot be determined with certainty. Calculations are based on such issues as persecution of the Jews, which seems to be mentioned and may be taken as some specific time of oppression or as persecution in general; the relation, or lack thereof, between Wis and Philo of Alexandria[§]; and literary style. Conjectures span a period from the third century B.C.E. to the first century C.E. On the basis of internal evidence, Deane felt he could arrive at a certain date of 217-145 B.C.E. Grimm took up where Deane left off and situated the book at 145-50 B.C.E. As in other matters a large number of scholars hover in and around the same time period as Grimm, and even Stein placed the final editing at 145-130 B.C.E.

Another group of scholars has opted for the first century B.C.E. as the date of origin. Among them is A. Holmes, who opined that the book was early enough to have been used by Paul[†§]. Harris (1929) placed it before Philo and after the Septuagint of Ecclesiastes, as have others who maintain Septuagintal dependence and New Testament use. Reese prefers this time period; but basing his conclusions on the education of the day and on the literary characteristics reflected in the text, he sees a time before the accession of Augustus as the proper situation for the book's protreptic literary form (1970, 146-51). Gilbert (312) also works from the point of view of literary form, calling it encomium, and places the book between 30 B.C.E. and the first decades of the first century C.E. Hadas accepts a time near 30 B.C.E. but reverts to the often-repeated themes of persecution and idolatry for determining his date.

Scholars who assign a date in the first century C.E. connect the writing with the tumults of Caligula's reign. Among these are Winston, who places it around 40 C.E.; and also Farrar, who on this point only took exception with Grimm and posited a date in the decade after the death of Christ. Because internal historical evidence is limited in Wis, various interpretations are possible; they recur repeatedly without the emergence of universal consensus on a date for the writing.

4. *Conclusion.* In all of the scholarship on Wis there is no definite certainty on most issues. The sage's reflections on Jewish traditions show wisdom to be active in creation and carrying history to its goal. From whatever frame of reference one views the book, it is an enriching contribution to evolving religious thought in the intertestamental period. For full treatment and bibliography see especially the works of B. J. Lillie, Reider, Winston, and Ziegler.

Recent commentaries on the Wisdom of Solomon include a linguistic commentary by P. Arzt, *et al.* (1997), Collins (1997), Engel (1998), Enns (2003), Hübner (1999), and Tanzer (1998[2]). Calduch-Benages and J. Vermeylen have edited a collection of essays on Wis (1999). Bergant interprets the book from a feminist, liberationist perspective (1997) and an ecological perspective (2000). Assorted recent theological studies of Wis include Cheon (1997), Collins (2002), Kepper (1999), McGlynn (2001), and Winston (2002).

Bibliography: **P. Arzt, et al.,** *Sprachlicher Schlüssel zur Sapientia Salomonis (Weisheit)* (Sprachlicher Schlüssel zu den Deuterokanonischen Schriften (Apokryphen) des Alten Testaments 1, 1997[2]). **D. Bergant,** *Israel's Wisdom Literature: A Liberation-Critical Reading* (Liberation-Critical Reading, 1997); "The Wisdom of Solomon," *Readings from the Perspective of Earth* (ed. N. C. Habel, Earth Bible 1, 2000) 138-50. **E. C. Bissell**, *The Apocrypha of the OT: With Historical Introductions* (THBW 15, 1880). **N. Calduch-Benages**

and J. Vermeylen (eds.), *Treasures of Wisdom: Studies in Ben Sira and the Book of Wisdom: Festschrift M. Gilbert* (BEThL 143, 1999). **S. Cheon,** *The Exodus Story in the Wisdom of Solomon: A Study in Biblical Interpretation* (JSPSup 23, 1997). **E. G. Clarke,** *The Wisdom of Solomon: A Commentary* (CBC, 1973). **J. J. Collins,** *Jewish Wisdom in the Hellenistic Age* (OTL, 1997); "Apocalyptic Eschatology in Philosophical Dress in the Wisdom of Solomon," *Shem in the Tents of Japhet: Essays on the Encounter of Judaism and Hellenism* (J. L. Kugel, ed., JSJSup 74, 2002) 93-107. **W. J. Deane,** *The Book of Wisdom* (1881). **J. G. Eichhorn,** *Einleitung in die Apokryphischen schriften des AT* (J. G. Eichhorn Kritische Schriften 4, 1795). **H. Engel,** *Das Buch der Weisheit* (Neuer Stuttgarter Kommentar. Altes Testament 16, 1998). **P. Enns,** "The Wisdom of Solomon," *NISB* (2003) 1419-49. **F. W. Farrar,** "The Wisdom of Solomon," *The Holy Bible with an Explanatory and Critical Commentary* (ed. H. Wace, 1888). **F. Focke,** *Die Entstehung der Weisheit Salomos: Ein Beitrage zur Geschichte des jüdischen hellenismus* (FRLANT 5, 22) 1913. **J. Freudenthal,** "What was the Original Language of the Wisdom of Solomon?" *JQR* 8 (1891) 722-53. **M. Gilbert,** "The Wisdom of Solomon," *Jewish Writings of the Second Temple Period* (ed. M. E. Stone, CRINT 2/2, 1984) 301-13. **L. L. Grabbe,** *Wisdom of Solomon* (Guides to Apocrypha and Pseudepigrapha 3, 1997). **K. L. W. Grimm,** *Das Buch der Weisheit* (1860). **M. Hadas,** "Wisdom of Solomon," *IDB* (1962) 4:861-63. **J. R. Harris,** "Stoic Origins of the Prologue to St. John's Gospel," *BJRL* 6 (1921-22) 439-51; "Athena, Sophia, and the Logos," *BJRL* (1922-23) 56-72. **C. Houbigant,** *Veteris Testamenti versio nova ad hebraicom veritatem facta; acedunt libri deutero-canonici ex Graeca editione translati* (1713); *Notae criticae in universos Veteris Testamenti libros* (1777). **H. Hübner,** *Die Weisheit Salomos = Liber Sapientiae Salomonis* (Alte Testament Deutsch, Apokryphen ; Bd. 4, 1999). **M. Kepper,** *Hellenistische Bildung im Buch der Weisheit: Studien zur Sprachgestalt und Theologie der Sapientia Salomonis* (BZAW 280, 1999). **W. Kohler,** *Beiträge zur Geschichte der Mystik in der Reformationszeit* (Archiv für Reformationsgeschichte, 1906). **M. Kolarcik,** "The Book of Wisdom," *NIB* (1997) 5:435-600. **B. J. Lillie,** "A History of the Scholarship on the Wisdom of Solomon from the Nineteenth Century to Our Time" (diss., Hebrew Union College, 1983). **D. S. Margoliouth,** "Was the Book of Wisdom Written in Hebrew?" *JRAS* (April 1890) 263-97. **M. McGlynn,** *Divine Judgement and Divine Benevolence in the Book of Wisdom* (WUNT 2/139, 2001). **B. Metzger,** *An Introduction to the Apocrypha* (1957). **J. K. C. Nachtigal,** *Koheleth, oder Die Versammlung der Weisen, gewohnlich genannt der Prediger Salomos* (1798). **R. H. Pfeiffer,** *History of NT Times, with an Introduction to the Apocrypha* (1949). **J. M. Reese,** "Plan and Structure in the Book of Wisdom," *CBQ* 27 (1965) 391-99; *Hellenistic Influence on the Book of Wisdom and Its Consequences* (1970). **J. Reider,** *The Book of Wisdom* (1957). **E. Schürer,** *HJPAJC* (1885). **C. A. Siegfried,** *Analecta Rabbinica ad NT et Patres ecclesiasticus spectantia* (1875). **E. M. Stein,** "Sefer Hokmah Shlomo," *Sefarim Ha-Hitzonim* (ed. A. Kahana, 1936) 463-514. **S. J. Tanzer,** "Wisdom of Solomon" *Women's Bible Commentary* (ed. C. A. Newsom and S. H. Ringe, 1998[2]) 293-97. **D. Winston,** *The Wisdom of Solomon* (AB 43, 1979); "Solomon, Wisdom of," *ABD* (1992) 6:120-27; "Philo and the Wisdom of Solomon on Creation, Revelation, and Providence: The High-Water Mark of Jewish Hellenistic Fusion," *Shem in the Tents of Japhet: Essays on the Encounter of Judaism and Hellenism* (J. L. Kugel, ed., JSJSup 74, 2002) 109-130. **A. G. Wright,** "Wisdom," *NJBC* 33 (1965, 1990) 510-22. **W. Wright,** *Apocryphal Acts of the Apostles* (1968). **J. Ziegler** (ed.), *Sapientia Salomonis: Septuaginta* (1962).

B. J. Lillie

APOCRYPHA

Ecclesiasticus, Book of
(or Wisdom of Jesus Ben Sira or Sirach)

In one sense the interpretation of Ecclesiasticus, or the Wisdom of Jesus Ben Sira, (also known as Sirach and usually abbreviated as Sir) begins within the work itself. From the prologue we learn that Ben Sira's grandson translated the book from Hebrew into Greek. The grandson also offers his opinion that Ben Sira wrote his teaching so that "those who love learning should make even greater progress in living according to the law." In addition, the reader learns that the grandson translated and published the book for the sake of "those living abroad who wished to gain learning." Whatever the original purpose of the book, Sir proved to be immensely popular and influential in both Judaism and Christianity.

There have primarily been three broad questions about the interpretation of Sir: its status within Christianity and Judaism, its textual history, and the person and perspective of Ben Sira within his historical context.

1. *The Book within Judaism and Christianity.* That Sir was highly regarded in the early church is suggested by its possible influence on the book of James and by the fact that it is quoted in the *Didache* (c. 130-160 C.E.). Moreover, it is quoted as Scripture by Clement of Alexandria[§], Origen[§], and Cyprian. Only Jerome[§] denied it the status of canonical Scripture by designating it as one of the "ecclesiastical" books, in contrast to the canonical books. Nevertheless, Augustine[§] accepted it as canonical, along with the other books of the LXX (Septuagint*[§]); and the Councils of Hippo (393) and Carthage (397 and 418) included it in the Canon[§] of the church.

During the Reformation Luther[§] revived Jerome's opinion that, although Sir was an edifying book, it did not have inspired, canonical status. Luther thus removed Sir along with those other books not found in the Hebrew Scriptures and placed them together in a distinct section between the Hebrew Bible and New Testament (1534). Consequently, in contrast to Roman Catholicism and the Eastern Orthodox Church, Protestantism has either followed the practice of placing these books (designated Apocrypha) in a separate section or excluding them altogether. Not surprisingly, Protestant scholars have not given Sir the same attention devoted to the books they consider to be canonical.

Judaism in the time of the *tannaim* and the *amoraim* reveals a degree of ambivalence toward the book. Numerous quotations in rabbinic literature and the Talmud*[§] demonstrate not only a familiarity with it but also a high regard for its teachings. Indeed, many of the rabbinic quotations of Sir begin with the expression "it is written," which is usually reserved for canonical works. In addition, the fact that the manuscripts found at Qumran (Dead Sea Scrolls[§]) and Masada are written in the stichometric style normally used for sacred texts may indicate that certain Jewish groups had given a special status to the book.

In light of the number and nature of the quotations from Sir, it is surprising to discover that no less an authority than Rabbi Akiba[§] (d. 135 C.E.) banned its reading and declared that those who read such "outside books" would have no share in the world to come. Attempts to reconcile Akiba's ban of Sir with the high respect for the book within Judaism were made within the Talmud (J. Sanh. 28a). An anonymous commentary found in the Cairo Geniza suggested that the ban resulted from the public's confusion of Sir with similar works. Others have suggested that the ban applied primarily to public, liturgical reading or to the serious study of the book. S. Leiman (1976) has argued that the ban on Sir was a measure directed against sects within Judaism that had granted it virtual canonical status. Once the canon was firmly established and the threat to normative Judaism had passed, the ban was relaxed or disregarded.

It is doubtful that normative Judaism ever considered Sir to be a part of its canon. It is described by the rabbis as a book that "does not defile the hands," i.e., that is not inspired (Inspiration of the Bible*§) or canonical. Since there is no evidence that the so-called Council of Jamnia seriously considered the status of Sir, it is safe to conclude that, although highly respected, the book was not considered to be inspired or to have the status of a canonical book. Indeed, the grandson of Ben Sira appears to refer to a more or less fixed, three-part canon at the time he translated the book into Greek (c. 120-117 B.C.E.).

2. *Text-History Issue.* A second important area of research on Sir has been the investigation of its Textual*§ history. The ban on reading Ben Sira, the fixing of the canon, and the emergence of the Talmud all contributed to the loss of the Hebrew text of the book, perhaps shortly after the time of Jerome, although it survived in both Greek and Syriac translations. The Greek manuscripts as well as the Syriac suggest that at an early date two different Hebrew *Vorlagen* had emerged. The Syriac version also shows evidence of a Christian revision before the middle of the fifth century (M. Winder 1977; D. Nelson 1988).

The textual situation changed dramatically between 1896 and 1900 with the discovery and publication of parts of four distinct Hebrew manuscripts, designated A, B, C, and D, that were found in the Geniza of the Ezra Synagogue in Cairo and dated to the tenth-twelfth centuries. In 1931 a fifth manuscript (E) was found in the Adler Collection of the Jewish Theological Seminary of America. Between 1958 and 1960 a few more leaves of manuscripts B and C were identified and published. Finally, in 1982 a fragment of manuscript C and a new leaf of another manuscript were identified in the Geniza materials of the Taylor-Schlechter Additional Series Collection at Cambridge. Although initially identified as part of manuscript D, it is now clear that the newly discovered leaf represents a previously unknown manuscript (F). Thus the Geniza material ultimately yielded fragments of six distinct Hebrew manuscripts.

Almost immediately after the initial discoveries of the Geniza manuscripts, their authenticity was challenged. In 1899 both D. Margoliouth and G. Bickell argued that the Geniza fragments were translations from the Persian and/or Syriac. Later these scholars would be joined by others, including C. C. Torrey§ (1950), E. Goodspeed§ (1939), and H. Ginsberg§ (1955), who believed that the Geniza manuscripts were translations from the Greek and/or Syriac. In each case the main objections to authenticity were the presence of both late Hebrew and poor idiomatic Hebrew in the manuscripts.

Although the challenges to the authenticity of the Geniza manuscripts were effectively and repeatedly refuted by various scholars, the decisive defense of their essential authenticity came only with additional manuscript discoveries. In 1956 two short fragments of a Hebrew manuscript of Sir dating to the early first century B.C.E. were found at Qumran (2Q 18). This discovery played a crucial role in establishing the authenticity of the Geniza manuscripts, since the text of the Qumran fragments is almost identical to manuscript A. Moreover, like manuscripts B and E, the Qumran manuscript is arranged stichometrically (each line contains a single clause).

A scroll containing Sir 51:13-20, 30b was also found (11QPsᵃ) at Qumran, and in 1964 a Hebrew scroll dating to the first century B.C.E. and containing Sir 39:27-44:17 was found at Masada (M). This scroll was crucial in demonstrating the general faithfulness of the Greek translation. No less important is the fact that the scroll proves the essential authenticity of the Geniza fragments, although it also demonstrates that a number of corruptions have entered the text of the Geniza manuscripts (Y. Yadin 1965). Similarly, the earlier discovery of a scroll containing Sir 51:13-20, 30b at Qumran (11QPsᵃ) also demonstrated both essential authenticity and the presence of corruptions in the Geniza fragments.

Although the authenticity of the Geniza fragments has been established, scholarship is still attempting to establish the textual history of the book. For example, A. Di Lella (1988) argues that many of the examples of poor or late Hebrew in the Geniza manuscripts indicate that the translator had to work from the Syriac at places where his *Vorlage* was corrupt or missing. In contrast, H. Rüger (1970) maintains that the readings in the Geniza fragments can all be explained in light of later developments of language, exegetical tendencies, and style. A third option is offered by T. Middendorp, (1973) who contends that the differences are due to oral transmission. Undoubtedly, scholarship will continue to attempt to define the nature and the relationships of the various Hebrew texts. Also important are similar efforts to establish the nature and development of other versions, including the Greek rescensions (J. Ziegler 1965) and the Syriac (Winder; Nelson).

3. *Sirach in Its Historical Context.* Much scholarly work on the book in the past century can be viewed as an attempt to understand the person and perspective of Ben Sira within his historical context. In particular, the book's place within Judaism and, vis-à-vis, Hellenism has been the focus of many studies. A number of earlier scholars located the book within the party of the Sadducees because of the author's praise of the priesthood and the conspicuous lack of references to Ezra (R. Moulton 1896; W. Oesterley 1912). Later investigations showed that it was historically impossible for Ben Sira to have been a Sadducee, although his thought has affinities with a conservative, nationalistic party that was replaced by the Hasmoneans (M. Hengel 1974).

Ben Sira's place within the wisdom tradition of Israel has been an important subject of study (H. Kieweler 1992). His equation of wisdom and Torah is a significant development within the wisdom tradition in Judaism. Some scholars have concluded that for Ben Sira the Torah has actually replaced the older wisdom point of view that norms of conduct were to be derived from observation and experience (Hengel). G. von Rad[§] (1972) took exception to this conclusion, however, and argued that a careful examination of the relevant texts shows that Ben Sira sought to legitimate and interpret Torah from the wisdom tradition.

In addition to an interest in Ben Sira's place within Judaism, the question of his attitude toward Hellenism has been the focus of a number of major studies. In 1906 R. Smend[§] characterized the book as a "declaration of war" against Hellenism. A number of subsequent studies found that a marked anti-Hellenistic *Tendenz* pervades and shapes the whole work. On the other hand, recent investigations have discerned a more complex and ambivalent attitude toward Hellenism; indeed, on a number of points Ben Sira is influenced by Hellenistic ideas and attitudes. Not only does he reveal a cautious attitude toward the Ptolemies, but he also borrows ideas and quotations from Greek literature and thought (T. Middendorp 1973; J. Marböck 1999; L. Prokter 1990). Recent work also raises the possibility that Ben Sira's presentation of Lady Wisdom/Sophia is influenced by Hellenistic hymns to Isis (E. Schuller 1992). In any case, a number of studies have shown that many of Ben Sira's concerns with such subjects as freedom of the will and the importance of human action and wisdom are a response to Hellenism in general and to Stoic and Epicurean philosophies in particular (G. Maier 1971; R. Pautrel 1963; Marböck 1975). Undoubtedly, the investigation of Ben Sira's relation to the wisdom tradition and to Hellenism will continue to be fertile ground for research in the years to come.

Recent commentaries on Sir include Bergant (2003), Eisenbaum (1998), Sauer (2000), and Schreiner (2002). Coggins (1998) gives a general introduction to the book. Recent reference works include Calduch-Benages and Reiterer's bibliography (1998) and Thompson's critical concordance (2002). Conference proceedings, *Festschriften,* and collected studies are in Beentjes (1997), Calduch-Benages and Vermeylen (1999), Egger-Wenzel (2002), Egger-Wenzel and Krammer (1998), Muraoka and Elwolde (1997, 1999, 2000), and Reiterer (1996). Recent text-critical studies include Nelson (1988), Wagner (1999). Theological studies include Argall (1995), Collins (1997), Corley (2002), Kaiser (2003), Marböck (2001), Reitemeyer

(2000), Schrader (1994), and Wicke-Reuter (2000). McKinlay (1996) presents a feminist analysis of Sirach's intertextual relationship to Proverbs and John 4.

Bibliography: E. N. Adler, "Some Missing Chapters of Ben Sira (7:20-12:1)," *JQR* 12 (1899-1900) 466-80. R. A. Argall, *1 Enoch and Sirach: A Comparative and Conceptual Analysis of the Themes of Revelation, Creation, and Judgment* (SBLEJL 8, 1995). W. Baumgartner, "Die literarischen Gattungen in der Weisheit des Jesus Sirach," *ZAW* 34 (1914) 161-98. P. C. Beentjes, "Recent Publications on the Wisdom of Jesus ben Sira (Ecclesiasticus)," *BTFT* 43 (1982) 188-98; *The Book of Ben Sira in Hebrew: A Text Edition of All Extant Hebrew Manuscripts and a Synopsis of All Parallel Hebrew Ben Sira Texts* (VTSup 68, 1997); ed., *The Book of Ben Sira in Modern Research* (BZAW 225, 1997). D. Bergant, "Sirach," *NISB* (2003) 1451-1519. G. Bickell, "Der hebräische Sirachtext eine Rückübersetzung," *WZKM* 13 (1889) 251-56. T. A. Burkhill, "Ecclesiasticus," *IDB* 2 (1962) 13-21. N. Calduch-Benages, F. Reiterer, et al. (eds.), *Bibliographie zu Ben Sira* (BZAW 266, 1998). N. Calduch-Benages and J. Vermeylen (eds.), *Treasures of Wisdom: Studies in Ben Sira and the Book of Wisdom: Festschrift M. Gilbert* (BEThL 143, 1999). R. J. Coggins, *Sirach* (Guides to Apocrypha and Pseudepigrapha 6, 1998). J. J. Collins, *Jewish Wisdom in the Hellenistic Age* (OTL, 1997). J. Corley, *Ben Sira's Teaching on Friendship* (BJS 316, 2002). A. E. Cowley and A. Neubauer, *Facsimiles of the Fragments Hitherto Recovered of the Book of Ecclesiasticus in Hebrew* (1897). J. L. Crenshaw, "Wisdom," *OT Form Criticism* (ed. J. H. Hayes, 1974) 225-64; "The Book of Sirach," *NIB* (1997) 5:601-867. A. A. Di Lella, "Recently Identified Leaves of Sirach in Hebrew," *Bib 45* (1964) 153-67; *The Hebrew Text of Sirach: A Text Critical Study* (Studies in Classical Literature 1, 1966); "The Newly Discovered Sixth Manuscript of Ben Sira from the Cairo Geniza," *Bib* 69 (1988) 226-38. R. Egger-Wenzel (ed.), *Ben Sira's God* (BZAW 321, 2002). R. Egger-Wenzel and I. Krammer (eds.), *Der Einzelne und seine Gemeinschaft bei Ben Sira* (BZAW 270, 1998). P. M. Eisenbaum, "Sirach," *Women's Bible Commentary* (ed. C. A. Newsom and C. H. Ringe, 1998²) 298-304. M. Gilbert, "The Book of Ben Sira: Implications for Jewish and Christian Traditions," *Jewish Civilization in the Hellenistic-Roman Period* (ed. S. Talmon, 1971). H. L. Ginsberg, "The Original Hebrew of Ben Sira 12:10-14," *JBL* 74 (1955) 93-95. L. Ginzburg, "Randglossen zum hebräischen Ben Sira," *Orientalische Studien T. Nöldeke gewidmet* (ed. C. Bezold, 1906) 609-25. E. J. Goodspeed, *The Story of the Apocrypha* (1939). D. J. Harrington, "Sirach Research Since 1965: Progress and Questions," *Pursuing the Text: Studies in Honor of B. Z. Wacholder on the Occasion of His Seventieth Birthday* (ed. J. Kampen and J. C. Reeves, JSOTSup 184, 1994) 164-76. J. D. Harvey, "Toward a Degree of Order in Ben Sira's Book," ZAW 105 (1993) 52-62. J. Haspecker, *Gottesfurcht bei Jesus Sirach: Ihre religiöse Struktur und ihre literarische und doktrinäre Bedeutung* (AnBib 30, 1967). M. Hengel, *Judaism and Hellenism: Studies in Their Encounter in Palestine During the Early Hellenistic Period* (2 vols. 1974). M. A. Jolley, *The Function of Torah in Sirach* (1993). O. Kaiser, "Die Begründung der Sittlichkeit im Buch Jesus Sirach," *ZKT* 55 (1958) 51-63; *Zwischen Athen und Jerusalem: Studien zur griechischen und biblischen Theologie, ihrer Eigenart und ihrem Verhältnis* (BZAW 320, 2003). C. Kearns, "Ecclesiasticus, or the Wisdom of Jesus the Son of Sirach," *A New Catholic Commentary on Holy Scripture* (ed. R. C. Fuller et al., 1969) 541-62. H. V. Kieweler, *Ben Sira zwischen Judentum und Hellenismus: Eine Auseinandersetzung mit T. Middendorp* (BEATAJ 30, 1992). T. R. Lee, *Studies in the Form of Sirach 44-50* (SBLDS 75, 1986). S. Z. Leiman, *The Canonization of Hebrew Scripture: The Talmudic and Midrashic Evidence* (1976). H. McKeating, "Ben Sira's Attitude to Women," *ExpTim* 85 (1973-74) 85-87. G. Maier, *Mensch und frier Wille: Nach den jüdischen Religionsparteien zwischen Ben Sira und Pauls* (WUNT 12, 1971). J. Marböck, "Sirachliteratur seit 1966: Ein überblick," *TRev* 71 (1975) 177-84; *Weisheit im Wandel: Untersuchungen zur Weisheitstheologie bei Ben*

Sira mit Nachwort und Bibliographie zur Neuauflage (BZAW 272, 1999); "Gerechtigkeit Gottes und Leben nach dem Sirachbuch: ein Antwortversuch in seinem Kontext," *Gerechtigkeit und Leben im hellenistischen Zeitalter* (ed. J. Jeremias, BZAW 296, 2001) 21-5 2. **J. E. McKinlay,** *Gendering Wisdom the Host: Biblical Invitations to Eat and Drink* (JSOTSup 216, Gender, Culture, Theory 4, 1996). **D. S. Margoliouth,** *The Origin of the "Original Hebrew" of Ecclesiasticus* (1899). **J. D. Martin,** "Ben Sira: A Child of His Time," *A Word in Season: Essays in Honour of W. McKane* (ed. J. D. Martin and P. R. Davies, JSOTSup 42, 1986) 141-61. **D. Michaelis,** "Das Buch Jesus Sirach als Typischer Ausdruck für das Gottesverhältnis des nachalttestamentlichen Menschen," *TLZ* 83 (1958) 601-08. **T. Middendorp,** *Die Stellung Jesus ben Siras zwischen Judentum und Hellenismus* (1973). **R. G. Moulton,** *Ecclesiasticus: The Modern Reader's Bible* (1896). **T. Muraoka and J. F. Elwolde** (eds.), *The Hebrew of the Dead Sea Scrolls and Ben Sira* (*STDJ* 26, 1997); *Sirach, Scrolls, and Sages* (*STDJ* 33, 1999); *Diggers at the Well: Proceedings of a Third International Symposium on the Hebrew of the Dead Sea Scrolls and Ben Sira* (*STDJ* 36, 2000). **D. N. Nelson,** *The Syriac Version of the Wisdom of Ben Sira Compared to the Greek and Hebrew Materials* (SBLDS 107, 1988). **M. D. Nelson;** *The Syriac Version of the Wisdom of Ben Sira Compared to the Greek and Hebrew Materials* (SBLDS 107, 1988). **W. O. E. Oesterley,** *The Wisdom of Jesus the Son of Sirach or Sir* (1912). **S. M. Olyan,** "Ben Sira's Relationship to the Priesthood," *HTR* 80 (1987) 261-86. **R. Pautrel,** "Ben Sira et le Stoicisme," *RSR* 51 (1963) 535-49. **E. Pax,** "Dialog und Selbstgespräch bei Sirach 27, 3-10," *SBFLA* 20 (1970) 247-63. **L. J. Prokter,** "His Yesterday and Yours Today (Sir 38:22)," *JSem* 2 (1990) 44-56. **G. von Rad,** *Wisdom in Israel* (1972). **M. Reitemeyer,** *Weisheitslehre als Gotteslob: Psalmentheologie im Buch Jesus Sirach* (BBB 127, 2000). **F. V. Reiterer** (ed.), *Freundschaft bei Ben Sira* (BZAW 244 1996). **H. P Rüger,** *Text und Textform in hebräischen Sirach: Untersuchungen zur Textgeschichte und Textkritik der hebräischen Sirachfragmente aus der Kairo Geniza* (BZAW 112, 1970). **J. A. Sanders,** *The Psalms Scroll of Qumran Cave 11* (11QPsᵃ) (DJD 4, 1965). **G. Sauer,** *Jesus Sirach, Ben Sira* (ATD, Apokryphen 1, 2000). **S. Schlechter and C. Taylor,** *The Wisdom of Ben Sira: Portions of the Book Ecclesiasti from Hebrew Manuscripts in the Cairo Genizah Collection Presented to the University of Cambridge by the Editors* (1899). **L. Schrader,** *Leiden und Gerechtigkeit: Studien zu Theologie und Textgeschichte des Sirachbuches* (BBET 27, 1994). **J. Schreiner,** *Jesus Sirach* (NechtB, Altes Testament 38, 2002). **E. M. Schuller,** "The Aprocrypha," *The Women's Bible Commentary* (1992) 235-43. **E. Schürer,** *HJPAJC* 3, 1 (1986) 198-212. **P. W. Skehan,** "Ecclesiasticus," *IDBS,* 250-55. **P. W. Skehan and A. A. Di Lella,** *The Wisdom of Ben Sira* (AB 39, 1987). **R. Smend,** *Die Weisheit des Jesus Sirach* (1906). **J. D. Thompson,** *A Critical Concordance to the Apocrypha: Sirach* (The Computer Bible 108, 2002). **C. C. Torrey,** "The Hebrew of the Geniza Sirach," *Alexander Marx Jubilee Volume* (1950) 585-602. **W. C. Trenchard,** *Ben Sira's View of Women: A Literary Analysis* (BJS 38, 1982). **C. Wagner,** *Die Septuaginta-Hapaxlegomena im Buch Jesus Sirach* (BZAW 282, 1999). **U. Wicke-Reuter,** *Göttliche Providenz und menschliche Verantwortung bei Ben Sira und in der frühen Stoa* (BZAW 298, 2000). **D. S. Williams,** "The Date of Ecclesiasticus," *VT* 44 (1994) 536-66. **M. M. Winter,** "The Origins of Ben Sira in Syriac," *VT* 27 (1977) 237-53, 494-507. **O. Wischmeyer,** *Die Kultur des Buches Jesus Sirach* (1995). **Y. Yadin,** *The Ben Sira Scroll from Masada* (1965). **J. Ziegler,** *Sapientia Iesu Filii Sirach* (Septuaginta 12, 2, 1965).

C. S. Shaw

APOCRYPHA

Baruch, Book of

This book of the Hebrew Bible Apocrypha claims to have been written by Baruch, the companion and secretary of the prophet Jeremiah (Jer 32:12, 16; 36:4), in the fifth year of the Babylonian exile (1:1-2). The opening verses specify that the book was first read to the exiles in Babylon and then sent to Jerusalem, where it served as part of the Temple liturgy (1:3-4, 14). In modern times, the book is often designated "1 Baruch" to distinguish it from other works attributed to the same author (*2 Baruch*, or the *Syriac Apocalypse of Baruch*; *3 Baruch*, or the *Greek Apocalypse of Baruch*; and *4 Baruch*, or *Paraleipomena Jeremiou*). It is extant in Greek and in a number of ancient versions based on the Greek: Latin, Syriac, Coptic, Armenian, Ethiopic (Ethiopian Biblical Interpretation[§]), and Arabic. In some manuscripts and versions, including the Vulgate*[§], the Letter of Jeremiah is attached to the book of Baruch as if it were a part of the same work.

Following an introduction explaining the ostensible circumstances of writing (1:1-14) are three sections so disparate in form, style, use of divine names, and point of view as to suggest independent origin. The first part (1:15–3:8), entirely in prose, reports a series of confessions and prayers by the exiled community. In language strongly reminiscent of Deut 28, Jer, and especially Dan 9:4-19, the exiles acknowledge that their misfortune is God's just punishment for their sins. Nevertheless, they appeal for forgiveness and express confidence that God will restore them to their homeland and renew the covenant with them. The second part (3:9–4:4), which begins with an abrupt shift to poetic form (Poetry, Hebrew Bible[‡§]), is a poem in praise of wisdom. Here the affinities are with Israel's wisdom tradition rather than with the prophetic writings (Prophecy and Prophets, Hebrew Bible[‡§]). Israel is "dead" in captivity because of having forsaken "the fountain of Wisdom." The people must therefore find life by returning to God, the only source of wisdom. The third section (4:5–5:9), also poetic, is a psalm of comfort and hope punctuated with the refrain "take courage" (4:5, 21, 27, 30). The poet represents Jerusalem as a widow lamenting the loss of her children, but also assuring the children that they will be brought back to her. Then four strophes are addressed to Jerusalem herself; like her sons, Jerusalem is to "take courage" in view of the certain return of her children and punishment of her oppressors. The language of the third section is heavily indebted to Isa 40–55. There are also strong affinities with *Psalms of Solomon* 11.

The fictional character of the book's claims about authorship and setting is evident not only from the disparity among the various sections but also from the improbability that Baruch was ever among the exiles in Babylon (see Jer 43:1-7), inaccuracies in the description of that historical period, and affinities with Jewish writings of a much later date. The compositional history of the work is complex and has been variously reconstructed. The three separate compositions dealing with the exile and return may have been compiled by the unknown redactor who added the introduction in 1:1-14. The date and place of origin of both the component parts and the final composition are unknown. Assigning a date after 70 C.E. to the finished work, as some have done, is necessary only if the ostensible setting described in 1:2 reflects an actual devastation of Jerusalem and deportation of its inhabitants in the author's own time. If the exilic setting is an expression for the oppression of Jews generally rather than a cipher for specific oppressors and calamities, then a much earlier date is possible. On the whole, a date in the second century B.C.E. during the Hasmonean period seems most likely. The Greek of the prose portion shows clear signs of having been translated from Hebrew; it is less certain but likely that the poetic sections were also originally composed in Hebrew.

Bar has been used far more widely in Christianity than in Judaism. It was not included in the Hebrew Canon[§] but is found in most manuscripts of the Septuagint*[§]. Late in the fourth century Jerome[§] indicated that the Jews did not use or even possess a Hebrew text of Bar. The Apostolic Constitutions (late fourth cent.) and a sixth-century text attributed to Ephraem the Syrian[§] may imply scattered liturgical use of Bar by Jews, but the evidence is problematic in both instances.

In early Christian circles, on the other hand, Bar was used widely and quoted as Scripture. The reference in 3:36-37 to the earthly appearance and existence of wisdom (or God; the subject is not specified and must be deduced from context) was a special favorite because of its christological potential. Quotations of this and other passages appear in Athenagoras[§], Irenaeus[§], Clement of Alexandria[§], Hippolytus, Origen[§], Commodian, and Cyprian. Often these quotes are attibuted to Jeremiah—a practice facilitated by the placement of the book of Bar as an appendix to Jeremiah in the Greek manuscript tradition. The book is included in several canonical lists by the Greek fathers (Athanasius, Cyril of Jerusalem, Epiphanius, Nicephorus), but never by the Latin fathers; the latter presumably shared Jerome's conviction that Bar and the other books in the Septuagint, but not in the Hebrew Bible, are non-canonical. The book nevertheless made its way into the Vulgate, was included in the canon drawn up by the Council of Trent in 1546, and was ratified by the First Vatican Council in 1870. However, Luther[§] and other Reformers denied the canonicity of Bar and the rest of the Apocrypha; thus Protestant Bibles either exclude these writings or distinguish them from their Hebrew Bible or Old Testament canon by categorizing them separately as "Apocrypha."

Recent work on Bar includes at least one commentary (Newsom 2003), text critical studies (Feuerstein 1997, Kabasele Mukenge 1998, the latter arguing for the book's unity), Baruch's place in the canon (Steck 1993), and a critical concordance (Thompson 2002).

Bibliography: R. **Feuerstein,** *Das Buch Baruch: Studien zur Textgestalt und Auslegungsgeschichte* (1997). **J. A. Goldstein,** "The Apocryphal Book of Baruch," *PAAJR* 46-47 (1979-80) 179-99. **A. H. J. Gunneweg,** "Der Brief der Jeremias" *JSHRZ* 3.2 (1975) 165-81. **A. Kabasele Mukenge,** *L'unité littéraire du livre de Baruch* (*Ebib* n.s. 38, 1998). **J. J. Kneucker**, *Das Buch Baruch, Geschichte und Kritik: übersetzung und Erklärung* (1879). **R. A. Martin**, *Syntactical and Critical Concordance to the Greek Text of Baruch and the Epistle of Jeremiah* (1979). **B. Metzger,** *An Introduction to the Apocrypha* (1957) 89-94. **C. A. Moore,** *Daniel, Esther, and Jeremiah: The Additions* (AB 44, 1977) 255-316; "Toward the Dating of the Book of Baruch," *CBQ* 36 (1974) 312-20. **C. A. Newsom,** "Baruch," *NISB* (2003) 1617-26. **G. W. E. Nickelsburg**, *Jewish Literature Between the Bible and the Mishnah* (1981) 109-14. **E. Schürer,** *HJPAJC* 3, 2 (1987) 733-43. **O. H. Steck,** *Das apokryphe Baruchbuch: Studien zu Rezeption und Konzentration "kanonischer" Überlieferung* (FRLANT 160, 1993). **H. St. J. Thackeray**, *The Septuagint and Jewish Worship: A Study of Origins* (1923) 80-111. **J. D. Thompson,** *A Critical Concordance to the Apocrypha. Baruch* (The Computer Bible 102, 2002). **E. Tov,** *The Book of Baruch: Also called I Baruch: (Greek and Hebrew)* (SBLTT 8, Pseudepigrapha Series 6, 1975); *The Septuagint Translation of Jeremiah and Baruch* (HSM 8, 1976). **J. Ziegler,** *Jeremiah, Baruch, Threni, Epistula Ieremiae* (Septuaginta, Vetus Testamentum Graecum 15, 1957) 450-67.

R. D. CHESNUTT

APOCRYPHA

Jeremiah, Epistle of

This apocryphal work purports to have been written by the prophet Jeremiah (Prophecy and Prophets, Hebrew Bible‡§; Jeremiah, Book of‡§) to Jews about to be exiled to Babylon. Its purpose is ostensibly to warn the captives of the danger of assimilation to Babylonian religion during the "seven generations" of their exile.

In spite of the title the work is neither a letter nor a writing of Jeremiah. The unknown author, who lived centuries later than Jeremiah, found his literary model in the prophet's letter to the Babylonian exiles in Jer 29. The apocryphon is nevertheless more an impassioned discourse on the folly of idolatry than a letter; the influence of biblical satires on idolatry (Pss 115; 135; Isa 44:9-20; Jer 10:1-16) is far more evident than is the letter format. The style of the tirade is rambling and repetitious. The recurring formula "therefore they evidently are not gods, so do not fear them" (v. 16, repeated with some variation in vv. 23, 29, 40, 44, 52, 56, 65, and 69) creates a superficial tenfold division, but there is no logical progression of thought from one section to the next. Rather, the author relies on repetition and biting satire to drive home his point that idols are lifeless, powerless, useless, and perishable products of human hands.

The Ep Jer is extant only in Greek and versions based on the Greek, but shows some signs of having been written originally in Hebrew or Aramaic. The date of composition is uncertain. Proposals range from the late fourth century to the late second century B.C.E. The place of writing is also unknown. The Babylonian flavor of certain cultic practices mentioned lends credibility to the superscription's indication of a Babylonian setting, but the caricature of idols is mostly generic and could reflect any location where idolatry posed a threat.

In most manuscripts of the Septuagint*§ the Ep Jer appears along with the other supposed writings of Jeremiah (Jer, Bar, Lam) as a discrete work. However, some manuscripts and versions, including the Vulgate*§, attach it to the book of Baruch. Under the influence of the Vulgate, most English versions of the Apocrypha print the letter as the sixth and final chapter of Bar, but others treat it as a separate composition since it has nothing to do with the book of Baruch.

Quotations and echoes of the Ep Jer in Christian literature are few. Aristides of Athens seems to have been influenced by the work in his apology of Christianity to the emperor Hadrian, and the fourth-century Sicilian rhetorician Firmicus Maternus quoted it extensively in his critique of paganism. Brief portions were quoted by Tertullian§ and Cyprian. The letter is included by name in several patristic lists of canonical writings (Origen, Athanasius, the Council of Laodicea, Hillary of Poitiers, Cyril of Jerusalem, and Epiphanius), and others not mentioning it by name no doubt included it as part of the other supposed Jeremianic writings to which it was attached. Jerome§ called the letter a pseudepigraphon (Pseudepigrapha†§) and regarded it, along with the other books found in the Septuagint but not in the Hebrew Bible, as non-canonical (Canon of the Bible§). For the most part, the Ep Jer has experienced the same mixed fate within Christendom as have the apocryphal writings generally. Thus during the Reformation canonical status was denied to the Ep Jer and the rest of the Apocrypha by Protestant leaders but was affirmed by Roman Catholics at the Council of Trent in 1546; this latter decision was confirmed by the First Vatican Council of 1870.

Recent work on Ep Jer includes four commentaries (Fitzgerald 1990, Harrelson 2003, Saldarini 2001, Tull 1998) and a critical concordance (Thompson 2002).

Bibliography: A. Fitzgerald, "Letter of Jeremiah," (=ch. 6 in commentary on Baruch) *NJBC* (1990) 367. **A. H. J. Gunneweg**, "Der Brief der Jeremias" (*JSHRZ* 3.2, 1975) 183-92. **W. J. Harrelson**, "Letter of Jeremiah," *NISB* (2003) 1531-35. **R. A. Martin**, *Syntactical and*

Critical Concordance to the Greek Text of Baruch and the Epistle of Jeremiah (1979). **B. Metzger**, *An Introduction to the Apocrypha* (1957) 95-98. **C. A. Moore**, *Daniel, Esther, and Jeremiah: The Additions* (AB 44, 1977) 317-58. **W. Naumann**, *Untersuchungen über den apokryphen Jeremiasbrief* (BZAW 25, 1913) 1-53. **G. W. E. Nickelsburg,** *Jewish Literature Between the Bible and the Mishnah* (1981) 35-42. **W. M. W. Roth**, "For Life, He Appeals to Death (Wis 13:18): A Study of OT Idol Parodies," *CBQ* 37 (1975) 21-47. **A. J. Saldarini,** "Letter of Jeremiah," *NIB* (2001) 6.985-1010. **J. D. Thompson,** *A Critical Concordance to the Apocrypha. Letter of Jeremiah* (The Computer Bible 106, 2002). **P. K. Tull,** "Letter of Jeremiah," *Women's Bible Commentary* (ed. C. A. Newsom and S. H. Ringe, 1998[2]) 309-10. **J. Ziegler**, *Jeremiah, Baruch, Threni, Epistula Ieremiae* (Septuaginta, Vetus Testamentum Graecum 15, 1957) 494-504.

R. D. CHESNUTT

APOCRYPHA

Daniel, Book of (Additions to)

The additions to the book of Daniel, which are considered apocryphal by Jews and Protestants but deuterocanonical by Roman Catholics and Orthodox Christians, comprise the Prayer of Azariah and the Song of the Three Young Men (also know as Hymn of the Three Jews) and the stories of Susanna and of Bel and the Dragon. These stories, haggadic folk tales like those in Dan 1-6, belong to a "Daniel cycle." Fragments found at Qumran indicate that several other stories of the cycle also circulated among the Jews in pre-Christian times (J.-T. Milik 1981), but these never became canonical.

1. *Place in the Canon and Canonicity*. In the LXX (Septuagint*§) form of Dan, extant in only three witnesses (Cod. 88, Syrohexaplar, Pap. 967), the Prayer of Azariah and the Song of the Three Young Men are found in chap. 3 between vv. 23 and 24 of the MT; in the Greek, Syriac, and Vulgate*§ editions these are given as 3:24-90. In Codex 88, Syrohexaplar, and Vulgate, the order of material is chaps. 1-12, Sus, and Bel. In prehexaplaric Pap. 967, the order is chaps. 1-12, Bel and Sus; the Syriac edition has a similar order, but with Sus appearing between Ruth and Esther. The text of so-called Theodotion§-Daniel is found in all the other Greek witnesses; in them the order is Sus, chaps. 1-12 (including 3:24-90) and then Bel (L. Hartman and A. Di Lella 1978, 26-28). Roman Catholic editions of the Hebrew Bible follow the same order as the Vulgate: chaps. 1-12 (including 3:24-90), Sus (chap. 13), and Bel (14:1-22) and the Dragon (14:23-42). Protestant editions that contain the additions relegate them to an appendix.

Until recently, the scholarly consensus was that the Greek Hebrew Bible represented the list of books accepted as sacred only by the Jews of Egypt, where the LXX had been translated from the third to the first century B.C.E. (Dan in c. 100). It is now widely accepted that Theod-Dan also had its origin in pre-Christian times in Asia Minor, Palestine, or Syria-Mesopotamia, hence in that region during the first century B.C.E. there were Jews who viewed the additions to Dan as sacred. Near the end of the first century C.E. the rabbis of Pharisaic Judaism, who fixed the Jewish Canon§, excluded the additions. But by the beginning of the fifth century when the Western church determined the limits of the Christian canon, it included the additions (Hartman and Di Lella 1978, 78-84).

2. *Contents and Literary Genre. a. Prayer of Azariah and Song of the Three Young Men.* In the fiery furnace Daniel's faithful companions Hananiah, Mishael, and Azariah sing and bless the Lord. Azariah in his prayer praises divine justice, confessing that God has been righteous in visiting disaster on the Israelites because of their sins. He begs for forgiveness and deliverance from their pitiful state. A narrative then tells of the stoking of the furnace, the burning up of the Chaldeans nearby, and the descent of the angel to drive out the flames, thereby protecting the loyal Jews. Finally, the three Jews sing their hymn to the Lord, urging all creatures, great and small, to join in the chorus of praise. Not part of the original story in chap. 3, the Prayer and Hymn are a pastiche of earlier biblical verses, as is the intrusive prayer in Dan 9. The Prayer contains many expressions and motifs found in Pss 44, 74, 79, and 80. The Hymn, echoing ideas and phrases of Ps 148, follows the structure of Ps 136 in that the refrain "praise and exalt him above all forever" occurs in the second colon of thirty-eight successive bicola of the Hymn (see the NAB).

b. Susanna. Susanna, transmitted better in Theod-Dan than in the LXX (but see Milik 1981), is a charming detective story that has been included in some modern anthologies. Its point is that fidelity to the law of conjugal chastity will win out in the end, thus foiling the schemes of the wicked (Deut 28:1-14). Susanna (the word means "lily") is the pious and lovely wife of Joakim, a prosperous Jew in Babylon. Two Jewish elders, seeing her on her daily walk in the garden, begin to lust after her. One warm day Susanna decides to take her bath in the garden. While her maids go to fetch soap and oil, the two lechers, hiding nearby, come forward and threaten to accuse her of adultery with a young man unless she consents to have intercourse with them. She refuses their advances and cries out for help. Making good their threat, the elders testify that Susanna had lain with a young man. Though innocent, she is condemned to death. When she is led to execution, God inspires a young man named Daniel to rebuke the people for condemning Susanna without thorough examination of the witnesses. In the clever cross-examination Daniel shows that the witnesses have perjured themselves. The assembly thanks God for intervening and then inflicts on the two elders the death penalty they had plotted against Susanna.

c. *Bel*. Like Sus, Bel is a well-crafted and entertaining detective story; its purpose is to mock paganism and the worship of lifeless idols that cannot see or hear, eat or smell, (Deut 4:28; Wis 13:1-15:17). In the reign of Cyrus the Persian, Daniel, the king's favorite, refuses to worship the Babylonian idol named Bel (Isa 46:1; Jer 50:2). Daniel says he worships only the living God who made heaven and earth. The king protests that Bel is a living god, for he eats and drinks so much every day. Daniel laughs, much to the king's annoyance. The king orders the priests to find out who consumes all the provisions. The priests tell the king to provide the usual food and wine for Bel; after everybody leaves the temple, he is to seal the door with his ring. If Bel does not consume everything, the priests agree to die; otherwise Daniel is to die. With only the king present, Daniel has ashes scattered over the floor of the temple, which is then sealed. During the night, the priests, their wives, and their children enter the temple through a secret door and eat and drink everything. The next morning Daniel and the king find the seals unbroken and the table empty. The king exclaims, "Great are you, O Bel; there is no trickery in you!" Daniel laughs again, then asks the king to examine the floor, where there are footprints of the priests and their families. Enraged, the king puts them all to death and hands Bel over to Daniel, who destroys it and the temple.

d. *The Dragon*. This story, which is not as well constructed as the other two, also has as its purpose to ridicule the paganism of the Gentiles and their abhorrent idolatry (Isa 44:9-20). Daniel is ordered to worship a great dragon, whom the king describes as a living god. Daniel refuses and then receives permission from the king to kill the dragon without sword or club. Making cakes of pitch, fat, and hair, Daniel feeds them to the dragon, and it bursts asunder. Daniel exclaims, "This is what you worshiped!" The angry Babylonians accuse the king of becoming a Jew and demand that Daniel be handed over to them. They throw Daniel into a den of lions for six days. Each day the lions had been fed two carcasses and two sheep, but now they receive nothing so as to find Daniel the more appetizing. But the lions do not touch him. An angel transports to the den a prophet, Habakkuk, who had prepared a substantial meal. He tells Daniel to eat what God has sent; Daniel praises God and eats. On the seventh day, the king comes to the den to mourn, only to discover that Daniel is alive and well. Amazed, the king confesses that the God of Daniel alone is God; he then removes Daniel and casts his enemies into the den, where they are quickly devoured. This story is clearly a variant of the one in Dan 6.

3. *Original Language and Date*. Although there has been considerable dispute in the past, most scholars today agree that, like the rest of Dan, the additions were composed originally in either Hebrew or Aramaic. Since the additions have the same vocabulary, style, and syntax as the Greek of the rest of the book, it is reasonable to conclude that the Semitic originals were written in the second century B.C.E. and then translated into Greek about the time of the Greek translation of Dan, c. 100 B.C.E. (C. Moore 1977, 25-29).

Recent work on the Add Dan includes a commentary on all three texts (VanderKam 2003), a commentary on Bel and the Dragon (Wysny 1996), a critical concordance (Thompson 2002), literary analysis of Sus and Bel (Handy 2000), and feminist studies of Sus (Brenner 1995, Spolsky 1996).

Bibliography: W. H. Bennett, "Prayer of Azariah and Song of the Three Children," *APOT* (1913) 1:625-37. **A. Brenner** (ed.), *A Feminist Companion to Esther, Judith and Susanna* (Feminist Companion to the Bible 7, 1995). **J. J. Collins**, *Daniel: A Commentary on the Book of Daniel* (Hermeneia, 1993). **T. Craven**, "Daniel and Its Additions," *Women's Bible Commentary* (ed. C. A. Newsom and S. H. Ringe, 1992) 191-94. **T. W. Davies**, "Bel and the Dragon," *APOT* (1913) 1:652-64. **M. Delcor**, *Le livre de Daniel* (SB, 1971). **H. Engel**, *Die Susanna Erzählung: Einleitung, übersetzung, und Kommentar zum Septuaginta-Text und zur Theodotion-Bearbeitung* (OBO 61, 1985). **A. A. Di Lella**, *Daniel: A Book for Troubling Times* (1997). **L. K. Handy**, *Entertaining Faith: Reading Short Stories in the Bible* (2000). **L. F. Hartman and A. A. Di Lella**, *The Book of Daniel* (AB 23, 1978); "Daniel," *NJBC* (1990) 406-20. **M. Heltzer**, "The Story of Susanna and the Self-government of the Jewish Community in Achaemenid Babylonia," *Annali* 41 (1981) 35-39. **D. M. Kay**, "Susanna," *APOT* (1913) 1:638-51. **K. Koch**, *Deuterokanonische Zusätze zum Danielbuch: Entstehung und Textgeschichte* (AOAT 38, 1987). **A. LaCoque**, *Feminine Unconventional: Four Subversive Figures in Israel's Tradition* (1990). **R. A. F. MacKenzie**, "The Meaning of the Susanna Story," *CJT* 3 (1957) 211-18. **J.-T. Milik**, "Daniel et Susanne à Qumrân?" *De la Tôrah au Messie à Mélanges H. Cazelles* (ed. M. Carrez et al., 1981) 337-59; "'Prière de Nabonide' et autre ècrits d'un cycle de Daniel: Fragments araméens de Qumran 4," *RB* 63 (1956) 407-15. **C. A. Moore**, *Daniel, Esther, and Jeremiah: The Additions* (AB 44, 1977); *The OT in Syriac According to the Peshitta Version*, 3, 4: *Dodekapropheton-Daniel-Bel-Draco* (1980). **G. Rinaldi**, *Daniele* (La Sacra Biblia, 4th rev. ed., 1962). **D. L. Smith-Christopher**, "The Additions to Daniel," *NIB* (1996) 7:153-94. **E. Spolsky** (ed.), *The Judgment of Susanna: Authority and Witness* (SBLEJL 11, 1996). **J. D. Thompson**, *A Critical Concordance to the Apocrypha. Additions to Daniel* (The Computer Bible 103, 2002). **J. C. VanderKam,** "Additions to Daniel," *NISB* (2003) 1537-50. **A. Wysny**, *Die Erzählungen von Bel und dem Drachen: Untersuchung zu Dan 14* (SBB 33, 1996). **J. Ziegler**, *Susanna, Daniel, Bel et Draco* (Septuaginta 16, 2, 1954).

A. A. Di Lella

APOCRYPHA

Maccabees, First Book of

Ta Makkabaika (The Things Maccabean) was the designation for both 1 and 2 Macc by the second century C.E. Clement of Alexandria[§] terms 1 Macc *to Biblion tōn Makkabaikōn* (The Book of Things Maccabean), and 2 Macc *hē tōn Makkabaikōn epitom?* (The Epitome of Things Maccabean). Most Greek manuscripts term the books *Makkabaiōn A'* and *Makkabaikōn B'*. These are certainly not the original titles. According to Origen[§] (Eusebius *Hist. eccl.* 6.25.2), the original Hebrew title of 1 Macc was *Sarbethsabaniel*. This title has been interpreted as *śar bêt 'ēl* (Official of the House of God), somehow corrupted, or *sfar bet sabanai' el*. In any case, it is difficult to interpret this title (for possible translations, see E. Schürer 1986, 182).

First Macc presents an account of the history of Judea from 175 to 135/34 B.C.E. It describes the background of the Maccabean revolt against the Seleucid Greeks, the revolt itself, the exploits of Judah the Maccabee, and the efforts of his brothers Jonathan and Simon to reestablish permanently Jewish nationhood and to strengthen religious practice.

The author was clearly a believing Jew who points to the piety of the Hasmoneans (the Maccabean family) and their trust in God. Judah's piety is especially emphasized in his prayers and speeches. At the same time the author gives full credit for the Hasmoneans' success to their sagacity and tenaciousness. He sees this family as specially selected by God to bring about the deliverance of Israel from the Seleucids, and he chronicles their lives as if he were an official historian of the dynasty (called "the state historian of the Maccabean dynasty" by A. Geiger[§], (1857). He represents the Maccabees as emulating various biblical figures, thus enabling them to provide charismatic leadership. In contrast to the heroes, the opponents of the Maccabees are "lawless men," motivated only by the basest of motives and allied against the way of God's Torah.

Numerous documents are included in this work to prove the authenticity of Hasmonean rule within the context of the Seleucid Empire and contemporary international law. In addition, the author has included various poetic extracts from contemporary compositions in circulation (G. Neuhaus 1974). Beyond this, the various theories regarding the sources of 1 Macc are speculative (for the debate, see K.-D. Shunck 1954 and Neuhaus).

The author of 1 Macc was certainly influenced by the style of biblical historiography, and he incorporated certain written sources into his composition. Further, he was extremely familiar with the practices of the Seleucid Empire. He regularly gives dates in accord with the Seleucid era (L. Grabbe 1991 for issues of chronology). On the other hand, he seems to exaggerate numbers greatly and takes the opportunity, like all historians of his period, to place speeches in the mouths of his heroes. It is generally agreed that 1 Macc is earlier and more trustworthy than 2 Macc, although in certain respects the evidence and approach of 2 Macc must be preferred (B. Niese 1900).

Virtually all scholars agree that the book had to have been written before the Roman conquest of Judea in 63 B.C.E., since the Romans are here presented as friends and allies of the Hasmonean Empire. The author's knowledge of the period of John Hyrcanus requires that he wrote not much before John's death in 104 B.C.E.. The most probable dating for the composition of 1 Macc, therefore, is the first decades of the first century B.C.E. J. Goldstein dates the composition to the reign of Alexander Janneus (103-76 B.C.E.) but not later than 90 B.C.E. (1976, 62-64). S. Zeitlin (1950, 27-33) argued that the last two chapters were late additions made after the fall of the Temple in 70 C.E..

First Macc was apparently composed in Hebrew in a style imitating that of biblical historiography. Jerome[§] reported seeing a Hebrew version ("Preface to the Books of Samuel and

Kings" NPNF 2, 6.489). Translated into Greek, it was known to Josephus[§], who used it as the basis of his account in Antiquities. Possibly the end of the book was not available to Josephus, since he seems to have lacked adequate sources for the reign of Simon. Knowledge of this book was widespread among the church fathers; yet, the contents of 1 Macc began to circulate among Jews only during the Middle Ages, indirectly through the Latin translation. The book, like 2 Macc, must be sharply distinguished from the medieval *Megillat Antiochus* (Scroll of Antiochus) or *Megillat Hashmonaim* (Scroll of the Hasmoneans) first mentioned by Saadia[§] Gaon.

The books of Maccabees were preserved in the Christian tradition in Greek and were never part of the Jewish Canon[§]. First Macc is missing from Codex Vaticanus but present in the other Greek uncial codices. It appears in an OL version in Vulgate*[§] texts not produced by Jerome and in two Syriac recensions.

First and Second Macc, along with Tob, Jdt, Wis, Sir, Bar, and the Add Daniel and Add Esther, part of the canon in Roman Catholic and Orthodox Bibles, are not in the Hebrew Bible and were never considered authoritative by Jews. Differences of opinion already existed in the early church over the issue of including writings in the Old Testament not found in the Hebrew Bible and reached a decisive point in the sixteenth century. In the early patristic period these works were quoted by Irenaeus[§], Tertullian[§], Cyprian, and others without distinguishing them from books found in the Hebrew Bible—that is, as Scripture. In the fourth century some Greek fathers (Eusebius, Athanasius, Gregory of Nazianzus, and others) raised questions about the works' status. Jerome came to distinguish the *libri canonici* (works in the HB) from the *libri ecclesiastici* (works not in the HB but found in the OL and OG Bibles). He applied the old term Apocrypha (hidden, secret) to the latter and indicated that these works should be read and used for edification but not for establishing doctrine (see his *Preface to Solomon's Books*).

In the Western church Augustine[§] (see *On Christian Doctrine* 2.8.12-13) was a strong supporter of the larger Old Testament canon that was recognized in regional councils at Hippo (393 C.E.) and at Carthage (397 and 419 C.E.). Acceptance of the inclusive canon was the dominant view throughout the Middle Ages, although a number of interpreters (W. Strabo, Hugh of St. Victor, Hugh of St. Cher, Nicholas of Lyra, J. Wyclif) had doubts about the Authority*[§] of the *libri ecclesiastici*. In spite of the confirmation of the inclusive canon by the Council of Florence in 1442, some scholars, e.g., T. Cajetan[§] and Jiménez De Cisneros[§], still placed the "apocryphal" writings on a secondary level. The latter wrote in the second preface (to the reader) of the Complutensian Polyglot[§] that these works were received by the church "only for the edification of the people rather than for confirming the authority of the church's teaching." Catholic Bibles published in Germany (1527) and France (1530) contained only the shorter Hebrew Bible.

Protestants broke with the dominant tradition and declared as canonical Old Testament only those works present in the Hebrew Bible (but in a different order). Luther[§], who opposed the concept of purgatory, and who was defended by J. Maier of Eck in their 1519 debates using texts from 2 Macc (see the following article), supported the shorter Old Testament canon. In 1520 A. von Karlstadt[§] wrote two works defending what came to be called the Protestant Old Testament canon. In its fourth session (Apr. 8, 1546), the Council of Trent declared 1 and 2 Macc along with the other *libri ecclesiastici* to be canonical and placed under anathema those who objected. Early Protestant Bibles generally contained but separated these works from the Old Testament and New Testament, often declaring them beneficial for the faithful to read but denying their authoritative status. (The 1648 Westminster Confession declared them of no more value "than any other human writings.") A Jewish convert to Christianity, Sixtus of Siena, in his 1566 *Bibliotheca sacra*, designated these disputed books as "deuterocanonical," a term widely used in modern times.

The books of Maccabees have not received much attention throughout most of history, although the Maccabean rededication of the Temple (1 Macc 4:36-59) forms the basis of the Jewish festival of Hanukkah, and Maccabean martyrs were commemorated in the Christian church. The first full commentary on Macc was written by Rabanus Maurus[§] (partially published in *PL* 109 1851, 1125-256) and was excerpted for the *Glossa Ordinaria*[§].

Luther actually held 1 Macc in high regard. In the preface to his 1536 translation he wrote: "This is another of those books not included in the Hebrew Scriptures, although in its discourses and description it almost equals the other sacred books of Scripture, and would not have been unworthy to be reckoned among them, because it is a very necessary and useful book for the understanding of the prophet Daniel in the eleventh chapter."

Between the Reformation and the twentieth century, the books of Maccabees (and the entire apocryphal/deuterocanonical material) received noticeably less attention than the other biblical writings. (For older bibliography, see Fürst 1861) During the 1740s, surprisingly, a lively debate on the historical trustworthiness of and the relationship between the two books led to a flurry of publications: E. Frölich, *Annales compendiarii regum et rerum Syriae* (1744); E. Wernsdorf, *Prolusio de fontibus historiae Syriae in libris Maccabaeorum* (1746); E. Frölich, *De fontibus historiae Syriae in libris Maccabaeorum* (1746); G. Wernsdorf, *Commentatio historico-critica de fide librorum Maccabaeorum* (1747); and the anonymous *Auctoritas utriusque libri Maccabaici canonico-historica asserta* [J. Khell?] (1749).

Protestant antipathy toward the Apocrypha led to the decision (May 3, 1827) by the British and Foreign Bible Society to omit it from English-language editions. This exclusion lasted for well over a century, during which the general Protestant readership of the Bible did not have ready access to the Apocrypha and thus to the books of Maccabees.

With the development of historical-critical study of the Bible, primarily Protestant, in the late nineteenth century, the Apocrypha came more into purview. J. D. Michaelis[§] published a translation and notes on 1 Macc in 1778; and J. G. Eichhorn[§] published an introduction to the Apocrypha in 1795, as did W. De Wette[§]. An English translation of all the Maccabean literature was published by H. Cotton in 1835. (What he called "fifth Maccabees" is a late compilation extant in Arabic.) The standard nineteenth-century commentary on 1-2 Macc was that of C. Grimm in the *Kurzgefasstes exegetisebes Handbuch zu den Apokryphen des Alten Testaments* (1851-60). C. Keil[§] produced a major commentary in 1875, but it did not replace Grimm.

Interest at the turn of the twentieth century in the religious background of the New Testament led to the production of major works on the Apocrypha and Pseudepigrapha[†§]: *Die Apokryphen und Pseudepigraphen des Alten Testaments* (2 vols., ed. E. Kautzsch, 1900) and *The Apocrypha and Pseudepigrapha of the Old Testament* (2 vols., ed. R. H. Charles, 1912-13). These works remained standard volumes until the last quarter of the twentieth century.

The discovery of the Dead Sea Scrolls[§] created a renewed interest in early Jewish life and thought and in the background to Christian origins. With this went a renewed interest in such writings as the Apocrypha and Pseudepigrapha and their dissemination in modern translations in several languages.

Williams (2003) is a recent commentary on 1 Macc. Keel (2000) discusses the commemoration of the Maccabees seen in 1 Macc 2. Williams (1999) discusses the literary structure of the book.

Bibliography: F. M. Abel, *Les livres des Maccabées* (EB, 1949[3]). **F. M. Abel and J. Starcky**, *Les livres des Maccabeés* (1961[3]). **J. R. Bartlett**, *The First and Second Books of the Maccabees* (1973); *1 Maccabees* (Guides to the Apocrypha and Pseudepigrapha 5, 1998). **E. J. Bickermann**, *The God of the Maccabees* (1937; ET, SJLA 32, 1979). **D. de Bruyne**, *Les anciennes traductions latines des Machabées* (Anecdota Maredsolana 4, 1932). **J. C. Dancy**, *A Commentary on*

I Maccabees (Blackwell's Theological Texts, 1954). **R. Doran**, "The First Book of Maccabees," *NIB* (1996) 4:1-178. **H. W. Ettelson**, "The Integrity of I Maccabees," *Transactions of the Connecticut Academy of Arts and Sciences* 27 (1925) 249-384. **T. Fischer**, "First and Second Maccabees," *ABD* (1992) 4:439-50. **J. Fürst**, *Bibliotheca Judaica* 2 (1861) 316-18. **A. Geiger**, *Urschrift und Übersetzungen der Bibel* (1857). **J. A. Goldstein**, *1 Maccabees* (AB 43, 1976). **L. L. Grabbe**, "Maccabean Chronology: 167-164 or 168-165 BCE?" *JBL* 110 (1991) 59-74; *Judaism from Cyrus to Hadrian* (2 vols. 1992) 439-50. **M. Hengel**, *Judaism and Hellenism: Studies in their Encounter in Palestine During the Early Hellenistic Period* (WUNT 10 1969, 1973[2]; ET 1974). **O. Keel**, "1 Makk 2: Rechtfertigung, Programm und Denkmal für die Erhebung der Hasmonäer: Eine Skizze" (O. Keel and U. Staub, *Hellenismus und Judentum: Vier Studien zu Daniel 7 und zur Religionsnot unter Antiochus IV,* OBO 178, 2000). **S. Meurer** (ed.), *The Apocrypha in Ecumenical Perspective* (UBS.MS 6, 1991). **G. O. Neuhaus**, *Studien zu den poetische Stücken in 1. Makkabäerbuch* (FzB 12, 1974); "Quellen im 1. Makkabäerbuch? Eine Entgegnung auf die Analyse von K.-D. Schunck," *JSJ* 5 (1974) 162-75. **B. Niese**, *Kritik der beiden Makkabäerbücher* (1900). **R. H. Pfeiffer**, *History of NT Times with an Introduction to the Apocrypha* (1949) 461-98. **A. Schalit** (ed.), *The Hellenistic Age: Political History of Jewish Palestine from 332 BCE to 67 BCE* (WHJP 6, 1972). **K.-D. Schunck**, *Die Quellen des I. und II. Makkabäerbuches* (1954). **E. Schürer**, *HJPAJC* 3.1 (1986) 180-85. **S. Stein**, "The Liturgy of Hanukkah and the First Two Books of Maccabees," *JJS* 5 (1954) 100-106, 148-55. **V. Tcherikover**, *Hellenistic Civilization and the Jews* (1966). **J. C. VanderKam**, "Hanukkah: Its Timing and Significance According to 1 and 2 Maccabees," *JSP* 1 (1987) 23-40. **D. S. Williams,** *The Structure of 1 Maccabees* (CBQMS 31, 1999); "1 Maccabees," *NISB* (2003) 1551-93. **S. Zeitlin and S. S. Tedesche**, *The First Book of Maccabees* (Jewish Apocryphal Literature, 1950).

L. H. SCHIFFMAN

APOCRYPHA

Maccabees, Second Book of

Second Maccabees opens with two letters (1:1-9; 1:10–2:18) and then presents a history of the Jewish community from the outbreak of the revolt against the Seleucids until the triumph of Judas over the general Nicanor in 161 B.C.E. (3:1–15:39). The book thus presents a parallel history to the first part of 1 Macc (chaps. 1–7). Based on its style and ancient tradition, it was originally written in Greek. Evidence from some OL, but non-Vulgate*[§], texts suggests translation from a text that differed from the standard LXX texts (Septuagint*[§]).

Early use of 2 Macc was somewhat limited. Hebrews 11:35 seems to allude to 2 Macc 6–7 (especially 6:19, 28). Josephus[§] apparently made no use of 2 Macc in his description of the period. Fourth Macc clearly builds upon the account of the martyrdoms in 2 Macc 7. Clement of Alexandria[§] cites 2 Macc 1:10 (*Strom.* 5.14.97).

Second Macc was used by early Christian exegetes as a mine for texts to support certain doctrines. Origen[§] appealed to 2 Macc 7:28 to support the idea of creation ex nihilo (*Com. Jn.* 1:17; *On First Principles* 2.1.5), and to 15:14 for the idea of the intercession of saints on behalf of the living (*Com. Jn.* 13:58; *Homilies on Canticles* 3). The death of the Jewish mother and her seven sons in 7:1-42 led to their extollment as Christian martyrs (4 Macc[†§], J. van Henten 1997).

The interpretation of 2 Macc in church history closely parallels that of 1 Macc. Luther[§] and other Protestants, however, were more critical of Second than of First Macc. In his 1536 preface to the German translation, Luther wrote: "We tolerate it because of the beautiful history of the Maccabean seven martyrs and their mother, and other pieces. It is evident, however, that the writer was no great master, but produced a patchwork of various books; he has likewise a perplexing knot in ch. xiv, in Razis, who committed suicide, which was also troublesome to Augustine and other fathers. For such example is of no use, and is not to be commended, though it may be tolerated and charitably explained. It also describes the death of Antiochus, in ch. i, differently from 1 Macc. To sum it all up: Just as 1 Macc deserves to be adopted in the number of sacred Scriptures, so 2 Macc deserves to be thrown out, though there is something good in it." The idea of offering prayers and sacrifices on behalf of the dead (12:40-45) was repudiated by most Protestants.

Since the rise of historical-critical approaches to the study of the Bible, 1 and 2 Macc have been the subject of extensive investigation because these two books, plus Josephus's *Jewish Antiquities*, constitute the primary sources for reconstructing the nature and course of the Maccabean revolt. Differences between the books further complicate matters and indicate that they were not dependent on each other. Second Macc claims to be a summary or epitome of a five-volume work by a Jason of Cyrene (2:19-32). Although the vast majority of scholars take this claim seriously, it was challenged in the nineteenth century by W. Kosters[§] (1878) and in the twentieth century by W. Richnow (1967, 41-42). The identity of this Jason remains uncertain, although some have proposed the Jason sent to Rome on a diplomatic mission by Judas Maccabeus (1 Macc 8:17). Also uncertain is how much of chaps. 3-15 derive from Jason and how much from the epitomizer.

Although sources probably underlie both books (as well as some eyewitness evidence), they are reconstructed only hypothetically (K.-D. Schunck 1954; J. Bunge 1971; and J. Goldstein 1983, 37-41). Goldstein has proposed that the two works were based on a common source. The various official documents quoted in 2 Macc are generally assumed to be genuine, though not necessarily correctly placed chronologically (see C. Habicht 1976).

Second Macc offers a fuller and different account of the origin and course of the revolt in 3:1-5:27 (L. Grabbe 1992, 1:247-56 surveys the theories regarding the causes and origin of the revolt). Most modern reconstructions of the times rely primarily on 1 Macc but recognize that 2 Macc, in spite of its strong supernaturalism and miraculous events, is a far better historical source than earlier commentators imagined.

The relationship of the two (or three) letters at the beginning of 2 Macc to each other and to the remainder of the book has been a matter of dispute (C. C. Torrey 1940; R. Pfeiffer 1949; B. Wacholder 1978). Their purpose was to encourage the observance of the festival of the rededication of the Temple (Hanukkah). The date in 1:9 (124/23 B.C.E.) indicates that the book was written after this date if the letter was incorporated by the epitomist, or else that the letter(s) was added by a later editor. A. Momigliano (1975) has proposed that the book was prepared about 124/23 B.C.E. and sent to Alexandria to encourage support for the Jerusalem community and Temple (see R. Doran 1981 for the work's emphasis on the Temple).

Early critical study sought to assign 1 and 2 Macc to particular parties in Judaism. A. Geiger[§] wrote that "the two books ... are party productions; the author of the first was a Sadducee, and a friend of the Maccabean dynasty, while the author or epitomizer of the second was a Pharisee, who looked upon the Maccabees with suspicion" (206). Modern scholars are not so convinced that one can determine party affiliation, although Goldstein argues that Jason wrote about 90 B.C.E. in an effort to counter the pro-Hasmonean tendency of 1 Macc.

Recent literature on 2 Macc includes the commentary by Williams (2003).

Bibliography: **E. J. Bickermann,** "Ein Festbrief vom Jahre 124 v. Chr. (II Macc 1:1-9)," *ZNW* 32 (1933) 233-54 = his *Studies in Jewish and Christian History* 2 (1980) 136-58. **A. Büchler,** *Die Tobianden und die Oniaden im II. Makkabäerbuche und in der verwandten jüdische-hellenistischen Litteratur* (1899). **J. G. Bunge,** "Untersuchungen zum zweiten Makkabäerbuch" (diss., Bonn University, 1971). **R. Doran,** "2 Maccabees and 'Tragic History,'" *HUCA* 50 (1979) 107-14; *Temple Propaganda: The Purpose and Character of 2 Maccabees* (CBQMS 12, 1981); "The Second Book of Maccabees," *NIB* (1996) 4:179-299. **T. Fischer,** *Seleukiden und Makkabäer: Beiträge zur Seleukidengeschichte und zu den politischen Ereignissen in Judäa* (1980). **A. Geiger,** *Urschrift und Übersetzungen der Bibel* (1857). **J. A. Goldstein,** *II Maccabees* (AB 41A, 1983); "The Origins of the Doctrine of Creation Ex Nihilo," *JJS* 35 (1984) 127-35. **L. L. Grabbe,** "Maccabean Chronology: 167-164 or 168-165 BCE?" *JBL* 110 (1991) 59-74; *Judaism from Cyrus to Hadrian* (2 vols., 1992). **C. Habicht,** "Royal Documents in Maccabees II," *HSCP* 80 (1976) 1-18; *JSHRZ* 1 (1976) 167-285. **J. W. van Henten,** *The Maccabean Martyrs as Saviours of the Jewish People: A Study of 2 and 4 Maccabees* (JSJSup 57, 1997). **U. Kellermann,** *Auferstanden in den Himmel: 2 Makkabäer 7 und die Auferstehung der Märtyrer* (SBS 95, 1979). **W. H. Kosters,** "De Polemiek van het tweede boek der Makkabeën," *Theologisch Tijdschrift* 12 (1878) 491-558. **R. Laqueur,** *Kritische Untersuchungen zum zweiten Makkabäerbuch* (1904). **A. Momigliano,** "The Second Book of Maccabees," *CP* 70 (1975) 81-88. **R. H. Pfeiffer,** *History of NT Times with an Introduction to the Apocrypha* (1949) 499-522. **W. Richnow,** *Untersuchung zu Sprache und Stil des 2. Makkabäerbuch* (1967). **K.-D. Schunck,** *Die Quellen des I. und II. Makkabäerbuches* (1954). **E. Schürer,** *HJPAJC* 3.1 (1986) 531-37. **C. C. Torrey,** "The Letters Prefixed to Second Maccabees," *JAOS* 60 (1940) 119-50. **B. Z. Wacholder,** "The Letter from Judah Maccabee to Aristobulus: Is 2 Maccabees 1:10b-2:18 Authentic?" *HUCA* 49 (1978) 89-133. **D. S.** "2 Maccabees," *NISB* (2003) 1595-1631. **S. Zeitlin and S. Tedesche,** *The Second Book of Maccabees* (JAL, 1954). See also bibliography for 1 Maccabees.

L. H. SCHIFFMAN

APOCRYPHA

Esdras, First Book of

The Greek book of 1 Esdras depicts the history of Israel during a pivotal period, tracing the major events from a high point of prosperity in Judah under King Josiah (d. 609 B.C.E.) to a nadir of destruction and exile (587/86 B.C.E.), followed by return and restoration in the Persian period under Zerubbabel and Ezra (538-458 B.C.E.). The first book in the Apocrypha, in the Septuagint*§ 1 Esdras appears as Esdras *a*, to be distinguished from Esdras *b* (i.e., the canonical Ezra-Nehemiah), which follows it. In the Vulgate*§ it is designated as 3 Esdras (or 3 Ezra). Although the most ancient Greek manuscripts include 1 Esdras, the book nevertheless has been excluded from the Christian Canon*§ (the only book consistently attested to in the Septuagint to suffer such a fate) and from the Hebrew Bible§. Since the Council of Trent (1546), many Roman Catholic Bibles append it after the New Testament as a supplement.

The earliest extant copies of 1 Esdras are in Greek. Most modern scholars concur, however, that the book goes back to a Hebrew or an Aramaic original. The translation comes from the second century B.C.E. and is independent of (and in many cases superior to) that of Ezra-Nehemiah in the Septuagint. The estimated date of the original remains controversial. Some scholars date some form of the original as early as the fifth (F. M. Cross 1975) or the third century B.C.E. (C. C. Torrey 1910), but most place it in mid-second century B.C.E. because its vocabulary largely corresponds to that of other second-century compositions, such as Ben Sira, Judith, and 1–2 Maccabees (J. Myers 1974, 6).

With very few (yet often telling) exceptions, 1 Esdras overlaps portions of the canonical books of 1–2 Chr and Ezra-Nehemiah, which explains why the dominant interpretive debates have concentrated on its scope and relations to these two books. In particular, scholars disagree as to whether 1 Esdras is a fragment of the original work of the chronicler or a later compilation from the canonical books. The following charts the relations:

1 Esd 1:1-22   =   2 Chr 35:1-19
(Josiah's Passover in Jerusalem)
1 Esd 1:23-24   =   without canonical parallel
(summary of Josiah's deeds and the nation's sins)
1 Esd 1:25-58   =   2 Chr 35:20-36:21
(decline and fall of Judah and Jerusalem to the Babylonians)
1 Esd 2:1-5*a*   =   2 Chr 36:22-23   = Ezra 1:1-3*a*
(Cyrus's edict calling for return to Judah and rebuilding the temple. End of Chronicles)
1 Esd 2:5*b*-15   =   Ezra 1:3*b*-11
(Cyrus's decree continues; the return to Judah during Cyrus's time)
1 Esd 2:16-30   =   Ezra 4:7-24
(hostile neighbors interrupt the building of the house of God)
1 Esd 3:1-5:6   =   without canonical parallel
(story of the three guardsmen)
1 Esd 5:7-73   =   Ezra 2:1-4:5
(return and rebuilding under Jeshua and Zerubbabel)
1 Esd 6:1-9:36   =   Ezra 5:1-10:44
(completion of the temple, the story of Ezra, and the separation from foreign wives)
1 Esd 9:37-55   =   Neh 7:72-8:13*a*
(Ezra's mission and the reading of the law in Jerusalem, followed by a celebration)

First Esdras contains the story of the three guardsmen (3:1–5:6) and the summary of King Josiah's deeds (1:23-24), which have no parallels in the canonical books. Another key difference from the canonical books involves when and where the reading of the law occurs. In Ezra-Nehemiah, this event takes place after Nehemiah rebuilds the wall (Neh 8). In 1 Esdras, which lacks the story of Nehemiah, the reading directly follows the expulsion of the foreign wives (leading some scholars to conclude that this represents the original version of the story). This and other details, some of them seemingly minor, significantly shape the material, offering a distinctive account of ancient Israel's history.

First Esdras begins and ends with grand celebrations in Jerusalem. The opening scene, set in seventh-century Jerusalem, focuses on Passover during King Josiah's reign, a high-water mark on which the narrator lavishes many details (1:1-24). After Josiah's sudden death, however, the nation plunges into apostasy and suffers divine punishment: The Babylonians destroy Jerusalem and exile or kill its people (587/86 B.C.E.), leaving the land desolate for a seventy-year sabbatical (1:25-58).

The longest part of 1 Esdras depicts the three stages of Jewish restoration. In the first stage (2:1-25), the Jews respond to Cyrus's edict and go up to rebuild the temple in Jerusalem. Their efforts, however, come to a halt when Judah's neighbors harass those who returned. In the second stage (3:1–7:15) more Jews return and this time successfully rebuild the temple under the leadership of Zerubbabel, a descendant of David. According to the story of the three guardsmen (3:1–5:3 and unique to 1 Esdras), Zerubbabel rises to prominence in King Darius's court. He wins the admiration of the Persian king with an eloquent exposition on the power of women and the even greater power of truth. As a result, Zerubbabel receives unstinting support for the reconstruction of the temple and for communal life in Judah. He leads a major return, culminating in the completion of the temple, full restoration of worship, and a grand celebration of Passover by all. In the third and final stage (8:1–9:55), Ezra the priest brings further support for the temple and implements the law during Artaxerxes' reign. Under his guidance the community separates from foreign influences (in particular from foreign wives). The final scene of 1 Esdras is the climactic public reading of the law in Jerusalem followed by yet another grand celebration (cf. 1 Esd 1:1-22).

1. *Ancient Interpretations.* The Jewish historian Josephus[§] provides the main witness for 1 Esdras in antiquity. His reliance on it for a rendition of the return from exile (*Ant.* 11) indicates that the book circulated and was granted importance in the first century C.E. Other ancient Jewish sources do not refer to 1 Esdras, although some talmudic teachings (see Talmud*[§]) about truth recall Zerubbabel's speech on truth in 1 Esd 4:33-40 (e.g., 'Abot 1:18 and Šabb. 55a).

The early church fathers widely used and quoted 1 Esdras but rarely commented on it (J. Myers 1974, 17). Origen[§] not only cited 1 Esdras but also may have used this book, rather than canonical Ezra-Nehemiah, in his Hexapla. Several Latin fathers also used 1 Esdras; e.g., Augustine[§] saw Zerubbabel's praise of truth as a possible Prophecy*[§] about Christ (*City of God*, 28.36). Jerome[§], however, rejected the work as apocryphal (see his *Preface to Ezra and Nehemiah*). Largely as a result of Jerome's objections, 1 Esdras was eventually taken out of the Vulgate and relegated to non-canonical status—the only book fully attested to in the various LXX manuscripts to be excluded. Although it appears in some fifteenth-century Latin Bibles, it was regarded as apocryphal by the sixteenth century and was ignored by Luther[§].

2. *Modern Interpretations.* Lack of canonical status may explain the long neglect of 1 Esdras. It gained attention during the nineteenth century with the rise of source criticism, when its nature, scope, and relation to the canonical books became a subject of controversy. Already H. Grotius[§] (seventeenth cent.) and J. D. Michaelis[§] (eighteenth cent.) had suggested that 1 Esdras preserves a more reliable account than MT Ezra-Nehemiah, but it was H. Howorth (nineteenth cent.) and later C. C. Torrey[§] who brought 1 Esdras into the limelight.

As advocates of what has been called the fragment hypothesis, these and other scholars maintained that 1 Esdras is a fragment from the original work of the Chronicler. Initially connected to the books of Chronicles, it preserves the original form of 2 Chr's account of the return and restoration. The canonical Ezra-Nehemiah, according to this view, is a later rearrangement of Ezra-Nehemiah. Arguments in support of this position include the use of 1 Esdras by Josephus[§] and the absence of comparable early witnesses to Ezra-Nehemiah. This hypothesis uses the separate traditions about Ezra and Nehemiah in the postexilic era (Ben Sira and 2 Maccabees mention only Nehemiah, not Ezra, and Josephus keeps them apart) to support the contention that the linking of the two men in Ezra-Nehemiah is later than 1 Esdras. J. D. Michaelis, A. Treuenfels, H. Howorth, J. Marquart, C. C. Torrey, G. Hölscher[§], and most recently K. F. Pohlmann, among others, have been supporters of the fragment hypothesis.

Torrey claimed that 1 Esdras is "simply a piece taken without change out of the middle of a faithful Greek translation of the Chronicler's History of Israel" (1910, 18). According to him, the original version of the Chronicler's history was written in the mid-third century B.C.E. and included the following: 1 and 2 Chr; Ezra 1; 1 Esd 4:47-56; 4:62–5:6; Ezra 2:1–8:36; Neh 7:70–8:18; Ezra 9:1–10:44; Neh 9:1–10:40; 1:1–7:69; 11:1–13:31 (1910, 30). A redactor later added the story of the three guardsmen and transposed certain chapters of the Ezra narrative. Further revisions had emerged by the first century B.C.E., out of which 1 Esdras grew. The canonical Ezra-Nehemiah only came into being in the second century C.E. First Esdras, however, remains "the one surviving fragment of the old Greek version of the Chronicler's history" (1910, 34). Torrey's thorough analysis and his reconstruction of a Semitic original underlying 1 Esdras have been influential.

Pohlmann, an articulate proponent of the fragment hypothesis, also claims that 1 Esdras is an older and better translation than LXX Esdras *b* (Ezra-Nehemiah). In addition, he argues that the original sequence of Ezra history, as far as it can be ascertained, corresponds to the account preserved in 2 Chronicles-1 Esdras. Pohlmann examines the beginning and end of 1 Esdras, the interpolation of the story of the three guardsmen, the Ezra narrative in 1 Esdras and its relation to Ezra-Nehemiah, and especially the evidence of Josephus. He concludes that all of these data support the fragment hypothesis.

A contrasting view, generally labeled the compilation hypothesis, maintains that 1 Esdras presupposes the canonical books of 1–2 Chr and Ezra-Nehemiah and was compiled from them. The most important evidence for the compilation hypothesis appears in studies by P. Bayer (1911) and B. Walde (1913), whose detailed textual analysis of variants supports the dependence of 1 Esdras on 1–2 Chronicles and Ezra-Nehemiah. Advocates of this position claim that 1 Esdras has been preserved largely as its author had intended (although some, like W. Rudolph, modify the ending somewhat). They maintain that the omission of Nehemiah is deliberate and that Josephus's reliance on 1 Esdras is understandable in light of his own apologetic reasons. Neither feature requires the priority of 1 Esdras over Ezra–Nehemiah. The LXX (which consistently presents 1 Esdras as a distinct composition) and the subsequent ancient lists and records lend further support to this theory. Advocates of the compilation hypothesis include L. Bertholdt, Bayer, Walde, Rudolph, and H. Williamson.

Williamson (1977) provides the most thorough contemporary expression of the compilation hypothesis by criticizing Pohlmann's version of the fragment hypothesis. He claims that, as 1 Esd 1:23-24 (which Pohlmann largely ignores) indicates a new beginning, not merely a continuation of 2 Chr, 1 Esdras is a distinct compilation (Williamson 1977, 18). He, like Pohlmann, recognizes it as an ancient and independent translation of an alternative reading or a misunderstanding of the Hebrew text (1977, 13); but he questions the plausibility of two different contemporary translations of the same work, both done in Egypt, as implied by Pohlmann's theory (1977, 15). Whereas Pohlmann argues that Josephus did not know Ezra-Nehemiah in its present form (1970, 114-26), Williamson turns the matter around. He points out that Josephus's account of Ezra breaks off just where 1 Esdras does, which suggests that Josephus's *Vorlage* ended as did the present version of 1 Esdras and implies, therefore, that the latter is a complete composition and not a fragment.

Although forms of the fragment and compilation hypotheses continue to be held (see Pohlmann 1980; G. Garbini 1988; Myers; R. Klein 1989), new interpretations have been proposed. Cross models his interpretation of 1 Esdras on approaches to the two recensions of Jeremiah, identifying one as Palestinian (i.e., Ezra-Nehemiah) and one as Alexandrian (i.e., 1 Esdras). Basing his findings on those of Klein, he argues for a more pristine *Vorlage* for 1 Esdras. Cross envisions three different editions of Chronicles. The first included 1 Chr 10— 2 Chr 34, plus a *Vorlage* of 1 Esdras 1:1-5:65 (= 2 Chr 34:1—Ezra 3:13, composed shortly after 520 B.C.E.). The second included 1 Chr 10—2 Chr 36:23, plus the *Vorlage* of 1 Esdras (composed around 450 B.C.E.). The third and final edition included 1 Chr 1–9, plus 10:1—2 Chr 36:23 and Hebrew Ezra-Nehemiah (composed around 400 B.C.E.). Cross concurs with D. N. Freedman (1961, 437-38) that the books of Chronicles—hence 1 Esdras—focus on "City and ruler, temple and priest—these appear to be the fixed points around which the Chronicler constructs his history and his theology." First Esdras (as part of the larger work of the Chronicler) was designed to support the restoration of the kingdom under Zerubbabel (Cross 1975, 13), but the third revision suppressed material concerning Zerubbabel in light of the changed political climate.

T. Eskenazi suggests that 1 Esdras is a compilation from the canonical Ezra-Nehemiah but claims that it was composed as a distinct and complete work by the school of the Chronicler, representing the Chronicler's ideology. Much as 1-2 Chronicles uses Samuel and 1-2 Kings for a retelling of the story of the preexilic era, 1 Esdras with the same point of view, uses Ezra-Nehemiah for the later era in Israel's history. She argues that omissions and additions to 1 Esdras shape the book to conform to the central emphases of 2 Chr: direct retribution (wherein persons and generations are responsible for their own fates); insistence on the decisive role of the prophets; and a more lenient attitude toward non-Jews than is found in Ezra-Nehemiah. But the most telling signs are the elevation of David's house and the temple. Whereas Ezra-Nehemiah ignores Zerubbabel's Davidic origin, 1 Esdras spells it out, exalting Zerubbabel with the story of the three guardsmen and the rearrangement of the chapters and making him uniquely responsible for the successful restoration. Eskenazi also links the ending of 1 Esdras and 2 Chr: Both books end, seemingly in mid-sentence, with a key word that sums up the important communal task: "going up" for 2 Chr and "gathering together" for 1 Esdras (author's translation). These and other details convince Eskenazi that 1 Esdras does have a thematic and ideological relationship to the books of Chronicles as the fragment hypothesis maintains; but, as the compilation hypothesis maintains, it is nevertheless a distinct composition, not a fragment of Chronicles.

Other contemporary contributions to the interpretation of 1 Esdras include Myers's linguistic analysis, which establishes a second-century B.C.E. date for the Greek translation, and his suggestion that the book may be an apologia for Jews who assisted Antiochus III. Myers relates the book's heightened emphasis on divine presence with the existence of competing temples (e.g., at Leontopolis), which may have necessitated special pleading on behalf of Jerusalem. A. Gardner (1986) links its purpose and date to the Maccabean era, reading it as a specific response to priestly abuses; and Garbini reasserts the priority of 1 Esdras over Ezra-Nehemiah, claiming that this independent second-century B.C.E. composition reflects reforms directed toward removing the rigid separation between clergy and laity and implementing a new popular liturgy. Klein (2003) provides a recent concise commentary, and Talshir discusses the text critical issues (1999, 2001).

Bibliography: D. Böhler, *Die heilige Stadt in Esdras und Esra-Nehemia: Zwei Konzeptionen der Wiederherstellung Israels* (OBO 158, 1997). **S. A. Cook,** "I Esdras," *APOT* (1913) 1:1-20. **F. M. Cross**, "A Reconstruction of the Judean Restoration," *JBL* 94 (1975) 4-18. **T. C. Eskenazi**, "The Chronicler and the Composition of 1 Esdras," *CBQ* 48 (1986) 39-61; *In an Age of Prose: A Literary Approach to Ezra-Nehemiah* (1988). **D. N. Freedman**, "The Chronicler's Purpose," *CBQ* 23 (1961) 436-42. **G. Garbini,** *History and Ideology in Ancient Israel* (1988). **A. E. Gardner**, "The Purpose of 1 Esdras," *JJS* 37 (1986) 18-27. **R. Hanhart,** *Text und Textgeschichte des 1. Esrabuches* (MSU 12, 1974). **R. W. Klein,** "Studies in the Greek Texts of the Chronicler" (diss., Harvard University, 1966); "1 Esdras," *The Books of the Bible* (ed. B. W. Anderson, 1989) 2:13-19; "1 Esdras," *NISB* (2003) 1633-54. **T. Muraoka**, *A Greek-Hebrew/Aramaic Index to I Esdras* (Septuagint and Cognate Studies 16, 1984). **J. M. Myers,** *I and II Esdras* (AB 42, 1974). **K. F. Pohlmann,** *Studien zum dritten Esra* (FRLANT 104, 1970); *Historische und legendarische Erzählungen: 3. Esrabuch* (FRLANT 104, 1980). **C. C. Torrey,** *Ezra Studies* (Library of Biblical Studies, 1910). **B. Walde**, *Die Esdrasbucher der Septuaginta: Ihr gegenseitiges Verhältnis* (BibS(F) 18, 4, 1913). **J. C. VanderKam,** *The Jewish Apocalyptic Heritage in Early Christianity* (1996). **H. G. M. Williamson,** *Israel in the Books of Chronicles* (1977).

T. C. ESKENAZI

APOCRYPHA

Manasseh, Prayer of

Second Chr 33:10-20 records that Manasseh, the most wicked of Judah's kings (see 2 Kgs 21:1-18; 2 Chr 33:1-9), repented while a prisoner in Babylon, prayed to God for mercy, and was restored to his throne in Jerusalem, where he labored to reverse his earlier abominations and promote the true worship of YHWH. The Chronicler indicates further that Manasseh's prayer is preserved in two literary records: the annals of the kings of Israel and the annals of *Hozai* (LXX, "the seers"). Lacking any such extra-biblical records, an unknown Jewish author of a much later time remedied the loss by composing a prayer appropriate for the occasion described in 2 Chr 33. The resulting composition, the pseudonymous Prayer of Manasseh, is a brief but beautiful Penitential psalm of fifteen verses.

The prayer has close affinities of form, language, and imagery with both the canonical psalms (Canon of the Bible*§) of penitence (especially Psalm 51 [LXX 50]) and apocryphal prayers like the Prayer of Azariah in the Additions to Daniel and that of Aseneth in *Joseph and Aseneth*. Following an ascription of praise to YHWH for the divine works of creation (vv. 1-4) and God's mercy to penitent sinners (vv. 5-8), there is a personal confession of sin (vv. 9-10), a plea for mercy and forgiveness (vv. 11-13), an expression of trust in God's mercy (v. 14), and a concluding doxology (v. 15). Permeating the prayer are two emphases: God's abundant mercy and the efficacy of true repentance. Most memorable is the vivid image of contrition in v. 11: "And now I bend the knee of my heart."

Though nothing specific is known of the time and place of writing, composition during the last two centuries B.C.E. or the first century C.E. seems likely. Since Manasseh's name appears only in the title and since the confession of sins is quite general, some have supposed that the prayer existed long before its attribution to Manasseh. However, several elements in it are reminiscent of the Chronicler's account of Manasseh's reign, and the manuscript tradition is consistent in ascribing it to Manasseh. It is likely, therefore, that the title is original and that the work was created to supply the missing prayer mentioned in 2 Chr 33. Linking the prayer with the biblical tradition of the wicked but penitent Manasseh enabled the author to ensure his own generation of forgiveness and restoration where there is true repentance. The work is too brief and general to allow a more precise determination of its occasion and purpose.

The Prayer of Manasseh is extant in Syriac, Greek, Latin, Armenian, Old Church Slavonic, Ethiopic, and Arabic. Whether it was composed in Hebrew, Aramaic, or Greek is unknown. If the extant form of the Greek text was translated from a Semitic original, it is a very free and idiomatic rendering. On the other hand, if Greek is the original language, it is heavily influenced by biblical modes of expression.

The work is first attested in the *Didascalia* (an early third-century church manual written in Greek) but is preserved only in a Syriac translation. From the *Didascalia* the prayer was included in the fourth-century *Apostolic Constitutions*, which provides our earliest Greek text. There is no evidence for the inclusion of the prayer in the early form of the Septuagint*§; clearly it was not in the manuscripts known to Origen§ and Jerome§. Probably from the *Apostolic Constitutions*, the prayer found its way into some manuscripts of the Septuagint, where it is positioned, not after 2 Chr, but among the fourteen canticles or odes appended to the psalter. Although not in Jerome's Vulgate*§, a Latin translation appears in some medieval Latin manuscripts and on this basis is appended to 2 Chr in some early printed editions of the Vulgate. However, since the work was not recognized as canonical by the Council of Trent in 1546, subsequent editions of the Vulgate relegate it to an appendix following the New Testament. Luther§ translated the prayer into German, first publishing it separately and then as the last work in his version of the Apocrypha*§. Beginning with the Matthew Bible of 1537, most English versions have included it among the apocryphal writings, and most Protestants consider it one of the Apocrypha, although it was not part of the Septuagint. The Roman Catholic Douai Bible of 1609-10 placed it in an appendix at the end of the Hebrew Bible.

Evidence of liturgical or other use is far more abundant in Christianity than in Judaism. Rabbinic legends about Manasseh are numerous but show no trace of the prayer. On the other hand, the appearance of the work in the third-century *Didascalia*, the fourth-century *Apostolic Constitutions*, the liturgical canticles appended to the psalter in some manuscripts of the Septuagint, and numerous versions from various times and places attests to its popularity in Christian circles. Other early Christian writers, among them Julius Africanus§ (third cent.) and G. Hamartolos (ninth cent.) made use of the prayer, but none cites it as Scripture. Thomas Aquinas§ quoted v. 8 in connection with the sacrament of penance, and Luther commended the prayer as a model plea for forgiveness. L. Andrewes, one of the translators of the KJV of the Bible, popularized the prayer in the seventeenth century by quoting it extensively in his book of private devotions.

Bibliography: W. Baars and H. Schneider (eds.), *The OT in Syriac According to the Peshitta Version* (1972) vol. 4.6 i-vii, 1-9. **J. H. Charlesworth** (ed.), *OTP* (1983-85) 2:625-33. **A. M. Denis,** *Introduction aux pseudépigraphes grecs d'Ancien Testament* (SVTP 1, 1970) 177-81. **B. Metzger,** *An Introduction to the Apocrypha* (1957) 123-28. **E. Osswald,** *Das Gebet Manasses* (JSHRZ 4.1, 1974) 15-27. **A. Rahlfs,** *Psalmi cum Odis* (Septuaginta, Vetus Testamentum Graecum 10, 1931, 1967²) 361-63. **H. Schneider,** "Der Vulgata-Text der Oratio Manasse: eine Rezension des Robertus Stephanus," *BZ* 4 (1960) 277-82. **E. Schürer,** *HJPAJC* 3.2 (1987) 730-33. **J. L. Trafton,** "Prayer of Manasseh," *NISB* (2003) 1655-58. **H. Volz,** "Zur überlieferung des Gebetes Manasses," *ZKG* 70 (1959) 293-307.

R. D. CHESTNUTT

APOCRYPHA

Psalm 151

Preserved in four ancient forms—Hebrew, Greek, Latin, and Syriac—Psalm 151 is distinctive, even unique, in three respects. First, although Jews, Protestants, and Catholics do not regard this composition as part of their canonical Psalter, the Greek and other Eastern Orthodox churches view it as canonical Scripture. For these churches (with some variations) the canonical Old Testament text is the Septuagint, in which the Book of Psalms concludes with Psalm 151.

Second, the single psalm found in the Greek, from which the Latin and Syriac forms derive, is an amalgamation of two separate psalms. This only became clear with the publication of the large Psalms scroll from Cave 11 at Qumran, which ends with Psalms 151A and 151B; components of both compositions are found in the Septuagint version of Psalm 151. It appears that the Hebrew psalms were composed well before the Christian era, most likely in the Hellenistic period, and that the translation into Greek was made at the beginning of the second century CE.

Third, Psalm 151 (or 151A and 151B) is the only psalm where both the superscription(s) and the content are clearly autobiographical with respect to David. Although the superscriptions of several other biblical psalms clearly refer to events in David's life (e.g. Psalm 50, "A Psalm of David, when the prophet Nathan came to him, after he had gone in to Bathsheba," in all these cases the body of the psalm is less specific, and can refer to pious or repentant people in general (cf. Ps 50:1, "Have mercy upon me, O God, according to your steadfast love . . ."). In contrast, events in David's life are unambiguously evident in the superscription(s) and content of Psalm 151 (151AB). For example, the Greek superscription includes "ascribed to David" and "after he had fought in single combat with Goliath," and the psalm itself refers to David's brothers ("I was small among my brothers"), his musical prowess ("my hands made a harp; my fingers fashioned a lyre"), his being chosen ("and took me from my father's sheep"), and his victory over Goliath ("I went out to meet the Philistine, ... But I drew his own sword; I beheaded him"). In the Hebrew original, the Goliath incident begins the new Psalm 151B: "At the beginning of God's power after the prophet of God had anointed him. Then I [saw] a Philistine uttering defiances from the r[anks of the enemy]"). Unfortunately, the rest of this psalm is not preserved in the Cave 11 Psalms scroll.

Editions: J. A. Sanders, *The Psalms Scroll of Qumrân Cave* 11 [11QPsa] (DJD 4, 1965) 49, 53-64, pl. 17; **A. Rahlfs**, *Psalmi cum Odis* (Septuaginta: Vetus Testamentum Graecum Auctoritate Societas Litterarum Gottingensis 10, 1979³) 339-40; **W. Baars**, "Psalmi Apocryphi," The Old Testament in Syrac According to the Peshiṭta Version (ed. Peshiṭta Institute, 1972) 4.6, i–x, 1-12, esp. 2-4; **J. A. Sanders**, *The Dead Sea Psalms Scroll* (1967) 88-89, 94-100

English Translations: M. G. Abegg, P. W. Flint and E. Ulrich, *The Dead Sea Scrolls Bible* (1999) 585-86; **F. G. Martínez**, *The Dead Sea Scrolls Translated. The Qumran Texts in English* (1996²) 310; **T. H. Gaster,** *The Dead Sea Scriptures* (1976³) 217-19; **A. Pietersma**, *A New English Translation of the Septuagint, and the Other Greek Translations Traditionally Included Under That Title: The Psalms* (2000) 147-48; **J. A. Sanders**, "Psalm 151," *The Harper Collins Study Bible: New Revised Standard Version (with the Apocryphal/ Deuterocanonical Books)* (ed. W. Meeks, 1993); **G. Vermes**, *The Complete Dead Sea Scrolls in English* (1997) 302; **M. O. Wise, M. G. Abegg, and E. C. Cook,** *The Dead Sea Scrolls. A New Translation* (1997) 447-48.

Bibliography: J. H. Charlesworth with J. A. Sanders, "More Psalms of David," *The Old Testament Pseudepigrapha* (ed. J. H. Charlesworth 1985) 2.609-24, esp. 612-15; **D. A. deSilva,**

Introducing the Apocrypha. Message, Content, and Significance (Grand Rapids: Baker, 2002) 301-303; **Peter W. Flint**, "The Book of Psalms in the Light of the Dead Sea Scrolls," *VT* 48 (1998) 453-72, esp. 467-69; "'Apocrypha,' Other Previously-Known Writings, and 'Pseudepigrapha' in the Dead Sea Scrolls," *The Dead Sea Scrolls After Fifty Years: A Comprehensive Assessment* (ed. P. Flint and J. VanderKam, 1999) 2.24-66; **D. J. Harrington, SJ,** *Invitation to the Apocrypha* (1999); **S. S. Pigué,** "Psalms, Syriac (Apocryphal)," *ABD* (1992) 5.536-37; **J. C. VanderKam and P. W. Flint,** *The Meaning of the Dead Sea Scrolls* (2002) 189-91, 447.

PETER W. FLINT

APOCRYPHA

Maccabees, Third Book of

This book relates the attempt of Ptolemy IV Philopator (221-205 B.C.E.) to enter the holy of holies of the Jerusalem temple on his way back from defeating Antiochus III (The Great) at Raphia (217 B.C.E.). Unable to dissuade Ptolemy from his course, the Jews prayed to God, who paralyzed Ptolemy as he attempted to enter. (This account resembles the story of Heliodorus in 2 Macc 3:9-39.) Ptolemy returned to Egypt determined to avenge this affront and immediately enacted a series of severe anti-Jewish measures, culminating in an organized plan to exterminate the Jews. They were imprisoned in the Hippodrome, where elephants were to be intoxicated and incited to trample them to death. The book describes in detail the organization of transport and the attempt to record carefully the names of the Jews to be killed as well as the cooperation of the native population in rounding them up. After some delay, when the plan was to be put into action the prayers of the Jews ascended to heaven and God sent two angelic apparitions to intervene. They turned the animals on the king's army, leading the king to command the release of the Jews, whom he then hosted for a seven-day feast. As a result, the Jews declared a permanent festival and were granted permission to put to death some 300 apostates.

Despite its name, the book, as the above summary indicates, has nothing to do with the Maccabees, who flourished several decades after Ptolemy IV. This provides some evidence that the book may have once borne the name *Ptolemaica* (matters ptolemaic), but the persecution theme led to its association with the Maccabees. The style and vocabulary indicate that the book was written in Greek. It is found in only one of the great uncial Greek manuscripts— Alexandrinus—but also appears in the important eighth-century Greek manuscript Venetus Graecus. It was early on translated into Syriac but not into Latin and thus was never part of the Vulgate*§. (The first Latin translation was prepared for inclusion in the Complutensian Polyglot. Both the Paris and the London polyglots reproduce the Syriac version.) The fourth-century apostolic canons (see Canon of the Bible*§) list it among the scriptural books (canon 85), and the 1672 Orthodox Synod of Jerusalem (actually convened in Bethlehem) declared 3 Maccabees to be canonical. The earliest English translation was produced by W. Lynne in 1550; but the book, like 4 Maccabees, is not well known. Later editions of the RSV and the NRSV contain it.

The narrative presented in 3 Maccabees seems to be a fictional expansion based on certain historical information, e.g., the account of the battle of Raphia and a story known from Josephus§ (*Contra Apion*, 2.50-55) to the effect that Ptolemy VIII Physcon (145-116 B.C.E.) attempted to incite intoxicated elephants against the Jews of Alexandria as punishment for their support of his enemy Cleopatra II. Instead, the elephants turned on the king's friends. The festival celebrating deliverance from this scourge probably served as the stimulus for the writing of 3 Maccabees, and credence is possibly to be given to the book's claim that full civil rights were offered to the Jews by Ptolemy IV in exchange for their abandonment of Judaism and acceptance of the Dionysian cult. In general terms, the author's characterizations of Ptolemaic Egypt and of Ptolemy IV indicate a familiarity that may have been based on accurate written sources.

The book presupposes the *Greek Additions to Daniel* (which, in their present form, were completed in the second century B.C.E.) and perhaps also the Greek translation and expansion of the book of Esther (completed by 77 B.C.E.). Certainly the book of Esther had an impact on the author. Some scholars have argued that the use of the Greek *laographia* for "census" requires a Roman date, probably between 20 and 15 B.C.E. (M. Hadas 1953; V. Tcherikover 1961; F. Parente 1988). This proposal is based on the census and poll tax undertaken in Egypt in 23/22 B.C.E. that discriminated between citizens of the Hellenistic cities and the native population. Other scholars would date the book much earlier and see its account as containing much historical material (A. Kasher 1985). At any rate, the book seems to have been written before 70 C.E. since it presumes that the temple is still standing and since it was taken over into Christianity. We cannot discount the possibility of a complex literary history, according to which different sections of the book are to be variously dated. Since the plot centers primarily around Alexandria, Egypt, it is likely that the book was composed there. Nonetheless, the Judaism of the book cannot be characterized as Hellenistic. A more recent discussion and commentary can be found in Williams (1995, 2003).

Jewish tradition preserves no mention of this book or direct use of its contents. Nevertheless, the style of the prayers of the Jews about to be martyred contains striking parallels to similar prayers recorded in the chronicles detailing the persecution of the European Jews during the crusades. Parallels may also be observed with Jewish penitential prayers. The reader cannot help feeling the uncanny similarities between the plan for systematic destruction of Egyptian Jewry and the Holocaust that ravaged the Jewish people in modern times.

Bibliography: H. Anderson, "3 Maccabees," *OTP* (ed. J. Charlesworth, 1985) 2:509-29. C. W. Emmet, *APOT* (1913) 1:156-73. C. L. W. Grimm, *Kurzgefasstes exegetisches Handbuch zu den Apokryphen des Alten Testaments* (6 vols. ed. O. F. Fritzsche and C. L. W. Grimm, 1851-60). M. Hadas, *The Third and Fourth Books of Maccabees* (JAL, 1953). A. Kasher, *The Jews in Hellenistic and Roman Egypt: The Struggle for Equal Rights* (TSAJ 7, 1985). F. Parente, "The Third Book of Maccabees as Ideological Document and Historical Source," *Hen*10 (1988) 143-82. A. Paul, "Le Troisième Livre des Maccabées," *ANRW* 2, 20-21 (1987) 298-336. E. Schürer, *HJPAJC* 3, 1 (1986) 537-42. V. A. Tcherikover, "The Third Book of Maccabees as a Historical Source of Augustus' Time," ScrHier 7 (1961) 1-26. David S. Williams, "3 Maccabees: A Defense of Diaspora Judaism?" *JSP* 13 (1995) 17-29; "3 Maccabees," *NISB* (2003) 1661-75. H. Willrich, "Der historische Kern des III. Makkabäerbuches," *Hermes* 39 (1904) 244-58.

L. H. Schifman

APOCRYPHA

Esdras, Second Book of

Second Esdras is the name given in the English Apocrypha*§ to an expanded version of an apocalypse (Apocalypticism*§) identified in Latin manuscripts as *4 Ezra*. That apocalypse is found in chaps. 3–14 of 2 Esdras. *Fourth Ezra* is part of a fairly extensive body of Ezrianic traditions, the breadth and importance of which are reflected in the wealth of extant manuscripts. Of the eleven Latin codices that survive, perhaps the oldest and most important is Codex Sangermanensis. Written about 822 C.E., this codex lacks some sixty-nine verses of chap. 7. In 1875 R. Bensly published a fragment that restored these missing verses, *4 Ezra* 7:36-105, which appear to deny the value of prayer for the unrighteous dead. B. Metzger (1957) and L. Gry (1938) also believed that this codex was the source of "the vast majority of extant manuscripts" of the book. An Armenian*§ text was published in 1805 by Zohrab (or Zohrabian) and later by Hovsepheantz (it was translated into English in 1901 by Issaverdens). Ezrianic material distinct from the more "mainline" Ezrianic traditions survives in Arabic; Ethiopic (Ethiopian Biblical Interpretation*§); Syriac; Coptic/Sahidic; Georgian; and, in fragmentary form, Greek. Important editions of the Ethiopic and related texts were published by A. Dillmann§ in 1894 and by J. Halévy§ in 1902.

With respect to the question of the text's original language, three languages are proposed: Greek, Aramaic, and Hebrew. While Metzger argued that all extant manuscripts derive from the Greek, he left open the possibility that the Greek may itself derive from a Semitic text. With the possible exception of the Armenian texts, differences between the various versions of *4 Ezra* can be explained "by presupposing corruptions in or misunderstanding of a Greek text underlying them" (1983, 1:520) A. Hilgenfeld§ used the Latin version to reconstruct the original Greek. Supporters of this position included G. Volkmar (1863), O. Fritzsche (1851), F. Rosenthal (1885), and H. Thackeray.

In 1633 J. Morin§ postulated that either Hebrew or Aramaic was the original language of *4 Ezra* (Gry 1938, 1:xxi). Accordingly, J. Wellhausen§ argued that the work's vocabulary, grammar, syntax and use of formulas were more consistent with Semitic usage than with Greek (Gry 1938, 1:xxii) and argued in favor of Hebrew (1899, 234, note 3). Later, however, he reversed himself and endorsed Aramaic as the original language (1911, 1:xxiii-lxxx). Likewise, Gry, C. C. Torrey§, and J. Bloch argued that the original language was Aramaic.

The presence of "notable Hebraisms" has led others—including G. Box (1912), A. Kaminka (1932), F. Zimmerman (1960-61), and G. Nickelsburg (1981)—to speculate that the original language was Hebrew. J. Schreiner offers a practical perspective: "Textual problems dissolve against the backdrop of Hebrew, but not against the backdrop of Aramaic" (1981, 295).

In light of 3:1 and the reference to the thirtieth year after the destruction of the city, most scholars argued that *4 Ezra* could not have been written before c. 100 C.E. Moreover, by the end of the Bar-Kokhba revolt, Christian and Jewish circles totally separated, making it unlikely that the original Hebrew dates much after 120 C.E. Nickelsburg places the date of authorship in the second century C.E.

How the present text came into existence remains an open issue. Most scholars fall into one of two groups: those who see it as a collection of independent sources woven together by a redactor and those who see it as essentially the work of a single hand. Those who ascribe to the first position include Box, Metzger (*OTP*, 1:517), M. Knibb (1979, 76), W. Oesterley§, and R. Kabisch§. Scholars who hold the second opinion include B. Violet (1910-24), Gry, D. Russell (1964), H. Gunkel§ (1900), J. Collins, J. Keulers (1922), W. Sanday§, and M. Stone (at least in later works). These scholars do not rule out the possibility that more than one source was used by the author; rather, they all argue in some shape or form that, however many independent traditions might be reflected in the text's present form, the book as it now stands is the work of one hand, although chaps. 3–10 or 14 may have existed as an independent work.

A number of scholars, including Violet, Collins, Box, and R. Charles[§] (1913, 2:476-77), have noted many similarities between *4 Ezra* and *2 Baruch*[§]. These parallels have led some of them, notably E. Ewald (1863) and M. James (1895), to speculate that these texts had a common author. For Charles, these points of convergence are matched by nearly as many points of divergence. Box regarded *4 Ezra* and *2 Baruch* as "twin" works that are at once related yet distinct. They are related in that they have been subject to a mingling of rabbinic and apocalyptic material, and distinct because each is the product of a different rabbinic school. They, therefore, do not share common authorship (*APOT*, 2.542; Box, lxii-lxvi, esp. lxv). Box noted other, less direct, parallels between *4 Ezra* and the *Psalms of Solomon*[*§] (Box, lxxiii). In addition, parallels to *1 Enoch*[*§], the *Testament of Napthali*, and the *Testament of Levi* have been noted.

Addendum

Recent discussion includes a study of the eagle vision in 2 Esd 11:1–15:2 (DiTommaso 1999), the interpretation and use of 2 Esdras from the Renaissance to the Englightenment (Hamilton 1999), a concise commentary (Harrington 2003), studies of apocalyptic motifs in 2 Esdras (Kerner 1998, Reese 1999), and the textual history of 2 Esdras (Bergren 1997).

Bibliography: R. L. Bensly, *The Missing Fragment of the Latin Translation of the Fourth Book of Ezra* (1875); *The Fourth Book of Ezra: The Latin Version Edited from the MSS* (1895). **T. A. Bergren,** *Sixth Ezra: The Text and Origin* (1997). **J. Bloch,** "Was there a Greek Version of the Apocalypse of Ezra?" *JQR* 46 (1956) 309-20; "The Ezra Apocalypse: Was It Written in Hebrew, Greek, or Aramaic?" *JQR* 48 (1957) 279-94; "Some Christological Interpolations in the Ezra-Apocalypse," *HTR* 51 (1958) 87-94. **G. H. Box,** *The Ezra Apocalypse* (1912); "4 Ezra" *APOT* (1913) 2.542-624. **R. J. Coggins and M. A. Knibb,** *The First and Second Books of Esdras* (1979) 76-305. **J. J. Collins,** "The Jewish Apocalypses," *Apocalypse: The Morphology of a Genre* (*Semeia* 14, 1979) 33-34, 53; *The Apocalyptic Imagination* (1984) 156-69. **A. M. Denis,** "Les fragments grecs de l'Apocalypse 4 Esdras," *Introduction aux Pseudepigraphes Grecs d'Ancien Testament* (SVTP 1, 1970) 194-200. **L. DiTommaso,** "Dating the Eagle Vision of 4 Ezra: A New Look at an Old Theory," *JSP* 20 (1999) 3-38. **E. G. A. Ewald,** *Das vierte Ezrabuch nach seinem Zeitalter, seinem arabischen Ubersetzungen, und einer neuen Wiederherstellung* (Abhandlungen der Koniglischen Gesellschaft der Wissenschaften zu Göttingen 11, 1863). **O. F. Fritzsche,** *Kurzgefasstes exegetisches Handbuch zu den Apokryphen des Alten Testaments* (1851). **J. Gildemeister,** *Esdrae liber quartus arabice e codice Vaticano* (1877). **L. Gry,** *Les dires prophetiques d'Esdras* (2 vols. 1938). **H. Gunkel,** "Das 4. Buch Ezra," *APAT* (1900) 2.331-401. **A. Hamilton,** *The Apocryphal Apocalypse: The Reception of the Second Book of Esdras (4 Ezra) from the Renaissance to the Enlightenment* (1999). **D. J. Harrington,** "2 Esdras," *NISB* (2003) 1679-1722. **R. Hanhart,** *2 Esdras* (1993). **A. Hilgenfeld,** *Messias Judaeorum* (1869) 36-113. **M. R. James,** *2 Esdras* (TS 3, 1895). **R. Kabisch,** *Das vierte Buch Ezra und seine Quellen untersucht* (1889). **A. Kaminka,** "Beiträge zur Erklärung der Esra-Apokalypse und zur Rekonstruktion ihres hebraischen Urtextes," *MGWJ* 76 (1932) 121-38, 206-12, 494-511; "Beiträge zur Erklärung der Esra-Apokalypse und zur Rekonstruktion ihres hebraischen Urtextes," *MGWJ* 77 (1933) 339-55. **J. Kerner,** *Die Ethik der Johannes-Apokalypse im Vergleich mit der des 4. Esra: ein Beitrag zum Verhältnis von Apokalyptik und Ethik* (BZNW 94, 1998). **J. Keulers,** "Die Eschatologische Lehre des vierten Esrabuches," *Bib* S20 (1922) 1-204. **B. W. Longnecker,** *2 Esdras* (Guides to Apocrypha and Pseudepigrapha, 1995). **B. M. Metzger,** "The `Lost' Section of II Esdras (= IV

Ezra)," *JBL* 76 (1957) 153-57; "The Fourth Book of Ezra," *OTP* (1983) 1.516-59. **G. T. Milazzo,** *The Protest and the Silence: Suffering, Death, and Biblical Theology* (1992). **G. W. E. Nickelsburg,** *Jewish Literature Between the Torah and the Bible* (1981) 287-94. **W. O. E. Oesterley,** "The Ezra Apocalypse (2 [4] Esdras)," *The Books of the Apocrypha: Their Origin, Teaching, and Contents* (1914) 509-33; *II Esdras (The Ezra Apocalypse), with Introduction and Notes* (1933). **G. Reese,** *Die Geschichte Israels in der Auffassung des frühen Judentums: eine Untersuchung der Tiervision und der Zehnwochenapokalypse des äthiopischen Henochbuches, der Geschichtsdarstellung der Assumptio Mosis und der des 4Esrabuches* (BBB 123, 1999) **F. Rosenthal,** *Vier apokryphische Bücher aus der Zeit und Schule R. Akiba's: "Assumptio Mosis," "Das vierte Buch Esra," "Die Apokalypse Baruch," "Das Buch Tobi"* (1885). **R. Rubinkiewicz,** "Un fragment grec du IVe livre d'Esdras (chapitres xi et xii)," *Mus 89* (1976) 75-87. **D. S. Russell,** *The Method and Message of Jewish Apocalyptic* (1964) 62-64. **J. Schreiner,** "Das 4. Buch Ezra," *JSHRZ* 5.4 (1981) 291-412. **E. Schürer,** *HJPAJC* (1986) 3:294-306. **M. E. Stone,** "Some Features of the Armenian Version of IV Ezra," *Mus* 79 (1966) 387-400; "Some Remarks on the Textual Criticism of IV Ezra" *HTR* 60 (1967) 107-15; "Apocryphal Notes" *IOS* (1971) 1:123-31; *The Armenian Version of IV Ezra* (Armenian Texts and Studies 1, 1979); *Features of the Eschatology of IV Ezra* (1989); *Fourth Ezra* (Hermeneia, 1990). **B. Violet,** *Die Esra-Apokalypse* (2 vols. GCS, 1910-24). **G. Volkmar,** *Second Esdras* (Handbuch der Einleitung in die Apokryphen 2, 1863). **J. Wellhausen,** *Skizzen und Vorarbeiten* (1899) 215-49. **F. Zimmerman,** "Underlying Documents of IV Ezra," *JQR* 51 (1960-61) 107-34.

G. T. MILAZZO

APOCRYPHA

Maccabees, Fourth Book of

Fourth Maccabees is essentially a philosophical tract expressing a Hellenistic approach to Judaism. It was written in the first person in the style of a discourse; its original title was probably "On the Sovereignty of Reason," as it was designated by Eusebius*§ (*Hist. eccl.* 3.10.6), the first writer to refer to the work. It is addressed directly to the Jewish people, "children born of the seed of Abraham" (18:1, author's translation), and maintains that reason must be the underlying guide for piety; only through reason can the passions be controlled. This point is illustrated through Jewish history, most notably through the story of the martyrdom of the elderly priest Eleazar and seven brothers and their mother during the persecutions of the Seleucid king Antiochus IV Epiphanes (175-164 B.C.E.) in connection with the Maccabean revolt. The author presents an expanded version of the material he found in 2 Maccabees (or in the original five-volume work of Jason of Cyrene, which is summarized in 2 Maccabees; see 2 Macc 2:23). This relationship to the Maccabees gave rise to the title 4 Maccabees.

The first section of the book (1:1–3:18) presents the basic concepts of reason and its rule over the passions, accomplished only through a life of wisdom. Several biblical examples are given: Joseph facing the advances of Potiphar's wife, Moses controlling his anger against Dathan and Abiram, etc. Then there is a description of the attempt of Apollonius to plunder the temple treasures and of the persecutions of the Jews (3:19–4:26) that led up to the Maccabean revolt (168-164 B.C.E.), all to set the stage for the description of the martyrs of the Maccabean period. The torture and martyrdom of Eleazar (5:1–7:23) and the seven sons (8:1–14:10) and their mother (14:11–17:6) are described in detail; they are all praised for their courage, virtue, and loyalty to their faith. A discussion follows of the blessings granted to the Jewish people by God on account of the dedication of its martyrs, emphasizing the atonement provided by their deaths (17:7–18:19). A short epilogue concludes the book (18:20-23).

The book's philosophical approach combines elements of middle Platonism and Stoicism. Emphasizing the need for reason to control the passions, the book mentions the four cardinal virtues: prudence, justice, courage, and self-control. The author's concept of reason, however, is a Jewish one—namely, fear of the word of God. This philosophical description of Judaism indicates only a surface Hellenization since the underlying concepts are Jewish. This fact also explains the eclecticism of the author, who felt free to derive his philosophical underpinnings from whatever sources were available, provided they supported the Jewish concepts he wished to teach.

The book praises the Maccabean martyrs for their adherence to the Torah. The author believed in the immortality of the soul, a view that (as in 2 Maccabees) is adduced to explain the willingness of the martyrs to give their lives. He consistently omitted any mention of bodily resurrection. Further, he saw the death of the righteous as atoning for the transgressions of the people. The author believed in the biblical concept of divine providence— that God takes an interest in human beings and their lives.

Fourth Maccabees, originally written in Greek, is not part of any Canon*§, although it appears as an appendix in the Orthodox Bible. It is included in two of the early biblical Greek manuscripts, Sinaiticus from the fourth century and Alexandrinus from the fifth, as well as in the eighth-century Venetus Graecus. None of the books of Maccabees is included in Codex Vaticanus. The work was early translated into Syriac; a Latin paraphrase (*Passio SS. Machabaeorum*) exists but there is no early Latin translation.

Eusebius and Jerome*§ (*De viris illustribus* 13) ascribed the book to Josephus*§; but this seems unlikely since the work is based on 2 Maccabees, which he did not use. The legend of the martyrs was well known among Christians (J. Freudenthal 1869, 29-34); their relics were revered at Antioch (J. Obermann 1931), and a feast in their honor held August 1 was widely observed in the church. Origen[§], in his *Exhortation to Martyrdom*, praised their heroic deaths, while Gregory of Nazianzus[§] in *Oratio* 15 (*Im laudem Machabaeorum*; *PG* 35.911-54) saw their deaths as anticipating Christian martyrdom, and the mother as a forerunner of Mary. Augustine's[§] Sermon 300 is entitled *In Solemnitate martyrum Machabaeorum* (further Chrysostom [PG 50.617-28; 64.525-50] and Ambrose [PL 14.627-30, 662-63]). Numerous Hebrew versions of stories of the Maccabean martyrs circulated in Judaism during the Middle Ages (see G. Cohen 1953; G. Stemberger 1992; and Hadas, 127-35), although no literary dependence on 4 Maccabees can be demonstrated.

Erasmus*[§] popularized the story by publishing a paraphrase of the martyr legend (1524) based on the early Latin paraphrase. The first printed version of the Greek text appeared in the Strasbourg Septuagint*[§] (1526), but scholarly study of the book did not begin until the nineteenth century. C. Grimm's (1851-60) was the first substantial commentary. De Silva (1998) provides a general introduction to 4 Maccabees. Trafton (2003) provides a recent concise commentary.

The work is most frequently dated to the first half of the first century. C. Bickermann argued for a date between 20 and 54 C.E., when Syria, Phoenicia, and Cilicia were under one governor (see 4 Macc 4:9), although other scholars have dated the book as late as the second century C.E. (A. Dupont-Sommer 1939; U. Breitenstein 1978). Various locations have been proposed as the place of authorship: Alexandria, Antioch, somewhere in Asia Minor, etc. About all that can be said is that it was written by a Greek-speaking Jew in the Diaspora. The work may have been written for some special occasion (see 1:10; 3:19; 14:9), such as the commemoration of the martyrs' death, but this too remains uncertain. The book has also been examined in terms of its narrative depiction of Jewish identity, heroic death, martyrdom, and vicarious suffering as well as the parallels to early Christian understandings of the death of Jesus[†§].

Bibliography: H. Anderson, "4 Maccabees," *OTP* (1983) 2:531-64. **R. L. Bensly,** *The Fourth Book of Maccabees and Kindred Documents in Syriac* (1895). **E. J. Bickermann,** "The Date of IV Maccabees," *L. Ginzberg Jubilee Volume* (vol. 1, 1945) 105-12 = idem, *Studies in Jewish and Christian History* (AGJU 9, 1976) 1:275-81. **U. Breitenstei**n, *Beobachtungen zu Sprache, Stil, und Gedankengut des Vierten Makkabäerbuchs* (1978). **G. D. Cohen,** "The Story of Hannah and Her Seven Sons in Hebrew Literature," *M. M. Kaplan Jubilee Volume* (1953) 109-22 (Hebrew section). **H. Cotton,** *The Five Books of Maccabees in English* (1832). **A. Dupont-Sommer,** *Le quatriéme livre des Maccabées* (Bibliothèque de l'École des Hautes Études 274, 1939). **C. W. Emmet** (tr.), *The Fourth Book of Maccabees* (Translations of Early Documents, ser. 2, Hellenistic-Jewish Texts 6, 1918). **J. Freudenthal,** *Die Flavius Josephus beigelegte Schrift über die Herrschaft der Vernunft (IV Makkabäerbuch): Eine Predigt aus dem ersten nachchristlichen Jahrhundert* (1869). **C. L. W. Grimm**, *Kurzgefasstes exegetisches Handbuch zu den Apokryphen des Alten Testaments* (6 vols. ed. O. F. Fritzsche and C. L. W. Grimm, 1851-60) 4:283-370. **M. Hadas,** *The Third and Fourth Books of Maccabees* (JAL, 1953; repr. 1976). **J. W. van Henten,** *The Maccabean Martyrs as Saviours of the Jewish People: A Study of 2 and 4 Maccabee*s (JSJSup 57, 1997). **M. de Jonge,** "Jesus' Death for Others and the Death of the Maccabean Martyrs," *Text and Testimony: Essays on NT and Apocryphal Literature* (ed. T. Baarda, 1988) 142-51. **H. J. Klauck,** *JSHRZ* 3, 6 (1989) 645-763. **S. D. Moore and J. C. Anderson,** "Taking It Like a Man: Masculinity in 4 Maccabees," *JBL* 117 (1998) 249-73. **J. Obermann,** "The Sepulchre of the Maccabean Martyrs," *JBL* 50 (1931) 250-65. **P. L. Reddith,** "The Concept of Nomos in Fourth Maccabees," *CBQ* 45 (1983) 249-70. **R. Reneham,** "The Greek Philosophical Background of Fourth Maccabees," *Rheinisches Museum für Philologie* 115 (1972) 232-38. **D. A. de Silva,** "The Noble Contest: Honor, Shame, and the Rhetorical Strategy of 4 Maccabees," *JSP* 13 (1995) 31-57; *4 Maccabees* (Guides to the Apocrypha and Pseudepigrapha 7, 1998). **G. Stemberger,** "The Maccabees in Rabbinic Traditions," *The Scriptures and the Scrolls* (ed. F. García Martinez et al., VTSup 49, 1992) 193-203. **E. Schürer,** *HJPAJC* 3, 1 (1986) 588-93. **R. B. Townshend,** *APOT* 2 (1913) 653-85. **J. L. Trafton,** "4 Maccabees," *NISB* (2003) 1723-44. **D. F. Winslow,** "The Maccabean Martyrs: Early Christian Attitudes," *Judaism* 23 (1974) 78-86. **R. D. Young,** "'The Woman with the Soul of Abraham': Traditions About the Mother of the Maccabean Martyrs," *"Women Like This": New Perspectives on Jewish Women in the Greco-Roman World* (ed. A. J. Levine, *SBLEJL* 1, 1991) 67-81.

L. H. SCHIFFMAN

PSEUDEPIGRAPHA

Pseudepigrapha

The history of biblical interpretation includes an examination of a large body of ancient apocryphal writings. The authors of these works frequently claimed them to be equal in Authority*§ to any book now canonized within the Bible. Understood in broad categories, the Old Testament Pseudepigrapha (OTP) comprises about sixty-five quasi-biblical documents. Many of these developed out of interpretations by Jews or Jewish Christians of earlier biblical books and were exegetical or expository expansions of biblical narratives or psalms. The most important of them were written between 250 B.C.E. and 200 C.E. in Palestine.

The interpretation of the OTP has been markedly diverse during the last 2,250 years. In essence, a large body of literature cherished in antiquity fell from favor for centuries but has been recovered by modern scholarship and restored to a position of significance.

1. *Early Period.* From approximately 250 B.C.E. to 200 C.E. Jewish and Christian scholars, many of whom were erudite and skilled scribes, composed apocalypses, testaments, psalms, odes, histories, and ethical tracts, attributing them to ancient biblical heroes or sages like Enoch, Noah, Abraham, Moses, David, Solomon, and Ezra. This literature was born out of biblical interpretation.

Reflection on Scripture demanded not only adoration but also creative dialogue with the text. Questions abounded. For example, the famous account of Jephthah's sacrifice of his beloved and only daughter raised numerous issues. Why did he kill her? What was her name? Did she resist? Pseudo-Philo*§, a Jewish Palestinian writing probably dating from the first century C.E., presents an expanded account of the incident. Her name is Seila, probably because in Hebrew the meaning would be "she who was requested." She accepts her father's vow obediently, requesting permission only to retreat to the mountains and vent her laments. For the author and his commentary these were prized and apparently authentic stories. For modern critics they are an example of first-century exegesis of Judg 11:30-40.

During the early period of interpretation many Jewish and Christian groups highly revered the documents in the OTP as authentically inspired writings equal in every way to other biblical works. Even some documents in the Christian Canon*§ reflect a high evaluation of some of the OTP. The classic example is Jude, which alludes to more than one of these writings and quotes from so-called *1 Enoch*§, prefacing the quotation by saying that Enoch "prophesied" these words. Later, perhaps under the influence of the developing orthodoxy, the author of 2 Pet quoted Jude but felt compelled to remove all allusions to, and the quotation from, the OTP.

2. *Medieval Period.* As in the early period, in the Middle Ages there was no collection of the OTP. Instead, the documents were treated individually. Jews no longer were characteristically interested in reading or interpreting it, and although a few works like *3 Enoch*§ show that, in some Jewish circles, the interest in Pseudepigrapha continued, the widespread fascination by Jews with the documents in the OTP ended before this period. Three main reasons for this paradigm shift in biblical interpretation seem obvious: First, the documents in the Mishnah*§ had been codified by Judah the Prince around 200 C.E., and it then came to dominate the life of the religious Jew. Second, the disastrous Jewish revolts against the Romans in 66-70 C.E. and 132-135 C.E. were judged to be caused in part by the apocalyptic fervor seen to be typical of many documents in the OTP. Third, this Apocalypticism*§ had given rise to rabbinic Judaism's rival, Christianity.

Many of the greatest thinkers in early Christianity—e.g., Tertullian§, Clement of Alexandria§, Origen§, Eusebius§—highly valued many of the OTP. The administrators of the church, however, were less interested in ancient writings than in the current social, political, ideological, and theological crises. They saw the need to combat heresy; to clarify, defend, and strengthen orthodox faith; and to define a closed canon of Scripture. During the early centuries C.E., works like Hebrews and Revelation (eventually included in the canon) and apocryphal works (see Apocrypha*§, New Testament*§) like the Shepherd of Hermas and the Birth of Mary, were intermittently shunted aside or away from the shelter of the canon's umbrella. During the same period, the documents in the OTP were falling out of favor or had ceased to circulate.

The relegation of the OTP to a very subordinate status was not the consequence of deliberate and overt action, but resulted from a preoccupation with the survival of what was perceived to be the purity of the holy apostolic faith. This orthodox faith was clarified through an exegesis and exposition of those works that slowly, and initially without any vote of the great councils, emerged as canonical. It is imperative to correct the fallacious notion that the synagogue and the church examined and then discarded the OTP.

The works in the OTP thus gradually were ignored in the major centers of rabbinic Judaism and Western Christianity. Fortunately, scribes in monastic centers throughout the world devoted years to copying ancient manuscripts that contained one or more of the OTP. For these scribes, worship and interpretation of holy Scripture involved preserving sacred writings; interpretation was repetition, and God's word was often defined in terms of a *prima facie* acceptance of the claims in the document lying open on the desk. No other description can explain the presence of the thousands of manuscripts in Greek, Latin, Ethiopic (Ethiopian Biblical Interpretation*§), Armenian*§, Syriac, Slavonic, and Coptic that now can be read in the major monasteries and European and American libraries. Copying one of the OTP, as we learn from the colophons at the end of manuscripts, was an act of devotion to God. The art and adoration poured into preserving God's sacred word, the canon, ebbed over into other related words.

3. *Renaissance and Reformation.* The Renaissance opened the eyes of Western European scholars and leaders to the world of antiquity and to the cultures of the Near East. It might be expected that a renewed interest in the OTP would result from this reawakening to antiquity and Eastern cultures, but this did not occur.

In spite of the emphasis on the Bible by the Protestant Reformers, the para-biblical books—the Apocrypha*§ and the Pseudepigrapha—were not rediscovered. Perhaps the emphasis on interpreting the New Testament, especially Paul's†§ letters, in terms of the concept of righteousness by faith alone may explain this fact. This explanation may also clarify Luther's§ desire to cast *4 Ezra* (2 Esdras) into the Elba River, but it does not explain why he was so attracted to the Prayer of Manasseh. Both documents are in the OTP.

4. *Enlightenment.* The OTP writings were rediscovered during the European Enlightenment of the seventeenth and eighteenth centuries. Some OTP were included in the famous Polyglots*§, especially the nine-volume Paris Polyglot (1629-42) and the six-volume London Polyglot (1655-57). For the first time in history a collection of the OTP was prepared and published. J. Fabricius's§ edition of the OTP in Latin translation, *Codex Pseudepigraphus Veteris Testamenti* (1713-14), rendered the OTP available to scholars and to the learned.

The interpretation of the OTP during this period was certainly precritical. No recognition of the composite natures of many Jewish Pseudepigrapha or of the Christian expansions of earlier Jewish documents accompanied attempts to understand such writings. No perception of the complex world of early Judaism supported interpretations, which were essentially literal. No clear distinction was drawn between the medieval pseudepigraphical titles and the pseudepigraphical intent of the authors. The tendency was to assume that if a document was attributed to Enoch, it had been written by him.

5. *Modern Period.* The modern study of the OTP occupies the nineteenth and twentieth centuries. Five periods can be isolated for examination.

a. Nineteenth century. The first phase began in the early nineteenth century. In 1812 F. Muenter discovered quotations from the lost *Odes of Solomon* in the *Pistis Sophia.* From 1819 to 1838 R. Laurence published translations or editions of the *Ascension of Isaiah* (the *editio princeps*), *4 Ezra* (the *editio princeps* of the Ethopic), and *1 Enoch* (first an English translation and then the *editio princeps* of the Ethiopic).

The perception arose that the documents in the OTP were composed by early Jews or Christians and did not predate 500 B.C.E. Laurence, for example, argued that Enoch did not write the Book of Enoch (= *1 Enoch*): "Its allusions to the Lord, or rather to the Son of man exalted on his throne of glory and of judgment by the Ancient of days, may demonstrate, that it was written after the book of Daniel; but not, surely, that it was the production of Enoch before the flood" (1833, xviii).

The rest of the nineteenth century witnessed an unprecedented preoccupation with the OTP. Vast advances were made from 1850 to 1900, especially in terms of the production of texts, Lexicons*§, Concordances*§, and grammars. In the middle of the nineteenth century, J. Migne, who was greatly indebted to Laurence, published the first modern collection of the OTP, *Dictionnaire des apocryphesé ou collection de tous les livres apocryphes relatifs a l'ancien et au nouveau testament* (1856-58). Since the work reflected the Roman Catholic view of the canon, which incorporates as deuterocanonical the Protestant Apocrypha, the Pseudepigrapha were labeled "apocryphes."

With editions, translations, and at least one collection of the OTP, scholars could now— virtually for the first time—focus on this amorphous corpus and attempt to interpret the documents within it. Gradually, recognition of the vast differences between the modern European and ancient Near Eastern cultures began to surface, undoubtedly inspired by the knowledge of the East that resulted from French and British conquests of Egypt (Egyptology and Biblical Studies*§) and Palestine. The interpreters of the biblical and apocryphal books, however, continued to attribute European norms to the ancient authors. As Jesus†§ was habitually portrayed as a teacher uninfluenced by the eschatological and apocalyptic movements in early Judaism, so also the authors of the Pseudepigrapha were assumed to think logically and systematically like Europeans influenced by the Enlightenment.

When the OTP were interpreted, they were considered inferior to the canonical works and important only because of the knowledge they provided of the intertestamental period and for an understanding of the sacred canon. This limited appreciation of the OTP was due to the fact that Christian scholars were interested in Christian Scriptures. An ignorance of Christian origins, therefore, impeded fruitful interpretation. Scholars did not take seriously the insights that Jesus was a Jew, that his earliest followers were Jews, and that for decades Christianity was only one of many groups within pre-70 C.E. Palestinian Judaism, an understanding that was widely shared only after 1970. Even more seriously, there was a tendency to deny that Jesus was a Jew. Christianity was considered distinct from and far superior to Judaism; thus it is no wonder that such beautiful Jewish Pseudepigrapha as *Joseph and Aseneth* and the Prayer of Manasseh were singled out and elevated as Christian and that the profound wisdom of early Judaism was minimized. Unfortunately (but understandably in such a *zeitgeist*) E. SCHÜRER, in his voluminous *A History of the Jewish People in the Time of Jesus Christ* (ET 1890-91), cast aspersions on early Jewish prayer and piety. Interpretation of the OTP was often warped by such polemics.

b. Early twentieth century. The twentieth century began on a very promising note with the first German collection of the OTP, published under the editorship of E. Kautzsch§ in 1900. This valuable work was followed in 1913 by the first English collection, under the editorship of R. Charles§. Now it was possible, or much easier, to read the great Jewish apocalypses like *4 Ezra, 1 Enoch, 2 Enoch**§, and related apocalyptic writings like the *Testaments of the Twelve*

Patriarchs*§. The presence of the OTP in individual translations, editions, or collections produced an awareness of—if not an appreciation of—Jewish apocalypticism. It is understandable that during this period numerous New Testament scholars, most notably A. Schweitzer§, stressed the importance of apocalypticism and eschatology in the life of Jesus and of his earliest followers.

The best interpreters of the documents in the OTP saw that they witnessed to a complex yet not chaotic or disoriented group of theologies. Charles tended to see two main types of early Jewish theology: apocalyptic Judaism and legalistic Judaism. One of his significant contributions is the insight that "to all Jewish apocalyptic writers the Law was of eternal validity, but they also clung fast to the validity of the prophetic teaching as the source of new truth and the right of apocalyptic as its successor in this respect" (1913, 2:vii).

c. Post World War I. After 1913, the feverish study of the OTP came to a temporary halt. World War I wracked Western culture, which had supported biblical studies since the time of the Reformation, draining it of energy and resources. Crises degenerated into chaos as world depression and the rise of Communism rocked the West, shattering the dream of achieving peace on earth through progress in industry and technology.

Biblical interpretation, too, was deeply affected by the resulting disorientation and disillusionment. One result was the demise of the study of the OTP. Another was a denigration of the importance of history in biblical interpretation and the correlative stress on existentialism. Jewish documents were no longer considered important. Anti-Semitism seeped into biblical interpretation, and an aversion to anything Jewish gripped many sectors in Europe.

The most influential and perhaps greatest New Testament scholar of the period, R. Bultmann§, stressed the need to remove Jewish myth (Mythology and Biblical Studies*§) from the New Testament and to interpret the message of the gospel in existential terms since the gospel was primarily a call to decision in the present. Bultmann was indeed preoccupied with history, but his interests were theological, not historical. Examples of his interpretation of the OTP and his theological reconstruction of Jewish history may be found in the following excerpts from his *Primitive Christianity in Its Contemporary Setting* (1949 [ET 1956]): "Israel (apart from Hellenistic Judaism) cut herself off from the outside world and lived in extraordinary isolation" (1956, 60). In early Judaism God "was a superior cosmic power, spatially distant and ontologically distinct from all worldly phenomena. The apocalypses provide fantastic pictures of his cosmic rule, with his hosts of angels and blinding glory of heaven" (1956, 61). The scribes' "method of exegesis was primitive, and, despite certain variations, stereotype" (1956, 64). For Bultmann, pre-70 C.E. Palestinian Judaism was intolerably burdened by a rigid legalism, yet he was far more sensitive to early Judaism than Schürer, who influenced him. Contrary to the popular sentiment in Germany, Bultmann placed Jesus squarely within Palestinian Judaism as a Jew. However, even though Bultmann was far more aware than his colleagues of the need for historical research in the study of earliest Christianity, he nevertheless devoted years to the Greek New Testament but little time to the Semitic OTP.

d. Post World War II. After World War II, interest in history and the OTP once again rose in biblical circles, partly due to the discovery of the Qumran manuscripts (Dead Sea Scrolls*§). Among these scrolls were found fragments of several documents of the OTP, notably early versions of at least two of the *Testaments of the Twelve Patriarchs*, fragments from more than a dozen manuscripts of *Jubilees**§, and numerous manuscripts of the *Book of Enoch*. At least these documents from the OTP clearly predate the destruction of the Qumran monastery in 68 C.E.

New sensitivities to the traditions and complexities of the New Testament Gospels, the refinement of New Testament Form Criticism*§, and the development of Redaction Criticism*§ cumulatively led to a "new quest of the historical Jesus." The call for research in this area was heard in France and Israel (P. Benoit), in Norway (N. Dahl), and especially in Germany among Bultmann's students (esp. E. Käsemann). A renewed interest in history and in ancient texts was in the air.

The study and interpretation of the OTP lagged behind as attention initially focused on the documents unique to and supposedly produced by the Qumran community. However, the interpretation of these scrolls eventually revolutionized the understanding of pre-70 C.E. Palestinian Judaism and paved the way for an unprecedented devotion to the study of the OTP.

e. 1970 to present. Beginning around 1970, the OTP was restored to a place of honor in biblical research. Groups were organized in the United States, Germany, Holland, and elsewhere for an intensive examination of these writings. In the 1980s, new collections appeared in English, German, French, Dutch, Danish, Spanish, Italian, modern Greek, and Japanese.

For the first time in over 1,500 years, the OTP is now recognized as a major witness to the origins of modern Judaism and Christianity. No longer are these documents interpreted only in terms of a closed Jewish or Christian canon. Pre-70 Palestinian Judaism is no longer denigrated as "Late Judaism" or "Intertestamental Judaism"; it is correctly labeled "Early Judaism." Moreover, it is increasingly difficult to distinguish between Jewish and Christian thought, and discussions turn on what makes an ethical tract like the *Testaments of the Twelve Patriarchs* Jewish or Christian. *First Enoch* 37-71, which J. Milik and some scholars interpreted to be Christian and perhaps from the third century C.E., is now acknowledged to be clearly Jewish and probably earlier than 70 C.E. Other documents are being similarly reinterpreted and redated. Significant reference works for the OTP include Denis (1987, 1993) and Lechner-Schmidt (1990). Recent compilations of OTP bibliography include Anderson (1987) and DiTomasso (2001). Kraft (1994, 2001) provides recent overviews of the state of OTP studies.

Hence, early Judaism is interpreted differently. It is no longer seen as orthodox, closed, and monolithic but is recognized to be diverse and creatively alive, open to the scientific, linguistic, and philosophical advances of other cultures. It is not seen as simply divided into four clearly defined sects but is characterized by more than a dozen groups and by many more subgroups, one of them the Palestinian Jesus movement. The documents in the OTP are no longer interpreted as if they were insignificant compositions by insignificant groups on the fringes of a dominant normative Judaism.

Formerly, the origins of Christianity were often thought to be tied to the pagan mystery religions and perhaps, in some ways, to some forms of Judaism. Now, the tide has turned. Both rabbinic Judaism and early Christianity are seen to have developed out of the same religion— actually, religions—namely, early Judaism. It is now recognized that while rabbinic Judaism tended to reject the apocalyptic elements in its forerunner (pre-70 C.E. Palestinian Judaism), it nevertheless preserved some elements from earlier Jewish apocalypticism, which profoundly affected the origins of earliest Christianity. The renewed appreciation and interpretation of the OTP has been the main catalyst for this paradigm shift.

Obviously, the interpretation of the OTP is just beginning. No systematic presentation of the materials is possible at present. The documents are diverse, often composite, even self-contradictory; however, their interpretation opens our eyes to the vast range of meanings of biblical interpretation and ushers us into the brilliant, informed, and creative reflections of early Jews and Christians.

Bibliography: F. I. Andersen, "Pseudepigrapha Studies in Bulgaria," *JSP* 1 (1987) 41-55. **R. H. Charles** (ed.), *The Apocrypha and Pseudepigrapha of the OT in English* (1913). **J. H. Charlesworth** (ed.), *The OT Pseudepigrapha* (2 vols. 1983-85); "A History of Pseudepigrapha Research: The Re-emerging Importance of the Pseudepigrapha," *ANRW* (1972-) II.19.1, 54-88. **A. M. Denis,** *Introduction aux pseudépigraphes grecs d'Ancien Testament* (SVTP 1, 1970); *Concordance Grecque des Pseudépigraphes d' Ancien Testament. Concordance, Corpus des textes, Indices* (1987); *Concordance latine des pseudépigraphes d'Ancien Testament* (1993). **A. Díez Macho** (ed.), *Apócrifos del Antiguo Testamento* (1982-).

L. DiTommaso, *A Bibliography of Pseudepigrapha Research 1850-1999* (JSPSup 39, 2001). **A. Dupont-Sommer and M. Philonenko** (eds.), *La Bible: Écrits intertestamentaires* (1987). **E. Kautzsch** (ed.), *Die Apokryphen und Pseudepigraphen des Alten Testaments* (1900; repr. 1975). **R. A. Kraft,** "The Pseudepigrapha in Christianity," *Tracing the Threads: Studies in the Vitality of Jewish Pseudepigrapha* (ed. J. C. Reeves, SBLEJL 6, 1994) 55-86; "The Pseudepigrapha and Christianity Revisited: Setting the Stage and Framing Some Central Questions," *JSJ* 32 (2001) 371-395. **R. A. Kraft and G. W. E. Nickelsburg** (eds.), *Early Judaism and Its Modern Interpreters* (1986). **W. G. Kümmel** (ed.), *Jüdische Schriften aus hellenistisch-römischer Zeit* (1973-). **R. Laurence,** *The Book of Enoch the Prophet: An Apocryphal Production* (1833). **W. Lechner-Schmidt,** *Wortindex der lateinisch erhaltenen Pseudepigraphen zum Alten Testament* (TANZ 3, 1990). **P. Sacchi** (ed.), *Apocrifi dell'Antico Testamento* (1981). **H. F. D. Sparks** (ed.), *The Apocryphal OT* (1984). **M. E. Stone** (ed.), *Jewish Writings of the Second Temple Period: Apocrypha, Pseudepigrapha, Qumran, Sectarian Writings, Philo, Josephus* (CRINT 2, 2, 1984).

J. H. CHARLESWORTH

PSEUDEPIGRAPHA

Baruch, Book of 2 (Syriac Apocalypse of)

Lost for nearly 1,200 years, the manuscript known as the *Syriac Apocalypse of Baruch* was rediscovered in the late nineteenth century by A. Ceriani (1871, 113-80). Until that time, only about nine and one half chapters survived in the Syriac Bible. This manuscript, found in a library in Milan, is the only source for the Syriac of chapters 1-77. The manuscript survives under the title "Epistle of Baruch," or something similar (*APOT*, 2.470; *AOT*, 835). Ceriani first published the text in Latin translation (1876-83) and later published the Syriac.

R. Charles[§] (1896) argued that the Syriac was a translation from Greek. However, the presence of a number of unintelligible phrases or expressions in the Syriac, which become intelligible when translated, not into Greek, but into Hebrew, suggest that Hebrew and not Greek was the original language. Charles dated the Greek to sometime between 120 and 130 C.E. (*APOT*, 2.473). L. Brockington noted that the title of the Syriac manuscript found by Ceriani claims to be a translation from the Greek. This was affirmed in 1897 by the discovery of the Oxyrhynchus fragments (Brockington 1984, 836). F. Zimmerman (1939, 151-56) and J. Collins (1984, 170) follow Charles's analysis, while A. Klijn (1976, 107-11) argues that the close parallels between *2 Baruch* and other Jewish texts suggest that either Hebrew or Aramaic was the original language (1983, 616). He does not exclude the possibility that a different textual tradition might be represented by the Greek.

Charles identified seven distinct redactional strata (*APOT*, 474), each the work of a different author (1896, liiiff). The earliest strata derive from three fragmentary apocalypses that date before 70 C.E. The remaining strata were written after 70 C.E. This distinction between earlier and later strata is reflected in distinctive eschatologies: an earlier, optimistic one that looks to the restoration of the temple, and a later, pessimistic one that looks toward final judgment. This stratification implies redaction by a single editor. Final redaction of the Hebrew may have taken place between 110 and 120 C.E. (*APOT*, 2.474-76); translation into Greek occurred sometime between 120 and 130 C.E. (*APOT*, 2.473).

V. Ryssel, P. M. Bogaert (1969; *AOT*, 836-37), and Collins have all found this analysis wanting. Collins points to the description of the fast in *2 Bar* 5:7: "And we sat there and fasted until evening." Unlike the remaining six fasts, this fast does not last seven days; it lasts only until evening. Thus, Collins concludes, this passage does not indicate a new section. Rather, *2 Bar* 5 must be viewed within the larger context of chaps. 1-8, which collectively form the opening section of the text. (G. Nickelsburg 1981 extends the introduction through chap. 9.) As such, this section provides the context for the rest of the book by describing the fall of Jerusalem to the Babylonians. Such narrative introductions are not unusual in apocalypses; as examples, Collins cites the *Apocalypse of Abraham* and Daniel 1-6. Collins finds Charles's hypothesis that there are two distinct eschatological perspectives in this text unfounded (1984, 171); no single layer or stratum of the text can be identified with the degree of certainty required by Charles's analysis. Here as in *4 Ezra*, Collins argues, diverse eschatological perspectives have been woven together into a single fabric. In the present shape of the text they appear without contradiction (1984, 172).

Bogaert suggests that *2 Baruch* might have been authored by R. Joseph ben Hananiah during the Domitian persecution (1969, 287-95), whereas B. Violet (1924) associates *2 Baruch* with Akiba's[§] circle. Klijn dates the work to early in the first or second decade of the second century C.E., basing his conclusion on the text itself and on its strong relationship to *4 Ezra*, Pseudo-Philo*[§], and the *Epistle of Barnabas**[§]. Focusing on three passages—*2 Bar.* 32:2-4; 67:1; and 68:5—he argues that *2 Bar.* 32:2-4 clearly mentions the first and the second destruction of the temple, which would indicate that the author lived after the second destruction of the temple in 70 C.E. *Second Bar.* 67:1, quoted in Barnabas 11:9, refers to Zion's present suffering. Read in the light of the reference to the second restoration of the temple in *2 Bar.* 68:5, which occurred c. 130 C.E. under Hadrian, this passage places the time of authorship in the early second century C.E. (*OTP*, 116-17). In contrast, Nickelsburg finds precise dating of this text impossible and suggests a date of composition shortly after 70 C.E., as did C. C. Torrey§ (1945). P. Volz§ (1903, 1934) suggested 90 C.E.

The relationship between *2 Baruch* and other texts is much debated. Charles, Klijn, and Ryssel have noted strong similarities between it and *4 Ezra*. Klijn also notes strong parallels to Pseudo-Philo and the *Letter to Barnabas*. However, Nickelsburg finds the relationship between *2 Baruch* and *4 Ezra* to be tenuous (1981, 287).

Bibliography: K. Berger (ed.), *Synopse des Vierten Buches Esra und der Syrischen Baruch-Apokalypse* (TANZ 8, 1992). **P. M. Bogaert**, *L'Apocalpse de Baruch: Introduction, traduction du syriac et commentaire* (SC 144, 145, 1969); "Le nom de Baruch dans la littérature pseudépigrapha: L'apocalypse syriaque et le livre Deutéonomique," *La Littérature juive entre Tenach et Michna* (ed. W. C. van Unnik, 1974) 56-62; "Le personnage de Baruch et l'histoire du livre de Jeremie: Aux origines du livre de Baruch," *BIOSCS* 7 (1974) 19-21. **L. H. Brockington,** "The Syriac Apocalypse of Baruch," *AOT* (1984) 835-95. **A. M. Ceriani**, *Monumenta sacra et profana* 5.2 (1871) 113-80; *Translatio Syria Pescitto Veteris Testamenti ex codice Ambrosiano sec. fere vi, photolithographice edita* (1876-83) 257a-267a. **R. H. Charles**, "2 Baruch, or the Syriac Apocalypse of Baruch," *APOT* 2.470-526; *The Apocalypse of Baruch* (1896, 1918). **J. J. Collins**, *The Apocalyptic Imagination* (1984) 170-80. **S. Dedering**, "Apocalypse of Baruch," *The OT in Syriac*, 4:3 (1973). **P. F. Esler**, "God's Honour and Rome's Triumph: Responses to the Fall of Jerusalem in 70 CE in Three Jewish Apocalypses," *Modelling Early Christianity: Social-Scientific Studies of the New Testament in its Context* (1995) 239-58. **L. Gry**, "La Date de la fin des temps, selon les revélations ou les calcula du Pseudo-Philo et de Baruch (Apocalypse syrique)," *RB* 48 (1939) 337-56. **J. F. Hobbins**, "The Summing up of History in 2 Baruch." *JQR* 89 (1998) 45-79. **R. Kabisch**, "Die Quellen der Apokalypse Baruchs," *JPT* (1891) 125-67. **R. Kirschner**, "Apocalyptic and Rabbinic Responses to the Destruction of 70," *HTR* 78 (1985) 27-46. **A. F. J. Klijn**, "2 (Syriac Apocalypse of) Baruch," *OTP* (1983) 1.615-52; "The Sources and the Redaction of the Syriac Apocalypse of Baruch," *JSJ* 1 (1970) 65-76; "Die syrische Baruch-Apokalypse," *JSHRZ* 5.2 (1976) 103-84; "Recent Developments in the Study of the Syriac Apocalypse of Baruch." *JSP* 4 (1989) 3-17. **M. Kmosko**, "Liber Apocalypseos Baruch Filii Neriae" and "Epistola Baruch Filii Neriae," *Patrologia Syriaca* I, II (1894) 1056, 1207-37. **A. Laato**, "The Apocalyse of the Syriac Baruch and the Date of the End," *JSP* 18 (1998) 39-46. **F. Leemhuis**, "The Arabic Version of the Apocalypse of Baruch: A Christian Text?" *JSP* 4 (1989) 19-26. **F. Leemhuis, A. F. J. Klijn, and G. J. H. van Gelder**, *The Arabic Text of the Apocalypse of Baruch* (1986). **J. R. Levison**, *Portraits of Adam in Early Judaism: from Sirach to 2 Baruch* (JSPSUP 1, 1988). **F. J. Murphy**, *The Structure and Meaning of Second Baruch* (SBLDS 78, 1985); "2 Baruch and the Romans." *JBL* 104 (1985) 663-69; "The Temple in the Syriac Apocalypse of Baruch," *JBL* 106 (1987) 671-683. **G. W. E. Nickelsburg**, "Narrative Traditions in the Paralipomena of Jeremiah and 2 Baruch," *CBQ* 35 (1973) 60-8. **N. Roddy**, "'Two Parts: Weeks of Seven Weeks': The End of the Age as Terminus ad Quem for 2 Baruch," *JSP* 14 (1996) 3-14; *Jewish Literature Between the Bible and the Mishnah* (1981) 281-87. **V. Ryssel**, "Die syrische Baruchapokalypse," *APAT* 2.404-46. **G. B. Sayler**, *Have the Promises Failed? A Literary Analysis of 2 Baruch* (SBLDS 72, 1984). **E. Schürer**, *HJPAJC* 3 (1986) 750-56. **M. E. Stone**, "Lists of Revealed Things in the Apocalyptic Literature," *Selected Studies in Pseudepigrapha and Apocrypha with Special*

Reference to the Armenian Tradition (SVTP 9, 1991*a*) 379-418; "Apocalyptic—Vision or Hallucination?" *Selected Studies in Pseudepigrapha and Apocrypha* (1991*b*) 419-28; "Reactions to Destructions of the Second Temple," *Selected Studies in Pseudepigrapha and Apocrypha* (1991*c*) 429-38. **C. C. Torrey,** *The Apocryphal Literature: A Brief Introduction* (1945). **B. Violet,** *Die Apokalypsen des Esra und des Baruch in deutscher Gestalt* (GCS 32, 1924) 203-36, 334-63. **P. Volz,** *Jüdische Eschatologie von Daniel bis Akiba* (1903, 1934²). **T. W. Willett,** *Eschatology in the Theodicies of 2 Baruch and 4 Ezra* (JSPSup 4, 1989). **J. E. Wright,** "The Social Setting of the Syriac Apocalypse of Baruch," *JSP* 16 (1997) 81-96. **F. Zimmerman,** "Textual Observations on the Apocalypse of Baruch," *JTS* 40 (1939) 151-6.

G. T. MILAZZO

PSEUDEPIGRAPHA

Baruch, Book of 3 (Greek Apocalypse of)

Third Baruch survives in Greek and Slavonic. The Slavonic text was found in a fifteenth-century Serbian manuscript. The longer of two fifteenth-century Greek texts was discovered in 1896 by E. Butler (*AOT*, 897; *APOT*, 2.527) and published by M. James in 1897. Until the latter discovery, only the Slavonic version of this apocalypse (Apocalypticism*[§]) was known to exist. The shorter Greek text was found by J. C. Picard among papers from the monastery of Hagia. The Slavonic was published in 1886 by S. Novakovic (*APOT*, 2.527). W. Morfill published an English translation in 1898 and N. Tikhonravov published the text of a second fifteenth-century Slavonic text in 1894. Since that time, another Greek text and additional Slavonic manuscripts have been discovered. There are at least twelve known Slavonic manuscripts. The differences between the Greek and the Slavonic versions of this apocalypse are extensive, as are the differences among the various Slavonic texts. The Greek texts, however, bear close similarity to one another (*AOT*, 898).

In his *De principiis* (2.3.6) Origen[§] refers to a "book of Baruch the prophet." This book, Origen recounted, offered a revelation that had as its centerpiece Baruch's journey through each of the seven heavens. None of the surviving manuscripts describes this exact journey, although the longer Greek text details a journey through five heavens. H. Hughes argues that this text, though incomplete, serves as the source for Origen's apocalypse (1913, 2.527). Tikhonravov's text details Baruch's journey through only two heavens.

Among more recent scholars, H. Gaylord argued that the Slavonic text is a translation of the Greek. He also held that there is no convincing argument that the Greek is a translation from any other language (1983, 1.655). Even though Semiticisms exist in the text, causing some scholars to argue for the existence of an original Semitic text, the presence of Semiticisms is not unknown in later Koine Greek. This position is shared by J. Collins (1979).

According to D. Russell (1964, 65-66), this text was originally written in Greek during the second century C.E. He contends that sections of the text show obvious Christian influence (*3 Baruch* 4:9-15; 11:1-9), although this opinion is not shared by all scholars. R. Charles[§], e.g., argued that the author of this text was influenced by "Hellenic-oriental syncretism" (*APOT*, 2.529). James (1899) was convinced that the author was familiar with the Pauline epistles (Paul[†§]) and with Christian apocryphal writings (Apocrypha, New Testament*[§]), among which he gave prominence to the *Paraleipomena of Jeremiah* (c. 136 C.E.; *Baruch 4*). This became the basis for James's dating of the text between 140 and 200 C.E. (*AOT*, 898). James ruled out the possibility that the distinctively Christian passages are the work of a later redactor, thus arguing for Christian authorship. Hughes was most critical of James's claim that the author of this apocalypse had knowledge of the Pauline epistles, while L. Ginzberg (1902) argued that the author was a Jewish Gnostic*[§].

Hughes maintained that the framework of this apocalypse is distinctively Jewish—including the story of the vine in chap. 4, which, according to Ginzberg, was the only element that showed Christian influence (*APOT*, 2.528; *AOT*, 898). Among other characteristics Hughes considered distinctively Jewish are the text's angelology and cosmic revelations. However, the hand of a Christian redactor is also clearly present: Hughes pointed to the apparent transformation of the story of the vine, where a narrative that originally equated the vine with the forbidden tree in Genesis now ties the image of the vine to the life-giving force of the Eucharist (*APOT*, 2.528). The Christian redactor's influence is most evident in chaps. 11–17.

This redaction of the text reflects an appeal to the Gentile church to be patient in its attempt to convert the Ebionites and the Jews. In effect, Hughes argued that this redaction reflects the plight of those Jews who attempted to be both Jewish and Christian and, in the end, failed to be either (*APOT*, 2.529-30). He maintained that the text received its current form sometime around 136 C.E. A. Argyle pressed Hughes's analysis a step further, saying that while this text is clearly a part of the Baruch literature, its author was a Christian: "Whatever Jewish material he may have used he certainly re-phrased and very thoroughly recast" (*AOT*, 900). Argyle restricted parallels to the Baruch tradition to the narrative setting in which this apocalypse takes shape. Such parallels arise "naturally" within that context and therefore do not necessarily reflect an appropriation of actual texts.

Following Picard (1970, 77-8; 1967, 61-96) and U. Fischer (1978, 75), Collins argues that this text originated in Hellenistic Diaspora. This conclusion is drawn on the basis of allusions to Greek and Egyptian Mythology*§ found in the text. Collins also notes the close affinities this text has to Egyptian Judaism. In addition, G. Nickelsburg (1981) supports the theory that this is a Jewish, if not Jewish Gnostic, text that shows clear Christian interpolation. The place of origin was probably Egypt; like Collins, Nickelsburg notes strong parallels with Egyptian and Greek mythology and also with the Septuagint*§ Deuteronomy. He dates this text toward the end of the first century or early in the second century C.E. Because the relationship between the Slavonic texts and the Greek manuscripts is unresolved, Picard did not include any of the Slavonic texts in his inquiry. Argyle, following Ginzberg, argued that there is indirect evidence for a Latin version of the apocalypse that circulated in Spain in the seventh century. Bauckham (1990) discusses *3 Baruch's* image of Hades. Harlow (1996) is the most recent comprehensive overview of the book's text, genre, setting, function, literary integrity, and original Jewish or Christian authorship.

Parallels with other apocalyptic texts, especially with the *Testament of Abraham, 2 Enoch, 2 Baruch, Apocalypse of Abraham,* and *4 Ezra,* have been noted by many scholars.

Bibliography: **A. W. Argyle,** "The Greek Apocalypse of Baruch," *AOT* (1984) 897-914. **R. Bauckham,** "Early Jewish Visions of Hell," *JTS* 41 (1990) 355-85. **J. J. Collins,** "The Jewish Apocalypses," *Apocalypse: The Morphology of a Genre Semeia* 14 (1979) 41-2, 55. **A. M. Denis and Y. Janssens,** *Concordance de l'Apocalypse grecque de Baruch* (Publications de l'Institute Orientaliste de Louvain 1, 1970); *Introduction aux pseudepigraphes greces d'Ancien Testament* (1970) 79-84. **U. Fischer,** *Eschatologie und Jenseitserwartung im Hellenistischen Diasporajudentum* (BZNW 44, 1978). **H. E. Gaylord,** "3 (Greek Apocalypse of) Baruch," *OTP* (1983) 1.653-80. **L. Ginzberg,** "Greek Apocalypse of Baruch," *JE* (1902) 2:549-551. **W. Hage,** "Die griechische Baruch-Apokalypse," *JSHRZ* 5.1 (1979) 17-44. **D. C. Harlow,** *The Greek Apocalypse of Baruch (3 Baruch) in Hellenistic Judaism and Early Christianity* (Studia in Veteris Testamenti Pseudepigrapha, 12, 1996). **H. M. Hughes,** "3 Enoch and the Apocalypse of Baruch," *APOT* (1913) 2.527-41. **M. R. James,** "The Apocalypse of Baruch," *Apocrypha Anecdota* 2 (Contemporary Theology Series 5.1. 1899) li-lxxi, 83-94. **E. Kautzsch,** *APAT* 2.446-57. **W. Lüdtke,** "Beiträge zu slavischen Apocryphen: 2 Apokalypse des Baruch," *ZAW* 31 (1911) 219-22. **G. W. E. Nickelsburg,** *Jewish Literature Between the Bible and the Mishnah: A Historical and Literary Introduction* (1981) 299-303. **J. C. Picard** (ed.), *Apocalypsis Baruchi Graece* (PVTG 2, 1967) 61-96; "Observations sur l'Apocalypse grecque de Baruch I: Cadre historique fictif et efficacite symbolique," *Sem* 20 (1970) 77-103. **D. S. Russell,** *The Method and Message of Jewish Apocalyptic* (1964). **V. Ryssel,** "Die griechische Baruchapokalypse," *APAT* (1900) 2.446-57. **E. Schürer,** *HJPAJC* 3 (1986) 789-92. **E. Turdeanu,** "Apocryphes bogomiles et apocryphes pseudo-bogomils," *RHR* 133 (1950) 177-181; "Les apocryphes slaves et roumains: Leur apport . . . la connaissance des apocryphes grecs," *Studi bizantini e neoellenici* 8 (1953) 47-52; "L'Apocalypse de Baruch en slave," *Revue des études slaves* 48 (1969) 23-48.

G. T. MILAZZO

Baruch, Book of 4

The Greek versions of this work bear the name *Paraleipomena Jeremiou*, "Things Omitted from Jeremiah"; the Ethiopic version (Ethiopian Biblical Interpretation*§) designates the work as "The Rest of the Words of Baruch." The writing exists in various forms of differing length in Greek, Ethiopic, Armenian, Slavonic, and Romanian. The Greek text was first published by A. Ceriani (1868) and the Ethiopic by A. Dillmann§ (1866). Modern English translations can be found in J. Charlesworth (1985, by S. Robinson); H. Sparks (1984, by R. Thornhill) (and Kraft-Purintum (1972, along with an eclectic Greek text).

Three human characters carry the story line of the book: the prophet Jeremiah, his scribe Baruch, and Abimelech the Ethiopian (= Ebed-melech, who rescued Jeremiah from his incarceration in a cistern; Jer 38:1-13). The plot centers on the fall of Jerusalem and the return from exile as well as the end of Jeremiah's life by stoning. According to *4 Baruch*, after Jerusalem was "surrendered" to the Babylonians and the city burned by divine messengers, Jeremiah was carried captive to Babylon (contra the account in Jeremiah 43, where Jeremiah is forcibly taken to Egypt by his fellow Judeans, and the account of his stoning in Egypt in *The Lives of the Prophets* 2). During the period of exile—some sixty-six years—Jeremiah's servant Abimelech had slept under a tree in the vicinity of Jerusalem, having napped after picking figs. When Abimelech finally awakened, his figs were still fresh, which was understood as a sign that the exiles were to return. The document has Jeremiah leading the exiles home from Babylon; the foundation of the city of Samaria is traced to those returnees who were denied access to the Jerusalem community because they refused to divorce their Babylonian spouses.

In its present form, the document is clearly Christian, since Jeremiah, in his final proclamation, announces the coming of the Messiah, Jesus[†§]. Most recent scholars, however, argue that the original document was of Jewish origin, probably written in Hebrew, which was subjected to Christian redaction and interpolation. G. Nickelsburg (1973) has argued that lying behind this work and *2 Baruch* is a no longer extant narrative that served as a source for both. Such a Jewish document could be read as an exhortation to Jews to prepare for a return to Jerusalem by divesting themselves of foreign influences. At any rate, it belongs to the rather extensive non-biblical literature associated with Jeremiah and his works around the fall of Jerusalem (see 2 Macc 2:1-8).

Fourth Baruch comes from the Roman period, as references to the property of Agrippa indicate. Most interpreters relate it to the destruction of the Jewish community in the Bar-Kochba war (132-135 C.E.) and see the reference to Abimelech's sixty-six-year sleep as pointing to c. 136 C.E.—that is, sixty-six years after the Romans' first destruction of Jerusalem in 70 C.E.

Bibliography: P. **Bogaert,** *Apocalypse de Baruch* (SC 144, 1969) 1:177-221. **A. Ceriani,** *Monumenta Sacra et Profana* 5, 1 (1868) 9-18. **J. H. Charlesworth,** *The Pseudepigrapha and Modern Research* (SBLSCS 7, 1976) 88-91. **M. De Jonge,** "Remarks in the Margin of the Paper 'The Figure of Jeremiah in the 'Paralipomena Jeremiae', by. J. Riaud," *JSP* 22 (2000) 45-49. **G. Delling,** *Judische Lehre und Frommigkeit in den Paralipomena Jeremiae* (BZAW 100, 1967). **A. M. Denis,** *Introduction aux pseudipigraphes grecs d'Ancien Testament* (SVTP 1, 1970) 70-78. **A. Dillmann** , *Chrestomathia Aethiopica* (1866) 1-15. **J. R. Harris,** *The Rest of the Words of Baruch* (1889). **J. Herzer,** "Die Paralipomena Jeremiae—eine christlich-gnostische Schrift? Eine Antwort an Marc Philonenko," *JSJ* 30 (1998, 25-39); "Direction in Difficult Times: How God is Understood in the Paralipomena Jeremiae," *JSP* 22 (2000) 9-30. **K. Kohler,** "The Pre-Talmudic Haggada: B. The Second Baruch or Rather the Jeremiah Apocalypse," *JQR* 5 (1893) 407-19. **R. A. Kraft** and **A. E. Purintum,** *Paraleipomena Jeremiou* (SBLTT 1,

Pseudepigrapha Series 1, 1972). **G. W. E. Nickelsburg,** "Narrative Tradition in the Paraleipomena of Jeremiah and 2 Baruch," *CBQ* 35 (1973) 60-68. **L. Prijs,** "The Figure of Jeremiah in the Paralipomena Jeremiae Prophetae: His Originality; His 'Christianization' by the Christian Author of the Conclusion (9.10-32)," *JSP* 22 (2000) 31-44. **S. E. Robinson,** *OTP* (ed. J. H. Charlesworth, 1985) 2:418-25. **B. Schaller,** "Paralipomena Jeremiou," *JSHRZ* (1998) 1.659-777; "Is the Greek Version of the Paralipomena Jeremiou Original or a Translation?" *JSP* 22 (2000), 51-89; "Paralipomena Jeremiou: Annotated Bibliography in Historical Order," *JSP* 22 (2000), 91-118. **H. Sparks** (ed.), *The Apocryphal Old Testament* (1984) 813-33. **M. E. Stone,** "Baruch, Rest of the Words of," *EncJud* 4 (1971) 276-77; "Some Observations on the Armenian Version of the Paraliepomena of Jeremiah," *CBQ* 35 (1973) 47-59. **R. Thornhill,** "The Paraleipomena of Jeremiah," *APOT* (1913) 813-833. **C. Wolff,** "Irdisches und himmlisches Jerusalem—Die Heilshoffnung in den Paralipomena Jeremiae," *ZNW* 82 (1991) 147-158.

J. H. HAYES

PSEUDEPIGRAPHA

Enoch, First Book of

Part of the Jewish Pseudepigrapha*[§], *1 Enoch* (also called the *Ethiopian Book of Enoch*) is falsely attributed to the Enoch of Gen 5:24. Modern scholarship recognizes *1 Enoch* as an anthology of five separate works: the *Book of the Watchers* (chaps. 1–36), the *Parables* or *Similitudes of Enoch* (chaps. 37–71), the *Astronomical Book* (chaps. 72–82), the *Book of Dreams* (chaps. 83–90), and the *Epistle of Enoch* (chaps. 91–105). It concludes with a short appendix about the birth of Noah (chaps. 106–107) and an exhortation (chap. 108). The *Astronomical Book* and the *Book of the Watchers* date to the third century B.C.E. The *Book of Dreams* comes from the time of the Maccabean revolt; the *Epistle* from some time in the second century B.C.E.; and the *Parables* probably from the first half of the first century C.E. Aramaic fragments of all of the major units of 1 Enoch except the *Parables* were found at Qumran (Dead Sea Scrolls*[§]). The Aramaic works were translated into Greek at an early date, although the provenance of the translations is unclear.

This Enochic literature, and especially the *Book of the Watchers*, exercised considerable influence on literature of the late Second Temple period. The later sections of *1 Enoch* involve interpretation and development of themes found in the earlier ones (on the *Book of Dreams* and the *Epistle*, see J. VanderKam 1984, 141-78; G. Nickelsburg 1981*a*, 190-94, 150-51; on the *Parables*, Nickelsburg 1981*a*, 214-21). The writer of Jubilees*[§] seems to have known the *Astronomical Book*, the *Book of the Watchers*, and the *Book of Dreams*, and *Jubilees* also reflects traditions about Enoch beyond those found in these works (VanderKam 1984, 179-88). The ascent to heaven in *2 Enoch* reinterprets the *Book of the Watchers'* account of Enoch's ascent (*1 En.* 14) and journey to the ends of the earth (*1 En.* 17–36) in relation to its schema of seven heavens; other parts of *2 Enoch* appear to be modeled on the *Epistle of Enoch* and the account of Noah's birth (Nickelsburg 1981*a*, 185-88; M. Himmelfarb 1993, 38-41). While the *Testament of Levi* in its present form is a Christian work (part of the *Testaments of the Twelve Patriarchs*[§] dating from the second century C.E.) it is appropriate to consider it with these Jewish pseudepigrapha because it clearly draws on the Aramaic Levi document, which is partially preserved at Qumran and in the Cairo Geniza. The ascent to heaven in the *T. Levi* 2–7 reworks the ascent in *1 En.* 14 (but not the journey to the ends of the earth) to fit a schema of seven heavens (Nickelsburg 1981*c*, 588-90; Himmelfarb 1993, 30-33). (For lists of references to Enochic traditions and Enochic books in early Jewish literature, see R. Charles[§] 1912, lxx-lxxix; and F. Martin, cvi-cxi. These should be used with caution; Charles especially displayed the parallelomania that was so often a feature of scholarship at the turn of the century.)

There is very little in classical rabbinic literature to suggest knowledge of *1 Enoch* or its traditions; the references to Enoch are few, and some are not altogether positive. The relative silence may be polemical. On the other hand, *3 Enoch*, a *hekhalot* text from perhaps the end of the talmudic period (Talmud*[§]), makes Enoch the hero of the greatest success story in human history: Upon his ascent to heaven, he is transformed into the angel Metatron, God's vice-regent. Thus *3 Enoch* represents a clear continuation of the traditions about Enoch's ascent found in *1* and *2 Enoch*, although the precise nature of the relationship between *3 Enoch* and these earlier works remains to be clarified (Himmelfarb 1978).

Christian literature in the first four centuries contains a number of quotations of Enochic texts, often regarded as authoritative. The letter of Jude (vv. 14-15) in the New Testament, for example, quotes the *Book of the Watchers* (*1 En.* 1:9) as a prophecy of Enoch. Not all of the quotations, however, can be matched to extant Enochic works. In addition to quotations there are many allusions to traditions drawn from the Enochic corpus, particularly the story of the descent of the angels and its aftermath. Among the early Christian authors and works that seem to know parts of *1 Enoch* are the *Epistle of Barnabas**[§], Justin Martyr[§], Irenaeus[§], Tertullian[§], Clement of Alexandria[§], Origen[§], Priscillian, Augustine[§], and Jerome[§]. (For more inclusive lists, see E. Schürer 1986, 3:1.261-63; and the extensive discussions in H. Lawlor 1897; VanderKam 1996; W. Adler 1978). Enochic literature appears to have been particularly popular among Christians in Egypt, with clear evidence of interest in North Africa and Syria-Palestine as well (Nicklesburg 1990; VanderKam 1996).

Despite the existence of some Latin fragments, there is very little evidence that *1 Enoch* as a whole was ever translated into Latin; the Latin authors who quote it may also have known Greek. It does not appear to have had wide circulation in the West, and it certainly did not have a long career there (Lawlor 1897, 223-25). In the Greek-speaking East it lived on in the work of the ninth-century Byzantine chronographer G. Syncellus, who did not know the work directly but rather through excerpts transmitted in compilations of texts relevant to antediluvian history (Adler 1989, esp. Gen 6:1-4). The channels through which the book reached Ethiopia (Ethiopian Biblical Interpretation*[§]) are poorly understood, but the Ethiopic version of the work was so highly valued that it was transmitted with the Hebrew Bible. It is only in Ethiopic translation that the complete contents of the anthology have been preserved.

The West rediscovered *1 Enoch* only in the late eighteenth century, when the English traveler J. Bruce brought back three manuscripts from Ethiopia. The first modern translation was the English version by R. Laurence in 1821. Laurence also edited the first edition, which appeared in 1838.

The newly discovered work provoked considerable discussion, including debate about whether it was Jewish or Christian. The *Parables*, of particular interest because of its description of a heavenly Son of Man, was sometimes considered a separate, Christian source in an otherwise Jewish work. There was, however, no consensus on the number of sources making up the larger work, on their boundaries, or on whether the original language was Hebrew or Aramaic. Dates proposed for various parts of the book ranged from the period of the Maccabean revolt to the second century C.E. (For an annotated listing of nineteenth-century work on *1 Enoch*, see Charles 1912, xxx-lviii.)

At the end of the nineteenth century, Charles (1893) proposed dividing the book into the five units recognized today. By the beginning of the twentieth century two great critical editions had appeared, one by the German scholar J. Fleming (1902), the other by Charles (1906). Charles's edition has not been fully replaced even today; the only major edition since Charles's, that of M. Knibb (1978), transcribes a single manuscript, although it provides an extensive critical apparatus. M. Black's translation and commentary (1985) is a thorough revision of Charles's 1912 translation; Black's work is the first to take full account of the evidence of the Aramaic fragments from Qumran.

Charles's edition marks the culmination of the pioneering stage of study of *1 Enoch*. Between Charles and the Qumran discoveries, Enochic studies slowed down sharply as part of the general decline of interest in the Pseudepigrapha. Nonetheless, a few contributions from that period are particularly worthy of note. G. Dix (1926), drawing on Charles's division of the book into five sections, argued that this structure represented conscious imitation of the Pentateuch (Pentateuchal Criticism*[§]). H. Ludin Jansen (1939) related the traditions of *1 Enoch* to ancient Mesopotamian parallels. E. Sjoberg (1946) argued that the Son of Man in the *Parables* is to be understood as a heavenly being, active only at the eschaton yet sharing many of the characteristics of the ancient Near Eastern *Urmensch*.

The discovery at Qumran of Aramaic fragments of all of the works contained in *1 Enoch*, except the Parables, and their publication by J. Milik (1976) has given a new impetus to Enochic studies. The question of the original language of the works represented in these fragments has been resolved in favor of Aramaic. Moreover, the impact of the fragments on the question of date has been particularly dramatic: The third-century date of the *Astronomical Book* and the third- or early second-century date for the *Book of the Watchers,* determined on the basis of paleography, make them the two earliest apocalypses (see Apocalypticism*§), earlier than Daniel, which can be dated to 167-164 B.C.E. and had previously been considered the earliest. On the basis of its absence at Qumran, Milik suggested a rather late Christian date for the *Parables.* He also took the presence at Qumran of another Enochic work, the *Book of the Giants* adopted by the Manicheans, as evidence for an Enochic pentateuch; this claim has been disputed (J. Greenfield and M. Stone 1977; D. Suter 1981).

The new dates for the *Astronomical Book* and the *Book of the Watchers* have led to a new interest in those aspects of apocalyptic literature more or less ignored in Daniel but so well represented in these earliest Enochic works: astronomical secrets, cosmology, the heavenly throne room, and the seer's journey to view them (M. Stone 1976, 1978; Nickelsburg 1981c; Himmelfarb 1993). This in turn has contributed to interest in the question of the definition of the genre of the apocalypses by making it clear that apocalypses are not defined by apocalyptic eschatology alone (Stone 1976; J. Collins 1979, 1983). By placing two apocalypses with comparatively little interest in eschatology at the beginning of the development of the genre, the new dates also have important implications for the origins of apocalyptic literature and the question of the contributions of Prophecy*§ and wisdom (Stone 1976, 439-44; VanderKam 1984, 52-75). Considerable attention has been focused on the Babylonian connections of the early Enoch traditions (Grelot 1958a, 1958b; VanderKam 1984). VanderKam has suggested that mantic wisdom in the form of Mesopotamian divination is an important source for the Enochic traditions and for apocalyptic literature more generally. The relations among the various Enochic works are complex, and the place of the Qumran community in the creation and transmission of this material requires further clarification (Nickelsburg 1983; Suter 1979).

Bibliography: W. Adler, "Enoch in Early Christian Literature," *SBLSP* 13 (1978) 271-76; *Time Immemorial: Archaic History and Its Sources in Christian Chronography from Julius Africanus to George Syncellus* (1989). M. Albani, *Astronomie und Schöpfungsglaube. Untersuchungen zum astronomischen Henochbuch* (WMANT 68, 1994). R. A. Argall, *1 Enoch and Sirach. A Comparative Literary and Conceptual Analysis of the Themes of Revelation, Creation and Judgment* (SBLEJL 8, 1995). M. Black, *The Book of Enoch of I Enoch* (SVTP 7, 1985); "A Bibliography on 1 Enoch in the Eighties," *JSP* 5 (1989) 3-16. D. Bryan, *Cosmos, Chaos and the Kosher Mentality* (JSPSup 12, 1995). R. H. Charles, *The Book of Enoch* (1893); *The Book of Enoch or 1 Enoch* (1912); *APOT* (1913) 2.163-281. J. J. Collins (ed.), *Apocalypse: The Morphology of a Genre* (Semeia 14, 1979); *The Apocalyptic Imagination: An Introduction to the Jewish Matrix of Christianity* (1984). M. J. Davidson, *Angels at Qumran. A comparative Study of 1 Enoch 1-36, 72-108 and Sectarian Writings from Qumran* (JSPSup 11, 1992). G. H. Dix, "The Enochic Pentateuch," *JTS* 27 (1926) 29-42. D. Dörfel, *Engel in der apokalyptischen Literatur und ihre theologische Relevanz. Am Beispiel von Ezechiel, Sacharja, Daniel und Erstem Henoch* (1998). J. Flemming, *Das Buch Henoch* (1902). I. Frölich, "The Symbolical Language of the Animal Apocalypse of Enoch (1 Enoch 85-90)," *RevQ* 14/56 (1990) 629-36. J. C. Greenfield and M. E. Stone, "The Enochic Pentateuch and the Date of the Similitudes," *HTR* 70 (1977) 51-65. P. Grelot, "La géographie mythique d'Hénoch et ses sources orientales," *RB* 65 (1958a) 33-69; "La légende d'Hénoch dans les apocryphes et dans la Bible," *RSR* 46 (1958b) 181-210. P. D. Hanson, "Rebellion in Heaven, Azazel, and Euhemeristic Heroes in Enoch 6-11," *JBL* 96 (1977) 195-233. M. Himmelfarb, "A Report on Enoch in Rabbinic Literature," *SBLSP* 13 (1978) 259-70; "The Temple and the Garden of Eden in Ezekiel, the Book of the Watchers, and the Wisdom of Ben Sira," *Sacred Places and Profane*

Spaces: Essays in the Geographics of Judaism, Christianity, and Islam (ed. J. Scott and P. Simpson-Housely; Contributions to the Study of Religion 30, 1991) 63-78; *Ascent to Heaven in Jewish and Christian Apocalypses* (1993). **R. V. Huggins,** "Noah and the Giants: A Response to John C. Reeves," *JBL* 114 (1995) 103-110. **E. Isaac,** *OTP* (1983) 1.5-89. **H. L. Jansen,** *Die Henochgestalt: Eine vergleichende religionsgeschichtliche Untersuchung* (1939). **M. A. Knibb,** *The Ethiopic Book of Enoch: A New Edition in the Light of the Aramaic Dead Sea Fragments* (1978); "Christian Adoption and Transmission of Jewish Pseudepigrapha: The Case of 1 Enoch," *JSJ* 22 (2001) 396-415. **R. Laurence,** *The Book of Enoch the Prophet* (Secret Doctrine Reference Series, 1821); *Libri Enoch Versio Aethiopica* (1838). **H. J. Lawlor,** "Early Citations from the Book of Enoch," *JP* 25 (1897) 164-225. **F. Martin,** *Le livre d'Hénoch* (1906). J. T. Milik, *The Books of Enoch: Aramaic Fragments of Qumran Cave 4* (1976). **G. W. E. Nickelsburg,** "Apocalyptic and Myth in 1 Enoch 6-11," *JBL* 96 (1977) 383-405; *Jewish Literature Between the Bible and the Mishnah* (1981*a*); "The Books of Enoch in Recent Research," *RelSRev* 7 (1981*b*) 210-17; "Enoch, Levi, and Peter: Recipients of Revelation in Upper Galilee," *JBL* 100 (1981*c*) 575-600; "Social Aspects of Palestinian Jewish Apocalypticism," *Apocalypticism in the Mediterranean World and the Near East* (ed. D. Hellholm, 1983); "Two Enochic Manuscripts: Unstudied Evidence for Egyptian Christianity," *Of Scribes and Scrolls: Studies on the Hebrew Bible, Intertestamental Judaism, and Christian Origins* (ed. H. W. Attridge, J. J. Collins, and T. H. Tobin, Resources in Religion 1, 1990) 251-60; "The Apocalyptic Construction of Reality in 1 Enoch." *Mysteries and Revelations: Apocalyptic Studies since the Uppsala Colloquium* (ed. J. J. Collins and J. H. Charlesworth, JSPSup 9, 1991) 51-64; "Scripture in 1 Enoch and 1 Enoch as Scripture," *Texts and Contexts: Biblical Texts in their Textual and Situational Contexts. Essays in Honor of Lars Hartman* (ed. T. Fornberg, D. Hellholm, et al., 1995) 333-54; "Enochic Wisdom: An Alternative to the Mosaic Torah?" *Hesed Ve-Emet. Studies in Honor of Ernest S. Frerichs* (ed. J. Magness and S. Gittin, 1998) 123-32; "'Enoch' as Scientist, Sage, and Prophet: Content, Function, and Authorship in 1 Enoch," *SBLSP* 38 (1999) 203-30; "Two Enochic Manuscripts: Unstudied Evidence for Egyptian Christianity," *Of Scribes and Scrolls* (ed. H. J. Attridge et al., 1990); "The Nature and Function of Revelation in 1 Enoch, Jubilees, and some Qumranic Documents," *Pseudepigraphic Perspectives: the Apocrypha and Pseudepigrapha in light of the Dead Sea* (ed. E. G. Chazon and M. E. Stone, 1999) 91-119; *1 Enoch 1: A Commentary on the Book of 1 Enoch, Chapters 1-36; 81-108* (Hermeneia, 2001). **D. C. Olson,** "Recovering the original sequence of 1 Enoch 91-93," *JSP* 11 (1993) 69-94. **A. A. Orlov,** "Overshadowed by Enoch's Greatness: 'Two Tablets' Traditions from the Book of Giants to *Palaea Historica*," *JSJ* 32 (2001) 137-58. **É. Puech,** "Les fragments 1 à 3 du Livre des Géants de la grotte 6 (pap 6Q8)," *RevQ* 19/74 (1999) 227-38; *Qumrân grotte 4 XXII Textes Araméns Première Parte 4Q529-549* (DJD 31, 2001) 9-115. **J. C. Reeves,** *Jewish Lore in Manichaean Cosmogony: Studies in the Book of Giants Traditions* (HUCM 14, 1992); "Utnapishtim in the Book of Giants?" *JBL* 112 (1993) 110-15; "Giants, Book of," *EDSS* (2000) 309-11. **E. Schürer,** *HJPAJC*, vol. 3.1 (rev. and ed. G. Vermes et al., 1986). **E. Sjöberg,** *Der Menschensohn im äthiopischen Henochbuch* (1946). **P. O. Skjaerv,** "Iranian Epic and the Manichean Book of Giants. Irano-Manichaica III." *Acta Orientalia Academiae Scientiarum Hungaricae* 48 (1995) 187-223. **M. E. Stone,** "Lists of Revealed Things in the Apocalyptic Literature," *Magnalia Dei* (ed. F. M. Cross et al., 1976) 414-52; "The Book of Enoch and Judaism in the Third Century BCE," *CBQ* 40 (1978) 479-92. **L. T. Stuckenbruck,** *The Book of Giants from Qumran: Texts, Translation and Commentary* (TSAJ 63, 1997); "The Sequencing of Fragments Belonging to the Qumran Book of Giants: An Inquiry into the Structure and Purpose of an Early Jewish Composition," *JSP* 16 (1997) 3-24; "The 'Angels' and 'Giants' of Genesis 6:1-4 in Second and Third Century BCE Jewish Interpretation: Reflections on the Posture of Early Apocalyptic Traditions" *DSD* 7 (2000) 354-77. **D. W. Suter,** "Fallen Angel,

Fallen Priest: The Problem of Family Purity in 1 Enoch 6-16," *HUCA* 50 (1979) 115-35; "Weighed in the Balance: The Similitudes of Enoch in Recent Discussion," *RelSRev* 7 (1981) 217-21. **E. J. C. Tigchelaar,** *Prophets of Old and the Day of the End: Zechariah, the Book of Watchers and Apocalyptic* (OtSt 35, 1996); "Eden and Paradise: The Garden Motif in Some Early Jewish Texts (1 Enoch and Other Texts Found at Qumran," *Paradise Interpreted: Representations of Biblical Paradise in Judaism and Christianity* (ed. G. P. Luttikhuisen, Themes in Biblical Narrative Jewish and Christian Traditions 2, 1999) 37-62. **P. A. Tiller,** *A Commentary on the Animal Apocalypse of I Enoch* (SBLEJL 4, 1993). **J. C. VanderKam,** *Enoch and the Growth of an Apocalyptic Tradition* (CBQMS 16, 1984*a*); "Biblical Interpretation in 1 Enoch and Jubilees," *The Pseudepigrapha and Early Biblical Interpretation_*(ed. J. H. Charlesworth and C. A. Evans, JSPSup 14, *SSEJC* 2, 1993) 96-125; *Enoch, a Man for All Generations* (1995); "1 Enoch, Enochic Motifs, and Enoch in Early Christian Literature," *The Jewish Apocalyptic Heritage in Early Christianity* (ed. J. C. VanderKam and W. Adler, CRINT 3.4, 1996) 32-100.

M. HIMMELFARB

PSEUDEPIGRAPHA

Enoch, Second Book of

Slavonic Enoch or *2 Enoch* draws on traditions about the antediluvian patriarch of Gen 5:24 related to those found in sections of *1 Enoch*, recasting them in the light of its own cosmology and ethical concerns (G. Nickelsburg 1981, 185; M. Himmelfarb 1993, 37-41, 83-87). The work first came to the attention of scholars outside Russia at the end of the nineteenth century. The two English editions of R. Charles[§] (1896; 1913) distinguish a long form and a short form of the work, offering a single manuscript for each. Both Charles and G. Bonwetsch (1896), the first German translator, considered the short version a condensation of the long, although Charles also argued that the long version contained many interpolations. In Charles's view, the author of the work was an Egyptian Jew who wrote in Greek while the temple was still standing; he thought some parts of the work, however, were originally written in Hebrew. Charles based his claims on parallels to the thought of Jewish writers in Egypt and native Egyptian elements; he dated the work by its reference to animal sacrifice. There are no clear ancient testimonies to the work, and the earliest manuscripts are late medieval. No Greek (or Hebrew) fragments survive.

In 1918 a strong challenge to Charles's views appeared in the unlikely forum of an astronomy journal. A. Maunder (1918) argued that the astronomy and calendrical system of the fourth heaven required a much later date than Charles proposed, the end of the fifth century at the earliest, as well as a Christian author. Taking seriously the absence of any clear traces of the supposed Greek original, she suggested that *2 Enoch* was composed in Slavonic by the dualist Bogomil between the twelfth and the fifteenth centuries. While Charles and later others (e.g., A. Rubinstein 1962; E. Turdeanu 1981) argued convincingly against the claim of Bogomil features, Maunder's astronomical arguments were accepted by the historian of ancient astronomy J. Fotheringham and by K. Lake[§].

The next era in the study of *2 Enoch* began several decades later with the 1952 French translation of A. Vaillant, who claimed the short version as the translation of the original Greek. (He was anticipated in his preference for the short version by N. Schmidt, who had argued for its priority in 1921, although on quite different grounds.) The long manuscripts form two groups representing different stages of recension, which took place in Slavonic. Vaillant argued that *2 Enoch* was a "Jewish-Christian" work, by which he meant a work written by an early Christian but containing Jewish traditions. The arguments Vaillant offered in favor of this view are not very compelling and were criticized even by Rubinstein, who concurred with the conclusion of Christian authorship. Unlike Charles and Bonwetsch, Vaillant treated the Melchizedek section at the end of *2 Enoch* as an integral part of the work.

All subsequent scholarship on *2 Enoch* has drawn on Vaillant's textual work. In his study of the Aramaic fragments of *1 Enoch* from Qumran, J. Milik (1976) accepts Vaillant's view of the short version as more original, but dates *2 Enoch* to the ninth or tenth century on the basis of astronomical considerations and other arguments that have not been widely accepted.

The two most recent translators of *2 Enoch* differ considerably in their approach to the textual problems. A. Pennington (1984) translates the short version from Vaillant's edition. F. Andersen (1983), on the other hand, argues that the textual situation is so complex that no conclusions are possible at this stage of study. He distinguishes four recensions: very long, long, short, and very short. His translation offers a synoptic presentation of a very long manuscript and a short manuscript. Both manuscripts include a form of the Melchizedek story.

Despite almost a century of scholarship that has called into question many of Charles's basic assumptions, most scholars continue to maintain his view that *2 Enoch* is the work of an Egyptian Jew writing in Greek before the destruction of the temple. This view may be correct, but it has not been adequately grounded. Progress in the study of the date and provenance of the work is linked to further progress on its central textual problems, but there is reason for optimism: Since the fall of the Soviet Union and the emergence of a new group of scholars of ancient Judaism and Christianity well-versed in Slavonic and familiar with the history of the Russian church, *2 Enoch* may receive the attention it deserves.

Bibliography: F. I. Andersen, "*2 (Slavonic Apocalypse of) Enoch,*" *OTP* (1983) 1:91-221. **R. Bauckham,** "Early Jewish Visions of Hell,"*JTS* 41 (1990) 355-385. **G. N. Bonwetsch,** *Das slavische Henochbuch* (Abhandlungen der königlichen Gesellschaft der Wissenschaften zu Göttingen, Philologisch-historische Klasse, NF 1, 3, 1896); *Die Bücher der Geheimnisse Henochs: Das sogenannte slavische Henochbuch* (TU 44.2, 1922). **C. Böttrich,** "Recent Studies in the Slavonic Book of Enoch," *JSP* 9 (1991) 35-42; *Weltweisheit— Menschheitsethik—Urkult. Studien zum slavischen Henochbuch* (WUNT II 50, 1992); *Adam als Mikrokosmos. Eine Untersuchung zum slavischen Henochbuch,* (Judentum und Umwelt 59, 1994); "Die Vögel des Himmels haben ihn begraben," *Überlieferungen zu Abels Bestattung und zur Ätiologie des Grabes* (Schriften des Institutum Judaicum Delitzschianum 3, 1995); "Beobachtungen zum Midrasch vom 'Leben Henochs', *Mitteilungen und Beiträge der Forschungsstelle Judentum an der Theologischen Fakultät Leipzig* 10 (1996) 44-83; "Das slavische Henochbuch," *JSHRZ* 5 (1995) 781-1040; "Astrologie in der Henochtradition," *ZAW* 88 (1997) 222-245; "Frühjüdische Weisheitstraditionen im slavischen Henochbuch und in Qumran," *The Wisdom Texts from Qumran and the Development of Sapiential Thought* (ed. C. Hempel, A. Lange, and H. Lichtenberger, BETL 159, 2002) 297-321. **R. H. Charles,** "The Date and Place of Writing of the *Slavonic Enoch,*" *JTS* 22 (1921) 161-63. **R. H. Charles** (ed.), *The Book of the Secrets of Enoch* (tr. **W. R. Morfill,** 1896). **R. H. Charles** (ed.), "*2 Enoch or the Book of the Secrets of Enoch,*" *APOT* (tr. **N. Forbes,** 1913) 2:425-69. **M. Delcor,** "La naissance merveilleuse de Melchiséedeq d'après l'Henoch slave," *Kecharitonene. Mélanges R. Laurentin* (ed. C. Augustin et al., 1990) 217-229. U. Fischer, *Eschatologie und Jenseitserwartung im hellenistischen Diasporajudentum* (BZNW 44, 1978) 37-70. **J. K. Fotheringham,** "The Date and Place of Writing of the Slavonic Enoch," *JTS* 20 (1919) 252; "The Easter Calendar and the Slavonic Enoch," *JTS* 23 (1922) 49-56. **C. A. Gieschen,** "The different Functions of a Similar Melchizedek Tradition in 2 Enoch and the Epistle to the Hebrews," *Early Christian Interpretation of the Scriptures of Israel: Investigation and Proposals* (ed. C. Evans and J. A. Sanders, JSNTSup 148, 1997) 364-379. **M. Himmelfarb,** *Ascent to Heaven in Jewish and Christian Apocalypses* (1993) 37-41, 83-87. **K. Lake,** "The Date of the Slavonic Enoch," review of *Die Bücher der Geheimnisse Henochs* by G. N. Bonwetsch, *HTR* 16 (1923) 397-98. **A. S. D. Maunder,** "The Date and Place of Writing of the Slavonic Book of Enoch," *The Observatory* 41 (1918) 309-16. **J. T. Milik,** *The Books of Enoch: Aramaic Fragments of Qumran Cave* (1976) 107-16. **G. W. E. Nickelsburg,** *Jewish Literature Between the Bible and the Mishnah* (1981) 185-88. **A. A. Orlov,** "Titles of Enoch-Metatron in 2 Enoch," *JSP* 18 (1998) 71-86. **A. Pennington,** *AOT* (1984) 321-62. **M. Philonenko,** "La cosmogonie du `Livre des secrets d'H‚noch,'" *Religions en Égypte hellénistique et romaine* (1969) 109-16. **S. Pines,** "Eschatology and the Concept of Time in the *Slavonic Book of Enoch,*" *Types of Redemption* (Numen Sup. 18, ed. R. J. Z. Werblowsky and C. J. Bleeker, 1970) 72-87. **A. Rubinstein,** "Observations on the *Slavonic Book of Enoch,*" *JJS* 13 (1962) 1-21. **N. Schmidt,** "The Two Recensions of *Slavonic Enoch,*" *JAOS* 41 (1921) 307-12. **A. Theocharis,** "La notion de la Sagesse dans le Livre des Secrets d'Henoch ou d'Henoch slave," *Kleronomia* 18 (1990) 95-100. **E. Turdeanu,** *Apocryphes slaves et roumains de l'Ancien Testament* (1981) 37-43, 404-35. **A. Vaillant** (ed. and tr.), *Le livre des secrets d'Hénoch* (Textes publiés par l'Institut d'Études slaves 4, 1952).

M. HIMMELFARB

PSEUDEPIGRAPHA

Enoch, Third Book of

The earliest evidence for interest in *3 Enoch* comes from the twelfth and thirteenth centuries when the German Hasidim studied and copied it along with other *hekhalot* texts. There are extensive quotations from *3 Enoch* in the work of Eleazar of Worms, one of the great exponents of German Hasidism[§].

The modern study of *3 Enoch* begins with H. Graetz[§] (1859), although Graetz did not know the book itself but only works dependent on it. Graetz understood Enoch/Metatron speculation to be closely linked to the *Shi'ur Qomah* literature—descriptions of the size of God's limbs and their names—because of the appearance of Metatron in the *Shi'ur Qomah*. For Graetz, the anthropomorphism of the *Shi'ur Qomah* was a "monstrosity" (1859, 115). He preferred to see it, not as an internal development of rabbinic thought, but as the result of the influence of certain strands of Islam (1859, 108, 115-18), pointing out that the idea of the transformation of Enoch into Metatron is in conflict with the much more negative view of Enoch in classical rabbinic literature. He saw the positive picture of Enoch as another result of Islamic influence, since Enoch was highly regarded in the Quran (107-8; Quranic and Islamic Interpretation*[§]). The influence of Islam, along with the *terminus ante quem* provided by quotations in Karaite[§] polemical works, led Graetz to a date in the early ninth century for these mystical texts (1859, 113).

The first extended treatment of *3 Enoch* itself was H. Odeberg's critical edition and English translation with introduction and notes (1928). It was Odeberg who gave the work the title *3 Enoch*; in the manuscripts it is usually called *Sefer Hekhalot*. In opposition to his predecessors, Odeberg placed the work in the second half of the third century and argued that, while the rabbis would not have looked on the composition with favor, the compilers of the work viewed themselves as rabbinic Jews. Odeberg saw the transformation of Enoch as a development of a theme found in the early Jewish apocalypses (Apocalypticism*[§]) and related the figure of Metatron to apocalyptic and Gnostic*[§] traditions.

G. Scholem, the great student of Jewish mysticism, was highly critical of Odeberg's choice of manuscript base for his edition but praised Odeberg's rejection of a date in the gaonic period (1929-30, 1930). Scholem dated *3 Enoch* later than did Odeberg, to the fifth or sixth century, since he saw it as one of the latest of the *hekhalot* texts. Although he recognized striking parallels to contemporary Gnostic literature and magical texts for *3 Enoch* as for other *hekhalot* texts, he also saw continuity with early Jewish apocalyptic traditions. Like Odeberg, he understood the transformation of Enoch into Metatron as a development of these traditions. Scholem also insisted on the "halakhic character" of the *hekhalot* literature, despite certain conflicts with the outlook of the classical rabbinic works (1954, 1965, 1974).

Perhaps the most thorough examination of *3 Enoch* since Scholem is that of P. Alexander (1977, 1983). Alexander concurs with Scholem on a fifth- or sixth-century date and suggests a Babylonian provenance. In terms not unlike Odeberg's, he locates the work on the fringes of rabbinic Judaism.

It has long been noted that, because of its use of Enoch traditions, *3 Enoch* is closer than the other *hekhalot* texts to the early Jewish apocalypses. Recent work on the *hekhalot* literature has shown that the work is unusual in other respects as well. In his articles (e.g., 1983) and his synoptic edition of the *hekhalot* texts (with M. Schlüter and H. von Mutius, 1981) P. Schäfer has called into question old assumptions about the limits and identity of individual *hekhalot* works by showing the fluidity of the forms they take in the manuscripts. *Third Enoch* stands out as a relatively well-defined redactional entity. Further, Schäfer (1992) and D. Halperin (1988) have challenged Scholem's view that heavenly ascent is the dominant theme of the *hekhalot* literature, emphasizing the central importance of the adjuration of angels for the revelation of magical secrets as well. Almost alone of the *hekhalot* texts, *3 Enoch* fits Scholem's model: It is an account of heavenly ascent, but it lacks adjurations completely (Schäfer 1992, 123-38, 147-48). Schäfer notes, however, that a Geniza fragment contains astrological material (1992, 137-38, 147-48; for the fragment, Schäfer 1984, 137). This fragment, which appears to come from an earlier stage of the text, raises interesting questions about the process by which *3 Enoch* reached its present form in which magical elements are absent. The process of the work's development, its place among the *hekhalot* texts, and its relation to earlier traditions will continue to occupy scholars.

Bibliography: P. Alexander, "The Historical Setting of the Hebrew Book of Enoch," *JJS* 28 (1977) 156-80; "*3 (Hebrew Apocalypse of) Enoch*," *OTP*, 1:223-315. **H. Graetz,** "Die mystische Literatur in der gaonäishcen Epoche," *MGWJ* 8 (1859) 67-78, 103-18, 140-53. **J. Greenfield,** "Prolegomenon," *3 Enoch or the Hebrew Book of Enoch* (ed. H. Odeberg; repr. 1973). **D. Halperin,** *The Faces of the Chariot: Early Jewish Responses to Ezekiel's Vision* (TSAJ 16, 1988). **H. Odeberg,** *3 Enoch or the Hebrew Book of Enoch* (1928; repr. 1973). **P. Schäfer,** "Tradition and Redaction in Hekhalot Literature," *JSJ* 14 (1983) 172-81; *The Hidden and Manifest God: Some Major Themes in Early Jewish Mysticism* (1992); (ed.), *Geniza-Fragmente zur Hekhalot-Literatur* (TSAJ 6, 1984). P. Schäfer (ed., in collaboration with M. Schlüter and H. G. von Mutius), *Synopse zur Hekhalot Literatur* (TSAJ 2, 1981). **P. Schäfer and K. Herman**n (eds.), *Übersetzung der Hekhalot-Literatur* (TSAJ 46, 1995) 1.1-80. **G. Scholem,** review of *3 Enoch or the Hebrew Book of Enoch* by H. Odeberg, *Kirjath Sepher* 6 (1929-30) 62-64; review of *3 Enoch or the Hebrew Book of Enoch* by H. Odeberg, *OLZ* 33 (1930) 193-97; *Major Trends in Jewish Mysticism* (1954[3]); *Jewish Gnosticism, Merkabah Mysticism, and Talmudic Tradition* (1965[2]); *Kabbalah* (1974).

M. HIMMELFARB

PSEUDEPIGRAPHA

Jubilees, Book of

The *Book of Jubilees* relates a divine revelation, mediated to Moses through an "angel of the presence," about events from the creation of the world to the law-giving on Mt. Sinai. Its name derives from the author's use of a chronological system (Chronology, Hebrew Bible*[§]) whose principal unit is a forty-nine-year period called a "jubilee." The book was known to and used by the community of the Dead Sea Scrolls*[§] (CD 16:2-4), and some of its extra-biblical stories, like the war between Jacob and Esau, are reflected in midrashic literature (A. Jellinek 1855; B. Beer 1856; A. Epstein 1890, 1891; R. Charles 1902; and K. Berger 1981). It also exercised a certain influence in some Christian circles. Several chronographers (e.g., G. Syncellus fl. c. 800) used material, particularly from its earlier chapters, to supplement information from Genesis and Exodus; and in the Abyssinian Church it achieved canonical status (Canon of the Bible*[§]) as part of the Hebrew Bible. It has also enjoyed high repute among the Jews of Ethiopia. At some point, however, the text of the book was lost in most centers of Jewish and Christian populations.

Western scholars were aware that a *Book of Jubilees* once existed because of references to and citations from it in Greek and Latin sources. (Many of these were collected already by J. Fabricius[§] in 1722; see also H. Rönsch 1874; R. Charles 1895, 1902; A. Denis 1970; and J. VanderKam 1989). Modern Western study of the text began when a missionary named J. Krapff had a copy made of an Ethiopic manuscript of *Jubilees* (called *kufālē* [division(s)]; Ethiopian Biblical Interpretation*[§]); this he brought to Tübingen, where H. Ewald[§] announced its existence in 1844. Ewald's student A. Dllmann[§] translated this very poor copy in 1850-51 and, in 1859, made this translation and a manuscript from the Bibliothèque Nationale in Paris the foundations for the first critical edition of the Ethiopic text. Charles[§] prepared the next critical edition in 1895, using Dillmann's edition for the evidence from his two manuscripts along with two other much better copies that had subsequently been identified. Those who translated the book after 1895 worked from Charles's text (e.g., E. Littmann 1900; C. Rabin, *AOT*; and O. Wintermute, *OTP*), with the exception of Berger, who had access not only to these manuscripts but also to other copies that were made available after Charles's labors. Charles personally published the most widely used translations of his edition (1902, 1913). A new edition and translation of the Ethiopic version has been published by VanderKam (1989), who based his text on collations of fifteen of the twenty-seven currently available Ethiopic manuscripts of *Jubilees*. The edition includes the Hebrew texts available at the time of publication and all of the other versional evidence.

Since the last quarter of the nineteenth century, additional textual data for the book have come to light, although the Ethiopic remains the only complete version extant. A. Ceriani (1861-63) published twenty-five sections of a very literal Latin rendering (fifth-sixth cent. C.E.) of the book; he found these in a palimpsest manuscript that was used for copying excerpts from Augustine's[§] writings. The sections preserve nearly one-third of the full text (for the text with notes, see Rönsch 1874; Charles 1895; VanderKam 1989). E. Tisserant (1921) later isolated a series of citations from *Jubilees* in an anonymous Syriac chronicle ad annum 1234. Fragments of fifteen manuscripts of the Hebrew of *Jubilees* have been found among the Dead Sea Scrolls, and all of these have been published (see VanderKam 1977 and VanderKam and Milik 1994). The Hebrew fragments indicate that the Ethiopic version is generally a faithful rendering of the original. From all of the extant textual data scholars have concluded that the book was composed in Hebrew, translated into Greek, and from Greek was rendered into Latin and Ethiopic. Whether there was ever a Syriac translation and, if so, whether it was based directly on a Hebrew base (as Tisserant argued) remain open questions.

There has been a long debate about the date of *Jubilees* and about the party affiliation of its author (the issue of the place where it was written is related to these). Although the earliest Western students of the book were aware that its views about legal and theological matters differed on many points (e.g., its 364-day solar calendar) from those of the Pharisees and Sadducees, there was uncertainty about the identity of the group to which the author belonged. Jellinek attributed it to an Essene author who opposed pharisaic calendrical views; Beer thought that the writer was a Dosithean who wrote in Egypt; Z. Frankel (1856) believed he was a Jewish Hellenist associated with the temple of Onias in Egypt; and A. Büchler (1930), who noted Jubilees' agreements with the LXX (Septuagint*§) and evidence of Hellenistic customs in the book, considered the author a descendant of one of the ten tribes who wrote in Greek and lived near Samaritan territory somewhere in Egypt or in a part of Palestine under Egyptian influence. The scholars who have devoted detailed analyses to the book's legal material have also insisted that the author could not have been either a Pharisee or a Sadducee but must have belonged to a sect (L. Finkelstein 1923; C. Albeck 1930).

During the latter half of the nineteenth century, most experts followed Dillmann (1851) in dating *Jubilees* to the first century C.E. Dillmann argued—from the book's dependence on the books of Enoch§, from the dependence of the *Testaments of the Twelve Patriarchs*§ on *Jubilees*, and from the fact that *Jubilees* presupposed an existing temple—that the book was written before 70 C.E. Rönsch and W. Singer (1898) accepted Dillmann's dating and added that anti-Christian elements could be detected in the book. A significant change in the dating discussion took place when F. Bohn (1900) defended a time of composition in the mid-second century B.C.E., drawing this conclusion, in part, from his belief that passages like the story about the battle between Jacob and Esau reflected events during the Maccabean wars. He also maintained that the author was one of the Hasidim.

Charles, however, preferred a date between 135 and 96 B.C.E. (1902) or 109 and 5 B.C.E. (1913). He too saw reflections of Maccabean events in the book but was convinced that the author was a Pharisee, giving him warrant for dating the book, which he considered pro-Maccabean, before the schism between Alexander Jannaeus and the Pharisees. His view, despite its obvious flaws, has dominated the field until the last decades of the twentieth century (VanderKam 1977 for bibliography), and some writers (e.g., M. Testuz 1960) still accept it. Nevertheless, two prominent scholars insisted for some time that *Jubilees* was written at a much earlier time. S. Zeitlin dated the book to the fifth-fourth centuries B.C.E. for several reasons, one of which was his assumption that its opposition to some Pentateuchal legislation would have been impossible once the Pentateuch achieved normative status. W. F. Albright§ (1957²) originally thought that the book was written in the fourth-third centuries B.C.E., but after the Qumran discoveries he lowered his dating to c. 175 B.C.E.

Since 1960, a growing number of scholars have returned to the date that Bohn had defended—the mid-second century B.C.E. (e.g., Berger, VanderKam). The Dead Sea Scrolls, which many experts think were written by Essenes, show very close affinities with *Jubilees* in many areas such as the 364-day solar calendar (Testuz; B. Noack 1957-58; VanderKam 1977), and one of the Qumran copies—4Q216 (4QJubilees[a])—may date to a time around 125 B.C.E. (VanderKam and Milik 1994). Yet the book does not appear to have been written by someone who had separated from Jewish society. This suggests that it was written before the Essene exodus to Qumran (perhaps before c. 135 B.C.E.). G. Nickelsburg (1981), J. Goldstein (1983), and M. Knibb (1989) have held that it antedates 167 since it shows no awareness of Antiochus IV's prohibition of Judaism (earlier, Finkelstein had opted for a similar time). It does seem likely, however, that the author knew the Enochic Book of Dreams (*1 Enoch* 83-90), which was written in the late 160s B.C.E. Judea now seems the only likely place of composition, while new insights into the variety of biblical texts in this area in the second pre-Christian century allow one to explain textual agreements between *Jubilees* and the LXX from the author's use of a Palestinian form of the biblical text.

The greatest subject of scholarly interest in the book since the discovery of the scrolls has been its calendar, which it shares with *1 Enoch* and several of the Qumran texts. *Jubilees'* statements about the number of days in the year (364), in each month (eight months of thirty days, four of thirty-one), and the dates for crucial festivals such as Weeks (month 3, day 15) are clear; but pre-Qumran scholars had a difficult time with some of them because of their assumptions about calendrical possibilities. The pivotal issue has been the date of the Festival of Weeks. Leviticus 23:15-16 places it on the fiftieth day after the presentation of "the sheaf of the wave offering." There was extensive discussion in ancient Judaism about precisely when the sheaf was to be presented, and several options were chosen by different groups. Epstein, who (from his knowledge of these ancient debates) thought that it could not have been presented later than the twenty-second of the first month, concluded that if Weeks was to be celebrated on 3/15, *Jubilees* must operate with a religious calendar that used months of twenty-eight days (so also Finkelstein) in addition to a civil arrangement consisting of twelve months of either thirty or thirty-one days that the book describes. A. Jaubert (1953), however, clarified the book's calendrical data and drew the proper conclusion that, in this system, the sheaf of the wave offering (which is not mentioned in *Jubilees*) was presented on 1/26, a date that is verified by some calendar texts from Qumran. There is now a large bibliography about this calendar and about the possibility that it was used as the official cultic calendar in Jerusalem early in the Second Temple period. To date, though, no decisive evidence for or against its official use has been found.

The religious teachings of *Jubilees* and some instances of the ways in which its author has edited biblical sections have received extended treatment. Testuz published a study of the book's views about creation and the world, the history of the world and Israel, the world of the spirits, the two moral ways, the revealed calendar, and the last times (with a chapter comparing *Jubilees* and the major Qumran scrolls). G. Davenport (1971) devoted a monograph to the book's eschatology in which he traced a development through what he concluded were the three stages of the book's evolution: from a largely non-eschatological "angelic discourse" (written in the early second cent.), through redaction 1 (which turned the original into an eschatological message of hope during the Maccabean revolt), to redaction 2 (between 140 and 104 B.C.E., which emphasized the sanctuary and looked for a cosmic renewal that would focus on Jerusalem and Zion). E. Schwarz (1982) has analyzed the book's teachings about Israel's separation from the peoples and traced the history of this tradition, which began with the Hebrew Bible commands that Israel was to form no treaties with the nations of Canaan. Studies of selected sections of the book include O. Steck's examination of the creation section in *Jub.* 2 (1977; cf. VanderKam 1994b) and J. Endres's monograph on the highly significant Jacob cycle (1986). The Levi expansions (*Jub.* 30-32) within the Jacob stories have elicited detailed analyses that relate them to the Levi-priestly tradition (J. Kugel 1993; R. Kugler 1996). The sabbatical chronological system, which applies the biblical legislation about the year of Jubilee to the nation rather than to the individual, has also been researched (VanderKam 1995).

The book's unity has been denied by Testuz, E. Wiesenberg (1961-62), and Davenport (for his view, see the preceding paragraph). Testuz, who agrees with Charles's dating of the book, thought that *Jub.* 1:7-25, 28; 23:11-32; and 24:28b-30—which manifest an "ardent hatred" for the nations—were added between the years 65-38 B.C.E., while Wiesenberg based his view of a subsequent Zealot reviser (first cent. C.E.) on chronological problems. These writers have failed, however, to convince other scholars of their positions (for brief reviews, see R. Pummer 1979; VanderKam 1981).

Although much exegetical work remains to be done (no commentary has ever been written on *Jubilees*), there is widespread agreement that the book was written by a single Jewish writer in Judea between 175 and 140 B.C.E. and that the author belonged to the religious movement, some of whose members later withdrew from Jewish society and produced the Dead Sea Scrolls.

Bibliography: M. Albani et al, (eds.), *Studies in the Book of Jubilees* (TSAJ 65, 1997). **C. Albeck,** *Das Buch der Jubiläen und die Halacha* (BHWJ 27, 1930). **W. F. Albright,** *From the Stone Age to Christianity* (1957²). **B. Beer,** *Das Buch der Jubiläen und sein Verhältniss zu den Midraschim: Ein Beitrag zur Orientalischen Sagen- und Alterthums Kunde* (1856). **K. Berger,** *Das Buch der Jubiläen* (JSHRZ II.3, 1981). **M. J. Bernstein, Moshe J.,** "'Walking in the Festivals of the Gentiles' 4QPHosea/a 2.15-17 and Jubilees 6.34-38," *JSP* 9 (1991) 21-34. **F. Bohn,** "Die Bedeutung des Buches der Jubiläen," *TSK* 73 (1900) 167-84. **A. Büchler,** "Studies in the Book of Jubilees," *REJ* 82 (1926) 253-74; "Traces des idées et des coutumes helénistiques dans le Livre des Jubilés," *REJ* 89 (1930) 321-48. **A. M. Ceriani,** *Monumenta Sacra et Profana* (2 vols. 1861-63). **R. H. Charles,** "The Book of Jubilees, Translated from a Text Based on Two Hitherto Uncollated Ethiopic MSS," *JQR* 5 (1893) 703-8; "The Book of Jubilees, Translated from a Text Based on Two Hitherto Uncollated Ethiopic MSS," *JQR* 6 (1895) 184-217, 710-45; "The Book of Jubilees, Translated from a Text Based on Two Hitherto Uncollated Ethiopic MSS," *JQR* 7 (1895) 297-328; *Maṣḥafa Kufālē or the Ethiopic Version of the Hebrew Book of Jubilees* (Anecdota Oxoniensia, 1895); *The Book of Jubilees or the Little Genesis* (1902); *APOT* (1913) 2:1-82. **G. L. Davenport,** *The Eschatology of the Book of Jubilees* (SPB 20, 1971). **A. M. Denis,** "Liber Jubilaeorum," *Fragmenta Pseudepigraphorum Quae Supersunt Graeca* (PVTG 3, 1970) 70-102. **A. Dillmann,** "Das Buch der Jubiläen oder die kleine Genesis," *Jahrbuch der biblischen Wissenschaft* 2 (1850) 230-56; "Das Buch der Jubiläen oder die kleine Genesis," *Jahrbuch der biblischen Wissenschaft* 3 (1851) 1-96; *Maṣḥafa Kufālē sive Liber Jubilaeorum* (1859). **J. Endres,** *Biblical Interpretation in the Book of Jubilees* (CBQMS 18, 1986). **A. Epstein,** "Le Livre des Jubilés, Philon, et le Midrasch Tadsch," *REJ* 21 (1890) 80-97; "Le Livre des Jubilés, Philon, et le Midrasch Tadsch," *REJ* 22 (1891) 1-25. **H. Ewald,** "Über die Aethiopischen Handschriften zu Tübingen," *Zeitschrift für die Kunde des Morgenlandes* 5 (1844) 164-201. **J. A. Fabricius,** "Parva Genesis," *Codex Pseudepigraphus Veteris Testamenti* (2 vols. 1722) 1:849-64, 2:120-22. **L. Finkelstein,** "The Book of Jubilees and the Rabbinic Halaka," *HTR* 16 (1923) 39-61. **Z. Frankel,** "Das Buch der Jubiläen," *MGWJ* 5 (1856) 311-16, 380-400. **J. Goldstein,** "The Date of the Book of Jubilees," *PAAJR* 50 (1983) 63-86. **B. Halpern-Amarnu,** "The Naming of Levi in the Book of Jubilees" *Pseudepigraphic Perspectives: the Apocrypha and Pseudepigrapha in light of the Dead Sea Scrolls* (ed. E. G. Chazon and M. E. Stone, 1999) 59-69. **M. Himmelfarb,** "Sexual Relations and Purity in the Temple Scroll and the Book of Jubilees," *DSD* 6 (1999) 11-36. **A. Jaubert,** "Le calendrier des Jubilés et de la sect de Qumran: Ses origines bibliques," *VT* 3 (1953) 250-64. **A. Jellinek,** *Bet ha-Midrasch* (Dritter Theil, 1855) ix-xiii. **M. Knibb,** "Jubilees and the Origins of the Qumran Community" (inaugural lecture in the Dept. of Bib. Stud., King's College London, Jan. 17, 1989). **J. Kugel,** "Levi's Elevation to the Priesthood in Second Temple Writings," *HTR* 86 (1993) 1-64. **R. Kugler,** *From Patriarch to Priest: The Levi-Priestly Tradition from Aramaic Levi to Testament of Levi* (SBLEJL 9, 1996). **E. Littmann,** "Das Buch der Jubiläen," *ABAPAT* (1900) 2:31-119. **G. W. E. Nickelsburg,** *Jewish Literature Between the Bible and the Mishnah* (1981); "The Nature and Function of Revelation in 1 Enoch, Jubilees, and some Qumranic Documents," *Pseudepigraphic Perspectives: the Apocrypha and Pseudepigrapha in light of the Dead Sea Scrolls* (ed. E. G. Chazon and M. E. Stone, 1999) 91-119. **B. Noack,** "Qumran and the Book of Jubilees," *SEA* 22-23 (1957-58) 191-207. **R. Pummer,** "The Book of Jubilees and the Samaritans," *EgT* 10 (1979) 147-78. **C. Rabin,** *AOT* (1984) 1-139. **H. Rönsch,** *Das Buch der Jubiläen oder die Kleine Genesis* (1874; repr.

1970). **J. Rook,** "The Names of the Wives from Adam to Abraham in the Book of Jubilees," *JSP* 7 (1990) 105—117. **G. Schelbert,** *TRE* 17 (1988) 285-89. **E. Schwarz,** *Identität durch Abgrenzung: Abgrenzungsprozesse in Israel im 2. vorchristlichen Jahrhundert und ihre traditionsgeschichtlichen Voraussetzungen. Zugleich ein Beitrag zur Erforschung des Jubiläenbuches* (1982). **W. Singer,** *Das Buch der Jubiläen oder die Leptogenesis* (1898). **O. Steck,** "Die Aufnahme von Genesis 1 in Jubiläen 2 und 4 Esra 6," *JSJ* 8 (1977) 154-82. **M. Testuz,** *Les idées religieuses du Livre des Jubilés* (1960). **E. Tisserant,** "Fragments syriaques du Livre des Jubilés," *RB* 30 (1921) 55-86, 206-32. **J. VanderKam,** *Textual and Historical Studies in the Book of Jubilees* (HSM 14, 1977); "The Putative Author of the Book of Jubilees," *JSS* 26 (1981) 209-17; (ed. and tr.), *The Book of Jubilees* (2 vols. CSCO 510-11, Scriptores Aethiopici 87-88, 1989); "Das chronologisches Konzept des Jubiläenbuches," *ZAW* 107 (1995) 80-100; "The Angel Story in the Book of Jubilees," *Pseudepigraphic Perspectives: the Apocrypha and Pseudepigrapha in light of the Dead Sea Scrolls* (ed. E. G. Chazon, M. E. Stone, 1999) 151-170; "Biblical Interpretation in 1 Enoch and Jubilees," in *The Pseudepigrapha and Early Biblical Intrepretation* (ed. J. H. Charlesworth and C. A. Evans, JSPSup 14, 1993) 96-125. **J. VanderKam and J. T. Milik,** "The First Jubilees Manuscript from Qumran Cave 4: A Preliminary Publication," *JBL* 110 (1991) 243-70; *DJD* 13 (1994) 1-140; "Genesis 1 in Jubilees 2," *DSD* 1 (1994) 300-21. **E. Wiesenberg,** "The Jubilee of Jubilees," *RevQ* 3 (1961-1962) 3-40. **O. Wintermute,** *OTP* (1983) 2:35-142. **S. Zeitlin,** "The Book of Jubilees: Its Character and Its Significance," *JQR* 30 (1939-40) 1-31; "The Book of Jubilees and the Pentateuch," *JQR* 48 (1957) 218-35.

J. C. VanderKam

PSEUDEPIGRAPHA

Psalms of Solomon

The so-called *Psalms of Solomon*, eighteen of which survive, exist in Greek and Syriac. The origin of these writings is obscure. First noted in Codex Alexandrinus (fifth cent. C.E.) under the title the "Eighteen Psalms of Solomon," they are listed sequentially after the Hebrew Bible, New Testament, and Clementine epistles; however, the actual text is missing from the codex. For instance, Codex Sinaiticus is missing twelve pages that might have contained these psalms (*OTP*, 2.639). Pseudo-Athanasius's *Synopsis Sanctae Scripturae* listed them with the *Odes of Solomon* after Maccabees and before Susanna as antilegomena of the Hebrew Bible (sixth cent C.E.). A similar account is offered in the *List of Sixty Books*. Anastasius Sinaita's *Quaestiones et Responsiones* lists this text among the Pseudepigrapha*§ between the *Assumption of Moses* and the *Apocalypse of Elijah* in the list of sixty books found at the end of that work. The *Stichometry of Nicephorus* (ninth cent. C.E.) lists the *Psalms of Solomon* with the Apocrypha between Esther and Ecclesiastes. According to G. Gray, the fifty-ninth canon of the Council of Laodicea and Ambrose*§ (*Preface to the Book of Psalms*) appears to argue against the use of these psalms by the church (1913, 2.627); however, this text is not mentioned in the Gelasian Decree. S. Brock notes (1984, 649) that the two surviving Syriac manuscripts begin with the *Odes of Solomon* and then proceed with the Psalms—under the name *Odes* and *Psalms of Solomon*—as though the *Odes* and the *Psalms* are two parts of one work. In these manuscripts, *Pss. Sol* 1 is Psalm 43.

The first edition of the *Psalms*, published c. 1626 by J. de la Cerda, was marred by the fact that it was based on a faulty copy of one of the principal Greek manuscripts. By the time Gray did his translation, eight Greek manuscripts were known to exist; ten manuscripts and one fragment are now known. Gray regarded Codex (Romanus) Vaticanus Gr. 336 as the oldest and noted that some of the Greek manuscripts appear to be copies of other extant manuscripts (1913, 2.626). Two manuscripts and two fragments are extant in Syriac. It is generally believed that the Syriac is based on the Greek, and Gray held that the Syriac manuscripts are an incomplete version of the Greek (1913, 2.626). Brock agrees, while R. Wright argues that the Syriac is closest to Greek MS 253, although the Syriac also shows close ties to Greek MSS 769 and 336 (1983,2.640). J. Trafton (1981) argues that the Syriac may descend from the Hebrew.

Likewise, on the basis of the Syriac text, Gray proposed that Hebrew and not Greek was the original language because (1) the Greek shows a number of "strange expressions" that characterize Greek versions of existing Hebrew texts; (2) some of these strange expressions can be explained as blunders in translation from Hebrew to Greek; and, (3) in some places, the rhythm of the Hebrew can still be heard in the Greek (1913, 2.627 and 625). In varying forms this analysis has been supported by Trafton, H. Ryle and M. James (1891), and R. Hann (1982). D. Flusser, following S. Holm-Nielsen (1977), also argued for a Hebrew original. Only A. Hilgenfeld§, on the basis of apparent quotes from the Septuagint§ in this text, argued for a Greek original.

Ryle and James, citing apparent parallels between *3 Baruch* and *Psalms of Solomon*, maintained that this text was translated into Greek before 70 C.E. (1913, 628). According to them, the author was an Essene. Gray dated the *Psalms* to the first century B.C.E. and is followed by D. Russell (1987), who cites apparent historical allusions in the text (2:3031, death of Pompey); Flusser; G. Nickelsburg (1981); and Brock. Flusser and Holm-Nielsen, argue that this text was authored in Jerusalem by a latter-day member of the Hasidim (Hasidism*§); Flusser submits that the critique of the Hasmoneans and Pharisees in the text supports this. Nickelsburg holds that the author was a Pharisee (1981, 203), and Brock suggests that the text was written in Palestine by an unknown author (1984, 651-52).

Following Russell, Wright points to allusions in the text to the death of Pompey in 48 B.C.E. Accordingly, he limits the date of authorship to between 125 B.C.E. and the first century C.E. in broad terms, in more narrow terms to between 70 and 45 B.C.E. (1983, 2.641). These psalms have been so edited that it is not possible to tell if they were originally written by one or many authors; thus Wright considers them the product of a community and concludes that the author was either an Essene or a Pharisee. His analysis is amended by J. Charlesworth, who argues that it is impossible to determine the special socioreligious group to which the author belonged, if the author belonged to one at all (1983, 2.642).

Because of strong similarities between *Psalms of Solomon* and the biblical psalter Wright holds that the *Psalms of Solomon* are a "conscious imitation" of the Davidic psalter (1983, 2.646). There are certain stylistic and formal parallels. For example the "patina" that is the mark of liturgical use is missing; instead, a thin veneer covers historical allusions. Furthermore, parallels to Pss 28 and 72, Isa, Ezek, Lam, Prov, and perhaps Luke have been noted. Following O. Eissfeldt* and A. Dupont-Sommer (1987), Wright maintains that there are strong parallels to Qumran (1983, 2.642; Dead Sea Scrolls*§) and points out that 1 Baruch*§ quotes these psalms. Gray has noted parallels to *Pistis Sophia*.

Bibliography: K. Atkinson, "Towards a redating of the Psalms of Solomon: Implications for understanding the *Sitz im Leben* of an unknown Jewish sect," *JSP* 17 (1998) 95-112. **W. Baars,** "A New Fragment of the Greek Version of the Psalms of Solomon," *VT* 11 (1961) 441-44; "An Additional Fragment of the Syriac Version of the Psalms of Solomon," *VT* 11 (1961) 222-23; "Psalms of Solomon," *The OT in Syriac According to the Peshitta Version* (1972) pt. 4, fasc. 6, i-vi, 1-27. **S. P. Brock,** "The Psalms of Solomon," *AOT* (1984) 649-82. **A. M. Denis,** "Les Psaumes de Salomon," *IPAT* (1970) 60-64. **M. Ehrmann,** *Klagephänomene in zwischentesta-mentlicher Literatur* (1997) 241-314. **D. Flusser,** *Bermerkungen eines Juden zur christlichen Theologie* (Abhandlungen zum christlich-jüdisch Dialog 16, 1984); *Jewish Sources in Early Christianity* (ET 1989). **O. von Gebhardt,** *Psalmoi Solomontos: Die Psalmen Salomo's zum ersten Male mit Benutzung der Athoshandschriften und des Codex Casanatensis herausgegeben* (TU 13.2, 1895). **G. B. Gray,** "The Psalms of Solomon," *APOT* (1913) 2.625-52. **R. R. Hann,** *The Manuscript History of the Psalms of Solomon* (SBLSCS 13, 1982). **J. R. Harris,** *The Odes and Psalms of Solomon, Now First Published from the Syriac Version* (1909, 1911). **J. R. Harris and A. Mingana,** *The Odes and Psalms of Solomon, Re-edited for the Governors of the John Rylands Library* (2 vols. 1916-20). **A. Hilgenfeld,** *Die jüdische Apokalyptik in ihrer geschichtlichen Entwickelung* (1857); *Novum Testamentum extra Canonem receptum* (4 vols. 1866). **S. Holm-Nielsen,** "Die Psalmen Salomos," *JSHRZ* 4 (1977) 51-112. **R. Kittel,** "Die Psalmen Salomo," *APAT* (1900) 2:127-48. **K. G. Kuhn,** "Die alteste Textgestalt der Psalmen Salomos" (BWANT 73, 1937). **J. La Cerda,** *Adversaria sacra . . . accessit . . . Psalterium Salomonis* (1626). **G. W. E. Nickelsburg,** *Jewish Literature Between the Bible and the Mishnah: A Historical and Literary Introduction* (1981) 203-12. **J. O'Dell,** "The Religious Background of the Psalms of Solomon (Re-evaluated in the Light of the Qumran Texts)," *RevQ* 3 (1961) 241-57. **A. Rahlfs,** *Septuaginta* (2 vols. 1935, 1952⁵) 2:471-89. **D. S. Russell,** *The OT Pseudepigrapha: Patriarchs and Prophets in Early Judaism* (1987). **H. E. Ryle and M. R. James,** *Psalmoi Solomontos: Psalms of the Pharisees, Commonly Called the Psalms of Solomon. The Text Newly Revised from All the Manuscripts* (1891). **E. Schürer,** *HJPAJC* (1986) 3:192-97. **S. von Stemm,** *Der betende Sünder vor Gott: Studien zu Vergebungsvorstellungen in urchristlichen und frühjüdischen Texten* (AGJU 45, 1999) 181-208. **J. L. Trafton,** "A Critical Examination of the Syriac Version of the Psalms of Solomon" (diss., Duke University, 1981);

The Syriac Version of the Psalms of Solomon: A Critical Evaluation (SBLSCS 11, 1985); "The Psalms of Solomon in recent research," *JSP* 12 (1994) 3-19. **J. Viteau,** *Les Psaumes de Salomon* (1911). **M. Winninge,** *Sinners and the righteous. A comparative study of the psalms of Solomon and Paul's letters* (1995). **R. B. Wright,** "Psalms of Solomon," *OTP* (1983) 2:639-70; "The Psalms of Solomon, the Pharisees, and the Essenes," *IOSCS* (SBLSCS 2, 1972) 136-47.

G. T. MILAZZO

PSEUDEPIGRAPHA

Pseudo-Philo

The *Liber Antiquitatum Biblicarum* (*L.A.B.*) of Pseudo-Philo is a retelling of the biblical narrative from Adam to Saul's death, focusing particularly on Israel's leaders. It is extant only in Latin; but its original language was Hebrew, which was translated into Greek and then into Latin (D. Harrington 1970). The text survives in eighteen full and three fragmentary copies dating from the eleventh to the fifteenth centuries. Harrington supplies a critical text and apparatus (1976), and this text has been translated into English (Harrington 1985) and French (J. Cazeaux 1976). Earlier translations were by M. James (Eng., 1971) and C. Dietzfelbinger (Ger., 1975). H. Jacobson (1996) presents a translation based on his reconstruction of the Hebrew original.

Scholars disagree over whether the extant text is complete. Since the narrative breaks off abruptly in the middle of a dialogue between Saul and the son of the Amalekite king in chap. 65, some scholars think that the original ending, perhaps including David's accession to the throne, has been lost. Others disagree. There are other places where text may be missing as well. There is general consensus that *L.A.B.* was written in the first or early second century C.E., with debate centering on whether it was written before or after the destruction of the temple in 70 C.E. In 1996 Jacobson argued that it was written after the destruction, while Harrington has consistently maintained that it was written before. It is most likely that *L.A.B.* was written in Palestine, given its use of a Palestinian text-type (Harrington 1971), the similarities of some of its ideas to those of *2 Baruch* and *4 Ezra* (both originating in Palestine at a time just after the destruction), and its knowledge of Palestinian geography.

The term Pseudo-Philo is due to the fact that the text was transmitted in a Latin translation of the works of Philo of Alexandria*§. Philo is not the author, however, since this document's approach to the Bible is very unlike his allegorical interpretation, conflicts with him on specific points, and seems to have been written in Palestine in Hebrew. The specific identity of the author is unknown, but it is clear that he was learned in biblical and extra-biblical traditions. There have been many attempts to assign Pseudo-Philo's work to a particular group within first-century Judaism, but such studies have not won acceptance. Thus Pseudo-Philo's importance is as a witness to the thought and methods of biblical interpretation of mainstream Palestinian Judaism, perhaps as found in Palestinian synagogues of the first century.

Pseudo-Philo's genre is a rewriting of the biblical story (G. Vermes 1961) similar to that of Josephus's§ *Antiquities* (see also *Jubilees*†§ and the *Genesis Apocryphon*). It was perhaps because of this similarity that the work was called *Liber Antiquitatum Biblicarum*, a title that is not original. Pseudo-Philo does not pursue later midrashic methodology (see Midrash*§) of providing verse-by-verse commentary on the biblical text; rather, he freely adapts the biblical story to its own purposes. In the process of retelling he liberally adds, subtracts, condenses, and rewrites, sometimes using existing traditions and at other times apparently exercising some creativity. The degree to which details of the retelling depend on the Bible is debated, with Jacobson and R. Bauckham (1983) seeing a maximum of such use. Pseudo-Philo is important as a source of extra-biblical Jewish traditions, some unique to this work, and as an example of how the Bible was interpreted by Palestinian Jews of the first century.

Modern interest in Pseudo-Philo was sparked in 1898 with the publication of L. Cohn's article. Important commentaries include L. Feldman's (1971) prolegomenon to James's 1917 work, C. Perrot and P. M. Bogaert (1976), and Jacobson. Literary and theological issues are treated by F. Murphy (1993) and E. Reinmuth (1994), who provide an extensive comparison with Luke-Acts.

Pseudo-Philo's main themes and concerns are assurance that God is faithful to Israel despite

321

its sins and despite Israel's sufferings; moral causality, where good is consistently rewarded and evil punished; condemnation of idolatry and of mixed marriages; repentance; leadership in Israel (G. Nickelsburg 1980); and eschatology, particularly as it bears on moral causality. There is no messianic interest.

Bibliography: R. Bauckham, *"The Liber Antiquitatum Biblicarum* of Pseudo-Philo and the Gospels as 'Midrash,'" *Gospel Perspectives III: Studies in Midrash and Historiography* (ed. R. T. France and D. Wenham, 1983) 33-76. **R. Burnette-Bletsch,** "At the Hands of a Woman: Rewriting Jael in Pseudo-Philo," *JSP* 17 (1998) 53 - 64. **L. Cohn,** "An Apocryphal Work Ascribed to Philo of Alexandria," *JQR* o.s. 10 (1898) 277-332. **J. E. Cook,** "Pseudo-Philo's Song of Hannah: Testament of a Mother in Israel," *JSP* 9 (1991) 103—114. **A. M. Denis,** *Concordance latine des pseudépigraphes d'Ancien Testament* (1993) 565-598. **M. T. DesCamp,** "Why are these women here? An examintion of the sociological setting of Pseudo-Philo through comparative reading," *JSP* 16 (1997) 53-80. **C. Dietzfelbinger,** "Pseudo-Philo: *Antiquitates Biblicae (Liber Antiquitatum Biblicarum),"* *JSHRZ* (ed. W. G. Kümmel, 1975) 2:91-271. **L. Feldman,** "Prolegomenon," *The Biblical Antiquities of Philo* (ed. M. R. James, 1971). **B. N Fisk,** "Scripture Shaping Scripture: The Interpretive Role of Biblical Citations in Pseudo-Philo's Episode of the Golden Calf," *JSP* 17 (1998) 3-23. **D. J. Harrington,** "The Original Language of Pseudo-Philo's *Liber Antiquitatum Biblicarum,"* *HTR* 63 (1970) 503-14; "The Biblical Text of Pseudo-Philo's *Liber Antiquitatum Biblicarum,"* *CBQ* 33 (1971) 1-17; "Pseudo-Philo," *OTP* (1985) 2.297-377; "A Decade of Research on Pseudo-Philo's Biblical Antiquities," *JSP* 2 (1988) 3-12. **D. J. Harrington and J. Cazeaux,** *Pseudo-Philon: Les Antiquités Bibliques,* vol. 1, *Introduction et Texte Critiques* (SC, 1976). **C. T. R. Hayward,** "The Figure of Adam in Pseudo-Philo's Biblical Antiquities," *JSJ* 23 (1992) 1-20. **H. Howard,** "The *Liber Antiquitatum Biblicarum* and Tammuz," *JSP* 8 (1991) 63-65. **H. M. Jackson,** "Echoes and Demons in the Pseudo-Philonic Liber Antiquitatum Biblicarum," *JSJ* 27 (1996) 1-20. **H. Jacobson,** *A Commentary on Pseudo-Philo's "Liber Antiquitatum Biblicarum"* (AGJU 31, 1996). **M. R. James,** *The Biblical Antiquities of Philo* (1971). **B. von Kienle,** *Feuermale: Studien zur Wortfelddimension "Feuer" in den Synoptikern, im pseudophilonischen Liber Antiquitatum Biblicarum und im 4. Esra* (1993). **F. J. Murphy,** *Pseudo-Philo: Rewriting the Bible* (1993); "The Martial Option in Pseudo-Philo," *CBQ* 57 (1995) 676-688. **G. W. E. Nickelsburg,** "Good and Bad Leaders in Pseudo-Philo's *Liber Antiquitatum Biblicarum,"* *Ideal Figures in Ancient Judaism: Profiles and Paradigms* (ed. J. J. Collins and G. W. E. Nickelsburg, 1980) 49-65. **C. Perrot and P. M. Bogaert,** *Pseudo-Philon: Les Antiquités Bibliques,* vol. 2, *Introduction Littéraire, Commentaire et Index* (SC, 1976). **E. Reinmuth,** *Pseudo-Philo und Lukas: Studien zum "Liber Antiquitatum Biblicarum" und seiner Bedeutung für die Interpretation des Lukanischen Doppelwerks* (WUNT 74, 1994). **E. R. Smits,** "Contribution to the History of Pseudo-Philo's *Liber Antiquitatum Biblicarum* in the Middle Ages," *JSJ* 23 (1992) 197-216. **G. Vermes,** *Scripture and Tradition in Judaism: Haggadic Studies* (1961). **M. Vogel,** "Geschichtstheologie bei Pseudo-Philo, *Liber Antiquitatum Biblicarum,"* (F. Siegert, J. U. Kalms, Vorträge aus dem Institutum Judaicum Delitzschianum, 1998) 175-195.

F. J. MURPHY

PSEUDEPIGRAPHA

Sibylline Oracles

These texts constitute a corpus of Jewish and Christian writings ranging from the second century B.C.E. to the seventh century C.E. Since they are presented as oracles of the pagan Sibyl, there is no overt appeal to Scripture; the degree of actual dependence on the Bible varies considerably. There is virtually none in books 11–14, which consist of political prophecy and commentary from the Roman period. In the earlier books, the influence of the Bible appears in three ways: paraphrase of biblical accounts; adherence to biblical ethical norms; and use of biblical motifs, especially in eschatological passages.

The most extensive biblical paraphrase is found in *Sib. Or.* 1, a Jewish work from around the turn of the era that was updated by a Christian in the second century. The Jewish stratum contains a lengthy paraphrase of Genesis, retelling the stories of Adam and Eve and, in greater detail, the flood. Two modifications of the biblical account are typical of the oracles: Noah is presented as a preacher of repentance (1:150-198), and the narrative contains some details that diverge from Genesis but correspond to Babylonian myth (1:233-257). The interest in primeval history is also typical: The flood is featured again in *Sib. Or.* 7:7-15, and *Sib. Or.* 3:97-109 tells of the tower of Babel, which is recalled again in *Sib. Or.* 8:4-5. In contrast, the summary of Israelite history in *Sib. Or.* 3:218-94 is exceptional. The Christian stratum contains a synthetic presentation of the life of Christ (1:324-84). Similar summaries of the gospel story are found in *Sib. Or.* 6, a short, twenty-eight-verse hymn to Christ, and in *Sib. Or* 8:251-336. There is a reference to the baptism of Christ in *Sib. Or* 7:66-67.

The ethics of the *Oracles* are representative of the Hellenistic Jewish Diaspora. Little attention is paid to the ritual requirements of Judaism. The primary emphasis falls on polemic against idolatry and against sexual abuses (adultery and homosexuality). The attacks on idolatry and the emphatic monotheism are often reminiscent of Second Isaiah (Isa 40–45; e.g., *Sib. Or.* 3:13-14; 6:29; 8:377) but are not so much indebted to specific biblical texts as to the common understanding of biblical law in Hellenistic Judaism. The oracles also contain a tradition of criticism of Rome on grounds of injustice (*Sib. Or.* 3:350-380; 5:162-178; 8:73-109), which is informed in a general way by the prophetic tradition (e.g., by allusions to Isa 14 and 47; Prophecy and Prophets, Hebrew Bible*[§]).

Biblical influence is also apparent in the eschatological passages of the oracles. *Sibylline Oracle* 3 draws on the motifs of the Gentile assault on Jerusalem (3:660-668; cf. Pss 2, 48), the eschatological transformation of the earth (3:785-795; cf. Isa 11), and the eschatological pilgrimage of the Gentiles to Jerusalem (3:710-723; cf. Isa 2; Mic 4). Other books adopt the apocalyptic belief (Apocalypticism*[§]) in resurrection. In *Sib. Or.* 2:221-226 and 4:181 the formulation echoes Ezekiel 37. *Sibylline Oracle* 2:154-213 has lengthy accounts of the signs of the end that partially parallel those of Mark 13, etc., while the scene of Christ enthroned for judgment, *Sib. Or.* 2:241-243, is reminiscent of Matt 25:31. In all these cases, however, the biblical references are intertwined with a wealth of other allusions to traditions attested in the Pseudepigrapha*[§] and in pagan sources. The sibyl speaks with an independent prophetic voice and is never simply an interpreter of inherited Scripture.

Bibliography: J. J. Collins, "Sibylline Oracles," *OTP* (1983) 1:317-472; "The Sibylline Oracles," *Jewish Writings of the Second Temple Period: Apocrypha, Pseudepigrapha, Qumran, Sectarian Writings, Philo, Josephus* (ed. M. E. Stone, CRINT 2, 2, 1984) 357-81; "The Development of the Sibylline Tradition," *ANRW* II.20.1 (1987) 421-59; "Sibylline Oracles," *ABD* (1992) 6:2-7. **L. Kreitzer,** "Sibylline Oracles 8, the Roman Imperial Adventus Coinage and the Apocalypse of John," *JSP* 4 (1989) 69-85. **H. Merkel,** "Sibyllinen," *JSHRZ* (1998) 5.1041-1148. **V. Nikiprowetzky,** "La Sibylle juive et le 'Troisième Livre' des 'Pseudo-Oracles Sibyllins' depuis Charles Alexandre," *ANRW* II.20.1 (1987) 460-542. **J. C. O'Neill,** "The Man from Heaven: SibOr 5.256-259," *JSP* 9 (1991) 87-102. **W. K. Whitney,** "The Place of the 'Wild Beast Hunt' of *Sib. Or.* 3,806 in Biblical and Rabbinic Tradition," *JSJ* 25 (1994) 68 -81.

J. J. COLLINS

PSEUDEPIGRAPHA

Testament of Moses

The *Testament of Moses* is a pseudepigraph (Pseudepigrapha*§) extant in a single poorly preserved, incomplete, and at times illegible Latin palimpsest discovered in the Ambrosian Library of Milan and published by A. Ceriani in 1861. The manuscript dates from the sixth century C.E., but orthography and style indicate that it is a copy of an early fifth-century writing. The Latin text is clearly a translation from a Greek document that may be as early as the late first or early second century C.E. Most early editors assumed that Greek was the original language, but it is now universally agreed that the Greek text available to the Latin translator was itself a translation of a Semitic writing. Whether the Semitic text was Aramaic or Hebrew remains a matter of dispute, but the latter is more probable.

Ceriani, on the basis of quotations in the *Acts of the Council of Nicea* and in scattered patristic references (Origen *De principiis,* 3.2.1), entitled the manuscript *The Assumption of Moses,* an account of Moses' being taken directly to heaven rather than dying a natural death. This story is well known in many Jewish writings and is probably referred to in the letter of Jude (v. 9). The present text, however, knows nothing of an assumption and clearly indicates that Moses died a natural death (1:15; 10:11-14). Some ancient quotations and stichometries (lists of books and the number of lines contained in each) refer to both an *Assumption* and a *Testament of Moses,* although the relationship between them is not clear. It has been proposed that they were two distinct works, a single work consisting of two sections, or two separate works that were subsequently joined together. It is more prudent, lacking manuscript evidence, to refer to the present manuscript as the *Testament of Moses* and leave open the question as to whether a section following the mutilated ending of 12:13 did contain an account of Moses' assumption.

The *Testament of Moses* belongs to the well-known testament genre, the last words of an ancient worthy to his people, family, or successor (*Testaments of the Twelve Patriarchs*). Moses reveals to Joshua the history of the community from his day until the end time, which, in the present form of the text, is the immediately post-Herodian age (the first half of the first century C.E.). The theology of the book is not particularly original, combining in a somewhat awkward fashion the apocalyptic emphasis (Apocalypticism*§) on God's predestination of all things with the Deuteronomistic formula that the fate of the community results from their obedience or disobedience to God's laws. The former is dominant, in accord with the pragmatic purpose of apocalyptic to give hope to people living in a dying age.

From the time of the manuscript's discovery, scholars have differed widely as to its date of composition and its religious provenance (R. Charles 1897 for nineteenth-century discussion). Dates from the time of Antiochus Epiphanes (175-164/163 B.C.E.) to the Bar Kokhba revolt (132-135 C.E.) and religious groups as varied as the Sadducees and the Samaritans have had proponents. Charles's§ conclusion that the work was written in the first half of the first century C.E. and represented a "quietistic Pharisaism" reflects a general consensus that prevailed until the recent contention for an Antiochan dating, with the consequent location of the work in the somewhat amorphous group of Hasidim (Hasidism*§) who figured in the Maccabean revolt (168-165 B.C.E.).

Both Charles's arguments for a first-century C.E. date and arguments for an Antiochian date must come to terms with an internal chronological inconsistency in the present form of the manuscript. Chapter 6 clearly alludes to Herodian times, but chaps. 7 and 8 are best understood within an Antiochian context. Charles solved the problem by assuming that there had been a dislocation in the transmission of the manuscript, while proponents of an essentially Antiochian dating maintain that chap. 6 is a first-century C.E. interpolation into an earlier document. Both dislocation and interpolation are well attested elsewhere, and no *a priori* conclusion may be drawn. It seems more prudent to suggest that the *Testament of Moses* is a first-century C.E. document, with the recognition that some of its contents may have had a considerable earlier history in either oral or written form. Increasing awareness of the complex nature of Judaism in this period mitigates against attempting to identify precisely the group within which the document arose. We may conclude, at most, that it has affinities most clearly with the Pharisees, the Essenes, and other groups that evolved from the broader circles of the Hasidim.

Some recent scholars, following J. Licht (1961), have proposed that a distinctive theological theme is to be found in the story of the Levite Taxo and his seven sons, who chose to die rather than abandon their faith (chap. 9), and in the following eschatological hymn depicting the divine visitation (10:1-10). They propose that the vow of martyrdom is designed to provoke God to intervene on behalf of his people and thus to inaugurate the eschatological era. This is a possible conclusion, but the story of Taxo and his sons may also be understood as a typical martyrdom story well known elsewhere in the literature of the period (e.g., 2 Macc 6:18–7:42).

The *Testament of Moses* may have been known and used by several New Testament writers. Attention is called most often to Matt 24:19-21 (with parallels); Acts 7:36-43; 2 Pet 2:13; and Jude 9, 12–13, 16. The clearest allusion is Jude 9, but it apparently refers to the assumption of Moses, which is not found in the extant testament. Although definite dependence cannot be proven, the possible use of the work in some Christian circles as scripture underlines the fluidity of Canon[§] in the late first and early second centuries C.E.

Bibliography: E. **Brandenburger**, "Die Himmelfahrt des Moses," *JSHRZ* 5.2 (1976) 57-84. R. **Carlson**, "Vengeance and Angelic Mediation in *Testament of Moses* 9 and 10," *JBL* 101 (1982) 85-95. R. H. **Charles,** *The Assumption of Moses* (1897); *"The Assumption of Moses,"* *APOT* (1913) 2:407-24. A.-M. **Denis**, *Introduction aux pseudepigraphes grecs d'Ancien Testament* (1970) 128-41; *Fragmenta pseudepigraphorum quae supersunt graeca* (PVTG 3, 1970) 63-67. E. M. **Laperrousaz,** *Le Testament de Moïse (généralment appel, "Assomption de Moïse" : Traduction avec introduction et notes* (*Sem* 19, 1970). C. J. **Lattey,** "The Messianic Expectation in *The Assumption of Moses,*" *CBQ* 4 (1942) 9-21. J. **Licht,** "Taxo, or the Apocalyptic Doctrine of Vengeance," *JJS* 12 (1961) 95-103. D. P. **Moessner,** "Suffering, Intercession, and Eschatological Atonement: An Uncommon Common View in the *Testament of Moses* and in Luke-Acts," *The Pseudepigrapha and Early Biblical Interpretation* (ed. J. Charlesworth, 1993) 202-27. G. E. W. **Nickelsburg** (ed.), *Studies on the "Testament of Moses"* (1973). J. **Priest,** "Some Reflections on *The Assumption of Moses,*" *PerR St* 4 (1977) 92-111; *"The Testament of Moses,"* *OTP* (1983) 1:919-34. H. H. **Rowley,** *The Relevance of Apocalyptic: A Study of Jewish and Christian Apocalypses from Daniel to the Revelation* (1963) 106-10, 149-56. E. **Schürer,** *HJPAJC* 3 (1986) 278-88. J. P. M. **Sweet,** *"The Assumption of Moses,"* *OTA* (1984) 600-616. J. **Tromp, Johannes:** *The Assumption of Moses: A Critical Edition with* (SVTP 10, 1993). D. H. **Wallace,** "The Semitic Origin of the *Testament of Moses,*" *TZ* 11 (1955) 321-28. S. **Zeitlin,** *"The Assumption of Moses* and the Bar Kokhba Revolt," *JQR* 38 (1947-48) 1-45.

J. F. PRIEST

PSEUDEPIGRAPHA

Testaments of the Twelve Patriarchs

1. *Introduction.* Since the discovery of Hebrew and Aramaic testamentary texts in the Cairo Geniza (*T. Levi*), in the medieval manuscripts of the *Chronicle of Jerahmeel* (*T. Naph.*), in the *Midrash Wa-yissa'u* (*T. Jud.*), and in the Qumran caves (*T. Levi, T. Naph.*, etc.), it has become increasingly important to distinguish between the composition and transmission of separate testaments and their compilation as the document known as the *Testaments of the Twelve Patriarchs* (*T. 12 Patr.*). Some of the testaments may have been composed at the same time they were compiled in the *T. 12 Patr.*; others appear to be redacted forms of earlier works.

2. *Interpretation of the Bible in the Testaments of the Twelve Patriarchs. a. The use of Genesis.* Some of the characteristics associated with each patriarch are derived from Jacob's blessing of his sons (Gen 49:2-27); e.g., Judah recalls Gen 49:10 in *T. Jud.* 22:3. Jacob's blessings are explicitly referred to in *T. Sim.* 5:6 (see Gen 49:7). More often the exhortation of each patriarch is linked to an incident narrated in Genesis; e.g., Reuben's act of immorality with Bilhah (Gen 35:22) is used as the basis for his instruction against sexual promiscuity. Several details in *T. 12 Patr.* reflect the Genesis traditions as they were adapted in other texts; e.g., the twelve trees to be presented to God are mentioned in *T. Levi* 9:12 (expanding Gen 28:10-11) and enumerated in *Jubilees* 21:12.

b. Other biblical interpretation. The *T. 12 Patr.* barely alludes to specific commandments of the law, being more concerned with universal values and virtues, which are sometimes expressed in phraseology that echoes the wisdom literature. Pentateuchal texts are occasionally used: e.g., *T. Levi* 8:2-10 adapts Exod 28:3-43 in its description of the priestly garments; and *T. Iss.* 5:2 echoes Deut 6:5 and Lev 19:18 in its formulation of what the law involves. There are some allusions to prophetic texts: e.g., the description of Joseph being in the cistern for three days and nights (*T. Zeb.* 4:4) recalls Jonah 1:17; and Naphtali's vision on the Mount of Olives (*T. Naph.* 5:1) recalls Zech 14:4-7. M. de Jonge (1953) has discerned two literary patterns in several of the testaments: One is sin-exile-return, an eschatological variant of the Deuteronomistic*[§] view of history; the other is the juxtaposition of Levi and Judah based on Gen 49:5-12 and prophetic texts that link priesthood and kingship (e.g., Jer 33:17-18; Zech 4:14).

c. Biblical models. The principal models within the Bible for the testaments are the farewell blessings of Jacob (Gen 49:2-27) and Moses (Deut 33:2-29); both of these also link all the tribes together, as does *T. 12 Patr.* In the Second Temple period the genre of testament, a farewell speech in a deathbed scene, began to emerge in its own right (Tob 4:2-21; 14:3-11; 1 Macc 2:49-70). It was very adaptable, providing a form for many kinds of exhortatory and predictive content.

d. The New Testament. Many of the allusions in the *T. 12 Patr.* to the prophetic books occur in passages that may be Christian interpolations, since similar prophetic passages feature in various New Testament writings: e.g., Joel's Prophecy*[§] of the pouring out of the Spirit (Joel 2:28-29; cf. Acts 2:17-21) is used in association with the star from Jacob and the shoot of God (*T. Jud.* 24:1-5; cf. Rev 22:16). Some possible allusions to the New Testament apart from the interpolations support the position of those who see the whole work as a Christian composition.

On the other hand, those who argue for Jewish authorship point to how phrases from the non-interpolated passages are cited in the New Testament. J. Grabe used the possible citation of *T. Levi* 6:11 in 1 Thess 2:16 to support his 1698 proposal that *T. 12 Patr.* was pre-Christian.

e. Enoch. Several times in *T. 12 Patr.* there are references to the books of Enoch*[§], which clearly possessed scriptural Authority*§ for the compiler. Yet few of the allusions can be matched to Enoch materials known in Aramaic, Greek, or Ethiopic; e.g., in *T. Dan* 5:6 Dan's sons are aligned with Satan, according to the *Book of Enoch the Righteous*, an association perhaps based on Judg 18:11-31 and Jer 8:16-17. R. Charles§ thought the phrasing might reflect *2 Enoch* 18:3, but this is unlikely. This use of Enoch drew the attention of several medieval and Renaissance scholars to *T. 12 Patr.* as they attempted to explain the similar authoritative use of Enoch in Jude.

3. *The Interpretation of the* Testaments of the Twelve Patriarchs. *a. Early redaction.* If the *T. 12 Patr.* is not regarded as a coherent composition by a single author, then its earliest interpretation is found in the process of redaction through which it assumed its present form. If some or all of the testaments were originally Jewish compositions, then it could be that the first stage of redaction was undertaken by Jews who added apocalyptic passages (Apocalypticism*§), perhaps to make the testaments relate more directly to their own religious and political experiences. These same passages contain the most explicit Christian material, which perhaps belongs to a second redactional stage in the early Christian period when Christian interpolations were added: e.g., *T. Jos.* 19:8 reads, "And I saw that a virgin was born from Judah, wearing a linen stole; and from her was born a spotless lamb"; *T. Ben.* 9:3 reads, "The Lord will be abused and will be raised up on wood. And the temple curtain shall be torn." J. Jervell has proposed (1969) that some of these Christian interpolations reflect a theological concern with the salvation of Israel and so should be dated to the first century C.E. Origen§ appears to cite from *T. 12 Patr.* in his *Homilies on Joshua*, thus providing a likely terminus *ad quem* for its composition, although the text known to him may have been different from the Byzantine one established by modern scholars. And *T. Dan* 7:3, which notes how Dan's predictions came true, may be an even later gloss.

b. Thirteenth to seventeenth centuries. M. Paris recorded how R. Grosseteste§, bishop of Lincoln, translated the *T. 12 Patr.* from Greek into Latin in 1242; Grosseteste probably acquired the Greek manuscript from the library of M. Choniates, who until 1204 was archbishop of Athens. Paris noted that the work had been hidden by the Jews but that Greeks had discovered and translated it from Hebrew.

R. Bacon§, writing in 1266-68, noted that each patriarch describes what Christ must fulfill and what should be believed about him. He believed that the testaments are not authentically patriarchal but have an authority based in their wide use as a non-Christian witness to Christian belief, particularly to convert Jews.

Although featured in several sixteenth-century collections, the *T. 12 Patr.* appears to have been commented on only seldom. In 1566 Sixtus of Siena, a converted Jew, referred to them to illuminate the use of Enoch in Jude and noted that they were very old (he may have considered them authentic) and had been translated from Hebrew.

J. Salianus used *T. 12 Patr.* to supplement his history of the period 1770-1625 B.C.E., published in Paris (1619-24). In 1631 the Puritan J. Selden§ commented on the priority of Levi over his brother Judah (*T. Jud.* 21:1-4) and noted that such disorders were clearly not just a recent phenomenon. In the mid-seventeenth century, S. Sgambati, a Jesuit from Naples, was the first to remark explicitly on the work's literary purpose as moral exhortation. The Zurich theologian J. Heidegger not only called into question Salianus's use of the testaments, arguing like several scholars before him that they were inauthentic, but also seems to have been the first to propose that *T. 12 Patr.* was a Christian work falsely ascribed in order to convert Jews, just as the Sibylline Oracles*§ were intended to convert non-Jews. Much of Heidegger's approach is paralleled in the seventeenth-century work of Dutch scholar J. de Mey, who also provided a four-page summary of the testaments and concluded that they were originally written in Greek, not Hebrew. R. Simon§, writing pseudonymously (1687; see H. de Jonge 1975), argued for the work's stylistic unity and for its composition by a Jewish Christian or sectarian; he was the first to propose that it had originally been written in Aramaic (reading Jamnia at *T. Naph.* 6:1 as Aramaic for "sea," preserved as a doublet in the Greek).

The first printed edition of the Greek text appeared in 1698. Its editor, Grabe, argued that the work was Jewish, composed in Hebrew, translated into Greek in the third century B.C.E., and subsequently (first or second cent. C.E.) interpolated by a Christian.

c. Eighteenth and nineteenth centuries. The interpretation of the *T. 12 Patr.* in these two centuries was dominated by consideration of its Christian authorship. In 1713 J. Fabricius[§] argued on stylistic grounds that the testaments were composed by a Christian in Greek and should be associated with the Shepherd of Hermas and the *Sibylline Oracles*; he was supported by A. Gallandi (1709-79). H. Corrodi (1781-83) proposed that *T. 12 Patr.* was a Jewish Christian document, since its militaristic messiah was similar to that of Revelation. This ascription was developed further by C. Nitzsch (1787-1868), who linked the work with early second-century Alexandria, and by I. Dorner[§], whose work provoked a flurry of studies on whether *T. 12 Patr.* was really Jewish Christian or Gentile Christian (or both). The most detailed study was by R. Sinker, who in 1869 published an extensive introduction, concluding that it was a product of Nazarene Jewish Christianity at Pella.

d. F. Schnapp. In 1884, through a rigorous application of Literary*[§] criticism, F. Schnapp proposed that the original *T. 12 Patr.* had consisted of brief narratives about the patriarchs together with corresponding exhortations on virtues and vices; that these had been redacted, first by a Jewish hand, at which stage several passages were added, largely of apocalyptic or messianic character; and second, by a Christian, who altered those same passages with Christian additions. A variation of this view has remained influential, partly because it was popularized by E. Schürer[§] (1886-90) and by Schnapp in E. Kautzsch's[§] German collection of Pseudepigrapha*[§] (1900), and partly because it appeared to be confirmed by F. Conybeare's work on the Armenian*[§] Edschmiadzen manuscript, by M. Gaster's[§] claim (1894) that the Hebrew original of *T. Naph.* was to be found in the *Chronicles of Jerahmeel*, and by the publication in 1900 of the Cairo Geniza Aramaic text parallel to *T. Levi* 9-13.

e. R. Charles and after. In 1908 Charles published both a critical text of *T. 12 Patr.* and the first complete commentary on it. His position was similar to Schnapp's, as refined especially by W. Bousset[§] (1900): He believed there had been an original coherent work authored by an early pro-Maccabean Pharisee into which were interpolated various Jewish additions, mostly from the first century B.C.E., many of which were anti-Maccabean; last, at various times the work was given dogmatic Christian additions.

For over forty years Charles was widely followed. Challenges to the theory of a Jewish origin came only from J. Hunkin and N. Messel. In his extensive literary-critical approach, J. Becker (1970) has outlined in theory what the original Jewish form of the *T. 12 Patr.* might have looked like; to that consistent base text (dated 200-175 B.C.E.) many additions were made, the last being the Christian elements. Through motif analysis A. Hultgard has described (1977-81) three stages: the first is based on anti-Hasmonean Levi material (c. 100 B.C.E.); the second, on additional levitical traditions (1st cent. B.C.E.); the third, on Christian traditions.

f. The Dead Sea Scrolls. The Dead Sea Scrolls*[§] stimulated some scholars, notably A. Dupont-Sommer (1953) and M. Philonenko (1960s), to associate the *T. 12 Patr.* directly with the Qumran community. No direct historical connection can be proved, but the scrolls show that many of the testaments' theological interests, e.g., certain forms of messianic expectation, eschatology, ethical dualism, and angelology, are at home in Judaism and need not be attributed to early Christianity. None of the extant Aramaic (*T. Levi, T. Jud., T. Jos.*) and Hebrew (*T. Naph., T. Jud.*) testaments among the scrolls is the Semitic source for its Greek counterpart in *T. 12 Patr.*, but each provides evidence for the likely Jewish source material available to the compiler and shows that some of the testaments may have had a long compositional and redactional history before all twelve were compiled and edited together. In particular, several different forms of testamentary material are associated with Levi (1Q21, 4Q213, 214, 540, 541), at least one of which is close to *T. Levi* from the Cairo Geniza.

g. *M. de Jonge*. In 1953 de Jonge showed that there was no textual basis for the removal of Christian interpolations. He proposed that *T. 12 Patr.* had received such thorough Christian redaction, with several major sections (e.g., *T. Levi* 3:5-9) being Christian compositions, that the whole is better described as the work of a Christian of the second century C.E. who used much Jewish material (especially in *T. Levi, T. Naph., T. Jud.,* and *T. Reub.*). Although he has revised his position somewhat, he and H. Hollander (1985) still deny the usefulness of literary criticism for understanding the history of the text's redaction. Rather, they insist on a formal approach to the Greek text as it is known now and stress that the diversity of the testaments is largely the result of the wide variety of source material used. De Jonge has also been the driving force behind a new critical edition of the Greek text (1978) in which the reclassification of the extant witnesses is supported by recent study of the Armenian version.

h. *Continuing research*. Further work on the Armenian manuscripts may provide information on the early transmission of the text. The eventual principal editions of all the Dead Sea Scrolls texts will aid in the study of the Jewish sources that indirectly lie behind the Greek *T. 12 Patr.* However, deciding whether *T. 12 Patr.* is a Jewish work with Christian additions or a Christian composition using Jewish sources, and determining its original language, provenance, and date will most likely be answered only after further study of all the Apocrypha*[§] and Pseudepigrapha.

Bibliography: J. **Becker,** *Untersuchungen zur Entstehungsgeschichte der Testamente der zwölf Patriarchen* (1970). R. H. **Charles,** *APOT* (1913) 2.282-367. J. J. **Collins,** "The Testamentary Literature in Recent Scholarship," *Early Judaism and Its Modern Interpreters* (ed. R. A. Kraft and G. W. E. Nickelsburg, 1986) 268-78. H. **Corrodi,** *Kritische Geschichte des Chiliasmus* (1781-83). A. **Dupont-Sommer,** *Nouveaux aperçus sur les manuscrits de la mer Morte* (Orient ancien illustré 5, 1953). L. J. **Eron,** "'That Women Have Mastery Over Both King and Beggar' (*TJud.* 15,5)—The Relationship of the Fear of Sexuality to the Status of Women in Apocrypha and Pseudepigrapha: 1 Esdras (3 Ezra) 3-4, Ben Sira and the Testament of Judah," *JSP* 9 (1991) 43-66. H. W. **Hollander and M. de Jonge,** *The Testaments of the Twelve Patriarchs: A Commentary* (SVTP 8, 1985). A. **Hultgard,** *L'eschatologie des Testaments des douze patriarches* (Acta Universitatis Upsaliensis 6-7). J. **Jervell,** "Ein Interpolator interpretiert: Zu der christlichen Bearbeitung der Testamente der zwölf Patriarchen," *Studien zu den Testamenten der Zwölf Patriarchen* (ed. W. Eltester, BZNW 36, 1969). H. J. **de Jonge,** "Die Patriarchtestamente von R. Bacon bis R. Simon," *Studies on the Testaments of the Twelve Patriarchs: Text and Interpretation* (ed. M. de Jonge, SVTP 3, 1975) 3-42. M. de Jonge, *The Testaments of the Twelve Patriarchs: A Study of Their Text, Composition, and Origin* (1953); "The Interpretation of the Testaments of the Twelve Patriarchs in Recent Years," *Studies on the Testaments of the Twelve Patriarchs: Text and Interpretation* (ed. M. de Jonge, SVTP 3, 1975) 183-92; review of *The Testaments of the Twelve Patriarchs*, by H. D. Slingerland, *JSJ* 9 (1978) 108-11; "The Main Issues in the Study of the *Testaments of the Twelve Patriarchs*," *NTS* 26 (1980) 508-24; "*The Testaments of the Twelve Patriarchs:* Central Problems and Essential Viewpoints," *ANRW* II.20.1 (1987) 359-420; "Levi in Aramaic Levi and the Testament of Levi," *Pseudepigraphic Perspectives: the Apocrypha and Pseudepigrapha in light of the Dead Sea Scrolls* (ed. E. G. Chazon and M. E. Stone, 1999) 71-89. H. C. **Kee,** "Testaments of the Twelve Patriarchs," *OTP* (1983) 1.775-828. M. **Konradt,** "Menschen- und Bruderliebe? Beobachtungen zum Liebesgebot in den Testamenten der Zwölf

Patriarchen," *ZNW* 88 (1997) 296-310. **E. Puech**, "Fragments d'un apocryphe de Lévi et le personnage eschatologique: 4QTestLévi^c-d et 4QAJa," *The Madrid Qumran Congress* (ed. J. Trebolle Barrera and L. Vegas Montaner, STDJ 11, 1992) 449-501. **H. D. Slingerland,** *The Testaments of the Twelve Patriarchs: A Critical History of Research* (SBLMS 21, 1977). **G. Vermes and M. Goodman,** *"The Testaments of the Twelve Patriarchs," HJPAJC* 2 (ed. E. Schürer, 1986) 767-81.

G. J. Brooke